Edited and produced by
DAVID AND PAT ALEXANDER
Lion Publishing

Consulting Editors

DAVID FIELD
Vice-Principal, Oak Hill Theological College, London

DONALD GUTHRIE
Formerly Vice-Principal, London Bible College

GERALD HUGHES
Formerly Education Officer for the Diocese of Coventry

HOWARD MARSHALL
Professor of New Testament Exegesis, University of Aberdeen

ALAN MILLARD
Rankin Senior Lecturer in Hebrew and Ancient Semitic Languages,
University of Liverpool

Outline-guide (Parts 2 and 3) by Pat Alexander

Graphics (charts) by Tony Cantale

Pictures by David Alexander and others
(see Acknowledgements)

LION PUBLISHING

THE LION HANDBOOK TO THE BIBLE

THE LION

Handbook
to the Bible

Copyright © 1973 Lion Publishing

Published by
Lion Publishing
Icknield Way, Tring, Herts, England
ISBN 0 85648 320 6
Albatross Books
PO Box 320, Sutherland, NSW 2232, Australia
ISBN 0 86760 271 6

First edition 1973
Reprinted 1974
Reprinted 1975
Reprinted 1976
Reprinted 1977
Reprinted 1978
Reprinted 1979
Reprinted 1981
Reprinted 1982
Second revised edition 1983
Reprinted 1984

Photoset in England
by Focus Photoset Ltd, London

Printed and bound in Hong Kong
by Mandarin Offset International (HK) Ltd

Preface

Over the ten years since this Handbook was first published it has sold more than a million copies and has been translated into a score of languages. This in itself is testimony to the universal appeal of the Bible. Today, as much as ever, people are turning to the Bible – some simply out of curiosity; many out of real interest, seeking help and inspiration. This Handbook has been designed as a stimulus and guide.

It is in four parts. The first sets the scene, giving help and information on the Bible as a whole, its setting, use and relevance today.

The second and third parts, on the Old and New Testaments, go through the Bible book by book, section by section.

The aim is to give information to help the reader understand it for himself, not to give thoughts on the passage or a commentary on it. A heading or brief description gives the main theme. Notes on difficulties aid understanding. Pictures, maps and charts help to build up a vivid and accurate picture of the setting of the passage. Brief articles by experts allow special interests to be followed up in more detail.

The fourth part provides reference material for those wanting to look up particular subjects or who seek help and want to know where in the Bible to find it.

The emphasis of the book is on sheer information, presented in a simple, helpful and visually interesting way. Many of the contributors are those who have previously written at a technical level on subjects which are here reduced to a page or so. The Editors are grateful to them for allowing their findings to be made known at a more popular level in this way.

Technical questions of date and authorship of more academic interest have not been tackled as such. The major concern is the content and meaning of the Bible rather than matters of introduction, and the text has been taken simply as it stands. Though positions have had to be assumed rather than argued, careful account has been taken of current scholarship, particularly of the findings from the Near East which help our understanding of the setting and meaning of the text.

Many may recognize the fruit of their work in these pages. The standard reference books at a more academic level have been a vital source of information. The Editors are grateful to all who have contributed to this book directly or indirectly, by sharing insights into the Bible's teaching, making their own material readily available, or simply by their own delight in the study of the Bible and their conviction of its relevance and power to transform life.

The Editors are also grateful to those who have helped in many other ways. Some are listed under 'Acknowledgements', though this hardly does justice to the enthusiastic assistance received from a wide variety of sources – from directors of specialist museums and collections to those who provided hospitality, help and information.

The work of revision for this second edition revealed surprisingly little 'dated' material. But in the past ten years at least two new English translations of the Bible – the Good News Bible and the New International Version – have come into wide use. This has particularly affected the notes on the text, though the Handbook is not linked to any one translation. We have also taken the opportunity to modernize the typography and to replace some pictures and graphics. We hope that with these changes the Handbook will continue its job of helping new generations of readers to understand the Bible afresh.

CONTENTS

 1

 2

3

 # 4

Contributors

Professor E. M. Blaiklock, Emeritus Professor of Classics, University of Auckland, New Zealand *(The Herod Family, The New Testament and History)*

The Rev. Robert Brow, Rector of St James Church, Kingston, Ontario, Canada, formerly missionary in India *(The Origin of Religion)*

The Rev. Dr J. Philip Budd, Lecturer, Westminster College, Oxford and Ripon College, Cuddesdon *(The Sacrificial System, Feasts and Festivals)*

George S. Cansdale, formerly Superintendent, Zoological Society of London *(Birds and Beasts, The Quail, Clean and Unclean Animals, Fishing in the Lake of Galilee)*

Sir Fred Catherwood, Member of European Parliament and Chairman of Committee on External Economic Relations *(The Bible and Society)*

David J. A. Clines, Reader in Biblical Studies, Sheffield University *(The Apocrypha)*

Peter Cousins, Editorial Director, The Paternoster Press *(The Bible is Different)*

The Rev. Arthur E. Cundall, Principal, Bible College of Victoria, Australia *(Unravelling the Chronology of the Kings)*

The Rev. David Field, Vice-Principal, Oak Hill Theological College, London *(The Bible and Christian Living, The Kingdom of God and the Kingdom of Heaven)*

Dr Richard T. France, Head of Department of Biblical Studies, London Bible College *(Jesus Christ and the Bible, The Religious Background of the New Testament, New Testament Quotations from the Old Testament)*

The Rev. Ralph R. Gower, Staff Inspector for Religious Education, Inner London Education Authority *(Everyday Life in Bible Times)*

Canon Michael Green, Rector, St Aldate's Church, Oxford *(Early Christian Preaching)*

The Rev. Geoffrey W. Grogan, Principal, Bible Training Institute, Glasgow *(Holy Spirit in Acts)*

Dr Donald Guthrie, formerly Vice-Principal, London Bible College *(Texts and Versions, The Letters: Introduction)*

Dr Colin J. Hemer, Lecturer in New Testament Studies, Sheffield University *(The Historical and Political Background of the New Testament)*

F. Nigel Hepper, Principal Scientific Officer, The Herbarium, Royal Botanic Gardens, Kew *(Plants of the Bible)*

Dr J. M. Houston, Chancellor, Regent College, Vancouver, Canada *(The Bible in its Environment)*

Kenneth G. Howkins, Senior Lecturer in Religious Studies, Hertfordshire College of Higher Education and Editor of *Religious Studies Today (Meeting Objections)*

The Rev. F. Derek Kidner, Formerly Warden, Tyndale House and Library for Biblical Research, Cambridge *(Poetry and Wisdom Literature: Introduction)*

Kenneth A. Kitchen, Dr and Reader in Egyptian and Coptic, School of Archaeology and Oriental Studies, Liverpool University *(Egypt)*

John P. U. Lilley, Chartered Accountant *(Times and Seasons)*

Dr I. Howard Marshall, Professor of New Testament Exegesis, University of Aberdeen *(The Bible and Christian Doctrine, The Gospels and Jesus Christ, The New Testament Miracles)*

Alan R. Millard, Rankin Senior Lecturer in Hebrew and Ancient Semitic Languages, University of Liverpool *(The Methods and Findings of Archaeology, Other Creation Accounts, Flood Stories, The Old Testament and the Ancient Near East, The Cities of the Conquest, The Temples, The Threat of Assyria, Exile to Babylon)*

Terence C. Mitchell, Deputy Keeper, Department of Western Asiatic Antiquities, British Museum *(Nations and Peoples of Bible Lands)*

Dr Leon Morris, formerly Principal, Ridley College, University of Melbourne, Australia *(The Gospels and Modern Criticism)*

The Rev. Alec Motyer, Vicar of Christ Church, Westbourne, Bournemouth *(The Names of God, The Tabernacle, The Meaning of Blood Sacrifice, The Prophets: Introduction)*

Dr Harold Rowdon, Senior Lecturer, London Bible College *(Pilate, Roman Soldiers in the New Testament)*

The Venerable John A. Simpson, Archdeacon of Canterbury *(The Virgin Birth of Jesus)*

The Rt Rev. John B. Taylor, Bishop of St Albans *(The Five Books: Introduction, The Historical Books: Introduction)*

Dr Gordon Wenham, Senior Lecturer in Religious Studies, The College of St Paul and St Mary, Cheltenham *(Criticism and the Old Testament, Covenants and Near Eastern Treaties)*

The Rev. John Wenham, Formerly Vice-Principal of Tyndale Hall, Bristol and Warden of Latimer House, Oxford *(The Large Numbers of the Old Testament)*

The Rev. Canon David Wheaton, Principal, Oak Hill Theological College, London *(The Accounts of the Resurrection)*

1

DISCOVERING THE BIBLE

A BIBLE FOR TODAY

THE BIBLE IN ITS SETTING

The Bible in its Environment

JAMES HOUSTON

Much of man's physical environment is of his own making. As Cicero makes Balbus say in his discourse: 'We enjoy the fruits of the plains and of the mountains, the rivers and the lakes are ours, we sow corn, we plant trees, we fertilize the soil by irrigation. We confine the rivers and straighten their courses. By means of our hands we try to create as it were a second world within the world of nature.'

Few areas of the earth have borne more human impact, for good and ill, than the lands of the Bible. In this pivotal land-bridge connecting the continents of Africa, Asia and Europe, early man first learned the rudiments of agriculture between say 12,000 and 8,000 BC, and domesticated some of man's most useful animals. Here too the first irrigation systems were developed and the first towns were created some time during the 5th or 4th millennia BC. But here man has also destroyed the vegetation cover, induced soil erosion, and possibly even climatic deterioration. Here then, where the oldest civilizations of the world first developed, in Mesopotamia and Egypt, the inter-relations of man, culture and physical environment have been most ancient and most complex.

THE ENVIRONMENT AND MAN'S VIEW OF THE WORLD

The great idolatrous cultures of Egypt and Mesopotamia closely reflected their physical environment. Their religion, like that of their neighbours the Hittites and Canaanites, focussed on nature. They had no real concept of a single, all-powerful Creator-God. And so they accounted for the vagaries of climate, agricultural events and the geography of the world around them by means of a whole array of gods. The distinctive geography of Egypt and Mesopotamia – particularly the great river-systems of the Nile and Tigris/Euphrates – to a large extent determined their contrasting ways of life.

Rainfall and religion

The Euphrates and the Tigris rise in the Armenian mountains and flow some 1400 miles down to the Persian Gulf. The Euphrates is the longer, gentler river. But the steep course of the Tigris leads to rapid floods. High water in lower Mesopotamia is in May and June, when melting snows combine with the maximum spring rainfall. The two do not always coincide, so flooding is variable and unpredictable. Mesopotamian rulers, in consequence, were unable to claim the power of prediction and were therefore never acclaimed as gods by their peoples.

By contrast, Egypt has only one river, the Nile. The great lake reservoirs of East Africa regulate its flow, and monsoon rains in the Ethiopian highlands provide a regular, predictable flow in the Blue Nile. There were three fixed seasons in the annual calendar of the lower Nile: 'Inundation', from mid-July to November; 'Coming Forth' (when the land emerged from the water and the seed grew), from mid-November to mid-March; and 'The Drought'. It may have been the regular rhythm of the Nile which gave the pharaohs a greater sense of confidence, raising them to the status of gods in the minds of the people. To his subjects it certainly seemed that the pharaoh possessed a power of control no Mesopotamian ruler ever felt he had over nature.

From the beginning of Egypt's 1st dynasty of kings, annual records of the

A 7th-century BC tablet from Nineveh containing omens derived from the flooding, colour and deposit of rivers.

height of the Nile were kept and yearly estimates made of the flood and probable yield of grain. The story of Joseph indicates that he understood the secrets of Egypt's river-science, but attributed his success, none the less, to the one God.

Nature and belief

The mixture of cultures has tended to mask the contrasts between the two great river-civilizations. Whereas Mesopotamia was exposed to invasion from both mountain peoples and desert nomads, Egypt was more secure in its greater isolation. The lower plain of Mesopotamia was also threatened by unpredictable floods, through climatic caprice and the occasional landslides which dammed up the major tributaries of the Tigris. The pent-up waters would then burst through, releasing an immense volume of water. The threat of salinity, making the soil infertile, may help to explain the general migration northwards to the middle Mesopotamian plain after the fall of the Sumerian civilization.

No wonder then that man felt Mesopotamia's destiny was decided year by year by the gods – no one god having absolute power. It was a society that needed the stability of laws and covenant-agreements. In contrast, Egypt considered her world to be the outcome of a single creative process, as the Nile was the sole factor in her economy. The king's rule was, in theory, absolute, as he was sole official intermediary between the gods and the people. Theoretically, therefore, law was issued as the will of the pharaoh, although in practice a body of law and usage was built up. Royal edicts could supplement this. History was measured against two standards: the distant golden age when the sun-god had ruled on earth, and *maat*, the ideal of the stable, just world-order to which gods, king and people should all conform. So 'progress' for the

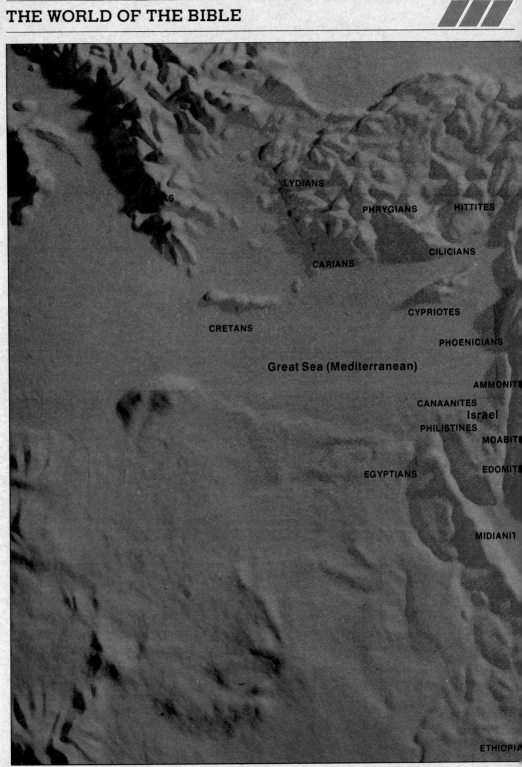

LYDIANS

PHRYGIANS   HITTITES

CILICIANS

CARIANS

CYPRIOTES

CRETANS

PHOENICIANS

Great Sea (Mediterranean)

AMMONIT

CANAANITES
PHILISTINES   Israel

MOABIT

EDOMIT

EGYPTIANS

MIDIANIT

ETHIOPIA

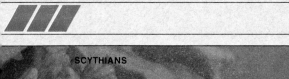

SCYTHIANS

CIMMERIANS

URARTIANS   HURRIANS

MEDES

ASSYRIANS

AMAEANS

AMORITES

AKKADIANS

BABYLONIANS

ELAMITES

SUMERIANS

PERSIANS

ARABIANS

EDANITES

Red Sea

ancient Egyptians was a return to ancient norms.

THE GOD OF NATURE

While these world-views were being evolved, there was general unrest in western Asia and the eastern Mediterranean. By the middle of the 2nd millennium the Harappan civilization in the Indus Valley and the Minoan civilization in the Aegean had both collapsed. A general desiccation of climate was the background to the movements of people in south-west Asia and resultant pressure on western Semitic tribes. Among these Habiru or 'Apiru' ('displaced persons') was Abraham, 'a wandering Aramean'. The later migration and rise to power of Joseph's family in Egypt reflects the period after the 12th dynasty (ended about 1786 BC), when related Hyksos (Asiatic) groups held control over Palestine and Egypt.

From nomads to managers of land

The presence of the Israelites in Palestine by the 13th century BC and the arrival of the 'Sea Peoples' (of whom the Philistines are the best-known) on the coast of Palestine, with their use of iron, are also significant events of the period. The transition of the Israelites from a semi-nomadic to a settled way of life in Palestine has often been recognized as a crucial event in the land. But the training that lay behind all this – weaning Abraham from the Mesopotamian world-view and emancipating Moses from the ways of Egypt – is even more crucial.

Man's view of nature determines his use of it. The Israelites' knowledge of God their Creator gave them a very different attitude to nature and the management of the land. 'The land which you are entering to take possession of it is not like the land of Egypt, from which you have come, where you sowed your seed and watered it with your feet, like a garden of vegetables; but the land which you are going over to possess is a land of hills and valleys, which drinks water by the rain from heaven, a land which the Lord your God cares for; the eyes of the Lord your God are always upon it, from the beginning of the year to the end of the year' (Deuteronomy 11: 10-12).

God in nature – and above it

Thus the Hebrews had no word for nature other than the idea of the activity of God himself. It was God who spoke in the thunderstorm. He blessed in the rainfall; he cursed in the drought. God breathed in the wind as he judged in the earthquake and manifested his glory in the heavens.

The Hebrew faith which saw God working in the activity and mysteries of nature understood that he was also above and beyond it. God was not limited by the environment, as the pagan Syrians thought. Israel's understanding of God and nature was not philosophical but born of faith and experience.

The sub-steppe climate of Palestine with its uncertain rainfall remained a vital challenge to the moral life of Israel. The Ras Shamra tablets have shown how Baal, god of fertility and rain, dominated the Canaanite pantheon. In this context, Elijah's victory against the priests of Baal on Mt Carmel was a triumphant vindication of God. As a later prophet said, 'Do any of the worthless idols of the nations bring rain? Do the skies themselves send down showers? No, it is you, O Lord our God. Therefore our hope is in you, for you are the one who does all this' (Jeremiah 14: 22). There was also the temptation to trust in the material provision of water-storage cisterns, carved out of the limestone. The invention of a waterproof mortar during the Bronze Age made such storage possible. This helps to explain the rapid expansion of Israelite settlement in the hills of Judea and Samaria, colonizing clearances in the woodland which formerly had not been settled. Jeremiah declared: 'My people have committed

The Canaanite god Baal was invoked in various forms: as the god of the weather, or war, or fertility. The prophet Elijah on Mt Carmel challenged Baal on his own ground: but the one true God, not Baal, was master of the elements.

two evils: they have forsaken me, the fountain of living waters, and hewed out cisterns for themselves, broken cisterns, that can hold no water.' The broken cisterns were no doubt the result of local seismic shocks which shattered the limestone so that the water stored for the emergency of summer drought leaked out.

CONSERVING LAND AND RESOURCES

If God cared for their land, his people as good stewards of his gifts should also have this sense of ecological responsibility. The Mediterranean climate, its flora and soils are delicately balanced. War places this whole balance in jeopardy. So at the conquest of the land God told the Israelites: 'I will not drive them out (i.e. the Canaanites) from before you in one year, lest the land become desolate and the wild beasts multiply against you. Little by little I will drive them out from before you, until you are increased and possess the land.'

Deforestation and removal of plant cover leads to soil erosion, possibly alluded to in Job 14: 18-19; and the 'slippery paths' so frequently mentioned in the Old Testament testify to the rapid dissection and sharp relief of the semi-arid highlands. By the first centuries AD there were Jewish laws against the raising of sheep and goats because of overgrazing and soil erosion. For example, Rabbi Akiba said, 'Those who raise small cattle and cut down good trees ... will see no sign of blessing.' The oppressor of the poor is likened in Proverbs 28: 3 to 'a beating rain that leaves no food' and the destruction of the mountain terraces which offset erosion is described by Ezekiel as a terrible calamity. 'The mountains shall be thrown down

and the cliffs (terraces) shall fall, and every wall shall tumble to the ground.'

Alongside careful use of the land went the democratic community of small landowners. The Jubilee Year was intended to preserve the system. The prophets resisted the formation of big estates, although even in David's time there were crown-domains and forced labour. Conquest by powers such as the Assyrians was disastrous to the delicate balance of Israel's environment.

THE GEOGRAPHY OF BIBLE LANDS

The Bible's references to the geography of the land are accurate and reliable. But the allusions are incidental, not central to the narrative. However, if we put together the data on plant-distribution, allusions to climate and other material in the Old Testament, we find the description fits. Indeed, the evidence is reliable enough to show that throughout biblical times climate has been stable, and the ecological zones we depict today are the same as in Old Testament times, the only differences being woodland cover, location of settlements and other such variables of human occupation.

The main geographical regions

The geographical divisions of Palestine can be seen in the map. We shall concentrate on those geographical features which influenced the course of political events in Old Testament times. The most striking distinctions are between 'the desert and the sown', the mountains and the coastal plains. South of a line from Aleppo to Hassetche in Syria the rainfall diminishes and turns the steppe into a 'desert, in a series of undulating plateaux' between 300 and 1,000 feet/90 and 300m. The southern

THE MAIN GEOGRAPHICAL REGIONS

◀ *The Negev desert, near Avdat.*
The hills of Judea: vines grow in the foreground.

The hills of Samaria: rocky hills, cultivated hillsides.

»

part of Palestine is also desert, the triangle-shaped Negev. The western part is a level or slightly undulating plain; the eastern sector is hilly, badly eroded, and stony hammada desert. The Negev and Sinai to the south were the scene of Israel's wanderings before their settlement in 'the land'.

The central backbone of folded limestone north of the Negev forms various low mountain chains from Judea through Samaria to lower Galilee. Upper Galilee consists of recent basalt lavas that break through the limestone cover. It is overlooked by Mt Lebanon with its peaks rising over 3,300 feet/1,005m and continued northwards into the Ansariye mountains. This hilly backbone was the nucleus of Israelite territory. East of these chains is the system of rift valleys, laced together by the Jordan Valley between the Lake of Galilee and the Dead Sea in the south, while the Orontes-Hama-Ghab depressions continue the geological fracture north into Syria.

The coast north of Gaza consists of a broad belt of shifting sand dunes that narrows progressively. From Jaffa/Tel Aviv northwards there is sufficient moisture to provide a vegetation cover that inhibits the further spread of dunes, and this stretch as far as the Yarkon River was Philistine territory. The Plain of Sharon between the Yarkon and Crocodile rivers was swampy, or heavily forested, and formed a buffer zone between Philistia and Phoenicia, in whose sparsely settled area the tribe of Ephraim obtained a foothold. North of Mt Carmel the coast is more rocky and indented, and here the Phoenicians established their power in the natural harbours of Tyre and Sidon.

The influence of geography on events

The ecological transition between 'the land' and 'the wilderness' was of great

The coastal plain.

Galilee: cultivated valleys among dry mountains, beside 'Kinnereth', the harp-shaped Lake of Galilee.

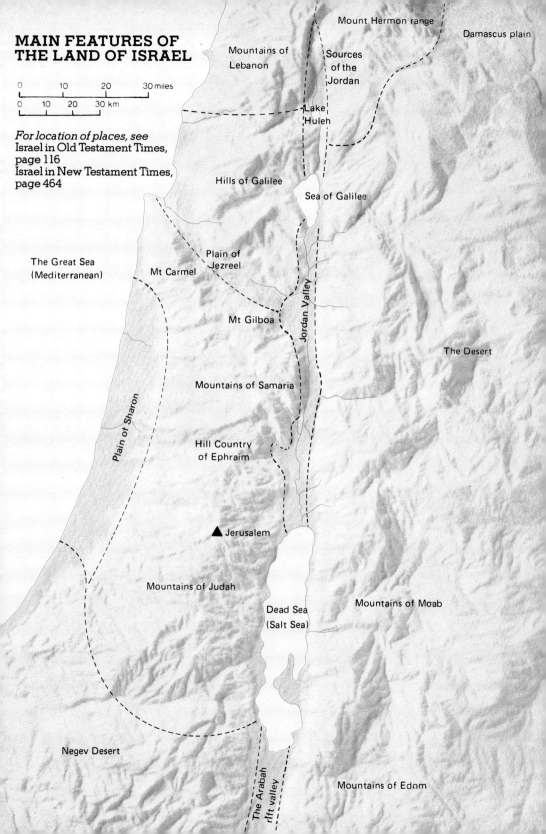

MAIN FEATURES OF THE LAND OF ISRAEL

0   10   20   30 miles
0 10 20 30 km

For location of places, see
Israel in Old Testament Times,
page 116
Israel in New Testament Times,
page 464

Mount Hermon range

Damascus plain

Mountains of
Lebanon

Sources
of the
Jordan

Lake
Huleh

Hills of Galilee

Sea of Galilee

The Great Sea
(Mediterranean)

Plain of
Jezreel

Mt Carmel

Jordan Valley

Mt Gilboa

The Desert

Mountains of Samaria

Plain of Sharon

Hill Country
of Ephraim

▲ Jerusalem

Mountains of Judah

Dead Sea
(Salt Sea)

Mountains of Moab

Negev Desert

The Arabah rift valley

Mountains of Edom

significance in the Bible. The contrast between the mountain 'spine' and the coastal plain was more widely important. The mountains had the slight advantage in higher rainfall, better drainage and in being more suitable for tree crops. There was a strong demand from Egypt and elsewhere for the oil, wine, raisins and dried figs this region produced. More important, the difficult terrain enabled every village to be a fortress and plenty of stone was available for building elaborate walled defences. But on the coastal plain there was no stone, the settlements were difficult to defend, and the international highway of Via Maris built by the Egyptians remained a long time under Egyptian control. The plain was indeed the eastern border of the Mediterranean world, rather than the western fringe of Asia and its steppe peoples.

The Philistines settled on the southern part of the coast with Egyptian consent, and they were the guardians of the maritime highway. But the Phoenician realm began when the road left the coast to cross the Carmel range into the Plain of Jezreel. The Phoenicians appear to have respected the Philistine-Egyptian sphere of influence and did not expand further south. When Egypt's influence waned, David and his generals deprived the Philistines of their conquests in the 'Shephelah' or foothill zone beyond the coast, and confined them to the southern coastal plain. Philistia never recovered her former power. But Israel respected the Phoenician sphere of influence, since

Wells were often simple affairs using buckets and ropes. More sophisticated versions used counter-balances. Various forms of mechanical aids, using donkeys or oxen, were contrived to raise water in buckets. This more recent example is at Ashkelon, Israel.

their trade was vital. Solomon was not equipped to rival the Mediterranean power of the Phoenician merchants, though he did benefit from the direct opportunities of trade in the Red Sea and the Indian Ocean, via his port at Ezion-geber on the Gulf of Aqaba.

But the penetration of the Indian Ocean by Israel, and through her the Phoenician traders, threatened a monopoly Egypt had closely guarded. So Egypt became a centre of intrigues against Solomon, later instigating the revolt of Edom on the trade-route. Later again Egypt backed Jeroboam's revolt which put an end to the united kingdom and terminated the menace of Judean trade in the Red Sea.

Greece, Rome and the New Testament

The rise of the Greek world in the conquests of Alexander the Great introduced a new factor. The thousand-year rule of Phoenicia was ruthlessly broken. To maintain its maritime interest, Alexander guaranteed all inland peoples their positions and rights. Greek settlers, Greek language and Greek civilization were now introduced on the Palestinian coast, and remained – slightly modified by the Romans – for a thousand years. With the fall of the Carthaginian Empire in the west, Roman rule struck a final blow at the Phoenician civilization, and the Roman occupation of Palestine followed.

In the New Testament we sense a contrast in atmosphere between the Judean interior with its rural village life (portrayed in the Gospels), and the civic atmosphere of Roman city life on the coast and beyond the Mediterranean Sea (depicted in the letters). The fall of Jerusalem in AD 70 saw the intensive occupation of the hill lands too, with a Roman road network and Roman camps in the interior grafted on to the Hellenized world of the coastlands.

In the dry lands of the Near East seasonal rainfall is soon lost unless efforts are made to catch and store it.

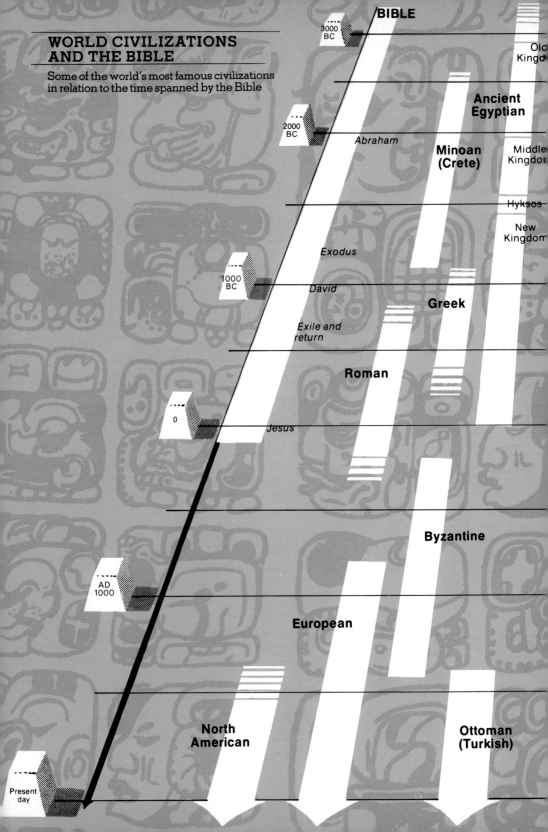

WORLD CIVILIZATIONS AND THE BIBLE

Some of the world's most famous civilizations in relation to the time spanned by the Bible

BIBLE

3000 BC

Old Kingd

Ancient Egyptian

2000 BC

Abraham

Minoan (Crete)

Middle Kingdor

Hyksos

New Kingdom

Exodus

1000 BC

David

Greek

Exile and return

Roman

0

Jesus

Byzantine

AD 1000

European

North American

Ottoman (Turkish)

Present day

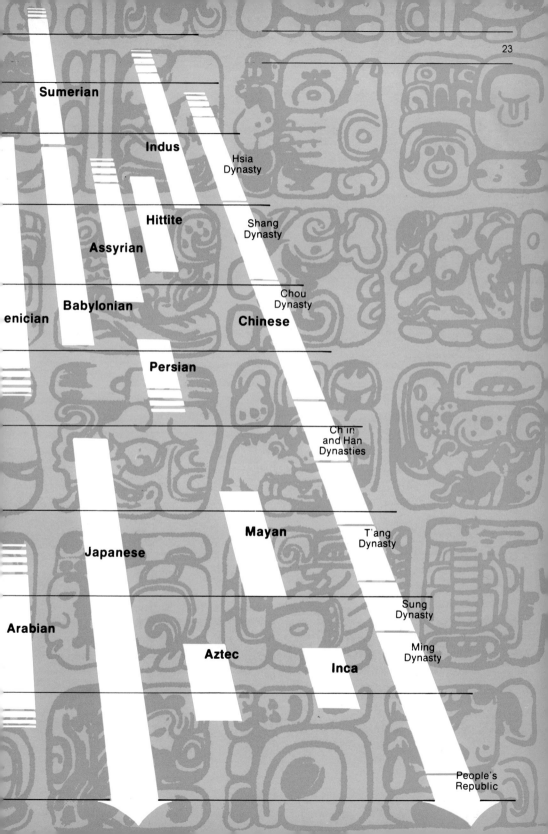

Sumerian

Indus

Hsia
Dynasty

Hittite

Shang
Dynasty

Assyrian

Chou
Dynasty

Babylonian

enician

Chinese

Persian

Ch'in
and Han
Dynasties

Mayan

T'ang
Dynasty

Japanese

Sung
Dynasty

Arabian

Ming
Dynasty

Aztec

Inca

People's
Republic

The Origin of Religion

ROBERT BROW

The origin of religion has often been largely a matter of guesswork. The usual guesses go something like this. The first creatures that stood erect must still have been animals at heart. We know that animals do not have a religion. We also know that two thousand years ago, by the time of Jesus Christ, man had attained a very high form of religion. Therefore in between there must have been a gradual evolution of religion upwards to the higher forms.

The next step is to assume that the lower forms of religion must have been something like that of stone-age tribes which are untouched by modern civilization. Such tribal people are afraid of the spirits of the dark jungles, they rely on witchdoctors to practise magic, and they think that the souls of the dead hover around for a time and then come back in other forms (Animism). It is then an obvious guess that the witchdoctors eventually became priests, with their sacrifices and temples and books of ritual. The next step is that it eventually dawned on people that loving one's neighbour is the main thing in religion, and the one who first taught that clearly was Jesus Christ, who founded the Christian or higher form of religion.

THE BEGINNINGS OF MANKIND

Now it is clear that if this kind of guess about the origin of religion is correct, the first few chapters of the Bible and many parts of the Old Testament are historically unreliable. This is why many people claim that they like the teachings of Christ but they cannot be bothered with the book of Genesis. In the heyday of evolutionary philosophy Old Testament scholars worked at trying to reconstruct what they took to be the true history that underlies the Old Testament according to their theories about the evolution of religion.

What does Genesis really say?

So we must look carefully at the account of man's first religion as it is given in the Bible. Much misunderstanding arises because people read into it much more than it actually says. In the first place the book of Genesis tells us that the human race began with one male and one female. Whether or not scientists are right in saying that we evolved from lower forms, there still had to be a first male that was truly human and a female that was truly human, and they had to be able to propagate a race of humans.

What were this first truly human pair like? Were they half-stooping gorilla-faced cave dwellers beginning the long ascent to civilization? The Bible is silent. We are not told whether they were black or white, stooping or erect, tall or small, with snub or Roman noses. We are, however, given three basic facts concerning their nature.

The first human pair were made from the 'dust of the earth' (Genesis 2:7). When the human body is analysed chemically it is no more than so much carbon, calcium, phosphorus, iron, water, and so on. Second, by zoological classification the first humans belonged to the class of animals in that they had the breath of life, a breathing apparatus of the same kind as the beasts of the earth, the birds and the reptiles (compare Genesis 2:7 and 1:30).

What made the first pair distinct from all the animals was that they were made in the image of God (Genesis 1:26-27). It is important to remind ourselves that in the Bible man is not defined by the fact that he walks upright, or has a certain sized brain, or uses language, or is particularly intelligent. After all, there have been humans who had bent backs, and smaller brains, and could hardly talk. Some animals on the other hand are extremely intelligent. The one thing that makes man peculiarly man is that he was made in the image of God.

Obviously man is not like God in his shape, or almighty power, or ability to be in more than one place at one time. But one thing the image of God in man does imply is that man can understand and choose to listen to the voice of God (Genesis 2: 16-17; 3: 9-13).

THE BEGINNINGS OF RELIGION

When we look for the origin of religion, then, we begin with humans who could respond to God's voice. At first they presumably loved him with all their heart and also loved each other. By the third

At Hazor, in northern Israel, were found these mute symbols of man reaching out to the unknown. This Canaanite shrine also contained a seated Baal.

and fourth chapters of Genesis we find that this first love for God and for one another is wrecked by sin.

In that first state humans did not need temples or priests, or sacrifice. It was only when sin had occurred that the necessity for sacrifice arose at all. In Genesis 4 we find Cain bringing an offering of the fruits of the ground, and Abel bringing an animal sacrifice. Abel's animal sacrifice was accepted by God but Cain's offering of fruit was rejected, for God knew their motives. Already the one way was shown by which sinful man could approach a holy God, the way of the shedding of blood, of death. For sin inexorably means being cut off from God, and that means death.

At first the head of the family or tribe would preside in the offering of sacrifice. After the exodus from Egypt Moses appointed a special line of priests descended from Aaron to supervise the morning and evening, weekly, monthly and special sacrifices. Later, in the time of Solomon, a temple was built for the same purpose, and the offering of animal sacrifice among

the Jews continued until AD 70, forty years after the death of Christ.

There was nothing particularly primitive or barbaric about animal sacrifice. In our cities thousands of animals are slaughtered every day for food. In the Old Testament period each killing of an animal was given a religious meaning, and that meaning only became fully clear in the death of Jesus Christ on the cross. (See John 1: 29; Hebrews 9: 11-14).

THE DEVELOPMENT OF RELIGION

So according to the Bible the first religion of man was monotheism, belief in one God, and animal sacrifice indicated that there was a way of forgiveness and acceptance before him. This helps us to understand the subsequent history of religion.
The Old Testament gives examples of how

A lamb about to be sacrificed at Mecca.

Witchcraft and animism have developed where man fears the supernatural and forces of nature. A witchdoctor appeases evil spirits and drives out sickness by incantations and magic potions.

again and again men were tempted from monotheism into polytheism (worship of more than one god). Laban was a typical polytheist and we know that at the time of Laban polytheism was already the main religion of India. The *Iliad* and *Odyssey* illustrate the complex polytheism of Greek gods at the time of Homer.

Priestcraft and magic

Similarly there is a constant temptation to change God's gracious provision of sacrifice into a ritual that has value in itself. The Brahmins of India and the priests of Egypt and Greece claimed that their sacrifices were pleasing to God, and could obtain blessings for the worshippers. This false view – not sacrifice in itself – is what the great prophets of Israel spoke against. From priestcraft it is only one step into magic and the religion of the tribal witchdoctor. There is thus a constant process of degeneration of religion into the lower forms of polytheism, priestcraft and magic.

It is against this background of degeneration that we must understand

A worshipper touches the arm of a priest to identify himself with the offering to the gods.

Abraham's call from the idolatry and magic of Ur of the Chaldees to worship the one true God with a simple faith based on God's way of sacrifice. Later, Moses had to teach the children of Israel, who had been corrupted in Egypt, to worship the one true God and offer sacrifice in a way which made it clear that no magic was intended.

Maintaining true religion

The Bible therefore illustrates the historical process of the degeneration of religion, and the sending of prophets to restore and reform true religion.

The night before he died, Jesus provided the symbols of bread and wine to remind us of his final sacrifice. Both among the Jews and among many other nations the practice of animal sacrifice ceased. This however did not end the tendency to degeneration. Both in the Christian church and in religions such as Hinduism priests are tempted to claim that by their ritual they can force God to give favours in this life and the next.

THE BIBLE AND ANTHROPOLOGY

■ Since the worship of one God based on animal sacrifice leaves no evidence for archaeologists, we should be suspicious of attempts to reconstruct primitive religion by guesswork based on a few skulls and cave drawings.

■ Long before Abraham, the ancient Egyptians, Sumerians and people of the Indus Valley civilization in India were building temples and using idols. These religions indicate that the process of degeneration had already taken place, and Abraham's task was to restore true religion, not take an upward step in its evolution.

■ In the 6th century BC Buddha, the founder of Buddhism, and Mahavir, the founder of Jainism, both taught that man could attain salvation by his own efforts, and they rejected the practice of animal sacrifice and in fact recommended vegetarianism. They were right in objecting to the priestly magic of the Brahmins, but they did not understand God's way of forgiveness.

■ It is often assumed that the stone-age tribes which have been discovered in the last hundred years give us examples of original primitive religion. This assumption has no basis in fact. For instance, research suggests that virtually all so-called primitive tribes have a memory of a 'High God' who is fatherly and good. There is also growing evidence to show that the sacrifices of witchdoctors for magical purposes are a degeneration from higher forms rather than a remnant of primitive religion.

On Mount Gerizim today the Samaritans still sacrifice the Passover. At the time of Jesus they were despised as a heretical sect. Today, though a tiny minority, they in turn despise the secular state of Israel for not practising the ancient sacrifices. See too page 497.

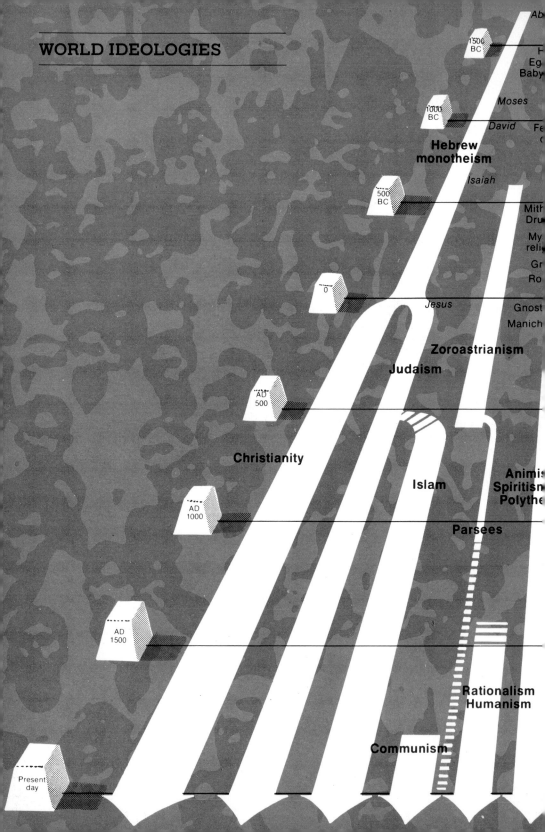

WORLD IDEOLOGIES

Hebrew monotheism

1500 BC

1000 BC

500 BC

0

AD 500

AD 1000

AD 1500

Present day

Ab

H
Eg
Baby

Moses

David

Fe
O

Isaiah

Mith
Dru

My
reli

Gr
Ro

Jesus

Gnost

Manich

Zoroastrianism

Judaism

Christianity

Islam

**Animis
Spiritism
Polythe**

Parsees

**Rationalism
Humanism**

Communism

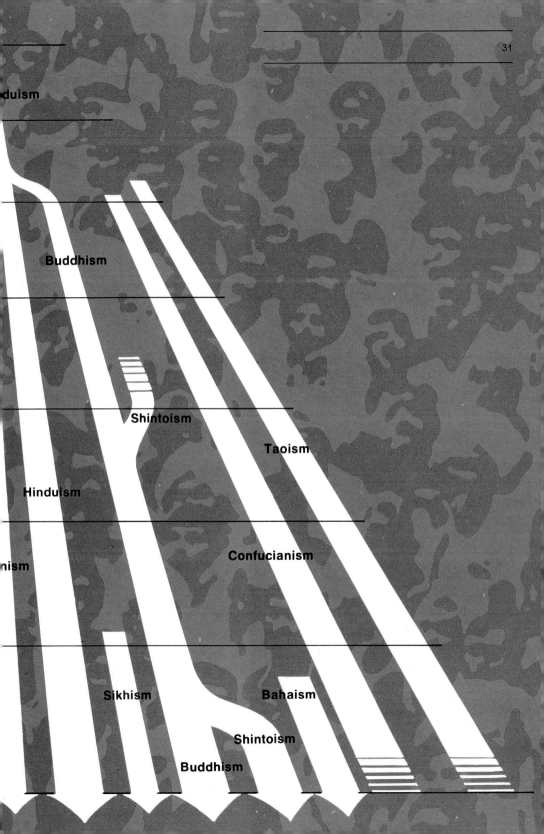

The Bible is Different
PETER COUSINS

Men have always stood in awe of creative power. We think of it as a gift bestowed on exceptional people. We call their work 'inspired' – because it inspires us, and because the artist himself somehow feels his work comes from beyond himself. It is more than just the result of his own conscious activity.

So when we say the Bible is 'inspired' this is how many people understand the word. But when we look at what the Bible claims for itself, we find its 'inspiration' lies deeper than this. It is inspired in a different sense from other works of art.

THE 'INSPIRED' MESSAGE

Hosea 1:1; Joel 1:1

2 Peter 1:21

1 Peter 1:10-12a

Jeremiah 23:28-29

△
**FOLLOW UP THE POINTS
IN THE BIBLE ITSELF**

The Bible does of course speak of its message as coming to men from beyond themselves. The words of the prophets are 'the word of the Lord (that) came to X'. Indeed, Peter clearly affirms that 'no prophecy ever came by the impulse of men, but men moved by the Holy Spirit spoke from God'. Not surprisingly, he also shows that the prophets were unable fully to understand all the implications of their own teaching. The source of their utterance lay beyond themselves; it was in fact 'the spirit of Christ within them . . . predicting the sufferings of Christ and the subsequent glory'.

Naturally, God's message produces a remarkable response in the hearers. To borrow Jeremiah's phrases, when the prophet speaks the word of God and not his own ideas, then men are fed (it is 'wheat' to them) or shattered by its impact (it is a 'hammer'). This has led some to conclude that the Bible's inspiration lies in its impact on them – on the fact that it inspires them.

But they are wrong. Admittedly such an experience points to the fact that the Bible is inspired. It may lead a man to study the Bible closely to see how it explains its own power. But the fact of its inspiration in no way depends on its being received by men. For at this point we are compelled to take note of what the Bible claims for itself. This must be our starting-point.

The biblical use of the word 'inspired' – a term used only once, in Paul's second letter to Timothy – shows that inspiration is grounded not in the response of the hearers, nor in the subjective experience of the

2 Timothy 3:16

writers, but in the fact that 'all Scripture is God-breathed'. This is the literal meaning of the word translated 'inspired'. The point is not that some of the scriptures are inspired and that these alone are useful in the ways listed there. It is a statement about 'scripture' in general, claiming not that it is inspiring in some general way, nor even that it was written by inspired men, but that the scripture itself is 'breathed out' by God.

THE NEW TESTAMENT ATTITUDE TO THE OLD

Acts 4:25; 28:25

Romans 9:17;
Galatians 3:8

See article 'Jesus Christ and the Bible'.

Clearly the New Testament writers treat the Old Testament as if they believed this. They do not argue the case, but simply take it for granted. For example, they speak of what the psalmist and prophet wrote as what God said by his Holy Spirit. 'Scripture says', for Paul, means the same as 'God says'. In doing this the New Testament writers are following the example and precept of Jesus himself. For them the Old Testament is far more than a series of 'stories with a meaning'.

God has chosen to convey his message to men through the medium of words, and the New Testament writers therefore take the actual words used seriously. This is not to say that they take the words in isolation, as if it were possible to communicate in words apart from phrases, sentences and paragraphs. But their example is sufficient to warn us against a casual, pick-and-choose attitude to the actual God-given words of Scripture.

Amos 3:7-8; Jeremiah 20:9;
Ezekiel 2:7

The New Testament attitude to the Old is paralleled by what the Old Testament says about itself. More than 3,800 times words are introduced by such formulae as 'The Lord spoke', 'Thus says the Lord' and 'The word of the Lord came'. Amos and Jeremiah claimed that they were compelled to speak for God; Ezekiel is under orders to give his people the divine message whatever the consequences.

See John 16:12-15

1 Corinthians 2:13
Galatians 1:12

1 Corinthians 14:37

In the nature of the case, the New Testament says little about its own inspiration. Generally the fact that it is backed by the apostles' own authority is in itself sufficient guarantee. But Paul clearly says he is taught by the Holy Spirit and supports the gospel he preached by saying that it was revealed to him by Jesus Christ. In 1 John 1: 5 the writer affirms that the message he is writing came from Christ himself. Elsewhere, Paul says he judges a man's spiritual insight by the way he responds to the contents of his letters. And he clearly believed that he and the apostles were empowered to

Ephesians 3:3-5

2 Peter 3:15-16

reveal truth beyond anything previously made known.

Most explicitly of all, Peter brackets together the letters of Paul with 'the other scriptures'. This last phrase almost certainly refers to the Old Testament and implies that at this time Paul's letters were being read in public worship with the same authority as the Old Testament.

A STUPENDOUS CLAIM

There can thus be little doubt what the Bible teaches about its own inspiration. The words originally written by the human writers were the words of God. This is a very different matter from general 'artistic' inspiration. Certainly God the Creator is the one who by his Holy Spirit gives all men made in his image the power to create beauty. In just the same way he enables them to care for their children and to govern wisely. But this grace given to all men, even those who hate God, is not to be confused with the saving power that is seen at work when God ensures that men can see and hear his words. In something of the same way it is true that God's image may be seen in all men, but that only one man, Jesus Christ, displays the divine likeness without distortion.

SOME MISUNDERSTANDINGS

To do full justice to the facts about the written word of God we are compelled to hold two truths at the same time, as we do in the case of Jesus, the incarnate word. The Bible is both divinely inspired and fully human.

The fact that God speaks directly and uniquely through the Bible does not, however, reduce the biblical writers to typewriters. Each book gives clear evidence of its human history. The writers and editors were plainly not automatic writing machines. Luke pains-

Luke 1:1-4

Joshua 10:13;
1 Kings 15:7,31

takingly collected material for his two volumes and did all he could to make them accurate records. The Old Testament writers also exercise powers of discrimination, omitting what they regard as irrelevant to their purpose, but using what is needed. Paul wrote his letters with specific situations in mind. There are as immense stylistic differences between him and John as between say Isaiah and Hosea.

On the other hand, the fact that the Bible is a human book does not automatically make it faulty. After all, it was God the Lord of all creation who shaped the characters and circumstances of those responsible for recording his revelation. He equipped them to carry out his purpose. We cannot deny him the ability, in his

An orthodox Jew reading the Torah, the law of God.

saving purpose and his infinite wisdom, to ensure the truth and reliability of the record.

The fact that the Bible is 'inspired' does not in any way relieve us of the spiritual and mental effort necessary to understand and interpret it aright. Nor does it imply that all parts of the Bible reveal God to the same extent. To say that Leviticus 3 and John 3 are both inspired means no more than that God has so directed the writing of both that the words used are those best adapted to conveying the saving truth he intends.

God has chosen, then, to make his message of salvation known by means of the written word – our Old and New Testaments. Precisely how and why he has done so is as difficult for us to understand as the doctrine of the Trinity, or how God became man in Jesus Christ. But in each of these cases the teaching of the Bible makes better sense than human theories or attempted compromises. By accepting the Bible's own word on the matter, we put ourselves in the best position to learn from God, saying with the psalmist: 'You Lord are all I have; I have promised to keep your word.'

The accuracy of the Bible on points of detail is illustrated by Luke's description of Philippi in the Acts. The official names translated 'rulers', 'magistrates' and 'police' were all correct to the particular time and place.

Jesus Christ and the Bible

RICHARD FRANCE

As a Christian I want to follow Jesus Christ. I want to do what he said, go where he leads, follow his example, enter into the life he offers.

To do so I must read the eye-witness accounts of those who knew him. I discover that he claimed to be the revelation of God himself, the One who shows us what God is like. And I discover too that he is the culmination of centuries of God's revelation recorded in documents going back hundreds of years before his time.

So I seek the authority of Jesus; and I am led on by him to see the authority of the Bible.

We cannot have one without the other. Certainly Jesus revealed God to man in a way the written Old Testament alone could never have done. Ordinary people saw him, heard him, touched him, lived with him. But we were not there ourselves. Nor can we know what Jesus was like, what he said and did, by consulting the secular historians of the time. They will only tell us that a Jewish prophet called Jesus lived, preached, fell foul of the authorities and was executed. One or two may also suggest some knowledge of his resurrection. But that is as far as it goes. If we are to know the revelation Jesus gave, we must turn to the New Testament to find it.

The fact that a book is necessary to know Jesus is not something to be regretted. It is in fact what Jesus intended. One of his top priorities was the selection and training of his apostles – that inner circle of his disciples who were to preserve and pass on his teaching. The church was founded on the apostles' teaching. The New Testament is the record of what they taught. It is a collection of those books which the early church accepted as written by the apostles themselves, or by their close associates, and which therefore set out the true apostolic faith.

Read the beginning of John's first letter.

THE BIBLE OF JESUS

See John 14:26; 15:26; 16:13-15

If we are to know Jesus and his teaching, then, we must turn to the New Testament, to the testimony of those he himself chose and trusted to pass on his teaching. To do so he himself sent the Holy Spirit to 'guide them into all the truth'.

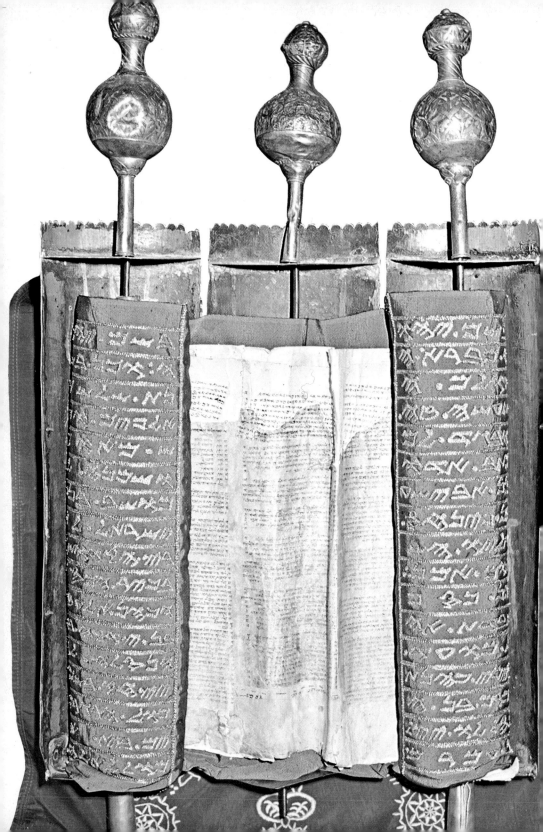

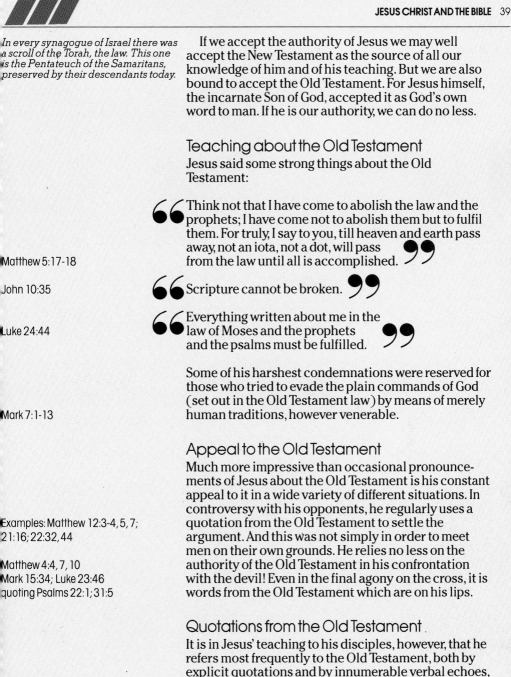

In every synagogue of Israel there was a scroll of the Torah, the law. This one is the Pentateuch of the Samaritans, preserved by their descendants today.

If we accept the authority of Jesus we may well accept the New Testament as the source of all our knowledge of him and of his teaching. But we are also bound to accept the Old Testament. For Jesus himself, the incarnate Son of God, accepted it as God's own word to man. If he is our authority, we can do no less.

Teaching about the Old Testament

Jesus said some strong things about the Old Testament:

66 Think not that I have come to abolish the law and the prophets; I have come not to abolish them but to fulfil them. For truly, I say to you, till heaven and earth pass away, not an iota, not a dot, will pass from the law until all is accomplished. **99**

Matthew 5:17-18

John 10:35

66 Scripture cannot be broken. **99**

Luke 24:44

66 Everything written about me in the law of Moses and the prophets and the psalms must be fulfilled. **99**

Some of his harshest condemnations were reserved for those who tried to evade the plain commands of God (set out in the Old Testament law) by means of merely human traditions, however venerable.

Mark 7:1-13

Appeal to the Old Testament

Much more impressive than occasional pronouncements of Jesus about the Old Testament is his constant appeal to it in a wide variety of different situations. In controversy with his opponents, he regularly uses a quotation from the Old Testament to settle the argument. And this was not simply in order to meet men on their own grounds. He relies no less on the authority of the Old Testament in his confrontation with the devil! Even in the final agony on the cross, it is words from the Old Testament which are on his lips.

Examples: Matthew 12:3-4, 5, 7; 21:16; 22:32, 44

Matthew 4:4, 7, 10
Mark 15:34; Luke 23:46
quoting Psalms 22:1; 31:5

Quotations from the Old Testament

It is in Jesus' teaching to his disciples, however, that he refers most frequently to the Old Testament, both by explicit quotations and by innumerable verbal echoes, so that some passages seem like a patchwork of Old Testament words and ideas. For instance, Jesus' prediction of the destruction of Jerusalem and of his own second coming is full of Old Testament language. The words of only three verses draw on no less than seven Old Testament passages.

Matthew 24; Mark 13; Luke 21

Matthew 24:29-31: from Isaiah 13:10; 34:4; Daniel 7:13; Zechariah 12:12; Isaiah 27:13; Deuteronomy 30:4; Zechariah 2:6

Fulfilment of the Old Testament

But it is not just a matter of language. The actual content of Jesus' teaching relies heavily on the Old Testament. His central ethical rules are drawn from the law of Moses. And if he differed from his contemporaries in ethical matters, it was only because he accused them of taking the Old Testament commands too lightly and superficially.

Matthew 19:18-19; 22:37-40 – see Deuteronomy 6:5; Leviticus 19:18

Matthew 5:21-22, 27-28, etc.

Above all, his teaching about his own role in the purposes of God depends entirely on the conviction that he must fulfil the Old Testament. His teaching after the resurrection, when 'beginning with Moses and all the prophets, he interpreted to them in all the scriptures the things concerning himself', was the climax of what he had been teaching them through the years of his ministry.

Luke 24:27

In a number of passages there are emphatic statements that he had come to fulfil the scriptures. But these are only the outcrops of a conviction which underlies all his teaching about his own mission. He had come 'to fulfil', and there was a divine compulsion about what was written. It *must* be fulfilled.

Luke 4:21; Mark 9:12-13; Luke 18:31; Mark 14:21, 27; Luke 22:37; Matthew 26:54; Luke 24:44-47

So the Christian is a follower of one for whom the Old Testament was the unquestionably authoritative word of God. Jesus believed its statements, endorsed its teaching, obeyed its commands, and set himself to fulfil the pattern of redemption which it laid down. It is clearly inconsistent for one who calls Jesus 'Lord' to think lightly of those scriptures which were to him the supreme revelation of God.

THE NEW TESTAMENT ENDORSES THE OLD

The rest of the New Testament, needless to say, fully endorses Jesus' view of the Old Testament. Constant Old Testament quotations and allusions show the same reliance on the Old Testament teaching for the disclosure of God's character and purposes. It was God who spoke through the prophets, declares the writer of Hebrews. Indeed, says Paul to Timothy, 'All scripture is inspired by God.' The Old Testament is the message of God.

Hebrews 1:1; see too 2 Peter 1:21; 2 Timothy 3:16 Romans 3:2

It is interesting that the New Testament makes no distinction between what 'Scripture' says and what God says. Old Testament quotations are given as what God said, even though God was not the speaker in the Old Testament context. Conversely, words spoken by God in the Old Testament narrative are ascribed to 'Scripture'. Where Jesus led the way in his acceptance of the Old Testament as the word of God, the New Testament

Matthew 19:4-5; Acts 4:24-25; Hebrews 1:6-12 Romans 9:17; Galatians 3:8

was content to follow. If we Christians set our own judgement or our inherited traditions above the Old and New Testament scriptures we part company with the Lord and the apostles, and cut ourselves off from our one source of knowledge of God.

DEALING WITH PROBLEMS

This is not to eliminate all problems in advance. The interpretation and application of the Bible's teaching poses many problems, and Christians may legitimately differ in their interpretation at some points. But where such differences occur, our aim must always be to discover, by the most careful and rigorous study of which we are capable, what the relevant passages really mean, whether this turns out to agree with our own previous ideas or not. Then, having discovered the true meaning, we must accept it as the word of God. It will not always be easy; it may sometimes be impossible; but that is the ideal.

We may be convinced in our minds of the Bible's authority: we will be even more convinced when we allow it to have its authority in our lives. We will know for ourselves the experience of God speaking through his written revelation to us. The Bible is God's word, what God has said. He still speaks to us through it today.

It was not only in ancient times that the Bible was treasured. This Rumanian woman reads from a 1968 edition of the Bible – a prized copy in a Communist country, where circulation of the Bible has been restricted.

Meeting Objections
KENNETH HOWKINS

Much of the Bible is in the form of history. It is not however *mere* history. If that is all we see, we miss the point. It is history from one point of view, history with an aim. Stories are recorded not simply because they happened, but because they reveal something of God and his activity in the world. So it is sometimes called a 'history of salvation'.

HISTORY WITH A DIFFERENCE

This alters the perspective. The secular historian may be amazed that an ancient Hebrew nomad, Abraham, occupies more than thirteen chapters, while a powerful despot, Omri, is dealt with summarily in less than a dozen verses. Archaeological records do not even mention Abraham, though his story fits well into what is known of his times; but Omri was known far and wide to later generations. In the Bible, Abraham was the founder of Israel, a man chosen by God, a man of faith, the recipient of God's promises, and a man of profound significance to both Jew and Christian; but Omri founded the city of Samaria and was an evil man. Thus he is dismissed from the story. As God's revelation of himself unfolded, and as his work of salvation continued, men and events in history assumed different proportions.

Discrepancies

It is easy to find historical problems in the Bible. But patient research has gradually solved many of them. Apparent discrepancies between different parts of the Bible are sometimes due simply to the lack of detail given, and we should not too hastily pounce on contradictions.

For example, in both Acts and Galatians there are references to Paul's visits to Jerusalem. It is difficult to fit the two together, and to know which visits in the two books correspond. But Acts is clearly not intended to give a complete account of Paul's activities, and he may well have visited Jerusalem on other occasions which are not recorded.

Again, there may be apparent discrepancies between the biblical version of a story and the version in other ancient records. It is strange that those who wish to discredit the reliability of the Bible sometimes seem to have such strong faith in the reliability of other ancient records! So first we need to be sure that the other record is in fact reliable and, second, we need to remember how little total evidence we have from the ancient past. The debate on the book of Daniel illustrates this. It is no longer possible just to dismiss Darius as 'unhistorical'. There are problems: but there are also possible solutions.

Problems with numbers

A difficulty arises on various occasions in connection with numbers in the Bible. Here we find that the manuscripts themselves may vary in the figures they give. It must be remembered that letters of the alphabet in both Hebrew (at least after the exile) and Greek served also as numerals. Because of the similarities of certain letters, errors in copying could easily creep in. Also different methods of reckoning were employed. A year may be reckoned by the sun, or by the reign of a king. Inclusive reckoning was also used. For example, midday on Sunday until midday on the following Sunday could be called eight days, rather than seven, as eight days were involved, even though the first and the last were incomplete. Again, there are problems, but some progress can be made with them.

Myth

An objection frequently heard today is that it is being unduly literalistic to discuss whether or not the Bible history is true. We are told that what matters is not whether a certain event happened, but what it means. This is the opposite extreme to the view that it is *mere* history; the claim is that the stories are not history but 'myth' – a term used in varying ways, and notoriously hard to define exactly. It does not imply that the story is completely untrue, but that it is not literally true. The term is brought in whenever there is anything supernatural or different from the ordinary course of nature.

Now the first question to consider is whether the biblical writers intended their words to be taken as history or as myth. It is clear that the accounts of miracles in the Bible are written just as factually as the accounts of other events. The second question, therefore, is whether we can accept them as history, or whether we must treat them as myth and 'demythologize' them, that is, assume that the miracle did not actually occur as a miraculous event, but that some spiritual truth is enshrined in the story in symbolic form.

The basis for this line of argument is that the bible was written in an unscientific age, when people thought of 'a three-decker universe', with a God who kept on interfering; but that now, in our enlightened scientific age, we know that their view of the world was quite wrong. Miracles are supposed to fit in with the unscientific views of the ancients, but not with our own scientific views. It is claimed that we now know that the world operates in accordance with laws, and so we do not need to bring God in to explain things.

Now this view of science is already out of date. Science, or rather scientists, no longer hold such a rigid view of the laws of nature. The laws are descriptions of what is observed to happen normally. If a law does not account for all that happens, then it has to be modified. Science, as such, does not rule out miracles, though some scientists may reject them.

We have been considering the subject of history. The question of whether miracles happened or not is a question of history and not of science. History deals with what happened, and then tries to find explanations. Science takes the knowledge of what happened and tries to systematize that knowledge.

THE QUESTION OF MIRACLES

The biggest miracle in the Bible is the resurrection of Jesus from the dead. Some would say that the universe is such that a resurrection could not take place, and they would base this assertion on 'science'. But in view of the historical evidence for the resurrection, it would be more scientific to ask what light is thrown on the nature of the universe by the occurrence of such a resurrection. In other words, science does not

A Hebrew text, with vocalized and accented Hebrew characters, accompanied by notes in the margin in Aramaic.

disprove the resurrection: the resurrection is one of the facts which science must take into account. And what is said of the resurrection may be said of other miracles.

Of course there are objections here which must be faced. If miracles were always taking place, there would be no order in the universe, and without the regularity of nature we should not know where we were. Moreover, if God were always intervening to get us out of difficulties or dangers, we should never learn to become responsible people. But the Bible does not give us a miracle on every page. It covers about two thousand years of history, but most of the miracles are clustered round a few persons and events:

■ Moses and the beginning of the nation of Israel;
■ Elijah and Elisha and the emergence of a line of prophets who called the nation back to their covenant-agreement with God;
■ Jesus and the final revelation of God and his salvation, followed by the apostles and the founding of the Christian church.

Thus most of the miracles occur in these three separate periods. They must be seen in perspective.

Complementary accounts

In science it is not always possible to find one theory which accounts for and describes every aspect of an event. It is sometimes necessary to have two or more theories, not as alternatives, but held together. Light can be described in terms both of waves and of particles. Neither description alone is sufficient; both are needed. There can be a number of different levels of explanation.

Now when a scientist investigates a 'miracle', he may, or may not, be able to offer a 'natural' explanation. This is the function of science. The account of the crossing of the Red Sea in the Bible refers to a strong wind. That is the natural

explanation. But the same account also ascribes the event to God. There are two levels of description. Both are true. One answers the question of *how,* the other the question of *why.* To say that God did it is to give the ultimate cause and to give meaning to it. The description given by science (where one is possible) explains *how* God did it.

In the Bible miracles are not as sharply divided from other events as they tend to be in our thinking. The ordinary events of nature, as well as the extraordinary, are ascribed to God. God is seen as active in all nature, and not only in miracles; they are simply his unusual way of working.

An experiment with laser beams. Light can be described as waves (and the waves re-aligned to make lasers). It can also be described as particles. The two accounts are complementary, not contradictory. In the same way science and the Bible can give complementary descriptions of the same facts.

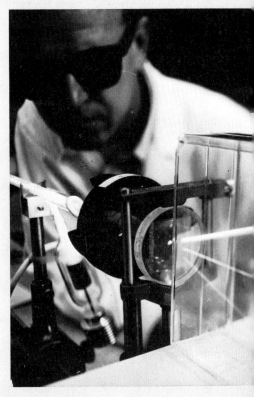

Religious and historical truth

On the philosophical level another objection is raised against taking the miracle stories as historically true. We are told that there are two categories which must be kept absolutely apart. Thus the objectors would want to say that it is a 'religiously' true statement that God raised Jesus from the dead, and this has a spiritual meaning; but that on the level of history, Jesus died and remained dead and buried. We are told that to say the body of Jesus actually lived again is 'to confuse the categories'. But what are those categories, and where do they come from? They exist solely in the mind of the man who invented them. They can be neither proved nor disproved. But there is something more important still. If we start off by accepting these categories, then we start off by saying that Jesus did not rise from the dead, in the ordinary sense of those words. No matter how strong the historical evidence for the resurrection, we shall never accept it. We shall simply look for some other explanation.

This philosophical objection is really the same as the so-called scientific objection that miracles just do not occur in this world or universe. In both cases the objection is simply assumed to be valid, without proof, and before the evidence has even been considered. Indeed, all 'evidence' is automatically discounted. This is a fine example of question-begging: it assumes the answer before it starts. To such objectors we simply put the question: what sort of evidence would you require to be convinced that miracles did occur?

Creation stories

A similar problem arises at the very beginning of the Bible, in the creation stories. Some dismiss these as myth in the sense of old wives' tales. Others call them myth, meaning to say that they contain truth, even though they are not literally and historically true. If this is the case, in what sense are they true? What is the real point of the stories?

Objections to the creation stories are made in the name of science. So it may be surprising to find how little there is which impinges on the realm of science. It is boldly shown that God is the Creator of all – the universe, man, and everything else. But it is not shown how God did it. If God made man from the dust of the earth, that tells us something about the nature of man, the creature, as compared with God, the Creator. We are mere dust, and live only because God has made us live. Therefore, apart from God, our lives have no meaning. But how did God make man from dust? That is a scientific question, and so we turn to science, not the Bible, for an answer, or a suggested answer. We shall not be satisfied with a theory which does less than justice to the biblical view of the nature of man, but at the same time we need to be sure that we really have grasped the biblical view, and not just read our own ideas into it.

THE VALIDITY OF THE OLD TESTAMENT

Some people reject the Old Testament, partly or wholly, as being non-Christian, or sub-Christian. This is no new idea. In the first place, the Christian's view of the Old Testament must be Christ's view of it. It is quite clear that he accepted its authority and its validity. The question is whether Christ and Christianity have presented a new and truer view of God which invalidates the Old Testament picture.

In certain respects the Old Testament *is* now invalidated. Sacrifices are no longer necessary, as Christ himself has offered the final sacrifice, once for all. The rest of the Jewish ceremonial law is similarly superseded. But that does not mean that those Old Testament rituals should now be completely ignored. They reveal something permanently true about the nature of God and man's relationship with him. The teaching is the same, but the practical outworking is different, because of Christ. God is still holy.

The parts of the Old Testament which cause greatest offence are those which depict God as a God of anger, who orders his servants to act in judgement for him. This, it is said, is a primitive view of God, and quite different from the New Testament picture, which proclaims that God is love. But there is no fundamental opposition between the Old and New Testaments. There is much about the love and forgiveness of God in the Old Testament, and much about his righteous anger and judgement in the New. Indeed some of the strongest words are found on the lips of Jesus himself. Those who reject the Old Testament picture are compelled to reject also parts of the New. The whole idea of God's righteousness,

A rock tomb of the 1st century AD, recently discovered under the Convent of the Sisters of Nazareth, Israel. The great stone was rolled across to seal the tomb. The accounts of the resurrection of Jesus in the Gospels are brought vividly to life by such actual examples of the type of tomb in which Jesus was laid.

anger against evil, and judgement is not pleasant, especially in a permissive age. But this does not make it any less true. (See Parts Two and Three for notes on particular moral difficulties.)

MEN OR MACHINES?

A final objection to a Christian view of the Bible is that it bypasses human thought, and makes men into machines. It is said that on this view the writers mechanically wrote what God said, and the readers do not need to think, because every bit of truth is presented on a plate. But this objection reveals a radical misunderstanding. Although the Bible's claim for itself is that God did directly speak through men, and that he so controlled them that they said what he wanted them to say, it is clear also that the men concerned used their own minds in the process. Their own personalities come through in the different styles of writing and their different approaches. (See article 'The Bible is Different'.)

Clearly also the Christian must use his own mind to receive the word of God. He must read carefully, compare one passage with another and use all the aids he can. Besides this he needs to seek the help of the Holy Spirit, through whom Scripture was written, to illuminate its meaning. As with the writers of Scripture, so with its readers, the mind and whole being needs to be dedicated to God. It is one of the remarkable features of the Bible that it contains enough to occupy the greatest intellects for a lifetime, and yet the simplest person can read and understand, and in reading with an obedient heart find God himself.

The Bible and Christian Living

DAVID FIELD

The Bible can be read as great literature, or as a history of Israel, or as a source-book of theological information. It is all of these things. But none of them does full justice to the purpose of Scripture as set out by the Bible writers themselves, or to the cumulative experience of Bible users through the centuries.

When Ezra the scribe read from the law of Moses to the returned exiles in Jerusalem, the people, we are told, not only 'understood the reading' but alternately 'wept when they heard the words of the law' and made 'great rejoicing'. And they came back the next day to build shelters for the Feast of Tabernacles, in obedience to the law's commands. The act of hearing and understanding the scriptures had aroused their emotions and stirred them to action.

Nehemiah 8

Centuries after Ezra, J. B. Phillips describes his similar experience in translating the New Testament. 'Although I did my utmost to preserve an emotional detachment,' he writes, 'I found again and again that the material under my hands was strangely alive; it spoke to my condition in the most uncanny way.'

These reactions accurately reflect the vivid metaphors we find in the Bible, used by its writers to describe the impact God's word made in their own experience. It is a fire to warm and a hammer to break, water to cleanse, milk to nourish, meat to invigorate, light to guide, a sword for the fight, and a mirror to reveal. It is 'at work in you believers', 'able to build you up', 'living and active...piercing...discerning'.

Jeremiah 23:29; 1 Peter 2:2;
Hebrews 5:13-14; Psalm 119:105;
Ephesians 6:17; James 1:23-25;
1 Thessalonians 2:13; Acts 20:32;
Hebrews 4:12

THE BIBLE IS RELEVANT

All this means that the reader who approaches the Bible in a purely detached way is in danger of failing to appreciate its primary purpose, which is a practical, dynamic one. Its aim is to *do something* in the life of the person who reads it, as well as to capture his aesthetic interest and supply him with historical and theological information. The huge cultural gaps which separate Bible times from our own make such a purpose all the more remarkable, but the Bible can justify its claim to contemporary relevance in two ways.

In the first place, it deals with those elements in *human nature* which are timeless. The men and women we read about in the Bible have aspirations and failings with which we easily identify, and even the heroes of Scripture are displayed in the cold light of truth. As Augustine put it, 'The sacred record, like a faithful mirror, has no flattery in its portraits.'

Then, secondly, the truths of the Bible are ever-relevant because *God himself* does not change, either in his nature or in his dealings with men. Through reading the Bible we discover fundamental truths about God, and see them demonstrated by events in the lives of his people which illuminate his character and illustrate his will for all men at all times. So it is that even events from the distant past 'were written down for *our* instruction' in order that in the present and for the future 'by the encouragement of the scriptures we might have hope'.

Corinthians 10:11;
Romans 15:4

THE BIBLE IS PRACTICAL

The Bible, then, retains its contemporary bite. What are the practical purposes it aims to achieve?

It points people to Jesus

The purpose of John's Gospel is clearly set out: 'Now Jesus did many other signs in the presence of the disciples, which are not written in this book; but these are written that you may believe that Jesus is the Christ, the Son of God, and that believing you may have life in his name.'

ohn 20:30-31

In writing with this frankly propagandist aim – to focus on Jesus Christ – the disciple was being faithful to the remarkable way in which his Master summed up the purpose of *all* Scripture. 'You search the scriptures', Jesus once replied to his critics, 'because you think that in them you have eternal life; and it is they that bear witness to *me*. If you believed Moses, you would believe me, for he wrote of *me*.'

ohn 5:39, 46

Not surprisingly, the listening disciples were slow to grasp the full meaning of these words. After the resurrection Jesus had to rebuke them for their dull-ness before showing them once again – and this time more explicitly – how, like the spokes of a wheel, the whole message of the Bible converged on himself. 'Beginning with Moses and all the prophets, he inter-preted to them in all the scriptures the things concern-

uke 24:27

Two oil lamps of the type used in Bible times. The Bible was often compared to a lamp, or a light for the way ahead.

ing himself'. And Luke goes on to tell us that Jesus drew special attention to those passages from the Old Testament which spoke of his death and resurrection, as a stimulus to repentance and the basis for forgiveness of sins.

Jesus clearly believed that the main aim of the (Old Testament) scriptures was to point people to himself; which meant in practice (if we add Luke's evidence to John's), that through repentance and faith men and women should find the forgiveness and life which he had died and risen to make possible for them.

By their preaching and writing, the apostles showed that they had finally grasped Jesus' point that the Bible's main practical purpose is to draw people to himself as their Saviour. 'To him', preached Peter, 'all the prophets bear witness, that every one who believes in him receives forgiveness of sins through his name.' James pleaded with his readers to 'receive with meekness the implanted word, which is able to save your souls'. Paul reminded Timothy 'how from childhood you have been acquainted with the sacred writings which are able to instruct you for salvation through faith in Christ Jesus'.

Acts 10:43

James 1:21

2 Timothy 3:15

It builds a relationship with God

In Martin Luther's words, just as a mother goes to the cradle only to find the baby, we go to the Bible only to find Christ. It is the Bible's primary purpose to bring men to their Saviour by arousing the beginnings of faith. But this is not the only practical function it aims to fulfil. Peter and the author of the letter to the Hebrews use the analogy of birth and growth to illustrate a further purpose of Scripture. Those who have put their trust in Jesus as Saviour 'have been born anew . . . through the living and abiding word of God'; but, like all new-born babes, they must 'long for the pure spiritual milk' of the word if they are to survive and grow; and once beyond babyhood they need solid food – which is the 'meat' of God's word.

1 Peter 1:23

1 Peter 2:2

Hebrews 5:12-14

This growth process is, above all, a growing up in relationship with God. It is the Bible's function to feed the personal knowledge of the Father which the Christian 'child' enjoys. And 'enjoy' is exactly the right word, because as the believer learns more about God his delight becomes more intense. That is why Bible study should never be dull for a Christian. 'Your words', cries out Jeremiah, 'became to me a joy and the delight of my heart; for I am called by your name, O Lord, God of hosts.' Any personal relationship is fostered by words, and through the pages of his Bible the Christian

Jeremiah 15:16

hears God speaking to him; an experience, says the Psalmist, that is 'sweeter than honey'.

Psalm 19:10

If this sounds like love-letter language we should not be surprised, because the relationship into which God invites believers is a love-relationship. His, however, is a love which makes exacting demands. The information about God and his will which the Christian receives through reading the Bible calls for a tough response that is anything but sentimental. 'If a man loves me', Jesus taught, 'he will *keep* my word, and my Father will love him, and we will come to him and make our home with him…and the word which you hear is not mine but the Father's who sent me.'

John 14:23-24

It equips for battle

Such a stern demand is appropriate because once a man becomes a Christian he finds himself enlisted on God's side in a lifelong battle. He is called upon both to defend his faith against stiff opposition and to spread it among his friends. For both operations, offensive and defensive, his chief weapon is the Bible. It is the 'sword of the Spirit', declares Paul, with which he can combat hostile ideas and cut a straight path for God's truth into the innermost strongholds of the human will.

Ephesians 6:17

Hebrews 4:12

Jesus himself set the pattern for this very practical use of the Bible in his own ministry. Honest enquirers, like the lawyer who asked him about the greatest commandment, were impressed and attracted by his Bible-based teaching (though, as with the rich young ruler, they did not all respond to it positively). On the other hand Jesus fought off false teaching, whether the arguments of men like the Sadducees or the insidious suggestions of the arch-enemy in the desert, with the words of his Bible. Bible words do not have magical powers in themselves, but because all words express ideas, and ideas lie behind action, the word of God is a mighty weapon to influence men's convictions and conduct. Jesus fought his battles with his own words and with the words of his Bible, and he sent his disciples out to preach both.

Mark 12:28-34

Matthew 19:16-22

Matthew 22:23-33

Matthew 4:1-11

This gives the Christian all the incentive he needs to fill his mind with Bible doctrine. Without (for example) a grasp of what the Bible teaches about human nature he will soon be speechless before the claims of twentieth-century humanism. If he is vague about the meaning of Christ's death and resurrection, he cannot hope to introduce others to Jesus as their Saviour. Hence the insistence of the later books of the New Testament that anyone who aims to serve Christ faithfully must make it his aim to know and conserve God's truth. 'Guard the truth that has been entrusted to you

Timothy 1:14; 2:2

by the Holy Spirit', writes Paul to Timothy, 'and what you have heard from me before many witnesses entrust to faithful men who will be able to teach others also.'

It guides conduct

Timothy 1:18-19

In his earlier letter to Timothy, Paul had already drawn attention to the importance of maintaining right standards of conduct alongside right beliefs. To 'wage the good warfare' involves 'holding faith *and a good conscience.*' The one cannot be made a substitute for the other; indeed, any failure in right conduct inevitably brings about a downfall in right beliefs. 'By rejecting conscience, certain persons have made shipwreck of their faith'. This is a major Bible theme. In the Old Testament, farmer Amos, with rustic bluntness, flays those who attempt to keep up a religious façade without matching conduct; and James, his outspoken New Testament counterpart, exposes those who are 'hearers of the word' but not 'doers' of it. Jesus makes the same point in his parable of the two builders.

ames 1:22

latthew 7:24-27

The same pressures which threaten to muddle his faith can seduce the Christian into moral laxity; but the Bible, which provides his main line of defence

against false teaching, is also an effective weapon against moral temptations. It sets out, by example as well as by direct command, the differences between right and wrong, so that the man who measures his conduct by Bible standards gains from it both 'reproof' when he is in the wrong and 'correction' to set him back on a right course. The Bible becomes his bastion against moral powerlessness, too, by reminding him constantly of the divine power that is available to overcome his weakness ('for God is at work in you, both to *will* and to *work* for his good pleasure'). The man who knows and claims the Bible's promises is empowered to live a kind of life which would otherwise be completely beyond his grasp.

The moral commands of the Bible are presented more as main guiding principles and ideals than as a set of meticulously detailed regulations for daily living. They reach behind right actions to right motives, and their application may differ from person to person according to circumstances. Goodness is defined as that which pleases God, so the Christian with a clear conscience is the one who is totally absorbed with pleasing him. And, as we have already seen, it is the Bible's function to feed and foster such a relationship.

2 Timothy 3:16

Philippians 2:13

See Romans 14

Hebrews 13:21

THE BIBLE IS FOR ORDINARY PEOPLE

The Bible is not written in a secret spiritual code which must be cracked if its message is to be understood. Provided it is read sensibly (see the section 'Understanding the Bible'), it is clear enough for the simplest Christian to live by, as well as being profound enough to exercise the mind of the brightest scholar for a lifetime. The decisive qualifications for profitable Bible study are spiritual rather than intellectual.

Among the qualities which the Bible itself suggests, the following are particularly prominent:

Families and groups in homes and churches throughout the world gather with one simple aim: to discover what the Bible says and apply it to their own situation today. The Bible is not just a book of the past. It is read by more people today than ever before.

A will to obey

John 7:17

'Whoever has the will to do the will of God', said Jesus, 'shall know whether my teaching comes from him.' This is a fundamental requirement, if the teaching of the Bible is going to make its full impact on any reader's life. It has been well said that 'the Bible is never mastered by the reader who refuses its mastery of him'.

Concentration

Timothy 2:15, Phillips

Words calling for sustained effort ('search', 'meditate', 'examine') are used in the Bible to describe the way the scriptures must be read for maximum benefit. *'Concentrate* on winning God's approval, on being a *workman* with nothing to be ashamed of, and who knows how to use the word of truth to the best advantage.'

Patience

Hebrews 6:12

ee Hebrews 11:17-19

It is 'through faith and patience' that the Bible's promises are to be obtained. Patient conviction that God's word is to be trusted will bring the believer through times of perplexity.

Persistence

uke 8:18

Jesus' promise and warning, 'To him who has will more be given, and from him who has not, even what he thinks that he has will be taken away', was made in the context of hearing the word of God. To the persistent seeker the Bible yields more and more of its riches.

Submission to the Holy Spirit

uke 24:45

When Jesus met his disciples after the resurrection 'he opened their minds to understand the scriptures', by relating what they read in their Bibles to what was happening around them. It is through the prompting of the Holy Spirit that the Bible reader gains the mind of Christ, which enables him to apply teaching given centuries ago to contemporary life.

e 1 Corinthians 2:9-16

It would be impossible to better Paul's summary of the practical and devotional potential of the Bible: 'Your mind has been familiar with the holy scriptures, which can open the mind to the salvation which comes through believing on Christ Jesus. All scripture is inspired by God and is useful for teaching the faith and correcting error, for re-setting the direction of a man's life and training him in good living. The scriptures are the comprehensive equipment of the man of God, and fit him fully for all branches of his work.'

Timothy 3:15-17, Phillips

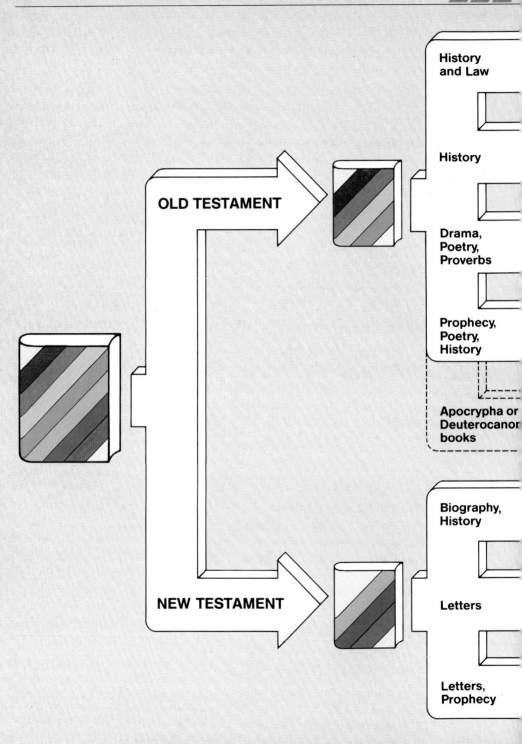

History
and Law

History

Drama,
Poetry,
Proverbs

Prophecy,
Poetry,
History

Apocrypha or
Deuterocanon
books

OLD TESTAMENT

NEW TESTAMENT

Biography,
History

Letters

Letters,
Prophecy

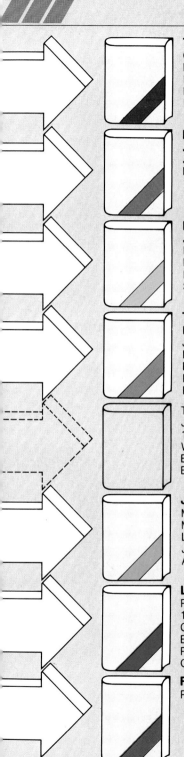

The Pentateuch
Genesis
Exodus
Leviticus
Numbers
Deuteronomy

History
Joshua
Judges
Ruth
1 and 2 Samuel
1 and 2 Kings
1 and 2 Chronicles

Ezra
Nehemiah
Esther

Poetry and Wisdom
Job
Psalms
Proverbs
Ecclesiastes
Song of Solomon

The Prophets
Isaiah
Jeremiah
Lamentations
Ezekiel
Daniel
Hosea

Joel
Amos
Obadiah
Jonah
Micah
Nahum

Habakkuk
Zephaniah
Haggai
Zechariah
Malachi

Tobit
Judith
1 and 2 Maccabees
Wisdom
Ecclesiasticus
Baruch

Jesus and the early Church
Matthew
Mark
Luke
John
Acts

Letters
Romans
1 and 2 Corinthians
Galatians
Ephesians
Philippians
Colossians

1 and 2 Thessalonians
1 and 2 Timothy
Titus
Philemon
Hebrews
James

1 and 2 Peter
1, 2 and 3 John
Jude

Revelation
Revelation

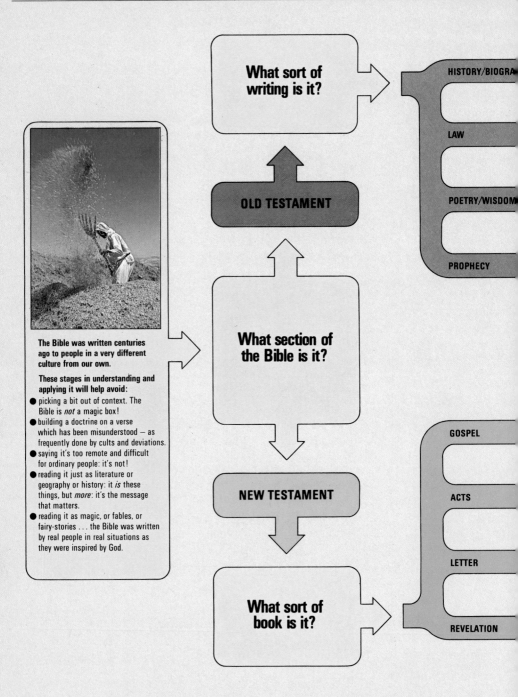

What sort of writing is it?

HISTORY/BIOGRA...

LAW

POETRY/WISDOM

PROPHECY

OLD TESTAMENT

The Bible was written centuries ago to people in a very different culture from our own.

These stages in understanding and applying it will help avoid:

● picking a bit out of context. The Bible is *not* a magic box!

● building a doctrine on a verse which has been misunderstood — as frequently done by cults and deviations.

● saying it's too remote and difficult for ordinary people: it's not!

● reading it just as literature or geography or history: it *is* these things, but *more*: it's the message that matters.

● reading it as magic, or fables, or fairy-stories . . . the Bible was written by real people in real situations as they were inspired by God.

What section of the Bible is it?

NEW TESTAMENT

GOSPEL

ACTS

LETTER

REVELATION

What sort of book is it?

What happened? Where? To whom? Why was the story told? Is this a story-with-a-point?

Is this moral law, for all time? Or matters of social or ceremonial law? If the latter, what point was being expressed, or general principle?

Don't read poetry as if it's prose! Expect imagery, picture language. Instead of rhyme, Hebrew poetry said things twice in different words.

What was the historical setting, the story behind the passage? Is the writing poetic, symbolic? What was the original purpose of the prophecy?

What did the passage mean to the original readers or hearers? How does the same message apply today?

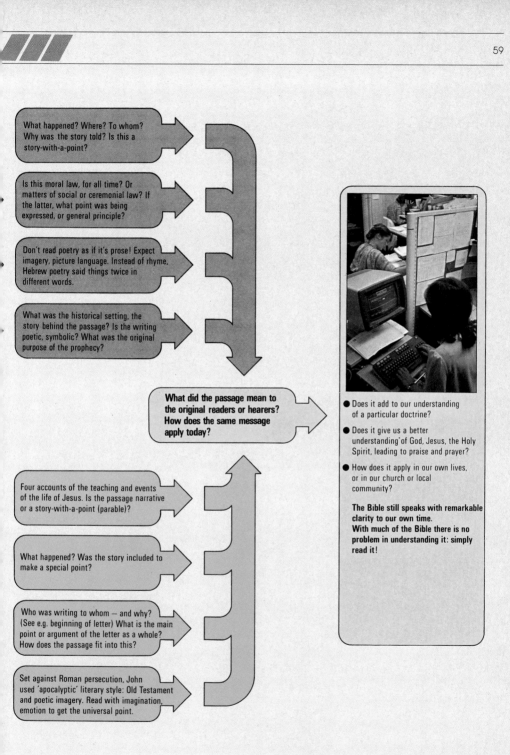

- Does it add to our understanding of a particular doctrine?

- Does it give us a better understanding of God, Jesus, the Holy Spirit, leading to praise and prayer?

- How does it apply in our own lives, or in our church or local community?

The Bible still speaks with remarkable clarity to our own time. With much of the Bible there is no problem in understanding it: simply read it!

Four accounts of the teaching and events of the life of Jesus. Is the passage narrative or a story-with-a-point (parable)?

What happened? Was the story included to make a special point?

Who was writing to whom — and why? (See e.g. beginning of letter) What is the main point or argument of the letter as a whole? How does the passage fit into this?

Set against Roman persecution, John used 'apocalyptic' literary style: Old Testament and poetic imagery. Read with imagination, emotion to get the universal point.

The Bible and Society
SIR FRED CATHERWOOD

God created the universe. He sustains it. He cares for the whole of mankind and has given us in the Bible a guide-book by which to live.

The Bible tells us how to conduct ourselves in relation to God and to our fellow men. And since God is timeless, the wisdom of the Bible is timeless too.

The Bible is not only relevant to individuals, it is relevant to society. Christianity is not just for private behaviour and public worship. It is a world system which competes with other world systems. It argues on more than equal terms with Marxism, Existentialism, Nationalism, Capitalism. Each of these systems is based on its own particular view of human behaviour, and all have their own standards of morals. The Christian believes that since the Christian teaching is true, it will be more useful and more relevant than that of any other system. The Bible offers to twentieth-century man the very thing he cries out for.

THE BIBLE ANSWERS FUNDAMENTAL HUMAN NEEDS

Deuteronomy 6:24

If there is no God, there can be no divine law. If there is no divine law men must try to agree among themselves what is right and what is wrong. But if they disagree, who is to have the last word? So classes and nations fight it out, and conflict escalates as external authority is removed.

The Bible declares that there is an external morality given by God for the good of all mankind. Rulers and ruled alike are answerable to him. His standards are binding on all men.

A basis for science

Other philosophies are said to depend on science. But science itself is based on Christian teaching. It was belief in a God of order, a God of reason, a God of unchanging decrees, which led to the development of the scientific method in the 17th century. When science forsakes this basis it loses its way. Some people have made a god of it. Many are now rejecting it altogether. Its hope lies in a return to its Christian basis.

A realistic view of man

Evil is all too apparent in our world. Education does

not eradicate it, nor does an improved environment.
Revolution and change of government all too often
mean simply exchanging one set of evils for another.
The Bible explains why. Evil is not simply external, it
is deep inside man himself. The initial disobedience to
the Creator has left human nature with a permanent,
in-born bias to evil. Neither reason nor force will
change this. The Bible also teaches that God provides
all men with certain common benefits – conscience, the
recognition of right and wrong, and certain institutions
(family, state, church) which encourage good and
discourage evil.

Humanity restored

The all-pervasive rationalism of our own century,
infiltrating our whole culture and philosophy, has
reduced man to an animal, condemned to a meaningless existence terminated by death. But men cry out
against this. They feel there is something outside the
box of time and space in which they find themselves.
And they grope instinctively after the Christian truth
that man is not just body, he is soul and spirit too. He
is not just a passing atom of an overwhelming universe,
but is of eternal significance.

THE BIBLE AND THE SOCIAL ORDER

The Bible's relevance is not confined to broad generalities. It enables us to understand and evaluate
ourselves and the world we live in. It provides us with
a world-view – a philosophy to live by. But it speaks
also to practical situations, to the way we run our lives
and order our society.

Much of the Bible's teaching goes back to the way
we are made; it goes back to creation itself. The same
basic principles were backed up in Old Testament law
and, in the New Testament, reinforced by Jesus himself.

The Old Testament ceremonial law came to an end
at the crucifixion, its purpose fulfilled. The civil law
applied directly only to Israel as a nation and cannot
be lifted out of its context, though many of the principles it embodies are still highly relevant to modern
society. But the moral law of the Old Testament retains
eternal validity. Men may be forced to change their
laws but God does not change his. This moral law includes the Ten Commandments. Christ came to fulfil
the moral law, not to destroy it. He pointed out its full
implications in the Sermon on the Mount and elsewhere. Not only was the act of adultery wrong, but even
a lustful look. The moral law had been covered with

Genesis 3; Jeremiah 17:9;
Matthew 15:18-19

Genesis 1:26-31
Psalm 8:3-8

Hebrews 9

Exodus 20
Matthew 5:17-48

Many of the Bible's laws applied the principles of love and concern for others to people in a rural economy. In many parts of the world they still apply in the same way today. But often in industrial societies the same principles have to be worked out in fresh ways for the teaching to be relevant.

Deuteronomy 23:19-20

Leviticus 25

Romans 13:1-7

Exodus 21-22

casuistry and hypocrisy. Christ ripped away the cover and put men's obligations to their fellow men on full view.

Not only is the Christian moral law valid for all time, it applies to all men. Though they may find the standards high, most people believe in right and wrong, truth and falsehood. The Christian law has wide support – and for good reason.

A law that protects the weak

The large mass of the world's population is open to exploitation of one kind or another. The Christian moral law is a bulwark against this, whenever men can be taught to respect it. It protects the weak against the strong, the poor against the rich, the women and children, fatherless and widows against those who would neglect and exploit them.

The intention of the Old Testament law on usury, for example, was to make a man use his good fortune to help tide his less fortunate neighbour over a bad patch until he could again become self-sufficient. The law protected farmers living near subsistence level who needed something to carry them over from one harvest to the next, especially if the harvest had been bad. Without some such law the rich could hold the poor to ransom. They could charge such a rate of interest that the poor farmer would have to sell his land to pay it. It was certainly not a prohibition on lending money at a rate of interest which can be earned by the recipient. Lending of unused savings is vital to economic development.

Most people agree that the moral law protects the weak. The trades unionist suspects that in competitive capitalism the weak go to the wall. The working man takes naturally to a creed which aims to help the weak.

Similarly, the principle of the law of Jubilee was that the rich should not be allowed to accumulate all property rights. Every fifty years there was a redistribution of land back to the original owners.

The concept of law and order

The Christian law protects society against chaos. The civil power, Paul tells the Romans, is ordained by God to uphold good and suppress evil.

When it comes to crime and punishment, the penalties laid down in the Old Testament for offences against the person are more severe than for offences against property. People matter more than things – an ideal we are often in danger of forgetting today.

Crime demands just punishment. But the criminal

must be treated with compassion. So the Christian stands between the 'hard' line on punishment and the 'soft'. The Old Testament laws endeavoured to ensure that punishment was no greater than the offence, and in any case was less than private retribution. Christ himself said to the woman caught in adultery – for which the punishment was death – 'Go, and do not sin again.'

At the other extreme, the Christian is not at liberty to base his view of crime and punishment on the pre-supposition that all crime is just another kind of sickness, and just as capable of cure. The Bible sees crime as a moral act for which the criminal is responsible, which sickness is not. The Christian's concern for the reform of the criminal should never make him either deny the offence or fail to protect society against the offender. But once the sentence has been paid, the criminal is entitled to society's help to become a good citizen.

One danger of treating all crime as sickness is that it makes the criminal a second-class citizen. A judge's sentence is normally limited by the nature of the offence, but a doctor can detain until he decides a

ohn 8:11

Initially the scientific method was based on Christian principles derived from the Bible. Many believe that science will be restored to a sure basis today if scientists return to the theism which gives it its true perspective.

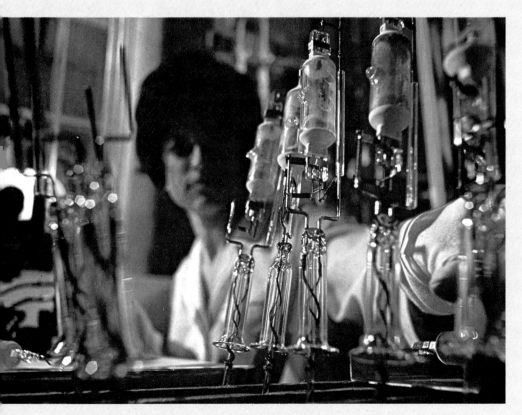

patient is cured. And if an objective moral standard is thrown over, what is to stop the majority in society – or even a minority in power – from putting away in a mental institution those who do not see eye to eye with them until they are 'cured'? It has been done.

Support for the family

The Christian law protects the basic institution of society – the family. The Bible has a great deal to say about the concept of the family, and the Christian ideal differs markedly from some current concepts.

Matthew 19:5-6

The idea of permanence is basic to Christian marriage. This gives security to both partners and children. Relationships can be far freer within a secure framework than when partners or children have to take into account the possible collapse of the whole basic structure. The strains arising from insecurity can often precipitate collapse. Whole new areas of jealousy and friction arise.

The Bible nowhere allows divorce on the grounds of incompatibility. There are some incompatibilities in every marriage. But the Bible sets marriage in a wider context. It is not just a romantic attachment between two individuals to the exclusion of the world at large. The wider family on both sides is involved. So too is society. The wider family protects husband and wife, as well as children, from the stresses and strains of today's tiny nuclear family, where all contact with uncles, aunts, cousins and even grandparents is limited to a weekly long-distance phone-call.

The Christian ideal is marriage between one man and one woman – a factor which has greatly raised the status of women in the world. Anyone inclined to question the advisability of monogamy should read of the troubles of Jacob, David and others who took more than one wife. The husband is to cherish his wife. He has no absolute rights over her. But he is, none the less, the head of the family, the final arbiter.

Ephesians 5:21-33

Strictly speaking, the Bible regards pre-marital sex as a contradiction in terms. Living together in physical union *is* marriage. The two partners become one flesh. But it cannot stop there. Marriage is social as well as physical. It involves leaving parents. It involves other people – society generally. The marriage ceremony gives recognition to this. The one ground of divorce seemingly allowed by Christ is the adultery of one or other partner with a third person.

Genesis 2:24;
1 Corinthians 6:16

Matthew 19:1-9

Sex, as seen in the Bible, is part and parcel of a wider relationship. It should be the expression of a lasting respect and self-sacrificing love. Within that relationship it increases the love and respect. Outside it, it

Samuel 13

the clash of ideologies today the Bible speaks with renewed force: philosophies which do not do justice to its basic teaching on the nature of man and society do not take account of man as he is and as he is designed to be.

seems to have the opposite effect. And the woman, because of her greater dependence, is usually the loser.

Promiscuity has always been with us. No one knows what society would be like if everyone acted on the advice of those who openly advocate it. Even so, the majority of mankind do not find this view practicable or desirable. The Christian view of marriage on the other hand is both practical and a good deal happier than any alternative.

THE OFFER OF NEW LIFE

Romans 3:9-26

These are simply illustrations of the Bible's relevance to present-day society, to modern man. They are based primarily on creation and a law which is true to man and society as they really are.

But the Bible does not limit itself to God's law for humanity. It recognizes that man is unable either to keep these laws, or to make reparation for his offences against a holy God. So the law is intended not simply to regulate conduct in an imperfect world, but to show up our imperfections and so lead us to Christ.

For Christ, by his death, has served sentence for our sin, and offers forgiveness and a new life to all men. To Christians of all generations for two thousand years and of all nations and races, this is the supreme reality. They know forgiveness. They know fellowship with God through prayer and worship. They know the presence of the Holy Spirit who changes their lives. They know that God's laws are good and true. For them the Bible is not just a realistic book about human nature. They have put it to the test and found it true.

The Bible and Christian Doctrine

HOWARD MARSHALL

What we believe determines how we live. So Christians cannot say, 'I have no time for doctrine.' Doctrine is not an optional extra. What we believe affects our whole way of life.

As Christians we are followers of Christ. We will want to do what he has told us to do. 'If you love me', he said, 'you will keep my commandments.' So this involves finding out what Jesus actually taught. It involves, too, finding out what his apostles taught, how they explained his coming and death and resurrection and how this works out for his followers and his church.

Jesus' view of the Bible must become ours, too, if we are to follow him. It will become our source-book, our inspiration, the source not only of our devotion but of our basic beliefs which will mould our characters and our lives. For our beliefs will be brought to bear on our society, our job, our whole system of values. It is vital that we should build a body of belief, a body of doctrine, that will be true to what is taught by Jesus and taught in the whole Bible.

THE SOURCE OF CHRISTIAN BELIEF

The Bible is the account of how God spoke to a variety of people in their own particular situations over a period of centuries. It is a historical record, not a systematic tabulation of doctrine.

So the teaching of the Bible on a particular subject, such as God, man, evil, the church, is built up by bringing together teaching from various parts of the Bible until we have the whole picture. We are looking for the sum total of a revelation given 'in many and various ways', as the writer to the Hebrews put it.

From Old Testament to New

An immediate practical question is the relation of the various parts of the Bible to each other. The Old Testament is incomplete without the New. There was a development in understanding and in the revelation God gave.

This means that the New Testament must clearly have the last word. What is said in the Old Testament must not be taken in isolation: it must be seen in the context of the total revelation of God.

The same kind of problem can arise in the New Testament as well. If we try to construct a doctrine of the Christian life solely from the Gospels, we will find that the main theme is the relation of disciples to their Master. But we would miss out on all the rest of the teaching of the New Testament: the teaching on our relationship with a crucified and risen Saviour.

In the same way it would be possible to concentrate wholly on the teaching in the letters about spiritual union with Christ, and to forget what the Gospels say about the very practical commands Jesus gave to his disciples during his earthly life. So we must balance our teaching from the various parts of the Bible, though making the New Testament regulative.

Text and context

We must also make sure that we do not lift texts out of context and make them mean what we want.

The Bible is not a collection of timeless truths which can be combined with each other forthwith without any regard for their original setting and purpose. We cannot simply cull them from all parts of the Bible and add them together to make a doctrine. The meaning of a statement is partly dependent on its context. We must make sure that a verse is understood in the light of the whole passage from which it is taken, when considering what it is saying about a particular doctrine.

WORDS AND THOUGHT-FORMS

When John wrote to the people of his time, 'the Word became flesh', he was sharing a common understanding of the terms 'word' and 'flesh'. So he could express his meaning in a way the readers could understand.

But these expressions may mean something rather different in modern speech. So we cannot build up our doctrines, or compile our theology, simply by repeating the biblical statements without regard for the meaning of the terms then and now. We have the added responsibility of re-expressing the statements so that their original meaning is clear to people today. If some of the biblical terms no longer make sense, we must try to find fresh ones

'Do not let the world squeeze you into its own mould,' wrote Paul to the Romans (12:2, Phillips). What we believe inevitably affects how we live. This relief from Roman times is shown beside the mould from which it was made.

which will get the meaning across without any loss of content.

A job for the expert?

All this may make it seem very difficult to use the Bible as our source for Christian doctrine. Certainly we need to be aware of the difficulties. But we must not exaggerate them.

First, the Bible was written to be intelligible to ordinary people. This is what the Reformers meant by the 'perspicuity' of Holy Scripture, and it is a principle which is accepted by other traditions today as well. The Bible is clear enough not to require the interposition of a priestly caste to explain its secrets to the uncomprehending layman. Nor do we need to have a new generation of scholars to take over from the priests, to mediate the essential message of the Bible to the ordinary person!

Second, there is an accumulated wisdom of biblical interpretation amassed over the centuries. It would be short-sighted and stupid of us to rest content with our own investigations and to bypass the results of much Christian study of the Bible. We will want to check our own findings with the body of agreed doctrine. Or we will want to take the agreed doctrine and make it our own by seeing how it is worked out from Scripture itself.

BIBLE DOCTRINE AND MODERN THOUGHT

Having worked out what the Bible teaches in a coherent, systematic form, a further step remains. The Bible presents the word of God spoken to men at particular periods of history and in the context of their problems and needs. It does not deal with the whole of human research and knowledge, and it would be unreasonable to expect it to do so.

So we have to relate what the Bible says to the rest of human knowledge, and the rest of human knowledge to what the Bible says.

Scientific knowledge

For example, the Bible speaks of God's creation of the universe, but the Bible is not a textbook of science. What the Bible says about creation has to be related to the discoveries of the scientist. All truth is God's truth. God, who speaks in 'special revelation' in the Bible, also speaks in 'general revelation' by means of scientific research and discovery. The Bible must have supreme authority if there is any apparent clash, for that alone does justice to the teaching of Jesus and to the claims of the Bible for itself. But God's truth will not be contradictory: we will seek further light on the problem.

Man is a fallen creature, whose mind has been blinded by sin. So what the scientist says may be false and inadequate, or based on false presuppositions. But we too are fallen creatures liable to error, so we shall try to evaluate every kind of statement in the light of the word of God. And we must do all we can to hear and understand the word of God clearly and correctly. Only in this way can we hope to bring together the knowledge of God and the universe given in the Bible and given through general revelation and so arrive at a unified picture.

FROM FAITH TO LIFE

God can be known to us only in so far as he reveals himself. We have no means of knowing him otherwise. We have no real knowledge of Jesus Christ except what we read of him in the Bible. We can know nothing of the joy of the Christian life, or the life and fellowship of the church, unless we go for an understanding of them to the Bible God has given us.

So every Christian must build up a clear understanding of what the Bible teaches on major themes (see Part Four). Only in this way will he have a Christian basis to living. For it is what we believe that will inevitably be expressed in our daily life.

exts and Versions

ONALD GUTHRIE

Our Bible is a collection of no fewer than 66 books. Their origins stretch back over hundreds of years. The story of how the Bible was written and handed down to us, and how the various books came to be selected, is a fascinating one. It is also vital for us, since the Bible is the basis of belief and teaching for the whole Christian church.

THE TEXT OF THE OLD TESTAMENT

It is difficult to investigate the history of the Old Testament text and the collection of the books simply because much of the material is so very old. There is also the added difficulty that the Hebrews destroyed old manuscripts when new texts had been made from them. Until the

remarkable discovery of the Qumran library – the Dead Sea Scrolls – in 1947, the earliest Hebrew manuscripts of any part of the Old Testament which we possessed were 9th-century AD copies of the Pentateuch, the first five books of the Bible, and of the historical and prophetic books. These manuscripts preserve what is known as the 'Massoretic text', which was edited into a fixed form about AD 500. All the later manuscripts agree closely with these 9th-century texts, which is a testimony to the remarkable care taken by the scribes who copied out the Hebrew text.

The evidence from Qumran takes us back a further 1,000 years, to the 1st century BC. Only a few complete texts of Old Testament books have been preserved, but even the fragmentary texts are of very great value in confirming the careful way in which the text was transmitted. These finds give us added confidence that it was preserved through earlier periods with equal care. Obviously, we should like older evidence still about the more ancient parts of the Old Testament. But the fact that the Jews preserved their scriptures so accurately over many centuries says much for the reliability of the text. Of course this does not mean there are no problems. There are a number of places where the original text is uncertain, and the editor or translator simply has to be guided by what is most likely.

In 1947 Bedouin shepherds, entering one of these caves, found a priceless treasure. Inside the caves were the Dead Sea Scrolls, manuscripts of Old Testament and other books dating back to before the time of Christ. Nearby are the ruins of Qumran, the 'monastery' of a community which must have hidden its library of scrolls in the caves because of the impending Roman invasion.

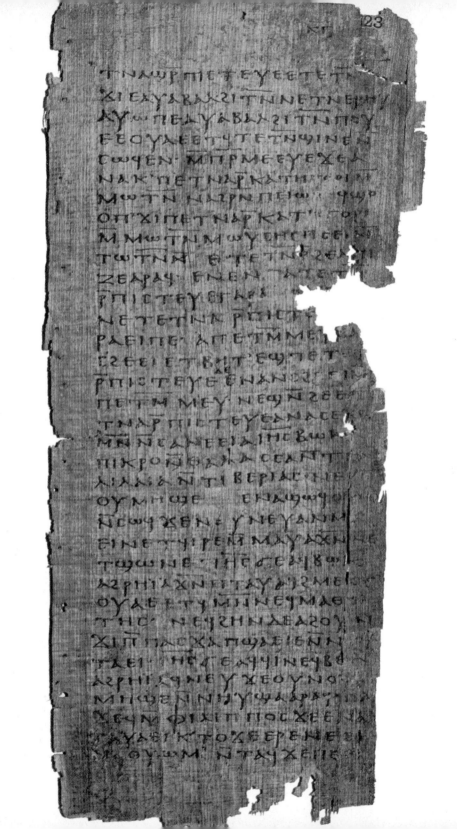

ⲧⲛⲁ̣ϣⲣ ⲡⲓⲥⲧⲉⲩⲉ ⲉ ⲧⲉⲧ
ⲭⲓ ⲉ ⲁⲩ ⲁⲃⲁⲗ ϩⲓⲧⲛ ⲛⲉⲧⲛⲉⲣ̣ⲏ̣ⲩ̣
ⲁⲩⲱ ⲡⲉⲗ ⲁⲩ ⲁⲃⲁⲗ ϩⲓⲧⲛ ⲡ̄ⲥⲟⲩ
ⲉ ⲟⲩ ⲁⲉⲉ ⲧⲩ ⲧⲉⲧⲛ ϣⲓⲛⲉ ⲛ
ⲥⲱ ϥ ⲉⲛ· ⲙⲡⲣⲙⲉ ⲉⲩ ⲉ ⲭ ⲁⲗ
ⲛⲁⲕ ⲡⲉⲧⲛⲁⲣ ⲕⲁ ⲧⲏⲧ̣ ⲟⲓⲛ
ⲙⲱⲧⲛ· ⲛⲗⲁⲣⲛ ⲡⲉ ⲓⲱ· ϭⲱⲣ
ⲟⲡ· ⲭⲓⲡⲉⲧⲛⲁⲣ ⲕⲁⲧ· ⲟⲩ
ⲙⲙⲱⲧⲛ· ⲙⲟⲩ ⲉ ⲏ ⲥ ⲉ ⲉⲓ ⲉⲓ
ⲧⲱⲧⲛⲁ· ⲉ ⲧⲉⲧⲛ ϫⲉ ⲭ ⲓ
ϩ ⲉ ⲁⲣ ⲁⲩ· ⲉⲛ ⲉⲛ· ⲡⲓⲉ ⲧ
ⲣ ⲡⲓⲥⲧⲉⲩ ⲉ ⲧ ⲁⲉⲓ·
ⲛⲉ ⲧⲉⲧⲛ ⲁ ⲣ ⲡⲓⲥⲧⲧ
ⲣⲁ ⲉ ⲓ ⲡⲉ· ⲁ ⲡⲉ ⲧ ⲙ ⲙⲉ ⲟ
ⲉ ϩ ⲉ ⲉⲓ ⲉ ⲧ ⲃ ⲏ ⲧ· ⲉ ϥ ⲡⲉ ⲧ
ⲣ ⲡⲓⲥⲧⲉⲩ ⲉ ⲉ ϩⲁ ⲛ ⲁ ⲥ ⲉⲓ ⲛ
ⲡⲉⲧⲙ ⲙⲉ ⲩ· ⲛⲉ ϥ ⲛ̄ ϩⲉ ⲉ
ⲧ ⲛ ⲁ ⲣ ⲡⲓⲥⲧⲉⲩ ⲉ ⲁ ⲛ ⲁ ⲥ ⲉ ⲟ
ⲙⲛ̄ ⲥ ⲁ ⲛ ⲉ ⲉ ⲓ ⲁ ⲓ ⲡ ⲉ ⲃ ⲱ ⲕ
ⲡ ⲓ ⲕ ⲣ ⲟ ⲛ ⲟ ⲃ ⲁ ⲗ ⲁ ⲥ ⲉ ⲁ ⲛ ⲧ
ⲗ ⲓ ⲗ ⲁ ⲛ ⲧ ⲓ ⲃ ⲉ ⲣ ⲓ ⲁ ⲥ ⲡ ⲉ ⲩ ⲧ
ⲟ ⲩ ⲙ ⲙ ⲟ ⲩ ⲉ· ⲉ ⲛ ⲁ ⲱ ⲱ ϫ ⲟ
ⲛ ⲉ ⲱ ϥ ϫⲉ ⲛ· ⲩ ⲛ ⲉ ⲩ ⲁ ⲗ ⲓ ⲛ
ⲉ ⲓ ⲛ ⲉ ⲧ ϥ ⲓ ⲣ ⲉ ⲙ ⲙ ⲁ ⲩ ⲁ ⲭ ⲛ ⲏ ⲉ
ⲧ ⲱ ϣ ⲱ ⲛ ⲉ· ⲓ ⲏ ⲥ ϭ ⲉ ⲝ ⲓ ⲃ ⲁ ⲗ
ⲁ ⲣ ⲏ ⲓ ⲁ ⲭ ⲛ ⲉ ⲓ ⲧ ⲁ ⲩ ⲁ ⲥ ⲙ ⲉ ⲓ
ⲟ ⲩ ⲁ ⲉ· ⲧ ⲩ ⲙ ⲏ ⲛ ⲉ ⲩ ⲡ ⲛ ⲉ ⲩ ⲙ ⲁ ⲑ
ⲧ ⲏ ⲥ· ⲛ ⲉ ⲩ ϩ ⲏ ⲛ ⲁ ⲃ ⲁ ⲗ ⲟ ⲩ ⲛ
ⲭ ⲓ ⲡ ⲛ ⲁ ⲥ ⲭ ⲁ ⲡ ⲱ ⲗ ⲉ ⲉ ⲛ ⲛ
ⲧ ⲁ ⲉ ⲓ· ⲡ ⲉ ϫ ⲉ ⲁ ⲩ ϣ ⲓ ⲛ ⲉ ⲩ ⲃ ⲁ
ⲁ ⲣ ⲏ ⲓ ⲉ ϭ ⲛ ⲉ ⲩ ⲭ ⲉ ⲟ ⲩ ⲛ ⲟ
ⲙ ⲓ ⲕ ⲩ ⲉ ⲛ ⲛ ⲏ ⲩ ϭ ⲱ ⲁ ⲣ ⲭ ⲓ ⲛ
ⲭ ⲉ ⲩ ⲛ̄ ϥ ⲓ ⲭ ⲓ ⲡ ⲓ ⲟ ⲥ ⲭ ⲉ ⲉ ⲛ ⲁ
ⲁ ⲩ ⲁ ⲉ ⲓ ⲕ ⲧ ⲟ ⲭ ⲉ ⲉ ⲣ ⲉ ⲛ ⲉ ⲉ ⲓ
ⲙ ⲟ ⲩ ⲱ ⲙ̄ ⲛ ⲧ ⲁ ⲩ ⲭ ⲉ ⲡ ⲉ

The first Bible translation

Even in these instances, though, it is not just a matter of guesswork. We have the help of the Greek version of the Old Testament, the Septuagint (LXX). This was the version used by Greek-speaking Jews at the beginning of the Christian era, and by the early Christians. Its origin is uncertain, but tradition traces the Septuagint back to the time of Ptolemy Philadelphus of Egypt (285-246 BC).

The Dead Sea Scrolls have also provided us with our earliest manuscripts of parts of the Old Testament in Greek. And again there is a close similarity with previously-known LXX texts – although variations have led some scholars to wonder whether the Qumran evidence reveals an earlier text. In principle, however, the Hebrew text carries more weight than the Greek, since the Greek editors took a good many liberties in translation. Even so, there may well be cases where the Greek text has preserved a more ancient text than existing Hebrew manuscripts.

In addition to the LXX, other Greek texts circulated during the early centuries of the Christian era. Origen of Alexandria compiled a book known as *Hexapla* in which he set out the Hebrew and LXX texts in parallel columns, together with texts by Aquila, Symmachus and Theodotion, and finally his own revision of the text. In only one instance did these other versions compete with the LXX: at an early date Theodotion's translation of the book of Daniel was substituted for the much poorer original in the LXX. After Origen, other editions were made by Christian editors (Lucian, Hesychius).

As the Christian church spread to parts of the world where Greek was not spoken, translations were made into Latin, Syriac, and Egyptian, alongside the developments in the New Testament text mentioned below.

THE FORMATION OF THE OLD TESTAMENT

The history of how the collection of acknowledged books ('canon') of the Old Testament came to be formed is also difficult to establish because of lack of information. But there is enough to show what the Old Testament contained during the period immediately before the Christian era. And this goes a long way towards establishing what Jesus and the apostles would have regarded as Scripture. There is a strong Jewish tradition that it was Ezra the scribe who arranged the canon, although collections of the Pentateuch and some of the prophets existed long before his time.

The books of the Hebrew canon were arranged in three groups – the Law, the Prophets and the Writings (which included the Wisdom literature, some historical works such as Ezra, Nehemiah and Chronicles, and one prophetic book, Daniel). The prologue to the apocryphal *Book of Sirach* or *Ecclesiasticus* (about 130 BC) contains evidence of this threefold grouping, but no indication of the contents of each section. The manuscripts of the Qumran library include texts or fragments of all the Old Testament books except the book of Esther (which may yet come to light).

Josephus, the first-century AD historian, acknowledged 22 books; the *Apocalypse of Ezra* (about AD100) acknowledged 24. If Josephus included Ruth with Judges and Lamentations with Jeremiah the two agree. The 24 books of the Hebrew canon are equivalent to the 39 books of the Greek canon (since Samuel, Kings, Chronicles, Ezra-Nehemiah and the twelve minor prophets counted as only one book each in the Hebrew list). Most of the books in our own Old Testament are quoted in the New Testament, which suggests that the Old Testament canon which Jesus used was identical to that generally used among the Jews and known to Josephus. The books known as

A papyrus of John's Gospel, written in Coptic in the 4th century. It contains 43 pages written on both sides – almost the whole of the Gospel.

the Apocrypha (Deuterocanonicals), which were included in the Greek canon but excluded from the Hebrew, were clearly not accepted on the same footing as Scripture in the age of the apostles. They are never quoted as authoritative in the New Testament. Later in certain circles there was a greater regard for these books, but where the Hebrew text was regarded as authoritative, the Apocryphal books were not regarded as canonical.

THE TEXT OF THE NEW TESTAMENT

When we turn to the New Testament text we are confronted with such a mass of evidence that the problem is to find some basic principle of editing. We possess thousands of manuscripts: a striking contrast to the very few extant manuscripts of classical Greek authors. Not only are there thousands of Greek manuscripts; there are also a great many manuscripts of translations into Latin, Syriac, Egyptian and other languages. We also have New Testament quotations in the writings of the early church fathers. But this evidence must be used with caution, since they are not all noted for their accuracy.

The great majority of the Greek manuscripts contain a text which became standardized in the 5th century. A few manuscripts seem to preserve a much earlier text, and textual editors attach much greater importance to these. The first printed edition of the Greek text was Erasmus's text, published in 1516. Before this there had been no thought of examining the history of the text. The complete authenticity of the standardized text – also supported by the Latin Bible (the Vulgate) – was assumed without question. Several editions published in the 16th and 17th centuries noted the evidence of manuscripts which differed from the standard text. The most notable of these were the editions of Stephanus, which formed the basis of the King James' Version in

England, and that of Elzevir, which became the standard continental text (it was this that claimed the name 'Textus Receptus', or Received Text).

The standard text itself, however, remained largely unaltered, until textual critics began to investigate its history in the 18th and 19th centuries. They discovered that many older manuscripts deviated from it. Bengel was one scholar who helped to establish the principle that the age and quality of a manuscript was more important than the sheer quantity of witnesses to a particular reading. Other scholars (Griesbach, for example) developed the idea of grouping manuscripts into families on the basis of certain characteristics. This resulted in the rejection of the 5th-century standardized text and the substitution of older groups, for example, the Alexandrian (or Neutral) text and the Western text.

Variations in manuscripts

Ancient methods of publishing were very different from today's. Manuscripts were usually reproduced by a group of scribes writing at the dictation of the chief scribe. Inevitably they occasionally misheard and made mistakes, but these are generally easy to detect. Where one scribe worked alone, producing a single copy of a manuscript, he might make the odd mistake through misreading his text. Because of the labour involved in producing handwritten manuscripts they were too expensive for general use and tended to be preserved for the use of groups – as they were in the Christian churches.

The form of manuscript used in the early church was the papyrus, leather or parchment scroll, which had been in use for centuries. But there is good reason to believe that quite early on (in the 2nd century AD) Christians began using the 'codex' or book form, for ease of reference. The whole New Testament would fill a number of scrolls, but could be included in one codex when the smaller cursive style of writing was used.

Manuscripts of the New Testament

Among the most important manuscripts now known are two groups of manuscripts written on papyrus – the Bodmer Papyri (one of which dates from the end of the 2nd century) and the Chester Beatty Papyri (which are generally dated in the early or mid-3rd century). Both of these groups are fragmentary. But we have two manuscripts, produced during the 4th century by professional scribes at Alexandria, which contain much more of the New Testament. In fact, Codex Sinaiticus contains the whole New Testament. And the slightly older Codex Vaticanus takes us as far as Hebrews 9:13.

Neither of these manuscripts was used in the preparation of the Authorized Version. But almost all authorities on the text agree that they preserve a better text than the standardized 5th-century one, which shows clear signs of having been edited. These two manuscripts formed the basis of the text prepared by the 19th-century scholars Westcott and Hort, and the parallel text used by the editors of the Revised Version. The papyrus manuscripts mentioned above were then unknown, but they have been used in the most recent editions of the text.

Two and a half centuries of careful work have established a New Testament text as near as possible to the original. In a few instances there is still some doubt about the precise form of the text, but these are of minor importance and none affects the essential teaching of the New Testament.

THE FORMATION OF THE NEW TESTAMENT

It is fascinating to trace the beginnings of the New Testament as we know it today. We have little early evidence, but it is easy enough to piece together what must have happened. The Old Testament was regularly read in early-church services, and it would be natural to add a reading from some authentic document about the life and death of Jesus Christ. At first the apostles themselves would provide a spoken testimony, but after their death the church needed a written record of what they had said. Their letters would have been added to the Gospels, because these gave guidance on Christian behaviour. The book of Acts would be included as a continuation of Luke's Gospel, the only authentic account of the beginnings of Christianity. The Revelation of John, too, would have had a strong appeal in a period of persecution.

But what evidence do we have of how the New Testament was formulated? We have sufficient to be able to construct a picture of the position at the close of the 2nd

A manuscript written in Syriac characters, dating from the early 13th century. It contains the Peshitta (or simple language) New Testament. It has a record not only of its owners, but also of its writer, 'the feeble man, the sinner Marcos of Yariya'.

century. By this time our four Gospels, and no others, were in official use. Irenaeus, an early-church father who had contacts with both eastern and western churches, leaves us in no doubt about the 'fourfold' Gospels. Tertullian and other church fathers of the time confirm this. Much spurious literature circulated (some of it the work of heretics) and this included 'Gospels'. But there is no evidence that any Gospel other than Matthew, Mark, Luke and John was received as Scripture within the orthodox church. By the end of the 2nd century the four Gospels and Acts were indisputably 'accepted' writings. There is also no doubt that the thirteen epistles of Paul were by this time accepted on the same level as the Gospels.

Meeting the needs of the church

There is less evidence about the remaining books apart from 1 Peter and 1 John. Indeed the history of the canon in the 3rd and 4th centuries revolves around the position of these remaining books. The book of Revelation was certainly used in the 2nd century, but it is not until the 3rd century that evidence for its use becomes widespread. The Epistle to the Hebrews was known and used at an early date (it is quoted by Clement of Rome, in about AD 95), but there was later more reluctance to receive it in the west than in the east. Origen did not believe it was written by Paul, but he did not reject it as an apostolic writing. It was not until the 4th century that it was generally received in the western church. Many churches regarded it as Paul's, but some church fathers (Augustine among them) adopted the same view as Origen. In modern times this view has been almost universally accepted.

The 'general' epistles – 2 Peter, 2 and 3 John, James and Jude – encountered resistance in some of the churches, but no reason is given. It would seem to have been doubt about the suitability of their contents, rather than doubt about their origin. The choice of 'approved' books was largely influenced by their suitability for public reading in church, and it is easy to see why these short letters were not much used for this purpose.

So far nothing has been said about church councils. The reason is that no church council made any pronouncement about the canon until long after it had been established and was in use in the individual churches. The books listed by the Council of Laodicea (AD 363) and the similar list agreed at the council at Carthage (AD 397) are identical with our New Testament, except that the former omitted the book of Revelation. It is clear that the New Testament canon was not the result of ecclesiastical pronouncements, but grew in accordance with the needs of the church. The major factor governing selection was 'apostolicity' – the conviction that the books represented the position of the apostolic age.

TRANSLATIONS

Some reference must be made to translations, if we are to bring the history of the Bible down to modern times. In the Middle Ages the Latin Vulgate was the church's official version. But following the Reformation there was a desire to translate the Bible into the national languages so that the people could understand it. There was also a new interest in the original languages, and a desire to base new translations on the 'original text' rather than on the Vulgate. Luther's version was officially adopted by the German Lutheran churches; and there were translations into several other European languages.

Translations into English

In England there had been many early attempts to translate parts of the Bible into English, notably by the Venerable Bede (who translated John's Gospel into Anglo-Saxon in the 7th century), King Alfred (in the 9th century) and Wycliffe.

LIGHT FOR THE WORLD

First translations of the Bible
into main languages
Partial or preliminary translations
are in brackets

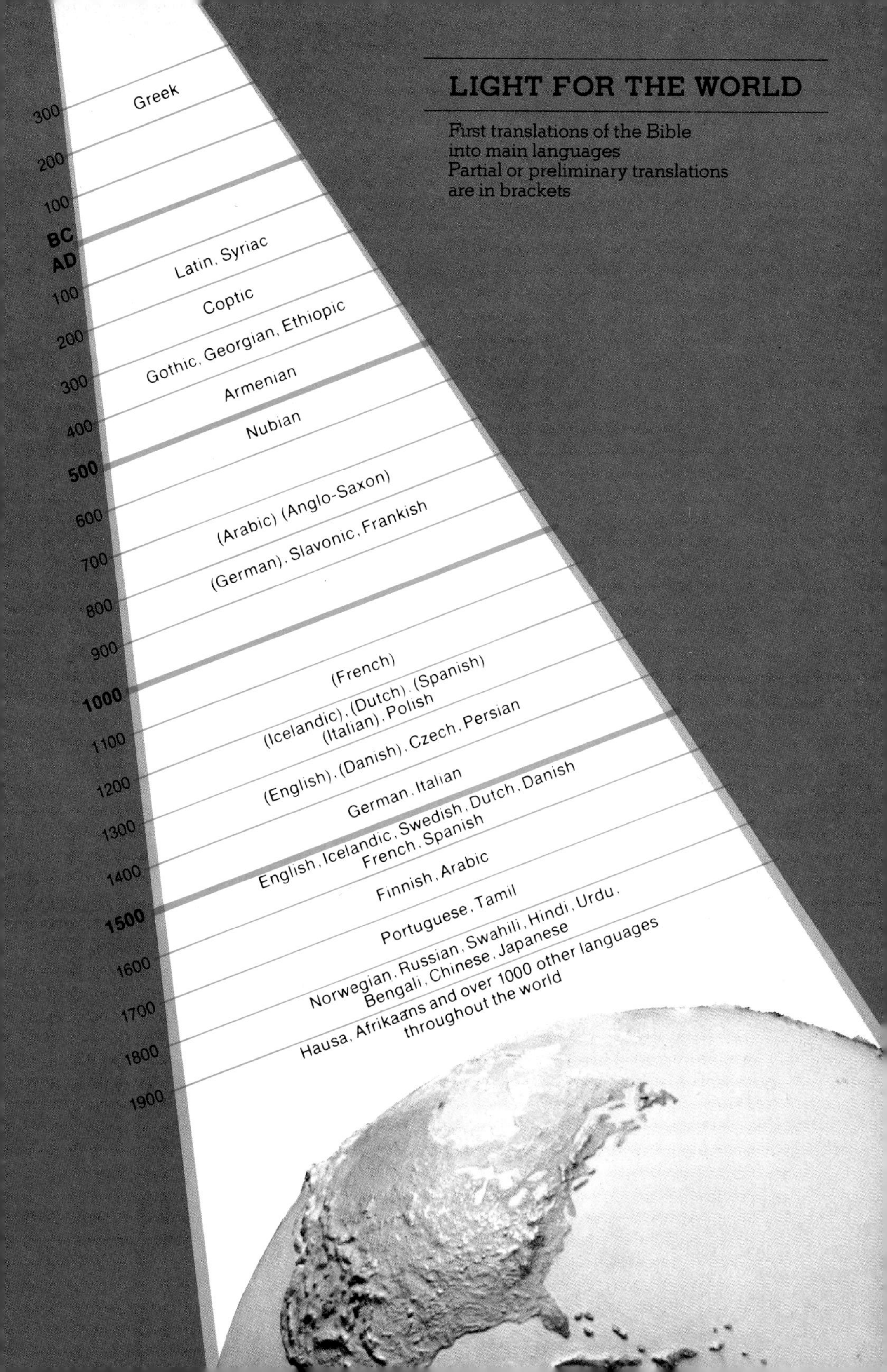

300 — Greek
200 —
100 —
BC
AD
100 — Latin, Syriac
200 — Coptic
300 — Gothic, Georgian, Ethiopic
       Armenian
400 — Nubian
500 —
600 — (Arabic) (Anglo-Saxon)
700 — (German), Slavonic, Frankish
800 —
900 —
1000 — (French)
1100 — (Icelandic), (Dutch), (Spanish)
        (Italian), Polish
        (English), (Danish), Czech, Persian
1200 — German, Italian
1300 — English, Icelandic, Swedish, Dutch, Danish
        French, Spanish
1400 — Finnish, Arabic
1500 — Portuguese, Tamil
1600 — Norwegian, Russian, Swahili, Hindi, Urdu,
        Bengali, Chinese, Japanese
1700 — Hausa, Afrikaans and over 1000 other languages
1800 —   throughout the world
1900 —

It was Tyndale who was responsible for the first printed New Testament in English, translated direct from the Greek. In 1535 Coverdale published the first full Bible in English.

Other versions followed before the publication of the Authorized, or King James' Version, in 1611. What distinguished this from the earlier printed Bibles was that it was produced by a committee of scholars. Not all the others were so representative.

In 1881 a Revised Version was produced, based on a more accurate text and aiming at a word-for-word rendering of the original. The result was not good from the point of view of modern idiom, which led to the production of other texts such as the Revised Standard Version, New English Bible and Good News Bible – these last two specifically setting out to use contemporary idiom. In addition, a number of individuals – Weymouth, Moffatt, Phillips, Taylor and others – have produced their own versions.

At the end of the 18th and the beginning of the 19th centuries, Bible Societies were founded to serve the missionary outreach of the churches. Their aim has been to prepare and print copies of the Bible (or parts of the Bible) in as many languages as possible. The number of versions they have prepared and circulated already runs into several hundreds, and specialist groups, such as the Wycliffe Bible Translators, are working to fill many of the gaps that remain.

The first complete Bible in English was the work of the Oxford scholar John Wycliffe and his followers. A renewed understanding of the gospel drove them to translate the life-giving Bible for ordinary people. This manuscript copy of the New Testament, dating from about 1420, is one of 170 surviving today.

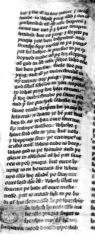

William Tyndale's translation of the Bible into English in 1526 had to be smuggled into Britain at first, such was the opposition to the idea of a version not only in the common tongue but also translated from the original Hebrew and Greek rather than Latin. This edition of his New Testament dates from 1535, and is thought to be the last revised by the translator himself, who was put to death for his efforts.

The earliest edition of the New Testament to be printed in a language of India is this version in Tamil. It was translated in 1714-15 by Bartholomäus Ziegenbalg, an early missionary to India, assisted by Johann Ernst Gründler.

The first Bible in Chinese was translated by Robert Morrison and his colleague William Milne and published in Canton in 1823. This edition of Acts (in 'High Wenli') was produced earlier, in 1810.

The first edition of the letter to the Romans in Yoruba, the language spoken in the south-western part of Nigeria. It was produced in 1850. One of the translators was Samuel Adjai Crowther who later became Bishop of the Niger.

FIRST ENGLISH TRANSLATIONS OF THE BIBLE

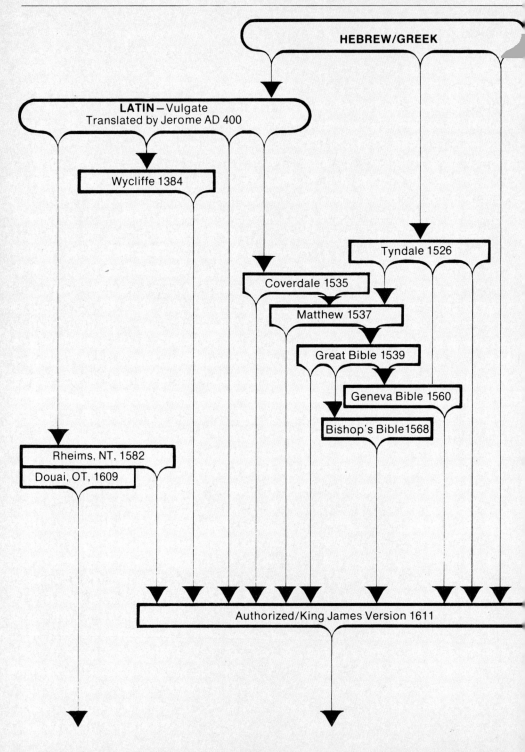

HEBREW/GREEK

LATIN—Vulgate
Translated by Jerome AD 400

Wycliffe 1384

Tyndale 1526

Coverdale 1535

Matthew 1537

Great Bible 1539

Geneva Bible 1560

Bishop's Bible 1568

Rheims, NT, 1582

Douai, OT, 1609

Authorized/King James Version 1611

Modern English Translations of the Bible

The **Authorized,** or **King James' Version** of the Bible was translated over 350 years ago. The **Revised Version** in the last century kept the same language but made revisions in the light of increased knowledge of the original Hebrew and Greek texts. In the 20th century there have been a number of new translations concerned not only to reflect an accurate text but also current English usage. Their main differences are:

■ Some are revisions (e.g. **The Revised Standard Version**), some wholly new translations from the original languages (e.g. **New English Bible, Jerusalem Bible, Good News Bible**).

■ Some use 'literary' language, including formal or academic words (e.g. **New English Bible, Jerusalem Bible**). Others use colloquial English (e.g. **The Living Bible**), or 'common' English (**Good News Bible**), the language common to both written and spoken English.

■ Some translations are concerned to keep the idiom and general force and meaning of the original; others to keep as closely as possible to the original words and sentence structure.

■ Some keep the literary forms of the original when possible, e.g. by printing poetry as such.

■ Some translations are produced by one man, others by a group.

■ Some translations are made to conserve particular theological or linguistic traditions.

THE MAIN 20th-CENTURY ENGLISH TRANSLATIONS

1903	**R. T. Weymouth,** *The New Testament in Modern Speech*	A classical scholar's translation of the New Testament into dignified modern English.
1913 and 1924	**James Moffatt,** *A New Translation of the Bible*	A free, vigorous, idiomatic translation which takes some liberties with the text.
1927	**E. J. Goodspeed,** *The Complete Bible: an American Translation*	A very readable version appreciated both in the United States and elsewhere.
1944 and 1949	**Ronald Knox,** *The Holy Bible*	A Roman Catholic translation based on the Latin Vulgate.
1946 and 1952	*The Revised Standard Version*	Revision of the American Standard Version of 1901, which was in turn a revision of the Authorized/King James' Version. Translated by a committee of 32 scholars, with the aim of producing a version which would retain the good qualities of the Authorized/King James' Version but take full account of modern scholarship.
1955	**H. J. Schonfield,** *The Authentic New Testament*	A translation by a distinguished Jewish scholar, emphasizing the Jewish background of the New Testament.
1958	*The Amplified Bible*	A version giving alternative words to suggest different possible meanings; produced by 12 editors in California.
1958	**J. B. Phillips,** *The New Testament in Modern English*	A fresh, vigorous, free translation of the New Testament; revised 1972.

1959	*The Holy Bible: The Berkeley Version in Modern English*	The New Testament is the work of a single scholar, the Old Testament the work of a team of 20, in the USA: a conservative revision concerned for accuracy.
1961 and 1970	*The New English Bible*	A completely new translation by panels of scholars taking into account the most accurate and up-to-date linguistic, textual and historical findings; sponsored by the main British churches and Bible Societies.
1963	*New American Standard Bible*	A revision of the American Revised Version by evangelical scholars; clear and readable.
1966	*The Jerusalem Bible*	Based on the textual studies of the Roman Catholic School of Biblical Studies, Jerusalem, this is a clear, accurate, scholarly translation.
1966 and 1976	*Good News Bible*	A completely new, fresh, straightforward translation in 'common' or non-academic English; produced by the American Bible Society.
1970	*The New American Bible*	A major Roman Catholic translation from the original languages, sponsored by the Bishops' Committee of the Confraternity of Christian Doctrine.
1971	**Kenneth Taylor,** *The Living Bible*	A colloquial, conservative American paraphrase designed for family reading and to help ordinary people understand the Bible.
1972 and 1979	*New International Version*	A new translation by an international team of evangelical scholars using the best results of recent research to produce a dignified version in the tradition of earlier English Bibles.
1973	*Common Bible*	American Revised Standard Version text with the Apocrypha/Deuterocanonical Books
1982	*New King James Version/ Revised Authorised Version*	A revision to deal with changes of language and the meaning of words since the 1611 edition.

The Methods and Findings of Archaeology

ALAN MILLARD

Archaeology came to birth with the scientific advances of the industrial revolution. Great quantities of earth were dug out for commercial purposes, or in the course of laying railways, and in the process different layers of soil were seen to contain different types of man-made objects. Obviously the things lying nearest the ground-surface were the most recent. In this way the study of prehistoric flint tools, especially, grew in Britain and northern Europe.

Meanwhile, the expansion of trade and rapid improvement of travelling conditions brought greater awareness of the lands where the Bible was written. Diplomats, merchants and travellers took note of the ancient remains they saw, as the fewer earlier ones had done, and some began to study them in earnest. Governments, museums and wealthy connoisseurs were eager for the prestige of owning ancient works of art and gave support to anyone able to bring back suitable pieces.

ARCHAEOLOGY: THE NEW SCIENCE

So it was that the great monuments, first from Italy and Greece, then from Egypt and Assyria, reached Europe and America. This had happened gradually through the 17th and 18th centuries, but became a large-scale business in the 19th century. Egyptology began with Napoleon's expedition to Egypt, which included a corps of learned men to survey the antiquities and remove some to France. Some of the men who proceeded to explore the Near East were no more than treasure-hunters, but many took pains to record the circumstances of discovery, planning and drawing sites, buildings and objects in detail.

Since that time the study of the past from its material remains has grown into a complex science involving more skills than a single man can command. To reap the greatest possible amount of information from ruined cities, tombs, and other ancient remains, help is sought from such varied sciences as atomic physics, bacteriology, botany, astronomy, and many more. This research is carried on in museums, universities and laboratories as much as in the actual unearthing of ancient objects. All has to be set side by side and compared with older findings before any valid results are obtained. Fresh advances in knowledge often result in a revision of earlier conclusions – a factor which should not be overlooked when archaeological discoveries appear to disagree with statements in biblical or other 'traditional' texts.

The dig

Most of the major cities named in the Bible can be identified on the ground, either by general geographical considerations, or by tradition (not always reliable), or by preservation of the ancient names among local people. In many cases it is possible to study the history of a place by digging into its ruins. But some important towns still occupy their ancient sites, and little can therefore be learnt of their material culture by this means (Damascus is a major example).

All over the Near East, mounds of debris mark the places where towns or cities once flourished (Arabic *tell*, 'mound', indicates this in place-names). Clearly, the excavation of an entire town is an impossible task. Archaeologists usually concentrate on the more rewarding parts, where temples or palaces stood, or lay out their trenches so that they probe each period of existence in the life of the place. To do this, a trench may slice right through the mound, producing a small amount of information at all levels. Each building, or time of occupation, will have left its mark on the mound in the form of floor surfaces, stumps of walls and heaps of rubbish. These will be sandwiched between earlier remains below and later remains above.

The most vital part of the excavation is to observe the features of the soil. Objects found on a hard earth floor belong roughly to the time the floor was last in use. Anything found underneath the floor is older than the floor. But if a rubbish pit was dug, cutting through older floors, things of much later date dropped into the pit may be confused with things lying in the floors it has cut through. So the archaeologist must learn to look for the tell-tale differences in the soil which show the pit's presence.

Building a picture of ancient times

On rare occasions in Palestine, more frequently in Egypt and Mesopotamia, written documents give the date when a building was in use. Failing that, the ordinary pottery of the people is a valuable guide. Fashions and processes in pottery-making varied from time to time and from place to place, so that a piece securely dated at one site by inscriptions or other means may make it possible to date a closely comparable piece found at another site where no other means of dating exists.

The pot or the inscription is of little value to the archaeologist once it is separated from its context in the soil, so it is of primary concern to note exactly where any object is found. All the notes made during excavation, the plans drawn, and photographs taken, are evaluated beside the reports from experts on particular matters. Then conclusions may be drawn about the history of the place, the daily life and cultural achievements of its people, and their religion. At this stage as complete and balanced a knowledge as possible is required. Neglect of a single section of the evidence can lead to a distorted picture. Written texts, especially, should not be interpreted apart from the material remains. Nor should the objects recovered from an excavation be

A gaming-board from about 2,600 BC, from the Royal Graves at Ur. It is made of wood decorated with a mosaic of blue lapis lazuli, shell, bone, red paste and limestone.

A 'tell' or mound – this one of the city of Lachish. The debris of successive periods of a city's existence gradually built up to form the characteristic shape of the tell.

Archaeologists at work: a trench through a tell shows the different levels, helping archaeologists piece together the history of the site.

explained without reference to written evidence when it is available.

The total knowledge drawn from a century's work on these lines would fill many volumes if it was all brought together. An impression of advances made in the past half century can be gained by comparing the new edition of the *Cambridge Ancient History* (1970 onwards) with the old one (1925) in a library.

THE ROOTS OF NEAR EASTERN CIVILIZATION

From 6,000 BC and long before – the dating rests mainly on a technique developed by atomic physics, known as Carbon 14 – people built townships depending upon their earliest attempts at cultivating edible plants, domesticating animals, and controlling the use of water. Even at this stage, people could not have carried out these projects without some sort of organized collaboration, although there is not enough evidence to tell us how society was arranged. Only a few of these early centres have been found – Jericho is the outstanding example – but they are sufficient to give a picture of slow development over the centuries.

Some time before 5,000 BC pottery came into use. Techniques of forming, firing and decorating improved over the succeeding ten centuries to reach a very high level indeed. With pottery in general use, things were often broken, and the broken pieces now show where the sites are. While there was much slow development, there were occasional spurts of progress. And there were sudden changes, too, brought about by drought, disease, or enemy action.

The oasis settlement at Jericho was

strongly defended by a stone wall and a tower over thirty feet high by about 7,000 BC. Defences of this kind can hardly have been intended simply as protection against wild animals. They indicate people's fear of one another even in so remote an age. A glimpse of their beliefs may be caught in the careful preservation of human skulls, their faces built up in clay. Whether they were revered ancestors, or trophies, or used as talismen to ward off ghosts, is not known. Human and animal figures were modelled in clay and carved in bone and stone, again for purposes now unknown. In Anatolia, vivid paintings on clay walls show, perhaps, the cult of the bull and other

Looking steeply down at an ancient tower at Jericho.

creatures. And worship of the mother-figure is found everywhere. How far any of the beliefs and rites survived into later ages can only be conjectured.

Temples and trinkets

Babylonia and Egypt saw the growth of their major cultures from 4,000 BC onwards. The need for centralized control of public works fostered larger kingdoms. The more powerful cities gradually gained wider powers. Their bureaucracies in turn encouraged the art of writing from before 3,000 BC. Trade grew in order, for instance, to bring stone for major buildings, in exchange for grain, dates or manufactured goods, or to import rare materials for the temples and the rulers. An example of these is the blue stone, lapis lazuli. This was mined in Afghanistan, but was known all over the Near East and Egypt by about 3,500 BC. The level of craftsmanship in the 4th millennium BC was very high both in Egypt and in Babylonia.

Of course, the fine objects were luxury articles, never handled by the peasants, whose humble reed and mud homes have left little to attract the archaeologist. Once the basic way of life was established in these lands, it changed little as far as the ordinary person was concerned until the industrial revolution reached them.

Bringing these roots of civilization to light is probably the most important of archaeology's findings as a whole. Many individual discoveries have given us outstanding examples of ancient skill; for example the wealth of gold and jewellers' craft in Tutankhamun's tomb and in the Royal Graves of Ur; the stupendous architecture of the pyramids, the temples of Baalbek, the city walls of Bogazkoy in Turkey or Tiryus in Greece; the carved walls of Egyptian temples and Assyrian palaces; the painted frescoes of Knossos in Crete. But the most illuminating results are always obtained by bringing together a whole range of discoveries. Perhaps two groups can be singled out

An ancient burial-cave at Jericho, with bones, and pottery for the dead to use in the next world; reconstructed at the Rockefeller Museum, Jerusalem.

for attention, objects relating to religion, and written documents.

RELIGION AND WRITING

The major beliefs and rites of state or city religions are known from texts, but the beliefs of the ordinary people – illiterate in the major centres of Egypt and Babylonia – can be recovered only from the remains of small chapels, household shrines, and the amulets and pottery figures kept to ward off evil. Some elementary medical discoveries enabled physicians to alleviate pain and effect cures for some complaints, but most illness was beyond treatment and had to be left with the gods. Demons and witchcraft could be a cause; magic would fight them. Equally, disease or any misfortune could be a divine punishment,

to be turned aside through acts of devotion and sacrifice. In a world where man's mortality was very evident, respect and fear of supernatural powers coloured every aspect of life.

Without the ruins of temples large and small, without the statues of gods and goddesses, the written documents dealing with religious affairs would be very dull, and sometimes unintelligible. And this is true of many types of text, despite their invaluable contributions. The recovery of ancient writings involves all the hazards of preservation. In Egypt the paper (papyrus) rolls only survive when they lie desiccated in the desert or uncultivated regions. Just occasionally they also survive in similar circumstances in other lands (e.g. the Dead Sea Scrolls). Babylonian clay tablets are more durable, although fragile when first found. But we have very few documents from countries such as Syria, Palestine and Greece, where paper and leather were normally used. They have simply decayed in the earth. Only when inscriptions were carved on stone for a king or state, or written on potsherds (broken pieces of pottery) by the poor who could not afford paper, did they stand a better chance of survival.

Ancient texts and daily life

As a result, some areas and periods are far better documented than others. Usually the last decades of life in a town leave more texts than the earlier ones, because

---

THE DEVELOPMENT OF WRITING

Written records go back more than 5,000 years. The earliest forms of writing were simple stylized pictures representing basic objects or ideas. The ancient Egyptians evolved the **hieroglyphic script** around 3,000 BC. This example dates from about 1,750 BC.

In Mesopotamia the early picture-writing gradually came to be represented by the wedge-shaped **cuneiform script** which was more easily impressed into clay, the readily available writing-material. This tablet was drawn up for the Royal Assyrian Library at Nineveh in the 7th century BC.

Writing took a major step forward with the development of a single symbol to represent each consonant (before 1,500 BC), greatly reducing the number of signs to be learnt. **Hebrew,** the language in which most of the Old Testament was written, has 22 consonants (the vowels were not represented at first), and reads from right to left. Later the letters came to denote numbers.

they were not thrown away. Occasionally a municipal rubbish dump is located containing the waste-paper, as has happened at a group of Graeco-Roman towns in Egypt. From these thousands of papyri (the Oxyrhynchus Papyri) sufficient information has been gleaned to make it possible to reconstruct government and local life in great detail. Where texts are absent from one region but exist in another through chance preservation, it is a fair assumption that the poorer region possessed similar texts, if its culture is in other respects at a similar level.

The accumulation of various findings over several decades points to the 2nd millennium BC as the period when the alphabet was invented. Stimulated by the

ncient Israel most cuments were written on rchment or papyrus and ve not survived in the np soil of Palestine. But s, receipts, notes and :ings of all kinds were de on the broken pottery gments, **potsherds,** which re always ready to hand. e potsherd pictured here itains a message to the nmander of the garrison at chish, about 586 BC. The iter sends a greeting in the ne of God (Yahweh).

Aramaic writing on papyrus from about the 5th century BC. The Aramaic language is closely related to Hebrew. Used for diplomacy as early as Sennacherib's time (705–681 BC), it became the official language of the Persian Empire after about 550 BC. The book of Daniel contains passages in Aramaic. In New Testament times Aramaic, rather than Hebrew, was the ordinary language of Palestine. It is still spoken today by the villagers of Malloula in Syria.

The New Testament documents were written in 'common' *(koine)* **Greek,** the international language of the Near East and Mediterranean countries throughout Roman times. The Greek alphabet was derived from the same original as the Hebrew. This is a Greek papyrus of the letter to the Hebrews, from the 3rd or 4th century AD.

»

Egyptian hieroglyphs, a simple scheme of 20-30 symbols developed over the centuries, reaching a standard form about 1,000 BC. This made the art of writing available to any man. It was no longer the scribe's privileged possession.

The efforts of archaeologists and the experts on whom they rely have contributed enormously to our knowledge of man's past. But whatever form the findings take, sadly, the overall conclusion is the same. Not all man's skills and labours, great and small, have changed his nature for the better. Great civilizations have come and gone, but man, shown in his daily life, his hopes, fears and religious aspirations, seems very much the same. God's message of faith and renewal was needed as much in the days of Abraham and David as it is in our own day.

The papyrus plant, from which paper was made, grew in marshy ground all over Egypt in ancient times (see page 100). **Papyrus** was widely used as a writing-material in Egypt. The paper was made from thin strips cut from the inner stem of the papyrus plant. A vertical layer of strips was covered by a horizontal layer, and the two were hammered together on a hard surface. The result was a durable sheet of whitish paper which tended to yellow with age. The writing here is Coptic – the end of Deuteronomy and beginning of Jonah, from the 4th century AD. Another example of papyrus is pictured on page 70.

The 'book' of Bible times was the **scroll** – a long roll of parchment or papyrus. It was written in columns on the inside, if necessary continuing on the back. The reader would unroll one end and roll up the other as he went. Parchment was made from specially prepared animal-skins. It was a more durable writing-material than papyrus, and readily available in Palestine.

In the 2nd century AD the scroll began to be replaced by the **codex** – the real predecessor of the modern book. The codex consisted of a number of written sheets, folded and fastened together at one edge, and often protected by covers. The picture shows John 21:1-25 in the 4th-century Greek Bible, Codex Sinaiticus. It is written on parchment (vellum).

veryday Life in Bible Times
ALPH GOWER

The patriarchs – Abraham and the rest – were semi-nomads. They lived in tents, and moved about with their flocks and herds in search of fresh pasture and water. Their life was very similar to that of the bedouin today. But after the exodus, the people of Israel settled in their promised land. And from that time on – through all the political scene-shifting, the rise of kings, the division of kingdoms – the life of ordinary people followed a pattern that changed surprisingly little.

DOMESTIC LIFE

Domestic life centred on the home, which was built to meet the demands of climate and the limitations of money and raw materials. For most of the year the weather was very hot and dry, this being broken by the former rains of autumn and the latter rains of spring. Water was scarce, especially in the southern, low-rainfall area. Homes were therefore built to keep out the heat. The poor lived in one-room houses, built of mud-brick on a stone foundation, later of limestone. The flat roof provided storage space and somewhere to sit out. It was approached by an external staircase. Windows were small – just a slit, or a latticed or shuttered aperture which kept out intruders while allowing the free passage of air.

Inside the house it was cool and shady. A raised platform at one end probably provided sleeping and eating quarters for the family, and the remainder of the earthen floor provided storage space for jars and utensils, including the hand-mill, and living space for the animals. Richer people had homes of better materials – dressed stone, and metal lattices to the windows. Some built their houses upwards to provide an 'upper room' while others built outwards to include one or more courtyards, many laid out with attractive gardens. The bedouin desert-dwellers were worst off, living in goatskin tents, traditional from the time of Abraham.

Inside the house, the poor sat and slept on mats, illuminated by an olive-oil lamp. By comparison, the wealthy sat at table, slept in beds and were waited on by servants who produced five-star food and music instead of the goats' milk, olives and barley bread which was the staple diet of others.

Food and clothing

The peasant family had to work in order to live. The man worked either in the fields or at a village craft, while the women and children worked to keep the

The bedouin today show the centuries-old life of the desert nomad.

home, drawing water from the village well in a goatskin bucket early in the day before it got too hot. Next the corn seeds were sorted to avoid any poisonous 'tares' and while some were 'popped' on a heated sheet of metal, most were ground at the hand-mill, and made into flat cakes before baking in the grass-fired oven. The bread was made to rise by using 'leaven', part of a previous day's dough allowed to ferment.

Clothes were conditioned by the climate. People wore long flowing robes in order to keep cool, but the material and texture was decided by wealth. The peasant wore a loincloth and/or tunic and cloak. The man's tunic was white and knee-length, and to work or run he tucked it up into the girdle round his waist – an action known as 'girding up the loins'. The woman's tunic was similar to the man's but probably more elaborate and colourful. When its wide sleeves were tied together and slipped up over her neck she was ready for work, arms bare. The outer garment, or cloak, was a long woollen garment of alternating dark and light brown stripes, slit at the shoulders for the arms. Since most Jewish looms were only some three feet wide, two pieces of cloth were sewn together side by side to give the required length to the garment – the seamless one worn by Jesus was something of an exception.

The wealthy could afford brightly dyed cloth, and used a short jacket over the tunic. Often the clothes indicated a man's profession – the special dress of the priests, for example, or the rabbi's blue-fringed robe. Footwear, when worn at all by the poor man, consisted of a cowhide sole fastened to the ankle by a leather thong passing between the large and second toe; though his richer friend might wear leather slippers. Because the head had to be protected from the sun, a turban was worn, or a square of cloth held on to the head by a cord. There were no such luxuries as night attire for the common man. He simply loosened his girdle and wrapped himself in his cloak.

Mud-brick houses and traditional rural working dress in a village in Northern Syria.

WORKING LIFE

The Israelites lived mostly as an agricultural community. Their work therefore tended to be either agricultural or one of the village crafts.

The farmer

Most important was farming. When the former rains (autumn) had softened the ground, furrows were made by a simple wooden plough pulled by an ox. The seed was scattered by hand and the latter rains (spring) brought on the crop. To reap they either pulled out the plants whole, or else

Winnowing: the grain is tossed into the air and the wind blows away the chaff.

cut the stalks with a wooden sickle which had sharp flints set into the cutting edge. The corn was carried to a hard level piece of ground known as the threshing-floor, where either the hooves of oxen or an ox-pulled wooden sledge was used to separate the straw from the grain. During the period of evening breeze the threshed corn was winnowed by tossing it into the air with a pronged fork. The wind blew the light straw away from the floor, where it could be picked up and tied into bundles later for firing domestic ovens. The winnowing was completed by the use of a shovel, by which means the dust was removed too. The pure grain was then measured and bagged for use or sale.

Other major crops were grapes, olives and figs. Most grapes were crushed for their juice in a winepress and the juice fermented in order to keep it. Olives were crushed too, for their oil – a vital commodity for cooking, lighting, cleaning and medicine.

The fisherman

There was a little fishing in Old Testament times but the Israelites were poor sailors, so fishing was limited to the few rivers and lakes, notably the Lake of Galilee. By Jesus' time there was a flourishing fishing industry in Galilee. The lake teemed with fish to such an extent that it was possible to catch them by throwing a weighted circle of net (the cast net) from the shore and then hauling it in. The more usual procedure was to suspend a seine net, with weights below and corks above, between two fishing-boats and either trap the fish in a circle of net in the centre of the lake, or else sail for the shore to trap the fish in the shallows. Some were sold straight away but others were salted.

Spear fishing and even rod and line were in use. The work was often dangerous because the lake could become stormy almost without warning. Sometimes this was caused by cold winds rushing down from the snow-covered slopes of

The flat-roofed houses, flocks and fields nearby, of a village in rural Syria.

Mt Hermon; sometimes by hot air rising from the below-sea-level lake and mixing with the cooler air coming over the hills from the Mediterranean.

The shepherd

From earliest times the work of shepherding was also very important. Since the shepherd had to feed as well as protect the flock, he travelled some distance, especially in the hot summer period. Each night he counted the sheep into an open fold, and himself lay across the opening, so becoming the 'door of the sheep'. He had to keep a keen watch for the wild animals which came up from the tangled 'jungle' of the Jordan Valley – including lions in Old Testament times and jackals. The shepherd usually had charge of a mixed flock of sheep and goats. He could drive the goats, but he led the sheep. Wool and goathair were both important for clothing. The goats gave milk, and both animals were a major source of meat.

Village crafts

All kinds of village crafts were practised, even in the early days. The carpenter made and mended farm tools – ploughs and forks and threshing-sleds – and the basic furniture for the home. But there was little wood to use, as trees were not plentiful. The mason quarried out the limestone which constitutes most of the bedrock of Palestine, roughly shaping it for building purposes. The potter used clay to make the utensils for the home, using a wheel (spun by hand at first; and later foot-powered), and a primitive oven. The tanner was also important, but his business was normally outside the village and near running water, because of the smell. Sandals, girdles and goatskin bottles for water were all made here.

SOCIAL LIFE AND CUSTOMS

Three days stood out in the memory of any Israelite family – those of birth, marriage and death.

Birth

In the East, childlessness was always regarded as a calamity, and one's happiness was proportionate (so it was said) to the number of children, particularly sons. When the firstborn son arrived, his mother became 'The mother of ...' instead of 'The daughter of ...' A daughter was not so welcome because of her subordinate position. She was an asset to the family only as a worker.

At birth, salt was rubbed into the baby's skin to make it firm, and it was closely wrapped in 'swaddling cloths' to make its limbs grow straight. The child received a carefully chosen name which indicated some presumed moral or physical property present in him. After eight days a boy was circumcised. The firstborn son was redeemed a month later by a payment to the priest. He was not weaned until he was two or three years old.

Marriage

Marriages were arranged by parents, and there was little social mixing between the

A woman making unleavened bread.

weep and wail. In such a hot climate the body had to be buried within 24 hours. It was washed and clothed – in New Testament times, anointed (rarely) and wrapped in special grave clothes, with a linen napkin bound round the head. Poor people were buried in common graves or in caves. The wealthy had tombs specially hewn out of rock and sealed with a boulder (in New Testament times, a flat, wheel-shaped stone door).

EDUCATION AND JUSTICE

In Old Testament times there was no 'school' for ordinary men's children. They were taught everyday skills by father and mother, who also explained the law and the religious festivals to them. By Jesus' time, a girl's education was still entirely in her mother's hands, but every boy went to the school attached to the synagogue when he was six. The Jewish scriptures were his only textbook as he learnt the history, geography, literature and law of his own people. If he was bright enough, he could be sent to Jerusalem, to sit at the feet of a learned rabbi and absorb his teaching.

In addition to knowledge of the law, the Jewish boy had to learn a trade. This, and the meaning of the festivals, remained the task of his father. When a boy was thirteen, he became 'Bar Mitzvah' – a son of the law – and for religious purposes he was counted a man. He qualified for the Minyan – the group of ten male adults without whom it was impossible to hold a synagogue service. On the first sabbath following, he read a portion of the law in Hebrew and received the Ruler's blessing.

Administering the law

There was no great division between civil and religious law in Israel. Priests, Levites and Elders worked to the same end, and shared the administration of justice. The gate of the city or village was the place where grievances were aired and cases formally judged.

The supreme court in New Testament

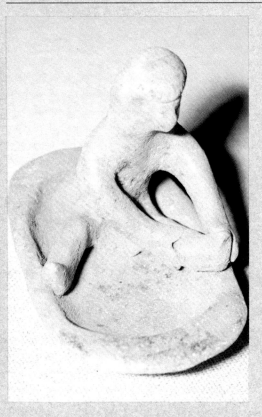

A woman washing: a Palestinian clay model from Bible times.

sexes. It was the duty of everyone to marry. Because the bride was a working asset, she had to be paid for.

First came the formal, and binding, ceremony of betrothal, with an exchange of gifts. When the wedding day came, the bridegroom and his friends went in procession in the evening to his bride's home, where she and her family were waiting. The couple were blessed, and the bridegroom led the bride through the village to his own home, the invited guests lining the way to make a torchlight procession. There followed a great feast which might last anything up to a week.

Death

A death in the household set in motion an elaborate ceremony of mourning. Professional mourners might be hired to

times was the Sanhedrin. This body of 70 men met in the temple. The Roman authorities allowed them to pass any sentence under Jewish law except the death sentence. Local quarrels continued to be settled in the 'gate' by the village elders.

RELIGIOUS LIFE

The religious life of Israel centred first on the tabernacle, then on the temple, and was determined by the regulations laid down in the law governing sacrifice and offering and the great annual festivals. These were administered by the priests and Levites.

The great day of the year was the Day of Atonement – the one occasion when the high priest entered the innermost shrine of the temple to atone for his own sins and the sins of the people. The other great festivals were Unleavened Bread or Passover, commemorating the escape from

Orthodox Jews wearing phylacteries (see picture and note on Deuteronomy 6:8).

Egypt; Weeks (later called Pentecost), celebrating the beginning of harvest; Tabernacles (the Harvest Festival); Trumpets; and Purim, commemorating Esther's deliverance of the Jews. The law required people to be present at the temple for the festivals three times a year, but those for whom the distance was too great came once. These were times of solemn assembly and of joyful celebration.

But the heart of the nation's religious life was the weekly sabbath, a day to stop work, recollect all God's goodness, and enter into the fruits of the week's labours. So important was this that the prophets took the nation's spiritual temperature, so to speak, by the way ordinary people valued and observed the sabbath.

Temple and synagogue

Between the end of the Old Testament and the beginning of the New there was considerable development in the formal religious life of the Jews. Regular worship now took place in the local synagogue – a practice evolved from the days in exile when there was no temple. Only the men took an active part in the synagogue service, the women and children being separated from them in a gallery. In charge was the Ruler of the synagogue – elected by the village elders. The service followed a pattern with creed, prayers and readings from the Law and Prophets. This was followed by a sermon and a time when the men could question the minister. Behind the pulpit, a curtained alcove contained the 'ark' of sacred scrolls, which only the doctors of law might open. Between the alcove and pulpit, the readers sat facing the congregation, together with the chief teachers, who sat on raised seats known as Moses' seats.

Whenever possible, visits were made to the temple at Jerusalem, which had been rebuilt by Herod. In plan it was similar to Solomon's, but on a much vaster scale. Basically, it was a large open area divided into courtyards by a series of walls. Non-Jews were confined to the outer courtyard which served also as a right of way into the city, a cattle market and money exchange. Jews might go through to the central courtyards. The men could watch the sacrifices from a courtyard alongside that of the priests, but the women were kept at a distance. If he was one of the fortunate ones, on just one day in his life the priest was allowed to offer incense in the holy place – the building at the heart of the temple area. As before, the high priest entered the inner shrine, the most holy place (empty in New Testament times), just once a year.

So the story of the Bible is played out against a background of traditional rural and family life, a way of life unchanged for centuries. It was also played out against the background of warring empires and the cosmopolitan life of the Roman Empire in the 1st century. Jesus came to share the life of both.

For further information on the background to New Testament times, see articles in Part Three.

Plants of the Bible

NIGEL HEPPER

Plants of one sort or another are frequently mentioned throughout the Bible. Most of them, such as fig, pomegranate, olive and vine are well known and easily identifiable. The exact nature of others, such as the 'lily of the field' and the rose, is a matter of opinion. Some of the interesting and important plants are illustrated here.

The well-known date is borne on the **date-palm** *(Phoenix dactylifera)* which grows in oases in Sinai and in the warmer parts of Palestine. It is a lofty palm-tree with a straight trunk surmounted by a tuft of huge leaves. The form of the leaves was often used to ornament the capitals of stone columns in Egypt. The palm also became one of Israel's national symbols. When Jesus made his triumphal entry into Jerusalem riding on an ass the people carried palm 'branches', which were really the leaves.

The **fig** was an important fruit in biblical times. Fig-trees *(Ficus carica)* were frequently found beside the road and near houses, as well as around vineyards. There are frequent references to figs in the Bible and Jesus used the fig-tree for several parables and illustrations. Its fruits ripen during the summer among the large lobed leaves which are shed in autumn. Another kind of fig is the **Sycomore** *(Ficus sycomorus)*. It was a sycomore Zacchaeus climbed to see Jesus (Luke 19: 4).

Cereals formed the major part of the people's diet in ancient Palestine. **Wheat,** shown here, made the best flour and bread, while barley was the food of the poorer peasant. The grain was sown when the rain had begun in the autumn and harvested during early summer: barley ripens before wheat. Wheat-flour was used in the Hebrew priestly offerings to the Lord.

The **myrtle** *(Myrtus communis)* is occasionally found in thickets in Palestine. Its glossy, evergreen leaves are fragrant and its numerous white flowers make it a delightful small tree. Traditionally Jews use it to make booths at the Feast of Tabernacles, as mentioned in Nehemiah 8: 15. Isaiah pictured it as one of the pleasant trees that would replace the thorns of the desert (Isaiah 41: 19; 55: 13).

The beautiful blossom of the **almond** *(Prunus dulcis)* is white or, less usually in Palestine, pink. It flowers early in the year, being the first fruit-tree to bloom. Almond nuts are delicious. The tree and its fruits are mentioned many times in the Bible, perhaps the most famous reference being Aaron's almond rod which flowered and fruited over night (Numbers 17: 8).

The **olive tree** *(Olea europaea)* was one of the principal tree crops of ancient Palestine. The olives were eaten pickled, but more important the crushed fruits yielded the valuable oil. Olive oil was used extensively for cooking and as fuel for lamps. In the dry Mediterranean climate it was also useful as soothing body ointment, and in the Bible oil was used for anointing, setting a man apart for special office — hence too the fact that it became symbolic of the anointing of the Holy Spirit.

Flax for linen cloth comes from the blue-flowered flax plant *(Linum usitatissimum)* which grows about 1½ feet (450mm) high. After the plants are pulled up the stem fibres are separated by standing them in water, a process called retting. The fibres were used not only for linen cloth, but also for string, nets and lamp-wicks.

The scarlet flowers of the **pomegranate** *(Punica granatum)* contrast with the deep-green leaves of this large shrub. The round pomegranate fruits are the size of an orange, with a hard yellowy-brown rind. Inside, the numerous seeds are each enclosed in a juicy pulp. In Exodus 28: 33 we read that the hem of the high priest's robe was to be embroidered with pomegranates. They were also used to ornament the pillars in King Solomon's temple (1 Kings 7: 20).

The **vine** *(Vitis vinifera)* is a trailing shrub which is widely cultivated in warmer countries in vineyards. It became a symbol of the Hebrew people, as grapes were abundant and characteristic of the promised land occupied by Israel. Grapes were eaten fresh or dried as raisins, but especially in the form of wine, which was the normal drink. Once the grapes were ripe they were gathered for pressing, which was often done with the feet in ancient times. The juice was left to ferment in earthenware jars or goatskins.

The famous **cedar of Lebanon** *(Cedrus libani)* is a huge coniferous tree restricted to the mountains of Lebanon. Scarcely any remain today. But in Old Testament times gangs of labourers man-handled the great trunks to the sea, where they were floated down the coast of Palestine before being hauled up to Jerusalem. There they were used as timber for King Solomon's temple (1 Kings 5:6-10). The interior was panelled with cedar and the beautiful carvings were overlaid with gold. Cedar beams supported the roof.

During Bible times there were considerable forests of **oak-trees** on the mountains of Palestine. This photograph shows Mt Carmel with the evergreen oak *(Quercus coccifera)* which was probably the one forming the 'groves' used for the idolatrous and immoral practices condemned by the prophets. There is another important oak, the Tabor or Vallonea *(Q. aegilops)*, which is deciduous and used to be common on the Plain of Sharon, but is now restricted to the foothills.

An **acacia** tree: see page 167.

Papyrus is the name given to the paper of the ancient world, and to the plant from which it was made. It is a sedge *(Cyperus papyrus)* which still grows in the Huleh swamp in northern Palestine and used to be common in the Egyptian Nile delta. Its greenish flower heads are like large mops and are held 10 feet/3m or more high. The three-cornered stems were sliced and hammered together in two layers to make paper. Much of the Bible would have been written on papyrus.

The trunk of the **frankincense-tree** *(Boswellia)* has thin peeling bark. Frankincense-trees grow in Africa, Southern Arabia and India. A cut into the trunk allows the pale-greenish resin to ooze out of the wound. When the resin is collected it is sold as frankincense which was burnt as incense in the worship of the ancient civilizations, including that of the Hebrews. An offering of frankincense, together with gold and myrrh, was brought to Jesus by the wise men. Myrrh is a shrub in Africa which also yields resin from its cut stems.

Thorns and thistles abound in dry lands such as Palestine. Their flowers, like this milk-thistle *(Silybur marianum)* may be beautiful, but their prickles are troublesome. Jesus may have had this plant in mind in his parable of the sower (Luke 8). It grows in masses at the edges of cornfields and quickly suffocates young wheat plants. The farmers collect the prickly plants fo burning, a picture often used in the Bible of the fate of wicked men.

Coriander *(Coriandrum sativum)* is an annual herb growing 1-2 feet/300-600mm high. The people of Israel also knew it in Egypt, since they described the manna in the desert as looking like coriander seed (Exodus 16:31). Coriander has long been used as a medicinal and culinary herb.

Rue *(Ruta graveolens)* grows about 2 feet/600mm high as a small shrub. Its grey-green leaves are very fragrant with oil, and it has been used since ancient times both as a disinfectant and as a coarse flavouring herb. The only biblical reference is when Jesus chided the Pharisees for tithing rue while they neglected more spiritual matters (Luke 11:42).

It is impossible to know exactly which plant Jesus had in mind when he said 'consider the lilies of the field' (Matthew 6:28). Any of the conspicuous wild plants of Palestine could be selected, such as anemone poppy, chamomile or the **yellow chrysanthemum** *(Chrysanthemum coronarium)* illustrated here.

Birds and Beasts

GEORGE CANSDALE

Because of its great range of habitats, and its position on one of the main migration routes, Palestine has a wealth of bird-life. The Bible reflects this, mentioning many different kinds, some of which are difficult to identify from their Hebrew names. Only the commonest are listed here. Animals listed are those which feature most prominently in the Bible.

Pigeons and Doves are the most familiar and important of all the birds in Scripture. The poor man, unable to afford a sheep or goat, would sacrifice two pigeons to the Lord. They were in fact widely kept as domestic birds. A number of different kinds inhabit Palestine, or come as winter visitors. The one shown is the Ring Dove or Wood Pigeon. The dove's soft call and gentle affection make it an apt term of endearment in the Song of Solomon.

Partridge. The same name probably covers three kinds: the Rock Partridge, as here, the Desert Partridge and the Black Partridge. The first of these is so good at concealment that it is far more often heard than seen. The partridge is a typical game bird, whose eggs have always been collected for eating. David, pursued by Saul, described himself as being hunted 'like a partridge in the mountains' (1 Samuel 26:20).

Eagles and Vultures. The term usually translated 'eagle' covers both the eagle proper and the Griffon-Vulture, pictured here. From a distance the two are very alike. It is vultures which cluster in the sky, ready to drop on a corpse – though the 'eagle' in Matthew 24:28 serves also to represent the forces of Rome. The eagle's vigour and strength lies behind two of the best-known references: 'They who wait for the Lord shall renew their strength, they shall mount up with wings like eagles' (Isaiah 40:31) and 'Your youth is renewed like the eagle's (Psalm 103:5).

Owl. Of the owls which inhabit Palestine the Eagle Owl is the largest. Commonest are the Tawny (Wood) Owl, the Barn (Screech) Owl, Little Owl (pictured here) and the small elusive Scops Owl. In the Bible, the owl's habitat is the epitome of desolation (Isaiah 34:15).

Stork. Both White and Black Storks pass through Palestine every year, flying north from their winter haunts in Arabia and Africa. The White Stork, which passes in the greatest numbers, is the one most often seen. Jeremiah (8:7) points a lesson from the fact that 'even the stork in the heavens knows her times'.

Serpent. The term 'serpent' translates four Hebrew and two Greek words. Varieties of snakes are found throughout Palestine, most of them harmless. But all the biblical references are to venomous snakes. The species most likely to have been the 'fiery serpent' of Numbers 21 is the Carpet or Saw-scaled Viper, which sometimes exists in large numbers and is notoriously aggressive. The picture here is of a Sand Viper.

The **scorpion** is most notable for its sting, used to paralyse or kill its victim, which lies in its tail. About twelve kinds exist in Palestine, none with a sting likely to kill a healthy person, though it can be unpleasant enough.

Deer and gazelle. Wild game no doubt provided a good deal of the meat eaten in country areas. The three common varieties were Fallow Deer, Gazelle and the Nubian Ibex. The gazelle (pictured here) has a pair of lyre-shaped horns and its sandy colouring makes it difficult to spot. Hart, hind and gazelle provide the biblical writers with ready imagery for swiftness, grace and gentleness (Song of Solomon 2:8-9).

Donkey (ass) and mule. The donkey is descended from the North African wild ass. The mule is cross-bred from a donkey stallion and horse mare, and combines the good qualities of each. Both ass and mule were pack animals – beasts of burden. They are sure-footed, capable of carrying heavy loads, and able to feed on much rougher terrain than horses. The Hebrews – even the wealthy – rode both asses and mules. The Messiah was to declare his peaceful rule by coming to his people riding an ass (Zechariah 9:9; Mark 11).

Cattle. Cattle were domesticated long before Abraham came down into Canaan, and they had become valuable as producers of meat, milk and leather. The ox was also an invaluable draught animal – to be harnessed to the plough, to pull the threshing-sled over the grain, or to draw carts and wagons. Both bullocks and heifers later became important for sacrifices, but mostly for special occasions, since few small farmers kept cattle. They were raised in certain regions with good pasture, notably Bashan in Trans-jordan.

Horse. Although the Hebrews had come across horses during their time in Egypt, it was not until late in David's reign that any were kept in Israel. As the result of a victory, David retained horses for 100 chariots. The horse is consistently used in Scripture as a symbol of martial power – the power men are tempted to rely on when they should be depending on God (Isaiah 31:1). It was the property of kings and nobles, never of the ordinary man.

Sheep and goats. Sheep and goats were vital to the economy of the nation and of individuals from earliest times. Both provided meat and milk and clothing. Goatskins were the standard water-bottle. Goathair was woven into strong cloth for tents. Wool shorn from the sheep was spun and woven into warm cloaks and tunics. Both animals were the mainstay of the sacrifices and offerings made in the tabernacle and temple. Sheep are mostly grazers, eating grasses. Goats prefer to browse the leaves of trees and shrubs, which they often climb to get tender shoots. By destroying shrubs whose roots hold the hillside soil firm, goats have caused immense damage by erosion throughout Bible lands. The flocks (often mixed) roamed free under the watchful care of the shepherd who warded off predators, led them to new grazing and watering, rounded up strays, and for much of the time lived with his flock. He knew each one, and they responded to his call (see John 10).

Camel. The camel featuring in most of the Old Testament narrative was the one-humped, Arabian camel that is most at home in hot deserts. But the two-humped, Bactrian camel is not unknown in Bible lands. We know that King Shalmaneser III of Assyria received them as tribute about 850 BC. There is some dispute over the camel's early history. It perhaps began to be used in patriarchal times and came into general use at the end of the 2nd millennium BC. It can live on poor food and go for several days without drinking. It has always been of major importance in and around the desert. In ordinary use it can carry a load of 400 lb/180 kg and its rider.

The predators: lion, bear, wolf, fox, jackal. Lions were widespread in Palestine and the lands around throughout Old Testament times. They could be a serious threat to both humans and their livestock. By New Testament times the lion was a rarity. Whereas the lions inhabited the thickets of the Jordan Valley, the Syrian bear (pictured here) lived in the hilly and wooded parts of Palestine. Bears live on fruit, roots, bees' and ants' nests, eggs – in fact almost anything. Hunger might drive them to seize a lamb from the flock (1 Samuel 17:34). In the half-light of evening the shepherd had also to keep a sharp look-out for prowling wolves. Jesus uses the familiar picture of 'ravenous wolves' to describe the false prophets who would raid the 'flock' of his people (Matthew 7:15). Foxes and jackals are the wolf's smaller cousins. The fox, which is a solitary hunter, has a weakness for fruit and was a threat in the vineyard. The jackal hunts in a pack and is basically a nocturnal scavenger. It was probably jackals, not foxes, that Samson used to fire the Philistine cornfields (Judges 15:4).

Other animals are as follows (see also the article on Clean and Unclean Animals under Leviticus, Part Two):

Raven. The name probably applies both to the raven and to the crow family as a whole. This would explain its inclusion in the list of 'unclean' birds (Leviticus 11:15) since crows are scavengers. After the flood, Noah sent out first a raven, then a dove, to see if the land was dry (Genesis 8:7).

Rock hyrax (Authorized Version, 'coney'; Revised Standard Version 'badger'). The rock hyrax is about the size of a rabbit, but with neat ears and no visible tail. Hyraxes are timid animals, and live in colonies in rocky places. Proverbs 30:26 aptly describes them: 'The conies are but a feeble folk, yet they make their houses in the rocks'.

Quail. See the special article, page 189.

WEIGHTS AND MEASURES

OLD TESTAMENT
Although David and Ezekiel (46: 10-12) both pronounced certain basic standards, these tended to vary. The purchaser often carried his own weights in a wallet (Proverbs 16: 11) so that he could check on the merchants. Both the law and the prophets take a strong line on just weights and measures. General standards in business dealings are a fair indication of the spiritual state of a nation.

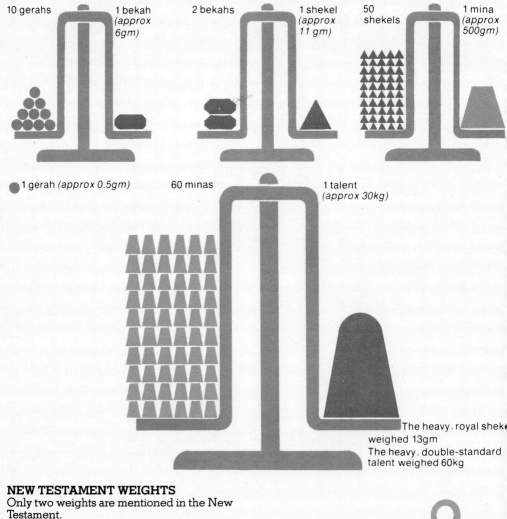

10 gerahs   1 bekah (approx 6gm)

2 bekahs   1 shekel (approx 11 gm)

50 shekels   1 mina (approx 500gm)

1 gerah (approx 0.5gm)

60 minas   1 talent (approx 30kg)

The heavy, royal shekel weighed 13gm
The heavy, double-standard talent weighed 60kg

NEW TESTAMENT WEIGHTS
Only two weights are mentioned in the New Testament.

The litra (pound): approx 327gm

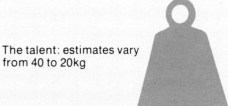

The talent: estimates vary from 40 to 20kg

c

a

b

d

OLD TESTAMENT
LINEAR MEASURES
Finger or digit (¼ handbreadth)
¾in/19mm
Palm or handbreadth (width of the
hand at the base of the fingers) 3in/76mm
Span (outstretched hand from thumb to
little finger): three handbreadths or
half a cubit 9in/230mm
Cubit (elbow to finger-tip) 17.5/445mm
The long cubit was a handbreadth
longer 20.4in/520mm
6 cubits = 1 reed

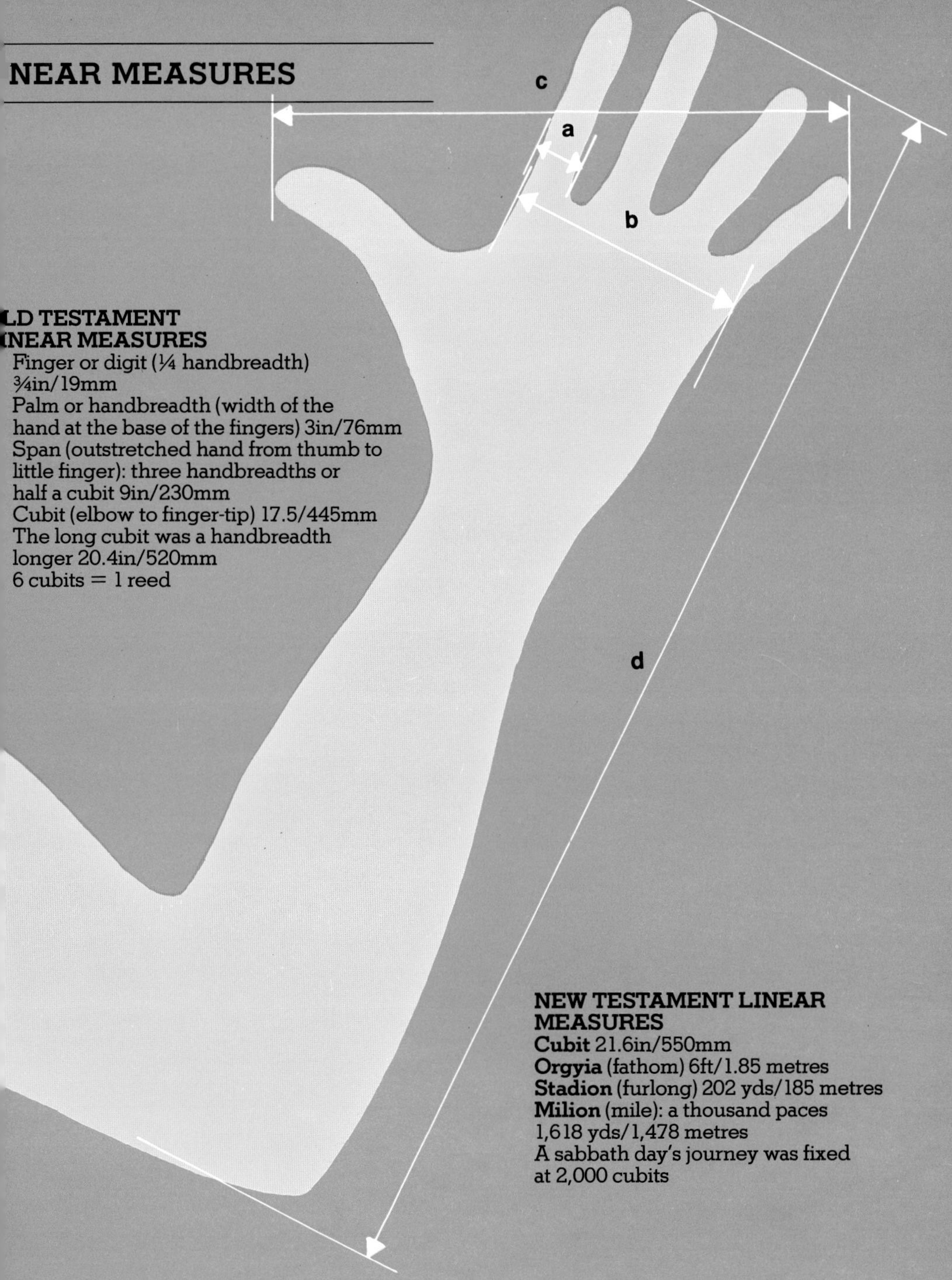

NEW TESTAMENT LINEAR
MEASURES
Cubit 21.6in/550mm
Orgyia (fathom) 6ft/1.85 metres
Stadion (furlong) 202 yds/185 metres
Milion (mile): a thousand paces
1,618 yds/1,478 metres
A sabbath day's journey was fixed
at 2,000 cubits

OLD TESTAMENT MEASUREMENTS OF CAPACITY

Terms derive from containers holding an agreed amount

LIQUID MEASURES

Bath *(22 litres)**

Hin *(3.66 litres)*

Kab *(1.2 litres)*

Log *(0.3 litre)*

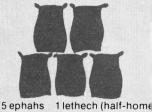

10 baths   1 homer (or kor)
'a donkey load' (220 litres)

DRY MEASURES

Ephah *(22 litres)*

5 ephahs   1 lethech (half-home
(110 litres)

Seah *(7.3 litres)*

Omer *(2.2 litres)*

Kab *(1.2 litres)*

Log *(0.3 litre)*

10 ephahs   1 homer
(220 litres)

**Approximate equivalents throughout*

EW TESTAMENT MEASUREMENTS OF CAPACITY

QUID MEASURES

os (or metretes): 'measure',
in', 'gallon' *(39.5 litres)**

tes *(0.3 litre)*

Y MEASURES

on: 'measure' *(13 litres)*

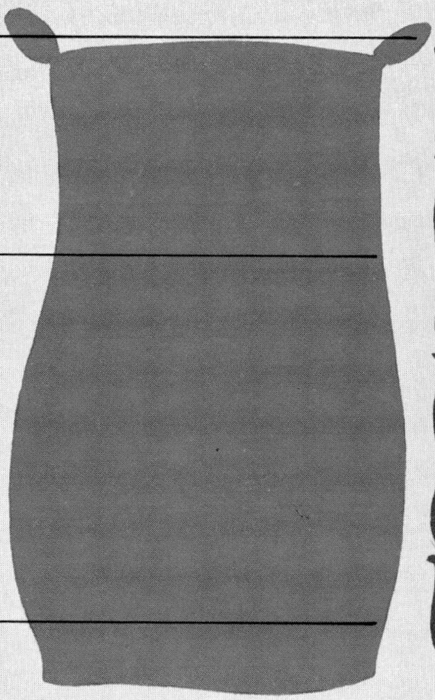

dios: 'bushel' *(8.7 litres)*

inix *(1.2 litres)*

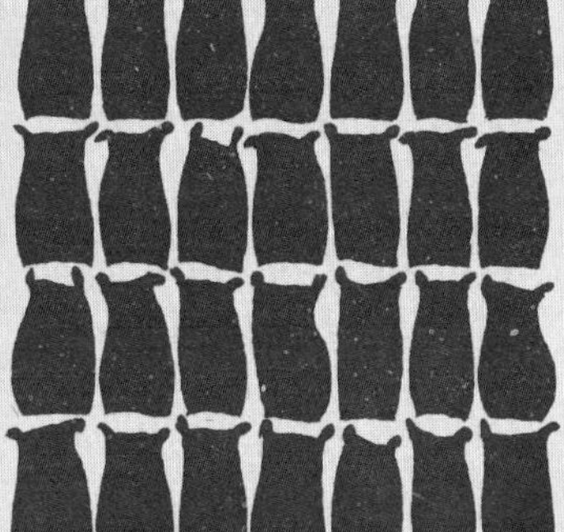

$40\frac{1}{2}$ satons 1 koros *(525 litres)*

proximate equivalents throughout

MONEY

OLD TESTAMENT TIMES

Coinage seems to have been introduced in the 7th century BC. Before that, metals and perishable and imperishable goods were exchanged – wool, barley, dates, timber, livestock, etc. Gold, silver and copper were weighed out and the quality checked. Some of the names for weights were taken over as coin names. Early coins were simply pieces of metal impressed with a seal. They seldom weighed more than 1 shekel in gold or silver.

NEW TESTAMENT TIMES

Money from three sources circulated in Palestine in New Testament times. Th[...] was the official, imperial money (Rom[...] standard); provincial money minted at[...]

JEWISH

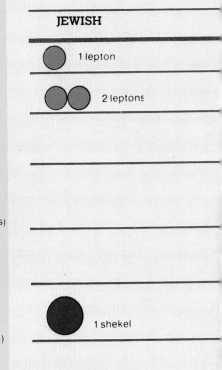

1 lepton

2 leptons

1 shekel

30 shekels

SILVER COINAGE

Shekel (weighs approx 11.4gms)

50 shekels    1 mina (approx 500gms)

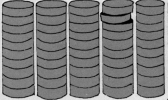

60 minas   1 talent (30 kg)

GOLD COINAGE

Shekel

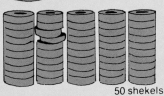

50 shekels   1 mina

60 minas   1 talent

tioch and Tyre (Greek standard); and local wish money, possibly minted at Caesarea. s not surprising that money-changers urished. Money was coined in gold, silver, pper and bronze or brass. The low-value Roman *as* and Jewish *lepton* were bronze coins. The commonest silver coins mentioned in the New Testament are the Greek *tetradrachma* and Roman *denarius,* which was a day's wage for the ordinary working man.

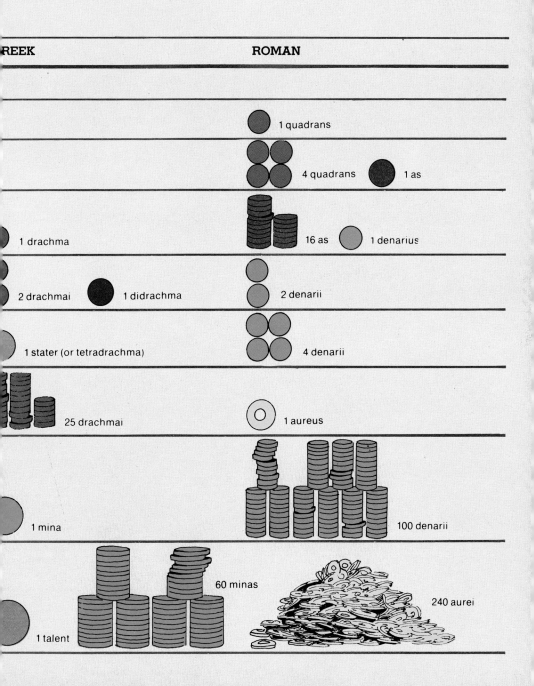

GREEK	ROMAN
	1 quadrans
	4 quadrans 1 as
1 drachma	16 as 1 denarius
2 drachmai 1 didrachma	2 denarii
1 stater (or tetradrachma)	4 denarii
25 drachmai	1 aureus
1 mina	100 denarii
1 talent 60 minas	240 aurei

Times and Seasons

JOHN LILLEY

A calendar is one of those essentials we all take for granted. The earliest calendars evolved around the seasons of the farmer's year, and the religious rites associated with them. Because of this link, and because the whole subject was so complex, the priests became the experts in managing the calendar. Trade and government made their own demands for accurate dating. So the great empires of Mesopotamia and the Nile Valley developed their varying systems to a high degree of accuracy.

We know little about the Old Israelite calendar, apart from the laws of the festivals. But the Mishnah (the collection of Jewish law made at the end of the 2nd century AD) fully describes the system which the Jews had worked out under Babylonian influence. This carried on alongside the Roman calendar so effectively reformed by Julius Caesar that it survives almost intact after 2,000 years.

WORKING OUT A CALENDAR

Basically, all calendars are determined by the sun, moon and stars. The sun gives us the basic unit of the day, and the seasons of the year. The waxing and waning of the moon divides the year roughly into 29/30 day periods. The great festivals were timed to coincide with the full moon. But in relatively cloudless Palestine it was easier to do the actual counting from the day the new moon first appeared – fourteen or fifteen days to the festival, and then on till the next new moon. From the dawn of civilization men also realized that the nightly pattern of the constellations changed in a cycle which matched the seasons of the year. Shepherds could often tell the seasons more easily by the

stars than by the sun.

The problem in all this was, of course, accuracy. Twelve lunar months are about eleven days short of a solar year. The Babylonians and Greeks eventually worked out that 19 years=235 lunar months – a fact borne out by modern astronomical measurements. So the question was how and when to absorb the

The 'Gezer Calendar', a simple aid for remembering the agricultural seasons, in Hebrew, from about 900 BC, found at Gezer.

extra months. Israel must have had a working arrangement from very early times, since the months were named and numbered, and the annual feasts kept in numbered months. When the new moon after the twelfth was due to come more than 14 days before the equinox, they decreed a repeat twelfth month (a second Adar) to straighten things out again. In this way they could make sure that the chief festivals, which were linked to the wheat and fruit harvests, matched the progress of the crops as closely as possible.

THE OLD TESTAMENT CALENDAR

The Old Testament calendar has its roots in two things: the system of festivals and the agricultural cycle.

The system of festivals, instituted by Moses, began with the Passover which commemorated the exodus. Nearly all Old Testament references to months are by number from this starting-point. The other festivals were based on the natural harvests (Exodus 23:14ff.; Deuteronomy 16:9-15), but for civilized life they had to be fixed by the lunar calendar (Leviticus 23; 1 Kings 8:2; 12:32).

The agricultural cycle culminated in the fruit harvest (Exodus 23:16b), and began again with the early rains which prepared the ground for ploughing. The 'first day of the seventh month' (Tishri) is still the Jewish New Year (see Leviticus 23:24). The kings of Judah probably counted their years from that date, until the Babylonian invasions at the end of the 7th century BC. Historical events were dated by the number of years from the accession of the reigning king – or by reference to great national events (the exodus, the exile, etc.).

The weekly sabbath (rest-day) presented its own problems, because the year does not contain a whole number of weeks, any more than a whole number of months. (This annoying fact makes trouble for accountants and government offices to this day!) Perhaps in early times the weekly sabbath was adjusted to coincide with major festivals, or even with new moons (see Leviticus 23). After the exile, the seventh-day sabbath was more strictly observed and became independent of the lunisolar calendar. So the orthodox Jews had problems over the relationship of the sabbaths and festivals.

IN THE NEW TESTAMENT

Most of the New Testament writers pinpoint events in relation to the current Jewish calendar. Occasionally they reckon dates by reference to non-Jewish rulers. Luke, for example, begins his history of the life of Jesus 'in the fifteenth year of the Emperor Tiberius'. Mostly the accounts are punctuated by the occurrence of the great annual festivals: Passover, Tabernacles, Pentecost. But even in this there was not absolute uniformity in New Testament times. There were minor differences between the calendar followed by the Pharisees and that of the Sadducees.

More significant was the 'sectarian' calendar put forward in the Book of Jubilees. This was a scheme for keeping all festivals permanently on the same day of the week. The year was to be divided into four quarters of 13 weeks, which were divided in turn into three months of 30 days, with an extra day each quarter. The year always began on a Wednesday, and no festival fell on a sabbath. (How a 364 day year could have been reconciled with the inexorable rhythm of the seasons after a generation or so remains a mystery.) The Qumran community may have adopted this calendar. They certainly kept festivals on different days from those observed in the temple. Practice may have varied in the days of Christ more than was once thought; this may help to explain why the Last Supper did not coincide with the day of Passover in the temple.

DIFFERENT CALENDARS COMPARED

**ASTRONOMICAL
STANDARD**

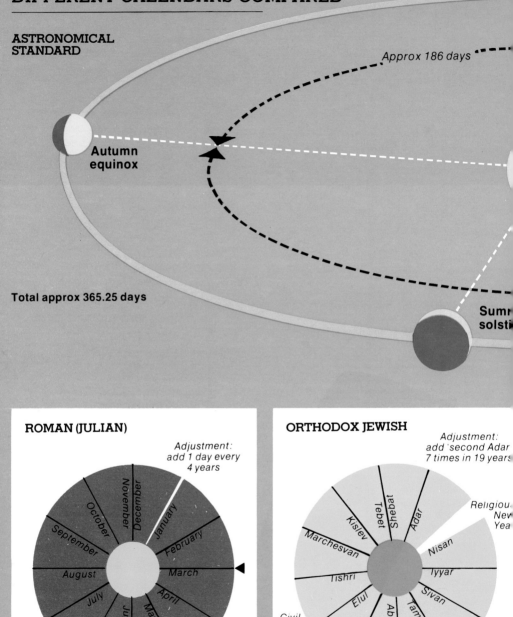

Approx 186 days

**Autumn
equinox**

Total approx 365.25 days

Sum
solsti

ROMAN (JULIAN)

*Adjustment:
add 1 day every
4 years*

November
December
January
February
March
April
May
June
July
August
September
October

*12 fixed months of 30/31 days
(February 28)*
Total 365 days

ORTHODOX JEWISH

*Adjustment:
add 'second Adar
7 times in 19 years*

Tebet
Shebat
Adar
Kislev
Marchesvan
Nisan
Religiou
New
Yea
Tishri
Iyyar
Elul
Sivan
Ab
Tammuz

Civil
New
Year

*12 lunar months beginning with
each new moon (visible crescent)*
Total approx 354 days

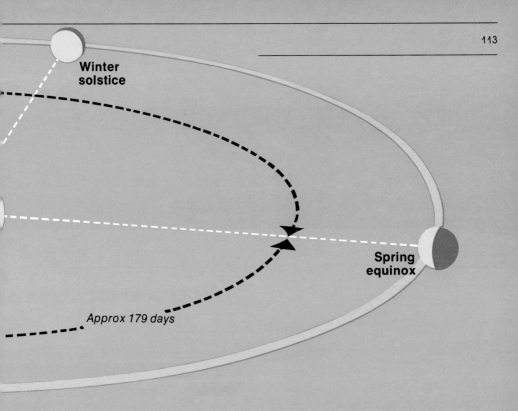

Winter solstice

Spring equinox

Approx 179 days

JUBILEES
(historical use uncertain)

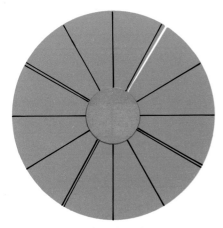

*12 fixed months of 30 days plus
1 extra day per quarter:
equivalent to 52 weeks
No adjustment*
Total 364 days

EGYPTIAN (FISCAL)

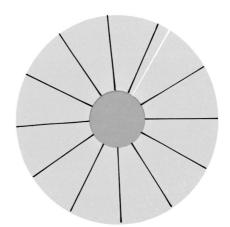

*12 fixed months of 30 days plus 5
additional days. Agricultural year
controlled by heliacal rising of Sirius (Sothis).
No adjustment: new year advanced
slowly in relation to agricultural
year in a 'Sothic cycle' of 1460 years.*
Total 365 days

THE CALENDAR IN ANCIENT ISRAEL

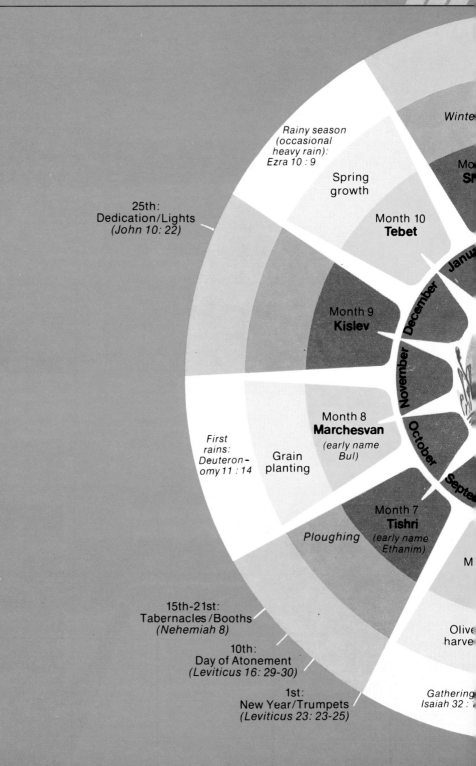

Winte

Mo
S

Month 10
Tebet

Janua

December

November

October

Septe

M

Rainy season
(occasional
heavy rain):
Ezra 10 : 9

Spring
growth

25th:
Dedication/Lights
(John 10: 22)

Month 9
Kislev

Month 8
Marchesvan
(early name
Bul)

First
rains:
Deuteron-
omy 11 : 14

Grain
planting

Month 7
Tishri
(early name
Ethanim)

Ploughing

Olive
harve

15th-21st:
Tabernacles/Booths
(Nehemiah 8)

10th:
Day of Atonement
(Leviticus 16: 29-30)

1st:
New Year/Trumpets
(Leviticus 23: 23-25)

Gathering
Isaiah 32 :

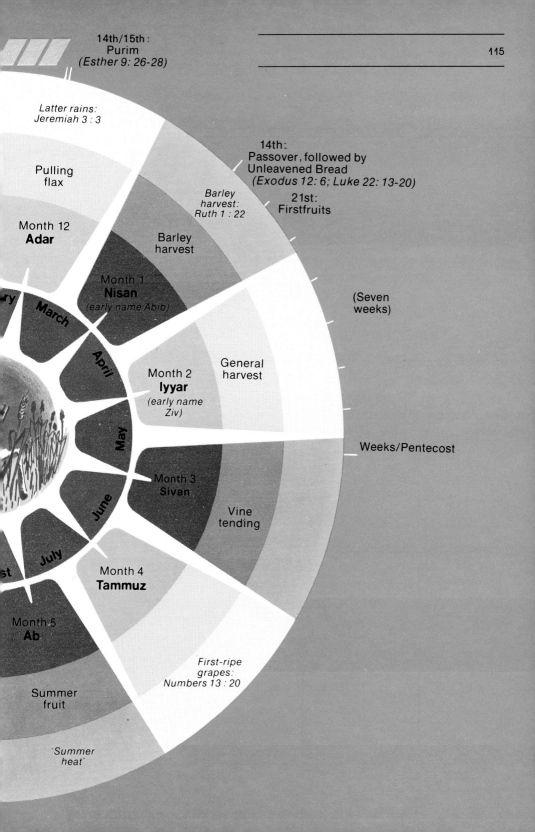

14th/15th :
Purim
(Esther 9: 26-28)

*Latter rains:
Jeremiah 3 : 3*

Pulling
flax

Month 12
Adar

Barley
harvest

Month 1
Nisan
(early name Abib)

14th :
Passover, followed by
Unleavened Bread
(Exodus 12: 6; Luke 22: 13-20)

*Barley
harvest:
Ruth 1 : 22*

21st:
Firstfruits

(Seven
weeks)

March

April

Month 2
Iyyar
*(early name
Ziv)*

General
harvest

May

Weeks/Pentecost

Month 3
Sivan

June

Vine
tending

July

Month 4
Tammuz

st

Month 5
Ab

*First-ripe
grapes:
Numbers 13 : 20*

Summer
fruit

*'Summer
heat'*

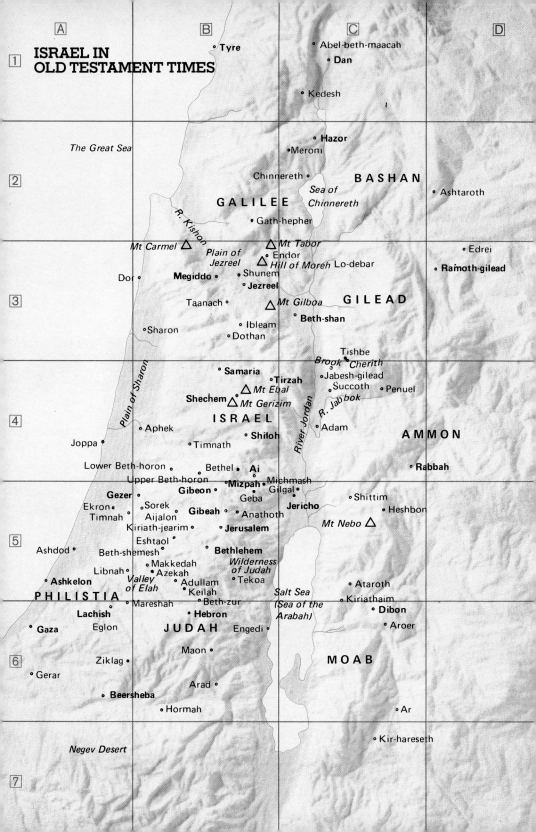

ISRAEL IN
OLD TESTAMENT TIMES

A | B | C | D

1

• Tyre

• Abel-beth-maacah

• Dan

• Kedesh

2

The Great Sea

• **Hazor**
• Merom

Chinnereth

BASHAN

Sea of Chinnereth

• Ashtaroth

GALILEE

R. Kishon

• Gath-hepher

3

Mt Carmel △

Plain of Jezreel

△ Mt Tabor
• Endor
△ *Hill of Moreh* Lo-debar

• Edrei

Ramoth-gilead

Dor •

Megiddo •
• Shunem

• **Jezreel**

GILEAD

Taanach •

△ Mt Gilboa

• Sharon

• Ibleam
• Dothan

• **Beth-shan**

Tishbe
Brook Cherith

4

• **Samaria**

• **Tirzah**

Shechem • △ Mt Ebal
△ Mt Gerizim

• Jabesh-gilead
• Succoth

• Penuel

ISRAEL

Plain of Sharon

R. Jabbok

River Jordan

• Aphek

• Shiloh

Joppa •

• Timnath

• Adam

AMMON

Lower Beth-horon •

• Bethel • **Ai**

Upper Beth-horon •

• Michmash

5

Gezer •
Ekron •
Timnah •

Gibeon •
• Sorek

• **Mizpah**
Geba •

• Gilgal

• **Jericho**

• Shittim

• Heshbon

Gibeah •
Aijalon •

• Anathoth

Mt Nebo △

Kiriath-jearim •

• **Jerusalem**

Eshtaol •

Ashdod •

Beth-shemesh •

• **Bethlehem**

Libnah •

• Makkedah
• Azekah

Wilderness of Judah

Ashkelon

Valley of Elah

• Adullam
• Keilah

• Tekoa

• Ataroth
• Kiriathaim

PHILISTIA

• Mareshah

• Beth-zur

Salt Sea (Sea of the Arabah)

• **Dibon**

6

Lachish •

• **Hebron**

• **Gaza**

Eglon •

JUDAH

• Engedi

• Aroer

• Gerar

Ziklag •

Maon •

MOAB

• **Beersheba**

• Arad

• Hormah

• Ar

• Kir-hareseth

7

Negev Desert

2

OLD TESTAMENT HISTORY AT A GLANCE

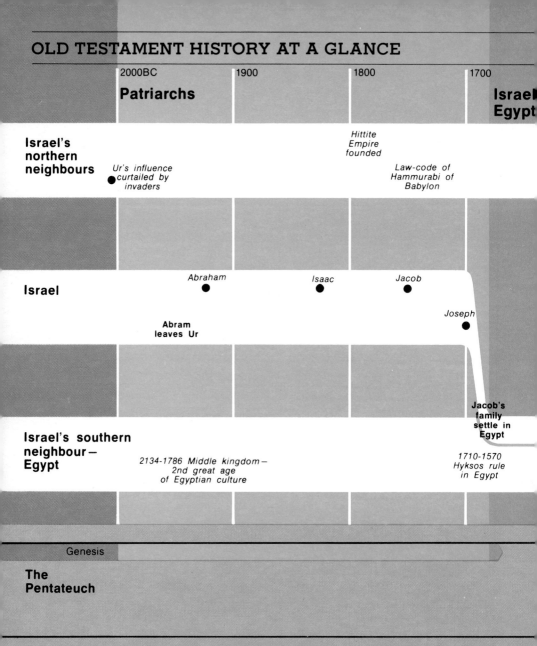

	2000BC	1900	1800	1700
	Patriarchs			**Israel** **Egypt**
Israel's northern neighbours	● Ur's influence curtailed by invaders		Hittite Empire founded Law-code of Hammurabi of Babylon	
Israel	Abraham ● **Abram leaves Ur**	Isaac ●	Jacob ●	Joseph ● **Jacob's family settle in Egypt**
Israel's southern neighbour – Egypt		2134-1786 Middle kingdom – 2nd great age of Egyptian culture		1710-1570 Hyksos rule in Egypt

Genesis

The Pentateuch

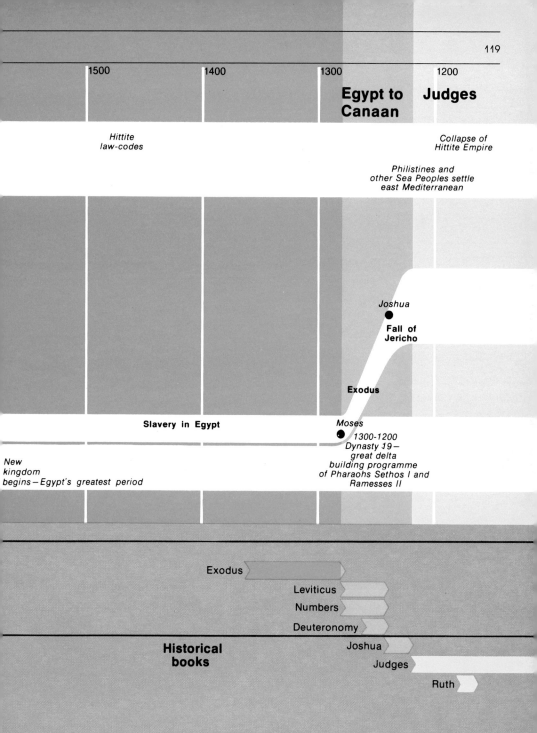

1500 1400 1300 1200

Egypt to Canaan **Judges**

Hittite law-codes

Collapse of Hittite Empire

Philistines and other Sea Peoples settle east Mediterranean

Joshua
●
Fall of Jericho

Exodus

Slavery in Egypt

Moses
● *1300-1200*
Dynasty 19 – great delta building programme of Pharaohs Sethos I and Ramesses II

New kingdom begins – Egypt's greatest period

Exodus

Leviticus

Numbers

Deuteronomy

Historical books

Joshua

Judges

Ruth

OLD TESTAMENT HISTORY AT A GLANCE

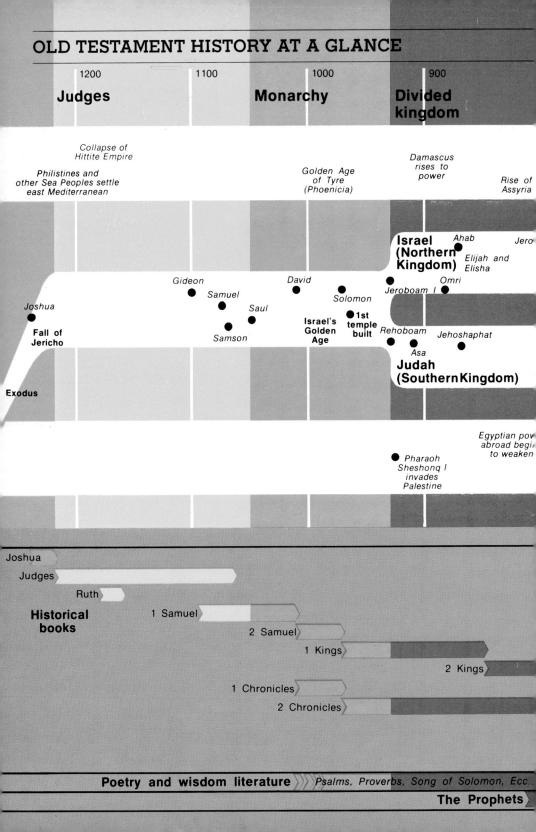

1200   1100   1000   900

Judges   **Monarchy**   **Divided kingdom**

Collapse of
Hittite Empire

Damascus
rises to
power

Philistines and
other Sea Peoples settle
east Mediterranean

Golden Age
of Tyre
(Phoenicia)

Rise of
Assyria

**Israel
(Northern
Kingdom)**   *Ahab*   *Jero*

*Elijah and
Elisha*

Gideon   *David*   *Omri*

Samuel   *Jeroboam I*

Joshua   *Saul*   *Solomon*

**Fall of
Jericho**

Israel's
Golden
Age

**1st
temple
built**

Rehoboam   *Jehoshaphat*

Samson   *Asa*

**Judah
(Southern Kingdom)**

Exodus

Egyptian pow
abroad begi
to weaken

● *Pharaoh
Sheshonq I
invades
Palestine*

Joshua

Judges

Ruth

**Historical
books**   1 Samuel

2 Samuel

1 Kings

2 Kings

1 Chronicles

2 Chronicles

Poetry and wisdom literature 〉〉 *Psalms, Proverbs, Song of Solomon, Ecc*

The Prophets 〉

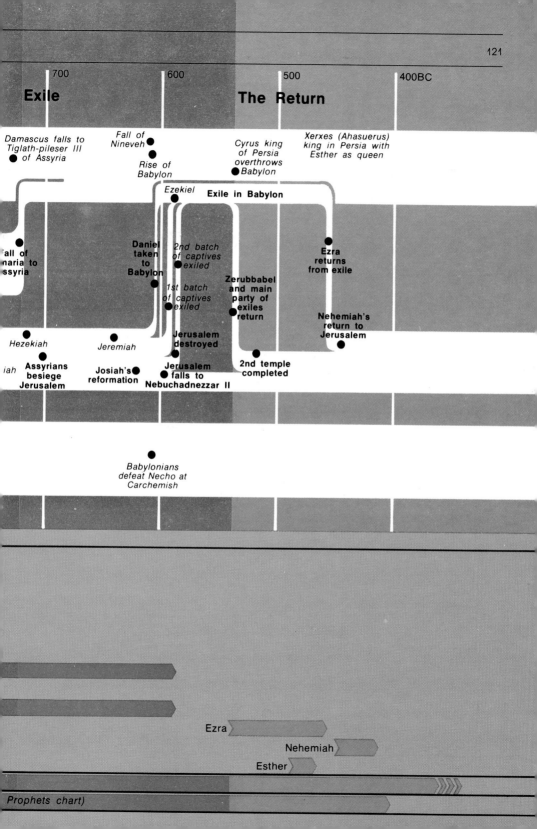

| 700 | 600 | 500 | 400BC |

Exile

The Return

Damascus falls to
Tiglath-pileser III
● of Assyria

Fall of
Nineveh ●

Rise of
Babylon

Cyrus king
of Persia
overthrows
● Babylon

Xerxes (Ahasuerus)
king in Persia with
Esther as queen

Ezekiel   **Exile in Babylon**

'all of
naria to
ssyria

**Daniel
taken
to
Babylon** ●

*2nd batch
of captives
● exiled*

*1st batch
of captives
● exiled*

**Ezra
returns
from exile**

**Zerubbabel
and main
party of
exiles
return**

**Nehemiah's
return to
Jerusalem**

Hezekiah

Jeremiah

**Jerusalem
destroyed**

iah **Assyrians
besiege
Jerusalem**

**Josiah's ●
reformation**

**Jerusalem
● falls to
Nebuchadnezzar II**

**2nd temple
completed**

●
*Babylonians
defeat Necho at
Carchemish*

Ezra >

Nehemiah >

Esther >

Prophets chart)

Introduction

JOHN TAYLOR

The name 'Pentateuch' is given to the first five books of the Bible. It comes from two Greek words meaning 'five scrolls'. But it is better to think of the Pentateuch as one book divided into five sections, rather than as five books rolled into one. In this way justice is done not only to its Hebrew origin, where it was called the 'Torah' (Law) or the 'Five fifths of Moses', but also to its own inherent unity.

That does not mean to say that the Pentateuch consists of an extended piece of narrative writing in strict chronological order. It is immediately obvious to the reader that it contains a wide variety of literary material – narratives, laws, ritual instructions, sermons, genealogies, poetry – which have been drawn together from different sources. It does mean, however, that the material has been carefully constructed within a narrative framework, with a clear purpose in mind and with recognizable objectives on the part of the author or editor.

THE FRAMEWORK

The framework of the Pentateuch consists of the story of God's people from the call of Abraham to the death of Moses. It spans a period of over 600 years, i.e. from about 1900 BC to about 1250 BC, though it is notoriously difficult to be sure of dates at this early stage of Israel's history. The story is in two sections. The first is dominated by the four generations of the patriarchs – Abraham, Isaac, Jacob and Joseph (Genesis 12-50); the second by the majestic figure of Moses (Exodus-Deuteronomy). It is preceded by a prologue (Genesis 1-11), consisting of ancient records and traditions, which serve not only to introduce the main themes of the narrative but also to relate them to God's purposes in the world of fallen mankind, of divided nations and of a created order which was originally good. It is best to look first at the main themes of the books as a whole, and then examine the significance of these introductory chapters.

FOUR IMPORTANT THEMES

Election

The Old Testament was written for the people of Israel – the people who looked back to Jacob (=Israel) as their common ancestor and to Abraham as the founder of their nation. Christians, too, look to Abraham as the father of all those who depend in faith on God rather than on anything they can do for themselves (see Romans 4:16). We therefore read the story of Abraham's call by God to become the ancestor of God's chosen people, not simply as an event in the distant past, but as something of present-day significance to us.

The idea of 'election' – God's special choosing of individuals – carries with it two subsidiary features: promise and responsibility. Genesis 12–22 is interspersed with words of promise spoken by God to Abraham. Abraham is promised descendants as countless as the stars of heaven. He is given the land of Canaan as his children's inheritance. He is promised a great name in days to come. And the Lord's special favour was to be shown not only to Abraham and his family but to all men through him.

So God's promises to Abraham were not just for the selfish enjoyment of a chosen few. They were to be used responsibly so that others might share in the benefits. Right at the heart of God's choice of Israel it is made plain that God has a missionary purpose. Israel's history must be read as the long story of their attempts to fulfil their responsibilities – with some successes, but with many conspicuous failures.

Covenant

To the modern mind a 'covenant' is simply a matter of legal documents and sealing-wax. But to the Hebrew mind it covered all human relationships. It was the bond which united people in mutual obligations, whether through a marriage contract, a commercial enterprise or a verbal undertaking. It was natural that people's relationship to God should have been expressed in covenant terms.

These covenant terms are used to describe three separate occasions in the Pentateuch:

■ God's promises to Noah that he would never again send a flood upon the earth (Genesis 9:9).
■ God's promises to Abraham (Genesis 15:18; 17:4).
■ The Sinai covenant established with Moses and summarized in the 'book of the covenant' (Exodus 24:7).

Though covenants were made between equals, the religious use of the term always referred to a relationship between a greater and a lesser partner. The form of the covenant between God and Israel in Exodus and Deuteronomy has been helpfully illuminated by recent discoveries of Hittite suzerainty-treaties made between a king and his vassal. They consisted of a historical introduction, a list of stipulations, curses and blessings invoked on the parties, a solemn oath and a religious ceremony to ratify the covenant. Most of these features can be found in the Old Testament pattern of covenants. (See 'Covenants and Near Eastern Treaties'.)

More important than the form of the covenant, however, was its theological significance.

It was based on the initiative of God. He acted in mercy and with sovereignty. He made an unconditional promise never to judge mankind with another flood (Genesis 9:11). He chose Abraham and his descendants to be the channels of his mercy to a fallen world. He cemented this election by committing himself to the Israelite nation with the words, 'I will take you for my people, and I will be your God' (Exodus 6:7).

It implied a new revelation of God. He appeared to Abraham as his shield (Genesis 15:1) and as God Almighty ('El Shaddai', Genesis 17:1). He appeared to Moses as 'Yahweh' ('I am who I am', Exodus 3:14), and later on as 'Yahweh your God, who brought you out of the land of Egypt' (Exodus 20:2). (See 'The Names of God', page 157.)

It made moral and ritual demands upon the people. The stipulations of the covenant included both these features. Ritual was represented by the rite of circumcision given to Abraham (Genesis 17:10), by the keeping of the sabbath, the day of rest (Exodus 20:8ff.) and by all the detailed requirements relating to worship and sacrifice found in the Pentateuch. At the same time the ethical requirements were spelt out in the Ten Commandments and other laws. Though at first sight these two demands seem strangely unrelated, they do in fact meet in the idea of God's holiness. A holy God requires his people to reflect his character both in worship and in behaviour.

Law

The idea of law is central to the Pentateuch and, as we have seen, it gave its name to the book as a whole. At its simplest, it covered the Ten Commandments (Exodus 20; Deuteronomy 5) but associated with these were various collections of laws which have been classified as:

- the book of the covenant (Exodus 21-23);
- the holiness code (Leviticus 17-26);
- the law of Deuteronomy (Deuteronomy 12-26).

Comparisons have been made with other ancient Near Eastern law-codes, especially the Code of Hammurabi, and many similarities noted. This illustrates the fact that Israel was a part of Eastern Mediterranean culture and shared in the ideas and experience of her neighbours. But what is so significant is not so much the similarities as the differences which made Israel's laws distinctive. These may be summarized as:

- their uncompromising monotheism (everything is related to the one God);
- their remarkable concern for the underprivileged: slaves, strangers, women, orphans;
- their community spirit, based on the covenant relationship shared by all Israel with the Lord.

It has also been pointed out that the laws in the Old Testament may be classified as either 'apodictic' in form ('thou shalt ...' or 'thou shalt not ...') or 'casuistic' ('when a man ..., he shall ...'). As most ancient law-codes consisted of the casuistic type, it may be that the apodictic was a peculiarly Israelite form, in which case the Decalogue (the Ten Commandments) was unique to Israel.

Some Christians have mistakenly seen Jesus' teaching in the Sermon on the Mount as a rejection of the Jewish law in favour of his new law of love. But Jesus' criticisms were in fact directed not at the laws, but at the way the rabbis had interpreted them. ('You have heard that it was said' was the traditional rabbinic formula for introducing their interpretation.) He was uncovering the inner motivation behind the commandments, which interpreters had failed to appreciate.

Some too have criticized the Ten Commandments for being negative. But they follow a positive assertion: 'I am the Lord your God ...' Those who have experienced deliverance by the hand of God, and who live under his sovereignty, must show it by distinctive behaviour. The Ten Commandments therefore began as God's charter for his liberated people. They consisted not of generalities but of specific commands for specific situations: worship, work, home life, marriage, respect for life and property, elementary justice and the personal realm of the will. To all these areas of human experience God had a word that was explicit and inescapable. Christ did not destroy it: he fulfilled and enlarged it.

The same cannot be said of the ceremonial and ritual laws which occupy much of Leviticus and other parts of the Pentateuch. The purpose of these laws was not only to provide guidance for the day-to-day running of the Israelite community, but to teach how a holy God was to be worshipped by a holy people. So, in addition to regulations for worship (festivals, sacrifices, etc.), detailed guidance was given for the preservation of ritual purity. The Israelite people had to be kept free of contamination from outside sources, especially the corrupting influence of Canaanite religion. They must approach God with a due sense of his moral and ritual distinctiveness.

These regulations no longer apply to the Christian church, though the underlying principles still have much to teach. And the elaborate sacrificial system has found its fulfilment in the one sacrifice of Christ – the perfect Lamb of God – through whom sins are forgiven and atonement is made for all men for ever (see Hebrews 10:1-18).

Exodus

The fourth major theme found in the Pentateuch, and recurring throughout the Bible, is the exodus from Egypt, described in Exodus 1-12. To the Jew this was the great saving act of God to which all later generations looked back with thankfulness. It was a miraculous intervention by God in response to the cries of his enslaved people (Exodus 3:7). It was essentially God's act – 'with mighty hand and outstretched arm'. It was a great victory over the gods of Egypt which demonstrated his total supremacy. It was a moment in history recalled every year in the Feast of the Passover. Later generations were frequently reminded that they were once members of a slave community whom the Lord had mercifully redeemed from bondage. They were encouraged to remember the past and warned of the danger of forgetting what God had done for them (e.g. Deuteronomy 6:12).

As a historical event the exodus was definitive. The fact that God had done it once meant that he could do it again. When Israel was in exile in Babylon the nation looked for a second exodus (Isaiah 51:9-11). And when Christ came, his work of deliverance was described in the language of the exodus (e.g. Luke 9:31).

These, then, are the four themes which are never far below the surface of the Pentateuch. They are the constant preoccupation of these five books. The only other theme – which recurs with depressing regularity – is the persistent sinfulness of the people of Israel. They were slow to accept Moses as their deliverer. They grumbled about the hardships of the journey. They even hankered after the old life in Egypt (suitably glamorized, Numbers 11:5).

They were daunted by the prospect of moving into the land of Canaan. And they wandered for 40 years in the wilderness of indecision. Not even Moses was immune, and he was punished by not being allowed to lead the people into their promised land. But sin was no new problem. To discover why, we must turn to the introductory chapters of Genesis.

THE PROLOGUE

The early chapters of Genesis were once regarded by some Christians as an embarrassment. But the old science-versus-faith controversies are increasingly a thing of the past. In fact, these chapters are now reckoned to be among the foremost theological statements the Bible contains. Once men were released from trying to defend them as scientific documents they were able to listen to what the text was actually saying.

The form of this message has often been described as 'myth'. But this is a misleading term, even when 'myth' is understood in the technical sense of a 'religious text designed to account for a custom, institution or other phenomenon'. It is also misleading because it is thought to be unhistorical and untrue. But in fact these early chapters of Genesis *are* historical, in that they bear witness to events which actually took place. The world was created; man and woman were made in God's image; the fall did take place in time. The problem is the degree of symbolism used in describing these events. On this, opinions will continue to vary considerably.

It is to these chapters that we turn for biblical guidance on the fundamental questions concerning God, man and the world. At every stage God is present. He is not simply presupposed; he is constantly and actively at work. This world is his world. Human history is the outworking of his plan. He is totally responsible for the world and all that is in it. All men are his creation, made 'in his image' – with spiritual capacities for goodness, worship and fellowship with him. There is no place whatsoever for other gods. Genesis 1 is all-embracing: sun, moon and stars are his handiwork, with duties to perform in his ordered universe; even the sea-monsters (the *tanninim* of ancient mythology) were created by him (Genesis 1:21).

Man is the climax of creation, superior to all else but subordinate to his Creator. Only when man aspires above his station and wants to be like God does he fall to a lowlier position in which all his relationships are soured. Sex, from being a good, companionable, shame-free relationship, becomes secretive, lustful, anomalous. Child-bearing is painful and hazardous. The noble art of husbandry becomes a drudgery. Even the ground is affected, and instead of producing food plentifully it has to be coaxed and sweated over. There is nothing that sin has not blighted. Its taint reaches out to family life, where religion turns to rivalry, brotherly love becomes murder, and justice degenerates into blood-lust (Genesis 4).

God's response to sin is, consistently, a blend of judgement and mercy. From the provision of skins for Adam and Eve, and the guarding of the way to the tree of life, to the confusion of tongues at Babel, God tempers justice with salvation. Beyond the immediate punishment of casting Adam out from the garden of Eden or Cain from human society, beyond the destruction of the flood and the scattering of the nations, there was always God's ultimate intention for man's well-being and blessing. Thus in a world of disorder and corruption, it was totally in keeping with God's nature that he should call out one man, Abraham, and through him his descendants the Jews, to be the channel of grace and revelation to all mankind.

It is this story which the Pentateuch tells.

The book of Genesis is an epic, a drama on a grand scale. It begins at the very beginning. God made the world, a world that was good. He made mankind, the apex of all creation.

The 'prologue' (chapters 1-11) provides us with a general history of mankind over some thousands of years. We see God's good creation progressively soured as a result of human sin in trying to become like God. Then everything is swept away in the great flood. A new beginning is made – only to end in the folly of Babel and the division and dispersion of the nations.

In chapter 12 the emphasis shifts. From the history of man in general we focus down to the story of a single individual, Abraham, and his descendants. God will not destroy his creation. Instead he begins to work, through one man of his choice, and one nation of his choice, for the renewing of the world. Genesis takes the story on through Isaac and Jacob to the death of Joseph in Egypt. And still the story of God's great purpose for mankind is scarcely begun. It continues on through the pages of Scripture to the very last words of the book of Revelation.

1—2:4
CREATION

The great drama of the beginning of all things starts with God. The language is simple but vivid. It evokes the wonder and richness of creation from formlessness to teeming life.

But it is more than poetic. It tells us what we need to know in order to understand ourselves and the world around us:

■ The origin of the world and of life was no accident. There is a Creator: God.

■ God made everything there is.
■ All that God made was good.
■ The high point of all God's creative acts was the making of mankind.
■ Mankind is distinguished from all other creatures in two respects: he alone is made in God's own likeness; and he is given charge over all the rest.
■ God's six 'days' of creative activity, followed by a 'day' of rest, sets the pattern for our working life.

Creation is described as taking place in six days. There are eight acts of creation, each introduced by the words 'and God said...'

Day 1 Light and darkness/day and night

Day 2 Earth's atmosphere (the firmament)

Day 3 Dry land and seas separated
Plants and trees

Day 4 Sun, moon and stars: seasons, days, years

Day 5 Sea creatures and birds

Day 6 Land animals
Mankind

Day 7 Creation completed, God rests

The events are described from the standpoint of an observer seeing the development of creation around him. The order is not necessarily chronological (a modern idea!) Light and darkness, for example, are described before the sun, moon and stars. The account is one which we can all understand – from the simplest peasant to scientifically educated 20th-century man.

This is not a treatise on geology, biology, or any other science. We are not told *when* creation took place. Nor are we given details as to *how* God brought the earth and life into being – nor how long it all took. The 'days' are taken by some to be periods of time. Others think that this pattern of seven days is simply the most vivid means of expressing the creative energy and satisfaction of God, the orderliness and simple majesty of the way he created all things.

The 'image' or 'likeness' of God (1:27): of all creation, only man (including both man and woman) is described as being made in God's likeness. However it is understood, the phrase sets people apart from the animals. It establishes them in a special relationship with God. God gives them control over the newly-made world and all its creatures. The 'likeness' is so basic to the human structure that the Fall did not destroy it. Sin has certainly spoiled and blurred it, but man remains a reasoning, moral, creative creature. He is still intended to be in control of his environment. To make him no more than animal is to make him less than man-in-God's-likeness.

2:5–3:24
MANKIND: TESTING AND DOWNFALL

2:5–25 Focus on people

This second description of creation is an enlargement of the first, which set the scene. It is written from a different point of view – this time focussing on people. It also uses a different name for God. In the first account it was *Elohim,* God the Creator, the great and lofty One who inhabits eternity. Now it is *Yahweh* (Jehovah) *Elohim,* God in relation to his people (see 'The Names of God', page 157). The two accounts may represent two different traditions or sources. But that is no reason for trying to make them contradict each other. Nor should this be an excuse to try to carve up Genesis to fit a theory – about the evolution of religion or anything else.

God creates man. (The Hebrew word translated 'Adam' means 'man'.) He plants a garden in Eden in the east, where man is to live. But man is not made for a solitary, self-sufficient

existence. Neither birds nor animals provide the kind of companionship he needs. So God creates woman, a new being, yet sharing man's own essential nature.

The pattern of chapter 1 shows the principle of one day's rest in seven. The account of chapter 2 sets the pattern for human marriage.

The two trees: the phrase 'good and evil' may well be a Hebrew idiom standing for the full range of moral knowledge represented by the two extremes. To eat of the tree of the knowledge of good and evil will therefore make man like God. The tree of life, inaccessible to man once he had sinned, appears again in the last book of the Bible. It stands beside the river in the city of the new Jerusalem, where God and his people once more live together – and its leaves are for 'the healing of the nations' (Revelation 22:2). True life is ultimately dependent on the presence of God.

3 Man and woman disobey God

The serpent questions what God has said, then calls God a liar. The woman has to set the enticing fruit, the desire to have knowledge like God himself, against God's plain command. The decision is deliberate, and fatal. Man has disobeyed God, rejected his authority, chosen to go his own way and become a 'god' himself.

The result is inevitable. A holy God cannot live with sin. The serpent is sentenced first (verse 14 does not mean that he had legs before). The woman is to experience suffering – in childbirth, the most fundamental human process. She is to know what it means for her husband to 'rule' over her. From now on Adam's work is to be sweat and toil.

Because of sin, access to the tree of life is now denied them. They are to leave the garden, and there is no return. Spiritual death, being cut off from God, is immediate. Physical death follows in the course of time. God's warning was true. Yet he continues to care for them, and clothes them before they go.

4

THE FIRST FAMILY – AND THE FIRST MURDER

Adam and Eve, after their expulsion from the garden, have two sons: Cain, the farmer, and Abel, the shepherd. In due course each brings his offering to God. Abel's is accepted, but not Cain's. It was not *what* Abel offered, but his faith, which made his gift acceptable (Hebrews 11:4). Cain's bitter resentment shows a very different spirit and ignores the remedy God gives in verse 7.

Cain kills Abel – it is a short step from rebellion to bloodshed – and God condemns him to a nomadic life, but provides protection against death. Verses 17-24 list some of Cain's descendants, and show the beginnings of civilized life. Enoch builds the first city. His successors learn to play and enjoy music – also to forge iron and bronze. If good things flourish, so do evil. Lamech takes two wives, and boasts to them of the murder he has committed, outdoing Cain.

The last two verses give a glimmer of hope. Seth is born to Adam and Eve, and men begin 'to call on the name of the Lord'.

Cain's wife: verse 17 and verses 14-15 give the impression of an earth already, to some extent, populated. The simplest way of accounting for this is to assume other, unnamed, children of Adam and Eve. Others would argue from the fact that the word adam = man, or mankind, that a race was created, not a single pair. However we resolve the problem we must never cut across the basic teaching of other scriptures, that one man's disobedience plunged the whole human race into sin, subjecting us all to death (see for example Romans 5:12ff.)

Other Creation Accounts

ALAN MILLARD

Creation stories belonging to other ancient peoples have given currency to the view that Genesis contains merely another version, adapted to suit Hebrew beliefs.

Folk-stories worldwide
Genesis 1 and 2 consist of a general account of the creation of the heavens and the earth, followed by a more detailed description of the making of man. Stories of cosmic and of human creation, either separately or as unities, are numerous, and many have several points in common: pre-existent deity; creation by divine command; man the ultimate creature; man formed from the earth as a pot is made; man in some way a reflection of deity. Almost all polytheistic faiths possess family-trees of their gods which can figure in creation stories. A primal pair or even a single self-created and self-propagating god heads the divine family, all of whose members represent or control natural elements and forces.

For some peoples, the physical universe or a basic element such as water or earth always existed, and the gods arose from it. For others it was the handiwork of a god or gods. These are simple concepts based on observation and elementary logic. For example, man as 'dust' is easily deduced from the cycle of death and decay.

However, common ideas need not share a common origin; it is misleading to reduce differing stories from all over the world to their common factors in order to claim that they do. A single source for all, or large numbers, of different stories is improbable.

Ancient Near Eastern stories
Nevertheless, it is quite in order to set Genesis beside other accounts from the world of the Old Testament. When we do so, we find that few of the ancient creation stories share more than one or two basic concepts – such as the separation of heaven and earth, and the creation of man from clay. The Babylonian literature, however, affords some striking resemblances. In the century since one was first translated into English, the Babylonian accounts have been cited as the ultimate source of the Hebrew's beliefs. Recently, the recovery of more texts and the re-assessment of those long known have »

shown that many of the accepted similarities are in fact illusory.

The famous *Babylonian Genesis,* usually linked with the Hebrew creation story, is one of several, and was neither the oldest nor the most popular. Written late in the 2nd millennium BC to honour Marduk, god of Babylon, who is its hero, it begins with a watery mother-figure, Tiamat, from whom the gods are born. (The name is related to the Hebrew word for 'the deep' through the pre-historic linguistic connections between Babylonian and Hebrew.) She is killed by Marduk in a battle with her children whose noise had angered her, and her corpse is formed into the world. Man is made to relieve the gods of the toil of keeping the earth in order, so the gods have rest.

There are clear indications that this story was made up from older ones, and earlier compositions have been found which contain some of these features. Only one theme recurs often, the relief of the gods from their labour by the making of man with a divine ingredient. The battle of the gods in the *Babylonian Genesis* has no Old

Tablet inscribed with a part of the Babylonian account of the creation. This version was copied about the 7th century BC but is dependent on other stories going back to the 3rd millennium BC.

Testament equivalent, despite attempts by many scholars to discover underlying references to it in the text of Genesis 1:2 and other passages which speak of God's power over the waters.

An epic of early man
One Babylonian poem, the *Atrakhasis Epic,* bears further comparison with Genesis. This is concerned with the infancy of man and the beginning of society, and hints at the order of the world without describing its creation. It starts with the minor gods working to irrigate the land, then rebelling at their lot, from which they are relieved by the creation of man who is to do the work instead. Man is a satisfactory substitute until his noise causes disturbance and leads to his destruction in the flood (see Flood Stories).

In outline, *Atrakhasis* (known from copies made about 1600 BC) has some similarity to parts of Genesis 2-8. Man is made from clay and a divine part ('breath' in Genesis, the flesh and blood of a god in *Atrakhasis*): man's task is to keep the earth in order (arduous labour in *Atrakhasis,* control of a paradise in Genesis); man is eventually destroyed by flood, all except one family. On the other hand, *Atrakhasis* has man toiling from the first, has no single 'Adam', no separate making of woman, no Eden, and no Fall – in fact no moral teaching at all. The sense is rather that this is how man's lot came to be, and he should accept it.

A Sumerian version names five important cities in the time before the flood, and they link with separately preserved lists of pre-flood kings whose ages far exceeded those of the patriarchs in Genesis 5. Babylonian writers looked upon the flood as a major interruption in their country's history. In their over-all coverage, therefore, Genesis and the tradition represented by *Atrakhasis* look back to the same events. Some of the themes in the Babylonian story – in particular, man's place as a substitute worker – can be traced in a Sumerian poem, *Enki and Ninmakh,* written before 2,000 BC.

Folk memory and revelation
These factual similarities only serve to emphasize the wide difference in moral and spiritual outlook between the Hebrew Genesis and its closest counterparts. There is no need to argue that Genesis was derived from the others, as critics of the Bible have hastened to do. The differences of standpoint and content are in fact so marked that they serve to highlight the divine inspiration of Genesis rather than undermine it.

5
FROM ADAM TO NOAH

Family-trees (genealogies) similar to this one are often given in the Bible attesting a line of descent. Many of them are selective, sometimes in order to give a pattern of a certain number of names (e.g. Matthew 1). So we cannot work out the length of the whole period simply by adding up all the figures given.

The life-span of these men is remarkable. It ranges from 777 years for Lamech to Methuselah's 969 years (apart from Enoch, whom God 'took' at 365). Many races have traditions of exceptionally long life amongst their early forebears. But none of the various attempted explanations has so far proved satisfactory.

Each of the ten records follows the same formula:

When A had lived x years he became the father of B. He lived after the birth of B y years and had other sons and daughters. Thus all his days were z years, and he died.

The sombre note of the final phrase 'and he died' is varied only in the case of Enoch, the man who 'walked with God'. For him God had other plans. Noah, the last of the ten, in his turn also 'walked with God' (6:9). And in his case, too, God intervened to save him from death.

The story of the garden of Eden is set in the well-watered valleys of ancient Mesopotamia.

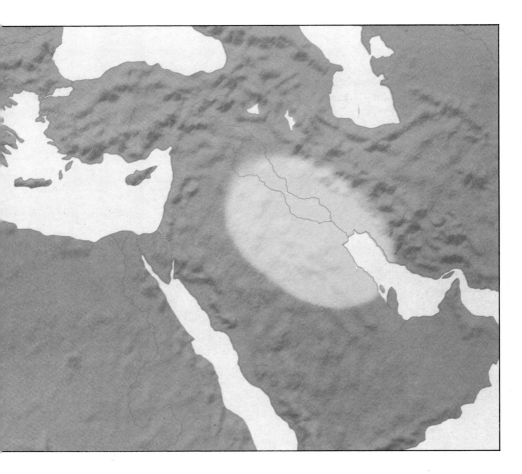

6—9
THE GREAT FLOOD

6—9:17 The rescue, and God's promise to Noah

Flood-stories have been handed down in many languages from most parts of the world. The Babylonian (Sumerian, and particularly Akkadian) accounts have considerable similarity with the story recorded here. This is not surprising, if both reflect memories of an actual event in the same general area. There is no need to assume the writer of Genesis must have drawn on the Babylonian stories for his information. Indeed, the crudeness of these (with their many bickering, capricious gods) makes this unlikely.

Extent and date of the flood: if we take the terms used in Genesis 7:19ff. in their modern sense, the flood must have been universal. But biblical writers use similar phrases in contexts where it is clear they are not speaking of the whole world as we understand it (Genesis 41:56-57; Acts 2:5). Taking the description at the very least, the flood covered a vast area, the 'whole world' of man's early history as recounted in Genesis 2ff.

Its universality as far as human life is concerned depends on when it actually happened, and we can do no more than guess at the date. The list of nations descended from Noah's sons (Genesis 10) makes it clear that the flood must have occurred very early indeed. It was certainly long before the various South Mesopotamian floods of which traces have been found in the course of excavation.

The ark ('boat', Good News Bible): the Hebrew word means 'box' or 'chest'. It is used elsewhere only for the watertight 'basket' in which the baby Moses floated on the Nile – an interesting parallel.

The ark is vast, designed to float, not sail – and there were no launching problems! An 18-inch cubit gives the measurements as 450 x 75 x 45 feet or 133 x 22 x 13 metres.

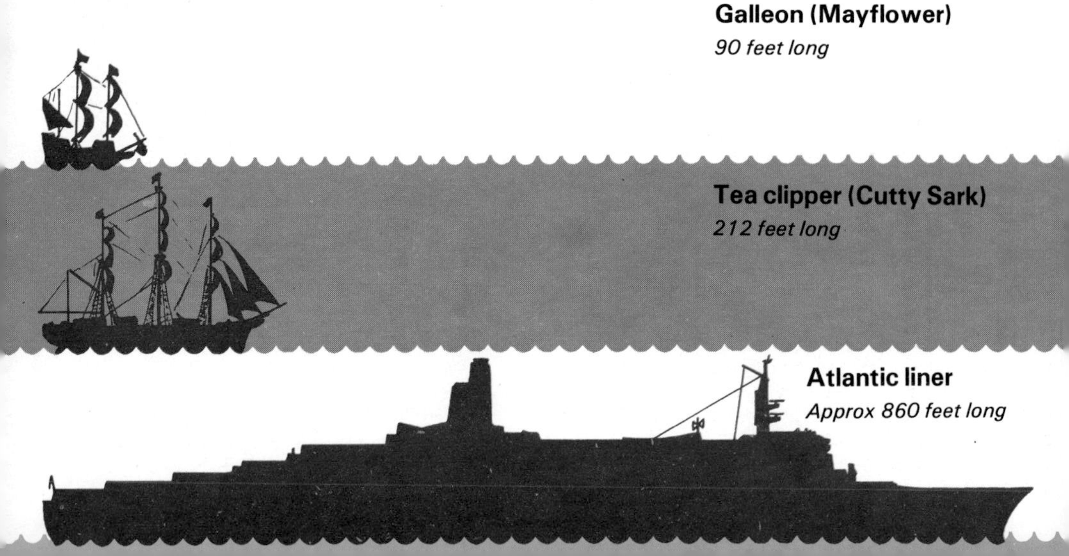

The Ark

Scholars have speculated for centuries over the shape of the Ark. Genesis 6: states the length was to be 300 cubits (approx 450 feet) long

Galleon (Mayflower)

90 feet long

Tea clipper (Cutty Sark)

212 feet long

Atlantic liner

Approx 860 feet long

Flood Stories

ALAN MILLARD

Memories of a great flood or floods are worldwide. As one would expect, they have such common features as escape by boat, animals taken aboard, and grounding on a high peak. Only Babylonia has given us a story so close to Genesis that the question of borrowing or of direct influence is seriously considered.

For a century this story has been known from the *Epic of Gilgamesh,* Tablet 11. Its theme is that man cannot hope for immortality, the only one who gained it being the Babylonian Noah. It was taken into the Gilgamesh series from an older work the *Atrakhasis Epic* (see 'Other Creation Accounts', page 129). Here it forms part of a longer account of man's history from his creation, as in Genesis.

Babylonian account

After the first men were made, it relates, the noise of their many children was so great that the god of the earth could not sleep. His schemes for reducing man's noise were thwarted when the pious Atrakhasis won the help of the god whose creature man was. Finally, the gods decided upon a catastrophic flood, all swearing to keep the plan secret. Again, Atrakhasis was warned, the god instructing him in a dream to build a boat, take on board his family and animals, and explain his action to his fellow men as a punishment inflicted upon him which would bring benefit to them. When all were aboard, the storm broke, and all mankind was swept away.

The gods themselves were also affected. With man destroyed, they lost the food and drink supplied in sacrificial offerings, and sat miserably in heaven until the seven days' tempest had ended. Then Atrakhasis sent out birds to learn whether the land was habitable again (an episode preserved only in the *Gilgamesh* version), and offered sacrifice on the mountain where his boat had come to rest. Eagerly, the gods gathered 'like flies', smelling the savour of the offering, swearing not to cause such destruction again. The mother-goddess swore by a necklace of blue stones. But the god whose sleep had been disturbed was not yet appeased, and after the unfairness of indiscriminate punishment had been discussed, a system was set up in which some women avoided childbirth by entering religious orders, while others lost infants through disease, thus limiting the population. (The terms used make it clear that this was an explanation of the social system of the author's time.)

A question of theology

The flood story in Babylonia is also known from a Sumerian text telling virtually the same tale, though more briefly, and many Sumerian compositions refer to the distant days of the flood or before.

The Genesis flood story has a recognizable background in Mesopotamia, and the numerous similarities suggest it is a record of the same event as the Babylonian. But its moral and theological content are obviously very different. God's revelation consists not only in the telling of the facts but also in their interpretation.

The eleventh tablet of the Assyrian version of the 'Epic of Gilgamesh', containing the Babylonian account of the flood, 7th century BC.

The covenant (6:18): an important and recurring theme in Scripture. God establishes his covenant (agreement) successively with Noah, with Abraham, with the nation of Israel (through Moses), and with David. Each covenant grows progressively richer in promise, until the coming of Christ ushers in the 'new covenant'.

In every instance God takes the initiative – this is no agreement between equal parties. God draws up the terms. He makes them known. And he alone guarantees their keeping. Men enjoy the blessings of the covenant in so far as they obey God's commands.

See 'Covenants and Near Eastern Treaties', page 98.

9:18-29 Noah's drunkenness

Even a completely fresh start does not change man – as this shameful little story makes plain. Ham dishonours his drunken father, and Noah curses him through his son Canaan. (His other sons are not named in the curse.) The Canaanites did indeed become subject to Shem's descendants, the Israelites.

10 – 11
FROM NOAH TO THE CALL OF ABRA(HA)M

10 The families of Noah's three sons

The genealogy is arranged in the following pattern:

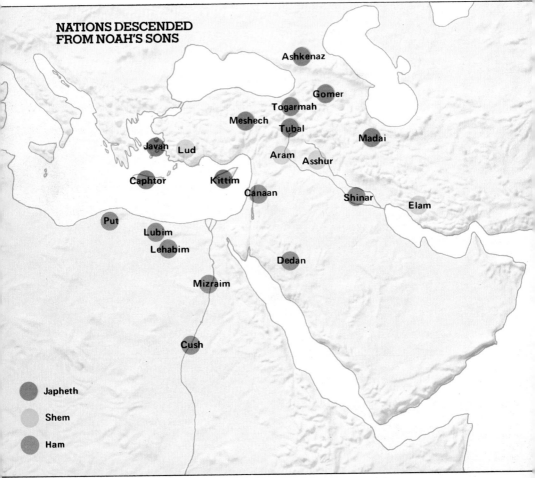

NATIONS DESCENDED FROM NOAH'S SONS

Ashkenaz
Gomer
Togarmah
Meshech
Tubal
Madai
Javan
Lud
Aram
Asshur
Caphtor
Kittim
Canaan
Shinar
Elam
Put
Lubim
Lehabim
Dedan
Mizraim
Cush

Japheth
Shem
Ham

Heading (1)
Japheth's descendants (2-4)
Extra detail on Javan (5a)
Summary (5b)

Ham's descendants (6-7, 13-18a)
Extra detail on Nimrod (8-12)
and Canaan (18b-19)
Summary (20)

Shem's descendants (22-29a)
Extra detail on Shem (21)
and Joktan (29b-30)
Summary (31)
Summary to the whole list (32)

Shem's family comes last, as these are the nations around which the next stage of the narrative develops.

11:1-9 Babel

In Shinar, kingdom of Nimrod the hunter (10:10), men get together on a great building project – a city and a tower with its top in the heavens. God looks down at this co-operative effort of man trying to make himself god-like, and sees it as the beginning of worse rebellion against him. So he divides men by language barriers, and scatters them abroad – the very thing they were trying to insure against. And the great tower remains unfinished.

The tower of Babel was in all likelihood a multi-storeyed temple-tower, or ziggurat, similar to those developed in Babylonia in the 3rd millennium BC.

11:10-32 Shem to Abraham

Here again the list of names is selective, probably abbreviating the total length of time involved. Noah's ancestors were considerably longer-lived than Terah's, and the age of parenthood is now much younger.

When Terah's name is reached the list becomes more detailed. This is the family we are to concentrate on. Terah's three sons are named, and their home-town given as Ur of the Chaldeans. After the death of Haran, Terah sets out for Canaan, with his grandson Lot and his son Abram and childless daughter-in-law Sarai. En route, however, they settle at Harran. Terah dies, and the stage is set for the story of Abraham (the new name records God's promise to make this man the father of many nations, 17:5).

A partially reconstructed ziggurat or temple-tower at Ur shows how the Tower of Babel may have been built, with stairways leading up from one level to the next. The house-walls recall the fact that Abraham was called from Ur when it was a thriving and prosperous city.

12—25:18
ABRAHAM: A NEW START

12:1-9 God's call, and the journey to Canaan

12:1 records God's call and promise to one man, Abram, and his obedient response. Yet the consequences of this simple beginning were to spread like ripples on a pond. As a direct result a new nation is born. And in course of time the whole world reaps the benefits.

'So Abram went . . .' He had already left Ur, a prosperous city with security and a high standard of living. Now he sets out on the second stage of the journey, with Sarai, his childless wife, and his nephew Lot, camping in tents.

At Shechem, in the midst of Canaanite country, God speaks again. 'This land' is to be the heritage of Abram's descendants. Yet the journey continues, down towards the Negev, a dry region of some 4,500 sq. miles, stretching south from Beersheba

to the Sinai highlands. Here there is pasture for nomadic flocks and herds.

12:10-20 Famine

Hunger drives Abram into Egypt. Under stress of fear and insecurity he adopts a pretence which puts God's whole plan at risk. God intervenes with plagues, and Abram is ignominiously deported.

Sarai's age: it seems surprising to find Sarai, at 65, described as 'very beautiful' (12:14). Presumably, since it is said that she lived to 127, her sixties would be equivalent to our thirties or forties.

13 The parting with Lot

Increasing flocks and herds precipitate the last break in family ties. Lot, generously given the choice by his uncle, selects the fertile pasture of the Jordan Valley.

14 War of the kings, and the meeting with Melchizedek

In Abram's day, although a semi-nomadic

Abraham's war with the tribal kings was followed by the fellowship meal with Melchizedek, king of Salem. This 'standard', buried in a royal tomb at Ur some centuries before Abraham's time, shows scenes of war on one side, and here the victory feast and parade of booty. The standard is a mosaic of shell, red limestone and lapis lazuli.

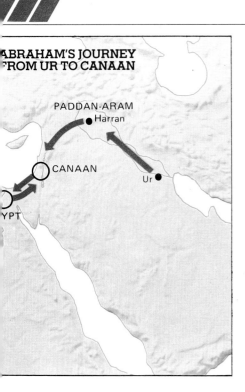

ABRAHAM'S JOURNEY FROM UR TO CANAAN

PADDAN-ARAM
Harran

CANAAN
Ur

YPT

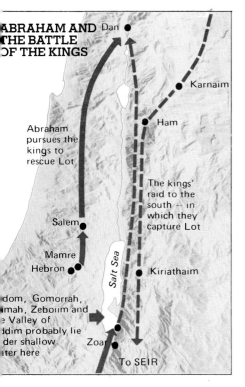

ABRAHAM AND THE BATTLE OF THE KINGS

Dan

Karnaim

Ham

Abraham pursues the kings to rescue Lot

The kings' raid to the south — in which they capture Lot

Salem

Mamre
Hebron

Salt Sea

Kiriathaim

dom, Gomorrah,
mah, Zeboiim and
e Valley of
ldim probably lie
der shallow
iter here

Zoar

To SEIR

existence was common, there was also settled life in villages and walled 'cities' (small towns). These were ruled over by local 'sheiks', who in turn were often vassals of more powerful kings.

Chedorlaomer of Elam (1): the overlords of the Dead Sea towns came from distant Elam and Babylonia. Trade-routes made for easy travel and communications between the land of Abram's birth and Canaan. The Elamites had considerable power in Babylonia. Ur was amongst the cities they conquered and sacked at this time.

Amorites (7): Abram's allies belonged to a tribe sharing the land with the Canaanites. They had good reason to support Abram, since their own people had been victims of the attack. Speed of pursuit and a surprise attack gave Abram victory.

Melchizedek (18): this is the only appearance of the rather mysterious king/priest of Salem (probably Jerusalem). Melchizedek's authority (the 'tithe' was God's portion, so by giving Melchizedek a tenth of everything Abram recognized him as God's representative), his lack of any named ancestors and descendants (extremely important for any man claiming kingship or priesthood), and his dual role as priest and king, led later writers to see in him a foreshadowing of the Messiah (see Psalm 110:4; Hebrews 7:1-10).

15 The covenant confirmed

Archaeology has shown that customs recorded here and in later chapters reflect the known social and cultural patterns of north Mesopotamia in the 2nd millennium (2,000-1,000) BC.

The heir: it was not uncommon practice at the time for childless couples to adopt an heir, sometimes, as here, a slave. The adoption contract might contain a proviso that if a natural son was born he would take precedence as the legal heir.

Verse 6: 'Abram believed the Lord, and he credited it to him as righteousness.' One of the most significant verses of Scripture, and in the circumstances a response

A bedouin sheik near Beersheba illustrates the life of the desert chieftain. Living in spacious tents, they are free to take their flocks to the best grazing-grounds.

the animals the parties to the treaty made it clear that the penalty for breaking the agreement was death. Here, significantly, it is only God who puts himself on oath by passing between the pieces. Darkness, smoke and fire mark the presence of God, as at Sinai (see Exodus 19:18; Hebrews 12:18).

Four hundred years (15:13)…the fourth generation (15:16): the word 'generation' may also mean 'lifetime', and the lifetime of Abram was well over a century.

Verse 16b: New English Bible 'for the Amorites will not be ripe for punishment till then.' This helps us understand the orders to destroy the Canaanite nations at the conquest. It was a matter of justice. God gave them more than four centuries to show a change of heart. By Joshua's time they had reached the point of no return. As with Sodom and Gomorrah, judgement could no longer be delayed.

16 A son by a slave-girl

The childless Sarai falls back on custom in giving her slave-girl to Abram. This provision could be written into the marriage contract. The resulting child would become the wife's. But human emotions in such a situation are complex, and the unhappy sequel is not surprising.

17 New names and a covenant sign

God's fifth affirmation of his covenant with Abram is marked by the giving of new names – Abram becomes 'Abraham'; Sarai becomes 'Sarah' – and the physical sign of circumcision. Twenty-four years after the departure from Harran the time of the promised son's arrival is announced.

Circumcision: this was no new rite. In the nations around it marked admission to adult status in the tribe. But for Israel it was the outward sign of a relationship: God was to be their God; they were to be his people. It was a mark of ownership,

of remarkable faith. Galatians 3:6ff. teaches that, as in Abram's case, our standing before God is entirely dependent on faith. We cannot win a place in heaven by good deeds – neither did he.

The covenant ritual: a typical procedure for the confirmation of a treaty (see Jeremiah 34:18). By killing and dividing

and a reminder of the covenant 'between me and you and your descendants after you' (17:7). Some stress the medical grounds for the practice and the choice of the eighth day, despite the dangers.

18 Three visitors, and Abraham's prayer for Sodom

Abraham welcomed a stranger and, all unknowingly, took the Lord himself into his home. The lavish welcome and provision (despite the inconvenience of the visitors' arrival during the midday siesta) are typical of hospitality amongst nomadic desert people even today. The 'morsel of bread' offered to the guests turns out to be a meal of fresh cakes, curds and milk, and the best veal. The words 'Is anything too hard for the Lord?' reveal the visitor's true identity, and Sarah's incredulous laughter changes to fear.

Abraham's prayer gives an insight into the quality of his relationship with God. No wonder 2 Chronicles 20:7 describes him as God's 'friend'. In the event, Sodom could not produce even ten good men, but we have seen something of the lengths to which God's mercy goes.

19 The destruction of Sodom and Gomorrah: Lot's rescue

'Where are the men who came to you tonight? Bring them out to us so that we can have sex with them' (verse 5). Every man in the city is implicated – not one supports Lot's protest against the infringement of the most sacred laws of hospitality (not to say humanity).
The destruction: the catastrophe was probably caused by an earthquake and explosion of gases. The shallow southern waters of the Dead Sea now cover the cities. Nothing could save the cities from God's judgement, yet for Lot's sake he

The Dead Sea is so far below sea-level that it has no outlet; the water evaporates, leaving a high concentration of salts which kill all life.

Salt rocks near the Dead Sea, and the acrid reek in the air, are silent reminders today of the fate of Lot's wife: reluctant to leave Sodom, she was overwhelmed in the catastrophe and rain of salt.

spares Zoar and delays the cataclysm till Lot is safe. 'I won't destroy that town. Hurry! Run! I can't do anything until you get there' (19:22). Even so Lot's wife drags behind, stopping to look, and dies. Local tradition calls salty crags by the Dead Sea after her still.

Moab and Ammon (37-38): both tribes were to prove a constant snare to Israel (see Numbers 25, and the frequent denunciations of the prophets).

20 Abraham and King Abimelech

A repetition of the same sin under similarly testing circumstances does not make this a duplicate of 12:10-20. Abraham is not the only man to be put to shame twice before those he considered to have 'no fear of God' to guide their actions. (On Abimelech, see 26:1.)

21:1-21 Isaac is born: Hagar and Ishmael leave

Twenty-five years have elapsed between the promise and its fulfilment. Isaac's elderly parents have reason to be overjoyed at his birth. Sarah's demand that Hagar and Ishmael should be sent away ran counter to custom. Abraham needs a word from God before he is willing to agree. Galatians 4:22ff. shows why the rift was inevitable.

The child (14): Ishmael was by now in fact about 16. Isaac would have been two or three years old by the time he was weaned.

21:22-34 A dispute over wells

Wells were precious to the herdsmen in the dry climate of southern Palestine, and disputes about ownership not infrequent (see 26:17ff.). Monthly rainfall in the area drops from 4 inches/100mm in January to nothing at all in the four summer months.

22 The supreme test

Abraham's previous experience of God would certainly not have led him to suppose child-sacrifice would please him. Nor was this general practice in Abraham's time. In addition, God has specifically promised descendants through Isaac, who was not yet married. It can only be, as Hebrews 11:19 says, that such was Abraham's faith in God's word, he believed him able to raise the boy to life again. This is implied in Abraham's 'we will come back to you' (verse 5). The parallel between Abraham's sacrifice and the greater sacrifice of God's own Son is striking – yet the lesson Hebrews draws from this chapter is one of faith.

The land of Moriah (2): Abraham's offering took place on one of the hills on which

An ancient water-skin in the Agricultural Museum, Jerusalem.

This portrayal of a ram's head, dating from near the time of Abraham, was found at Açana, Turkey.

Jerusalem now stands (possibly the temple hill itself – see 2 Chronicles 3:1). The journey of about 50 miles/80 km took him three days.

23 The death and burial of Sarah

These Hittites may have been early migrants from the Hittite Empire in Turkey (founded about 1,800 BC). The whole transaction conforms in detail to known Hittite law (the mention of the trees, the weighing of the silver by current standards, and the proclamation in the presence of witnesses at the city gate). Family-tombs, often caves or cut from rock, were also customary. The traditional site of the burial-cave at Hebron is today covered by a mosque.

24 A wife for Isaac

This is one of the loveliest and most beautifully told stories in the Old Testament. It reflects the traditional Eastern arranged marriage. The steward's gifts in verse 53 seal the betrothal. It is a fitting conclusion that God, who has so clearly

Watering flocks of sheep and goats at a well in the hills of Judea.

guided at every stage, should set his seal on the marriage in the deep love of Isaac for Rebekah.

25:1-11 Abraham's last days

Keturah's sons became the ancestors of a number of north Arabian peoples. Isaac remained his father's sole heir, and on Abraham's death the blessing of God became his.

25:12-18 Ishmael's descendants

'Havilah to Shur' – the tribes occupied Sinai and north-west Arabia.

25:19—26:35
ISAAC'S UNHAPPY HOUSEHOLD

Once again the line is continued by the direct action of God. After 20 years' waiting Esau and Jacob are born.

The birthright (25:31): as firstborn son Esau would succeed Isaac as head of the

Rebekah was given silver and gold ornaments: a traditional silver necklace and headdress are worn here by a Yemenite Jewish girl in present-day Israel.

family, and inherit a double share of the estate. When he sells his birthright he forfeits all title to the blessing which goes with it.

There is no commendation of Jacob's

A contract tablet for the sale of a plot of land and (right) its envelope which bears a duplicate text and seals of 11 witnesses. Old Babylonian, about 1750 BC.

cool calculation – but Scripture openly censures Esau's attitude. He was 'worldly minded' (Hebrews 12:16-17) – 'he sold his birthright for a single meal'. 'Thus Esau showed how little he valued his birthright' (25:34, New English Bible).

Abimelech, the Philistine king (26:1): the name is probably a family or throne-name. This is therefore likely to have been a later king than the one Abraham encountered (20-21). The Philistines (one of the trading Sea Peoples, many of whom settled the east Mediterranean coast-lands), who gave their name to Palestine, invaded the area in force in the 12th century BC. The group met by the patriarchs would have been amongst earlier settlements of Aegean traders.

27–35
DECEIT AND SHARP PRACTICE: JACOB'S EXILE AND RETURN

27 The blessing
Not one of the family comes out well in this story. Isaac's plan goes against what God revealed before the boys were born (25:23). Esau, in agreeing to the plan, is breaking his oath (25:33). Jacob and

Hebron, site of the traditional burial-place of the patriarchs, is over 3,000 feet/1,000m up in the hills of Judea. The building over the burial-cave goes back to the time of Herod, with additions in Byzantine and Crusader times.

Rebekah, although in the right, make no reference to God, but cheat and lie to achieve their ends.

Isaac relies completely on his senses, each of which lets him down – even the sense of taste on which he prided himself. When his ears tell him the truth, he will not listen. The blessing is Jacob's, as God always intended – but at a heavy price. Esau is ready to do murder. The relationship between Isaac and Rebekah is spoilt. And Rebekah will never again see her favourite son. Jacob, the home-lover, goes into exile.

28 The fugitive
Isaac's parting blessing recognizes Jacob as heir to God's promise.
Paddan-aram, or Aram-naharaim, 'land of the two rivers' **(2):** Rebekah's homeland,

Camels, in use in patriarchal times, became a major means of transport in peace and war by the times of Solomon and Ahab.

Paddan-aram, lay between the upper Euphrates and Habur rivers. The Aramaeans later penetrated south and east, settling in Syria and Mesopotamia.

Bethel, 'house of God' **(19):** Jacob reaches Bethel, 60 miles north of Beersheba, as darkness falls. In this desolate spot, at a moment of unutterable loneliness, God stands beside Jacob. He repeats to this unpromising man the promise made to Abraham and Isaac. And he adds his personal guarantee of company and protection, with the assurance of eventual safe return.

The 'ladder' of older translations is in fact a stairway (perhaps like that of the ziggurat, see page 135), since angels are going up and down it (compare Jesus' words to Nathanael in John 1:51).

The 'pillar' – not very large – consecrated by the oil is set up to commemorate the vision.

29 – 31 The years with Laban: Jacob meets his match

These three chapters cover the 20 years of Jacob's exile: 14 years' service for his two wives, 6 for flocks of his own. The years hold little joy for Jacob, who meets a crooked dealer after his own kind in his uncle Laban. The deceit over Leah leads to an intolerable home life. The unloved wife hopes with each new son to win her husband's affection. Rachel, lovely and loved, is embittered by continuing childlessness. And Jacob finds himself traded between the two. Small wonder the law later forbade a man to marry his wife's sister during the wife's lifetime.

29:14: 'You are my own flesh and blood.' The implication may be that Laban is adopting Jacob as his son – particularly as no son of his own is mentioned at this time. Marriage to a sister by adoption was quite customary.

29:18: Jacob offers service in place of the usual marriage gift. Laban is not slow to exploit the generosity of the offer. The gift of a slave-girl to his daughter (verse 24) may have been part of the dowry.

29:26: the custom Laban refers to is not otherwise known.

29:28: after the week's festivities Rachel was given to Jacob, on condition he served another seven years for her.

30:3: this reflects the same custom as Sarah observed (16:1-2).

30:14: mandrakes were thought to induce fertility – which makes Leah's subsequent pregnancy ironic.

30:37ff.: Jacob thought the sight of the rods during gestation would affect the unborn lambs. In fact he owed his flocks to the overruling of God, and to the practice of selective breeding which the dream revealed.

31:14: Leah and Rachel were entitled to part of the wealth their marriage-gifts brought Laban.

31:19: Rachel acted, so she thought, in Jacob's interest. The possession of household gods would support the legality of her claim to an inheritance.

31:44: the non-aggression pact made by Laban and Jacob has many contemporary parallels. The covenant meal seals it.

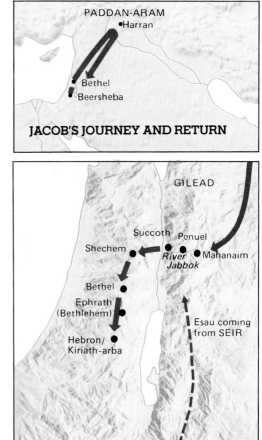

JACOB'S JOURNEY AND RETURN

32 God meets Jacob

Although Esau has settled in Seir in the far south, the meeting between the two brothers is inevitable. The news that Esau is coming at speed, and with a force, strikes terror into Jacob. This time, though, he plans *and* prays.

Alone, and sleepless, Jacob's lifetime struggle against God culminates in this strange wrestling-bout. At the end of it, Jacob is crippled, but a new man. The next altar he erects will be, not to the God of his fathers, but to 'God, the God of Israel' ('El Elohe Israel', 33:20).

33 Jacob meets Esau

Esau's welcome to the brother who had wronged him is so amazingly generous that Jesus may have had him in mind when he told the story of the prodigal son (see Luke 15:20). Jacob's gift, and Esau's acceptance of it, seal the reconciliation.

Verse 14: Jacob has no intention of going to Seir, as the next stage of the journey shows. Even now he cannot be straight-forward about it.

34 Dinah and Shechem: rape and massacre

The city of Shechem has a long and important history. Jacob's stay there cost him dear – and the treacherous vengeance of Simeon and Levi was not forgotten (see 49:5ff.).

35 The return to Bethel: Benjamin is born: Rachel and Isaac die

This chapter rounds off the section of Genesis centring on Jacob. Foreign gods are put aside. God reaffirms his covenant with Israel. Rachel dies near Bethlehem (Ephrath) giving birth to the last of Jacob's 12 sons. Esau and Jacob come face to face again at the death of the aged Isaac.

Standing stone in the ruins of Shechem, some of which date from Canaanite times.

36
ESAU AND HIS DESCENDANTS

Once again, before starting a new stage in the story, we catch up on the other branch of the family.

Seir/Edom (8): the valley between the Dead Sea and the Red Sea (Gulf of Aqaba) and the mountainous area on either side. The king's highway, an important trade route, ran down the eastern plateau. In later days there was little love lost between Edom and Israel.

37–50
JOSEPH, THE FAMINE AND THE MIGRATION TO EGYPT

37 Joseph sold into Egypt

The final section of Genesis, centring on Joseph, now begins.

Joseph's special robe (3): Joseph's brothers saw this as a sign that Isaac intended to pass them by and make Joseph his heir (see 48:21-22 and 49:22ff.).

Verse 24: the pit, here mercifully dry, was intended for water storage.

Ishmaelite and Midianite merchants (28): both these groups of desert-dwellers were descended from Abraham. The names are interchangeable (compare verses 28 and 36; Judges 8:24). The use of alternative names is a characteristic feature of Near Eastern writing. The 'balm' of Gilead (an area roughly east of the Jordan and north of the Jabbok) was famous, and the spice-trade an important one from earliest times. Spices had many uses – in food preparation and the manufacture of incense and cosmetics. The trade-route from Damascus to the coast ran past Dothan.

Verse 28: despite the way the verse reads in the Revised Standard Version, and the New English Bible's interpretation, verse 27 and 45:4 make it far more likely that Joseph was sold by his brothers. Reuben's absence is not improbable – there were

Vegetables for sale are spread on the ground at the bedouin market in Beersheba.

flocks to be seen to. Neither this, nor the matter of Ishmaelite and Midianite merchants, makes it necessary to see the story as a combination of two different traditions.

Officer (36): the word is usually translated 'eunuch', as in the New English Bible, but it may also have the more general meaning of 'court official', which is more likely here in view of Potiphar's marriage.

38 Judah's sons

This none-too-creditable story is probably

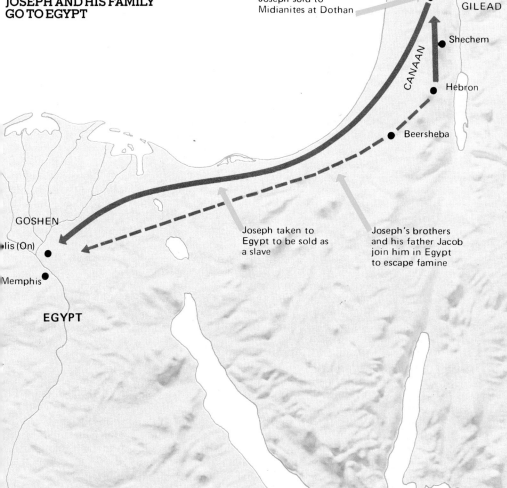

JOSEPH AND HIS FAMILY GO TO EGYPT

Joseph sold to Midianites at Dothan

GILEAD

Shechem

CANAAN

Hebron

Beersheba

GOSHEN

Iis (On)

Memphis

EGYPT

Joseph taken to Egypt to be sold as a slave

Joseph's brothers and his father Jacob join him in Egypt to escape famine

included because it forms part of the family-tree of the (later) royal house, from which the Messiah himself was descended (Matthew 1:3; Luke 3:33).
Verses 8-10: if a man died childless, his brother was duty bound to raise heirs to him by his widow (set out as the Levirate law, Deuteronomy 25:5).

39 Joseph accused and imprisoned

The account of Joseph's life in Egypt given in chapters 39-50 fits perfectly into the background of Egypt under the

Semitic Hyksos pharaohs. They ruled from about 1710-1570 BC, from a capital (Avaris) in the eastern part of the Nile delta. Goshen was also somewhere in this region.

The Egyptian *Tale of Two Brothers* narrates similar incidents to those in this chapter – underlining the unfortunate fact that such things do happen.

40 The dreams of the butler and baker

The story brings out the significance of

Measuring grain for taxation purposes; from the Tomb of Menna, west Thebes, about 1,400 BC.

Statuette of an Egyptian high official of the time Israel was in Egypt.

dreams and their interpretation at this time. Egyptian sages had dream-manuals to help them make their interpretation. Joseph, by contrast, depends completely on God to make the meaning clear.

The 'butler' (1, Revised Standard Version**):** Pharaoh's cup-bearer or wine steward, an important official (compare Nehemiah 2:1).

41 Pharaoh's dream and Joseph's promotion

Two years later Pharaoh himself has a dream which defeats his magicians and wise men, despite all their training and a whole library of reference books. When the cup-bearer at last remembers Joseph, he not only proves able to explain God's message, but comes up with a clear-cut

plan of action.

Verse 14: Egyptian custom dictates that Joseph must be shaven and dressed in linen for an appearance at court.

Verses 40-43: Joseph's investiture follows Egyptian tradition – the ring (his badge of authority), fine linen (court dress) and a gold chain or collar in reward for his services. Horses and chariots had helped the Hyksos pharaohs to gain ascendancy in Egypt. After 13 years as a slave, Joseph becomes governor of all Egypt.

Verse 45: On =Heliopolis, 10 miles north-east of Cairo, the centre of Egyptian sun-worship.

Verse 54: severe famine was not unknown in Egypt. But it was rare for famine to hit Egypt and Palestine simultaneously.

42—45 Famine, and family reunion

These chapters give a moving account of Joseph's meeting, testing and eventual reunion with his brothers. Behind his apparent harshness lies complete and

An Egyptian dream-manual probably composed about the time of Joseph. Good and bad dreams are listed in columns, with their interpretations.

generous forgiveness of the wrong done him, and a deep understanding of the way God controls human destiny (45:5ff.). Under each new stress the brothers show a genuine change of attitude from the old days. Twenty years have not obliterated their sense of guilt (42:21-22). They will not behave towards the new favourite (Benjamin) as they did towards the old.

43:32: the Egyptians probably considered that the presence of foreigners at the table defiled their food. For the same reason, later, Jews would not eat with Gentiles.

44:2, 5: Joseph may have used his silver cup for divination (interpreting events by the movement of drops of oil on water; Good News Bible, New International Version). Or the steward may be implying the impossibility of escaping detection by his wise and powerful master.

45:10: in times of famine nomads from Palestine are known to have been allowed pasturage in the eastern delta.

46—47 Israel settles in Egypt

Jacob's household numbers 70 on entry to Egypt (the 66 of 46:26 excludes Jacob, and Joseph and his two sons were there already). With all the wives and servants the company would be much larger.

46:34: the Egyptian dislike of the nomadic shepherds is probably no different from the feelings of most settled people towards wandering gypsies. Here the dislike serves a useful purpose in keeping the family as an isolated unit. Otherwise the group's identity might quickly have been lost.

47:16-19: under Joseph's economic policy Pharaoh gains ownership of the land, and the people become his tenants. Only the priests keep their estates.

48—49 Jacob's blessing

The blessing of Joseph's sons was an act of faith (Hebrews 11:21). How simply Jacob's hands cross over to convey God's blessing to the younger son. What a contrast to the story in chapter 27.

Joseph enjoys a double inheritance through Ephraim and Manasseh.

Jacob's dying blessing focusses on the distant future, when the descendants of these twelve will occupy the promised land.

49:4: the outrage recorded in 35:22 costs Reuben his birthright as firstborn son.

49:5-7: Jacob's judgement of Simeon's and Levi's conduct at Shechem (34:13ff.) is clear. Both tribes were to be scattered, but Levi's as the nation's priesthood.

49:10: from Judah came the royal line of Israel, from which the Messiah would eventually be born.

49: 13: although near enough to acquire wealth from maritime trade, Zebulun's territory did not stretch to the sea.

49:19: such raids are recorded on the 9th-century Moabite Stone.

50 The death of Jacob to the death of Joseph -- the end of the beginning

Jacob joins Leah in the family tomb at Hebron – the last member of the family to be buried in Canaan for more than 400 years. The huge canvas of Genesis, begun with the great strokes of creation and pulsating life in Eden, continued through destruction, promise, and the birth of a new nation in Canaan, is finished with the death of Joseph in Egypt.

Verses 2-3: it was normal to employ professional embalmers – but perhaps Joseph wanted to avoid religious entanglements. Two centuries later the normal embalming period was 70 days. The mourning observed for Jacob was only two days shorter than that for a pharaoh.

Verse 22: Joseph's life-span of 110 years was the Egyptian ideal, a token of God's blessing. His dying request sums up the faith of a lifetime.

Verse 26: the coffin would be of wood, with a painted head.

Egypt

K. A. KITCHEN

THE LAND

The real Egypt is not the blank square of modern political maps. It is the 600 miles of narrow valley north from Aswan culminating in the broad delta where the River Nile reaches the Mediterranean Sea. On a landmap, the delta and valley appear like a lotus-flower on a curving stem; the small 'bud' is the Fayum lake-province.

The sole source of life is the annual flooding of the Nile. Before the modern high dams, a 'good Nile' meant prosperity, leaving a new layer of silt and abundant water for crops. But a low Nile spelt doom by starvation and an excessive Nile widespread destruction. Wherever its waters reach, there is lush green plant-life; all else is dry, dead, tawny-yellow desert.

Flanked by deserts, inhabited Egypt on the ribbon of valley cultivation and broad delta plains was isolated but not insulated from her neighbours. Internally, the Nile was a major highway. Beyond, routes across north Sinai led to Palestine, and through the eastern desert valleys to the Red Sea. The Nile provided an agricultural economy, and the deserts yielded stone and metal.

HISTORY AND CULTURE

Egypt's history – like that of Sumer and Babylon – is a rich panorama covering 30 centuries. It began about 3,000 BC, when the valley and delta were united under a single king, soon after the invention of the hieroglyphs (a partly-pictorial writing-system). The long line of Egyptian kings or 'pharaohs' form 30 royal families or 'dynasties'. But the whole period from 3,000 down to 300 BC is more easily viewed in seven epochs: a beginning ('Archaic' age), three ages of greatness (Old, Middle, New Kingdoms) separated by 1st and 2nd 'intermediate' periods of dissension, and the Late Period of final decline.

Throughout most of Egyptian history, the real capital was at the junction of valley and delta, usually Memphis. In the New Kingdom, Thebes – 300 miles further south – became the southern capital; it long remained a religious centre as the city of the god Amun. In the Late Period, Memphis shared its role with various delta cities. Throughout, the pharaoh was the keystone of society, as the intermediary between gods

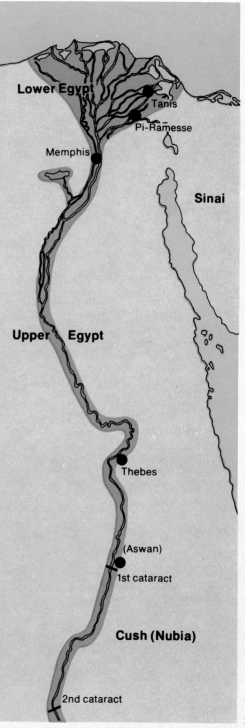

Lower Egypt

Tanis

Pi-Ramesse

Memphis

Sinai

Upper Egypt

Thebes

(Aswan)

1st cataract

Cush (Nubia)

2nd cataract

»

The secular side of pharaoh's rule was in practice shared with high officers of state: grand viziers for south and north, chief treasurers, superintendents of granaries, even chief taxation-masters! These departments were supported by a central and local bureaucracy of scribes in the capital and the provinces. The great priesthoods had their own estates and administrations. From the New Kingdom onward, pharaoh also led and maintained a standing army of chariotry and infantry. Education was based on scribal training in the civil administration and temple schools. Egypt developed a rich literature of stories, wisdom-books (similar to Proverbs), religious and lyric poetry, some of which became classics and 'set texts' for students. The base and foundation of the social pyramid was the toil of the peasant farmers. The magnificence of its monuments – from giant pyramid-tombs and temples to delicate frescoes and tiny signet-rings – came from the skills of a large body of artists and craftsmen who served pharaoh, the temples and the leading men of each major epoch.

Stimulated by the preservative qualities of the dry deserts around them, the Egyptians developed abundant theories of the after-life. In all of these, the body was mummified (embalmed) at death, to serve as the abode for the soul at night, as the tomb housed the body. Commonly, the hereafter was envisaged as a counterpart to earthly life, in the realm of Osiris, god of the dead. By magic means, the equipment and pictures in tombs were to serve their owners in that existence.

The dress of a princess is shown in this wall-painting of Queen Ahmes-Nefertari (about 1,550 BC), from Thebes about 1,150 BC.

and men. The gods were often embodiments of the powers of nature, or its phenomena (sun, moon), or of concepts (just order). The great temples maintained the official cult (the daily ritual of offerings) to which only pharaoh, the priests and higher dignitaries had access. Only at the spectacular processional festivals did the man-in-the-street share in honouring the great gods whose blessing on Egypt was sought through the temple-rites. Ordinary people worshipped their household gods, at lesser shrines of forms of the great gods, and at 'oratories' by gateways to the great temples. Magic flourished as an aspect of religion. On the positive side it was, to use the terms of King Merikare's teacher, an arm to ward off life's blows. But 'black' magic was a punishable crime.

EGYPT AND THE BIBLE

From Abraham to Joseph

Egypt's first major role in the Bible, is as a haven from famine for the patriarchs (Genesis 12:10ff.; 42-47). Since Egypt had the Nile, she could prosper independently of the Mediterranean rains which were vital to Syria-Palestine. Many others besides the Hebrew founding fathers sought famine-relief in Egypt. Back in the Old Kingdom, starving foreigners appear in sculptured scenes, while a thousand years later (about 1,230 BC) Edomite tribesmen are admitted to the pools of Pithom, 'to keep them alive, and to keep their cattle alive, through the great provision of pharaoh'. Egypt maintained frontier guards and officials on her eastern border, visitors sometimes being escorted into the land (like Sinuhe in the *Story of Sinuhe*) or out of it (like Abraham in Genesis 12:20).

The pharaohs of Abraham's and Joseph's time probably belonged to the 12th and

13th/15th dynasties respectively (Middle Kingdom and after), when many foreigners found employment in Egypt at various levels, from slaves to high stewards (like Joseph under Potiphar, Genesis 39:1-4). And like Joseph (Genesis 41:45), many of his non-Egyptian contemporaries were given Egyptian second names. In all walks of life, amongst high and low, dreams were considered meaningful–so much so, that learned scribes wrote textbooks to help interpret them. The motif of seven cows occurs not only in Pharaoh's dream (Genesis 41:18ff.) but also in Spell 148 of the *Book of the Dead,* which is concerned with food in the hereafter.

On the economic plane, the Egyptian authorities kept detailed registers of land-holdings, and measured off standing crops on the eve of harvest for tax purposes. With such a system, the measures Joseph proposed could readily have been carried out (Genesis 41:34-35, 48-49; 47: 23ff.). Also, the delta was a preferred area for pasturing cattle (Genesis 46:34), a fact evident from an inscription of about 1,600 BC.

The fine linen garments worn by Joseph as a high official (Genesis 41:42) are familiar from countless Egyptian paintings, while the mummification and coffins of Egypt (Genesis 50:2-3, 26) as well as her tombs (Exodus

Fowling-scene from an Egyptian tomb.

14:11) have been proverbial from those days till now.

Moses and the exodus

Four centuries later, many Hebrews had become slaves in the brickfields of New Kingdom Egypt for the great building-projects of that era. Their labours culminated in work on the cities Pithom and Raamses (Exodus 1:11), the latter being the famous east-delta residence of Pi-Ramesse, built by Ramesses II. In contemporary papyri, we read of Apiru (peoples who include the ➤➤

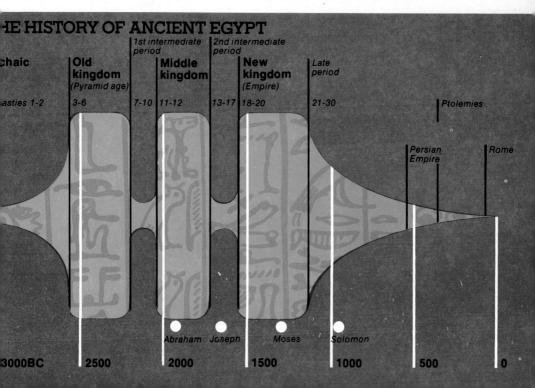

THE HISTORY OF ANCIENT EGYPT

chaic	Old kingdom (Pyramid age)	1st intermediate period	Middle kingdom	2nd intermediate period	New kingdom (Empire)	Late period			
asties 1-2	3-6	7-10	11-12	13-17	18-20	21-30	Ptolemies	Persian Empire	Rome

Abraham Joseph Moses Solomon

| 3000BC | 2500 | 2000 | 1500 | 1000 | 500 | 0 |

Hebrews) 'who drag stone for the great pylon-gateway of...(a temple of) Ramesses II'; of men 'making their quota of bricks daily'; and of officials having neither men nor straw for producing bricks (see Exodus 5:7). Conditions in Exodus 5 are echoed in Egyptian documents of that day. In western Thebes the village of the workmen who cut the royal tombs has yielded up 'work sheets' scribbled on potsherds (pottery fragments which were the ancient equivalent of memo-pads). These record in detail days worked and days 'idle', sometimes giving specific reasons for the absenteeism of individuals: 'his wife is ill', or 'brewing beer with the boss', or (very sad!) 'stung by a scorpion'. Most interesting are the entries for a man 'offering to his god', or for the whole gang having several days off for a local religious festival. (Compare Exodus 5:1-5, where Moses seeks leave for the Hebrews, but Pharaoh is unwilling to concede further public holidays or to recognize Moses' God.)

That a princess in an east-delta harem should care about a foreign child, as in Exodus 2, is not surprising in the cosmopolitan society of New Kingdom Egypt. We know that youngsters from Canaan were brought up in harems elsewhere. Foreigners featured at every level of society from the most insignificant slave to the cup-bearer at pharaoh's right hand; a Moses was no anomaly here. The magicians and wise men of Exodus (7:11; 8:7, 18; 9:11) were the chief lector-priests and learned scribes. The Egyptians themselves told entertaining stories of the reputed exploits of such men.

When Israel left Egypt, the pharaoh – probably Ramesses II – sent his chariotry in pursuit. Six hundred chariots (Exodus 14:7) was a sizeable force but perfectly feasible, as much larger musters are known at that period. In the wilderness period, the tabernacle – in essence, a prefabricated building – utilized techniques long-established in Egypt for structures needing to be readily erected and dismantled for secular and religious purposes. That Israel was out of Egypt and into Western Palestine by the late 13th century BC is confirmed by the only known Egyptian mention of Israel (in context with Gezer and Ascalon), in the Libyan victory-poem of Merneptah (about 1,220/1,210 BC), successor of Ramesses II.

Later periods
Egypt reappears in biblical history at the time of David and Solomon. Solomon married a daughter of a pharaoh who conquered Gezer and gave it him as a dowry (1 Kings 9:16). That pharaoh was most likely to have been Siamun (about 970 BC), who probably raided the Philistines and southwest Palestine, to judge from a broken triumphal relief found at Tanis, the capital of his dynasty (biblical Zoan).

The literary layout of Proverbs – largely a 'wisdom-book' of Solomon – shows affinity with other such works of the biblical Near East, a number of them being Egyptian. However, the oft-repeated statement that Proverbs in part derives directly from the Egyptian work by Amenemope is without adequate foundation.

Siamun's line was soon replaced by a new king and line: Sheshonq I, founder of the 22nd dynasty, the biblical 'Shishak' (1 Kings 11:40; 14:25). He saw Solomon's Israel as a political and commercial rival. And when Rehoboam succeeded Solomon, by using Jeroboam he successfully broke that kingdom up into two warring factions, and briefly subdued the divided Hebrew monarchy to his own material profit. A vast triumph-scene in the Karnak Temple of Amun at Thebes commemorates his campaign, besides inscriptions set up at Karnak and at Megiddo, in Palestine itself.

Thereafter, Egypt's real power swiftly sank. The Hebrew prophets rebuked their kings for relying on Egyptian support (see Isaiah 30, 31; Jeremiah 46). Egypt was no match for Assyria or Babylon, and with the rise of the Persian Empire indeed became a 'lowly kingdom' (Ezekiel 29:15), losing her real national independence for ages to come.

The book of Exodus is the story of the birth of Israel as a nation. It is an epic dominated by the central figure of Moses. It was he who led the people out from Egypt, the 'exodus' (exit) which gives the book its name. Through him God gave the law. The book falls into two main parts:

1. Israel's escape from slavery in Egypt (chapters 1-19).
2. The giving of the law and construction of the 'tabernacle' (God's tent) at Sinai (chapters 20-40).

The existence of such a large (see 12: 37) alien group in his borderlands has for some time made Pharaoh uneasy. Here is his chance to ensure they keep out of mischief. The people are organized into gangs, under taskmasters, to dig out mud and make the bricks for building the new cities.

But no matter how hard they are worked the population explosion continues. Pharaoh decides to tackle the problem in more direct ways (15-22), only to be defeated by the midwives' faith.

1 — 12:36
ISRAEL IN EGYPT; MOSES, GOD'S LIBERATOR

1 The scene is set
Nearly 300 years have elapsed since the death of Joseph, and the end of Genesis. Jacob's people have been in Egypt some 370 years. Their old privileged status is gone. Now they are a slave nation under a new pharaoh, of a dynasty which has long forgotten Egypt's debt to Joseph (see Genesis 41).

Things have changed in Egypt. The power of the Hyksos pharaohs has been broken and the Upper and Lower kingdoms once again united. The nation is at the height of its military power, ruled from Thebes and Memphis by a new dynasty of pharaohs. But with the accession of Sethos I (probably the 'new king' of 1:8) attention once again focusses on the fertile delta region. A great building programme is begun, including store-cities for Pharaoh. One is named after Sethos' successor, Ramesses II (who was mainly responsible for building it). And there is a large, ready-made, economic labour-force resident in the area – the Israelites.

2 Moses, prince and refugee
So now all Hebrew boy-babies are to be cast into the Nile. That is Pharaoh's decree. But the water which drowns can also be used to float a watertight basket (the same Hebrew word as Noah's 'ark') – and Moses' life is saved by his mother's resourceful action.

Moses was 40 when he tried to strike his first blow for freedom (2:11-12), which ended in disaster. A further 40 years passed before the events of chapter 3 (Acts 7:23 and Exodus 7:7).

Pharaoh's daughter would probably be a daughter by one of his concubines, not a princess of blood-royal. She would have taken Moses back to the harem where he would be brought up with others, learning to read and write the Egyptian hieroglyphic and 'cursive' scripts (see Writing illustrations, page 86), and gaining expertise in various skills and sports (see Acts 7:22). It was not unknown for foreigners to be brought up in this way, and trained for responsible posts in the army, priesthood or civil service.

Midian (15): the Midianites were descendants of Abraham through his second wife, Keturah. They were desert-dwellers, so Moses could scarcely have had better preparation for the wilderness journeys with Israel than these years of nomadic life.

3—4 The burning bush: God calls and equips his man

Moses is actually at Sinai (Horeb), the very place where he will later receive the law, when God's call comes. God has a stupendous commission for Moses – he is to be God's messenger to Pharaoh, and lead his people to freedom – but the missionary is most reluctant. He raises one objection after another, and each is countered by God:

■3:11: 'I am not up to the job.' But 'I will be with you', says God.
■3:13: 'How am I to explain to people who you are?' God reveals himself as the God of their ancestors, and God of the present: 'I am.'
■4:1: 'The people won't believe me.' God gives him three signs with which to convince them.
■4:10: 'I am no speaker.' God made him; he will enable him to speak.
■4:13: 'Please send someone else.' This God will not do, but he will allow him Aaron as spokesman.

Mt Horeb (3:1): the precise location is uncertain, but long tradition identifies it with Gebel Musa (7,363 feet/2,244m) at the southern tip of the Sinai peninsula.
The spoil from Egypt (3:21f.): see 11:2-3; 12:35-36. It was from this that the tabernacle was furnished (35:20ff.).
4:19: Pharaoh's death was recorded in 2:23.
Aaron (4:14): three years older than Moses (7:7), presumably born before Pharaoh's edict. Miriam would have been older than both.
Circumcision (4:24-26): Moses failed to circumcise his son – and God cannot overlook disobedience, even in one he has chosen. Zipporah puts the matter right and Moses' life is spared.

5—6:13 The first round goes to Pharaoh

The first request to Pharaoh merely aggravates the situation. The people turn against their 'deliverer'. Moses in his frustration turns once again to God.
The request (5:1): this seems less than the whole truth; but it is in the nature of a test-case. Israel had to leave Egypt in order to sacrifice because the nature of their sacrifice was offensive to the Egyptians (8:26). Pharaoh's reaction reveals his implacable hostility, already predicted by God (3:19).
Access to Pharaoh: Ramesses II is known to have made himself available even to

Egyptian model of a man digging or hoeing.

ordinary petitioners (compare 5:15ff.).
Moses, brought up in the harem, had a
special claim to Pharaoh's attention.

6:14-27 The family-tree of Moses and Aaron

As so often in Scripture, the list is
selective. Moses and Aaron are shown to
have descended from Jacob through the
line of Levi. The list covers the period of
Israel's stay in Egypt.

6:28 – 10:29 The contest with Pharaoh: the nine plagues

Pharaoh has heard and rejected Moses'
request. He has shown the sort of man he
is: 'Who is the Lord ...? I do not know the
Lord and I will not let Israel go' (5:2).

    Now God begins a series of judgements
to teach Pharaoh and his people who the
Lord is, and to show them the extent of
his power over all creation (7:5, 17; 8:10,
22; 9:14). Nine times God acts, and
Pharaoh, his magicians and all the gods
of Egypt are powerless to reverse his
judgements. The magicians may counter-
feit, but they cannot countermand.

1. The Nile – heart of the nation's
economy and worship – turns to blood,
its polluted waters killing the fish
(7:14-24).
2. Seven days later, frogs, driven from the
river banks by the rotting fish, seek
shelter in the houses (7:25 – 8:15).
3 and 4. First gnats and then flies,
breeding amongst the carcases of fish
and frogs, plague the land (8:16-32).
5 and 6. Disease strikes the cattle, and
skin infection breaks out on man and
beast, carried by the frogs and insects
(9:1-12).
7. Hail and thunderstorms ruin the flax
and barley crops – but not wheat and
spelt, which have not yet grown. And those
Egyptians who take note of God's
warning remain safe (9:13-35).
8. The wind blows in a plague of locusts
from Ethiopia which strip the country

The Names of God
ALEC MOTYER

THE WORDS AND THE NAME
Two Hebrew words are translated 'God':

EL 'The Deity', God in the power and distinctiveness of
his divine nature.
ELOHIM Plural in form signifying not 'gods' but the One
who completely possesses all the divine attributes.

ADON 'Sovereign', 'master' is used in the
form ADONAI, 'Sovereign', 'Lord' to refer to
God. In distinction from these nouns, there is
also the personal name Yahweh. To avoid
using this divine name (out of supposed
reverence) Adonai, 'Lord' was substituted in
public reading. English Bibles perpetuate
this scruple by representing Yahweh as
'Lord', or where the Hebrew has Adonai
Yahweh ('the Sovereign Yahweh') as 'Lord
GOD'. Much is lost if we forget to look
beyond the substitute word (always printed in
capitals) to the personal, intimate name of
God himself.
    By telling his people his name, God
intended to reveal to them his inmost
character. As a word, Yahweh is related to the
Hebrew verb 'to be'. This verb goes beyond
'to exist'; it means rather 'to be actively
present'. Yahweh (Exodus 3:13-16) is the God
actively present with his people – but the
moment he chose to make this known was
when they, as doomed slaves, needed to be
redeemed.
    In other words, the idea of 'active presence'
tells us that God is with us but not what sort of
God he is. In choosing the time of the exodus
to reveal the meaning of his name, he
identifies himself as the God who saves his
people and overthrows his adversaries.
    The holiness of God lies at the root of his
self-revelation as Yahweh (Exodus 3:5). This
works out in the holy redemption and holy
wrath of the Passover (Exodus 12).
    The Old Testament's understanding of the
character which the name reveals is well seen
in passages such as Exodus 34:6ff.; Psalms
103; 111; 146; Micah 7:18-19.

THE PROGRESS OF REVELATION
The name Yahweh appears in the Bible from
the earliest times (Genesis 4:1) and in such
ways as to imply that men both knew and
used it (e.g. Genesis 4:26; 14:22). How then **»**

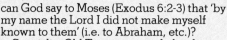

can God say to Moses (Exodus 6:2-3) that 'by my name the Lord I did not make myself known to them' (i.e. to Abraham, etc.)?

Specialist Old Testament study has long answered this question by saying that we have differing traditions of the early history of the people of God: one tradition in which the divine name was known from the earliest times, and another – contradictory – tradition that it was first revealed to Moses.

Influential as this theory has proved, it is neither inescapable nor necessary. 'To know' in the Old Testament goes beyond the mere possession of information, to the active enjoyment of fellowship with the person known. For instance, the sons of Eli certainly knew the name as a divine 'label' but they 'had no regard for (literally, 'did not know') the Lord' (1 Samuel 2:12; compare 3:7; Exodus 33:12-13). So Exodus 6:2-3 is telling us that what had hitherto possessed only the significance of a 'label', a way of addressing God, now became significant as a statement of the character possessed by the God who was so named – that he is the holy Redeemer and Judge, ever present with his people.

This view of the meaning of Exodus 6:2-3 is borne out by the evidence of Genesis. If Abraham had been asked 'Who is Yahweh?' he would undoubtedly have replied 'God Almighty' or one of the other titles of God used by the patriarchs:

EL SHADDAY Shadday probably means 'mountain', used symbolically of changelessness and enduring strength, contrasted to the helplessness of man. See for instance Genesis 17:1f.; 28:3f.; 35:11; 43:14; 48:3; 49:25.
EL ELYON 'God Most High', Genesis 14:18.
EL ROI 'God of Seeing', Genesis 16:13.
EL OLAM 'The Everlasting God', Genesis 21:33.
EL BETHEL 'God of Bethel', Genesis 31:13.
EL ELOHE YISRAEL 'God, the God of Israel', Genesis 33:20.

So when Yahweh is said to be 'the God of your fathers' in Exodus 3 (verses 6, 13, 15, 16), all this richness of meaning is added to the revelation of the holy Redeemer.

'WHO IS A GOD LIKE THEE?'
God in himself
Some attributes of God so express the heart of his divine nature that they are used as titles:

THE HOLY ONE The most centrally important title of all: see Joshua 24:19; Isaiah 5:16; 10:17; Habakkuk 1:12.
THE HOLY ONE OF ISRAEL A variation used especially by Isaiah, e.g. Isaiah 1:4.
THE GOD 'WHOSE NAME IS JEALOUS' shows his passionate love for his people: see Exodus 34:14.

THE LORD OF HOSTS is often repeated and points to the 'hosts' of potentialities and powers in the divine nature, conveying something very much like 'omni-potent'. See, for instance, Jeremiah 32:18b-23.

Furthermore, he is the *true, living* (Jeremiah 10:10) *high* (Micah 6:6) and *rewarding* (Jeremiah 51:56) God.

God of all the world
Such a God cannot be confined to one people. He is:

CREATOR Isaiah 40:28.
JUDGE Genesis 18:25.
KING Jeremiah 10:7.
GOD OF ALL FLESH Numbers 16:22; Jeremiah 32:27.

The God of Israel
He is the God who specially reveals himself to one people:

THE ANGEL OF THE LORD Without diminishing his deity, he accommodates himself to speak to man: Genesis 16:7f.; Judges 13:16f., etc.
THE GOD OF THE HEBREWS Exodus 5:3.
THE GOD OF ISRAEL Joshua 24:2.
He is also, as if to stress the grace and condescension involved, **THE GOD OF JACOB** (Psalm 81:4), in holiness (Isaiah 1:4) and power (Psalm 132:2).

The God of the individual
Within his chosen people, he is the God of the individual: 'my beloved' (Isaiah 5:1), 'the God of my salvation' (Psalm 18:46). The richness of personal awareness of God in the Old Testament is hardly better seen than through the wealth of metaphors for the God who was known and loved in daily life:

ROCK A title stemming from Exodus 17:1-7. See especially Deuteronomy 32.
SHEPHERD Psalm 23:1.
SHIELD, STRONGHOLD Psalm 18:2.
LIGHT Psalm 27:1.
STRENGTH Psalm 28:7.
REFUGE Psalm 37:39.
SUN Psalm 84:11.
FATHER Psalm 89:26; Isaiah 63:16.
MOTHER-BIRD Psalm 91:4; compare Isaiah 31:5.
HELP Psalm 115:9.
SHADE Psalm 121:5.
PORTION Psalm 142:5.
SONG Isaiah 12:2.
REDEEMER Isaiah 41:14.
WARRIOR Isaiah 42:13.
POTTER Isaiah 45:9.
HUSBAND Isaiah 54:5.
FOUNTAIN Jeremiah 2:13.
DEW Hosea 14:5.
LION, LEOPARD, BEAR Hosea 13:7-8.

bare of greenstuff (10:1-20).

9. For three days the light of the sun is blotted out by 'thick darkness' (probably a khamsin duststorm) (10:21-29).

The plagues probably occurred over a period of about a year. In each case God chose to use natural disorders to confound Pharaoh and the gods of Egypt (12:12). He caused the 'Nile-god' to bring ruin, not prosperity; the frogs to bring disease instead of fruitfulness; and the power of Re, the sun-god, was blotted out. The whole sequence of events follows a logical pattern which could have started with unusually high flooding of the Nile, bringing down red earth and microcosms which polluted the water. But however it happened, this was no mere 'chance' – God was demonstrating his absolute control. He distinguished between his people and

Egyptian magic: the 'Book of the Dead', written for the high priest of Amun, about 1,000 BC.

A locust; see too the picture in the section on Joel.

the Egyptians. He controlled the extent and the areas affected by each plague. He announced the timing of each, and could call a halt at any time in answer to prayer.

The hardness of Pharaoh's heart: several times in these chapters God is said to have hardened Pharaoh's heart and made him stubborn (4:21; 10:1, 20, 27). But this was not done against Pharaoh's will. Rather, where God could have softened Pharaoh's heart (as he did Paul's) he simply let him be. God gave him up (see Romans 1;

9:17)–let him be what he himself wanted, let him have his own way–so that in the end God's power would be plain for all to see.

11 – 12:36 The death of the firstborn, and the Passover

Preliminaries are over: God's warning of 4:22-23 is about to be realized. This is the end of the road for Pharaoh and his people. But for Israel it is the beginning. This is a day to remember down the ages: when God dealt death to the firstborn sons of Egypt, but spared and freed his own people. A new feast is instituted, and a new (religious) year begun. The Passover lamb or kid speaks of God's protection and provision for his people–Israel is his firstborn. The bitter herbs remind them of all their suffering in Egypt. The flat unleavened bread recalls the haste of their departure (no time to use yeast and wait for the bread to rise). Even so, they do not go empty-handed. The years of slavery are in some measure paid for by the clothes and jewellery heaped upon them by the Egyptians, now only too anxious to see them go.

12:37 – 19:25
OUT OF EGYPT: ON TO SINAI

12:37 – 13:21 The journey begins; instructions about the Passover, Unleavened Bread and the firstborn

Just as God foretold (Genesis 15:13-14), after four centuries in a foreign land (from the 18th century BC to about 1,300 or 1,290 BC) Israel is free. The journey to the

The pharaoh Ramesses II in action: this wall-painting shows him in his chariot pursuing fleeing Nubians.

A colossal statue of Ramesses II, pharaoh at the time of the exodus.

a total of some two million people – a high (though not necessarily impossible) figure which presents some problems. Subsequent chapters make it plain that their number was certainly too great for the wilderness to support – hence God's special provision of manna. They were also at times short of water, although they no doubt learnt to manage on very little, and their encampments would have been spread out to take advantage of several watercourses at each halt in the journey. **Joseph's bones (13:19):** see Genesis 50:24-25.

14 Pursuit and disaster

Hemmed in between sea and mountains, with water before them and Pharaoh's forces at their backs, the people of Israel meet their first big test of faith – and they panic. As God drives back the waters so that they can cross in safety, and as he sends the wall of water rushing down upon Pharaoh's forces, Israel learns the truth of Moses' words: 'The Lord will fight for you; there is no need for you to do anything' (14:14).

border begins. But first there are further instructions about how the Passover is to be celebrated, who may join in, and where it is to take place. The events are to be further commemorated in two ways:
■ For a seven-day period after Passover the people are to eat unleavened bread as a reminder of the hasty departure from Egypt.
■ As Israel's freedom has been purchased by the death of the firstborn of Egypt, the nation's firstborn belong in a special sense to God and are to be 'bought back' from him.
600,000 men (12:37): counting the women and children this would amount to

'Cattle in great numbers' were taken out of Egypt by the Israelites. This Egyptian painting is from the Tomb of Nebamun at Thebes, about 1,400 BC.

15:1-21 Moses' triumph-song

If ever a victory deserves to be recorded
for posterity this one does. Moses leads
the people in a great paean of triumph:
God has saved Israel; he has destroyed
their enemy. Miriam and all the women
take up the refrain, and dance for joy. The
song is a fine example of ancient Semitic
poetry (see 'Poetry and Wisdom Literature', page 316).

15:22—17:7 The grumbling begins, but God provides

It is not long before the complaints start.
There were plenty of fish to eat in Egypt,
and fruit and vegetables – and no shortage
of water. But in the desert the people are
soon thirsty and hungry – and mutinous.
God's method of provision is designed to
teach them obedience, and daily dependence upon him.

Quails (16:13): see page 189.

Omer (16:16): a bowl holding about 4
pints/2 litres.

Manna (16:31): various natural
phenomena have been identified with the
description given here, but none fits
exactly. This substance was Israel's staple
food for 40 years, ceasing abruptly when
they entered Canaan.

Water from the rock (17:6): Sinai
limestone is known to retain moisture.
This incident, and the names Massah and
Meribah, became a byword for rebelliousness (see Hebrews 3:7ff.).

*A woman playing a tambourine is depicted in this
model at the Rockefeller Museum, Jerusalem.*

*The amount of gold taken by the Israelites has
been thought exaggerated, but a surprising
amount of gold from the time has been found.
This is an electrotype of a gold dagger and
sheath found in the Royal Graves at Ur, dating
from much earlier, about 2,600 BC.*

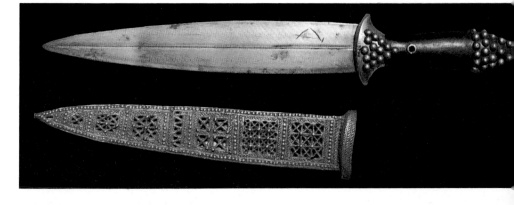

Egyptian jewellery from the time of Moses: the people of Israel's 'plunder' included 'jewellery of silver and gold'.

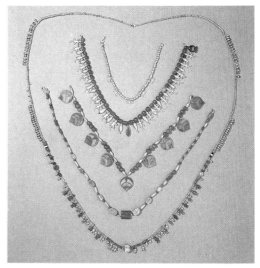

The route of the exodus. This is not absolutely certain. They did not take the direct coastal route (13:17) because they were unready to encounter the Philistine forces. Instead they journeyed south to Succoth, turned north before crossing the sea, and then south again down the west of the Sinai peninsula. The 'Red Sea', or 'sea of reeds', can refer to the Bitter Lakes region or to the Gulf of Suez. The actual crossing probably took place somewhere between Qantara (30 miles south of Port Said) and just north of Suez – over the papyrus marshes.

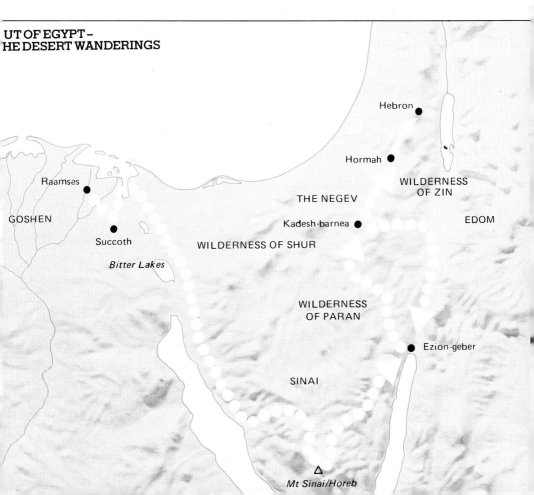

UT OF EGYPT –
HE DESERT WANDERINGS

Hebron

Hormah

WILDERNESS
OF ZIN

Raamses

THE NEGEV

GOSHEN

EDOM

Kadesh-barnea

Succoth

WILDERNESS OF SHUR

Bitter Lakes

WILDERNESS
OF PARAN

Ezion-geber

SINAI

△
Mt Sinai/Horeb

17:8-16 Battle with the Amalekites

Joshua (Moses' successor) leads a picked force against this nomadic tribe descended from Esau. But it is God who gives the victory, through Moses' intercession.

18 Jethro's advice

The burden of leadership is heavy, and Jethro's practical suggestion for reorganization and delegation is a sound one. Jethro, although a non-Israelite, is reckoned a godly man. He is welcomed and his advice taken. In religious matters, however, he learns from Moses (8-11), not vice-versa as some suggest. It is not clear when Zipporah returned home – perhaps soon after the incident recorded in 4:24-26.

19 The camp at Sinai

As God promised (3:12), Moses brings God's people to him at Mt Sinai, where he will establish his covenant with the nation. Thunder, fire, earthquake and lightning herald God's presence and demonstrate his power (20:20 explains why; compare Elijah's experience in the same place – 1 Kings 19:8ff. – and the contrast drawn in Hebrews 12:18-25). The Lord God, holy, awesome, unapproachable, speaks.

20–40
GOD'S LAW FOR ISRAEL; THE SETTING UP OF GOD'S TENT, THE 'TABERNACLE'

20:1-21 The Ten Commandments

This summary and climax of God's covenant-agreement with his people sets out a basic ethical norm applicable to all men in all ages (since they are in fact the 'Maker's instructions'). The first four commands concern our relationship to God, the remaining six our relationship to one another. Hence Jesus' two-clause summary of the law in Matthew 22:37-40.

The commandments show God's concern for the whole of life. He sets out standards governing family relationships, regard for human life, sex, property, speech and thought. God made us: he alone can show us how we are designed to behave.

Written on stone tablets, preserved in the ark (box) of the covenant, the ten 'words' were the basis of Israel's law. In form they follow the standard pattern of Near Eastern treaties current in the 13th century BC, particularly those between vassals and their overlords (see 'Covenants and Near Eastern Treaties' page 198):

■ Title: identifying the author of the covenant (2a).
■ Historical prologue: describing past relations of the two parties (2b).
■ Obligations imposed on the vassal (3-17), accompanied by 'blessings' (e.g. 6,12b) and 'cursings' (5,7b).

20:22—23:33 God's law-code for Israel

This section, known as 'the book of the covenant', is the oldest record we have of Jewish law. It consists of 'judgements' – i.e. case-laws – and 'statutes', straightforward commands. Although similar in form to other ancient law-codes of Western Asia, the Jewish code has several distinctive features:

■ The whole code rests on the authority of God, not of a king.
■ There is no division between civil and religious law. Most oriental codes deal with legal matters only: morals and religion belong elsewhere. In the Bible legal, moral and religious laws are inseparable, showing God's concern for life as a whole.
■ There is one law for all, whatever a man's status. Regulations protecting the weak and helpless (slaves, orphans, widows, foreigners) are particularly striking.
■ A high view of human life is demonstrated by fixed, limited penalties – one crime, one punishment.

The Sinai mountains.

The legislation looks forward to the settled agricultural life of Canaan – Israel's rebelliousness had not yet condemned her to 40 years in the Sinai peninsula. The section may be summarized as follows:

■ General instructions about worship (20:22-26)
■ Civil laws (21:1–23:13)
the rights of slaves (21:1-11)
manslaughter and injury to human life (21:12-32)
injury, theft and damage to property (21:33–22:15)
social and religious obligations (22:16-31)
justice and human rights (23:1-13)
■ Laws for the three main feasts – Unleavened Bread, Firstfruits and Harvest (23:14-19)

■ God's undertakings for his obedient people (23:20-33)
These regulations fill out in detail the summary of 20:1-17.

24 The covenant is ratified

The people's assent to the covenant is formally sealed by a special sacrifice, and by the covenant meal eaten by their representatives in the presence of God. The blood sprinkled on the people and on the altar unites the two parties to the agreement. In effect, each is swearing to keep it on pain of death.

Nadab and Abihu (1): two of Aaron's sons who later died after committing sacrilege (Leviticus 10:1-2).

They saw the God of Israel (9-11): having a meal with someone is the essence of fellowship in the Near East. Here the writer gropes for words to describe the indescribable communion which followed the sacrifice and fulfilled the covenant.

Hur (14): obviously a man of standing in Israel. He and Aaron held up Moses' hands in prayer during the battle with Amalek (17:12).

Forty days and nights (18): certain numbers have special significance in the Bible. The round number '40' occurs at almost every new stage in Israel's history: e.g. at the flood, the time of the spies in Canaan, Elijah's journey to Horeb, Jesus' time in the wilderness, and the time between his resurrection and ascension.

25–27
Instructions for making and furnishing the tabernacle

God has brought the nation out of Egypt.

He has set out the terms of his covenant and they have been agreed. Now, as a visible sign that these are his people with whom he will always be present, he gives Moses instructions to build a special tent for him. He is to have a home amongst them like their own homes. He will guide and accompany them wherever they go – and they will know that he is no local deity whose power is limited to Sinai. Portable, prefabricated tent-shrines similar to the tabernacle were constructed in Egypt even earlier than this. Here, although the description is detailed, some practical points are missing – it is not a complete workman's blueprint. The roof of the tent, for example, may have been flat or

A reconstruction of the tabernacle by the Rev. L. Schouten at the Bible Museum, Amsterdam.

Detail of the reconstruction of the tabernacle, with the coverings pulled back to show the different materials used.

The Tabernacle

ALEC MOTYER

The people of God were encamped at Mt Sinai. Every day they gazed with trembling at the cloud covering the mountain (Exodus 19:16-20), for it signified God's coming down to speak with them. But during their stay, at Moses' instruction, they provided materials for the construction of the very complex tent which has come to be called the tabernacle. On the day when it was finally completed and erected, as they watched, 'the cloud covered the tent of meeting, and the glory of the Lord filled the tabernacle' (Exodus 40:34). The Lord in his glory had actually come to dwell amongst his people. This is the supreme significance of the tabernacle.

Sinai
The law had been given at Mt Sinai. But there was more to it than that. The ceremony described in Exodus 24 places the law-giving in its correct context. It included the following elements:

■ The altar with its twelve pillars (verse 4) stands for the bringing of the whole people of God into his presence (for there were twelve tribes of Israel). This truth is represented in stone: the relationship is a permanent one.
■ Dashing half the blood of sacrifice (verse 6) against the altar signifies that it is by means of shed blood that the people can come into the presence of God. Sin inevitably means death, being cut off from God. But when the death penalty has been satisfied, the people can be brought to God and established permanently in his presence.
■ Next, Moses goes through the law of God, the pattern of obedience which God requires from his blood-bought people (verse 7).
■ The people commit themselves to a life of obedience, and Moses sprinkles the remainder of the blood over them (verse 8) – identifying them with the sacrifice made on their behalf, both initially and for the failures and sins of everyday life.

So Mt Sinai stands for the fulfilment of one half of the covenant promise of Exodus 6:7: 'I will take you for my people.' God has brought them to himself, and in the shed blood has provided a way for them to live and walk with him.

raised with a ridge-pole. The picture shows the basic structure and the position of the furnishings. The framework of the actual tent was hung with linked curtains of linen, over which was a cover of cloth made from goat-hair, topped by two weatherproof coverings (of rams' skins dyed red, and of fine hide).

Many of the materials used were brought by the Israelites from Egypt (11:2-3) and willingly given, so that God's tent might be as worthy of him as they could make it. Before the days of banks it was practical to convert wealth into jewellery, which could be worn and carried round easily. Wood is scarce in the Sinai desert, but the acacia is one of the few trees which grow there. Their own herds provided skins, and the hides came from the Red Sea.

The peoples of the ancient Near East were skilled in spinning, weaving and using natural dyes (scarlet from the cochineal insect; purple, for the wealthy, from the murex shellfish). Fine embroidery was also produced. Precious and semi-precious stones were rounded, polished and engraved (as those for Aaron). Gold and silver were beaten and worked into elaborate designs. All these skills God called into play for the construction of his tent.

»

The indwelling God

But what about the other half of the covenant promise? God had also said 'and I will be your God' (Exodus 6:7). By taking up residence amongst them, pitching his tent in the midst of their tents, the Lord makes this second sort of identification with his people. He is indeed their God. The tabernacle represents the completion and climax of God's redemption of his people. Everything he had done was for this final purpose, 'that I might dwell among them' (Exodus 29:43-46).

There is great emphasis on this fact of God's indwelling throughout the tabernacle narrative. It is stressed in two specific ways. First there is a whole series of verses with this as their topic (e.g. 25:8, 22; 29:42ff.; 40:34-38). It was God's intention that his people should always carry with them the values learnt at Mt Sinai. There God dwelt among them and they saw the visible manifestation of his presence. But God was not just providing a memory to cling to. He is determined to live amongst his people, to travel with them. The tabernacle represents something even more intense than the experience at Sinai (compare 24:18 with 40:35). They are not left with the diminishing glow of a receding experience. Instead, by living among them, God will himself guarantee the unabated reality of his personal presence.

The story of the tabernacle is interrupted and marred by the incident of the golden calf (Exodus 32-34). On the one side of this act of rebellion lie the details of the plan for the tabernacle (Exodus 25-31), and on the other side the details of the execution of that plan, point by point (Exodus 35-40). Why are we taken through the process of construction in such detail? Why is the summary statement of 40:16ff. not sufficient? Why must each separate moment of the work be dwelt upon? It is surely to emphasize this great truth: that not even the most audacious acts of human wilfulness and rebellion can deflect the Lord from his chosen purpose to dwell among his people. He has set his hand to it along lines dictated by his own will, and nothing can deter him. Man may impatiently rebel, but God will patiently continue.

God-centred religion

The general truth expressed by the tabernacle, then, is that the Lord determined to live among his people and the will of God – what he wants – equally governs the whole plan of the great tent and its construction. From 25:10 onwards the description moves from the inside to the outside: first the furnishings, the ark, table and lampstand (25:10-40), then the tent-covering (26:1-37), then beyond it to the altar and the court (27:1-19). It is an ordered story, but on reflection the order is striking and unexpected. One might reasonably have expected that the 'building' would come first and then the things it housed. But this would have been to start from the visible, and the whole tabernacle exists as the necessary 'wrapping' for the invisible God when he comes down to be with his people. God and his nature determines all, not man and his needs.

In this way the tabernacle sums up a basic biblical truth about religion: it must conform to the will and nature of God. Much in the Bible exists to expose man's tendency to make religion suit his own pleasure, or (as might be said) match what he finds 'helpful'. But if religion does not match the will of God it is ultimately futile (see, for example, Isaiah 29:13).

The ark of the covenant

At the very centre of this whole divinely-dictated religion was the ark. Everything pointed to it. Three matching entrances (26:31, 32, 36, 37; 27:16, 17) led to it – for the purpose of entering the court of the tabernacle was to enter the presence of God himself. Along the path leading to the ark lay the altar of burnt-offering (27:1-8), the altar of incense (30:1-6), and the mercy-seat (the cover or lid of the ark) where the blood of sacrifice was finally sprinkled (25:17ff.; Leviticus 16:14) – showing that it was only by sacrifice, prayer and the effectiveness of the shed blood that man could come to God.

Inside the ark were the tablets of the law – the supreme verbal statement of God's holiness (25:16); at one and the same time the reason why God dwelt alone (for none can match his holiness), and why by means of blood a sinner might enter his presence (for the blood speaks of life laid down in payment for sin).

The whole structure of the tabernacle, therefore, speaks clear and splendid truths. It provides a visible summary of the central affirmations of the Bible: that God indwells his people (see 1 Corinthians 3:16; Ephesians 2:19-22); that he intends his people to worship him according to his will and not their own whim (see Mark 7:6-13); and that only by means of sacrifice and shed blood can sinners ever come to live with the Holy One (see Ephesians 2:11-18; Hebrews 10:19-25).

28–30 The priests and their duties

If God's tent is to be a place of beauty and splendour, his priest must also be fittingly robed. His garments are intended 'to give him dignity and honour' (28:2)–not on his own account, but as befits the One he serves and represents. The precious stones engraved with the names of the twelve tribes point to his other function, as representative of his people, making atonement for their sin.

Urim and Thummim (28:30): two objects which stood for 'yes' and 'no'. Just how they were used to discover God's will is not known.

The bells on the hem of Aaron's robe (28:33-34): perhaps to ensure he does not enter God's presence unannounced.

The consecration: everything about this elaborate ceremonial points to the 'otherness' of God. He will be with his people, but there can be no familiarity. He is to be approached only in the ways he lays down. Sin disqualifies everyone from entering God's presence. The priests and every item of equipment must be specially set apart for his service. So Aaron and his sons must be cleansed, robed and their sins expiated by sacrifice before they may take office. The living God is no impotent image to be worshipped as man thinks fit. He lays down the only terms on which it is possible for him to take up residence with his people.

31:1-11 God chooses his craftsmen

When God selects individuals for a particular job he also equips them to do it. Verse 3 is one of the earliest references to the work of the Holy Spirit.

A model of the high priest (at the Bible Museum, Amsterdam) showing the blue robe fringed with bells and pomegranates; the shorter tunic (ephod) tied with a girdle; and the breastplate with its 12 precious stones, one for each of the 12 tribes. In the high priest's hand is Aaron's rod of almond (Numbers 17).

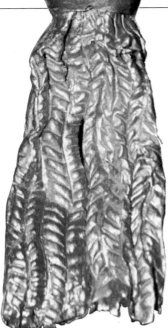

A golden tassel as worn by the high priest. This one is from Carchemish, 14th century BC.

Egyptian polytheism, shown in the worship of the golden calf, had widespread influence. This Egyptian bronze figure of an apis bull was discovered at Ashkelon, Israel.

31:12-18 Sabbath law

The way the sabbath day of rest is kept is an index of the nation's spiritual health. Obedience in this is a test of their obedience to God in other ways too.

32 The worship of the golden calf, and its aftermath

Only six weeks after making their solemn covenant-pledge with God the people are clamouring for a replica of the old gods of Egypt. And God's high priest not only makes the bull-calf, but identifies it with God. Death is the penalty for those who break covenant – but Moses' selfless intercession prevents Israel's extermination. The broken tablets dramatically proclaim the broken covenant. Such sin cannot go unpunished: Moses' own tribe, the Levites, mete out God's judgement.

33 Moses prays again, and sees God's glory

God will not go back on his promise, but Israel has forfeited his presence. And without that, the promised land is nothing. Again Moses pleads for the people at a time of crisis. God's answer encourages him to press a personal plea for a revelation of God in all his splendour.

34 The covenant is renewed

The tablets are engraved afresh in token of God's renewal of the covenant. This particular selection of laws is influenced by Israel's recent idol-worship, also by the coming temptations of Canaanite religion. Israel's firstborn belong to God, but are 'bought back' from him – there is to be no child-sacrifice as in Canaan. They must not forget sabbath law in the coming busy seasons of sowing and harvest. The firstfruits are to be brought to God, since it is he who makes the land fruitful. Israel is not to resort to the Canaanite practice of boiling a kid in its mother's milk to increase fertility.

Moses' long communion with God shows in his face when he returns to the people: he begins to reflect something of God's own glory (see 2 Corinthians 3:18).

Nomadic children in the Mt Sinai area illustrate the Israelites' struggle for survival in the desert.

35—40 The setting up of the tabernacle

These chapters record how the instructions given in chapters 25-31 are carried out to the letter. The craftsmen set to work, the people pour in their gifts, and the tabernacle, its fittings and the priests' robes are all completed exactly as God has laid down. When the work is finished, God gives Moses his instructions for setting up and arranging the tabernacle, and for its consecration. Aaron and his sons are anointed for service. When all is done, God signifies his satisfaction. The cloud, the visible token of his presence, rests on the tabernacle, and the place is filled with the dazzling light of his glory. For 300 years, until it is replaced by the temple in Solomon's day, God's tent will remain the focal centre of the nation's worship.

Leviticus

Leviticus is essentially a rule-book – the book of laws given by God to his people through Moses at Sinai. The laws cover ritual and worship and many aspects of life – but all seen in relation to him. The book takes its name from the fact that it was the Levitical priests (Aaron and his sons and descendants, helped in the practical work of the tabernacle by the rest of the Levites) who administered the laws. But the book is not for the priests alone. God intended all his people to know and keep his law. Again and again Moses is told to 'speak to the people of Israel'.

To many modern readers Leviticus may seen a strange book, perhaps even a repulsive one with all its blood-sacrifices. Some see it as reflecting only an odd set of ancient taboos. Yet take it away and whole areas of Scripture become inexplicable. Without the message of Leviticus the key event of all time, the death of Jesus Christ, is an enigma. The ritual and the rules were never simply an end in themselves. As the sacrifices were performed day after day, year after year, as the Day of Atonement came and went, Israel was constantly reminded of the sin which cut them off from God's presence. They had broken covenant with God by disobeying his laws and were under sentence of death. But God in his mercy showed them that he would accept a substitute – the death of an animal, perfect and blameless, instead of the offender. God was holy – a moral holiness unknown in the gods of the nations around. He demanded holiness in his people. The laws on ritual purity hammered this home in practical everyday experience.

Yet the book has value apart from its vital role in God's message of salvation. The laws in Leviticus show God working in harmony with his own natural laws for the good of his people. Although Israel had to obey the laws in blind trust (when they chose to do so at all), we can see how those laws were actually working for the nation's health and well-being. Because we know more today about the sources of infection and pollution, about quarantine and isolation, hygiene and preventive medicine, we can watch Israel's obedience actually fulfilling God's promise to take away their sickness (Exodus 23:25). And this not by magic, but by the natural working of principles we now, at least in part, can understand.

Many of the laws which seem strangest to us fall into place, too, when we look at them in relation to the contemporary religions of Egypt and Canaan. Against this dark backcloth the morality and religion of Israel shines like a star. Only God himself can account for it.

1—7
THE SACRIFICES

Priests and people are given instructions about five different offerings:

1. The burnt-offering (chapter 1 and 6:8-13): the only one in which the whole animal was burnt; a token of dedication.

2. The cereal- or grain-offering (chapter 2 and 6:14-18); often an accompaniment to burnt- and peace-offerings.

3. The peace- or fellowship-offering (chapter 3 and 7:11-36): re-establishing fellowship between the offerer and God; or it could be a thank-offering.

4. The sin-offering (4:1—5:13 and 6:24-30) made in order to obtain forgiveness. The relationship between this and the guilt-offering is not clear. Generally speaking the sin-offering seems to have referred to offences against God, and the guilt-offering to social offences. (But even sin against others is seen as sin against God, as 6:2 plainly states.)

5. The guilt- or repayment-offering (5:14–6:7 and 7:1-10).

There was a standard pattern of ritual. The worshipper brought his offering (a physically perfect animal from his herd or flock, or, in the case of a poor man, doves or pigeons) to the forecourt of the tabernacle. He laid his hand on it, implying that it represented him, and slaughtered it. (If it was a public offering the priest did this.) The priest took the basin of blood and spattered it against the altar. He burnt a specified part with certain portions of fat (or the entire animal in the case of the burnt-offering). The remainder was then eaten by the priests, or by the priests and their families, or (in the case of the peace-offering) by priests and worshippers together.

Sacrifice of some sort was almost universal practice amongst ancient peoples, and Israel's sacrifices have some similarities with those of their neighbours. Nonetheless, certain features are unique:

■ Israel's absolute monotheism – belief in the one true God – and the ritual as a direct revelation from him.
■ The emphasis on ethics and morality, stemming from God's own absolute moral holiness; sin as a bar to communion; the need for repentance and atonement; the insistence on obedience to God's law (moral as well as ceremonial).
■ The complete absence (and prohibition) of associated practices in other religions; no magic or sorcery.
■ The high tone of the sacrificial system: no frenzy, or prostitution, orgies, fertility rites, human sacrifice, etc.

Example of an altar with four 'horns': this one was found at Megiddo, Israel.

An aroma pleasing to the Lord (1:9): a human way of expressing God's satisfaction with the offering. The people knew God did not need to be fed by them – *he* was feeding *them* with manna.

No leaven (yeast) nor honey . . . you shall offer salt (2:11ff.): yeast or honey caused fermentation. Perhaps the part played by wine in the excesses of Canaanite religion lay behind this ruling. Salt, on the other hand, is a preservative and a reminder of the solemn covenant meal.

You must not eat the blood (7:26): the reason is given in 17:10-14; and see 'The Meaning of Blood Sacrifice', page 178.

8 – 10
THE CONSECRATION OF AARON AND HIS SONS

8 The investiture

Now that the priest's sacrificial duties have been listed, Moses implements the instructions given in Exodus 29. In an elaborate and impressive ritual Aaron and his sons are instituted to the priesthood. Moses performs the priestly duties on their behalf. The blood on Aaron's ear, hand and toe indicate the dedication of the whole man to God's service.

9 Aaron and his sons take office

The order of their first sacrifices is significant:

1. A sin-offering: obtaining cleansing and forgiveness.
2. A burnt-offering of dedication to God.
3. A peace-offering: fellowship and communion with God is restored and enjoyed.

10 Sacrilege

The rejoicing is short-lived. In no time Aaron's sons are deciding to do things *their* way: and God reduces the priesthood to three. Perhaps they were under the influence of drink (10:9). Whatever the reason, God's terrifying holiness cannot allow disobedience in those dedicated to his highest service. His commands are absolute; no man may tailor them to suit his fancy.

Verse 6: the uncombed hair and torn clothes are signs of mourning (see Good News Bible).
Verse 9: God's priests are to avoid the excesses of Canaan, where wine featured prominently.

The Sacrificial System

PHILIP BUDD

The offering of sacrifice was a regular feature in ancient Near Eastern religion. Israel appears to have shared many of the techniques and conceptions of sacrifice of her neighbours, but her own observances were set firmly in the framework of God's revelation at Sinai. The procedures set out in Leviticus presuppose a sanctuary, an altar, and an officiating priesthood, though the historical use and development of these rituals remains obscure.

Burnt-offering (Leviticus 1)
The distinctive feature was the burning of the whole animal. The Hebrew name for the sacrifice conveys the idea of 'going up', and the phrase 'an aroma pleasing to the Lord' is common. These points taken together suggest that the burnt-offering symbolized the worshipper's homage and total dedication to God. In laying his hand on the animal he identified himself completely with the sacrifice. The offering had to cost him something – one of his herd of cattle or flock of sheep and goats (a bird was permitted for the poor), and it had to be of the best – 'a male without blemish'.

Peace-offering (Leviticus 3)
The outstanding feature is the sharing of the sacrifice. Part was burnt in acknowledgement of God, part belonged to the priests, and part was eaten by the offerer and his family. The Hebrew name indicates 'peace' or 'well-being', and these sacrifices are sometimes seen as communion or fellowship rites. On the whole they are best regarded as expressing a desire to maintain and demonstrate right relations between God, man and his neighbour. This harmony might be expressed as an offering which accompanied a vow of some kind (Leviticus 22:21), or as a thank-offering (Leviticus 22:29) or free-will offering (Leviticus 22:21). The offerings expressed the individual's gratitude to God for his goodness, or were simply spontaneous expressions of devotion.

Grain-offering (Leviticus 2)
The Hebrew word has the sense of 'gift' or 'tribute'. No distinct meaning is evident; the offering probably expressed homage and thankfulness.

Sin and guilt-offerings (Leviticus 4–6:7)
The procedure is similar for both these sacrifices, and it is difficult to pin-point a difference of meaning. It may be that the sin-offering deals with infringements of God's laws, whereas the guilt-offering, since

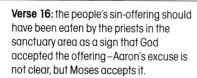

Verse 16: the people's sin-offering should have been eaten by the priests in the sanctuary area as a sign that God accepted the offering – Aaron's excuse is not clear, but Moses accepts it.

11 — 15
LAWS FOR DAILY LIFE: PURITY AND IMPURITY

Today we are better able to understand and appreciate the sound principles of diet, hygiene and medicine which these laws express. God works in and through the processes he has built into the natural world.

11 Food-laws: clean and unclean creatures

Israel may eat:

- Animals which chew the cud *and* have cloven hoofs.
- Sea creatures with both fins and scales.
- Birds not listed as forbidden.
- Insects belonging to four classes of the locust family.

Amongst those banned are:

- Carnivorous animals – which readily transmitted infection in a warm climate where flesh decayed rapidly.

---

it raises the question of compensation, deals with situations where human injury is involved. Both offerings demonstrate the need for sin to be dealt with objectively, and give prominence to the use of the blood. Both sacrifices deal with unwitting or unavoidable breaches of law. Hence 'sin' in these contexts often has a purely ritual meaning – as with the sin-offering after childbirth (Leviticus 12:6). In this case the sacrifice brings the offerer back to full membership of the holy community.

In various parts of the Bible all these offerings are said to 'atone' – to cover sin – indicating that any act of worship was set squarely in the context of God's forgiving grace.

The sacrificial system was clearly open to abuse, and on more than one occasion was criticized by the prophets (e.g. Amos 5:25; Isaiah 1:11-12; Jeremiah 7:22) probably in the light of contemporary attitudes. And a number of other texts stress the fact that obedience counts for more then sacrifice (e.g. 1 Samuel 15:22-23; Psalm 40:6-8). It was only too easy to assume God's acceptance of the offering and neglect the moral obligation to obey him. By making sin a purely external thing its seriousness was minimized.

On the other hand the sacrificial system did demand a right inward attitude. The sin-offering had to be accompanied by confession, and, where possible, a genuine attempt to put things right (Leviticus 5:5; Numbers 5:7). On the Day of Atonement the high priest confessed the sins of the whole community before the scapegoat was released (Leviticus 16:21). Furthermore the law provides no sacrifice for wilful and deliberate sin (Numbers 15:27-31).

Each sacrifice, upheld by God's promise and power, had real effect and potency, but this was not a power that could be manipulated by man. On the contrary, it was recognized that the system was divinely appointed from beginning to end. It was a God-given area of contact between God and man, bringing man into fellowship with God. Viewed in this light, a meticulous observance of these laws could inspire confidence in God. In any case, human activity was not the only factor in the observances. The priests, as God's representatives, were required to declare God's acceptance or rejection of the worshipper and his offering.

The letter to the Hebrews makes it clear that the Old Testament sacrifice was at best an incomplete answer to the problem of sin. The sacrifices themselves have disappeared, but they go far to help us understand the meaning of the cross, the sacrifice of Jesus Christ.

See too
'The Meaning of Blood Sacrifice', page 178.
'The Origin of Religion', page 24.
'Feasts and Festivals', page 180.

■ Pork – specially dangerous in this respect, as the old British saying about eating it only when there is an 'r' in the month (i.e. the cold months) bears out. Pigs are also hosts to various parasites.
■ Vermin and predatory birds – likely disease-carriers.
■ Shellfish – even today these often cause food-poisoning and enteritis.

Verses 32-40 set out measures to prevent contamination of food and water supplies. The same principles govern present-day public health regulations.

12 Purification after childbirth

In Canaan, prostitution and fertility rites were all mixed up with worship. In Israel, by sharp contrast, anything suggesting the sexual or sensual is strictly banned from the worship of God – as this chapter and chapter 15 make plain. The intention is not to write off this side of life as 'dirty', as is plain elsewhere in Scripture. The purpose is to ensure its separation from the worship of God. The rule of strict cleanliness in all sexual matters was also a positive safeguard to health.

Clean and Unclean Animals
GEORGE CANSDALE

The lists of clean and unclean animals in Leviticus 11 and Deuteronomy 14 (largely a repetition of the Leviticus list) have a significance often ignored. Far from being a catalogue of food taboos based on fad or fancy, these lists emphasize a fact not discovered until late in the last century and still not generally known – that animals carry diseases dangerous to man.

Five rough groups are recognized – mammals, birds, reptiles, water animals and insects – though not in these precise terms.
1. The clean furred animals belong to one type only, whether domesticated or wild. They are known as ruminants, or animals that chew the cud, and are still our most important meat-producers. Some others are considered edible, but it was safer to have a simple rule – any clean mammal was both cloven-hoofed and a chewer of the cud. Those that were one or the other were ruled out, and three such are named: the hare, hyrax and pig. The main purpose was probably to exclude the pig, now known to be host to several serious human parasites. Pork is safe only when thoroughly cooked. Further, the pig is a scavenger and may spread other diseases mechanically.
2. Birds are so much more varied that they cannot be classified by rule-of-thumb, and the forbidden kinds are named; all others

may be eaten. Some of these names are very difficult, with no help in the context, and translations vary widely. But there is general agreement that these are the birds of prey, crows and other scavenging and carnivorous birds.
3. The list in Leviticus 11:29-30 is thought to consist mostly of reptiles, all of which are forbidden. A snake is banned under verse 42 for 'going on its belly'.
4. Although fish are not actually named in any list they are included in the wider class 'anything living in the water' (9). In fact the qualification in this group is that the 'clean' ones should have fins and scales, so only ordinary fish could be eaten. All crustaceans, shellfish, etc., are wisely excluded.
5. In spite of their great numbers, few kinds of insects are eaten, even in countries short of animal protein. Termites (white ants) may be locally useful, but the grasshopper family – easily recognized by the pair of jumping-legs – is by far the most important. These are the only clean insects in the Mosaic Law. Locusts are best termed gregarious grasshoppers. They are wholly vegetarian and are useful food because of their high protein and calorie content. In warmer countries locusts have been a standard food since early times and it is likely that they were eaten regularly on the desert march.

13 — 14 Uncleanness due to skin diseases

Although the word 'leprosy' is used throughout in many versions, true leprosy as we would define it is only one of the skin diseases mentioned here. Chapter 13 is written in technical jargon – a professional textbook on diagnosis for the priest-physician, enabling him to distinguish between 'acute' and 'chronic' forms of the various diseases. This is the earliest formulation of quarantine regulations and preventive medicine relating to these diseases so far recovered from the ancient Near East.

As far as clothing and buildings are concerned, the 'disease' is a mildew, or fungus.

14:34ff.: we have a similar system of house inspection and treatment for dry-rot today.

Cedarwood (14:49): contains a substance used in medicine for skin diseases.

Hyssop (14:49): a herb, possibly marjoram, containing a mild antiseptic.

15 Uncleanness due to bodily discharge

See under chapter 12. Regulations are given for both normal (seminal and menstrual) and abnormal, possibly malignant, discharges. Washing is prescribed both to prevent and to sterilize infection.

16
THE DAY OF ATONEMENT

The 10th day of the 7th month (Tishri – September/October) was to be the annual Day of Atonement ('at-one-ment') for the nation. Only on this occasion was Aaron allowed into the innermost part of the tabernacle, where the ark of the covenant was housed. He must first obtain forgiveness and cleansing for his own sin. Only then might he cleanse the tabernacle and offer on behalf of the people's sins. For a New Testament look at the Day of Atonement, see Hebrews 9 and 10.

Azazel (8,10): a place in the wilderness to which the scapegoat was sent, symbolically carrying away the sins of Israel. The meaning is uncertain, but it cannot refer to an offering to a demon, as some suggest, for this was strictly forbidden (see, e.g., 17:7).

Outside the camp (27): neither offering might be eaten, since no one was to eat any of his own sin-offering, and Aaron identifies himself with the people in their sin-offering.

17
FURTHER REGULATIONS ABOUT SACRIFICE

As a safeguard against sacrificing to idols (17:7), sacrifice might be offered only in the proper place, and to the proper Person. On 17:10ff. see 'The Meaning of Blood Sacrifice', page 178.

18 — 20
ETHICAL AND MORAL LAWS

18:3 provides a key to these chapters. From what we know of Canaanite and Egyptian religions it is clear that many of these laws are directed against the specific practices of Israel's neighbours.

18 Sexual offences

6-18: marriage between those closely related by blood or by marriage is forbidden in Israel. In Egypt, which had no marriage-laws, such marriages were common.

19-30: adultery, child-sacrifice, homosexual relations, bestiality (perhaps a hangover from animal cults) were all part of the indescribably debased religions of Canaan. Israel is to shun behaviour which is bringing God's judgement on the land (compare Genesis 15:16).

19 Various laws

19:2 stands at the heart of the moral law for Jew and Christian alike (see 1 Peter 1:15-16). God's holiness, the holiness we are to reflect, shows itself in concern for the underprivileged (9-10, 14, 20), in honesty, fair dealing and impartial justice (11, 13, 15) and in respect for life and reputation (16-18).

Verses 23-25: the likelihood of heavy cropping is greatly increased by this practice.

Verses 26b-31: these are all heathen practices.

20 Serious offences and crimes punishable by death

Verses 6-21 list the penalties for dis-

obedience to laws in chapters 18 and 19 (compare, e.g., 6 with 19:31, 9 with 19:3; 10 with 18:20). That such a wide range of offences should be punishable by death seems incredibly harsh to the modern reader. It is worth noting, however, that the offences listed are either in deliberate defiance of God's holy law, or offences against people – not property.

Molech (2-5): an Ammonite god. Amongst the Phoenicians live infants were placed in the arms of an idol, and died in the flames burning inside it. Some equally horrible practice is in mind here.

The Meaning of Blood Sacrifice

ALEC MOTYER

The practice of sacrifice, the shedding of the blood of animals, goes back to the very beginning of God's dealings with sinful man (see Genesis 4:4). It pervades the whole of the Bible. In the New Testament it provides the terms in which the death of Jesus Christ is explained (see for instance Hebrews 9:11ff.).

The key verse, Leviticus 17:11, says that sacrifice is something that God has given to man: it is his provision for human need. It is a contradiction of this to say (as many Old Testament specialists do) that the basic meaning of sacrifice is an offering or gift to God. The word translated 'offering' certainly means gift. So, it is said, the person bringing the offering gains possession of the life, the blood, of the sacrificed animal, and can give it to God. By this means he injects new life into his relationship with God. Or else he is able to interpose a living screen between himself as a sinner and God the holy One. But how can that which God gives to man be interpreted as something man gives to God?

Leviticus 17:11 gives us two great clues to the meaning of blood and sacrifice. First: the purpose of the blood is to make atonement. Whenever the word translated 'atonement'– a ransom price. So it is not sufficient to say that the blood 'screens' the offender. One must say that it does so by providing a price sufficient to pay off a debt of sin before God.

So here, as always in the Bible, 'the wages of sin is death'. No sin, no sinner, can come

into the presence of an utterly holy God. To be cut off from God is death. Only if this price can be paid, the penalty taken, the sentence borne, can sinful man hope to be forgiven and come again into God's presence. This, says Leviticus 17:11, is precisely what the blood does.

We are told, second, that the blood can do this 'by reason of the life'. 'By reason of' (Revised Standard Version) translates a Hebrew preposition regularly used to express price or expenditure (e.g. 1 Kings 2:23; Proverbs 7:23; Lamentations 5:9). It is found in a basic legal passage on the necessity for exact justice, in the phrase 'life for life' (Deuteronomy 19:21), i.e. 'life in payment for life'. So in Leviticus 17:11, just as 'to make atonement' means 'to pay the atonement/ ransom price', so 'by reason of the life' means 'by reason of the payment of life'.

In other words 'blood' means death – the termination of life – just as it does in ordinary metaphorical usage (see, for instance, Genesis 9:5; 37:26; etc.). In the sacrifice, life was terminated. The flowing blood was the symbol and proof that life had been taken in payment for the sins of the guilty and as a substitute for his own guilt-stained life.

Animal sacrifice expressed the principle. The full reality took place in the death of the Lord Jesus Christ. In the Old Testament the people had a God-given preview of the shed blood of Jesus, his substitutionary death on our behalf, for our sins, the just for the unjust, once and for all.

Reconstructions of objects in the tabernacle: the altar for burning incense, seven-branched lampstand, table for the bread offered to God. See too page 173.

21—22
RULES FOR THE PRIESTS

Because of their position and duties the priests are subject to particularly stringent regulations on ritual purity. Any defilement disqualified them from contact with the holy things. The rules for the high priest (21:10-15) are even stricter (compare 11 with 1-2; 13-14 with 7). No one with any physical defect may serve as priest, though he may share in eating the offerings. Only the best we can give – whether in the priesthood or sacrificial offerings – is in any measure worthy of God.

23
THE SET FEASTS

Israel's special festivals, like the weekly sabbath, reflect a pattern of sevens – pointing back to God setting the seventh day apart as a special day at creation.

1. The sabbath: one day of rest in seven.
2. Passover, followed by the seven-day Feast of Unleavened Bread (March/April).
3. Firstfruits (April), followed seven weeks later by

4. The Feast of Weeks (Pentecost): the harvest festival (June).
5. The Feast of Trumpets: the New Year Festival and first of three festivals in the seventh month (September/October); the others being
6. The Day of Atonement; and
7. The Feast of Tabernacles or Shelters: a perpetual reminder of the nation's tent-dwelling days following the deliverance from Egypt.

24
THE LAMP, BREAD OFFERED TO GOD, AND THE SIN OF BLASPHEMY

Chapter 24 turns from special festivals to two regular duties: the lamps which must be kept burning, and the weekly offering of 12 loaves. The loaves remind the tribes of their complete dependence on God's provision. They are not put there for God to eat (as in pagan religions). Aaron and the priests are openly instructed to eat the bread themselves.

Verses 10-23 record the ruling about a breach of the third commandment. The emphasis is on one law for Israelite and resident foreigner alike.

Feasts and Festivals

PHILIP BUDD

From very early times the Jewish year was punctuated by the great festivals – the 'feasts of the Lord'. Some were timed to coincide with the changing seasons, reminding the people of God's constant provision for them, and providing an opportunity to return to God some token of all that he had given. Others commemorated the great events of Israel's history, the occasions when in an unmistakable way God had stepped in to deliver his people. All were occasions of whole-hearted delight and enjoyment of God's good gifts, and at the same time sober gatherings to seek his forgiveness and cleansing.

They were never intended to be observed out of mere formality and empty ritual. The prophets had sharp words for those who reduced them to this level. The purpose of the festivals was spiritual: a great and glorious meeting of God and his people.

There were probably many local festivals (Judges 21:21), but on three occasions in the year all the men were required to attend great national celebrations:

1. Passover and the Feast of Unleavened Bread (Exodus 12:1-20; 23:15). These two feasts, combining pastoral and agricultural elements, were observed together to commemorate Israel's departure from Egypt (see on Exodus 11-12). The observance began on the fourteenth day of the first

month and lasted for a week.
2. The Feast of Weeks (Harvest) (Exodus
23:16; Leviticus 23:15-21). Later known as
Pentecost, it was celebrated 50 days after the
beginning of Passover. It was essentially an
agricultural celebration at which the firstfruits of the harvest were offered to God.
3. The Feast of Ingathering (Tabernacles)
(Exodus 23:16; Leviticus 23:33-43). An
autumn festival at the end of the fruit-
harvest. The people lived for seven days in
shelters made of branches – essentially as an
agricultural thanksgiving, but also as a
reminder of their tent-dwelling days in the
wilderness (Leviticus 23:43).
 All of these festivals were regarded as
'holy', occasions when all ordinary work
stopped. There were also other celebrations
(all connected with the number seven).
4. Sabbath. On the seventh day all work was
forbidden and the daily sacrifices were
doubled. This observance was connected
with the completion of God's work of
creation (Exodus 20:11), the deliverance from
Egypt (Deuteronomy 5:15), and man's simple
need for rest and refreshment (Exodus
23:12). After the exile the sabbath rules were
strictly enforced (Nehemiah 13:15-22), and
their observance became one of the
outstanding features of Judaism.
5. New moon. This is often mentioned along
with the sabbath (e.g. Isaiah 1:13). Special
sacrifices (Numbers 28:11-15), and the
blowing of trumpets (Numbers 10:10) were
distinctive features of the new moon festival.
There were also special meals and family
sacrifices in early times (1 Samuel 20:5, 24),
and sometimes prophets were consulted
(2 Kings 4:23). On the new moon of the
seventh month there was a special **Feast of
Trumpets** (Numbers 29:1).
6. Sabbatical year. By law, every seventh
year the land lay fallow (Leviticus 25:1-7),
and every fiftieth year was a **Jubilee Year**
(Leviticus 25:8-34) when mortgaged property
was returned to its owners and Hebrew
slaves were freed.
7. Day of Atonement (Leviticus 16). On the
tenth day of the seventh month there was a
special annual ceremony of confession and
atonement for sin.
 There were other feasts not mentioned in
the biblical laws. One was the **Feast of
Purim** (Esther 9) to commemorate the Jewish
deliverance from Haman, and later the **Feast
of Dedication** (John 10:22) celebrating the
purification of the temple after its desecration
by Antiochus Epiphanes in 168 BC.

*A modern Jewish family celebrate Passover;
see also page 492.*

**The law of retaliation (lex talionis, verses
15ff.):** the principle this law expresses is
of exact public justice, as opposed to
individual revenge. In the event, compensation for injury often took the form of a
fine (as the exception made in the case
of murder implies – Numbers 35:31ff.).
The fact that literal retaliation by bodily
mutilation was legally allowed does not
necessarily mean it was practised. It was
a strict, legal statement against such
practices as family blood-feuds (the evils
of which are shown, for instance, in Greek
drama).

25
THE SEVENTH AND FIFTIETH YEARS: SABBATH AND JUBILEE
The pattern of sevens reflected in the
festivals (chapter 23) is now extended
to the land. One year in seven it is to lie
fallow: a year in which the people, freed
from much of their ordinary work, are
to be taught and trained in God's law
(Deuteronomy 31:10ff.). The fiftieth
year, following the seventh seven, is an
extra fallow year for the land, which
reverts to its original owner. It is a time
when those who have fallen on bad
times have their freedom and property
restored. Jubilee, the year of restoration,
serves a dual purpose. It reminds the
people that the land belongs to God;
and it prevents the wealthy from
amassing land.

26
PROMISE AND WARNING: BLESSING AND CURSING
The reward of obedience is pictured as
an idyll of peace and plenty. Best of all,
God will walk amongst his people, as he
walked in the garden with the first man
and woman. This is Eden restored.
Disobedience, on the other hand, will
bring calamity on the nation: fatal
disease, famine, wild beasts ravaging
the land, and war leading to exile. The
cursings are more detailed than the
blessings: human nature being

what it is, fear brings a readier response than love. Yet even after all the disobedience, God still promises to respond to the call of genuine repentance.

27
VOWS AND TITHES

Firstborn sons, the firstlings of flocks and herds, and firstfruits of the field are God's by right (he accepts part for the whole). One-tenth of all cattle and produce are also his due. Over and above this, men might vow individuals or possessions to God as a dedication or thank-offering. Normally these would be redeemed for their set valuation, plus one-fifth.

'Devoted' to the Lord (28): deliberately dedicated and set apart for God and therefore no longer available to man. Verse 29 presumably refers to someone 'set apart' under a death sentence.

Verse 34 brings us back to the source of authority for these and all the laws in Leviticus. The commands are God's, given through Moses, at Sinai.

Criticism and the Old Testament

GORDON WENHAM

'Criticism' is an indispensable aid to interpreting the Old Testament. In everyday speech it is a decidedly negative word. But in the specialized sense it covers a range of disciplines which apply to most types of literature, and it has made a very positive contribution to the understanding of the Bible.

The seven main branches of biblical criticism are textual, source, tradition, redaction, form, literary and historical criticism. The first six are basically concerned with the structures of literature and the various ways in which an author expresses himself. The last, historical criticism, is more concerned with the meaning and truth of the author's statements.

Textual criticism
Textual criticism is concerned with recovering the original text of a document. Mistakes are liable to creep into every document copied by hand, and it is the task of the textual critic to spot these errors and – wherever possible – correct them. By studying numerous manuscripts, textual critics have been able to work out a set of principles which can be applied to many different sorts of document.

For the most part the scribes who copied the Pentateuch were very careful, and it would seem that very few errors crept into the Hebrew text. In the case of other Old Testament books – notably Samuel and Jeremiah – there are passages where it is more difficult to re-establish the original text.

The discovery of the Dead Sea Scrolls was therefore very important, since they give us a Hebrew text of much of the Old Testament about a thousand years older than anything we had before. The scrolls have already shed a great deal of light on the history of the Old Testament, and helped scholars establish its original form.

Source criticism
Source criticism is the attempt to discover and define the written material on which the different biblical writers drew. It has important bearings on the reliability of the Bible books. Some Old Testament books describe events that occurred many years before they were written. The book of Kings, for instance, must have been written after the last event it mentions – the release of King Jehoiachin from prison in 562 BC – yet it also relates the accession of Solomon, some 400 years earlier, as well as numerous events in between. Stories simply handed down by word of mouth over that length of time are likely to be less accurate than those written down from the beginning. But source critics, prompted by the recurring refrain, 'And the rest of the deeds of King X, are they not written in the Book of the Chronicles of the Kings of Judah/Israel?' have concluded that much of the early material in the book has in fact been taken from royal annals and other trustworthy contemporary records.

It is extremely difficult to distinguish different literary sources within a document unless some of those sources have actually survived. In that case the source material may be subtracted from the document in question to leave the author's own contribution or material taken from another source. In the Bible we rarely possess two or more parallel documents where we can see how one writer used another as his source. The Synoptic Gospels (Matthew, Mark, Luke) in the New Testament and the Old Testament book of Kings with its parallel in Chronicles are the exceptions.

Elsewhere, though it is a reasonable assumption that the biblical writers used sources, there is little or no objective evidence that this is so. More subjective, less dependable criteria, such as variation in style or vocabulary, have to be used to distinguish the sources. Using such criteria it has become customary to distinguish at least four sources in the Pentateuch (commonly designated J,E,D and P). More recently, however, it has been argued that the differences in Hebrew style which are used to define the pentateuchal sources have no significance in the light of ancient literary conventions, and that a fresh approach to this aspect of the criticism of the Pentateuch is required.

Tradition criticism

Tradition criticism attempts to trace the development of a biblical story or tradition from the time it was first told to the time it was written down. For instance, the stories of Abraham were probably passed on by word of mouth for several generations before being incorporated in a written source later used by the author of Genesis. A historian concerned to reconstruct the life of Abraham as exactly as possible wants to know what changes the story of Abraham went through in the process of retelling. Tradition criticism tries to pin-point and explain such changes. However, except where the precise means and circumstances in which a story was transmitted are known, the results of tradition criticism are open to question and must be treated with caution.

Redaction criticism

The task of redaction criticism is to determine how the editor (redactor) of a biblical book utilized his sources, what he omitted and what he added and what his particular bias was. Only when the critic has access to all the sources which were at the disposal of the editor can his findings be absolutely certain. And in the Old Testament the critic has, at best, only some of the sources (e.g. the book of Kings used by the author of Chronicles). Elsewhere the sources are precariously reconstructed out of the edited work itself. Then redaction criticism is of limited value, but its methods can help to bring out the special interests of the editor and so lead to a fuller appreciation of the theology expressed in his work. For example, though it is hard to reconstruct the sources used in the book of Deuteronomy or Joshua, redaction criticism makes it possible to see what the aim of the editors was.

Form criticism

Form criticism is concerned with the study of literary form in the Bible. Different writings have different forms. An essay differs in form from a poem. The form of a law differs from that of a psalm. Often the form of a piece of literature may throw light on the nature of the piece and its background, or 'life-setting'. The basic method of form criticism is to compare like with like, to determine the characteristic features of a particular type of literature, and then to suggest reasons for these features.

Form criticism has been most profitably used in the psalms and has revolutionized our understanding of them. The psalms fall into different categories, such as hymns, thanksgivings, laments, royal psalms, pilgrimage songs, etc. It used to be held that most of the psalms were personal poems of pious Jews after the exile. Now, thanks to form criticism, it is recognized that most of the psalms were sung in the public worship of the temple prior to its destruction in 587 BC.

Literary criticism

Literary criticism attempts to identify and understand the literary conventions and styles which the biblical writers used. Recent work has paid special attention to Hebrew narrative, though some studies have also been devoted to Hebrew poetry.

The Old Testament contains some of the greatest stories in all of world literature. Their greatness resides not just in the content and their theological outlook, but in the way the tales are told and presented. The vivid graphic narratives of the books of Genesis and Samuel, when read aloud as they were intended to be, still have power to seize the listener's imagination. When contrasted with the dull annalistic style that characterizes earlier Near Eastern literatures the techniques of the biblical writers are truly revolutionary and a dazzling achievement. And of course biblical storytelling has continued to exercise a powerful influence on Western prose narrative.

The Old Testament writers achieve their effects with great economy of words; even the longest books take only a few hours to read aloud while sometimes covering centuries of historical events. The individual episodes are also very succinctly related, contain little straight description, yet are amazingly vivid and gripping (e.g. Genesis 22; 1 Samuel 17; 2 Samuel 18). Notice how dialogue is used in these episodes, Abraham and Isaac, David, his brothers, Goliath and so on. The narratives move forward in a series of scenes, e.g. in 1 Samuel 17 – battle front, David's home, battle front, Saul's tent, battle front. The stories frequently make use of repetition: sometimes mere phrases ('Here I ➤➤

am', Genesis 22:1,7,11), sometimes whole situations, recur (e.g. the pairs of dreams in the Joseph story, Genesis 37,40,41). Even the careers of the patriarchs Abraham, Isaac and Jacob, run in parallel at many points. The biblical writers manage to convey a great deal about the personality of their characters without using psychological description. Much is left unsaid, or merely hinted at, so that in fact the attentive listener supplies it himself thereby involving himself in the story.

Rarely do the writers give any clue to their identity, and this is highly appropriate, for usually they tell the stories from an omniscient perspective. Occasionally this is made explicit, when the narrator discloses God's attitudes or thoughts, but this viewpoint characterizes most of the historical books of the Old Testament. For this reason Jews call these books the former prophets, because their essential purpose is to explain God's will, why he chose one king and rejected another, why Israel prospered at certain times and suffered at others. Such an interpretation of history is quite beyond the competence of any ordinary historian, and the assumption by the biblical writers that their viewpoint is identical with God's is an implicit claim to the inspiration of their work.

One branch of literary criticism, sometimes called rhetorical criticism, concentrates on the surface features of biblical writing. Among the commonest devices of Hebrew prose are inclusion, i.e. beginning and ending a passage with the same word or phrase (e.g. Genesis 1:1; 2:3); repetition, both doublet and triadic patterns are possible (e.g. Numbers 22:23-28); and chiasmus, the ABBA pattern (Genesis 2:4). Palistrophic writing is also common in the Old Testament. Palistrophes are an extended form of chiasmus in which the second half of the story is structurally a mirror image of the first. The most spectacular example is the flood story in Genesis 6-9, in which the names of the actors, events (e.g. entry/exit from ark, covering/uncovering of the mountains), periods of time (7, 7, 40, 150 days), mentioned in the first half of the story reappear in reverse order in the second half. At the mid-point of the structure and of the narrative occur the keywords 'God remembered Noah', thereby reminding us that Noah's deliverance turned on the mercy of God.

Historical criticism

Historical criticism is a very broad discipline covering all aspects of history writing. There are two aspects of it which are of particular concern to biblical studies.

First, historical criticism has determined the techniques used for dating a document. How do we know when it was written, and the date of the copy we possess? Unless we have the original, the date of composition will of course always be earlier than a copy. The latter is relatively easy to determine with modern methods in palaeography and archaeology. However, our earliest manuscript of Exodus dates from about 250 BC, and all agree that it is not an original and that Exodus must have been composed much earlier. To discover that date is a much more involved process. If its author were named in the text, this would help. But a forgery could always claim to be written by Moses in the same terms as an authentic Mosaic document. A second clue to the date of a book lies in the events it records. Obviously its date of composition must be later than the last event mentioned – in the case of Exodus, the erection of the tabernacle. But this only tells us the earliest date at which the book could have been written, not the latest date, which is of more interest.

If there are no explicit statements in the text itself about its date of composition, we have to rely on indirect evidence, such as the assumptions of the writer. The author of the book of Judges shows when he was writing by remarking several times, 'In those days there was no king in Israel; every man did what was right in his own eyes.' The obvious implication is that the writer had experienced the order a just king could create, and was writing after the establishment of the monarchy.

The second important task of historical criticism is to verify information found in the biblical sources. When a document says something, how do we know it is telling the truth? This basic question may be broken down into a number of smaller ones. How close is the document to the events it describes? Are its statements backed up by other sources, biblical or non-biblical, or by archaeology? Could the events have occurred just as they are described? In trying to answer these questions the historian will be able to build up a fuller and richer picture of what happened. Discovering the author of a source may greatly illuminate the meaning of a narrative; and non-biblical sources can often fill in the background to the biblical account. In these various ways biblical criticism has been of use in interpreting the Old Testament and defending its integrity against those who question its truth. Only too often Old Testament criticism, especially historical criticism, has been marred by the introduction of unjustified rationalistic assumptions (e.g. that miracles do not happen). But on the whole, the value of criticism has been proved by its generally positive conclusions. Certainly all who believe in the value of the Old Testament must take criticism seriously, as they will be the first to want to establish an accurate text and be sure of its meaning.

umbers

Numbers covers 38 years in the history of Israel: the period of desert wandering in the Sinai peninsula. It begins two years after the escape from Egypt. It ends on the eve of entry into Canaan. The title comes from the 'numbering' (census) of Israel in the early chapters and chapter 26. The book might have been called 'The grumblings of a nation'. It is one long sad story of complaining and discontent. As a result, of the entire generation that had seen the marvels of God's deliverance from Egypt, only three men – Moses, Joshua and Caleb – survive to the end of the book. And only two – Joshua and Caleb – were to enjoy the promised land.

God's miraculous provision. Even so, 2-3 million would equal the entire population of Canaan, and other passages imply that the Canaanites were more numerous than the Israelites (Deuteronomy 7:7, 17, 22). For this reason, various attempts have been made to reduce the numbers. Some believe, for example, that the word translated 'thousands' should be 'captains'; others that it should be 'families'. It is also possible that the numbers are used as symbols of power and importance, rather than a literal count of heads. See further 'Large Numbers of the Old Testament', page 191.

1 – 10:10
ISRAEL IN THE SINAI DESERT

1 The general census
The purpose of the census is to list all men over 20 fit for military service. The Levites, by virtue of their other duties, were exempt. Moses and Aaron, the civic and religious heads, are in charge of the count, assisted by one representative from each tribe. In the second census (chapter 26), taken 38 years later, after Aaron's death, his son Eleazar takes his place. The later total, 601,730, is slightly less than the figure here, 603,550. In Egypt Israel's population rose rapidly, but now the tough desert conditions and the judgements their disobedience brings upon them keep the figures static.
The problem of high numbers: a military force of over 600,000 would mean a total population of some 2-3 million. The Bible account makes it plain that the numbers involved were considerable. Israel could not have survived in the desert without

2 The encampment
When the nation moved, the three eastern tribes, headed by Judah, led the way. 10:17 gives a slightly different order for the middle section – Gershonites and Merarites carrying the tabernacle, then Reuben, Simeon and Gad, followed by the Kohathites with the 'holy things'. The northern tribes, Dan, Asher and Naphtali bring up the rear. The tribal leaders are the same as those who helped in the census. Ramesses II of Egypt (Moses' contemporary) used this same hollow rectangular formation in his Syrian campaign, so it looks as if Moses was making a good use of his earlier Egyptian military training.
The standards (2:2): according to Jewish tradition, a lion for Judah, a human head for Reuben, an ox for Ephraim and an eagle for Dan.

3 God chooses the Levites for special service
God's claim to the firstborn goes back to

A gold dish dating from the latter part of the 2nd millennium BC illustrates the vessels of gold and silver brought by the chief men of Israel.

the night of the Passover (Exodus 12). Now God accepts the Levites instead of the firstborn of all Israel. The first census pairs them off man for man, leaving a surplus of 273 who are redeemed by money.
Shekel of the sanctuary (3:47): a weight of about 10gms, not a coin.

4 The Levitical families are assigned their jobs

The second census of Levites lists those between 30 and 50, eligible for the service of the tabernacle. (The age-limits varied at different times: see 8:24; 1 Chronicles 23:24.)

Verses 1-20: the **Kohathites** are responsible for carrying the sacred objects of the sanctuary after the priests have dismantled and covered them.

Verses 21-28: the **Gershonites** are in charge of transporting the curtains and coverings of the tabernacle and forecourt under Ithamar's supervision.

Verses 29-33: the **Merarites** are to look

after and transport the framework – pillars, pegs, cords – also under Ithamar's supervision. Wagons drawn by a yoke of oxen are provided for the Gershonites and Merarites (7:7-8).

5 Various laws; the jealousy ordeal

Verses 11-31 describe the trial by ordeal for suspected infidelity. Trials of this kind were not uncommon in ancient times, and they are also well known today from Africa and India. This one is mild by some standards – and also less heavily weighted than many towards a verdict of guilty. It is not clear whether the water contained some herb which would induce miscarriage if the woman were guilty and pregnant, or whether it worked simply by psychological suggestion.

6: 1-21 The Nazirite

A special vow gives the Nazirite his (or her) spiritual status. The outward marks of consecration to God are:

■ abstinence from wine and strong drink;
■ uncut hair;
■ special care to avoid defilement through contact with a dead body (see on chapter 19).

The vow was usually for a limited time, but Samson (a somewhat unorthodox Nazirite) had a lifelong vow (Judges 13-16). Samuel may also have been a Nazirite. It is not known how or when these practices originated.

6: 22-27 Aaron's benediction

7 The tribes bring their offerings

The dedication of the altar preceded the events of Numbers 1 by a month. On successive days the leader of each tribe brings a silver plate and silver basin filled with a cereal offering, a golden dish of incense, and animals for burnt-offering, sin-offering and peace-offering (see on Leviticus 1-7).

8 Consecration of the Levites

Those who serve God must be clean through and through. Washing and shaving ensure outward cleanliness. The blood of sacrifice cleans man of the inward stain of sin.

9: 1-14 Rulings about the Passover

No one may opt out of celebrating the Passover (see Exodus 12). But the absentee and anyone ritually unclean at the time may observe the feast one month later.

9: 15-23 The cloud and the fire

God's guidance in the wilderness was a clear and visible reality. Cloud by day and fire by night marked his presence at the tabernacle, which was quite literally in their midst. When the cloud lifted they moved on. Where it settled again, they encamped: no movement of the cloud, no movement of the people.

10: 1-10 The silver trumpets

These sounded the alarm, summoned the assembly, and announced the feasts and new months. Long trumpets like these were common in Egypt about 1400-1300 BC. Some were buried with the Pharaoh Tutankhamun (about 1,350 BC).

10:11 — 12:16
FROM SINAI TO KADESH

10:11-36 The journey begins

About three weeks after the census they strike camp and leave Mt Sinai. (See on chapter 2 for the marching order.)

Moses' brother-in-law goes with them as guide. The direction and company of the Lord is a very real thing (33-36).

11 Complaints about the monotonous diet

The first delicious taste of manna (see Exodus 16) was like wafers made with honey. Now sheer monotony makes it stick in the gullet like sawdust. Mouth-watering thoughts of all the fish and vegetables that abounded in the Egyptian delta soon produce an irresistible craving. God gives them what they want – till they are sick of it! And with it comes judgement for the attitude which lay behind the outcry.

Verse 29: a remarkable attitude in a leader – power without a streak of corruption (see 12:3).

Quails (31): as in the previous year (Exodus 16), this was a migratory flight returning in spring to Europe. See article page 189.

Homer (32): 'a donkey load'; 10 homers (Good News Bible, 1,000 kilogrammes) is the measure of their gluttony.

12 Miriam and Aaron challenge Moses' leadership

The real bone of contention is not Moses' marriage, but his position. As Miriam is the one to be punished, presumably she was the instigator. Moses is silent, but God's answer is a remarkable tribute to the man (6-8).

Cushite (1): may be Midianite or Sudanese.

A silver trumpet, as used for summoning the people and for breaking camp.

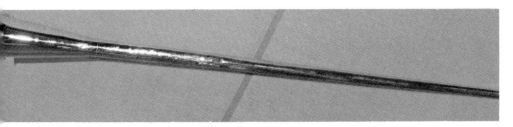

13—20:21
IN THE KADESH AREA

Details are few, but it seems that the best part of 38 years – a whole generation – was spent around here.

13—14 The twelve spies and their reports; mutiny

From Deuteronomy 1:19-25 it seems plain that Moses intended to go straight on into the promised land at this point; it was the people's suggestion that they should send spies ahead. No doubt Moses afterwards wished he had not listened. The two men of faith put the true interpretation on the facts (Numbers 13:30), but the people listened to the ten prophets of doom, with their tales of giants and grasshoppers. God, and the good land, was forgotten. Within sight of the goal, a whole generation cut itself off from all that was promised. Moses' prayer at this point is staggering. Only God's intervention has saved him from death by stoning. Yet here he is, pleading for the life of the stubborn nation that caused him nothing but trouble! Time and time again he stands between Israel and utter destruction (Exodus 32:7-14; Numbers 11:1-2; 16:41-48; 21:5-9). Now his plea involves him in sharing their sentence with them.

The Anakim (13:22)…the Nephilim (13:33): see Genesis 6:4. Nothing is known of them outside the Bible, but they were evidently a race of Goliaths.

Caleb never lost his whole-hearted trust in God. Forty-five years later, at the age of 85, he chooses Anakim territory to conquer as his possession (Joshua 14:6-15).

15 Various laws

Verses 1-31: offerings to be made after the conquest of Canaan.

After the long years in the desert the fertile gorge found by the spies, with its grapes, pomegranates and figs, must have seemed a luxuriant foretaste of the promised land. The picture here is of Ein Avdat, on the northern side of the Negev desert.

Verses 32-36: the seriousness of sabbath-breaking.

Verses 37-41: the border of tassels to remind forgetful Israel of God and his commands.

16 The rebellion of Korah, Dathan and Abiram

This unholy alliance has a two-pronged attack. Korah the Levite's grievance is Aaron's monopoly of the priesthood (10b). Dathan and Abiram challenge Moses on the grounds of high-handedness and his failure to bring them into the promised land (13-14). But at root the attack is on God (11), and it is God who puts the rebellion down.

Put out the eyes (14): New English Bible 'hoodwink' gives the right sense. Our equivalent of the Hebrew idiom is 'to pull wool over the eyes'.

The earth split open and swallowed them (32): God makes use of natural forces to execute judgement (as in the nine plagues of Egypt). The phenomenon here may be the breaking up (perhaps by storm) of the hard crusty surface which forms over deep lakes of liquid mud in the Arabah rift valley where this incident occurred.

17 Aaron's rod produces the fruit

Like all biblical miracles, this one has a very practical point. Everyone can see

The Quail
GEORGE CANSDALE

The quail is one of the few biblical birds that can be identified with certainty. Quails are the smallest of the game bird family and the only ones with migratory habits. The common quail, *Coturnix coturnix,* breeds in many parts of West Asia and Europe, including Great Britain, and flies south in winter, reaching North Africa and south-west Asia. It is about 7 inches/180 mm long, and heard much more often than seen, since its mottled brown colouring makes it inconspicuous.

Twice a year the common quail's migration route takes it across the region through which the Israelites journeyed at the time of the exodus. And this natural phenomenon was used by God to provide the people with meat. Two specific occasions are mentioned. The first (Exodus 16:13) was some six weeks after the Israelites left Egypt, when they had reached the Wilderness of Sin. The second (Numbers 11) was a year later at Kibroth-hattaavah, in the same general area. Each time, it was about the latter half of April, as the birds flew north.

The narrative makes it clear that very large numbers were involved. But the figures are admittedly difficult. It has been calculated that if the family unit is assumed to be ten

homers, the total kill would have been some nine million birds. Annual exports from Egypt during the past 100 years have in fact been of this order. For many years the kill was over two million, sometimes reaching three million, but this continued slaughter so reduced the breeding stocks that by about 1920 it had put a stop to the mass migration that had been going on since before the time of Moses.

The mention of 2 cubits (3 feet/900 mm) in Numbers 11:31 has caused confusion. It is best taken as referring to the height they were flying above the ground. Quail are at least partly dependent on the wind for their migration journeys and it is stated that they came in with the wind, also that they came in during the evening, which is still usual with the much smaller flocks today. Collection went on for two days, which fits the fact that the birds are sometimes so exhausted that they must rest for a day or two before flying further. Numbers 11:32 states that the people spread them out all around the camp. Centuries later Herodotus reported that the Egyptians were still preparing quail in this way, first cleaning them and then drying them in the sun.

where God's choice falls, and there is no more room for dispute.

18—19 Duties and dues of the priests and Levites; the purification ritual

Neither priests nor Levites share in the inheritance of the land. Instead, God gives the priests the remainder of all the sacrificial offerings, firstfruits and firstlings. The Levites are given the nation's tithes (one tenth of all the flocks and herds and produce), of which they in turn give one tenth to the priests.

The ritual with the red heifer (19:1-10) is the remedy for defilement by contact with a dead body, described in verses 11-22. To minimize the risk of accidental defilement, tombs were later painted white (see Matthew 23:27).

20: 1-13 Miriam's death; water from the rock

Miriam, Aaron (20:25ff.; 33:38f.) and Moses (Deuteronomy 34:5-8) all died in the same year – on the brink of entry into Canaan. The best part of 38 years has passed since 13:1.

Verses 2-13: Moses' sin seems to be his failure to give God credit for the water-supply. It cost him the land he had so longed to enter. Even the greatest of God's servants, after a long lifetime of trust and obedience, can fall. Nothing seems to cure the people's grumbles. They were moaning when they first left Egypt. They are moaning still, after all the years of God's providing.

Water out of the rock: Sinai limestone is known to retain water (see on Exodus 17:6). Moses struck the rock in the place God indicated.

20:14-21 Edom refuses a safe-conduct

Your brother Israel (14): not just a manner of speaking, the Edomites were descendants of Esau, Jacob's brother.
King's Highway (17): see map, page 196. Edom's refusal to let Israel pass involves them in a long detour south and round.

20:22—21:35 DETOUR TO AVOID EDOM

20:22-29 The death of Aaron

Mt Hor may be Jebel Madeira, north-east of Kadesh, on the north-west border of Edom.

21 Victories over Arad and Sihon; the incident of the poisonous snakes

Complaints begin again on the trek south to the Gulf of Aqaba (the 'Red Sea' here) to clear Edom's territory. Jesus used the incident of the bronze serpent to explain his own death in his discussion with Nicodemus (John 3:14). In the wilderness the people had only to look, and they lived.

The well (16): water lies close to the surface in some parts of the Sinai peninsula and southern Transjordan. The Israelites often had only to dig shallow pits to find it.

22—36 ISRAEL IN THE PLAINS OF MOAB

22—24 Balak and Balaam: the blessing of Israel

With the Israelites encamped on his doorstep, the king of Moab sends to Pethor (probably Pitru, near Carchemish) on the Euphrates for Balaam the diviner to come and curse his enemies. It was a routine business arrangement for the prophet, in a day when everyone believed in the power of words (especially formal 'blessings' and 'cursings') to influence events. What is surprising is the disclosure that the source of Balaam's knowledge is God himself. And neither bribe nor threat will budge him from the truth as God reveals it to him.

Three times they go through the same ritual (22:41-23:10; 23:13-24; 23:27-24:9). Three times Balaam blesses Israel, to the increasing anger of Balak. The fourth oracle tops all (24:15-24) – a remarkable prediction of Israel's future.

The Large Numbers of the Old Testament

JOHN WENHAM

The Old Testament at various places records numbers which seem impossibly large. It has often been assumed that these figures were simply invented, and are evidence that the Bible is historically unreliable. But who would make up figures which are patently absurd? Would any man in his senses invent a story of a bus crash in which 16,000 passengers were killed? It is much more likely that these Old Testament numbers were faithfully copied out, despite the fact that they did not seem to make sense. Invention does not satisfactorily account for them. The explanation must lie elsewhere. And in fact patient research has gone a long way towards resolving this knotty problem.

The corruption of numbers

There is evidence that the Old Testament text is on the whole marvellously well preserved. There is also evidence from the parallel passages in Samuel, Kings and Chronicles and (especially) in Ezra 2 and Nehemiah 7 that numbers were peculiarly difficult to transmit accurately. We have instances of extra noughts being added to a number: 2 Samuel 10:18 reads '700 chariots', 1 Chronicles 19:18 reads '7,000'. A digit can drop out: 2 Kings 24:8 gives the age of Jehoiachin on accession as 18, whereas 2 Chronicles 36:9 gives it as 8. An entire numeral can drop out: 1 Samuel 13:1 says 'Saul was years old'. In Ezra 2 and Nehemiah 7 the digits often vary by one unit. And there are other errors of copying, many of which are easily explained.

The confusion of words

In the modern Hebrew Bible all numbers are written out in full, but for a long time the text was written without vowels. The absence of vowels made it possible to confuse two words which are crucial to this problem: 'eleph and 'alluph. Without vowel points these words look identical: 'lp. 'eleph is the ordinary word for 'thousand', but it can also be used in a variety of other senses: e.g. 'family' (Judges 6:15, Revised Version) or 'clan' (Zechariah 9:7; 12:5, 6, Revised Standard Version) or perhaps a military unit. 'alluph is used for the 'chieftains' of Edom (Genesis 36:15-43); probably for a commander of a military 'thousand'; and almost certainly for the professional, fully-armed soldier.

Military statistics

At certain periods warfare was conducted by two sharply distinguished types of fighting men – the Goliaths and the Davids – the professional soldiers who were fully armed, and the folk army, whose only weapons were those of the peasant shepherd. It seems clear that in a number of places the word for professional soldier has been misunderstood as meaning 'thousand'. Take, for example, the attack on the little town of Gibeah in Judges 20. Verse 2 says that 400,000 footmen 'that drew the sword' assembled. If these were in fact 400 fully armed foot-soldiers, the subsequent narrative makes excellent sense. The Benjamite forces (verse 15) consist of 26 soldiers armed with swords, together with 700 men armed only with slings. At the first attack (verse 21) the Israelites lose 22 of their crack soldiers, the next day (verse 25) they lose a further 18; on the third day (verses 29, 34) an ambush is set, consisting of, or led by, 10 of them. (Could 10,000 men take up their positions undetected?) The losses begin again (verse 31) 'as at other times' – and in this case the scale of loss has been clearly preserved, for about 30 Israelites (not apparently sword-armed soldiers), 25 Benjamite soldiers and 100 others are killed. Eighteen of them were killed in the first stage of the pursuit, 5 were later 'cut down in the highways' and 2 more at Gidom. The remaining 600 slingers took refuge in the rock of Rimmon. Similarly, in the assault on Ai (Joshua 7-8) the true proportions of the narrative become clear when we realize that the disastrous loss of 36 men is matched by the setting of an ambush, not of 30,000 men of valour, but of 30.

David's feast in Hebron in 1 Chronicles 12 appears to be attended by enormous numbers, not of ordinary men, but of distinguished leaders – some 340,800 of them. In this case it looks as though in fact there were 'captains of thousands' and 'captains of hundreds', and that by metonymy or by abbreviation 'thousand' has been used for 'captains of thousands' and 'hundreds' for 'captains of hundreds'. 'Thousand' and 'hundred' have been treated as numerals and added together. When these figures are unscrambled we get a total of roughly 2,000 'famous men', which seems eminently reasonable.

Along these lines most of the numerical »

problems of the later history fall into place. In 1 Kings 20:27-30, the little Israelite army killed 100 (not 100,000) foot-soldiers, and the wall of Aphek killed 27 (not 27,000) more. The Ethiopian (Sudanese) invasion had a thousand, not a million, warriors (2 Chronicles 14:9). 10 (not 10,000) were cast down from the top of the rock (2 Chronicles 25:12).

The size of the Israelite nation

The most interesting, most difficult and (from the historian's point of view) the most important question is the size of the Israelite population at the different stages of its history. The present texts indicate that the 70 souls of Joseph's day had risen to two or three million at the time of the Exodus (Numbers 1) and to at least five million in the time of David (2 Samuel 24:9; 1 Chronicles 21:5). With regard to the latter, R. de Vaux rightly says: '(2 Samuel) lists 800,000 men liable for military service in Israel, and 500,000 in Judah . . . The lower total, in 2 Samuel, is still far too high: 1,300,000 men of military age would imply at least five million inhabitants, which, for Palestine, would mean nearly twice as many people to the square mile as in the most thickly populated countries of modern Europe.'

The solution of the problem of the Exodus numbers is a long story. Suffice it to say that there is good reason to believe that the original censuses in Numbers 1 and 26 set out the numbers of each tribe, somewhat in this form:

Simeon:

57 armed men; 23 'hundreds' (military units).

This came to be written:
57 'lp; 2 'lp 3 'hundreds'.

Not realising that 'lp in one case meant 'armed man' and in the other 'thousand', this was tidied up to read 59,300. When these figures are carefully decoded, a remarkably clear picture of the whole military organization emerges. The total fighting force is some 18,000 which would probably mean a figure of about 72,000 for the whole migration.

The figures of the Levites seem consistently to have collected an extra nought. The mystery of Plato's Atlantis has been solved

by recognition of this same numerical confusion. Plato obtained *from Egyptian priests* what now turns out to be a detailed account of the Minoan civilization and its sudden end. But as all the figures were multipled by a factor of ten, the area was too great to be enclosed in the Mediterranean, so he placed it in the Atlantic; and the date was put back into remote antiquity, thousands of years too early. This same tenfold multiplication factor is found in the figures of the Levites in the book of Numbers. When it is eliminated Levi fits into the pattern as a standard-size tribe of about 2,200 males. These figures agree remarkably well with the other indications of population in the period of the conquest and the judges.

David's census

The discrepancy between the two sets of figures for David's census can be accounted for by recognizing at different stages in transmission, first, the addition of noughts, and then, a misunderstanding of 'lp. If we postulate original figures: Israel: 80,000 plus 30 'lp; Judah: 40,000 plus 70 'lp, the present text of both Samuel and Chronicles can be accounted for thus:

CHRONICLES

Stage	Israel	Judah
1	80,000 + 30 'lp	40,000 + 70 'lp
2	800,000 + 300 'lp	400,000 + 70 'lp
3	1,100,000	470,000

SAMUEL

Stage	Israel	Judah
1	80,000 + 30 'lp	40,000 + 70 'lp
2	800,000 + 30 'lp	470,000

At this stage it would seem that the copyist was perplexed by the floating '30 'lp', which he took to be 30,000. He wrongly combined it with the Judah figure, so producing:

Stage 3	800,000	500,000

If the original figures totalled 120,000 men of military age, together with 100 professional soldiers, the entire population would have been nearly half a million, which again tallies well with other indications in the text.

By the use of these methods a very large proportion of the numerical difficulties can be resolved.

The incident of the ass: God's purpose seems to be so to impress Balaam, that no matter how hard Balak works on him, the prophet will stick to the truth.

The origin of these oracles: it is not known how these oracles came to be included in Numbers. But linguistic and other factors indicate that the oracles were written down by the 12th century BC.

25 Idolatry at Peor

It was on Balaam's advice (31:16, Revised Standard and more recent versions) that the Midianite women brought Israel low at Peor. And he paid for it with his life (31:8).

Verse 1: sexual relations with the Moabite women led the men of Israel to break faith with God and worship Baal.

Baal of Peor (3): the local deity of the place. 'Baal' (meaning 'master') gradually became a proper name for the great fertility god of the Canaanites. The events

Looking across to the mountains of Edom from the Negev desert.

described here already show a blend of sexual and religious practices.

Moabite...Midianite: the interchange of terms sounds confused, but from late patriarchal times on, there was in fact a good deal of overlap in the use of the terms 'Midianite', 'Ishmaelite', 'Medanite', 'Moabite'.

26 The second census
See on chapter 1.

27:1-11 The right of daughters to inherit
Women could not normally inherit in other ancient Near Eastern countries, but in Israel the ruling is given that brotherless daughters may inherit. However, to safeguard the tribal inheritance, they must marry within their own tribe (see chapter 36).

27:12-23 Joshua appointed as Moses' successor
Moses' life is almost over. Joshua, his right-hand man (Exodus 17:9ff.; 24:13; 33:11; Numbers 11:28) and one of the two faithful spies (14:6ff.), is now invested with authority to lead the nation in his place.

Mt Abarim (12): the name of the mountain range. Mt Nebo, overlooking Jericho, was the actual summit from which Moses viewed the land.

You rebelled against my command (14): see on 20:2-13.

28–30 Rules for public worship and vows
28:1-8, daily offerings; 9, 10, sabbath offerings; 11-15, offerings for each new month; 16-25, offerings for Passover and Unleavened Bread; 26-31, the Feast of Weeks (Firstfruits).

Chapter 29: the feasts of the seventh month. Verses 1-6, offerings for the Feast of Trumpets; 7-11, for the Day of Atonement; 12-38, for the Feast of Shelters.

For feasts, see Leviticus 23, and page 180. For offerings see on Leviticus 1-7, and page 174.

Chapter 30: vows. Men in Israel are unconditionally bound by vows of any kind (1, 2,). Verses 3-15: the terms under which vows made by women are binding.

31 Vengeance on the Midianites; dealing with the spoil
The Midianites are punished for their sin in inducing Israel to worship false gods (see chapter 25 and notes). Army and nation divide the spoil fify-fifty. One five-hundredth of the army's share goes to the priests; one fiftieth of the nation's share to the Levites. Verses 48-54 record the army's special offering given in gratitude for their safe return.

32 Reuben, Gad and half Manasseh settle east of the Jordan
See map. This is permitted only on condition that they help in the conquest of Canaan before returning to a settled life.

33 A list of the stages of the journey from Egypt to the plains of Moab
See map and caption.

Verse 52b: the intention is to wipe out everything associated with idolatrous religions – the carved images and places of worship ('high places' where shrines were built).

34 The ideal boundaries of Israel
See also Joshua 13-19.

35 Cities and pasture for the Levites: the six cities of refuge for those who cause death by accident
See also Joshua 20-21.

36 Safeguards in the case of daughters' inheritance
See on 27:1-11.

euteronomy

Deuteronomy is the record of Moses' farewell addresses to Israel, given about 1,260 BC on the plains of Moab, on the eve of entry to the promised land. The title, which comes from the Greek translation, implies a second law-giving, but in fact the book contains a restatement and reaffirmation of the Sinai covenant. It follows a specific treaty-pattern (see 'Covenants and Near Eastern Treaties', page 198):

1 Introduction 1:1-5
2 Historical prologue 1:6—4:49
3 Stipulations 5:1—26:19
4 Curses and blessings 27:1—30:20
5 Succession arrangements and public reading 31:1—34:5

The laws recorded in Exodus, Leviticus and Numbers are brought together and applied specifically to the settled life of Canaan which is about to begin.

1:1-5
INTRODUCTION
Time and place are carefully specified. Forty years after the exodus, at the end of the desert wanderings, in the plains beyond Jordan, Moses gives God's message to Israel.
Eleven days' journey (2): the journey from Jebel Musa (traditional site of Mt Sinai/ Horeb) to Dahab on the east coast of Sinai, up the coast and across to Kadesh (the Ain Qudeirat area) has recently been shown to take just this time.

1:6—4:49
HISTORICAL PROLOGUE: MOSES LOOKS BACK

1:6-46 Sinai to Kadesh; the spies and the revolt
Verses 9-18: Moses recalls how he found relief from the solitary burden of leadership in delegating responsibility. The wise advice to do so came from his father-in-law, Jethro (see Exodus 18:13-26).
Verses 19-46: see on Numbers 13-14, and map, page 163.
Verse 19: 'wilderness' (now more often translated 'desert') simply means uninhabited land. North of Sinai the land is barren and desolate, with rugged peaks and the earth covered with stones and flints. But there are oases, with a surprising amount of vegetation after the winter rains.
Amorites (44): Numbers 14:43 uses the wider term 'Canaanites'.

2 Edom, Moab, Ammon; war against the Amorites
Verses 1-8: see Numbers 20:14-21. Although the Edomites refused Israel passage along the main road, the King's Highway, it seems that some were willing to sell them food. The friendliness shown to Edom (Esau's descendants), Moab and Ammon (Lot's descendants, see Genesis 19:36-38) on grounds of kinship is characteristic of patriarchal and Mosaic times. God keeps his word down the ages, and he expects his people to keep theirs.
Verses 26-37: see Numbers 21:21-35.
Seir (8): the mountains of 'Seir', i.e. Edom, rise to the south and east of the Dead Sea.
Made stubborn/obstinate (30): the Old Testament sees no conflict between God's sovereignty and man's freedom. God is never described as 'hardening the heart' of a good man. See also on Exodus 6-10.

3 War against King Og; settlement of the two and a half tribes
See Numbers 21:33-35, and chapter 32.

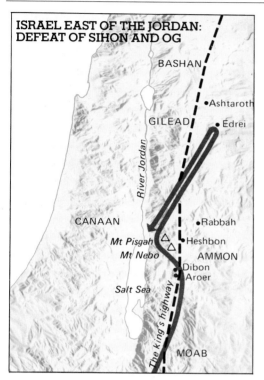

ISRAEL EAST OF THE JORDAN: DEFEAT OF SIHON AND OG

BASHAN

•Ashtaroth

GILEAD • Edrei

River Jordan

CANAAN •Rabbah

Mt Pisgah △ •Heshbon
Mt Nebo △ AMMON
Dibon
Aroer

Salt Sea

The king's highway

MOAB

Og's land was part of the Amorite kingdom. Bashan, famed for its cattle, with the area around was an attractive proposition to the stockmen of Reuben, Gad, and Manasseh.

His bed (11): probably a coffin (Good News Bible). The 'common cubit' was about 18 inches/450mm – so 4m x 2m.

The Arabah (17): the rift valley which runs from the Sea of Galilee south to the Gulf of Aqaba. 'Kinnereth' is Galilee: the word comes from the harp shape of the lake. The 'Salt Sea' is the Dead Sea.

Verses 23-26: the price of disobedience was a heavy one. What Moses longed for above all was to lead his people into the promised land. 'Because of you' is not merely an attempt to shift the blame. It was the people's provocation which stung him to anger.

4:1-40 Moses' warning and call to obedience

Moses has recounted the history of God's dealings with Israel over the past

40 years. Now he reminds them of God's character as shown in his acts, and warns of the inevitable consequences of disobedience to him. 'The Lord is God in heaven above and on earth below; there is no other . . . Keep his statutes . . . then all will be well with you.'

Baal-peor (3): see Numbers 25.

Verse 8: permanent rules of conduct; case-laws and judicial decisions.

4:41-43 Three cities of refuge for Transjordan

4:44-49 Historical and geographical setting of the covenant restated

5—11
BASIC COMMANDMENTS

5 The Ten Commandments and the law-giving at Sinai

See also Exodus 19:16-20:21 (and the notes on Exodus 20 above). Moses does not hesitate to modify the application, so that it relates more closely to a settled life (14-16, 21).

6 The great commandment; instruction to teach future generations

Jesus said that the whole law could be summed up in the words of verse 5 and Leviticus 19:18 (see Matthew 22:37-40).

You shall write them (9): ordinary people possessed no copy of the law, so it was to be taught by word of mouth, and important parts written down where they could not fail to see it. The whole law was also engraved on plastered stones and set up in public places (see 27:1-10; Joshua 8:32).

Cisterns (11): pits for storing water collected from rainfall or from a spring. The inside was coated with waterproof mortar. The pits narrowed at the top to reduce evaporation. Good News Bible and New International Version translate 'wells'.

An orthodox Jew with a phylactery – passages from the law in a small box – bound to his forehead in literal obedience to Deuteronomy 6:8.

Massah (16): see Exodus 17:6-7.

7—11 Moses calls the nation to faith and obedience

Moses turns from the past to the present and future. Israel will soon be right in amongst the pagan nations. They will taste the heady glory of victory (chapter 7). Prosperity will bring an unprecedented rise in the standard of living. There will be much to enjoy (chapter 8). And all these things bring dangers: the danger of losing their identity as God's people; the danger of false pride (chapter 9), of patting themselves on the back for all they have achieved; the danger of leaving God out of account.

But if they will let it, the past can keep them on the right lines for the future. So Moses urges them: 'Remember'; 'Do not forget'. Remember Egypt (7:18). Remember the desert years (8:2). Remember what you were really like (9:7). Remember God's love, his power, his provision, his law, his judgements. And let that memory keep you humble, faithful, obedient (chapters 10-11).

Not like the land of Egypt (11:10): there the vegetable crops depended on irrigation, using water from the Nile.
Blessing and curse: Gerizim . . . Ebal (11:26ff.): see on chapter 27.

12—26
DETAILED LAWS

12—13 Idols to be destroyed; the place for offerings; dealing with offenders

12:1-14: all the places where the Canaanites practised their depraved rites are to be wiped out. Israel is not to use them. When the nation is settled God will select a specific place for the sacrifices.

12:15-32: meat was not a staple food for the ordinary Israelite, but all enjoyed it at feasts and sacrifices. On the matter of the blood, see Leviticus 17:10ff. and 'The Meaning of Blood Sacrifice', page 178.

13:1-18: the danger of being enticed away to false religions was very real. Anyone encouraging this must be summarily dealt with. It was a case of drastic action to prevent contagion.

Jewish households have traditionally put in a 'mezuzah', a box attached to the doorpost, the text of Deuteronomy 6:4-9 and 11:13-21.

14 Clean and unclean animals; tithes

Verses 3-21: see on Leviticus 11, and 'Clean and Unclean Animals', page 176.

Verses 22-29: see also Leviticus 27 and Numbers 18. All man's wealth is God's gift. To remind him of this, a proportion is regularly set aside. Jewish writers generally see the tithe (one tenth) here as a 'second tithe', the first being given to the Levites. It provides an occasion for enjoyment, for entering into the result of one's labour, and for generous sharing with others.

15 The seventh year

Every seventh year is a year of release for Hebrew slaves, and cancellation of debts contracted by fellow-Israelites. See on Leviticus 25.

Verses 19-23: see on Leviticus 27.

16 The three main feasts

See the full list, Leviticus 23, and 'Feasts and Festivals', page 180. Three times each year – Passover, Weeks (Pentecost), Shelters (Tabernacles) – all Jewish men were required to present themselves at

Covenants and Near Eastern Treaties

GORDON WENHAM

Hebrew uses the same word for an international treaty and a covenant between God and his people. Study has shown that similarities between ancient Near Eastern treaties and Old Testament covenants extend much further than this, and considerable light has been shed on the characteristics of Old Testament covenants, and our understanding of the Old Testament generally, by comparing them with treaties.

Most of the ancient treaties discovered this century date from about 1500 to 600 BC, a period in which much of the Old Testament was composed. It therefore seems likely that the writers would have been familiar with the way in which treaties were drafted. Furthermore their use of treaty terms and ideas shows that they found the relationship between treaty-partners an apt picture for that between God and his people.

The earliest covenant recorded in Scripture was made with Noah (Genesis 9). Covenants were also made with Abraham (Genesis 15, 17). But by far the most important covenant in the Old Testament is the covenant of Sinai (Exodus 19ff.). Though Sinai is commonly thought of as the occasion when God's law was made known to Israel, in fact the law-giving was only one part of a much larger event, the call of Israel to be a holy nation owing exclusive allegiance to the Lord. The new relationship was termed a covenant.

The covenant made at Sinai was the decisive step in the creation of Israel as a nation; all subsequent covenants looked back to Sinai as their model, and in a sense were regarded as renewals of it.

Covenants resemble treaties in three principal respects: in language, form and ideology.

Language

The purpose of a treaty is to secure the entire allegiance of a vassal-king or state to the other partner in the treaty, whether it be a king or an empire. To this end florid and rhetorical language is used in the treaties to stir the emotions of the vassal and impress on him the importance of obedience. Rhetorical style has long been regarded as characteristic of Deuteronomy, a work that in other respects bears a close resemblance to a vassal treaty. Certain terms are used in treaties to describe an obedient vassal's behaviour. A good vassal should 'go after', 'fear', 'love', 'hearken to the voice of' his lord. A rebellious vassal 'sins'. This phraseology is often echoed in the Old Testament.

Form

The most striking similarity between treaties and Old Testament covenants is in their form, in their basic outline structure. The classical Near Eastern treaty used by the Hittites had six parts:

the chosen place of assembly.
Asherah...pillar (21-22): wooden images, and symbols of pagan deities.

17 The death-penalty for idolatry (1-7); legal problem-cases (8-13); the future king (14-20)

Verses 14-20: God permits the monarchy, but does not set it up. The dangers foreseen here – military aggression, and sensuality leading to idolatry – became an uncomfortable reality in Solomon's reign, 300 years later.

18 Revenue for priests and Levites (1-8); witchcraft (9-14); the future prophet (15-22)

Verses 1-8: see also Numbers 18.
 Verses 9-14: compare Leviticus 18:3, 24-30; 20:1-6.

A prophet like me (15): God raised up many prophets in succeeding centuries. But the New Testament seems to see in this a reference to the prophet 'par excellence', Jesus himself (John 5:46; Acts 3: 22-26).

---

1. **A preamble** naming the author of the treaty.
2. **A historical prologue** setting out the relations between the parties prior to signing the treaty.
3. **Stipulations** explaining the mutual responsibilities of the partners.
4. **A document clause** describing the treaty document and arranging for the vassal to read it at regular intervals.
5. **A list of gods** witnessing the treaty.
6. **Curses and blessings,** threatening the vassal with illness, death, deportation, etc. if he breaks the treaty, but promising him prosperity and blessing if he remains faithful.

Old Testament covenants have a similar though not identical structure. For instance, believing in one God, they omitted the list of gods as witnesses. Deuteronomy contains most elements of the treaty form:

1-3 Historical prologue
4-26 Stipulations
27 Document clause
28 Blessings and curses.

Exodus 19-24, Joshua 24, and I Samuel 12 are other shorter examples of the treaty form in the Old Testament, though here the form is modified a little by its incorporation into narrative.

Ideology
■ Treaties and covenants both begin with history and both insist on the grace and mercy of the author of the covenant. The Hittite king can remind his vassal of his

kindness in allowing him to continue as king of the vassal state in spite of his recent rebellion. God in similar tones reminds Israel of his mercy, 'I am the Lord your God, who brought you out of the land of Egypt' (Exodus 20:2).
■ In both treaties and covenants, the basis of the stipulations is the undeserved favour of the overlord. Stipulations or laws come after the vassal has been reminded of what the treaty-lord has done for him. He is expected to obey the stipulations out of gratitude. Similarly in the Old Testament, law follows grace. Because of the way God has saved them, Israel is encouraged to obey.
■ Blessing and prosperity are promised if the vassal remains obedient, but curses are invoked on him if he rebels. Drafters of treaties and the authors of the Old Testament, well knowing the human heart, tend to dwell much more on the curses than the blessings. Appalling pictures are drawn of the sufferings the people will endure if they disregard the demands of the covenant (see Deuteronomy 28:15-68). Prophetic threats of coming judgement often echo these covenant curses. The prophets remind the people that the covenant relationship involves responsibility as well as privilege (e.g. Amos 3:2).

The Dead Sea Scrolls show that covenant ideas continued to be important in Jewish theology up to the New Testament era. Jesus himself clearly assumed that his disciples were familiar with covenant thinking, when he referred to his death as inaugurating the new covenant (Mark 14:24).

19 Cities of refuge (1-3); provisions covering accidental death and murder (4-13); prohibition of acquiring property by fraud (14); witnesses (15-21)

Three cities of refuge in Canaan are added to the three in Transjordan (4:41-43). Joshua 20 lists them as: Kedesh, Shechem, Kiriath-arba (Hebron), Bezer, Ramoth and Golan.

Avenger of blood (6): the dead man's next of kin, whose duty it was to avenge his death. The regulations here are designed to prevent the development of a blood-feud.

Landmark (14): a stone inscribed with the boundaries of the property.

The law of retaliation (21): see on Leviticus 24.

20 Rules for war

Those who have built a new house or planted a new vineyard, the newly married, and the fainthearted are excused military service. Verses 10-18 make a distinction between the treatment of Canaanite nations and those further afield.

Completely destroy (17): in contrast to the compassion and humanitarianism of verses 1-11 and the concern for conservation in verses 19-20 this ruling seems incredibly harsh. But there is nothing arbitrary about it. The evil and corrupt religious practices of the Canaanite nations – child sacrifice, prostitution and much else – were highly contagious and therefore highly dangerous to the new nation of Israel. And God, in his patience, had given these nations long centuries in which to change their ways (Genesis 15:16).

21 Murder by an unknown hand (1-9); women captives (10-14); the right of the firstborn (15-17); sons beyond parental control (18-21); execution by hanging (22-23)

God sets a basic value and dignity on

A contemporary boundary-stone, showing a Babylonian king with bow.

every human life – even of the individual society sets least store by.
Shave her head (12): either a sign of purification from heathenism, or of mourning.
Right of the first son (17): already ancient custom. The trouble in Jacob's family stemmed from this kind of favouritism.
The stubborn and rebellious son (18): was casting off the authority not only of his parents but of God himself.
Under God's curse (23): see Galatians 3:13-14.

22 Lost animals and lost property (1-4); keeping the sexes distinct (5); birds-nesting (6-7); building, farming, clothing (8-12); sexual relations (13-30)

These are rules which encourage attitudes of mutual help and care, and a concern for purity.
Verse 5: a rule intended as a protection against perversion and immorality.
Verses 9-11: man should not obliterate the clear distinctions God has made in nature.
Tassels (12): see on Numbers 15:37-41.
Proof of virginity (14): a bloodstained cloth from the wedding-night is still displayed as proof of the bride's chastity in some places in the Near East.

23 Membership of the congregation (1-8); social rules (9-25)

The Lord's community is both inclusive (7-8) and exclusive (1-6). It is marked by purity and holiness (10-14, 17-18) and practical humanity (15-16, 19-20).
Verses 1 and 17-18: a protest and safeguard against Canaanite cultic practices.
Verse 2: a condemnation, not of the individual concerned, but of the illicit sexual relationship in which he was conceived.
Balaam (4): see Numbers 22-24.
Verse 15: Paul's letter to Philemon provides an interesting New Testament comment.

24 Divorce (1-4); humanitarian laws (5-22)

Verses 1-4: Moses is not instituting divorce, but regulating ancient practice, first by insisting on a definite grievance, and second by issuing a formal document.
Verses 5-22: even in exercising their rights, God's people are to be thoughtful of others. To take away one millstone, for example, left the other useless for grinding flour to make the day's bread.
Leprosy (8): the term includes various skin diseases, as recent translations make clear. See on Leviticus 13-14.
Miriam (9): see Numbers 12.

25 Corporal punishment (1-3); compassion for working animals (4); the Levirate marriage law (5-10); fights (11-12); fair weights (13-16); punishment of the Amalekites (17-19)

Verses 1-3: the lash is to punish guilt, not extract confession. It must never take away human dignity or self-respect. The 'forty stripes' later became 39, for fear of inadvertently overstepping the limit (see 2 Corinthians 11:24).
Verses 5-10: the Levirate ('husband's brother') law was intended to prevent the calamity of the family name dying out. See Ruth (and for the sandal custom, Ruth 4:7).
Muzzling the ox (4): the New Testament extends this principle – see 1 Corinthians 9:3-14.

26 Firstfruits and tithes (1-15); concluding plea (16-19)

See on 14:22-29. The firstfruits ceremony includes the recital of a lovely prayer of remembrance and praise summarizing Israel's career.
Verses 16-19: blessing comes through obedience.
A wandering Aramaean (5): after leaving Ur, Abraham stayed in Aram-naharaim, where part of his family settled (becoming

Aramaeans) while he journeyed on to Canaan.

27–30
CURSES AND BLESSINGS

The curses and blessings are an integral part of the ancient Near Eastern covenant. See page 198.

27:1-10 The law is recorded
See on 6:9.

27:11-26 The curses

Gerizim and Ebal are the two most prominent hills in the natural centre of Palestine. With six tribes on either side, the Levites are to pronounce a curse on twelve infringements of the law, and the people to add their assent. See Joshua 8:30-35.

28:1-14 Blessings

Obedience will bring the benefits of victory, peace, fruitfulness, prosperity.

28:15-68 Solemn curses

Disobedience will result in disease, famine, defeat, subservience, and ultimately exile, loss of homeland and all the joys of life. This is no idle threat, as events later proved, even to the horrors of siege (see 2 Kings 6:24-30; Lamentations 2).

Powder and dust (24): 'duststorms and sandstorms' (Good News Bible) in place of rain.

29–30 Moses calls the nation to a new commitment

Moses' life is fast drawing to a close. He puts his whole heart into this final appeal. He pleads (29:2-15). He warns (16-28). He encourages (30:1-14). He confronts them with the choice: life or death, blessing or curse (15-20).

Moist and dry alike (29:19): New English Bible, 'this will bring everything to ruin' catches the spirit of the proverb.

Sodom and Gomorrah, Admah and Zeboiim (29:23): cities at the southern end of the Dead Sea engulfed in the catastrophe of Genesis 19:24ff.

Israel's law reflects (in form and detail, if not in basic motive and aim) other law-codes of the ancient Near East, including that of Hammurabi, king of Babylon, pictured here.

Secret things (29:29): certain matters of eternal significance are known only to God (see also Acts 1:7).

30:11-14: Moses speaks of the accessibility of God's word. Paul (Romans 10:5-8) takes the thought and applies it to Christ, the Word made flesh.

31
THE COVENANT PLACED IN SAFE-KEEPING: THE SUCCESSION ASSURED

The law is safely deposited with the Levites, and provision made for regular public reading. Throughout their subsequent history, Israel prospered in so far as they listened to God's word and obeyed it. Joshua is formally appointed as Moses' successor (see Numbers 27:12-23).

Go out and come in (2, Revised Standard Version): New English Bible 'move freely' gives the sense. The phrase is used of citizens who 'go in and out' of a city, etc.

32:1-47
MOSES' SONG

God is the best of teachers. He instructs

Moses to warn his people of their future treacherous disloyalty in song, to make it unforgettable (31:19).

Apple of his eye (10): the pupil, on which sight depends.

Jeshurun (15): a poetic name for Israel – 'The Lord's people', Good News Bible.

32:48 – 34:12
MOSES' BLESSING AND DEATH

32:48-52 Moses receives his last orders

33 Moses blesses the tribes

After all the warnings, this last blessing looks forward to a great and glorious future for Israel. Simeon is omitted from the tribes: his people were later absorbed by Judah. (Compare Jacob's blessing in Genesis 49.)

Verses 2-5: the law-giving at Sinai is pictured as an eastern sunrise.

Let Reuben live (6): the tribe's numbers were reduced through the rebellion of Dathan and Abiram (Numbers 16).

Thummim and Urim (8): two objects kept in the high priest's breastplate by which he ascertained God's will (see Exodus 28:30). **Massah, Meribah:** see Exodus 17 and Numbers 20.

Between his shoulders (12): either a picture of God as Shepherd, carrying his lamb, or a reference to God's house at Jerusalem, which would be built on Benjamite territory.

Choicest fruits (14): the valleys of Ephraim and Manasseh were laden with fruit, year by year.

Verse 18: Zebulun's success was in commerce, Issachar's in agriculture and domestic life, as Good News Bible makes clear.

Verse 23: the fertile land south and west of the Sea of Galilee.

Oil (24): Asher's territory was famous for its olives.

34:1-8 The death of Moses
At last Moses sees the land he has for 40 years longed to enter. Israel sees him no more. But we meet him once again in Scripture – on a mountain, talking to the Lord (Mark 9:2-4).

34:9-12 Conclusion
The action now passes to Joshua – but the book closes with a simple and moving tribute to the greatest of all Israel's leaders. There would be no prophet to match him until Elijah; no one to surpass him but Christ himself.

THE HISTORICAL BOOKS

Introduction
JOHN TAYLOR

In the Hebrew Bible the account of Israel's history was in two separate sections:
■ *The Prophets* included Joshua, Judges, 1 and 2 Samuel, 1 and 2 Kings;
■ *The Writings* included 1 and 2 Chronicles, Ezra and Nehemiah.

PROPHETIC HISTORY

The historical narrative from Joshua to 2 Kings was in fact given the title 'The Former Prophets' in Hebrew. This was to distinguish the books from the Latter Prophets – Isaiah, Jeremiah, Ezekiel and the twelve minor prophets. What is interesting is that it was called prophecy at all.

There are two possible reasons for this. Either it was because the main aim of the books was to teach; or else because they are the history not so much of the nation as of the way God's message was fulfilled in the nation's life.

This group of six books (not counting Ruth, which belongs to 'The Writings' in the Hebrew Bible) has been regarded by many scholars as one complete historical work. Some call it the 'Deuteronomic history', because the theological viewpoint expressed is similar to that of Deuteronomy.

Formation of the 'prophetic history'
If the books are treated as a basic unity in this way, the earliest date that could be given to the entire work would be shortly after the last event in 2 Kings – the release of King Jehoiachin from prison in 561 BC. However, this would apply only to the latest editorial work. Most of the material is much earlier and contemporary sources were often used.

Sources quoted in the text include the Book of Jashar (perhaps an ancient national song-book of Israel), the Book of the Acts of Solomon and the Chronicles of the Kings of Judah and Israel (unconnected with the Books of Chronicles in our Bibles). These were court archives, or popular histories based on them. They illustrate two things: the amount of historical writing that had gone on in Israel during the monarchy; and the number of written sources which were available to the biblical authors. It is fair to assume that the sources quoted were not the only ones used, and that other writings – such as a Court-history of David and a collection of Elijah-Elisha stories – were also freely drawn upon.

Content of the 'prophetic history'
The period covered by these books extends from Joshua's entry into the land of Canaan until the middle of the exile. Most scholars prefer the late 13th century date for the conquest to an earlier one (1,400 BC has been suggested on the basis of 1 Kings 6:1) and would see the events of Joshua and Judges as taking place between 1,240 and 1,050 BC.

Joshua covers the life-span of Moses' successor and describes the conquest of Canaan from the crossing of the River Jordan to the covenant-renewal ceremony at Shechem which established the tribes in a united allegiance to the Lord. Space is also given to a detailed description of the apportionment of Canaan among the twelve tribes (Joshua 13-21).

Judges begins with a reminder that the conquest under Joshua was by no means complete and that almost every tribal allotment still contained pockets of enemy resistance. In fact, this was the setting for the whole book, for throughout the period of the Judges individual tribes suffered from the incursions of hostile neighbours (or former residents!) and the judges, or 'liberators', were raised up to lead the tribes against them in open battle or guerilla warfare.

Chief among these were *Deborah and Barak,* who led the combined forces of Zebulun and Naphtali against the Canaanites under Sisera; *Gideon* of Manasseh who defeated the Midianites and Amalekites; *Jephthah* the Gileadite who subdued the Ammonites; and *Samson* the Danite who successfully baited the Philistines. The book ends with two bizarre episodes. The first describes the establishment of a new sanctuary for the tribe of Dan (Judges 17-18). The second deals with the punishment of Benjamin for an outrage committed by the people of Gibeah (Judges 19-21).

So far the historical element in the writings has been relatively small: the style has been episodic, occasionally moralistic, and owing a good deal to the art of story-telling. With **1 and 2 Samuel** (the division between them is artificial and probably due only to the length of a scroll) we begin to have a more chronological record of events, and this is particularly true of the story of David. *Samuel* is an important figure at the start, being judge and prophet combined, but the interest is really focussed on the question of kingship, and Samuel fades

into the background as first *Saul* and then *David* dominate the scene. Saul probably reigned from shortly after the defeat at Aphek in 1,050 BC, when the ark was captured by the Philistines, until about 1,011 BC. David reigned from then until 971 (from Hebron for the first seven years and then from Jerusalem).

1 and 2 Kings continue the record, from the accession of *Solomon* to his father's throne, through the break-up of the kingdom 40 years later, and the continuing rivalry between the northern and southern kingdoms of Israel and Judah. This lasted until Israel became absorbed in the Assyrian Empire after the fall of Samaria in 722 BC. After that, Judah survived precariously for over a century, experiencing a miraculous deliverance from an Assyrian siege in the reign of *Hezekiah* and enjoying the extensive reforms of *Josiah's* reign (640-609). Then came collapse before the combined weight of God's displeasure and Nebuchadnezzar's armies, and exile in Babylon. The gloom of defeat is alleviated only by the concluding words of 2 Kings which tell of the release of King *Jehoiachin* from his Babylonian prison-cell. The hope of a survivor from David's line had not been totally extinguished.

Key themes of the 'prophetic history'

As we have seen, one of the main points of interest in this prophetic or 'deuteronomic' history is **kingship,** and in particular King David's dynasty. In Judges 9 there was the abortive attempt of Gideon's son, Abimelech, to establish himself as hereditary monarch in Shechem. In Judges 17-21, the evils of the day were attributed to the fact that 'there was no king in Israel; every man did what was right in his own eyes'. In 1 Samuel, five chapters (8-12) are devoted to the setting up of a monarchy. It appears to have been rather grudgingly accepted by the historian, since Israel was a theocracy, and the Lord her only rightful King. But with the rise of David all such hesitations disappear, even though his personal morality often left much to be desired. The high point of his reign was God's promise of a lasting succession (2 Samuel 7). The fulfilment of this word can be traced in the lives of all the subsequent kings of Judah.

A second main interest was prophets and **the word of the Lord.** The writer's treatment of Deborah and Samuel, Nathan and Gad, Ahijah and Micaiah, Elijah and Elisha, bears witness to the importance he accorded to the office of prophet. These men could make and break kings. They acted as court advisers and political watchdogs. They were the men of power because they in turn were controlled by the word of God. And, in the view of the writer, it was the word of God which controlled history. A word once spoken – the curse on the house of Ahab, for instance – inexorably worked its way to fulfilment.

A third interest of the writer was the **temple** at Jerusalem: From the beginning of 1 Samuel we can trace a special concern about the welfare of the ark of the Lord as it moved from Shiloh to Philistia, back to Kiriath-jearim and eventually was brought to Jerusalem. It was David's desire to build it a more permanent home that provided the occasion for Nathan's prophecy of the hereditary kingship. And in Solomon's time the temple was finally erected as a permanent house for it.

Finally, there was the fixed standard against which all kings were assessed. This was primarily a matter of **worship.** Was the Lord worshipped at Jersulem in purity, or were foreign, idolatrous influences allowed in? Were high places (the old, pagan shrines) stamped out or allowed to continue? By the nature of the evaluation, all the kings of Israel came short because they perpetuated worship at the Bethel and Dan sanctuaries which Jeroboam had set up. Kings of Judah also were found wanting when for political reasons they incorporated the religious practices of a foreign overlord as a mark of submission to him. Only Hezekiah and Josiah receive unqualified commendation. So it is reasonable to conclude that the historian's own theological standpoint was influenced by their reforms.

THE WORK OF THE CHRONICLER

The second part of the account of the history of Israel, included in 'The Writings' in the Hebrew Bible, was originally one book. The author or compiler is often called the Chronicler. The period before the exile was covered by 1 and 2 Chronicles, and the first hundred years after the exile by Ezra and Nehemiah. At first only the second section was incorporated into the Hebrew Bible, probably because of the overlap between Chronicles and Samuel-Kings, but subsequently 1 and 2 Chronicles were admitted. That is why in the Hebrew Bible Ezra-Nehemiah precedes Chronicles. In order to make their original unity apparent, the opening verses of Ezra were tacked on to the end of 2 Chronicles.

The period covered

A summary of contents clearly shows the Chronicler's particular interests and the ground covered in these four books:

1 Chronicles 1-9: genealogies from Adam to Saul.
1 Chronicles 10-29: the reign of David.
2 Chronicles 1-9: the reign of Solomon.
2 Chronicles 10-36: the history of Judah from Rehoboam to the exile.
Ezra 1-6: the rebuilding of the temple after the exile.
Ezra 7-10: Ezra's arrival in Jersulem and reforms.
Nehemiah 1-7: Nehemiah's rebuilding of the walls of Jersulem.
Nehemiah 8-13: Ezra's reading of the law and Nehemiah's reforms.

From this it can be seen that the northern kingdom, Israel, is ignored, and that most space is given to David and Solomon and matters to do with the Jerusalem temple. To this extent the author was following in the same steps as the deuteronomic historian. He was a strong advocate of David's dynasty and did not regard the northern kingdom after its secession from Judah as belonging any more to the true people of God. Similarly, when rebuilding operations were in progress on both the temple and the city walls, he was careful to note that the Samaritans – descendants of the mixed Israelite population – were debarred from participating in the work, or were actively hostile to it.

The Chronicler's concerns

The Chronicler was also a devotee of David as the chief architect of the temple, its worship and its organization. Even though Solomon was the builder, the ideas were all from David's mind. This resulted in what some have called an idealized picture of David, very different from the fallible guerilla-leader-turned-

monarch of the Samuel-Kings version. But it is not fair to accuse the Chronicler of deliberately whitewashing David. He was not writing a political history of Israel. He ignored events and records which had no bearing on the temple. His prime concern was to trace the temple and its worship back to its earliest origins and to tell as much of David's and Solomon's contributions as would enhance its glory.

Unlike the author of Samuel-Kings, however, the Chronicler was fascinated by the part played by priests and Levites, and their importance was frequently emphasized. So too was the uniqueness of their position as cultic officials.

The Chronicler was interested in Uzziah's leprosy, brought on through entering the temple unlawfully to burn incense; and in the care taken not to involve any but priests and Levites in the dethroning of Athaliah, which also took place in the temple.

The evaluation of the individual kings of Judah tallies with that of 1 and 2 Kings. But the Chronicler was keen to give

Megiddo, sited on the edge of the Plain of Jezreel by the entrance to the pass through the Mt Carmel range, has been the scene of many battles. This model, made to demonstrate the different archaeological levels, is in the museum there.

reasons for unusual features where a strict law of retribution did not appear to work out – for instance in the tragic death of a good king such as Josiah, or the long reign of a bad king such as Manasseh. Again, there is no evidence to show that he twisted or invented the facts to make his point, but he clearly used his material selectively because he was writing as an ecclesiastical, not a political, historian.

His interest in things priestly did not cut him off from the world of prophecy. For in addition to his extensive use of the annals – e.g. 'the book of the kings of Israel and Judah' and many similar records – he also made use of many collections of the sayings of prophets,

such as Samuel, Nathan, Gad and Iddo. This encourages us to respect the painstaking care with which he assembled and selected his material.

In the Ezra-Nehemiah period he was able to use memoirs of both these men (notice the use of the first person singular in Ezra 7:27-9:15 and Nehemiah 1:1-7:5; 13:6-31). Indeed Jewish tradition has held that Ezra was himself the Chronicler, and this is by no means impossible. Otherwise we can say at least that the Chronicler was almost certainly on the temple staff, that he was a man of deep piety (witness the many fine prayers that his work contains), and that he wrote in the late 5th or early 4th century BC.

Joshua

The book of Joshua takes the story of Israel's history on from the death of Moses, through the conquest of Canaan, to the death of Joshua. Chapters 1–12 cover the first five or six years after Moses' death. The events recounted in the last two chapters probably took place about 20 years later. The conquest probably began somewhere about 1,240 BC, according to recent archaeological and other evidence. It seems likely that this account was written down in the early days of the monarchy (1,045 BC), during Samuel's lifetime, and before David captured Jerusalem (see Joshua 15:63).

Joshua himself was born in Egypt. He became Moses' right-hand man during the exodus and desert wanderings. He was a fine military commander (Exodus 17:8ff.). In the law-giving at Sinai he was Moses' companion (Exodus 24:13). Joshua was one of the 12 spies sent by Moses to reconnoitre the land. He and Caleb alone had the faith and courage to recommend advance (Numbers 14:6ff.)– and in consequence were the only ones to survive the 40 years of wandering. When Moses died, Joshua was an obvious choice to succeed him in leading the nation (Deuteronomy 34:9).

1—4
ISRAEL ENTERS THE PROMISED LAND

1 Joshua takes over as leader

This account of Joshua's accession is one of the great chapters of the Bible. Moses is dead: but God's purpose for the nation continues. The keynote of this prelude to the conquest is the repeated call to be strong and take courage (6, 7, 9, 18).

This book of the law (8): see Deuteronomy 31:24-26. Joshua was with Moses when the law was given at Sinai.
Three days (11): either the events of chapter 2 have already taken place, or the meaning is simply 'soon'.
Verse 13: see Numbers 32.

2 Rahab and the spies

Jericho, the 'city of palm trees', lies just west of the River Jordan. Joshua's intention was to make his first thrust into the centre of Palestine, driving a wedge between north and south. Jericho stood directly in his path, an obvious first target. See 'The Cities of the Conquest', page 213.

Rahab's action in harbouring the spies stemmed not from fear, but from belief that Israel's God is the *true* God (see Hebrews 11:31, which commends her faith, not her immorality). Rahab's house was built on or into the city walls, with a flat roof on which produce could be spread out to dry – in this case flax, from which she would spin linen thread. Her house was somewhere the spies might go with no questions asked; and no doubt a good place to pick up information. The Israelites kept their promise to her (6:22ff.). Rahab was naturalized, married Salmon, and through her son Boaz (see Ruth 2-4) became an ancestress of David, and of Jesus himself (Matthew 1:5).

3 The Israelites cross the Jordan

It was spring, and the river swollen with

Jericho, 'city of palms', is a green, sub-tropical oasis on the edge of barren hills. For a picture of the excavations of ancient Jericho, see page 84, also page 272.

melted snows, when God took his people across Jordan. As the priests stepped into the flood-water, a blockage at Adam, 16 miles up river, dammed the stream, leaving 20 or 30 miles of river-bed dry. (In 1927 earth tremors caused a collapse of the high clay river-banks at the same spot, and the Jordan was dammed up for over 21 hours.)

The ark of the covenant (3 'Covenant Box', Good News Bible): containing the tablets inscribed with the law. It was a visible symbol of God's presence with his people – and of his leading and guidance.

Sanctify/consecrate/purify (5): i.e. 'prepare yourselves before God', by ritual purification and moral self-scrutiny.

4 The memorial stones

Two piles were made. One where the priests had stood in the eastern edge of the river, the other at Gilgal, their base-camp on the west. Both were to serve as a perpetual reminder of the greatness of God. (This is the same stretch of Jordan where John the Baptist's ministry and Jesus' baptism took place.)

For you … for us (23): not many of those who had crossed the Red Sea now remained. Of the over-20s at the time the spies were sent out, only Joshua and Caleb still lived.

5:1-12
GILGAL: ISRAEL CIRCUMCISED

The rite of circumcision had not been practised because the covenant itself was, so to speak, in suspension for 40 years as a result of the people's disbelief and disobedience (Numbers 14). Now the circumcision of the new generation marks the renewal of the old relationship between God and his people.

Flint knives (2): bronze tools had superseded stone by this time, but the traditional tools are used for the religious rite.

The manna stopped (12): see Exodus 16: 13ff. This special provision of God had

never failed through all the years in the wilderness. Now it was no longer needed.

5:13—6:27
THE FALL OF JERICHO

The conquest of Canaan was a holy war. God was at the head of the army. No one knew this better than Joshua, after his experience of 5:13ff. Israel knew it, as the ark of God's presence led the forces. And Israel's enemies knew it, and quaked (2:10-11; 5:1). It was a war of nerves for the men of Jericho; day after day the encircling troops, the trumpet-blasts, the silent army, building up to the great climax of the seventh day.

Devoted things (6:18): the city and all its contents are dedicated utterly to God. It

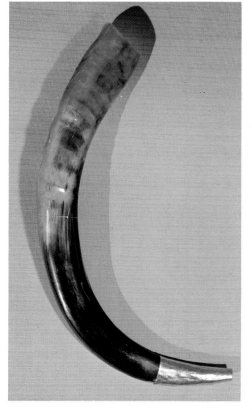

A 'shofar', or ram's horn, the trumpet of ancient Israel.

becomes sacrilege then, for anyone to
take anything for himself.
Outside the camp (23): until such time as
they were 'cleansed' by a period of
purification.
The curse (26): the mound lay in ruins for
400 years, until Ahab's reign. Then Hiel
rebuilt Jericho – and fell heir to the curse
(see 1 Kings 16:34).

7
ACHAN'S DEFIANCE
Because of Achan's sin (see on 6:18) 36
men died at Ai, and the whole nation was
shamed before their Canaanite enemies.
God requires absolute obedience; and
the disobedience of one individual
affects the whole people of God.
Ai (2): 'The Ruin'. See 'The Cities of the
Conquest', page 213.
Sanctify yourselves (13): see on 3:5.
Which the Lord takes (14; not Good News
Bible): the guilty man was discovered by
means of the sacred lot, the two stones
kept in the high priest's breastplate. It is not
now known exactly how this was done.
Stoned him . . . burned them (25): it would
seem that Achan's family were also in the
know and therefore to blame (see
Deuteronomy 24:16).

8
AI CONQUERED
The evidence of the mound at Et-Tell is
difficult to accord with the biblical
record here – which suggests that this
may not in fact be the correct site of Ai.
But see page 214. Joshua's flight and
ambush strategy makes capital out of
Israel's previous defeat.
   From Ai, Joshua moves north to
establish himself at Shechem, in the
valley between Mts Ebal and Gerizim. In
God's name he takes possession of the
land. And the covenant is sworn as Moses
had commanded (Deuteronomy 27).
30,000 (3): this may refer to the total
force, unless there were two ambushes
(12). But high numbers in the Old

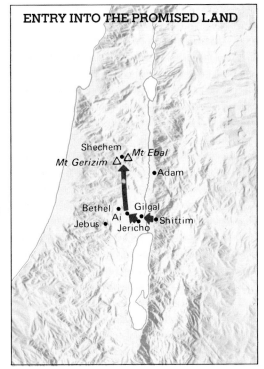

ENTRY INTO THE PROMISED LAND

Shechem • Mt Ebal
Mt Gerizim △△
• Adam

Bethel • Gilgal
Jebus • Ai • • Shittim
Jericho

Testament present a real problem. See on
Numbers 1, and page 191.
Bethel (9): the place where Jacob had his
vision. A well-fortified and prosperous city
during Israel's early days in Egypt;
somewhat declined by Joshua's day. Either
on this campaign (Bethel and Ai were only
1½ miles apart) or later, the king of Bethel
was defeated (12:16).

9—10
THE CAMPAIGN IN THE SOUTH

9 Gibeon tricks Israel into a treaty
Gibeon was an important city about six
miles north of Jerusalem. The treaty
obtained by such cunning (even to the
pretence that news of the recent
victories at Jericho and Ai had not
reached them, 9-10) also included
three other cities (17). Israel could not
draw back from a treaty sealed in friendship (the meal eaten together, 14).

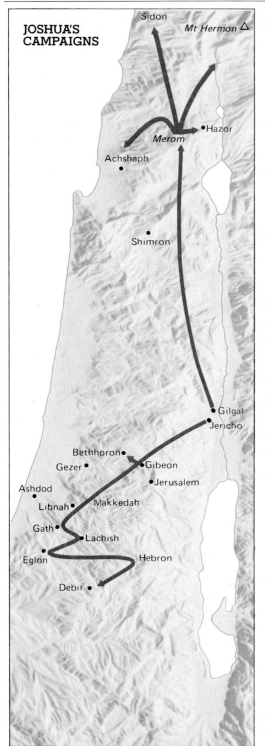

JOSHUA'S CAMPAIGNS

Sidon

Mt Hermon △

Hazor

Merom

Achshaph

Shimron

Gilgal

Jericho

Bethhoron

Gezer

Gibeon

Ashdod

Jerusalem

Libnah

Makkedah

Gath

Lachish

Eglon

Hebron

Debir

It still held good in David's day. The worst they could do was reduce the Gibeonites to slave status (21).

10 Alliance of the five Amorite kings; the 'long day'

The treaty with the Gibeonites promptly involves Israel in war. All five Amorite kings are killed at Makkedah and their city-states (all except Jerusalem) destroyed in the campaign following the rout at Beth-horon. All the strategic cities of the south fall before Joshua's army. Israel now controls the land from Kadesh-barnea in the south to Gaza on the west, and as far north as Gibeon.

The long day (12-14): usually taken as an extension of daylight (not necessarily by a literal standing still of the sun). But it may be a prolongation of *darkness*. Recently it has been suggested that there may have been an eclipse of the sun. Joshua's surprise attack was at dawn (as the positions of sun and moon in verse 12 also indicate) and the hailstorm increased the gloom and consequent confusion.

Book of Jasher (13): a book of songs praising national heroes.

Put your feet on the necks (24): customary gesture of total subjection.

Goshen (41): a town south of Hebron, not Goshen in Egypt.

11 THE NORTHERN CAMPAIGN

The powerful king of Hazor, commanding his vassals, assembles an even more formidable alliance than that of the south. But with no more success. Although the strategic cities were in Israel's hands within a short time of their entry into Canaan, mopping-up operations took a great deal longer (18).

Hazor (1): a vast metropolis of 40,000 people, many times the size of Jerusalem

The Cities of the Conquest

ALAN MILLARD

The Bible's accounts of Israel's entry into Canaan record the actual destruction of only a few cities. Throughout, they emphasize that Israel drove out the former inhabitants and took over (inherited) their property. A desolate land with its towns in ruins would be of little benefit to the Israelites, just emerging from 40 years of semi-nomadic life. What *had* to be destroyed were the pagan shrines of the Canaanites with their cultic paraphernalia.

Jericho was a special case. The city was an offering to God, a 'firstfruit' of the conquest. Ai and Hazor were also sacked. But again they were exceptional cases, perhaps as focal points of opposition. If the biblical record is to be believed, then, we shall not expect to find much physical evidence of the Israelite conquest. The change of ownership probably left few recognizable marks except in the religious sphere. More cities may have been sacked at that time than Joshua and Judges indicate, but the Hebrew accounts do not demand it.

So it is misleading to try to link all signs of destruction in Canaanite cities of the Late Bronze Age with the Israelite invasion. Excavations at the sites of Bethel, Beth-she-mesh, Hazor, Lachish and others have all revealed signs of violent destruction during the 13th century BC, but the dates are only approximate and the cities may not all have been destroyed at the same time. After their destruction the cities were deserted, or else reoccupied on a less elaborate scale.

It is important to realize that Israel was only one of the Canaanites' enemies, although ultimately the worst. The history of the 13th century BC includes major military actions, invasions, and a general decline in cultural standards. Egypt's pharaoh was lord of Canaan, and of Lebanon and Damascus. His governors and officials resided in major cities (e.g. Gaza, Megiddo), and other places served as garrison towns. There were periodic rebellions which were quelled by loyal neighbours or by Egyptian forces. Following a period of Egyptian weakness, Pharaoh Seti I campaigned in Canaan and east of the Jordan about 1,300 BC. Archaeologists often identify his invasion

with destruction levels in ruined cities, as at Hazor. Shortly afterwards, his son, Ramesses II, had to curb a revolt following an unsuccessful battle with the Hittites in Syria. He penetrated as far as Moab at this time (about 1,285 BC).

Perhaps as a result of these firm measures, once Ramesses had made peace with the Hittite king (in about 1,270 BC), there was no further invasion from Egypt for over half a century. Trouble came again in the reign of Merneptah, Ramesses' son. Little is known beyond the fact of Egyptian intervention in Canaan, and indirect evidence of continuing Egyptian control there. One record supplies the oldest non-biblical reference to Israel, as one of a number of defeated foes. Merneptah had halted a wave of invaders from the north-west, the 'Peoples of the Sea'. Egypt was safe until another wave repeated the threat, marching through Syria and Canaan **»**

Amongst the extensive excavations at Hazor is this Canaanite altar or 'high place'. Hazor, the main city of the whole area in Joshua's time, was one of the few cities which were completely destroyed.

as well as coming against Egypt by sea.

This wave was stemmed by Ramesses III who destroyed the fleet and stopped the advance before it reached the frontier, re-establishing his control of Canaan for a while. But many of the invaders remained, some seizing certain cities. The Philistines, for example, took over Ashdod, Ashkelon, Ekron, Gath, and Gaza; and another group took control of Dor. All these events, and others unknown to us, brought pillage and destruction to the towns of Canaan around the time of the conquest. Neighbouring princes could create as much devastation as an invading force.

Nevertheless, we are told that three cities – Jericho, Ai and Hazor – were set on fire by Israel. At Hazor in Galilee, there is evidence that the last city of the Late Bronze Age was violently destroyed at some time in the 13th century BC. The ruins of the last Canaanite city were not well preserved, partly because of exposure to the elements and damage by ploughing. But enough remained to show a city of importance, even if past its zenith. Other towns of the same date are closely similar. All were well fortified, although the city walls often incorporated (or were renovations of) earlier defences. Cities on the main roads – Megiddo, for example – tended to be far wealthier. On the other hand the relative poverty of such sites as Tell Beit Mirsim (Debir?) concentrated the excavators' attention on details of pottery styles, on which Palestinian archaeology depends for its comparative chronology.

At Jericho, the site where the clearest evidence of Israel's attack might have been expected, nothing has been found to show the existence of a city there in the middle of the 13th century BC. Severe erosion of the mudbrick ruins has left little trace of some earlier periods in the city's life. For this reason, the possibility of a fortified city standing there later in the century cannot be discounted. Its ruins would have disappeared during the long desertion of the site from Joshua's time to Ahab's (about 400 years; see 1 Kings 16:34). The city walls, thought at one time to be evidence of Joshua's attack, in fact date from a much earlier period; the excavations show a city which had already been frequently destroyed and rebuilt before the time of Joshua.

Ai also presents a problem. Excavations have revealed that the city was derelict from about 2,500 BC until after 1,200 BC, although it was important in the earlier period. The name Ai means 'ruin', and many see the Joshua story simply as an attempt to explain the very impressive ruins. But even

accepting the archaeological evidence, it is still possible that a group of Canaanites made use of the old fortifications of this strategic stronghold in their fight against the Israelites. Such a brief occupation would have left little or no trace.

In short, we need not expect to find widespread and unmistakable signs of a specifically Israelite conquest in the ruins of Canaan. Israel's mission was in any case not totally destructive. And there were other causes of destruction. Towns may have lain deserted as a result of general turmoil, or have been only partially inhabited, until the Israelites were established in the land and able to exploit it. This they could not do fully while they were menaced by the Philistines and enemies from across the Jordan. The poor remains in several post-Canaanite (early Iron Age) sites attest this situation.

Many scholars have explained Israel's possession of the promised land in terms of a gradual infiltration by nomadic herdsmen. Or they see it as a combination of infiltration and a movement of a few tribal groups from Egypt, perhaps on more than one occasion and over several generations. Or they even envisage a general revolt of the people of the land. These widely varying opinions are all connected with theories involving the documentary analysis of the Pentateuch. These assign stories to a number of different sources, so proposing separate origins for them, and fostering views of unrelated tribal histories. Closely linked with this is a theory that the concept of Israel as a nation was formed long after the 'conquest', and read back into early times by later Israelite historians.

The idea of a gradual process is supported by analogy with other invasions and movements with peoples. It is emphasized that the occupation was limited. (Judges 1 for example lists the main Canaanite cities on the major roads as unconquered, or only occupied jointly with the native citizens.) The stories in Joshua are attributed to tribal or cultic sources. They are thought to describe what were really small, local events, or to relate folk-tales woven around the origin of ruined cities whose real history was forgotten.

It always pays to be cautious in arguing from analogies, and this is certainly so in the case of the 'conquest'. The analogies of nomadic infiltration are used in order to fit Israel into a known pattern. But all her records claim that Israel was different. At best such approaches should be regarded as experimental, not factual. To rule out the account actually given in the Bible on the grounds that it is unusual is prejudiced and unscientific.

in David's day. The lower city which Joshua destroyed was never rebuilt. See 'The Cities of the Conquest' opposite.

As far as Greater Sidon (8): Tyre had evidently not yet risen to prominence.

The Anakim (21): the colossal race who struck fear into the hearts of the spies (Numbers 13:33).

Gaza, Gath, Ashdod (22): all Philistine strongholds. Gigantic Goliath came from Gath (1 Samuel 17:4).

12
LIST OF THE DEFEATED CANAANITE KINGS

Thirty-one kings are listed, including those defeated under Moses. The list rounds off the section on the conquest.

13–21
DIVISION OF THE LAND

Not all the land allocated had been completely subdued – and not every tribe realized its ideal by conquering all its allotted territory. In several places the writer comments on the situation in his own day (e.g. 15:63).

13:1-7 Land still unconquered

13:8-14 The land east of Jordan

13:15-23 The tribe of Reuben

13:24-28 The tribe of Gad

13:29-33 The half-tribe of Manasseh

14:1-5 The land west of Jordan
The inheritance of each tribe is decided by lot, by the high priest.

14:6-15 Caleb claims Hebron
Forty-five years after the spy episode

DIVISION OF THE LAND AMONG THE TRIBES

ASHER
NAPHTALI
ZEBULUN
ISSACHAR
MANASSEH
GAD
EPHRAIM
BENJAMIN
DAN
REUBEN
JUDAH
SIMEON

A clay tablet written in Ugaritic cuneiform, listing fields with their owners' names. From Ras Shamra, ancient Ugarit, in N. Syria, 14th century BC.

(Numbers 13-14) Caleb remains a man of unwavering faith. Despite 10:21ff. there are still Anakim survivors to deal with (15:14; Judges 1:10-15, 20). Hebron became Levite property (21:11-13), but Caleb retained the surrounding land and villages.

15 The tribe of Judah

Judah's inheritance included Caleb's lands – and also Jerusalem, or part of it (18:28). But the city remained unconquered when Joshua was written (63).

16 — 17 Joseph's sons: the tribes of Ephraim and Manasseh

They were to have extended their territory by clearance and conquest. But the horses and chariots of the Canaanites holding the plains deterred them.

Smaller towns and villages, with mud-brick houses, would have offered little resistance to Joshua's army.

18:1-10 The move to Shiloh; the land survey; the inheritance of the seven remaining tribes

18:11-28 The tribe of Benjamin
Jerusalem seems to have been partly on Judah's land, partly on Benjamin's (15:63; Judges 1:8, 21).

19:1-9 The tribe of Simeon
Simeon's people, whose land was part of Judah's territory, became absorbed into the larger tribe.

19:10-16 The tribe of Zebulun

19:17-23 The tribe of Issachar

19:24-31 The tribe of Asher

19:32-39 The tribe of Naphtali

19:40-48 The tribe of Dan

19:49-51 Joshua's city

20 The cities of refuge

See Numbers 35:6-34; Deuteronomy 19:1-13. The cities were a safeguard against vengeance and blood-feud, protecting those who caused accidental death.

21 The cities of the Levites

The Levites receive no tribal inheritance: God is their inheritance. But they are given 48 cities, with pasturage, by the other tribes. This ensures that the leaders of the nation's faith and worship are dispersed amongst the tribes.

22

THE TRIBES SETTLED ON THE EAST OF THE JORDAN RETURN HOME; THE ALTAR OF WITNESS

Reuben, Gad and Manasseh have fulfilled their obligations to help in the conquest. Now they return home, with Joshua's blessing, and a share of the spoil. Fear that, once across Jordan, Israel may at

Fortified towns had stone walls and strong gates. This is the east gate at Shechem, about 1,650-1,550 BC.

some future time disown them prompts the building of the altar which caused such misunderstanding. This was neither a sign of idolatry, nor a second sanctuary. It was a token of solidarity with the rest of Israel to whom they were bound by faith and worship of the one God.

The sin at Peor (17): when Israel worshipped Baal (Numbers 25).

Achan (20): for his sin 36 men died (chapter 7).

The Mighty One, God, the Lord (22): a solemn oath, twice repeated, and using all three names of God: El, Elohim, Yahweh. (See page 157).

23—24
JOSHUA'S LAST DAYS

23 Joshua counsels the leaders
Some years have elapsed since the division of the land. Joshua has reached the end of a long life, and is appointing no single successor. It is therefore vital to ensure that the leaders keep the law and remain faithful to God – the God who keeps his promises (23:14; see 21:45).

24 Joshua and the nation renew the covenant
Here, as in Deuteronomy, the covenant pattern follows that of contemporary treaties (see article, 'Covenants and Near Eastern Treaties', page 198). The King's title (2a) is followed by a rehearsal of his past favours (2b-13). The stipulations are made in 14-15, with warnings on the consequences of disobedience (19-20). Joshua's own readiness to commit himself wholly to God remains unwavering at the end of a long life. The eagerness of the people to follow him in renewing the covenant is in itself sufficient tribute to his leadership. Verse 31 is an indication of the strength of this man's influence for good.

Balak…Balaam (9): see Numbers 22-24.

I sent the hornet (12): a vivid image of the panic (Good News Bible) and confusion into which God threw Israel's enemies.

Judges covers the period in Israel's history between Joshua's death and the rise of Samuel – roughly 1,220 to 1,050 BC. It was a time of transition, when the scattered tribes were held together only by their common faith. Loyalty to God meant a strong united nation. Turning to the gods around brought weakness and division.

The writer looks back, probably from the days of Israel's first kings – Saul or David – to the time when the nation had no king. He wrote after the destruction of the sanctuary at Shiloh (18:31), but before David captured Jerusalem (1:21). He weaves together the stories of the nation's heroes; and Deborah's song, written just after the battle, he quotes verbatim. Six of the 12 judges mentioned are described in some detail: Othniel, Ehud, Deborah/Barak, Gideon, Jephthah, Samson. These 'judges' of Israel were not simply legal advisers. They were men of action who delivered tribe or nation from subjection to the nations around and became local or national rulers.

The human scene in Judges is a depressing one. The nation's fortunes follow a monotonous, repetitive cycle. Israel deserts God for the heathen gods. In consequence God allows them to suffer at the hands of the Canaanites. Israel cries to God for help. God sends a deliverer. All is well until his death: then the old pattern of infidelity reasserts itself. Nowhere in Scripture is man's essential bias to sin more graphically portrayed – a bias which shows itself even in those who know God.

The wonder is God's constant love and concern in the face of all this. Despite their past unfaithfulness, and what he knows will happen again, as soon as Israel turns to him he answers. And he uses the most unpromising people: Jael, who breaks all the sacred laws of hospitality; Ehud, who stoops to assassination; Samson, who leads a life of sexual promiscuity; a nation that gloats over acts of cruel revenge against the enemy. *And the Bible nowhere commends these things* or whitewashes the individuals who committed them. God took and used them because of their faith (Hebrews 11:32ff.), and despite their morals. So, because God is a God like this, there is hope for sinful man.

Chronology. Eastern writers do not show the same preoccupation with precise time-order as modern western historians. Added together, the figures in Judges total 390 years. Yet, with the most probable date for the conquest at about 1,240, the period covered must be under 200 years. One of the reasons for this seeming discrepancy is the overlap between the periods of the different judges. We know, for example, from 10:7 that the Ammonite oppression in the east and the Philistine oppression in the west occurred at the same time. It is likely there is considerable overlap elsewhere. A further factor is the frequent use of 'forty years' as a round figure for 'a generation' rather than a precise length of time.

A.E. Cundall suggests the following approximate chronology:

1200	Othniel
1170	Ehud
1150	Shamgar
1125	Deborah and Barak
1100	Gideon
1070	Jephthah
1070	Samson

THE 12 JUDGES AND THEIR VICTORIES

1. **Othniel** of Judah (3:9): victory against Cushan-rishathaim.
2. **Ehud** of Benjamin (3:15): victory against Eglon of Moab.
3. **Shamgar** (3:31): victory against the Philistines.
4. **Deborah** (Ephraim) and **Barak** (Naphtali) (4:4-6): victory over Jabin and Sisera.
5. **Gideon** of Manasseh (6:11): victory over the Midianites and Amalekites.
6. **Tola** of Issachar (10:1).
7. **Jair** of Gilead (10:3).
8. **Jephthah** of Gilead (11:11): victory over the Ammonites.
9. **Ibzan** of Bethlehem (12:8).
10. **Elon** of Zebulun (12:11).
11. **Abdon** of Ephraim (12:13).
12. **Samson of Dan** (15:20): victory against the Philistines.

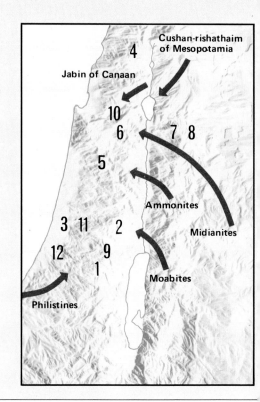

1—2:5
EXTENT AND LIMITS OF THE CONQUEST FOLLOWING JOSHUA'S DEATH

1:1-21 Campaigns in southern Canaan
Verses 10-15: see Joshua 15:13-19.
City of palms (16): Jericho.
Chariots of iron (19): this was the beginning of the Iron Age. The Philistines introduced and controlled the iron industry in Palestine and guarded it jealously (see 1 Samuel 13:19-22). Until the days of David, Israel were at a disadvantage against the superior iron weapons and chariots of their enemies.

1:22-26 Capture of Bethel

1:27-36 Unconquered cities

2:1-5 God's judgement on disobedience
The angel of the Lord (1): mentioned a number of times in Judges (here and in the stories of Gideon and Samson) as well as in other Bible passages. He always comes as God's representative, with a special message from God. He speaks in God's name, and is virtually identified with God by those to whom he appears (see e.g. 13:22). Sometimes he shows himself as an ordinary man, sometimes as an awesome heavenly being (see chapter 13). But none who see him are left in any doubt of his authority.

2:6—16:31
ISRAEL UNDER THE JUDGES

2:6—3:6 Introduction
Verses 11-23 set out the repeated pattern

of events which began once the
conquest generation had died out (10).
As a result of disobedience the
surrounding nations are not driven out.
They remain to test Israel and keep her a
fighting nation (2:20–3:6).

Baals and the Ashtaroth/Astartes (2:13):
local male and female fertility/vegetation
gods.

3:3: the five Philistine city-states were
Ashdod, Ashkelon, Ekron, Gaza, Gath (see
the Samson story, chapters 13 – 16, and
1 Samuel 17:1-54). Judah did not hold
her three cities for long (1:18).

3:7-11 Othniel

If Cushan-rishathaim was indeed king of
'Mesopotamia' (8: i.e. modern east Syria,
north Iraq) the attack must have come
from the north – which makes his defeat
at the hands of a southern champion
surprising. But some would emend the
name to 'Cushan chief of Teman' (in
Edom).

The Spirit of the Lord came upon him (10):
the same phrase is used of Gideon,
Jephthah and Samson. The might of these
champions was a special gift from God.

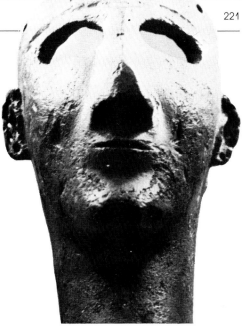

*Mask of a Canaanite god, perhaps Baal. See also
p.235.*

3:12-30 Ehud

Eglon of Moab headed an eastern
alliance which included Ammonites and
Amalekites. They not only overran the
land east of Jordan, but crossed the river
to set up an outpost at Jericho.

Like Ehud, many of the Benjaminites
were left-handed or ambidextrous – the
tribe's left-handed slingers had a high
reputation (see 20:16; 1 Chronicles 12:2).
On this occasion it meant that the
movement aroused no suspicion.

3:31 Shamgar

This isolated action did not restrain the
Philistines long. See chapters 13–16.

4—5 Deborah and Barak

Deborah is the judge in the judicial sense,
Barak the military leader. Deborah's song

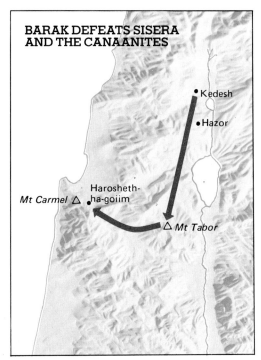

**BARAK DEFEATS SISERA
AND THE CANAANITES**

Kedesh

Hazor

Harosheth-
Mt Carmel △   ha-goiim

△ Mt Tabor

– one of the most ancient pieces of writing in the Old Testament – provides the clue to the victory. A cloudburst changed the Kishon to a raging torrent (5:21). Many of the chariots were swept away, the rest completely bogged down in the mud.

Hazor (4:2): Joshua defeated an earlier Jabin, and destroyed the city. The lower part was never rebuilt, but the mound (tell) was re-fortified by the Canaanites, and later by Solomon.

6–8:28 Gideon

Bedouin from the east, the Midianites, swept through southern Israel as far as the Philistine city of Gaza. The terror spread by these fierce camel-riders is vividly pictured in 6:11. Gideon is forced to thresh his meagre grain harvest secretly, in the confines of the wine press. The faith of this man, for all his initial caution, is seen in his prepared-

Barak charged down the slopes of the steep, rounded Mt Tabor, to attack the armies of Sisera.

ness to face the Midianite hordes with a force of only 300 men. Gideon used his wits in the surprise attack, but the victory in the ensuing rout is God's.

The Asherah (6:25): a wooden image of the Canaanite mother-goddess.

An ephod (8:27): probably an image of God, which the law forbade, though Good News Bible translates 'idol'. The place then became a rival to Israel's official sanctuary.

8:29-35 Gideon's later years

9 The rise and fall of the usurper Abimelech

Gideon, with some claim to kingship, firmly rejected it. Abimelech, his brutal and ambitious son, shows no such scruples.

Shechem (1): in the heart of Palestine; see map. Shechem was the central sanctuary of Israel in Joshua's day. But now it had a temple to Baal (for 'house', verses 4 and

GIDEON'S DEFEAT OF
THE MIDIANITES

NAPHTALI

ASHER

ZEBULUN

ISSACHAR

Mt Tabor △

Hill of Moreh △   Ophrah

Jezreel   Valley
Spring of Harod   of Jezreel

River Jordan

MANASSEH

GAD

EPHRAIM

Succoth

46 read 'temple' with recent versions). The city's history goes back to Jacob's day and earlier.

Scattered salt (45): symbolically consigning the city to permanent desolation. It was in fact rebuilt 150 years later in the time of Jeroboam 1.

Upper millstone (53): grain was ground between two heavy circular stone slabs about 18 inches across.

10:1-2 Tola

10:3-5 Jair

10:6— 11:40 Jephthah

Southern Israel is now caught in a vice between the Philistines on the west and the Ammonites on the east. Against Ammon, the new champion is the brigand-chief, Jephthah. Numbers 20-21 describes the events referred to in the parley of 11:12-28. Moab in fact had the better claim to the land, as part of it had been theirs until Sihon dispossessed them.

Three hundred years (11:26): i.e. it was now the third century since the events described (in fact about 160 years).

Jephthah's vow, and other moral problems in Judges: the vow is an indication of how little the Israelites understood God at this time. Human sacrifice might please the heathen gods, but never the God of Israel. Yet, though ignorant and mistaken, the vow was made in good faith, and kept, though it cost Jephthah his only child. And the New Testament writer of Hebrews commends this man's faith – as he commends the faith of Samson, Gideon and Barak (Hebrews 11:32). This instance of child-sacrifice, Jael's hideous murder of Sisera, Ehud's assassination of Eglon,

The scene of Gideon's surprise attack on the Midianites.

Gideon's camp at the spring of Harod   Midianite camp

Hill of Moreh

Samson's selfish, sensual and irresponsible behaviour (see Introduction, page 219) are a real source of embarrassment to many Christians. How can people like these be commended for their faith? How could God use them? There can be no completely satisfactory answer to questions like these. The 'heroes' of Judges are people of their age – an age which the Bible plainly shows was one of religious decline, falling far short of the standards of the Old Testament law, let alone those which Christ sets. The fact is – the wonder is – that God did and still does use men whose lives are far from blameless, who may even be acting from completely wrong motives. We are not meant to

imitate their shortcomings. Their immorality is neither condoned nor glossed over in Scripture. Only their faith and courage are commended. God does not permit his ultimate purposes to be thwarted even in an age of seemingly hopeless decadence. The dark ages of a period like that of Judges may be followed by a time of real spiritual advance.

12:1-7 Ephraimite jealousy

Where Gideon used softs words to placate these touchy tribesmen (8:1-3), Jephthah takes up the sword. At the fords the men's dialect pronunciation of 'Shibboleth' gives them away.

12:8-10 Ibzan

12:11-12 Elon

12:13-15 Abdon

Remains of Ashkelon – scene of Samson's exploits – dating mainly from Roman times.

13:1 — 16:31 Samson

The champion against the enemy in the west (see 10:7) is set apart for the task from the moment of his conception. For Samson the Nazirite vow (see Numbers 6) was lifelong. Yet he treats it with a casualness amounting to contempt, eventually allowing Delilah to shave off the long hair which was the sign of his dedication to God. Moral weakness robs the strong man of both spiritual stature and physical prowess – since his strength is God-given for a specific purpose.

Samson's marriage: not the usual Jewish type, although formally arranged by the parents. Instead of the bride returning to Samson's home she stayed with her family and her husband visited her, bringing gifts. Because of the deceit over the riddle there was no consummation at the end of the seven-day feast. A hasty second marriage to the best man was an attempt to lessen the bride's disgrace.

Three-hundred foxes (15:4): more probably jackals, who hunt in packs and would

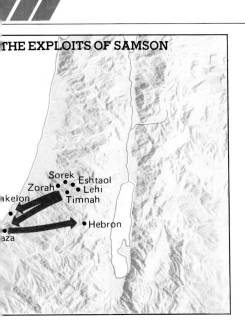

THE EXPLOITS OF SAMSON

Sorek · · Eshtaol
Zorah · · · Lehi
ikelon · · Timnah
· · Hebron
aza

therefore be easier to catch in large
numbers than the solitary fox.

17—21
APPENDICES

This closing section differs from the
rest of Judges. The writer turns from
Israel's heroes to two incidents which
illustrate the low state of religion and
morality in the days when Israel had no
central government and everyone 'did
as he saw fit'.

17—18 Micah, the Levite and the Danite migration

This story relates to the time when
Philistine pressure on their southern
territory led to the mass migration of
the Danites to the far north of Israel.
The image set up by Micah was strictly
forbidden by the law the Levites were
supposed to administer. 'Ephod and
teraphim' were used as means of
divination – equally strictly prohibited.

19—21 Rape of the concubine at Gibeah; punishment of the Benjaminites

When the Benjaminites refuse to hand
over the men of Gibeah – their fellow
tribesmen who committed the outrage –
civil war results. The outcome is the
near-extinction of Benjamin, and great
national grief. Chapter 21 relates the
lengths to which the tribes go to
circumvent the rash oath made at
Mizpah (21:1).

The writer has no need to point a
moral. The simple statement of verse 25
is sufficient. The whole book makes
plain the disastrous consequences of
breakdown of authority, when men
become a law unto themselves, setting
their own standards of permissiveness.

Ruth

This quiet tale of ordinary life stands in strong contrast to the war and strife of Judges, which relates to the same general period. No doubt many people lived just such a normal peaceful life during this age. And although religion generally was at a low ebb, the book of Ruth makes it clear that the personal faith of many in Israel remained strong. The most striking feature of this simple and beautiful story is the sense of God's intimate concern in humble affairs. He is the One who orders all the circumstances of daily life, even for the most unimportant people. And so the new-found faith of a Moabite girl, and her sacrificial love for her mother-in-law are woven into the great tapestry of God's plan of salvation. For descended from Ruth is King David, and from the line of David comes the Messiah himself.

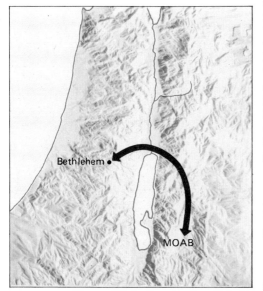

1:1-5 Elimelech takes his family to Moab

The journey was about 50 miles, to the far side of the Dead Sea.

1:6-22 The widowed Naomi returns to Bethlehem with Ruth, her daughter-in-law

The famine is over: God has again shown his care for his people. Orpah, sorrowfully, returns home to the hope of a second marriage. But Ruth will not leave Naomi to a lonely old age. Her choice is Naomi's people and, significantly, Naomi's God. The two reach Bethlehem in April.

2 Ruth goes gleaning and wins Boaz' protection

There were not many ways for widows to earn a living, and Ruth and Naomi were poor. But the law (Leviticus 19:9-10) laid down that the gleanings of the harvest must be left for the poor. By 'chance' in the common open field, Ruth gleans in the part belonging to Boaz, Elimelech's kinsman. His kindness goes far beyond the law's demands (9, 14-16).

An ephah of barley (17): the ephah was a large container holding about 22 litres. Ruth had gleaned about ½ cwt of barley ('nearly ten kilogrammes', Good News Bible) by her own hard work and Boaz' generosity.

3 The threshing-floor; appeal to Boaz as next of kin

Under the Levirate law (referred to by

As the grain was cut, Ruth gleaned what was left.

Naomi in 1:11-13), when a man died childless his brother was bound to raise an heir to him by the widow. This law extended to the next of kin, hence Naomi's plan. Ruth, by her action in verse 7, was claiming this right. It is complicated by the fact that Boaz is not in fact Elimelech's closest kinsman, but he promises to take up her case.

4:1-12 The transaction between the kinsmen

The city gate was the place for important assembly. It was also the place where legal business could be publicly transacted, as here. The elders acted as witnesses. In addition to his obligation to raise an heir to carry on the dead man's name, the next of kin also had to buy his land, to keep it in the family. Boaz discusses the land first, then the widow. The kinsman would have bought the land to add to his own inheritance. But when he hears it will in fact go to Ruth and her son, and that he will have Ruth to provide for, he declares himself unable to purchase.

Perez (12): ancestor of Boaz; son of Tamar by her father-in-law, Judah, because of his refusal to honour the custom later formalized as the Levirate law.

4:13-22 Ruth marries and becomes the great-grandmother of King David

So Boaz fulfils his own prayer of 2:12. God rewards Ruth with the gift of a husband and a son. And Naomi finds solace for her grief in this grandson. When God steps in, the ordinary events of life take on extraordinary significance. The child Obed became grandfather to the founder of the royal line of Israel from which Christ himself took human flesh, in another birth at Bethlehem.

The Old Testament and the Ancient Near East
ALAN MILLARD

The Bible is an ancient text, a historical record. As such it is very helpful to study it in the light of our knowledge of the world in which it was written.

There is nothing un-Christian in doing this. The Christian faith depends on historical events, things which actually happened. The events recorded and explained in the Bible can be set alongside other events known from other historical sources. The Bible itself consists of documents as ancient and as historically verifiable as any others.

Checking the accuracy of the Bible
Its accuracy can also be tested and checked against other known historical sources. However, this is not always as simple as it may seem. Documents are often damaged or incomplete. Archaeological evidence is in many cases open to more than one interpretation. We possess very few ancient writings which describe the same events the Bible describes, and in any case two observers will rarely describe the same event from an identical standpoint.

The Hebrews were a relatively insignificant people. Their career made little impact on the major powers whose records we possess. Hardly any of the biblical characters appear in other writings, apart from some of the later kings of Israel and Judah. None the less, where we are able to make comparisons, the accuracy of the biblical writers is impressive. Although we seldom find parallel accounts of the same events, we often find examples of customs and occurrences very like those described in the Old Testament, even though they are in no way connected. A superficial similarity can of course be misleading, so we have to be cautious. And a knowledge of the ancient Near East can help, even when it provides neither direct nor circumstantial evidence of the Bible's historical accuracy: the study of Israel's neighbours – customs, culture, literature, history – gives us an idea of what to expect in the case of the Hebrew nation.

These three types of evidence – direct

evidence, circumstantial evidence and the evidence of analogy – must be taken in turn to show how they shed light on the Bible.

Direct evidence

As we have seen, direct references to Israel are rare, and almost solely limited to royal names. Amongst those we do have is the record of an invasion by Shishak who was king of Egypt – he ruled about 945-924 BC (1 Kings 14:25f.). His inscription at Thebes, badly preserved, lists many towns conquered in Palestine – evidence of his campaign there. Tiglath-pileser III (about 745-727 BC) re-established Assyrian rule over Syria and Palestine following some decades of weakness, when Jeroboam had made Israel prosperous and Uzziah had built up Judah. The Assyrian records the tribute paid by Menahem of Samaria and claims to have been responsible for replacing Pekah by Hosea (2 Kings 15:19-20, 30). In 2 Kings 15:19 (see also 1 Chronicles 5:26) Tiglath-pileser is called Pul and he was known by that name to Babylonian chroniclers of the 6th century BC, when it is believed 1 and 2 Kings were finally compiled. Subsequently Assyrian rule in Samaria involved Judah as a vassal, but her kings preferred to struggle for independence, seeking Egypt's aid. So Hezekiah rebelled, and Sennacherib brought his forces to overwhelm Judah and lay siege to Jerusalem. The Assyrian tells of this in many inscriptions. He relates how Hezekiah sent tribute to him in Nineveh (the amounts seem to differ slightly from 2 Kings 18:14ff.), yet lays no claim to the capture of Jerusalem, nor, naturally enough, does he mention his army's fate.

In the account of Solomon's building projects, 1 Kings 9:15 names three major cities besides Jerusalem – Hazor, Megiddo and Gezer. Excavations at each one have uncovered city walls of the 10th century BC, all of the same pattern. Each city wall is pierced by a massive gateway, and all are identical in plan and in measurement, to within a few inches. Here is a material record demonstrating the truth of the biblical text. Here also are physical signs of an over-all planning authority, a central power. Indeed Solomon's glory, fabulous though it may appear, becomes more and more credible when set in its ancient context.

Circumstantial evidence

Most of the discoveries which feature in books of archaeology and the Bible fall into the class of circumstantial evidence – matters which make no direct reference to biblical events, but supply examples of practices or incidents apparently comparable with passages in the Bible. In this way we learn that Abraham's marriage to the slave-girl Hagar because of Sarah's childlessness, and his later refusal – until reassured by God – to send her from his household, agree with requirements in the contemporary Laws of Hammurabi of Babylon. The names of the patriarchs of Israel also accord with names generally used in the 2nd millennium BC, now known from thousands of contemporary documents.

Another of Solomon's glories gains evidence from Egyptian sources. According to 1 Kings 9:16, he married the pharaoh's daughter. Yet two or three centuries earlier, in Egypt's heyday, the princesses of Egypt did not leave the court, and when an important foreign king requested one as his bride he was refused. In the 10th century BC however, under the less glorious 21st dynasty and its successor, this rule was broken. So it was that Solomon received his bride.

A little before Solomon's time, the hero Gideon called on a boy to write down the names of trading men in Succoth – apparently just a boy who happened to be available (Judges 8:14). That names could be easily written and recognized then is shown by copper arrowheads, found near Bethlehem, and in other places, inscribed with their owners' names and dated to the 12th and 11th centuries BC.

The evidence of analogy

The fact that we have virtually no written record of ancient Hebrew life, thought and history apart from the Old Testament means that many aspects of life can hardly be known at all. Normal processes of decay have destroyed any documents on leather or papyrus buried in the cities of Palestine along with furniture and clothing. Where such items are preserved in neighbouring cultures, it is possible sometimes to attribute similar usages to ancient Israel. Each case needs thorough testing to ensure that the circumstances really are parallel, but some are sufficiently clear to help us evaluate the Old Testament.

No literature has survived from Israelite towns, but there is no doubt it existed. The Old Testament itself is witness to that, although scholars debate just how old its written form is. In Egypt and Babylonia the complicated writing-systems gave the scribes a monopoly. In Israel (and adjacent states) the simple 22-letter alphabet was **»** learnt easily by any who wanted, so writing was more widespread amongst the population, although professional scribes still had an important role. Evidence from various minor written documents demonstrates this fact for ancient Israel. If writing was used for daily affairs, this implies it could be used for works of literature, too. The written word was treated with respect. Valuable old books were copied with great care. They could be revised or edited, but the way this has been done is seldom detectable unless the older copies survive for comparison.

Egypt, Assyria and Babylonia, the Hittites and Canaanites all had elaborately-arranged religious rites, sacrifices, and priestly orders. Their temples were finely built and lavishly furnished, especially by successful kings. If Israel had been different in this they would have been the odd ones out, but in fact they were not. These analogies show that the tabernacle, Solomon's temple, and the Levitical regulations were Israel's counterparts. As in neighbouring nations, moreover, the mass of the people toiled and suffered to provide for the magnificence demanded by the king.

We would expect Israel, as a nation among nations of related stock, to share similar modes of thought and expression. When Babylonian or Egyptian literature shows features strange to modern thought, we take great pains to understand them – to account for inconsistencies, paradoxes, and apparent contradictions without impugning the accuracy of the texts which are our only sources of information (unless there are firmly-founded objective reasons for doing so). Israel's literature may be expected to contain similar quirks, and they too should be treated with respect. Some are clear, for instance narration of events out of chronological order, or the collecting of items without evident relation to the context.

Similarities and differences

These examples are sufficient to show the value of gathering, studying and applying whatever the ancient Near East affords by way of background to the Bible. The direct and indirect evidence agrees so strikingly

with the Old Testament that it makes attempts to discredit its picture of Israel's culture and career very dubious indeed. No discovery has been proved to contradict the Hebrew records. There may be discrepancies, uncertainties, unanswered questions. The incomplete nature of all our evidence makes this inevitable. New discoveries solve old problems, frequently revealing false premises in modern theories. At the same time they may raise fresh questions and stimulate deeper study, new approaches, and better understanding.

If the similarities between Israel and their neighbours form the bulk of the contribution made by biblical archaeology, the differences merit attention as well. The Old Testament proclaims an unbridgeable gap between Israel and their neighbours. Whereas their language and culture shared so much, their faith stood apart. To find material traces of Israel's monotheistic faith, imageless worship, centralized cult, is difficult. Israel's neighbours reckoned their God as no more than a national god like their own (Chemosh of Moab, or Milcom of Ammon), unaware of his unique place. To make things more complicated, Israel never remained entirely faithful, so pagan religious objects can be found in the ruins of their cities.

It is in comparing biblical teaching with contemporary texts that the distinctions are best seen. The absolute demands of the Ten Commandments, the exclusive devotion to Israel's electing God, the equality of individuals balancing their corporate responsibility, the altruism of the prophets – all these, and many others, find no true echo in the world of the Old Testament.

Some may find them incredible, yet we possess actually preserved manuscripts which guarantee them an antiquity of over 2,000 years.

Some may find them unacceptable, but although so old they still speak sense to modern man.

If the historical and cultural aspects harmonize with our knowledge of ancient times, as in fact is the case, the ethical and religious distinctions need explanation. The Old Testament gives one: God spoke.

These two books were originally one volume in the Hebrew Bible. They provide a history of Israel from the end of the Judges period to the last years of David, the nation's second and greatest king – roughly 100 years (about 1,075-975 BC). This is essentially religious history: the story of God and the nation – particularly, God and the nation's leaders. Samuel gives his name to the books, not as author, but as the dominating figure of the early chapters, and Israel's 'kingmaker' under God's direction. It was he who anointed first Saul and then David as king.

The historian may well have drawn his material from Samuel's own writings (1 Samuel 10:25) and those of the prophets who followed him (1 Chronicles 29:29). He certainly knew some of David's poems (which he quotes in 2 Samuel 1:19-27; 22:2-51; 23:1-7). And he was himself a born storyteller and master of suspense. He must have written some time after the division of the kingdom. (He several times refers to the separate kingdom of Judah, but the nation was not yet in exile: see, e.g. 1 Samuel 27:6.) 900 BC is therefore the earliest likely date for the books as we know them. Critics have argued for several authors, largely because of the 'duplicate' accounts of various events (e.g. the two sparings of Saul's life; the two occasions when Samuel announced God's rejection of Saul). On closer inspection, however, most of the so-called duplicates emerge quite clearly as two separate if similar events, recounted by the author in order to emphasize certain points. Repetition is a feature of his literary technique.

1 SAMUEL

1—3
SAMUEL'S BIRTH AND EARLY YEARS

1 God answers Hannah's prayer for a child

In the Old Testament, when God has a special purpose for a man there is often something special about his birth. Like Hannah, Sarah and Rebekah in the Old Testament and Elizabeth in the New experienced the bitterness of being childless. Like Samuel, Isaac and Jacob and John the Baptist were the God-given answers to many years of prayer. Each had a special role to play in the great plan of God. When God gave Hannah the son she longed for he also gave Israel the last and greatest of the judges, and the first (after Moses) of the great

prophets – the man who was to usher in the kings.

To sacrifice . . . at Shiloh (3): the centre of worship in the Judges period; the place where Joshua had set up the tabernacle (Joshua 18:1). (The 'temple' proper – verse 9 in most versions – was not built till Solomon's day.)

I will give him . . . (11): the child is dedicated to God for life under a Nazirite vow (see Numbers 6, and compare the vow made by Samson's parents in Judges 13).

Only her lips moved (13): it was usual to pray aloud. Eli is quick to jump to the wrong conclusion. Religious life must have been at a low ebb if worshippers came drunk to God's tent. Compare the conduct of Eli's own sons, 2:12ff.

When she had weaned him (24): Samuel would have been two or three years old.

The site of Shiloh is now no more than a ruin of fallen stones. By the time of Eli and his sons the sanctuary there had become a regular structure for Israel's worship, the tent being replaced with a 'temple' with door and door-posts.

2:1-10 Hannah's song of thanksgiving

Hannah's song is echoed by Mary in the New Testament (Luke 1:46-55). In the small mirror of her own experience Hannah sees reflected all the wonder of God's character. God has reversed her fortunes (1). Peninnah's taunts have been silenced (3, 5). Emptiness, misery, shame are gone – in their place, life, joy, honour. And what God can do for one, he can and will do for all his people.

Sheol (6): the shadowy land of the dead.
His King (10): this is either inspired prophecy on Hannah's part, or verses 2-10 are part of a psalm added by the narrator, as being singularly appropriate to her experience.

2:11-36 Eli the priest and his no-good sons

The priests were entitled to a share in the sacrificial offerings (see Numbers

18:8-20; Deuteronomy 18:1-5). But what is going on here is a travesty of the law. Eli's sons seize the best bits before the offering has even been given to God (15). What is more, they are bringing prostitution into the worship of God, in the worst traditions of Canaanite religion (22). On his death these two will be the nation's 'archbishops' – and all Eli can do is reason with them!

Verses 27-36: the prophet's prediction is fulfilled in the death of Eli's sons in battle at Aphek (4:11). The priesthood passed from Eli's family to the line of Zadok in David's day (2 Samuel 8:17).

A linen ephod (18): a tunic worn by the priests (see verse 28).
It was the will of the Lord to slay them (25): the writer puts it this way because God is sovereign in every circumstance. It is equally true that their death is a direct outcome of their own free choice to disobey God. The Bible sees no conflict between God's sovereignty and man's free will. See on Exodus 6:28 – 10:29.

3 Samuel hears God's call

In the early hours (before the oil for the lamp ran out, as it would at dawn), when he is on duty near the ark, inside the taber-

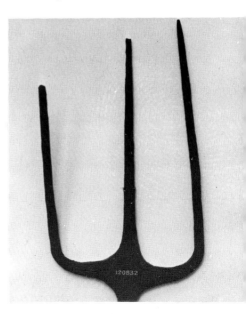

A three-pronged fork was used for spearing the meat from the cauldron; this one was found at Ur.

nacle, Samuel hears God speak to him for the first time – a message of judgement for Eli. From this time on, Samuel is God's messenger, and the whole nation knows it, from Dan in the far north to Beersheba on the edge of the southern desert.

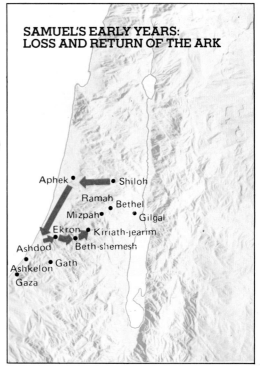

**SAMUEL'S EARLY YEARS:
LOSS AND RETURN OF THE ARK**

4:1 — 7:1
THE PHILISTINES AND THE ARK OF GOD

4:1-11 The Philistines defeat Israel and capture the ark

The ark or Covenant Box (see Exodus 25–27) was Israel's most precious possession, the focal point of the tabernacle. A copy of the law was kept inside it. Its lid was the mercy seat, symbol of the presence of God.

But now the nation wants to use it as a talisman, the ultimate protection against the Philistines. The result is total disaster: the army defeated, the ark in enemy hands.

Philistines (1): see 'Nations and Peoples', Part Four.

4:12-22 Death of Eli

The ark never returned to Shiloh. Although there is no mention of it here, the Philistines probably followed up their victory by destroying this city (see Jeremiah 26:6). These verses record the fulfilment of God's judgement on Eli's family (2:27-36; 3:11-14).

He had judged (18): 'led', New International Version. Most of Israel's judges were warrior-leaders (see Judges). But the last two, Eli and Samuel, were religious leaders and administrators of justice.

5 The ark in Philistine hands

To the Philistines' way of thinking, Dagon, their god, has given them victory. So they place the ark as a war-trophy at his feet. But Dagon is not in the same class as the God of Israel. God is no man-made idol. He treats the figure of Dagon as they

This relief from the temple of Pharaoh Remesses III at Thebes shows captive Philistine soldiers, kilted and wearing plumed helmets.

might have treated a captive king (see Judges 1:6-7). As a further demonstration of his power there is an outbreak of plague (bubonic plague, carried by the rat-flea; see verse 6 and 6:4, New English Bible). Moving the ark simply spreads the disease.

6 – 7:1 Return of the ark

After seven months of this, the Philistines have had enough. The religious leaders advise the ark's return – but in a way which will show, once for all, whether or not Israel's God is responsible for the disasters. The cows, not trained for the yoke, are unlikely to pull together. In the nature of things they would also be expected to stay near their calves. Yet they respond to the yoke like a team of oxen, and head straight for the border.

Verse 19, with 70 men killed 'because they looked into the ark', sounds a sombre note in all the rejoicing. Even Israel must learn not to overstep the mark. It is not safe to treat God as an object of idle curiosity.

7:2-17
NATIONAL REVIVAL: SAMUEL AS JUDGE

Twenty years pass, and there is a genuine turning to God (verse 2). The old idols – to Baal and Ashtoreth, the Canaanite fertility gods – are destroyed. And Samuel, judge and religious leader in Eli's place (see 15-17), leads the nation in an act of repentance and cleansing. Immediately the test comes. The Philistines are advancing, and God uses the occasion to show Israel just what he will do for a people who keep faith with him. Israel is needed only for the mopping-up operation. The name of the place of a former defeat (4:1) is chosen to mark the present victory (12). It is God's help which makes such a dramatic reversal possible.

Throughout Samuel's lifetime (13): this includes most of Saul's reign. War continued, but Saul and David kept the Philistines at bay until the great battle of Gilboa when Saul and Jonathan lost their lives.

From Ekron to Gath (14): the two inland Philistine city-states. Israel won back their border towns.

Bethel, Gilgal, Mizpah, Ramah (16-17): Samuel did an annual circuit of the four sanctuary towns.

8 – 12
SAUL BECOMES ISRAEL'S FIRST KING

8 The people ask for a king; Samuel's warning

History repeats itself in the case of

The ark remained for 20 years at Kiriath-jearim, usually identified with the village of Abu Ghosh, about 10 miles west of Jerusalem.

Samuel's sons. They turn out little better than Eli's (2:12). This provides the people with a ready-made excuse to ask for a king, like the nations around. Samuel warns of the cost. They have only to look at their neighbour states to see that having a king means conscription, forced labour, taxation, and loss of personal liberty. But even this does not deter them.

9 – 10:16 Saul becomes king: the private anointing

A search for lost donkeys, of all things, brings Israel's future king from Gibeah to Ramah, and the meeting with Samuel. All Israel knows the prophet, but not, apparently, this young provincial. The oil (10:1) sets Saul apart for his high office. The detailed fulfilment of Samuel's predictions assures Saul of the prophet's authority. Saul goes home a new man (10:9).

The high place (9:12): 'altar on the hill', Good News Bible; the phrase has not yet acquired the idolatrous associations of later times.

A bed...on the roof (9:25): a pleasantly cool place in the summer heat.

To Gilgal (10:8): the instruction seems to relate to mustering for battle. When this took place (chapter 13) Saul disobeyed.

When they came to Gibeah (10:10): Saul's ecstatic experience took place in his own home town.

10:17-27 The public proclamation

God chooses Israel's king; it is not left to the people.

11 Saul's first victory melts the opposition

God moves Saul to make his appeal (6) and the people to respond (7). For perhaps the first time since Joshua the nation is united: a good beginning to the new king's reign.

Figure of Baal: the people of Israel were constantly recalled by prophets such as Samuel from turning to the local pagan gods of weather, war and fertility.

12 Samuel cautions the people at Gilgal

Samuel has always been alert to the dangers of monarchy (8; 10:17ff.). Politically the move to choose a king was no doubt wise. Religiously, it was a

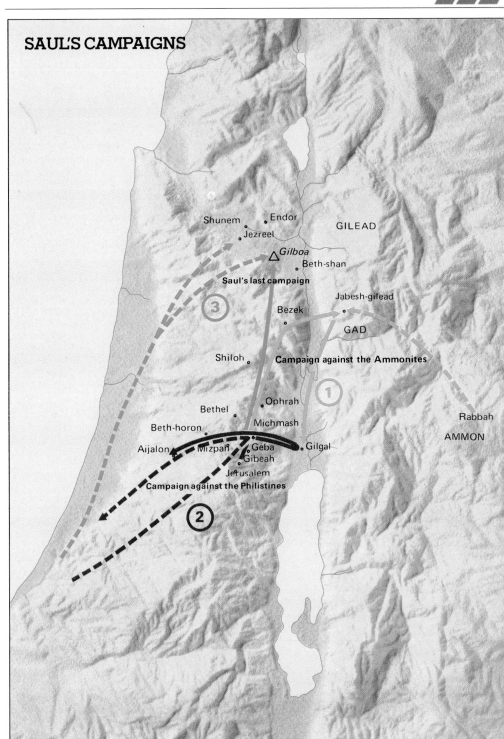

SAUL'S CAMPAIGNS

Shunem

Endor

GILEAD

Jezreel

△ *Gilboa*

Beth-shan

Saul's last campaign

Jabesh-gilead

3

Bezek

GAD

Shiloh

Campaign against the Ammonites

1

Ophrah

Rabbah

Bethel

Michmash

AMMON

Beth-horon

Aijalon

Mizpah

Geba

Gilgal

Gibeah

Jerusalem

Campaign against the Philistines

2

step in the wrong direction, a step away from the ideal of God alone as Israel's King. And if God ceases to be King for his people, both nation and monarchy will be swept away (25).

Verse 9: 'Sisera' defeated by Deborah and Barak (Judges 4-5); 'the king of Moab' – Eglon, assassinated by Ehud (Judges 3:12-30).

Verse 11: 'Jerubbaal' – i.e. Gideon (Judges 6-8); 'Jephthah' – Judges 11-12; 'Samuel' – this seems odd coming from his own lips. Perhaps we should read 'Samson' (New English Bible; Judges 13-16).

13 — 15
SAUL DISOBEYS AND IS REJECTED

13 — 14 War with the Philistines: Saul's disobedience and stupidity

Saul musters his troops and waits seven days, during which time the army steadily dwindles. But he fails to see the seventh day out. And his disobedience and arrogance in taking over the function of the prophet costs him his dynasty.

Chapter 14: Jonathan and his armour-bearer seem to have been taken for deserters, so they were able to catch the Philistines on the hop. Earth tremors add to the panic and confusion. And Israelite deserters change sides to help Saul to victory. Jonathan is seen as a man of outstanding faith and courage. By contrast, the narrative begins to bring out those flaws in Saul's make-up which later developed into serious mental disorder.

13:1: the text is incomplete. Acts 13:21 puts Saul's reign in round figures at 40 years. Possibly a tens-unit has dropped out here and the text should read 32 years (but see 'Unravelling the Chronology of the Kings', page 269). We know from 9:2 that Saul was a young man when he came to the throne. By this time he must be in his thirties since he has a son old enough to fight. When he died, a younger son,

Ishbosheth, was himself 40 (2 Samuel 2:10).

Thirty thousand (13:5): more probably 3,000 – see 'The Large Numbers of the Old Testament', page 191.

The Israelites hid (13:6): the atmosphere is much the same as it was in Gideon's day, when the people went in fear of the Midianites (Judges 6:2).

Bring the ark (14:18): perhaps in view of Saul's command to the priest in verse 19, New English Bible and Good News Bible translate 'ephod' rather than 'ark'. This was the tunic with the breastpiece containing the Urim and Thummim (41), the lots which were cast to discover God's will.

Sinning…by eating meat with the blood (14:33): forbidden in Leviticus 17:10ff.

Ishvi (14:49): short form of Ishbosheth.

Abner (14:50): he later set up Ishbosheth as king in opposition to David (2 Samuel 2:8-3:39).

15 God orders the destruction of the Amalekites; Saul again disobeys

This time the disobedience is deliberate (9). Saul is personally rejected by God as king, and Samuel pays him no more official visits. The prophet had foreseen trouble. He might well have relished Saul's downfall. Instead he went home grieving.

Amalek (2): the Amalekites were old enemies whose punishment had long been forecast (Exodus 17:8-16; Deuteronomy 25:17-19). Even so, we find it hard to swallow the order to destroy them completely – notwithstanding the unparalleled atrocities of our own century. In the more realistic, less individualistic world of Saul's day the whole community was held responsible for the misdeeds of its members, and suffered the consequences. Saul's disobedience (for the lowest of motives) left his people open to continued harassment from the Amalekites.

Kenites (6): a nomadic Midianite tribe into which Moses had married. The Kenites acted as Israel's guides in the desert (Numbers 10:29-33).

David's harp was a 'kinnor', as in this reconstruction at the Haifa Music Museum. It is the first musical instrument mentioned in the Bible (Genesis 4:21); David's was made of cypress wood (2 Samuel 6:5).

To obey is better than sacrifice (22-23): Samuel's declaration became a major theme of later prophets.

16—31
SAUL AND DAVID

16:1-13 Samuel anoints David king

With the anointing, as in Saul's case, comes spiritual power (13). Again God chooses his man and prepares him long before he becomes a national figure.

16:14-23 David finds a place at court

When the Spirit of God leaves Saul, evil forces take charge. Saul is at the mercy of his own ungovernable temperament. His disordered mind plunges him into black depression and violence. But music can push back the shadows, and so Saul's need becomes David's opportunity.
An evil spirit from God (15): to the observer, Saul is 'possessed' by a spirit sent by God in punishment.

17 David and Goliath

The Philistine champion is ten feet (nearly three metres) tall, fully armed and mailed. But David's time in the hills alone with the sheep has taught him faith – and deadly accuracy with the sling. The giant doesn't stand a chance.
Verses 55-58: this is difficult to tie in with 16:18ff. The events of chapter 17 may have taken place while David was still attending court only occasionally, when Saul's black moods came on him. 16:21-22 then refer to a later time. Or possibly the enquiry is a purely formal one concerning David's family background. The victor had, after all, been promised the king's daughter in marriage (17:25).

18 The friendship with Jonathan; Saul grows jealous

David was to look back on his friendship

with Jonathan as one of the best things in his life (2 Samuel 1:26). Nothing could shake the amazing bond between the king's son and the man who, humanly speaking, was to rob him of the throne.

As David's prestige grows, Saul's jealous suspicion increases, and he plots David's death. David's poverty gives Saul the chance to suggest a bride-price which is likely to cost him his life. Such a toll could be exacted only from the Philistines, Israel's number one enemy; the other nations practised circumcision. David doubles Saul's demand and returns unharmed, to claim his royal bride.

19—20 Attempts on his life force David to leave Saul's court

Jonathan's first attempt at reconciliation succeeds (1-7). But one of Saul's black moods follows and only Michal's deception saves David's life (8-17). For a time he joins Samuel and his school of prophets at Ramah (18-24). Jonathan tries to secure David's safe return, but his father only turns on him (20:30-33).

Shepherd-boy with a sling.

An example of contemporary armour; a helmet from Assyria.

And the two friends are forced to part (35-42).

Has Saul become a prophet? (19:24): compare 10:10-13. So irresistible is the power of the Spirit of God that not only is Saul's evil plan frustrated, but the king himself becomes 'infected'. Like his messengers, he too – for the time at least – turns prophet.

Tomorrow is the new moon (20:5): the first day of each new month was a feast day.

21 Ahimelech helps David to escape

The priest pays dearly for David's deception (22:11-19). But David is fed and armed, and makes good his escape to the Philistine city of Gath. In danger of recognition he feigns madness and plays the part so effectively that Achish is completely convinced (see also 27:5-12).

Nob (1): Israel's central shrine at that time.

Sacred bread (4): each sabbath twelve fresh loaves were placed on the altar and the twelve stale ones removed. Only the priests were entitled to eat them.
Verse 5: Israelite soldiers abstained from sexual intercourse during campaigns. If Uriah had not steadfastly stuck to the rules, David would have had no occasion to resort to murder (2 Samuel 11:11).

22 David the outlaw; Saul's revenge on Ahimelech
He left them with the king of Moab (4): for safety. David had Moabite blood in his veins (see Ruth).
Doeg (9ff.): the Hebrew title of Psalm 52 relates it to this episode.

23 The hunt is on: Keilah, Ziph, Maon
David welds his band of outlaws into an effective military force. But Saul's relentless pursuit keeps them continually on the move.
The ephod (6): see on 14:18.

24 David spares Saul's life in the cave at Engedi
Saul is completely at David's mercy. His refusal to take a short-cut to the throne brings the king to his senses. But Saul's word cannot be relied on.

25 The death of Samuel; David and Abigail
Not until Elijah will there be another religious leader to equal Samuel. The old prophet had anointed Israel's greatest king, but did not live to see him reign.

David's request to Nabal is not unreasonable. He is not demanding protection money, but asking some

In the hills and caves around Ein Gedi there were plenty of hiding-places for a man on the run. The fresh water from the spring flows down a gorge into the Dead Sea, allowing luxuriant vegetation to grow in an otherwise desert and barren area.

return on past services (15-16). After all, the man was rich and it was sheep-shearing, a feast time. Abigail's quick action saves the lives of her husband and household (22). She evidently made a good impression on David (see verse 39). God attends to Nabal's punishment. He dies of a double stroke.

26 David again spares Saul's life

The pro-Saul Ziphites again lay information against David. And once again it is Saul who finds himself at David's mercy and is shamed into repentance. No doubt Macbeth would have seen this as a heaven-sent opportunity for advancement. David knew God could and would put him on the throne without any assistance from him.

Abishai the son of Zeruiah (6): Abishai, Joab, and Asahel, David's military leaders, were all sons of his step-sister. Though

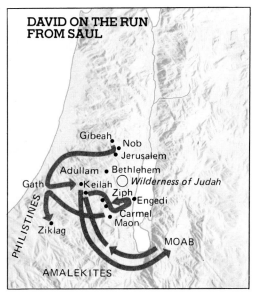

DAVID ON THE RUN FROM SAUL

Bedouin desert-dwellers, with their black tents, are the only sign of life in this picture of the Judean Desert.

brave, they caused him a great deal of trouble when he was king (2 Samuel 3:39; 18:14; 20:10).

27 Back in Philistine country

Achish is once again completely taken in (see 21:10-15). While pretending to raid Israel and her allies (10), David in fact wipes out enemy cities (8), leaving no one alive to tell the tale (11).

28 Saul consults a medium

Saul can get no reply from God (6). Witchcraft had always been forbidden in Israel (Leviticus 19:31). But in desperation he sets out at night and in disguise on a dangerous journey, close to the enemy camp at Shunem, to consult the medium at Endor. However, he finds Samuel no more reassuring in death than he had been in life.

29 David is not trusted

The other Philistine overlords are less gullible than Achish, so David is spared the awkward predicament of facing his

fellow countrymen in battle. This chapter refers to earlier events than chapter 28. The Philistines muster at Aphek. They have not yet moved north to Shunem.

30 The Amalekite raid on Ziklag; David's successful reprisal

David's return is well-timed, and the slave's information more than a stroke of luck. All is recovered. And Judah and the Calebites, also victims of the raid (14), share in the spoil.

31 The battle of Gilboa; death of Saul and Jonathan

The writer of Chronicles (1 Chronicles 10) found this account of Saul's death more credible than the Amalekite's story (2 Samuel 1:4-10). The latter may well have adjusted the facts to suit his own ends. Fittingly, it is the men of Jabesh who rescue the bodies. They have not forgotten what they owe to Saul's first great victory (chapter 11).

2 SAMUEL

The reign of David; also recorded in 1 Chronicles 11-29.

1—4
THE EARLY YEARS OF DAVID'S REIGN

1 News of Saul's death; David's lament

The Amalekite's story differs from the account of Saul's death in 1 Samuel 31. If he twisted the facts in hope of a reward, he did not know David. After the Amalekite raid on Ziklag (1 Samuel 30) David had no cause to love this race. But it was his strong conviction that the king's life was sacred (14; and see

1 Samuel 24 and 26), not racial discrimination, that led to the death sentence.

The lament for Saul and Jonathan is one of the most moving and beautiful of all David's poems. His regret for the king seems wholly sincere; his distress at the loss of Jonathan, deep and genuine.
On the third day (2): it was 100 miles from Gilboa to Ziklag.
The book of Jashar (18): a lost anthology (see Joshua 10:13).
The shield ... rubbed with oil (21): the shield was leather; oil prevented it drying and cracking.

2 Civil war; Abner kills Asahel

Only Judah (by this time probably including Simeon) acclaims David as

Saul and Jonathan lost their lives on the mountains of Gilboa, seen in the distance in this picture. Their bodies were brought here to Bethshan, and hung on the walls. Remains of temples found in the course of extensive excavation could have been those where Saul's armour was displayed.

king. The other ten tribes follow the lead of Abner, Saul's army commander, and give allegiance to Ishbosheth, Saul's son. For two years the nation is divided.

An attempt to settle the issue by representative single combat (14) at Gibeon is inconclusive, and full-scale civil war follows.

Sons of Zeruiah (18): see on 1 Samuel 26:6.

The butt of his spear (23): Abner did not intend to kill Asahel. But the butt was sharp so that it would stick in the ground, and the blow proved fatal.

The Arabah (29): the long rift valley from Galilee to the Dead Sea and beyond; here, the Jordan Valley.

3 Abner makes terms; Joab avenges his brother

Ishbosheth is not the man his father was. Abner is the real power. If he transfers his support to David, he carries the nation with him. But he reckons without the implacable hatred of Joab. David leads the nation's mourning for Abner. Despite a public declaration of innocence, the taint of the murder remains with him all his life (1 Kings 2:5).

Saul had a concubine (7): a king's harem normally passed to his heir, which makes Abner's action tantamount to a claim to the throne. Compare Absalom's action, 16:20ff. Rizpah appears again in chapter 21.

A dog's head of Judah (8): i.e. 'one of David's contemptible supporters'.

Dan to Beersheba (10): the whole country, north to south (in Britain one would say from John o' Groat's to Land's End).

My wife Michal ... (14): see 1 Samuel 18:20-27. Saul had given David's wife to another man.

One who has a discharge ... (29): who is defiled and therefore disqualified from religious service; 'holds a spindle': fit only for women's work.

4 The assassination of Ishbosheth

A second incident (compare 1:1-16) which shows the complete failure of David's supporters to understand his attitude to Saul and the royal family. Ishbosheth is given honourable burial, the two murderers are publicly disgraced.

5—12
DAVID'S KINGDOM ESTABLISHED

5 David, king of all Israel; the new capital at Jerusalem

The writer makes it clear that David is no usurper. God has given him his title to the throne: a fact recognized by Saul

(1 Samuel 24:18-20), by Abner (3:9-10) and finally by the whole nation (5:2).

Although part of Jerusalem fell to Judah at the conquest (Judges 1:8), the fortress itself had never been taken (Joshua 15:63; Judges 1:21). The Jebusites had some ground for their boast that a garrison of blind men and cripples could hold it (6). But they underestimated David. Jerusalem was held by Judah until Nebuchadnezzar destroyed it 400 years later. It was a first-rate choice of capital.

The Millo (9): part of the fortifications.
Hiram, king of Tyre (11): contemporary with David and Solomon (1 Kings 5). Hiram reigned about 979-945 BC. The sea-port of Tyre was capital of the Phoenician kingdom. Hiram's reign was a golden age of political expansion and commercial prosperity, when arts and crafts flourished. His craftsmen helped to build the temple.

6 The ark is brought to Jerusalem

See also 1 Chronicles 13, 15-16. After the Philistines returned the ark (1 Samuel 4-6), it remained at Kiriath-jearim (Baalah in Judah; see 1 Chronicles 13:6). Now David brings it to his new capital.

The occasion is marked with all the exuberance of Jewish worship. Even the king dances for joy. Only Michal stands aloof and outside it all, cold and unmoved by the presence of God.

Uzzah took hold of the ark (6): which not even the Levites might touch. David blames himself for not following the instructions Moses laid down (1 Chronicles 15:2-15). At the next attempt the Levites carried the ark on poles.

7 The house of God and the throne of David

David is not the man to build God's temple – that is for his son, a man of peace, not a warrior (1 Chronicles 22:7ff.). But God compensates for the disappointment by promising a 'house' for David, a dynasty which will be 'for ever' (16). On this promise rests a hope which runs right through the Old Testament, the hope of a Messiah. And when he came, the promise was fulfilled. Christ was born in David's birthplace, Bethlehem, and 'of the house and lineage of David' (Luke 2:4). The angel tells Mary: 'The Lord God will give to him the throne of his father David, and he will reign over the house of Jacob for

Hebron, which was David's capital before he took Jerusalem.

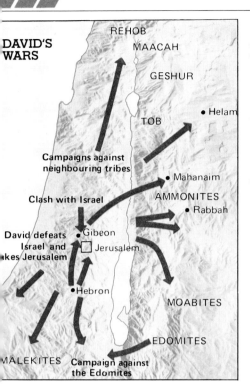

DAVID'S WARS

REHOB

MAACAH

GESHUR

• Helam

TOB

Campaigns against neighbouring tribes

• Mahanaim

Clash with Israel

AMMONITES

• Rabbah

David defeats Israel and takes Jerusalem

• Gibeon

□ Jerusalem

•Hebron

MOABITES

EDOMITES

MALEKITES Campaign against the Edomites

ever; and of his kingdom there will be no end' (Luke 1:32-33).

Your son . . . shall build (12-13): Solomon did build (1 Kings 5-7). But David contributed a great deal: he drew up the plans and provided materials (1 Chronicles 28:11ff.; 22:2ff.).

8 David's victories

See sketch-map above. This chapter pre-dates the events of chapter 7 (see 7:1).

Moab (2): previously David was on good terms with them (1 Samuel 22:3-4).

Valley of Salt (13): probably in the barren section of the great rift valley south of the Dead Sea.

Kerethites . . . Pelethites (18): Philistine mercenaries.

David's sons were priests (18): although not from a priestly family, David was himself something of a priest-king (see chapter 6), like Melchizedek, a much earlier king of Jerusalem (Genesis 14:18).

9 David and Mephibosheth, Jonathan's son

The events of chapter 21 may pre-date this chapter. If so, no doubt the king's summons terrified Mephibosheth. But David's motives are wholly good, 'for Jonathan's sake' (see 1 Samuel 20:42). He restores the family estates (7) and treats the young man as his own son (11).

Lo-debar (4): in north Gilead, not far from Jabesh.

Verse 10: this sounds contradictory, but being at court would mean an increase in general expenses, even if meals were provided.

10 Defeat of the Ammonite/Syrian alliance

See also 1 Chronicles 19. Hanun provoked the war by his outrageous treatment of the ambassadors. But no doubt neighbouring nations were suspicious and afraid of Israel's powerful king.

The campaign in verses 16-18 may be the one mentioned in 8:3ff.

11 David's adultery with Bathsheba

His army is fighting the Ammonites, but this spring the king is not with them. He is taking an after-siesta stroll in the cool, on the palace roof. And from his vantage-point he can see down into the open inner courtyard of a nearby house, where Bathsheba is going through the purification ritual. The events that follow – adultery and murder – are the watershed in David's life. From this point on he reaps the bitter harvest of his sin.

Rabbah (1): present-day Amman, capital of Jordan.

Uriah the Hittite (3): to make matters worse, Uriah was one of David's special guard (23:39), away on the king's war.

Verse 11: the army is on campaign, under canvas, and the rule is that the men abstain from sexual intercourse. Had Uriah been a man of less principle he would have gone home to his wife. The

The old city of Jerusalem from the Mt of Olives; the Kidron Valley is between.

child could then have passed as his and he would not have been killed. But maybe he already suspected the truth.

Jerubbesheth (21): i.e. Jerubbaal/Gideon (Judges 9). 'Baal' being a pagan name, the scribes later substituted the word 'bosheth'/'besheth', 'shame'. So Jerubbaal became Jerubbesheth; Eshbaal became Ishbosheth; Meribbaal, Mephibosheth, and so on.

12 Nathan's visit; death of the child

Uriah is dead; the wedding over; the child born. It all seems to have blown over very nicely – until Nathan arrives. And then the whole sordid episode is exposed. David is made to see himself as God sees him: a humbling experience for a king (see Psalm 51). God forgives him, but he is punished, and the child dies.

Pay four times over (6): see Exodus 22:1.
Verses 10-11: the prophecy was fulfilled. Three of David's sons were murdered, two by their own brothers. And in the rebellion

Absalom took over his father's harem (16:22).
Sent a message (25): presumably to reassure David that this child would not die.
A talent of gold (30): about 66lb/30kg.

13—20
DAVID AND HIS ELDEST SONS: ABSALOM'S REBELLION

13 Amnon and Tamar; Absalom's revenge

Faced with the appalling rape of his daughter by her half-brother, David does nothing at all. The strong king is a fatally weak father (see 1 Kings 1:6). Had David taken action he might have prevented both the murder and the later rebellion.
Speak to the king (13): Tamar does not think marriage out of the question (though in view of Leviticus 18:11 they would have needed a special dispensa-

tion). The 'impossibility' of verse 2 lies in her careful seclusion – Amnon only wanted to satisfy his lust, he had no thought of marriage.

14 The woman from Tekoa; Absalom forgiven

Joab pierces the king's defences much as Nathan had done (chapter 12), but with a fake law-suit. This time the appeal is to waive the next-of-kin's obligation to avenge his murdered relative. The application to David is obvious. He is willing to overrule in the case of one of his subjects; why not for his heir?

Joab wins his point, and Absalom returns from exile. But two long years pass before he is admitted to his father's presence.

Verse 26: it was Absalom's hair which eventually brought about his death (18:9). The weight is about 5lbs/2.3 kilos.

15 Absalom's rebellion; David leaves Jerusalem

With Amnon out of the way, and Abigail's son dead, Absalom is next in line to the throne. But Solomon is David's chosen heir. For four years Absalom lays his plans (1-6), gradually winning the people over. When he does come into the open (7-12) the challenge to David is extremely serious.

The King is caught unprepared. To save the city, and gain time, he leaves Jerusalem. But he organizes a spy-ring. And Hushai is sent back to outwit Ahithophel, whose far-sighted council is otherwise likely to win the day for Absalom.

The gate (2): where the city's business and legal transactions took place (see Ruth 4:1ff.).

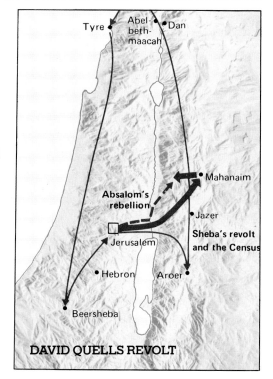

DAVID QUELLS REVOLT

(map labels: Tyre, Abel-beth-maacah, Dan, Mahanaim, Absalom's rebellion, Jazer, Sheba's revolt and the Census, Jerusalem, Aroer, Hebron, Beersheba)

The old titles to the Psalms link many of David's psalms to events in his life

Escape from the palace: 1 Samuel 19:11ff.: Psalm 59

David feigns madness: 1 Samuel 21: Psalm 34 (though the difference in names may indicate a further occasion not recorded in Samuel)

David in hiding in the cave: 1 Samuel 22:1ff.; 24:3ff.: Psalms 57, 142

Doeg's betrayal of the priests at Nob: 1 Samuel 22: Psalm 52

The Ziphite informers: 1 Samuel 23:19ff.: Psalm 54

David in the Judean desert: 1 Samuel 24:1-2, 22; and again in 2 Samuel 15ff.: Psalm 63

Defeat of the Edomites: 2 Samuel 8:13: Psalm 60

David's sin over Bathsheba: 2 Samuel 11-12: Psalm 51 (and probably 32)

Absalom's rebellion: 2 Samuel 15:13ff.: Psalm 3

David's song of deliverance: 2 Samuel 22: the same poem as Psalm 18

Hebron (7): David's former capital, in Judah.

The Mount of Olives (30): the place where Jesus spent the night of his betrayal.

Ahithophel (31): Bathsheba's grandfather; wisest of all David's advisers.

16 Ziba and Shimei; Hushai and Ahithophel

Ziba (1-4) clearly has an eye to the main chance. Mephibosheth later denies the charges made against him (19:24-30). Shimei (5-14) takes a vindictive pleasure in the downfall of the man who robbed his family of the throne (5-8).

In Jerusalem (15-19) Hushai succeeds in convincing Absalom of his loyalty. Verses 20-23 provide an example of Ahithophel's political strategy. By taking over David's harem, Absalom will convince his followers that reconciliation with his father is impossible. No king could forgive such a public insult.

17 Absalom rejects Ahithophel's plan

Ahithophel's advice is to strike quickly, and only against the person of the king – so avoiding civil war. But Hushai gains time for David by a scheme which appeals to Absalom's vanity (11ff.). Ahithophel has the foresight to realize the probable consequences – hence his suicide (24). Meantime Jonathan and Ahimaaz, on their way to David with the information, narrowly escape discovery by hiding in a dry well (17-20).

18 – 19:8 Defeat and death of Absalom; David's grief

Joab is shrewd enough to see that only the death of the pretender – or the king – can settle the issue. But David still loved his son, and he did not forgive Joab for ignoring orders (see 19:13). It was ironic that Absalom's beautiful hair (14:26) should tangle in the oak and leave him a helpless prey to Joab.

18:33 – 19:8: grief and remorse (see 12:10) blind the king to the effect of his

conduct on the people. Joab's harsh words bring him to his senses and save him from political disaster.

Pile of stones (18:17): a cairn marked the grave of a criminal

No son (18:18): presumably those mentioned in 14:27 died young.

Ahimaaz and the Cushite (18:19-32): Joab chooses the Sudanese slave to take the bad news. The king would naturally have assumed (as he does in 27) that the priest's son brought good news. Joab may also have been thinking of the fate of earlier messengers (1:11-16; 4:9-12). But the direct hill-route proved slower than the route Ahimaaz took along the Jordan Valley (23).

19:9-43 The aftermath of rebellion

Judah had backed Absalom. David's attempt to win them back, and his appointment of Amasa (Absalom's army commander, and his own nephew) in Joab's place lead to further trouble (41-43 and chapter 20). David is in effect

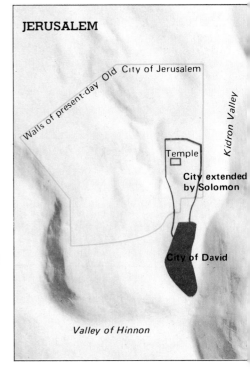

JERUSALEM

City of Jerusalem

Walls of present-day Old City of Jerusalem

Kidron Valley

Temple

City extended by Solomon

City of David

Valley of Hinnon

punishing loyalty and rewarding rebellion. Now that the king is back in power, there are some who are anxious to get back into favour (Shimei, 16-22, see 16:5-14; Mephibosheth, 24-30, see 16:1-4; on Shimei and Barzillai, see also 1 Kings 2).

20 Sheba's revolt; Joab kills Amasa

Despite the statement in verse 2, those who actively supported Sheba, when it came to it, were few (14ff.). Joab is as quick to kill Amasa (a member of his own family) as he was to kill Abner, when his own position was threatened before. In both cases his treachery is despicable. The kiss and the sword thrust bring to mind Judas' betrayal of Jesus. David did not forget, or forgive (see 1 Kings 2:5-6).
Your master's servants (6): the men of David's special guard (7 and 23:18ff.), led by Abishai.

It fell out (8): into Joab's hand.
Adoram (24): in a post not likely to win friends! He was stoned to death in the reign of Solomon's son.

21—24
RECORDS OF EVENTS IN DAVID'S REIGN

With Sheba's death, the nation is once more united and at peace. The writer now brings together events and information belonging to various periods of David's reign.

21 The appeasement of Gibeon; defeat of the Philistine giants

Verses 1-14 probably precede Mephibosheth's welcome at court (chapter 9). The story of Israel's pact with Gibeon is told in Joshua 9:3-27. Saul had broken

e temple area

The Kidron Valley

Site of David's city

The Valley of Hinnom

the treaty, despite close family connections with the city (1 Chronicles 8:29ff.).

That you may bless (3): and so remove the curse that brought the famine.

Hang (6): 'kill', New International Version; the Hebrew does not specify the manner of death.

Merab (8): the daughter who had been promised to David as wife.

Used sackcloth to make a shelter (10): Rizpah may have been there as long as six months. The coming of rain brought an end to the famine, and to the curse, leaving David free to act.

Elhanan…killed Goliath (19): this seems to conflict with 1 Samuel 17. The text here may be confused. R. K. Harrison suggests it should read, 'Elhanan, the son of Jairi the Bethlehemite, slew the brother of Goliath', which ties in with 1 Chronicles 20:5. Another possibility is that a new champion took the name of the one killed by David.

22 David's victory song

This is virtually identical with Psalm 18, and can be compared with Moses' song in Deuteronomy 32. It belongs to the period of David's great early victories. Verses 21-25 contrast with the deeper self-knowledge which followed the Bath-sheba/Uriah episode, expressed in Psalm 51.

23:1-7 David's 'last words'

These may be the last words he set down in poetry (see 1 Kings 2 for his final charge to Solomon). His thoughts centre on what makes a good ruler, on his own standing before God, and on the promised dynasty – a fitting close to the life of the king who was 'a man after God's own heart'.

23:8-39 Annals of the men of David's special guard

The exploits of 'The Three' against the Philistines (8-12) are followed by an incident from the campaign described in 5:17-25 (13-17; Bethlehem was David's home town). Then come the exploits of two leaders (Abishai, leader of 'The Thirty', and Benaiah, leader of the Philistine mercenaries), followed by a list of the special guard. The group was probably formed at Ziklag, and helped to put David on the throne (1 Chronicles 12:1; 11:10). More than thirty are listed – those killed (e.g. Asahel, Uriah) were replaced by others.

Ariel (20, Revised Standard Version**):** 'lion of God'; either lions of exceptional size, or a metaphor for great warriors.

24 The census and the plague

It is not clear why it was wrong to take the census. Perhaps it indicated reliance on numbers, instead of on God. Satan does the inciting in 1 Chronicles 21:1. Here it is God, since all is ultimately under his control.

Verses 8-25: the first readers did not need to be told the tremendous significance of David's purchase, explicitly mentioned in 1 Chronicles 21:18 – 22:1. On this threshing-floor the temple was built, close to the place where Abraham offered up Isaac (2 Chronicles 3:1; Genesis 22:2).

and 2 Kings

Four centuries of Israel's history are covered by the books of Kings. We move from the close of David's reign, through the golden age of Solomon and the rift between Israel and Judah, to the fall of Samaria in 722 BC and the destruction of Jerusalem in 587 BC. The account begins with a stable, united kingdom under a strong king and ends with total collapse and mass deportation to Babylon. It is a sombre story, and one in which the writer sees a clear moral. God is the Lord of history, actively involved in the affairs of men. When the nation and its leaders look to him and obey his laws, peace and prosperity follow. Political and economic disaster overtake Israel and Judah as a direct consequence of the weakening of the nation's moral and religious fibre.

The writer is unknown; probably a prophet in Babylon during the exile, about 550 BC. He mentions a number of his sources (e.g. 1 Kings 11:41; 15:31): court and official records and cycles of stories about the prophets. He wrote his account as one volume, to be read through from beginning to end. Much of the material is paralleled in Chronicles.

1 KINGS

1—2
DAVID'S LAST DAYS: SOLOMON'S ACCESSION

1 Adonijah and Solomon; rivals for the throne

King David is now an old man. Thoughts turn to his successor. With his three elder brothers dead, Adonijah is heir apparent. He has the backing of Joab, the army commander, and Abiathar, one of the two chief priests. But the throne has been promised to Solomon (1:13, and see 1 Chronicles 22:9). And thanks to some quick thinking by the prophet Nathan, and even quicker action by the old king, Adonijah is out-manoeuvred. Solomon is made king, co-regent with David.

Abishag (3): from Shunem near Nazareth. Although Abishag is sometimes identified with the heroine of the Song of Solomon, there are no real grounds for this.

Knew her not (4, older versions): did not have sexual intercourse with her. The verb 'know' often has this sense in the Old Testament (Genesis 4:1).

Verses 7-8: Zadok and Abiathar, see 2 Samuel 15:24ff.; Benaiah, 2 Samuel 23:20-23; Nathan, 2 Samuel 12. The mighty men: David's special guard, 2 Samuel 23:8-39.

Gihon (33): a spring just outside the eastern wall of Jerusalem, in the Kidron Valley.

Gezer was one of the cities rebuilt by Solomon after it had been destroyed by the Egyptians. The stone pillars belong to a Canaanite high place.

Kerethites and Pelethites (38): foreign (Philistine) mercenaries.
The tent (39): in which the ark was kept.
Horns of the altar (50): curved pieces at the four corners. See picture, page 173.

2:1-12 Last instructions to Solomon; David's death

High-toned advice (1-4) is abruptly followed by worldly wisdom of doubtful morality (5-9).
Joab (5): see 2 Samuel 3:26-30; 20:8-10.
Barzillai (7): see 2 Samuel 17:27-29; 19:31-40.
Shimei (8): David did not regard his pledge to Shimei as binding on Solomon. See 2 Samuel 16:5-14 and 19:16-23.

2:13-46 Solomon secures his position

This time Adonijah pays dearly for what may have been an unthinking request. Solomon interprets it as a claim to the throne, since possession of his predecessor's harem was part of the

eastern king's title to the throne (compare Absalom's action, 2 Samuel 16). Abiathar and Joab are dealt with at the same time. And Shimei, another potential trouble-maker, is put on parole in Jerusalem to keep him away from fellow-Benjaminites. When he breaks parole, even though for an innocent reason, Solomon has him killed.
The word ... about Eli (27): see 1 Samuel 2:27-36.

3 — 11
THE REIGN OF SOLOMON

3:1-15 Solomon's dream; the gift of wisdom

Solomon is at Gibeon, the town six miles from Jerusalem where the tabernacle and altar are kept, when God appears to him. His reign is outstanding for wise judgement, economic prosperity and fame – the very things God promised.
Verse 1: 'the city', i.e. the citadel on Mt Zion. See also article, 'Egypt'.
High places (2): the old Canaanite shrines (often, but not always, on hill-tops) which the Israelites took over. It was not long before the worship of God in these places became mixed with crude pagan practices. The later prophets condemned them.
Burnt offerings (4): for sacrifice generally, see on Leviticus 1 – 7.

3:16-28 Solomon the wise judge

We are given one example to illustrate Solomon's God-given gift. Where it is a case of one woman's word against another, special insight into human nature is needed to uncover the true facts. The incident shows the king's accessibility to ordinary folk, even two prostitutes.

King Hiram of Tyre provided Solomon with the materials and craftsmen for the building of the temple. The Israelites were not seafarers, and the Phoenicians to the north, from Tyre (pictured here) and Sidon, owed their importance to their role as international traders.

The Temples
ALAN MILLARD

In the journey through the wilderness, when the nation was living in tents, Israel had a 'tent' shrine, the tabernacle. The basic idea of a portable pavilion is attested in Egypt from before 2,000 BC. Surviving examples have a framework of wooden beams and rods, plated with precious metal and made with joints and sockets for easy erection. Ancient pictures show how they were once hung with curtains. (See page 167.)

Israelite craftsmen trained in Egypt would have known how to make such a structure, and all the materials used were obtainable in Sinai, or already in their possession (the gold and silver, for example).

The tabernacle was built to a simple plan. A courtyard contained the two-roomed holy place, the altar for burnt offerings and the basin for ritual washings. The two rooms were about 15 feet wide. The inner one, the 'holiest place', was square; the outer about 30 feet long. After the conquest of Canaan, the tabernacle was moved from one place to another until Solomon laid it up in the temple.

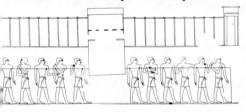

An Egyptian equivalent of the tabernacle: a 'Tent of Purification', an ink drawing on the wall of one of the rock tombs of Meir, dating from about 2,200 BC.

It was David's great ambition to build a temple, though this was only realized by his son. It was natural for a powerful king to honour his God in this way, and the existing tabernacle provided the pattern for a simple central sanctuary. The hill-top David bought is the site now covered by the 'Haram es-Sherif', the Mosque of Omar, in Jerusalem. The central rocky crust was perhaps the site of the altar of burnt-offering.

The detailed descriptions in 1 Kings 6—7,

The temple was built of stone and cedarwood from Lebanon; this grove of cedars is one of the few remaining in Lebanon today.

Solomon's craftsmen, decorating the temple, used motifs similar to this ivory carving of the period.

>>

and 2 Chronicles 3—4, give a fairly complete picture of the temple. This is supplemented by evidence from archaeological discovery. The tabernacle plan was extended by an entry porch, the resulting three rooms forming a scheme similar to some Canaanite temples (e.g. at Hazor and Ras Shamra). This may have been the work of the Phoenician builders whose skill Solomon utilized. A series of storage chambers three storeys high ran round the outside of the holiest place and the middle room (the 'holy place'). The doorway was flanked by two giant free-standing pillars whose function is uncertain.

Comparison with Ezekiel's temple suggests that the whole building stood on a platform above the level of the courtyard. An officiating priest would have crossed the courtyard, passing the great bronze altar for the sacrifices (about 33 feet/10 metres square, 10 feet/3 metres high) and the enormous bronze basin for water supported by twelve bronze bulls, before climbing the steps to the shrine. Apparently the porch had no doors; gates may have closed the passage, but he would have faced a pair of folding doors at the entrance to the 'holy place'. These were made of cypress wood, carved with flowers, palm-trees, and cherubim, and plated all over with gold, as was all the wood-work. In this room he would see the golden incense altar, the table for the sacred bread, and five pairs of lampstands. Additional light came from a row of windows high in the wall. Beneath his feet was a golden floor. And if he could see into the 'holiest place' the whole room would have shone a dim gold in the light admitted through the doorway. But these doors were opened rarely, perhaps only for the annual Atonement ceremony. The decorative motifs are well known from Phoenician ivory-carvings and bronze-work of the centuries around Solomon's time. And Egyptian and Babylonian kings boast of ornamenting their temples with gold wall-coverings, doors and furnishings.

Solomon's temple was destroyed by Nebuchadnezzar in 587 BC. Much of its glory had already been torn away and paid as tribute when foreign conquerors menaced Judah. The disconsolate exiles in Babylonia were heartened by Ezekiel's vision of a new temple (Ezekiel 40—43), described with minute attention, and including facts about the courtyard which hardly occur in the account of Solomon's work. This sanctuary was never built, but the exiles who returned about 537 BC, after some delay, completed the rebuilding of the old one in 515 BC. The little we know about it shows it followed the old design closely, however inferior its appearance. Nothing has survived from the first temple. But a length of stone walling above the Kidron Valley, on the east of the site, may be a part of the platform on which this second temple was erected, and which Herod incorporated into his walls.

The cosmopolitan nature of Jerusalem after the exile caused trouble to Nehemiah by bringing non-Jews into the sacred precinct (Nehemiah 13:4-9). It probably resulted in dividing off an outer courtyard from an inner one which only Jews could enter. This was certainly true of Herod's temple. Two stone blocks (one is shown on page 567) have been found inscribed with a warning to non-Jews that they passed in at their own risk (see also Acts 21:17ff.).

Herod's temple was the Idumaean king's attempt to curry favour with his Jewish subjects. Most of it was built between 19 and 9 BC, although work continued until AD 64. The Romans destroyed it in AD 70. Parts of its massive substructure are still visible on the west (the 'Wailing Wall') and east sides. Recent excavations have uncovered a flight of steps leading to the southern gates, and carved stone blocks from the parapets and porches.

Descriptions by the Jewish historian Josephus, and notes in rabbinic writings, supply us with information about this splendid building. The great courtyard was surrounded by a portico where schools were held, and business transacted (John 10:23; Luke 19:47; John 2:14-16). Beyond the barrier mentioned was the Women's Court where the money-boxes stood (Mark 12:41-44), then the Court of Israel, and finally the Priests' Court in which the altar and the temple proper stood. This last was a larger version of Solomon's design.

The 'holiest place', however, was empty, as in the second temple. The ark holding the terms of the covenant, upon whose covering lid (the 'mercy-seat') God had appeared, was no longer in existence. Significantly, the temple, too, disappeared with the establishment of the new covenant and the new Israel.

4 State officials: arrangements for provisioning the court

Solomon's harem alone was enormous (11:3). His court – which included not only the royal family, but ministers, civil servants and domestics – must have numbered several thousand. No wonder elaborate arrangements are necessary for their maintenance (7-28).

The king outshone his greatest contemporaries in wisdom, which he expressed, as they did, in proverbs and songs and sayings based on natural and animal life (see, for example, Psalms 72 and 127, both of whose titles ascribe them to Solomon, and Proverbs 10:1–22:16).

Verses 1-6: Azariah was head of inland revenue, in charge of those who collected taxes (in kind). 'King's friend' (Revised Standard Version, etc), i.e. king's councillor.

Every man under his vine . . . (25): a proverbial phrase indicating idyllic conditions of peace and plenty.

5 The trade-pact with Hiram; work on the temple begun

Friendship with Tyre (see on 2 Samuel 5:11) is further cemented by the agree-

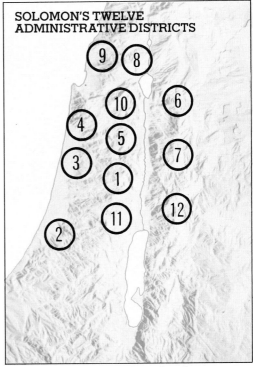

SOLOMON'S TWELVE ADMINISTRATIVE DISTRICTS

Deep below the old city of Jerusalem these great quarries extend 200 yards/65 metres into the rock. The marks of the picks used to dig out the building material for the temple can still be seen. See on 1 Kings 6:7.

ment that Hiram should supply raw materials for the temple in return for foodstuffs.

Cedars from Lebanon (6): the finest timber available. Few of these great trees remain today, but Lebanon was once densely forested. See pictures, pages 253 and 330.

Cor (11): a measurement of capacity. A cor of wheat: a donkey-load. A cor of oil: 48 gallons. Good News Bible translates, 2,000 metric tons of wheat and 400,000 litres of olive oil.

6 The building of the temple

In size the temple was a chapel rather than a cathedral. It was intended as a house for God, not a building to hold vast gatherings of people. It measured about 90 feet long x 30 feet wide x 45 feet high (Good News Bible gives 27 x 9 x 13.5 metres), divided into two sections, with part of the inner section curtained

A reconstruction of Solomon's temple, at the Bible Museum, Amsterdam.

off to form the sanctuary. In front was a 15 feet (4.5 x 9 metres) entrance porch, and along the sides were store-rooms.

480th year (1): the exodus probably took place something over 300 years before Solomon built the temple. The figure here (12 x 40) may indicate twelve generations rather than a precise number of years.

No noise (7): even at this stage the place was regarded as holy. The stone was quarried close to the site, but so deep underground that no sound would carry.

7 Other building projects; cast bronze furnishings for the temple

Verses 1-12: Solomon builds the House of the Forest of Lebanon (possibly an armoury, see 10:17; Isaiah 22:8), the Hall of Pillars, Hall of Judgement, and palaces for himself and for pharaoh's daughter (his queen; it may also have housed the rest of the harem).

Verses 13-51: Hiram, the craftsman from Tyre, supervises the casting in bronze of two decorative pillars for the entrance to the temple (15-22); a huge bowl able to hold nearly 10,000 gallons (Good News Bible, 40,000 litres) of water (23-26); ten wheeled stands to support more bowls (27-39), and numerous smaller items of equipment (40).

8 Dedication of the temple; Solomon's prayer

Work complete, the ark is brought from the citadel and installed in the inner sanctuary. And the whole building is filled with the glory of God's presence – the cloud that once rested on the tabernacle in the desert (Exodus 40:34-38).

Solomon's prayer, for the royal house (23-26) and for the nation (27-53), echoes the language of Moses. He asks that God will hear the prayers and forgive the sin of his people when they focus on the temple – even though no building on earth could ever contain the God of heaven.

Prayer is followed by blessing (54-61); blessing by sacrifice (62-64); sacrifice by feasting throughout the land (65; see on 2 Chronicles 7).

My name (16): God himself is present in a special sense in the temple, as he was in the tabernacle. But in contrast to the heathen temple, Israel's contained no statue to represent their God.

An oath (31): in which he solemnly swears his innocence.

9:1-9 God once again speaks to Solomon

He speaks in promise (3-5) and in warning (6-9).

As ... at Gibeon (2): when Solomon was given the gift of wisdom: 3:3-14.

The incense altar on wheels may have resembled this bronze stand from 1,200-1,100 BC.

9:10-28 Trade and commerce; building and public works

For all his wealth, Solomon has his balance of trade problems. On this occasion (10-14) he makes 20 cities over to Hiram of Tyre as security against a loan.

Verses 15-22: the vast labour force needed for new building and defence works is raised from two sources. Native Canaanites provide permanent slave-labour. And the Israelites are pressed into short-term forced labour.

Verses 26-28: Solomon is the first of Israel's kings to create a merchant navy. His ships traded with Arabia and beyond.

Ophir (28): suggestions include South Arabia, East Africa, and even India.

Winged creatures were used to decorate the border of this gold epaulette from the 7th century BC.

10:1-13 The visit of the Queen of Sheba

Intriguing reports of Solomon's wisdom and splendour bring the queen from the Yemen to Jerusalem. Unlike the people of Christ's day (Matthew 12:42) this woman was prepared to undertake a long journey to find out for herself the truth of what she had heard.

Almug wood (11): possibly the red sandalwood of Ceylon and India. Good News Bible has 'juniper'.

10:14-29 Solomon's wealth and power

Solomon's revenue through trade and taxes (including a lucrative tourist trade, 24-25) is enormous. But consumer spending more than keeps pace. The country's position made him a convenient middleman for chariots from Egypt and horses from Turkey (Kue=Cilicia).

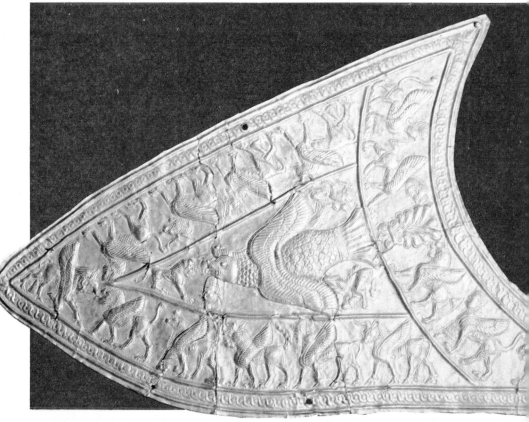

Using the Bible – in Archaeology

Professor Yigael Yadin, Professor of Archaeology at the Hebrew University of Jerusalem, describes how he used ancient records, especially the Bible, to help him recover the history of a lost city – Hazor.

At the foot of the great mound, Yadin uncovered the lower city, a built-up area of 170 acres; the largest city in the Holy Land dating from Canaanite times; the city the Bible describes as 'the head of all those kingdoms' (Joshua 11:10). A thick layer of ash remained, probable evidence of Joshua's destruction of the city in the latter half of the 13th century BC.

❝ The lower city was never rebuilt. The fields of today just cover the ruins of the last Canaanite city. But the Bible tells us that Solomon rebuilt the city. So where was that . . .?

In fact we did find Solomon's city – on the tell proper. When we dug under the later strata we discovered Solomon's fortifications. This was what we call a casemate wall: a double wall with an outer and inner wall divided into rooms. Nearby we found Solomon's city gate. We were struck by the fact that it was very similar in plan to a gate discovered many years ago in Megiddo, and also attributed to Solomon. The reason was, of course, that Solomon rebuilt three cities: Gezer, near Jerusalem, Megiddo and Hazor. So we copied the plan of the Megiddo gate just before proceeding with the excavation. We marked it on the ground and said to our workers, 'Dig here and you will find a wall. Dig here and you will find a room.'

Of course, when things turned out exactly as we'd said, they thought we were wizards! However, the workers who knew their Bible – when I re-read the Bible passage to them – realized how we arrived at this solution. Our prestige went down tremendously; that of the Bible was never higher.

So in Megiddo and Hazor gates were found of exactly the same plan, the same dimensions. What about the third city – Gezer – mentioned in that passage in the book of Kings . . .? Because of the biblical passage I decided to unearth the three-volume report of Macalister's much earlier excavations there. To my great surprise and delight, in the first volume I found what Macalister called a plan of the Maccabean castle, which looked identical to our gate and casemate wall. He had excavated only half the gate, and because of that it was not visible. But I published an article suggesting that this was in fact Solomon's gate and fortifications . . .

In recent years an American expedition from the Hebrew Union College went to Gezer, and one of their aims was to test my theory. They were very cautious. But they did find the second half of the gate, and what is more important, on the floor of the gate they found pottery from the 10th century – Solomon's time. So in all three cities mentioned in the Bible as rebuilt by Solomon, identical fortifications and gates were found. **❞**

Solomon's city gate at Hazor – dramatic support for the Bible's historical accuracy.

Egyptian warship

Merchant ship from King Solomon's fleet

Verse 14: Good News Bible gives 23,000 kilogrammes. The purchasing-power of the bullion is not known.
600 shekels (16): 'almost 7 kilogrammes'.
3 minas (17): 'almost 2 kilogrammes'.

House of Joseph (28): the tribes of Ephraim and Manasseh.
Book of the annals of Solomon (41): otherwise unknown.
Verses 41-43: this formula, with slight variations, is repeated throughout Kings at the end of each reign.

Bronze lion-weights from Assyria. The large one is inscribed '3 shekels'; the small '15 minas'.

11 Solomon's folly, and his enemies

Verses 1-13: Solomon's political marriage-alliances no doubt contribute to the country's peace and security. But foreign wives bring with them foreign gods. And Solomon in his old age turns from God to worship idols – a sin which costs his son the greater part of his kingdom and divides the nation.

Solomon's reign is not wholly trouble-free. In the south there is trouble from Hadad of Edom (14-22; a story reminiscent of Joseph's); in the north from Rezon of Damascus (23-25); and within his own nation there is Jeroboam (26-40), the man destined by God to rule over the ten breakaway tribes after the king's death.

Ashtoreth, Milcom, Chemosh, Molech (5, 7): worship of these gods involved perverted and gruesome practices – child sacrifice, fertility rites, prostitution, sexual deviations.
One tribe (13): the southern state of Judah also included the much smaller tribe of Benjamin (12:21). The other ten tribes broke away to form the northern kingdom of Israel.

12 – 14
THE KINGDOM SPLITS IN TWO

It was never easy to hold the twelve tribes together. Ephraim, in particular, envied Judah's power. A split had threatened in David's day (2 Samuel 20). The secret of national unity and strength always lay in the bond of common worship of the one God. The monarchy in itself was no substitute. Without the religious tie, king and people would go down together, as Samuel so clearly foresaw at Saul's coronation. 'If both you and the king ... will follow the Lord your God, it will be well; but if you ... rebel against the commandment of the Lord, then the hand of the Lord will be against you and your king' (1 Samuel 12:14-15). The nation's history as recounted in Kings fully bears this out. The division is a direct consequence of Solomon's idolatry. And as Israel strays further and

The Seal of Shema, who served King Jeroboam II of Israel, inscribed:
'(belonging) to Shema,
Servant of Jeroboam'
This is a bronze cast of the jasper original.

THE DIVISION OF THE KINGDOM

Dan

ISRAEL

Shechem

Penuel

Bethel

Jerusalem

JUDAH

PHILISTIA

resulted in the near-extinction of the royal house of Judah at the hands of Queen Athaliah.

Scorpions (11): barbed whips used on slaves.

Adoram (18): the Adoniram of 4:6; 5:14.

180,000 (21): the figure seems too high. See 'The Large Numbers of the Old Testament', page 191.

12:25-33 Jeroboam king in Israel; a new capital and new religious centres

Jerusalem had been the religious centre of the united kingdom. Jeroboam now creates two new sanctuaries for the northern kingdom to counter its draw and prevent the people from going to Jerusalem and coming under the influence of the king of Judah. But his action encouraged idolatry, and as time went by Israelite worship became more and more degenerate.

One of the centres of Jeroboam's rival religion was Dan, pictured here. The phrase 'Dan to Beersheba' referred to all Israel, from Dan in the far north to Beersheba in the south.

further from the law and worship of God, things go from bad to worse. Internal strife weakens both kingdoms. The nation becomes prey to stronger neighbours, and is eventually devoured by the great powers.

12:1-24 Rehoboam succeeds Solomon; the revolt

The northern tribes find a leader and spokesman in Jeroboam. But negotiations break down in face of Rehoboam's strong-arm tactics. The rebel tribes declare independence and set up the rival kingdom of Israel, but this kingdom never enjoyed the stability of a single dynasty as did Judah.

The division is permanent, with a constant state of hot or cold war between the kingdoms. Only in the reigns of Ahab-Ahaziah-Joram in Israel and Jehoshaphat-Joram-Ahaziah in Judah was the breach temporarily healed through a marriage alliance. And that

13 The man of God from Judah

The man of God from Judah is wrong to accept the old prophet's word when it contradicts God's own word to him. His death is a sign to Jeroboam and Israel of the severity with which God deals with disobedience. But there are none so blind as those who will not see (33).

Josiah (2): the king who initiated the most thoroughgoing reform in Judah. See 2 Kings 23.

Dried up/shrivelled (4): paralysed.

A lion (24): lions roamed Palestine, particularly the Jordan Valley, until the Middle Ages. Here the strange sight of the lion standing by its prey but leaving both the body and the ass untouched marks the event as having special significance. It is a 'sign' to Israel.

14:1-20 Ahijah's prophecy against Jeroboam

Ahijah had predicted Jeroboam's rise (11:29ff.). Now he announces his downfall.

Lion killing a man: an ivory from an Assyrian palace at Nimrud (ancient Kalah), 9th century BC.

This bracelet may have been made from gold plundered from the temple. It belonged to Nemoreth, son of Pharaoh Shishak who conquered Rehoboam and stripped the temple of gold.

Properly buried (13): meaning that all the rest will die violently.

Scatter them beyond the Euphrates (15): Israel was taken into exile by Assyria after the fall of Samaria (2 Kings 17).

Tirzah (17): capital of Israel in Baasha's day (15:33).

Book of the Chronicles, (19, some versions**):** not the same as Chronicles in the Bible.

14:21-31 Rehoboam's reign in Judah

The southern kingdom also turns back to pagan gods. The weakened state loses the temple treasures to the invading Egyptian pharaoh. See 2 Chronicles 12:1-12.

Shishak (25): Sheshonq, Libyan founder of the Egyptian 22nd dynasty. He left a record of his campaign carved on a temple in Karnak, Egypt.

15 — 16:28
KINGS OF ISRAEL AND JUDAH

The dates for the kings of Judah in this section include a number of periods of co-regency between one king and his predecessor. Almost all the dates given can only be approximate. See 'Unravelling the Chronology of the Kings', page 269.

15: 1-24 Abijam (Abijah) and Asa of Judah

The writer of Kings defines a good king as one who promotes the worship of God; a bad king as one who strays into idolatrous practices. On this definition, Abijam's three-year reign (about 913-911) was a bad one (see 2 Chronicles 13). Asa, by contrast, was a good king. He ruled for 41 years, about 911-870. The war with Israel continued but he made an alliance with Syria. See 2 Chronicles 15-16.

The case of Uriah the Hittite (5): see 2 Samuel 11.

Maacah (10, 13): Asa's 'grand'mother.

Ramah (17): only a few miles north of Jerusalem.

15:25—16:28 Kings of Israel

All Israel's kings were automatically bad by the writer's definition, though some were worse than others. After ruling for two years (910-909) Nadab (15:25-32) was murdered by Baasha.

15:33-16:7: Baasha introduces a new dynasty and rules Israel for 24 years, about 909-886.

16:8-14: his successor, Elah, rules for two years (886-885) before his assassination by Zimri.

16:15-20: Zimri introduces a shortlived new dynasty (885) and commits suicide when under siege by Omri.

16:21-28: although only briefly mentioned here, Omri was one of Israel's most powerful kings politically. He introduces a new dynasty and rules for 12 years, about 885-874, fortifying Samaria as his new capital. For 150 years from this time, Assyria refers to Israel as 'the land of Omri'.

According to the word of the Lord (15:29): see 14:6-16.

Jehu (16:1): a prophet, not the later king.

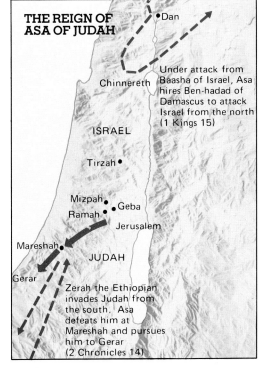

THE REIGN OF ASA OF JUDAH

Dan

Chinnereth

Under attack from Baasha of Israel, Asa hires Ben-hadad of Damascus to attack Israel from the north (1 Kings 15)

ISRAEL

Tirzah

Mizpah
Geba
Ramah
Jerusalem

Mareshah

JUDAH

Gerar

Zerah the Ethiopian invades Judah from the south. Asa defeats him at Mareshah and pursues him to Gerar (2 Chronicles 14)

16:29—2 KINGS 1
KING AHAB AND THE PROPHET ELIJAH

Religious life in Israel reached an all-time low in Ahab's 22-year reign. He and his thoroughly evil wife, Jezebel of Tyre, introduced the corrupt worship of the Phoenician god Melqart (the 'Baal' of these chapters). Into this crisis situation God sent Elijah, the greatest of all the prophets (see Matthew 17:3 and 10-13).

16:29-34 Ahab of Israel 874-853
Verse 34: see Joshua 6:26.

17 Elijah predicts drought; the widow of Zarephath

Baal was worshipped as a weather-god. God therefore stages a demonstration to show that he alone has power over sun and rain. And he provides for Elijah in

Palestinian woman making bread; a pottery model.

A short way down a track from the top of Mt Carmel lies a natural amphitheatre, littered with stones. The track leads on down to the brook below. At the top of the hill there is a view across to the sea.

Baal's own country, at Zarephath near Sidon!

Verse 21: Elijah may have used the 'kiss of life'; but the cure was the result of his prayer, not just a particular method of resuscitation.

18 The contest with the prophets of Baal on Mt Carmel

After three years, in which Jezebel has done her best to eliminate the worship of God in Israel (4), Elijah returns with a challenge. Baal should have been able to produce fire as readily as rain. But the result of the contest provides tangible evidence that God is God, and Baal is impotent. Even so, there was no deep and lasting religious reform.

He ran ahead of Ahab (46): 17 miles to the summer palace at Jezreel.

19 The escape to Sinai; Elisha's call

Elation passes. Spiritual and physical strain leave Elijah in the grip of depression, fear, disappointment. Jezebel still holds the whip hand. Elijah escapes south to the desert and Sinai (Mt Horeb). In the place where God made himself known to Moses, he speaks to Elijah, out of the stillness. Self-pity is dealt with, a sense of proportion restored, and the path ahead mapped out. Elijah had felt himself intolerably alone, his work finished. He is given a companion and successor, Elisha. God's work goes on.

Anoint Hazael ... and Jehu ... and Elisha (15-16): Elisha is 'anointed', called to become a prophet, by Elijah's symbolic action in throwing his cloak around him. But Elijah leaves the anointing of Hazael and Jehu to Elisha (2 Kings 8-9).

20 War between Israel and Syria

Benhadad of Syria and the allied kings of 32 city-states attack Samaria. The diplomatic exchange (2-9) is difficult to follow. But Benhadad has to eat his words in face of Israel's double victory. Ahab spares his life, but in doing so stores up trouble for Israel. (Israel and Syria fought as allies against Shalmaneser III of Assyria at Qarqar in 853, but later fell out – see 22:1-2.)

All the people/the rest (15): the Israelite army.

ELIJAH

Zarephath

Mt Carmel △

Jezreel • Tishbe
Brook Cherith

• Samaria

• Beersheba

To Horeb (Sinai)

WARS WITH SYRIA

SYRIA

1st Syrian attack on Israel

2nd Syrian attack

Israel defeats Syrians at Aphek

• Ramoth-gilead

Jezreel

Samaria •

ISRAEL

Ahab and Jehoshaphat set out to take Ramoth-gilead but are defeated by the Syrians (1 Kings 22)

Jerusalem •

JUDAH

The contest with the prophets of Baal on Carmel challenged them on their own ground: Baal as a weather-god is depicted here holding axe and thunderbolt; 8th century BC, from Syria.

100,000 ... 27,000 (29-30): the figures seem exaggeratedly high. See 'The Large Numbers of the Old Testament', page 191.
My father ... your father (34): meaning ancestor, not actual father.

A vineyard, with the flat-roofed house of its owner.

21 Ahab takes Naboth's vineyard; Elijah pronounces judgement

Seizure or compulsory purchase of land was illegal in Israel. A man's heritage had to be handed on to the next generation. But other people's rights do not bother Jezebel. While her husband sulks like a spoilt child, she quietly arranges for Naboth's liquidation. She has only to contrive a blasphemy charge – backed of course by the statutory number of witnesses – and the 'criminal's' lands are forfeit. Elijah, the old prophet of doom, is the only fly in the ointment. But Elijah speaks true (see 22:37; 2 Kings 9:30-37).

22:1-40 The alliance with Judah; Micaiah's prophecy; Ahab's death

See also 2 Chronicles 18. Jehoshaphat's son Jehoram has married Ahab's daughter Athaliah. Israel and Judah are, temporarily, allies against Syria. It is Jehoshaphat's request which brings Micaiah to the king with his fateful prophecy. The warning is ignored, and Ahab meets his death in battle at Ramoth-gilead, east of the Jordan. (For true and false prophets, see on 2 Chronicles 18).

22:41-50 Jehoshaphat of Judah 873-848

See 2 Chronicles 17-20. Jehoshaphat was a 'good' king. He reigned 25 years.
Verse 48: see on chapters 9 and 10. The strong north winds may have blown the fleet on to the rocks.

22:51—2 Kings 1, Ahaziah of Israel 853-852

Ahaziah reigned two years during which time Moab seized independence. Ahaziah consults the Philistine god after a fall and Elijah pronounces God's judgement on his idolatry. It takes three military posses to bring Elijah to the king. But nothing can alter the sentence.
Baalzebub (1:3): 'Lord of the flies', a derogatory pun on the god's real name, Baalzebul.

Ivory of a woman in the style of the period.

Unravelling the Chronology of the Kings

ARTHUR CUNDALL

At first glance there seems to be quite enough data on the kings of Israel and Judah to construct an accurate time-chart.

The reign of each king is clearly given (except for Saul: 1 Samuel 13:1 is uncertain); and during the period after the split between Israel and Judah, the accession of each king is related to the reign of the king in the other kingdom.

There are also 'check-points', where one event simultaneously affected both kingdoms, such as Jehu's slaying of Joram of Israel and Ahaziah of Judah on the same day (2 Kings 9:21-28). The historian has carefully integrated the chronologies of the two kingdoms. He keeps both histories parallel by dealing with the whole reign of one king from his accession until his death, and then returning to deal with the kings of the other kingdom whose reigns *began* during this period. The only exception is in 2 Kings 8-9 where Jehu's murder of Joram and Ahaziah made it necessary for the historian to mention Jehoram and Ahaziah of Judah (2 Kings 8:16-29), who would not normally have been dealt with until after the death of Joram of Israel.

Problems
However, serious problems arise on closer inspection. For instance, in Judah, the total from Rehoboam to Ahaziah's death is 95 years, whereas the identical period of Israel, from Jeroboam to Joram's death, totals 98 years.

A greater discrepancy appears in the period from Jehu's coup to the fall of Samaria. There the combined total for Judah's kings is 165 years and that for Israel is only 144 years. A further minor problem is that although we are told Queen Athaliah the usurper reigned for six years (2 Kings 11:3), she was not included in the normal chronological scheme.

We have another headache in the apparently conflicting dates for the accession of Jehoram of Israel (2 Kings 1:17 and 3:1). It is reasonably certain that Solomon's death cannot have been earlier than 930 BC, which makes the period between this event and the fall of Jerusalem in 587 BC about 343 years. But the lowest total we can set to the biblical figures supplied for this period is about 372 years.

Clues
Three factors, however, greatly increase our understanding of the apparent problems of the chronology of the period and go a long way towards resolving them completely.

- **Two different methods of reckoning the reigns of the kings were used in the ancient Near East.** One was the 'non-accession-year' method, the other the 'accession-year' method.

In the non-accession-year (or ante-dating) system the death of a king meant that a year was counted twice, since the portion of the year falling to the king who died was counted as a full year to him, whilst the re-mainder of the year was counted as a full year to his successor. To reduce this system to an accurate chronological reckoning, one year must be deducted for each king who reigned.

The accession-year (or post-dating) system did not count any *portion* of a year in the total years of a king's reign. The portion of the year falling to a king *before* his first, full calendar-year, was regarded as his accession year. This system allowed for an accurate chronological reckoning.

It is clear that, in the early period of the divided monarchy Israel used the first method and Judah the second. The discrepancy in totals between the two kingdoms corresponds to the greater number of Israelite kings in this period. A possible further complication is evidence suggesting that the year in Judah (in the earlier part of the period at any rate) began in the month of Tishri (September/October), whilst the year in Israel began in the month Nisan (March/April).

- **Some reigns overlap because of the practice of co-regencies.** The precedent for this is found in the case of David and Solomon, which effectively prevented Adonijah seizing power (1 Kings 1). Another clear instance is the case of Jotham, who acted as co-regent when his father Uzziah was smitten with leprosy (2 Chronicles 26:21). No doubt this practice, which appears to have been confined to Judah, lent stability to David's dynasty.

Most scholars accept co-regencies between Asa and Jehoshaphat, Jehoshaphat and Jehoram, Amaziah and Uzziah, Jotham and Ahaz, Ahaz and Hezekiah, and Hezekiah and Manasseh. In certain cases »»

Ahab's administrative organization is illustrated by the size of storage buildings at Megiddo. He supplied 2,000 chariots and 10,000 men to an anti-Assyrian alliance.

Hitching-posts and water-trough for donkeys carrying goods to the storehouses at Megiddo.

the younger man (for example, Hezekiah) outshone his father (Ahaz) and this has led to events being dated by reference to the co-regent rather than to the actual king (e.g. 2 Kings 18:9-10).

An awareness of this custom means a reduction of the over-all total of the reigns of Judean kings, and also helps us to understand the significance of the biblical figures. For example, Manasseh of Judah reigned from 687 to 642 BC. 2 Kings 21:1 says he reigned for 55 years, which leads us to assume a co-regency from 697 to 687, made the more plausible by Hezekiah's severe illness (2 Kings 20:1).

■ **Some reigns may have taken place at the same time as each other.** This is probably what happened in the northern kingdom of Israel during the last turbulent decades after the death of Jeroboam II. The combined reigns of the six kings of this period is 41 years 7 months, whereas historically the period cannot have been more than 31 years; indeed, most scholars hold that it was only about 24 years. The probability is that, in a period of near-anarchy, there were occasions when rival kings were 'ruling' over different parts of the kingdom at the same time.

External checks
By a careful application of these factors, the chronologies of Judah and Israel can be integrated. But the process of relating the resultant chronology to the events of the surrounding world, to obtain an absolute rather than a relative chronology, has been made possible largely by archaeological discovery. The most significant finds are as follows:

■ **The Assyrian Limmu or Eponym lists.** In Assyria an official holding annual office gave his name to that particular year. Remarkably complete lists of these officials have survived covering the period 892-648 BC, and significant events during their period of office were noted down. An eclipse of the sun is mentioned in the month Simanu when Bur-Sagale was *Limmu,* which astronomers have fixed as occurring on 15 June 763 BC. This provides a reliable basis for determining all other dates in the *Limmu* lists. Since biblical and Assyrian histories converge at various points, biblical events can also be dated accurately.

■ **The Khorsabad king list.** This, and duplicate copies, gives a complete list of Assyrian kings until 745 BC, often including the length of their reigns. This list agrees with the *Limmu* list.

■ **The Canon of Ptolemy.** Although this work dates from the 2nd century AD, its accuracy has been demonstrated beyond any reasonable doubt. It preserves the names and

Numerous ivories from Ahab's period have been found – including many from Samaria itself. This one is of a winged creature, typical of the decoration of the period.

The remains of Ahab's palace on the top of the fortified hill of Samaria.

lengths of reign of the Babylonian kings from the accession of Nabonassar in 747 BC.

■ **The Babylonian Chronicle.** These tablets, some only recently published, deal with Babylonian history during the period from Hezekiah to the fall of Jerusalem. They are of special interest to biblical scholars for the period when Judah was subject to Babylon, i.e. after 605 BC. Many facts which before were not clear have now been resolved. For instance, it was not known what encouraged the Judean king, Jehoiakim, to rebel against the Babylonians in 601/600 BC, or why the revolt was not put down until 598/597 BC. The Babylonian Chronicle tells us that in November/December 601 BC there was a fierce encounter between Babylonia and Egypt on the borders of Egypt. Although the battle was indecisive, Babylonian losses were great and meant a withdrawal from the area and a regrouping of the army. It was this apparent weakness which led Jehoiakim to rebel. The Chronicle gives the only exact date for an event in Old Testament history, the capture of Jerusalem on 15-16 March 597 BC.

One minor problem remains. It is not certain whether the Hebrew civil year uniformly followed the Babylonian pattern. This makes for an uncertainty of one year in dates during the reign of Zedekiah, the last king of Judah. The fall of Jerusalem, for example, is given as either 587 or 586 BC. The two modes of reckoning appear in Jeremiah 52:12 and 29, where, on first sight, the prisoners were taken from Jerusalem a year before it was captured!

■ **Numerous contemporary inscriptions** also relate to particular events: such as the battle of Qarqar in 853 BC, fought between Assyria and a coalition of small states including Israel under King Ahab; or Jehu's payment of tribute to the Assyrian king, Shalmaneser III, in 841 BC; or the fall of Samaria to the Assyrians in 722/721 BC. These records supply reliable pegs on which to hang the biblical information.

By carefully applying the principles underlying the biblical chronologies, and correlating them with the fixed chronology made possible by contacts between Judah and Israel and contemporary world-powers, we can establish an absolute chronology, including all the biblical data, which is accurate to within a year for the greater part of the period of the kings. The reign of Saul remains an exception. The 40 years given in Acts 13:21 is probably a round figure, and seems to be too high. Since '2' is the only figure remaining in the Hebrew text, most scholars accept that a tens-unit has dropped out and suggest a reign of 12, 22 or 32 years. Twenty-two is probably the most acceptable since it fits in best with other chronological data, such as the period of the Judges.

2—8:15
STORIES OF ELISHA

2 Elijah's dramatic exit

Elijah seems to want to face this last
experience alone. But Elisha stays with
him right through the journey. The final
scene – the whirlwind which catches up
the prophet, and Elisha's vision of a fiery
chariot and horses – is played out east of
the Jordan, close to the place where
Moses died. It is a remarkable end to a
remarkable life. Elijah's reappearance at
the transfiguration of Jesus (Matthew
17) underlines the unique position of
this man amongst all the prophets of
God. Elisha, left alone, takes up his task
straight away.

Prophets (3): groups possessing ecstatic
gifts; not always men of high spiritual
calibre.

A double share (9): i.e. the portion which
fell to the heir, the eldest son, who
inherited twice as much as anyone else.
So Elisha asks, not for twice Elijah's
spiritual power, but, as the Good News
Bible makes plain, for the share which
would mark him out as the prophet's
spiritual heir.

Chariots of Israel (12): Israel's defender;
Elijah was of more value to the nation
than its armed forces.

Some boys (23): Young men – local louts,
yelling abuse at the prophet and his God,
telling him to 'Go up' like Elijah.

3 Jehoram (Joram) of Israel, 852-841, and the Moabites

Jehoram reigned 12 years. A punitive
expedition against Moab by the allied
forces of Israel, Judah and Edom is made
hazardous by drought. Elisha, his
faculties stimulated by music (a
common prophetic custom), promises
an end to the drought, and victory.

Who poured water (11): i.e. who served
Elijah; 'Elijah's assistant', Good News Bible.

*Jericho, city of palms, still depends on its springs;
the mound of ancient Jericho (with the white hut)
rises behind.*

Verse 27: the sacrifice of the king's son so heartened the Moabites, or so terrified the Israelites, that the advance was halted.

4 Four of Elisha's miracles

Elisha's miracles, like those of Jesus, show God's care for ordinary people and their needs. Verses 1-7: the widow whose children were to become slaves to discharge her debts; 8-37 the childless woman of Shunem who gave Elisha generous hospitality; 38-41 and 42-44 the feeding of the hungry. These are not necessarily recounted in chronological order.

My head (19): the child had sunstroke.
Neither new moon nor sabbath (23): special times of religious observance when it would be natural to visit a holy man. The woman did not tell her husband the child was dead.
Wild gourds (39): in the famine one man gathered colocynths, a powerful laxative, bitter and poisonous in large quantities.
Bread from the first-ripe grain (42): the offering normally made to the priests at the beginning of the harvest.

5 The healing of Naaman the leper

God's concern is not limited to Israel (see Luke 4:27; Syria was often at war with Israel, and Naaman was the army commander). A young Israelite slave-girl, captured in a border raid, tells her Syrian master of Elisha's power. A visit is arranged through diplomatic channels. The prophet's instructions are not what Naaman expected. But his staff persuade him to try, and he is healed. Deeply impressed by the cure and Elisha's refusal of payment, the army chief of Syria becomes a follower of the God of Israel. Gehazi's greed might have undone it all, and could not go unpunished.

Talents, shekels (5): there were no coins

The Jordan river is certainly unpretentious compared to the rivers of Naaman's home-country; here it winds through Galilee.

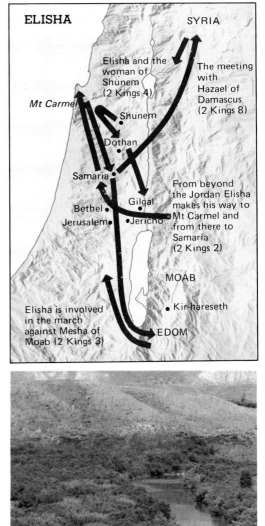

ELISHA

SYRIA

Elisha and the woman of Shunem (2 Kings 4)

The meeting with Hazael of Damascus (2 Kings 8)

Mt Carmel

Shunem

Dothan

Samaria

Gilgal

Bethel

Jerusalem

Jericho

From beyond the Jordan Elisha makes his way to Mt Carmel and from there to Samaria (2 Kings 2)

MOAB

Kir-hareseth

Elisha is involved in the march against Mesha of Moab (2 Kings 3)

EDOM

as yet; these were weights: see page 104.
Verse: 17: he took soil from the land of Israel's God so that he could worship him in his own land, not realizing his character as God of the whole world.

6:1-23 Elisha and the Syrian army

Verses 1-7: the floating axe-head. The thick woods of the Jordan Valley provide a ready source of timber for the new community building needed by the prophets. Elisha's miracle was simply an act of disinterested kindness.

Verses 8-23: God's people are under his protection, and this is a very real thing. Elisha seemed at the mercy of the Syrian army. In fact he has them in the palm of his hand – and shows *them* mercy.
Dothan (13): ten miles north of Samaria.

6:24 — 7:20 The siege of Samaria

The peace secured by Elisha (23) did not last for ever. Samaria is besieged by the Syrians and reduced to starvation and cannibalism. The king blames Elisha for telling him to hold out and promising deliverance (33). The lepers, who depended on gifts of food, are worse off

The defences of Samaria, overlooking the surrounding country occupied by the besieging army.

than most. Their desperate hunger makes them the first to discover the truth of Elisha's prediction. The Syrian army fled at the approach, so they thought, of a relief force.
6:25: the ass was an 'unclean' animal, forbidden food; dove's dung, some kind of weed. In the famine, both fetched astronomical prices.

8:1-15 Elisha and Hazael of Damascus

Verses 1-6 belong in time after 4:8-37 and before Gehazi's leprosy, 5:25-27.

Verses 7-15: Elisha fulfils God's commission to Elijah (1 Kings 19:15). Hazael, like Macbeth, resorts to murder to turn prediction into fact and seize the throne.

8:16 — 17:41
KINGS OF ISRAEL AND JUDAH TO THE FALL OF SAMARIA

The writer returns to the history of the kings which has been interrupted by the stories of Elisha.

8:16-24 Jehoram of Judah 853-841

Jehoram was a 'bad' king, influenced by his wife Athaliah, daughter of Ahab and Jezebel. He reigned eight years plus a co-regency, during which time successful revolts by Edom (to the south-east) and Libnah (on the Philistine border, south-west) crippled Judah. See 2 Chronicles 21.

8:25-29 Ahaziah of Judah 841

Ahaziah was another king who turned from God and went his own way. He reigned only one year. See 2 Chronicles 22.

9 Jehu anointed king of Israel (841-814); death of King Joram and Jezebel, the queen mother

Elisha carries out the last of Elijah's commissions (1 Kings 19:16) while the armies of Israel and Judah are defending Ramoth-gilead against Syria. With the king conveniently recovering from his wounds at Jezreel, 35 miles away, the time is ripe for Jehu's coup.

This mad fellow (11): the man's ecstatic state enables the army officers to recognize him as a prophet.

The property of Naboth (21): the vineyard seized by Ahab, 1 Kings 21.

Verse 26: see 1 Kings 21:19.

She painted her eyes (30): women's makeup, even in those days, was sophisticated: black kohl to outline the eyes; blue eyeshadow from lapis lazuli; crushed cochineal to serve as lipstick; and scarlet henna to paint finger- and toe-nails. There were also powders, and an array of perfumes and ointments.

You Zimri (31): King Elah's assassin, 1 Kings 16:8-10.

The word of the Lord...by...Elijah (36): 1 Kings 21:23.

10 Jehu's purge

Jehu's reign opens with a blood-bath in which all Ahab's family (1-11), many of the royal house of Judah (12-14), and the prophets, priests and worshippers of Baal (18-27) lose their lives. Objects connected

The Black Obelisk

The Assyrian King Shalmaneser III erected an obelisk in honour of his own victories. It includes a panel which reads:

66 The tribute of Jehu, son of Omri. Silver, gold, a golden bowl, a golden vase, golden cups, golden buckets, tin, a staff for the royal hand (?), **99** *puruhati*-fruits.

The scene from the Black Obelisk specifically mentioning Jehu. Here Jehu, or his envoy, brings tribute.

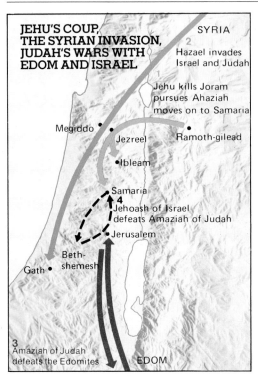

**JEHU'S COUP,
THE SYRIAN INVASION,
JUDAH'S WARS WITH
EDOM AND ISRAEL**

SYRIA
2
Hazael invades
Israel and Judah

Jehu kills Joram
pursues Ahaziah
moves on to Samaria

Megiddo

Jezreel   Ramoth-gilead

•Ibleam

Samaria
4
Jehoash of Israel
defeats Amaziah of Judah

•Jerusalem

Beth-
shemesh

Gath •

3
Amaziah of Judah
defeats the Edomites   EDOM

with Baal-worship are destroyed. But Jeroboam's shrines at Bethel and Dan are left and God's law neglected. Jehu reigned 28 years, starting a new dynasty. During his reign, territory east of Jordan was lost to Syria.

11:1-20 Queen Athaliah of Judah 841-835

Athaliah reigned six years. See 2 Chronicles 22:10–23:21. These are some of the darkest days in the nation's history. The royal line of David is all but wiped out; only the baby Joash survives. The priest Jehoiada (husband of princess Jehosheba, who rescued Joash) leads the well-planned and virtually bloodless coup which puts Joash on the throne. The constitutional monarchy is restored, and loyalty to God reaffirmed in the swearing of a new covenant-pact.

11:21—12:21 Joash of Judah 835-796; the temple repaired

Joash was one of Judah's best kings,

ruling for 40 years. See 2 Chronicles 24. Under Jehoiada's guidance Joash rules well. But for some years money intended for temple repairs gets no further than the priests. A new method of collection is devised and the work put in hand. Funds come from tax (2 Chronicles 24:6; Exodus 30:11-16) and freewill offerings. Joash's later years see a decline in political (17ff.), moral and religious spheres (2 Chronicles 24:17ff.). Syria makes inroads into Judah and threatens Jerusalem. The king dies at the hands of his servants.

13:1-9 Jehoahaz of Israel 814-798

Jehoahaz reigned 17 years during which time Israel fell under Syrian domination.
The deliverer (5): various suggestions have been made: Adad-nirari of Assyria, who took tribute from Damascus and from Jehoash of Israel; Jeroboam II; Elisha.
Verse 7: contrast Ahab's 2,000 chariots.

13:10-25 Jehoash of Israel 798-782

Jehoash reigned 16 years. There was war with Judah. Elisha's last prediction of victory over Syria is realized. The prophet dies.
Chariots of Israel (14): see on 2:12.

14:1-22 Amaziah of Judah 796-767

Amaziah was a 'good' king who reigned 29 years. See 2 Chronicles 25. Victory over Edom goes to his head. The disastrous challenge to Jehoash brings the forces of Israel right into Jerusalem, looting the temple and other treasures. The people make Azariah co-regent. A further conspiracy against Amaziah ends in his death at Lachish.
In the book of the law of Moses (6): Deuteronomy 24:16.
Valley of Salt (7): the area south of the Dead Sea.
A thistle on Lebanon (9): Joash replies in sneering parable to Amaziah's foolhardy challenge to battle
Elath (22): Ezion-geber on the Gulf of

A relief of Tiglath-pileser III, king of Assyria, from the Palace at Nimrud.

Dramatic evidence of Tiglath-pileser III's invasion of Hazor is this hurriedly-built wall, put up on the eve of the invasion.

Aqaba, naval base of Solomon's Red Sea fleet. The port fell into the hands of the Edomites but was recovered by Amaziah's victory.

14:23-29 Jeroboam II of Israel 793-753

Jeroboam II ruled for 41 years, including a time as co-regent. He was politically strong, dominating the land from north of Lebanon (Hamath) to the Dead Sea (Sea of Arabah). He defeated a weakened Syria. Jeroboam's reign is Israel's Indian summer. After his death the nation falls apart. Amos (2:6ff.) and Hosea reveal the corruption within Israel: extremes of wealth and poverty: the grinding down of the poor and the weak.

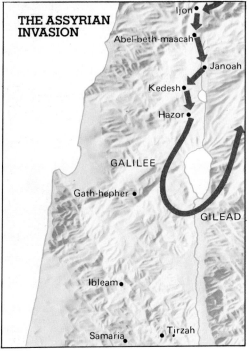

THE ASSYRIAN INVASION

Ijon

Abel-beth-maacah

Janoah

Kedesh

Hazor

GALILEE

Gath-hepher

GILEAD

Ibleam

Tirzah

Samaria

Menahem's tribute was reckoned by scribes, as in this Assyrian relief of the conquests of Tiglath-pileser III from Nimrud.

How he...are they not written (28): the meaning of the text is not clear.

15:1-7 Azariah (Uzziah) of Judah 791-740

Azariah, a 'good' king, reigned 52 years, including a time as co-regent. See 2 Chronicles 26. Azariah was a strong king who defeated the Philistines and Arabs and reduced Ammon to a vassal state. But pride brought him to an unpleasant end (5; 2 Chronicles 26:16ff.).

15:8-31 The succession of Israel 753-732

Verses 8-12: Zechariah son of Jeroboam rules six months and is assassinated by Shallum, 753-752.

Verses 13-16: Shallum rules only one month before his assassination by Menahem.

Verses 17-22: Menahem introduces another new dynasty, rules 10 years (752-742) and becomes vassal to the powerful Tiglath-pileser III (Pul) of Assyria.

Verses 23-26: Pekahiah son of Menahem rules two years and is overthrown by an army coup led by Pekah, 740.

Verses 27-31: Pekah introduces a new dynasty and rules 20 years, dating his reign from Menahem's accession, 752-732. His anti-Assyrian policy leads to mass deportation of the people by Tiglath-pileser. He is assassinated by Hoshea.

15:32-38 Jotham of Judah 750-732

Jotham was a godly king. During his 16-year reign (and co-regency) he encountered opposition from Syria and Israel.

16 Ahaz of Judah 735-716

Ahaz was one of Judah's worst kings. See 2 Chronicles 28; Isaiah 7. During his 16-year reign and co-regency Judah was under attack from all quarters: Syria and Israel to the north; Edom and Philistia to the south. The temple was stripped of silver and gold to pay the heavy tribute demanded by Assyria in return for help. Some of Isaiah's prophecies date from this time.

17 Hoshea, last king of Israel, 732-723; Samaria falls to Assyria

Hoshea reigned nine years as Assyria's vassal. An attempt to win Egyptian support proved fatal. Samaria fell after a three-year siege, and the whole remaining population was deported. Israel's fate is seen as the direct consequence of long-standing idolatry, of pursuing heathen practices, disobeying the law, and ignoring the prophets (7-18).

Assyria repopulated the land with other conquered peoples, each with its own religion. But troubles are attributed to their failure to placate the local god, and an Israelite priest is sent back as a missionary. From this strange hotchpotch of religions a purer form of worship emerged amongst their descendants, the Samaritans.

Verse 6: the people were deported to

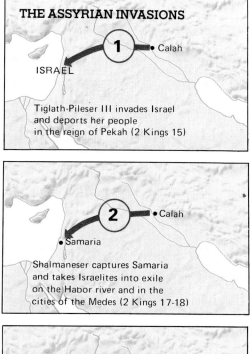

THE ASSYRIAN INVASIONS

1 — Calah — ISRAEL

Tiglath-Pileser III invades Israel and deports her people in the reign of Pekah (2 Kings 15)

2 — Calah — Samaria

Shalmaneser captures Samaria and takes Israelites into exile on the Habor river and in the cities of the Medes (2 Kings 17-18)

3 — Nineveh — Jerusalem

Sennacherib attacks the fortified cities of Judah and besieges Jerusalem (2 Kings 18-19)

north and east Mesopotamia (Halah, Gozan, Media): i.e. north-east Syria/Turkey and Iran.

18—25
KINGS OF JUDAH TO THE FALL OF JERUSALEM

18:1-12 Hezekiah's reign begins

Hezekiah was one of Judah's finest kings, and ruled for 29 years plus a co-regency, 729-687. See 2 Chronicles 29-32.

The bronze snake (4): see Numbers 21:4-9. This goes to show how easily an object which is innocent in itself can be misused once it has served its purpose.

Sennacherib's Prism

King Sennacherib of Assyria's own views about the siege of Jerusalem may be read on this hexagonal clay prism, inscribed with the details of his eight campaigns. It is also known as the 'Taylor Prism', and stands 15in/375mm high.

66 But as for Hezekiah, the Jew, who did not bow in submission to my yoke, forty-six of his strong walled towns and innumerable smaller villages in their neighbourhood I besieged and conquered by stamping down earth-ramps and then by bringing up battering rams, by the assault of foot-soldiers, by breaches, tunnelling and sapper operations. I made to come out from them 200,150 people, young and old, male and female, innumerable horses, mules, donkeys, camels, large and small cattle, and counted them as the spoils of war. He himself I shut up like a caged bird within Jerusalem, his royal city. I put watch-posts strictly around it and turned back to his disaster any who went out of its city gate. His towns which I had despoiled I cut off from his land, giving them to Mitinti, king of Ashdod, Padi, king of Ekron, and Sillibel, king of Gaza, and so reduced his land. Moreover, I fixed upon him an increase in the amount to be given as *katre-* presents for my lordship, in addition to the former tribute, to be given annually. As for Hezekiah, the awful splendour of my lordship overwhelmed him, and the irregular and regular troops which he had brought in to strengthen Jerusalem, his royal city, and had obtained for his protection, together with 30 talents of gold, 300 talents of silver, precious stones, antimony, large blocks of red stone, ivory (inlaid) couches, ivory arm-chairs, elephant hide, elephant tusks, ebony-wood, box-wood, all kinds of valuable treasures, as well as his daughters, concubines, male and female musicians he sent me later to Nineveh, my lordly city. He sent a personal messenger to deliver the tribute and make a slavish obeisance. 99

18:13-37 Sennacherib attacks Jerusalem

Eight years after the fall of Samaria, the Assyrians turn their attention to rebel Judah. Lachish, in the lowlands 30 miles south-west of Jerusalem, is besieged, and messengers sent to Hezekiah. The three Assyrians (the king's 'supreme commander, his chief officer and his field commander') are masters of psychological warfare. They refuse private talks with Hezekiah's cabinet, and insist on a public harangue. And they play on the people's fears by speaking Hebrew – not the diplomatic language, Aramaic – so that everyone understands. But their boast that God cannot save Judah from Assyria seals their fate.

Relief of Assyrian archers and slingers.

19 Hezekiah consults Isaiah; death in the Assyrian camp

See Isaiah 36-39; 2 Chronicles 32:9-23. Crisis brings out the best in the king. God answers his prayer and vindicates his trust. Isaiah's prophecy is fulfilled. Jerusalem is saved.

Isaiah (2): one of the great prophets of Judah. According to Isaiah 1:1 he prophesied during the reigns of Uzziah, Jotham, Ahaz and Hezekiah. His home was in Jerusalem. See further under the book of Isaiah.

Libnah (8): ten miles north of Lachish.

Tirhakah (9): Pharaoh Taharqa, of Sudanese descent; in charge of the army, but not yet on the throne.

Gozan (12): in north-east Syria; *Eden:* the Aramaean city-state of Bit-Adini on the Euphrates.

My hook (28): God will lead them meekly

captive as a man leads a bull or a horse.
The Assyrians drove rings through the
noses of captive kings.
The angel of the Lord went (35): it is not
clear what happened, possibly an outbreak
of bubonic plague. See 2 Chronicles
32:21; Isaiah 37:36.

20 Hezekiah's illness; the embassy from Babylon

Verses 1-11: to the people of the Old
Testament hope of life after death was
vague. The prospect of death fills
Hezekiah with distress (see also his
poem, recorded in Isaiah 38:9-20).
   Verses 12-21: Babylon at this time was
a small state south of Assyria, looking
for allies. Isaiah predicts its future
power, and the fate of Judah.
A poultice of figs (7): the routine
treatment for ulcers and boils.
Verse 11: 'made the shadow go back ten
steps on the stairway set up by King
Ahaz'– a staircase used as a form of
sundial.

*Siege of a walled city by Sennacherib – a
relief from Sennacherib's Palace at Nimrud.*

21:1-18 Manasseh 696-642

Manasseh was to Judah what King Ahab
had been to Israel. He reigned 55 years,
part of the time as co-regent, and
brought Judah to the point of no return;
a degradation worse than that of the
Canaanite nations the Israelites had
destroyed. The prophets declare God's
inevitable judgement. Jerusalem will
share the fate of Samaria. See also
2 Chronicles 33, which records a
complete change of heart before the end
of Manasseh's life (33:10-13).

21:19-26 Amon 642-640

Amon was another evil king. After ruling
two years he was assassinated by his
own house servants. See 2 Chronicles
33:21-25.

22 Josiah 640-609; Hilkiah discovers the book of the law

Josiah reigned 31 years. He was the best
of Judah's kings, carrying out thoroughgoing religious reform. See 2 Chronicles
34-35. A book of the law (probably a
copy of Deuteronomy) is found in the
course of repairing the temple. Reading
it shows just how far short of the
standards Judah has fallen – and the
penalty.

23:1-30 Josiah's reformation

Public reading of God's law is followed
by renewal of the covenant-pact with
God (1-3). Then comes a purge of public
places, ridding the land of objects
associated with pagan worship (4-14).
The clean-up extends beyond Judah to
former Israelite territory (15-20). The
neglected Feast of Passover is celebrated
once more (21-23; see 2 Chronicles 35),
and private malpractices dealt with
(24-25). God's judgement is delayed but
not reversed: the nation's heart is not
changed by an official reformation.
Josiah dies in futile conflict with
Pharaoh Necho, who was marching

to join forces with Assyria, after the Assyrian capital (Nineveh) had fallen to the Babylonians.

23:31-35 Jehoahaz 609

Jehoahaz was on the throne for an evil reign of three months. Then he was deported to Egypt by Necho. See 2 Chronicles 36:1-4.

23:36—24:7 Jehoiakim 609-597

Josiah's son Eliakim, renamed Jehoiakim as a sign of his subjection, was put on the throne by Pharaoh Necho. He ruled for 11 years. At first subject to Egypt, Jehoiakim became Babylon's subject after Egypt was defeated at Carchemish in 605. Judah remained a vassal of Nebuchadnezzar for three years, then defected to Egypt again. This brought more attacks from the Babylonians, and repeated warnings from the prophet Jeremiah. See also 2 Chronicles 36:5-8.

24:8-17 Jehoiachin 597

Jehoiakim's son, Jehoiachin, was removed from the throne after three months by Nebuchadnezzar. He was taken to Babylon with the treasures of Jerusalem and all the leading men of Judah.

24:18—25:30 Zedekiah 597-587; the destruction of Jerusalem

See also 2 Chronicles 36:11-21; Jeremiah 37-39. The new puppet king also rebels. Jerusalem suffers a terrible 18-month siege. Zedekiah attempts to escape south but is caught and taken to Babylon. The city falls to the Babylonian army, is looted and utterly destroyed. All but the poorest people, left under the governor, Gedaliah, are taken into exile. But Gedaliah is murdered and the people escape to Egypt to avoid the inevitable wrath of Babylon. 25:27-30 conveys a glimmer of hope. Under a new king in Babylon 35 years later, Jehoiachin, the deposed king of Judah, is released from prison and kindly treated.

BABYLONIAN ACCOUNT OF THE FALL OF JERUSALEM

The capture of Jerusalem is described on a Babylonian tablet as follows:

> In the seventh year, in the month of Kislev, the Babylonian king mustered his troops, and, having marched to the land of Hatti, besieged the city of Judah, and on the second day of the month of Adar took the city and captured the king. He appointed therein a king of his own choice, received its heavy tribute and sent (them) to Babylon.

An enemy's view of the 'tell', or mound, of Lachish. Extensive archaeological discoveries there include a mass grave and unmistakable signs of burning on the walls.

KINGS OF ISRAEL AND JUDAH

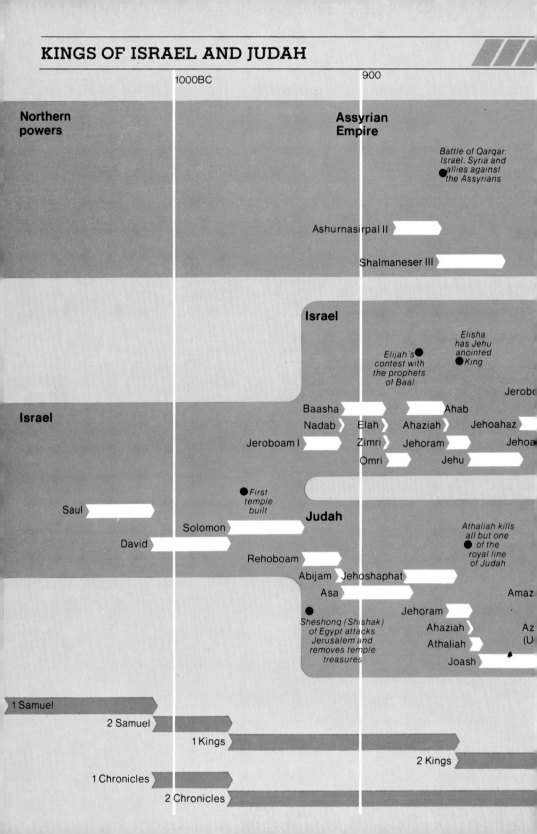

1000BC

900

Northern powers

Assyrian Empire

Battle of Qarqar: Israel, Syria and allies against the Assyrians

Ashurnasirpal II

Shalmaneser III

Israel

Elisha has Jehu anointed King

Elijah's contest with the prophets of Baal

Baasha
Nadab
Jeroboam I
Omri

Elah
Zimri

Ahab
Ahaziah
Jehoram
Jehu

Jerobo
Jehoahaz
Jehoa

Israel

Saul

First temple built

David

Solomon

Judah

Athaliah kills all but one of the royal line of Judah

Rehoboam
Abijam   Jehoshaphat
Asa

Amaz

Sheshonq (Shishak) of Egypt attacks Jerusalem and removes temple treasures

Jehoram
Ahaziah
Athaliah
Joash

Az
(U

1 Samuel

2 Samuel

1 Kings

2 Kings

1 Chronicles

2 Chronicles

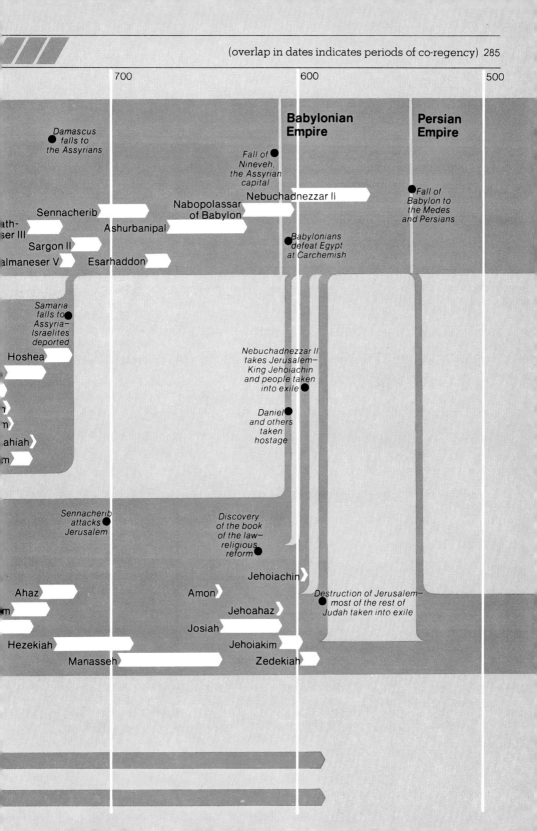

700

600

500

Babylonian Empire

Persian Empire

Damascus falls to the Assyrians

Fall of Nineveh, the Assyrian capital

Nebuchadnezzar II

Nabopolassar of Babylon

Fall of Babylon to the Medes and Persians

Sennacherib

Ashurbanipal

ath-
ser III

Sargon II

Babylonians defeat Egypt at Carchemish

almaneser V

Esarhaddon

Samaria falls to Assyria— Israelites deported

Hoshea

Nebuchadnezzar II takes Jerusalem— King Jehoiachin and people taken into exile

n
m

Daniel and others taken hostage

ahiah

m

Sennacherib attacks Jerusalem

Discovery of the book of the law— religious reform

Jehoiachin

Ahaz

Amon

Destruction of Jerusalem— most of the rest of Judah taken into exile

m

Jehoahaz

Josiah

Hezekiah

Jehoiakim

Manasseh

Zedekiah

1 and 2 Chronicles

On the face of it, Chronicles seems to repeat in duller and more moralistic fashion what we already have in 2 Samuel and Kings. In fact, the Chronicler was writing for those who knew the earlier books. He had no need to repeat, except in so far as it suited him. He was free to follow particular themes within a roughly chronological historical framework. And he was specially interested in two themes – true worship and true kingship in Israel – so he selected his historical material accordingly. (After the division of the kingdom, for example, he follows the fortunes of the kings of David's line only, ignoring the northern kingdom. And even in the introduction – the family-trees of chapters 1-9 – he concentrates on the southern tribes, Judah and Benjamin, and the tribe of Levi, which gave Israel her priests and ministers.) This is not to say, as some have done, that the Chronicler twists the facts of history to suit himself. A book does not have to be a history text-book to be historically reliable.

The Chronicler chose these particular themes with his original readers in mind – the men who had returned from exile to rebuild Jerusalem under Ezra and Nehemiah. (He may have written about 400 BC;

and his books form part of the longer series, Chronicles-Ezra-Nehemiah.) The new community needed to be linked with the past. They needed to know the right lines on which to re-establish patterns of worship. And, if history was not to repeat itself, they needed most of all to be reminded of the greatest lesson their history had to teach: that prosperity and well-being depend absolutely on faithfulness to God. Idolatry and neglect of God's law always has and always will result in judgement and disaster.

To assert the essential historical reliability of Chronicles is not to deny that there are problems. The Chronicler does not mind 'modernizing' – describing events in terms the people of his own day would understand. His high statistics are also a difficulty to modern (though not ancient) man. See 'The Large Numbers of the Old Testament', page 191. And names are often spelt differently in Chronicles from the earlier books, though changes made by those who copied the text must account for some at least of these. (It does no harm to remind ourselves of the wide variety in English spelling before Johnson compiled his dictionary – witness the various ways of spelling 'Shakespeare'.)

1 CHRONICLES

1—9
SKELETON FAMILY-TREE OF ISRAEL: ADAM TO THE EXILE AND AFTER

The lists are not intended to be complete. In line with his purpose the Chronicler gives most attention to the family of David, and the tribes of Judah, Benjamin and Levi (see introduction above). The family-trees provide a lead-in to the history which begins at chapter 10 and a link with those for whom the book was first written.

1:1 — 2:2 Adam to Israel and his family

1:1-27: Adam to Abram; Noah's descendants through Japheth, Ham and Shem. The list is drawn from Genesis, though the spelling of many names is slightly different here. (This is not reflected in some modern versions.)

1:28-54: Abraham, Isaac, Israel (Jacob); descendants of Ishmael and Esau. Attention narrows down to the father of the nation.

2:1-2: the twelve sons of Israel.

2:3 — 3:24 The royal line

2:3-55: the descendants of Judah: David's ancestors.

3:1-16: David's dynasty to the exile.
3:17-24: the royal line from the exile on.

Achar (2:7): Achan. See Joshua 7.
Kelubai (2:9): Caleb. Not necessarily Joshua's contemporary, who was not an Israelite, although he was adopted into the tribe of Judah.
Father of Kiriath-jearim (2:50): i.e. founder of the town.
Bathshua (3:5): Bathsheba.
Elishama (3:6): Elishua.
Johanan (3:15): not a king of Judah.
Zerubbabel (3:19): a leader in the return from exile. See Ezra.

4 — 7 The tribes of Israel

4:1-23 Judah; 4:24-43 Simeon; 5:1-10 Reuben; 5:11-22 Gad; 5:23-26 the half-tribe of Manasseh.

6 Levi. Verses 2-15: the line of the high priests; 16-30 the families of Gershom, Kohath and Merari; 31-48 families of the singers; 49-53 descendants of Aaron; 54-81 list of Levitical cities.

7:1-5 Issachar; 7:6-12 Benjamin (this does not tie in with chapter 8; it has been suggested that 6-11 is Zebulun and 12 is the end of an otherwise lost list of Dan); 7:13 Naphtali; 7:14-19 Manasseh; 7:20-29 Ephraim; 7:30-40 Asher.
Reuben (5:1): the reference is to Genesis 35:22.
Tilgath-pilneser (5:5): Tiglath-pileser.

5:26: Pul and Tiglath-pileser are one and the same, as modern versions make plain.
6:27: 'Samuel his son' should be inserted after Elkanah. The reference is to the prophet Samuel.

8 The line of Benjamin; Saul's family

9:1-34 Those who returned from exile to live in Jerusalem

9:35-44 Saul's family-tree

10 — 29
THE REIGN OF DAVID

10 The death of Saul

See on 1 Samuel 31 and 2 Samuel 1. The story of Saul's rise and fall is told in 1 Samuel 9ff. For the Chronicler the history of the monarchy begins with David – 10:13-14 is sufficient comment on Israel's first king.

11 — 12 David made king

11:4-9: the capture of Jerusalem. Verses 10-47: David's special guard – see on 2 Samuel 23. 12:1-22: David's supporters at Ziklag. Saul's own kinsmen went over to David, and the warriors from Gad were so eager to join him that they crossed the River Jordan when it was in spate. Verses 23-40: the troops who made David king at Hebron.
12:21: see 1 Samuel 30.

13 The first attempt to bring the ark to Jerusalem

See on 2 Samuel 6. In line with his purpose of outlining the *religious* history of the nation, the Chronicler assigns this event first place in the record of David's reign. In actual point of time it came somewhat later.

14 Foreign affairs

See 2 Samuel 5. David was well able to

handle the nations around. His family life was his weak point, as the other records make plain (2 Samuel 13ff.; 1 Kings 1:6).

15—16:6 The Levites bring in the ark

See also 2 Samuel 6. After three months, David brings the ark to Jerusalem and installs it in the tent he has had made. The original tent (the tabernacle) and altar remain at Gibeon. The Chronicler details the role of the Levites in the ceremony. Proper worship is characterized by both orderliness and joy. From earliest times music has held a special place in worship.

16:7-43 A call to praise; regular offerings reinstituted

Extracts from various psalms are brought

David formed a choir and orchestra from the Levites, the assistants to the priests; this model is at the Bible Museum, Amsterdam.

together in verses 8-36. These may be typical of what Asaph's choir sang before the ark, rather than the actual words. At Jerusalem and at Gibeon provision is made for daily sacrifices and praise to God in words and music.

17 David's request to build the temple

See on 2 Samuel 7. It seems wrong to David that he should have a palace to live in while the ark of God is still housed in a tent. And his attitude is right (contrast Haggai 1:4). God refuses the request, none the less. But he expresses his love and approval of David in the promise of a dynasty which will never die out, and in allowing Solomon to build the temple. David does not let disappointment shadow his glad acceptance of God's answer.

18 David's victories; expansion of the kingdom

See on 2 Samuel 8 for sketch-map.
Verse 4: the numbers are large. This problem is not unique to the Old Testament. Other contemporary documents give similarly large numbers of soldiers and chariots. Statistics given by the opposing sides in a war rarely tally – even today! See further 'The Large Numbers of the Old Testament', page 191.
Chief officials (17): the writer of Samuel calls them 'priests', but by the Chronicler's time the word priest had acquired a technical meaning, hence the change.

19—20 Wars with the Ammonites, Syrians and Philistines

Chapter 19: see on 2 Samuel 10. The Bathsheba and Uriah episode took place between 20:1 and 20:2. This is not an attempt to whitewash David; the Chronicler regularly omits details of private life, in line with his purpose. In any case, these incidents were already known from the earlier records.

A threshing-floor near a village in northern Syria.

19:18: 2 Samuel 10:18 says 700 chariots, a more likely figure. But the word chariot here can mean simply 'mounted men.' The foot-soldiers here are the 'horsemen' of Samuel, since at this time in the ancient Near East horsemen dismounted to fight.

21—22:1 Census and plague: the purchase of the temple site

See on 2 Samuel 24. For the Chronicler the census and plague are significant simply as the lead-in to David's decision (22:1) to build the temple on the site of Ornan's threshing-floor, a fact not even mentioned in Samuel.

Satan (21:1): 'God' in 2 Samuel. Satan has power only within the limits set by God (see Job 1-2). His existence in God's world, and God's use of him, remain a mystery.

The whole nation guilty (3): national solidarity is a fact. When the king as leader sins the people suffer.

Verse 5: these numbers differ from 2 Samuel 24:9. The Chronicler may have taken his figures from a different source.

Verse 18: the threshing-floor was a flat open space where the sheaves could be spread out. Oxen pulling studded sleds

loosened the grain, which was then winnowed by tossing it into the wind. 'Ornan' is the 'Araunah' of Samuel. Difficulty may have arisen because it was a foreign name.

Hid (20): perhaps in the cave beneath the rocky floor, which now lies under the Dome of the Rock mosque, erected on the temple site.

Verse 25: 2 Samuel records the price paid for the threshing-floor, this verse apparently the price paid for the whole site.

22:2-19 Preparations for the temple

This section has no parallel in Samuel. It follows naturally from the mention of the temple in verse 1. In point of time it probably belongs to the period of Solomon's co-regency with his father (23:1; 1 Kings 1), which may have lasted some years. David never stopped longing to build God a house fit for him. He accepted the set-back of God's refusal and turned all his energy and enthusiasm to the things he *could* do: selecting the site; amassing materials; deciding the plan.

Foreigners (2): the Canaanites who remained in the land were pressed into a permanent slave-force of navvies.

You have shed much blood (8): this does not imply that Solomon was morally better than David, or that David's wars were not justified (God is often stated to have been with him in his campaigns). These very wars bought Solomon's reign of peace in a strong kingdom, and with it the freedom for king and nation to concentrate at last on the great task of building God's temple.

Verse 14: taken literally, this would make David far richer than Solomon. The meaning is clear: David had laid up colossal supplies: a fortune in gold; fantastic wealth of silver; a vast mass of bronze and iron.

23 The duties of the Levites

Chapters 23-27 record David's organization of the nation's religious and civil administration.

From the earliest days of desert-wandering, the job of the Levites had been the care and transport of the tabernacle. They had also served the priests – in later times at the many shrines scattered throughout the land. Now the ark was to have a permanent home, and worship was to be centralized in the temple at Jerusalem. So David allocates new duties to the Levites: the care-taking and maintenance of the temple; appointments as magistrates, janitors, musicians and choristers; and general assistance of the priests.

Verses 3, 27: the age at which a Levite qualified to serve had been 30. David ordered that once the temple was completed it should be 20.

Verse 13: the sons of Amram were descendants of Aaron and Moses.

24 Divisions of priests

Twenty-four groups of priests were to be in charge of the temple sacrifices, each serving for two weeks a year. The order was decided by lot.

Nadab, Abihu (1): see Leviticus 10.

Verse 4: the fact that Eli's family was descended from Ithamar partly accounts for the reduced numbers. Because of the sins of Eli's sons, many of their descendants met a violent death (see 1 Samuel 2:30ff.).

25 The musicians

Music, both instrumental and vocal, was important in Jewish worship, as it was in social life generally. The temple musicians were 'leaders in inspired prophecy' (25:1, 3, New English Bible). Asaph,

Contemporary relief of musicians; from Carchemish, 8th century BC.

Heman and Jeduthun were amongst the famous: they are named in the Psalms. But status does not come into the temple service. Teacher and pupil alike share an equal place (8). David, himself a skilled musician (1 Samuel 16:15ff.; 2 Samuel 23:1), must have taken special delight in this part of the arrangements, over which he exercised personal supervision (2, 6).

26:1-19 The janitors

These were to take turns on guard outside the temple and store-house.
Verse 18: the meaning of 'parbar' is not known; it is variously translated 'court', 'colonnade', 'pavilion'.

26:20-32 Temple treasurers, clerks and magistrates

The temple treasuries – gifts and taxes from the people, and the spoils of war – were vast.

27 Army commanders, tribal leaders, civil service and government officials

All twelve army chiefs seem to have come from David's special guard of 'mighty men' (see chapter 11). Verses 26-31 list those in charge of the royal estates, each specializing in a particular branch of agriculture.
Below twenty (23): under-twenties were not eligible for military service and were never counted in the census.
Verse 32: Jonathan and Jehiel were tutors to the king's sons.
Verse 33: Ahithophel and Hushai both appear in the story of Absalom's rebellion, 2 Samuel 15:31ff. 'King's friend' is an official title.

28–29 The government passes to Solomon; plans and instructions for the temple

A formal public assembly marks Solomon's official coronation, after the hasty affair of 1 Kings 1 (see 29:22).

David presents his son to the people (1-8) and gives him a solemn charge (9, 10) before committing the plans for the temple to his care (11-19). The design is God-given, closely following the pattern given to Moses for the construction of the tabernacle. At the same time, David hands over the lists of temple duties (21; see chapters 23-36).

Chapter 29: in addition to all he has put by over the years, David makes a last

A worshipper, from Egypt.

lavish personal gift for the temple building fund (1-5). His example and appeal (5) calls forth a willing, joyful response from the people, and the gifts pour in (6-9). Deeply moved, David thanks God from his heart that such giving is possible from men who apart from God's goodness have nothing. His prayer is one of the greatest in the whole of the Old Testament. It shows, as perhaps no other passage does, just why this man could be described as 'a man after God's own heart'.

Verse 4: see on 22:14.

Darics (7): a Persian gold coin; anachronistic for David's day, but a clue to the date at which the Chronicler wrote.

All the sons of King David (24): earlier, Adonijah had attempted to wrest the throne from Solomon (1 Kings 1); later, Solomon put him to death. But for the present there was concord.

The southern wall of the temple area of Jerusalem, the site of David's city in the foreground. The ground slopes down to the Kidron Valley to the right. See too the picture on page 249, and key.

2 CHRONICLES

1—9
THE REIGN OF SOLOMON

1 Solomon established on the throne

See on 1 Kings 3 and 10.
Shephelah/foothills (15): the low hills between Judea and the Philistine coastal plain.

2 Trade arrangements with Huram over building materials for the temple

See on 1 Kings 5.
Huram (3): the 'Hiram' of Kings. See also on 2 Samuel 5.
Huramabi (13): elsewhere shortened to Huram or Hiram.

3 The construction of the temple

See on 1 Kings 6–7, and illustrations.
Mt Moriah (1): it was on a mountain in the
land of Moriah that Abraham was told to
offer up Isaac (Genesis 22:2).
Parvaim (6): not known; possibly in Arabia.
The veil/curtain (14): the sanctuary in
which the ark was kept was divided off
from the main part of the building by this
curtain.

4–5:1 The temple furnishings

See on 1 Kings 7.
3,000 baths (5): i.e. about 14,500 gallons
(Good News Bible, 60,000 litres), on the
usual reckoning of 4 gallons 6¾ pints/
22 litres to one bath. 1 Kings 7:26 gives
2,000 baths (10,000 gallons).

5:2–6:11 The dedication of the temple

See on 1 Kings 8. The ark is installed with
joyful music and singing and great
thanksgiving. The glory of God's
presence fills the temple (2-14). Solomon
speaks to the people (6:3-11).
The Levitical singers (12): see on
1 Chronicles 25.
Verse 2: in the desert days, when they
themselves lived in tents, the people made
a tent for God (the tabernacle). Now that
they are settled in houses, the temple is
built as a house for God. It was not a
cathedral in which they met for worship.
Assemblies took place in the open, in front
of the temple, where the altar and great
basin stood.

6:12-42 Solomon's prayer

See on 1 Kings 8. The ground for this·
prayer, and all prayer, is the fact that God
and his promises are utterly dependable.
The requests are based on other vital
facts about God: his love for his people;
his absolute moral standards; his
readiness to hear and forgive those who
genuinely turn away from sin.
Verses 41-42: a free quotation of Psalm
132:8-10.

Gate into the ancient temple area today.

7 The dedication feast; God's answer to Solomon

See on 1 Kings 8–9. Flame burns up the sacrifices in token of God's presence and approval. The seven days of festivity run on into the week-long Feast of Tabernacles, with a final day of solemn meeting before they all disperse (this clarifies 1 Kings 8:65-66).

Verses 11-22: God agrees to all Solomon's requests. But in return he expects loyal obedience.

8 Solomon's building and trading operations

See on 1 Kings 9:10ff.

Verse 2: the cities of 1 Kings 9:10-14, redeemed from Hiram by Solomon.
Verse 10: the 250 officers plus 3,600 overseers (2:18) add up to the same total as the 550 plus 3,300 of 1 Kings 9:23; 5:16.
Law of Moses (13): for the set feasts see Leviticus 23; the sacrifices, Leviticus 1-7.
Verse 14: David's instructions are given in 1 Chronicles 23-26.

9:1-12 The visit of the Queen of Sheba

See on 1 Kings 10. The Chronicler includes the visit as an illustration of Solomon's widespread fame and reputation.

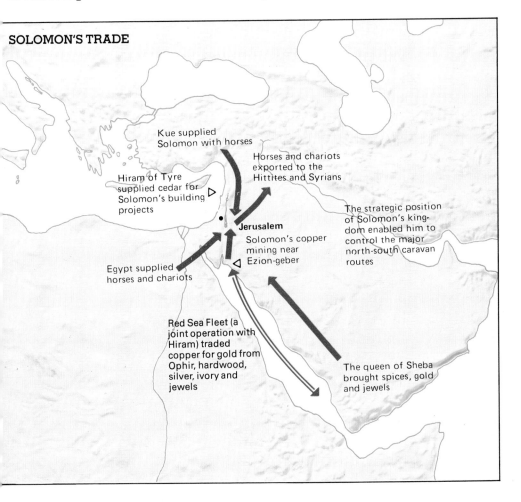

SOLOMON'S TRADE

Kue supplied Solomon with horses

Horses and chariots exported to the Hittites and Syrians

Hiram of Tyre supplied cedar for Solomon's building projects

The strategic position of Solomon's kingdom enabled him to control the major north-south caravan routes

Jerusalem

Solomon's copper mining near Ezion-geber

Egypt supplied horses and chariots

Red Sea Fleet (a joint operation with Hiram) traded copper for gold from Ophir, hardwood, silver, ivory and jewels

The queen of Sheba brought spices, gold and jewels

Algum (10): a foreign word, the 'almug' of 1 Kings; Good News Bible, 'juniper'.

9:13-31 Solomon's wealth and glory

See on 1 Kings 10:14-29.
Verse 21: 'ships plying to Tarshish' (Tartessus) in Spain is highly unlikely. Probably 'ocean-going ships' as in Kings.
Prophecy of Ahijah (29): this source is now lost, but two of Ahijah's prophecies are recorded in 1 Kings 11 and 14.

10—36
THE KINGS OF JUDAH

The dates and length of reign of each king are given in the parallel sections of 1 and 2 Kings. Many of them include a period of co-regency with a predecessor, so there is often some overlap. See 'Unravelling the Chronology of the Kings', page 269. See also the chart on page 284.

The Chronicler does not recognize the kings of Israel. Only David's descendants are the nation's true kings. From the time of the split he therefore largely ignores the northern kingdom, and frequently refers to Judah as 'Israel'. Even so, the ten tribes are still considered part of the Israelite nation, and contain elements which continue loyal to God and to the rightful king.

10 King Rehoboam and the split between Israel and Judah

See also 1 Kings 12. Rehoboam inherited from Solomon a wealthy kingdom beginning to show signs of weakness. By the time of his death only a fraction of that land and income remained to be handed down to his successor.
In Egypt (2): see 1 Kings 11:26ff.
The word spoken by Ahijah (15): 1 Kings 11:30-39.
Hadoram (18): the Adoram (Adoniram) of Kings.

11 Rehoboam strengthens Judah's defences

A timely word from Shemaiah averts civil war (1-4). Instead, Rehoboam concentrates on fortifying his tiny kingdom against attack from her larger and stronger neighbours, particularly Israel and Egypt. Refugee priests flock to Judah from Israel following Jeroboam's measures to break the religious ties with Jerusalem (see 1 Kings 12:26-33).
Satyrs (15, Revised Standard version): the goat-like desert-demons of the old nature worship.
Abijah (20): the Abijam of Kings.
Daughter of Absalom (20): the Old Testament often uses 'son of', 'daughter of' in the wider sense of 'descendant'. Maacah was Absalom's granddaughter (see 13:2).

12 Rehoboam turns unfaithful; Shishak's invasion

Invasion, here and later, is seen as a direct consequence of disloyalty to God. National repentance limits its effects, but

Above the excavations of ancient Shechem rise Mt Gerizim (left) and Mt Ebal (right).

Judah remains under Egyptian domination for some years. See also 1 Kings 14.

All Israel (1): the Chronicler means the true Israel, i.e. Judah.

Shishak (2): Sheshonq I, Libyan founder of the 22nd dynasty of Egypt.

13 King Abijah; full-scale war with Israel

See also 1 Kings 15:1-8. The fuller account here enlarges on what constitutes 'proper' worship, and on the reason for Judah's victory.

Micaiah (2): Maacah (11:20; 1 Kings 15:2).

Covenant of salt (5): salt had a ceremonial use in the ratification of treaties. It stood for faith, loyalty and long-lastingness (particularly in 'pacts' made with God).

500,000 (17): best taken as meaning simply 'a large number'.

14 Peace under King Asa; Zerah's invasion

See also 1 Kings 15:9-24.

Zerah (9): Ethiopia/Cush is modern Sudan. Zerah was probably an Egyptian or Arabian chieftain (the earlier identification with Pharaoh Osorkon has now been abandoned).

A million (9): best taken to mean simply 'an enormous number'.

15 Azariah's message from God encourages religious reform

Ephraim, Manasseh and Simeon (9): loyal men from the two northern tribes migrated to Judah. But Simeon's territory had always been in the south, and the tribe had been assimilated long ago by Judah.

Maacah (16): Asa's grandmother. See on 11:20.

Verse 17: on the face of it, a contradiction of 14:3. But Asa probably destroyed the shrines where foreign gods were worshipped and left the others.

16 The alliance with Syria against Israel

Asa's faith weakens under test in his later years. He calls in foreign aid. And he turns to medicine-men whose cures were effected by magic. Nonetheless, in death, his people honour him.

Fire (14): not a cremation, but the burning of spices (see Jeremiah 34:5).

17 Jehoshaphat: a king to be reckoned with

See also 1 Kings 15:24; 22:1-50.

Jehoshaphat builds up a strong army and defences. He arranges for the people to be taught the law. And he is much respected by the surrounding nations.

The Arabs (11): former nomads settling in Edom and Moab.

Verse 14: as they stand, the figures for the muster are over-high. It is possible that the term 'thousand' is a group term rather than a numeral. See 'The Large Numbers of the Old Testament', page 191.

18 Military and marriage alliance with Ahab; battle at Ramoth-gilead

A repetition of the story in 1 Kings 22.

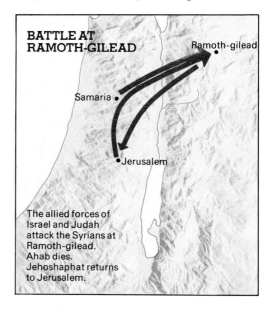

BATTLE AT RAMOTH-GILEAD

Ramoth-gilead

Samaria

Jerusalem

The allied forces of Israel and Judah attack the Syrians at Ramoth-gilead. Ahab dies. Jehoshaphat returns to Jerusalem.

The marriage alliance (1): Jehoshaphat's son Jehoram married Athaliah, Ahab's daughter. Far from reuniting the kingdom, this link brought near-disaster to Judah in later years (22:10).

True and false prophets (4ff.): it was never easy to distinguish between the two. Here Jehoshaphat senses from the shallow optimism of their message that these prophets are merely telling Ahab what he wants to hear. The false and the true can only be distinguished by their life and message, not by methods or manner (see Deuteronomy 18:17-22). No true prophet made a prediction which failed to happen; practised or encouraged immorality; or led people away from God and his law.

19 Reform of the legal system

After Ramoth-gilead, Jehoshaphat concentrates on home affairs. He appoints civil judges, sets up local law-courts and a mixed court of appeal in Jerusalem.

Jehu (2): probably grandson of the Jehu in 1 Kings 16:1. It was not unknown for names to alternate like this within families.

Law of the Lord (8): cases covered by the law of Moses; the other lawsuits ('disputed cases', Revised Standard Version) are civil matters.

Verse 10: 'fellow citizens', not kinsmen as in New English Bible.

20 War with the allied forces of Ammon, Moab and Edom

Judah's trust in God is amply vindicated. The invaders quarrel among themselves and leave the spoil to Judah. Only the alliance with Israel spoils the good record of Jehoshaphat's reign.

Meunites (1): from a district of Edom near Mt Seir.

The Sea (2): the Dead Sea.

Verse 33: this agrees with 1 Kings 22:43; but contradicts 17:6. (See on 15:17.) The high places (often but not always on hills) were simply platforms on which cult objects stood. As the places themselves were regarded as holy, nothing short of the desecration carried out by Josiah could stop people using them.

Tarshish (36, some versions): see on 9:21.

21 King Jehoram

See also 2 Kings 8:16-24. The evil influence of Jehoram's wife (Athaliah was the daughter of Ahab and Jezebel) proved stronger than his father's good example. Jehoram lost control over Edom and Libnah (on the Philistine border), and led the nation into idolatry. No one regretted his death (20): a terrible epitaph.

Elijah's letter (12): it would appear from 2 Kings 3:11 (in Jehoshaphat's reign) that Elijah was no longer alive, though we cannot be certain. Possibly, foreseeing how things would go, the prophet left a written message which was delivered by a successor.

Jehoahaz (17, some versions): an alternative way of writing Ahaziah (22:1). Both are a compound of 'Ahaz', meaning 'he has hold', or 'possession' and the name of God (written Jeho- or Jo- as a prefix; -iahu or -iah as a suffix). The whole name thus means 'God has possession'. Most of Judah's kings have names compounded in this way.

22:1-9 King Ahaziah

See also 2 Kings 8:25-29. Ahaziah learnt nothing from his father's horrible end. Friendship with Israel led directly to his death in Jehu's purge.

Verse 2: 42 (some versions) should be 22, as 2 Kings 8:26.

Verse 9: this seems to be at variance with 2 Kings 9 and 10, where Ahaziah dies at Megiddo, and before his nephews' deaths. It is possible that 'Samaria' is used here of the kingdom rather than the city itself.

22:10—23:21 Athaliah seizes the throne; the rising in favour of Joash

See also 2 Kings 11. Ahaziah's infant son Joash is the rightful heir. But so many of

the royal family have been wiped out
(21:17; 22:8) that the queen mother is able
to make her bid unchallenged. After six
years the usurper is overthrown. The
Chronicler lays his stress on the role of
the priests and Levites in restoring the
rightful monarch to the throne.

24 King Joash; the repair of the temple

See also 2 Kings 11:21–12:21. Under
Jehoiada's influence, Joash began well.
After the priest's death the king came
under less healthy influences, till he sank
to the murder of Jehoiada's son for his
outspoken criticism. In consequence his
own life ends in ignominious defeat and
assassination.

The tax (6): see Exodus 30:12ff.

25 King Amaziah

See also 2 Kings 14. Amaziah's cruel
victory over Edom leads to his downfall.
He brings home the foreign gods. And in
his bumptious pride he throws down the
gauntlet to powerful Israel. Defeat turns
the people against him. It seems that
Uzziah, the 'Azariah' of 2 Kings, was made
co-regent. And an eventual conspiracy
succeeded in ending Amaziah's life.

Verse 4: Deuteronomy 24:16.

100,000 (6): a round figure indicating a
large number.

Israel … Ephraimites (7): the Chronicler
makes it clear that in this instance he
means the northern kingdom.

26 King Uzziah

See also 2 Kings 15:1-7. A strong king,
Uzziah begins well, seeking God and
extending his sovereignty as far south as
the Red Sea. He loves the land and
protects the cattle from desert raiders
(10). He sees that his army is well-
equipped and armed with the latest in
guided missiles (14-15). But as with
many a good man before and since,
power and success are his undoing. In his

*A Canaanite 'high place', or sanctuary, discovered
by archaeologists at Megiddo, deep below the
present ground-level.*

pride he takes on the role of priest. God
strikes him with leprosy, a visible token of
that unseen defilement of sin which
made him unfit for God's presence.

27 King Jotham

See also 2 Kings 15:32-38. Jotham proves a
good king. He maintains and increases
his father's power, adding Ammon to his
tributary-states. But the religion of the
people remains mixed.

28 King Ahaz

See also 2 Kings 16; Isaiah 7. The terrible
apostasy of Ahaz brings Judah near to
destruction. God even uses the
idolatrous northern kingdom to punish
his people – and to show them up by
almost unheard-of clemency to the
prisoners-of-war. There were still some
'Good Samaritans' in Israel. Crisis brings
some people to deeper faith, but not
Ahaz.

Valley of Hinnom (3): the Valley of Gehenna, south of Jerusalem.
King of Syria (5): Rezin, see 2 Kings 16.
Tilgath-pilneser (20): Tiglath-pileser. This is not an invasion, but the imposition of crushing tribute.
Altars (24): to pagan gods.

29 King Hezekiah

See also 2 Kings 18-20. Hezekiah's first concern is to restore the temple to its proper use. The detailed account of the cleansing and rededication of the desecrated temple is characteristic of the Chronicler. When the building has been made ready, king, priests and people are themselves made clean from sin by the offering of sacrifices.
Verse 25: see 1 Chronicles 25. Gad and Nathan were both prophets of David's day.
The song to the Lord (27): many of the psalms were written for use in the temple on various occasions.

30 The great Passover celebration

(For the origin and meaning of Passover see on Exodus 11-13.) Samaria had fallen to Assyria in the reign of Ahaz (when Hezekiah was co-regent)–see 2 Kings 17. Most of the northern Israelites had been taken captive and their land re-settled. Hezekiah's appeal is to the few remaining Israelites to join with Judah for the feast (9). Despite the poor response, there had been no Passover to equal this since Solomon's day. And such was the general rejoicing that they extended the feast an extra week.
Verse 3: the normal date was the 14th of the first month, but Numbers 9 also allows the later date.
Verse 15: many priests and Levites were slow to return to the reformed worship (29:34).
Verse 19: the Chronicler, who set great

store by proper forms of worship, makes it clear that it is the attitude of heart that matters most.

31 The priests resume their functions; tithes and offerings brought in

The old laws governing worship and the support of the priests are reintroduced. The sheer volume of produce raised by the tithe takes everyone by surprise. Special care is taken to see that it is properly distributed.
Verse 7: people began to give in May/June at the grain harvest and continued to the end of the fruit and vine harvests in September/October.

32 Sennacherib's invasion

See also 2 Kings 18-19. Having wiped out the northern kingdom, the Assyrians make inroads into Judah, who have shown signs of independence. But Sennacherib fails to take Jerusalem. The reason, says the Chronicler, is that in the crisis Judah's king put his trust wholly in God.
Verse 12: the Assyrian emissary misunderstood Hezekiah's reforms.
Verse 18: they used Hebrew. The people would not have understood Aramaic, the diplomatic language.
Verse 31: see 2 Kings 20:12ff. 'Left to himself' Hezekiah exhibits his treasures with foolish pride.

33:1-20 Manasseh's evil reign

See also 2 Kings 21:1-18. For almost all of his long reign Manasseh was one of Judah's worst kings, responsible for desecrating the temple and practising human sacrifice. But the Chronicler relates a change of heart not mentioned in Kings. Possibly Manasseh was caught up in the revolt of Ashurbanipal's brother, vassal-king of Babylon, and was called to account there after Ashurbanipal was victorious. God answered the king's desperate prayer, and his

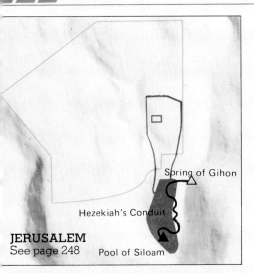

Spring of Gihon

Hezekiah's Conduit

JERUSALEM
See page 248　　Pool of Siloam

Hezekiah's Conduit

To secure his water-supply from the invaders, Hezekiah channelled the water from the Spring of Gihon to the Pool of Siloam. The tunnel is over 1,700ft/620m long, and winds to follow the lie of the rock.

In 1880 a boy who had been bathing in the Pool of Siloam found an inscription which tells its own story:

> 66 ... And this is the story of the piercing through. While (the stone-cutters were swinging their) axes, each towards his fellow, and while there were yet three cubits to be pierced through, (there was heard) the voice of a man calling to his fellow, for there was a crevice (?) on the right ... And on the day of the piercing through, the stone-cutters struck through each to meet his fellow, axe against axe. Then ran the water from the Spring to the Pool for twelve hundred cubits, and a hundred cubits was the height of the rock above the head of the stone-cutters. 99

The Spring of Gihon, from which Hezekiah's Conduit was channelled.

Detail of the inscription. This shows Hebrew writing as the prophet Isaiah knew it.

The Siloam tunnel.

release and return changed him, but not the people.

Verse 6: the Valley of Gehenna.

Hooks (11): kings conquered by the Assyrians had hooks or rings driven through their noses.

33:21-25 Amon

See also 2 Kings 21:19-26. Amon reigned two years, 642-640. He followed Manasseh's evil example and was murdered by his servants.

34 Josiah: Judah's last and greatest reformer

See also 2 Kings 22-23. Josiah desecrates and demolishes places and objects of pagan worship, and repairs the temple. During his reign the book of the law is discovered, and a measure of true repentance follows. But, despite the king's lead, the people's response is too

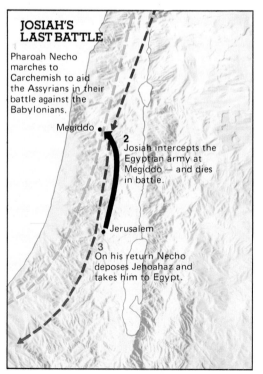

JOSIAH'S LAST BATTLE

Pharoah Necho marches to Carchemish to aid the Assyrians in their battle against the Babylonians.

Megiddo •

2 Josiah intercepts the Egyptian army at Megiddo — and dies in battle.

Jerusalem

3 On his return Necho deposes Jehoahaz and takes him to Egypt.

little and too late to avert judgement. There are some differences between the accounts in Kings and Chronicles, mainly in the order of events, but neither writer is primarily concerned with chronology. The real significance of the events lies in what they teach.

Verse 3: Assyrian power was declining, and Scythian hordes attacking her in the north, so Josiah became gradually freer to take the politically dangerous step of ridding his land of the Assyrian gods.

35 Josiah's Passover; the tragic end to his reign

See 2 Kings 23:21-30. Passover had been neglected during the monarchy. Now the celebration forms the climax to the reforms. The nation remember their deliverance from slavery in Egypt – within a few short years of a second slavery, to Babylon.

Verse 20: Necho was marching north in 609 to help Assyria fight off Babylon. On his way home he deposed and deported Josiah's successor, Jehoahaz. But in 605 he was defeated by Nebuchadnezzar of Babylon at Carchemish.

Jeremiah (25): the prophet's lament has not been preserved.

36:1-4 Jehoahaz

See also 2 Kings 23:31-35. See on 35:20.

36:5-8 Jehoiakim

See also 2 Kings 23:36 – 24:7. Jehoiakim began as a puppet of Egypt, and ended as a captive in Babylon.

36:9-10 Jehoiachin

See also 2 Kings 24:8-16. After only three months Jehoiachin was deposed and taken captive to Babylon. (He was 18 when he became king, not 8; and Zedekiah was his uncle.)

36:11-21 Zedekiah; the destruction of Jerusalem

See also 2 Kings 24:18 – 25:30. God gave Zedekiah and the nation many warnings

Ashurbanipal, king of Assyria, is represented in this relief from Babylon in a ritual act of labouring as a slave.

through Jeremiah and the other prophets, but they were all ignored. The judgement that came spelt death or exile for the whole nation. The exile lasted until the Persians took over the Babylonian Empire.

Sabbath (21): the Chronicler implies that these sabbaths were not kept under the kings. See Leviticus 25:1-7; 26:34-35.

36:22-23 New hope

When the book of Ezra was detached from Chronicles, these verses were retained at the end of Chronicles and repeated at the beginning of Ezra. Chronicles could not end at verse 21. God had not utterly abandoned his people. Jeremiah had spoken scalding words of God's judgement and condemnation. But he had also spoken of God's continuing love for his exiled people, and of their eventual return (Jeremiah 24:4-7).

THE FOUR EMPIRES

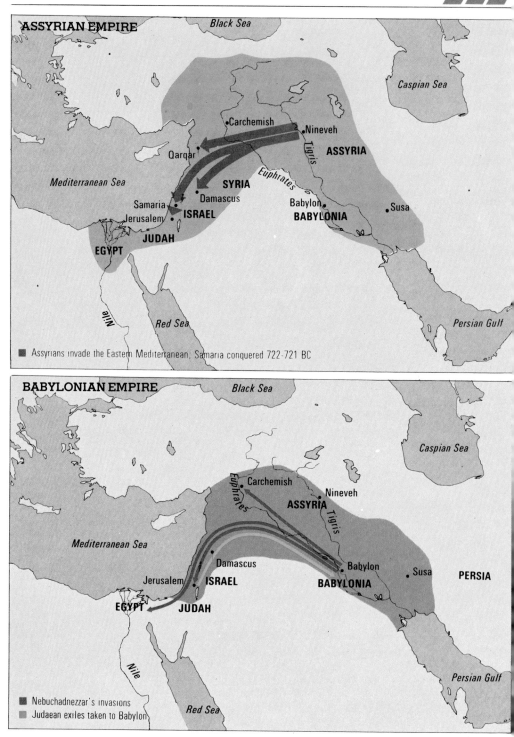

ASSYRIAN EMPIRE

Black Sea

Caspian Sea

Carchemish

Nineveh

ASSYRIA

Qarqar

Tigris

Euphrates

Mediterranean Sea

SYRIA

Damascus

Babylon

Susa

Samaria

ISRAEL

BABYLONIA

Jerusalem

JUDAH

EGYPT

Nile

Red Sea

Persian Gulf

■ Assyrians invade the Eastern Mediterranean; Samaria conquered 722-721 BC

BABYLONIAN EMPIRE

Black Sea

Caspian Sea

Euphrates

Carchemish

Nineveh

ASSYRIA

Tigris

Mediterranean Sea

Damascus

Babylon

Susa

PERSIA

Jerusalem

ISRAEL

BABYLONIA

EGYPT

JUDAH

Nile

Persian Gulf

■ Nebuchadnezzar's invasions
■ Judaean exiles taken to Babylon

Red Sea

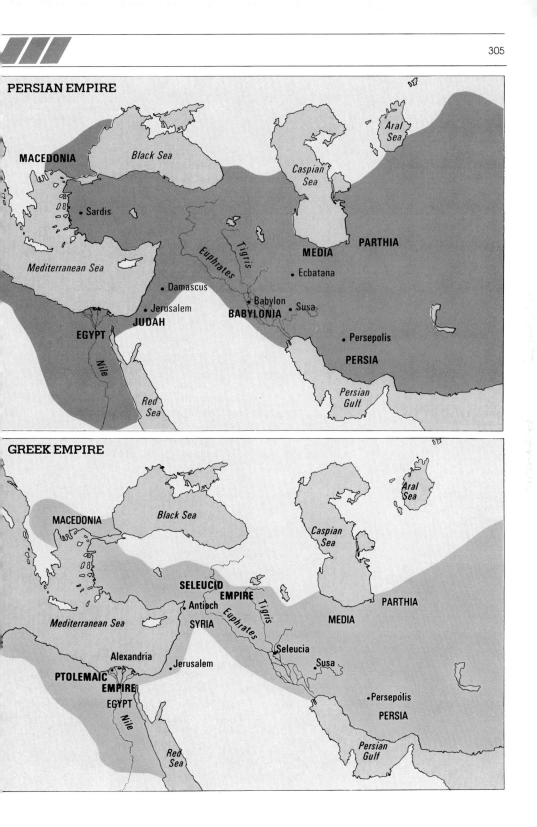

PERSIAN EMPIRE

MACEDONIA

Black Sea

Aral Sea

Caspian Sea

• Sardis

PARTHIA

MEDIA

Euphrates

Tigris

Mediterranean Sea

• Ecbatana

• Damascus

• Babylon

• Susa

• Jerusalem

BABYLONIA

JUDAH

EGYPT

• Persepolis

Nile

PERSIA

Red Sea

Persian Gulf

GREEK EMPIRE

MACEDONIA

Black Sea

Aral Sea

Caspian Sea

SELEUCID EMPIRE

PARTHIA

• Antioch

Euphrates

Tigris

MEDIA

Mediterranean Sea

SYRIA

Alexandria

• Seleucia

• Susa

• Jerusalem

PTOLEMAIC EMPIRE

• Persepolis

EGYPT

PERSIA

Nile

Red Sea

Persian Gulf

Ezra

Ezra, Nehemiah and Esther cover the last century of Old Testament Jewish history, roughly 538-433 BC. Ezra follows on from Chronicles (2 Chronicles 36: 22-23 and Ezra 1:1-3 are identical), which ended with the destruction of Jerusalem and the people being taken into exile in Babylon by Nebuchadnezzar (587). Ezra and Nehemiah describe the three-stage return: the main party, who returned with Zerubbabel in 538/7; the party that returned with Ezra 80 years later, in 458 (on the traditional dating – but this does raise some major problems, and debate on the subject continues); and Nehemiah's party in 445. Esther's story belongs to the time between the rebuilding of the temple at Jerusalem and Ezra's return (Ezra 7:1).

On the wider plane, the Jewish events belong to the time following the overthrow of the Babylonian Empire by Cyrus, king of Persia, in 539. Ezra and Nehemiah span the reigns of five Persian kings.

It is not clear who wrote what, or when.

The compiler may have been the Chronicler. But it seems plain that the personal memoirs of Ezra and Nehemiah make up the bulk of the books named after them.

1—2
THE EXILED JEWS RETURN TO JERUSALEM

1 Cyrus' proclamation
The policy of the Babylonian kings had been to deport the peoples they conquered. But Babylon has now fallen to Persia (as the prophets predicted). And one of Cyrus' first actions is to repatriate the exiled peoples, and allow them to reinstate their national gods. Among those who benefit from the change of policy are the Jews. (See Isaiah's remarkable prophecy, Isaiah 44:26-28; 45:1-13.)
Verse 1: see on 2 Chronicles 36:22-23.
Verse 6: God saw to it that the exiles did

CYRUS 559-530	The return from exile. Ezra 1	End of Daniel's life (1:21;10:1)
CAMBYSES 530-522	Not mentioned	
DARIUS I 522-486	The temple rebuilt. Ezra 4:5, 24:5	Haggai and Zechariah
XERXES I 486-465 (AHASUERUS)	Ezra 4:6. The king who made Esther his queen and Mordecai his grand vizier	
ARTAXERXES I 464-423	Ezra 4:7-23; 7:1ff.; Nehemiah 2:1. The king who sponsored the return of Ezra and of Nehemiah. Jerusalem rewalled. Reforms.	Malachi

not return empty-handed, as he had done at the exodus (Exodus 12:35-36).

2 The list of those who returned

See also Nehemiah 7.

Jeshua (2): the Joshua of Haggai 1:1.

Nehemiah (2): not the same individual as the later governor.

Verse 59: family-trees were reckoned of great importance. Those unable to prove their ancestry were barred from the priesthood.

Barzillai (61): 2 Samuel 17:27; 19:31ff.

Verse 64: the figures given do not add up to this total. There may have been mistakes in copying or interpreting the numbers.

3—6
REBUILDING THE TEMPLE

3 The foundation is laid

The first thing to be rebuilt is the altar, so that worship and sacrifice may begin again, on the pattern laid down by Moses (Leviticus 1–7). Lebanon again provides choice cedarwood for the building (see 2 Chronicles 2). But the work makes little progress beyond the foundations.

Verses 10-11: see 1 Chronicles 25. There are two choirs (or choir and soloist) singing alternately.

Verse 12: the older men wept for the glories of the temple that had been destroyed.

4 Work is halted

Verses 1-5, 24: the opposition succeeds in bringing the work to a standstill for 15 years, until Darius is king. Verses 6-23 interrupt the chronological sequence to carry the account of the opposition through to the time of Ezra and Nehemiah. Here the bone of contention is the rebuilding of the city walls (12).

Judah and Benjamin (1): it was mainly exiles from the southern kingdom who returned. Their 'adversaries' are the mixed

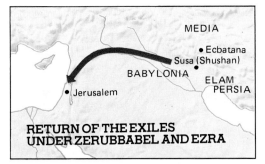

RETURN OF THE EXILES UNDER ZERUBBABEL AND EZRA

people Esarhaddon settled in the land, later known as Samaritans. They worshipped God, but alongside other 'deities' (2 Kings 17:24-41).

Verse 7: Aramaic was the international diplomatic language of the Persian Empire.

Osnappar (10, some versions): an Aramaic version of Ashurbanipal. 'Beyond the River'/'Trans (or West) Euphrates': title of the fifth 'satrapy' or province, which included all Palestine and Syria.

Eat the salt (14, some versions): i.e. they were maintained by the king; his paid officials.

Verse 23: this is the situation recounted in Nehemiah 1:3.

5—6 The temple completed

Urged on by the prophets Haggai and Zechariah, the people again start building. This time an attempt to get the new king, Darius, to stop it has the opposite effect. In four years the temple is finished and the people are able to celebrate Passover. For a nation recently delivered from a second 'bondage', this must have had special meaning.

6:11: a common form of execution in Persia; in effect crucifixion.

King of Assyria (22): i.e. king of what was once Assyrian territory.

7—10
EZRA'S RETURN TO JERUSALEM

Nearly 60 years separate 7:1 from 6:22, during which time Esther is able to avert a complete massacre of the Jewish people and, indirectly, to save the lives of Ezra and Nehemiah. Artaxerxes is favourably disposed towards the Jews, and Ezra the scholar and teacher (direct descendant of the high priests) is given official sanction to teach the law and appoint magistrates in his homeland, to offer sacrifices and beautify the temple. (Ezra's own memoirs, written in Hebrew, begin at verse 27.)

Verse 9: the 900-mile journey took four months.

8 The men who accompanied Ezra

Ezra's party of over 1,700 includes priests, people and, somewhat reluctantly, Levites. With them they take gifts valuing more than $1,000,000. Ezra is faced with a long and dangerous journey at a time of great unrest. And having boasted his confidence in God, he can hardly now apply to the king for an escort! His prayer is heartfelt, and his faith rewarded by God's own safe-conduct.

Satraps (36): Good News Bible, 'governors'; usually only one to each 'satrapy' or province, with several subordinates.

9 — 10 The problem of mixed marriages

Since their return, priests and Levites, rulers and people alike have intermarried with the heathen peoples around, a thing forbidden by God (Deuteronomy 7:1-5), not out of racial prejudice but because it led to idolatry. This very practice had been a major factor in the nation's downfall under the kings. Yet even the horrors of defeat and exile have not taught the people their lesson. Small wonder Ezra's bitter distress at the disclosure. His close identification with the offenders and the deep grief of his prayer move the nation to prompt action, despite the time of year (heavy December rains, 10:9). His lead saves the whole nation from extinction. The blame for all the unhappiness of broken marriages rests not on Ezra, but on those listed in 10:18-44 – the men who contracted those marriages in defiance of God's law. And some of them (as Malachi 2:10-16 makes clear) had even broken former marriages to Jewish wives in order to marry pagans. See also under Nehemiah 13.

A street in old Jerusalem.

Nehemiah

See introduction to Ezra.

1—2
NEHEMIAH RETURNS TO JERUSALEM

1 Bad news; Nehemiah's prayer

In December 446, Nehemiah's brother
Hanani (see 7:2) brings sad news of the
colony in Jerusalem (see Ezra 4:23).
Nehemiah holds the trusted position of
king's cup-bearer at the Persian court, at
that time resident in the winter capital
of Susa. It is his job to taste the king's
wine, in case it is poisoned. Although far
from his homeland, he is so concerned
for his people that for four months he
continues to grieve and pray over the
situation. And, characteristically, when
the opportunity comes he has a
practical plan to put to the king.
Remember the word (8): e.g. Deuteronomy
30:1-5.
This man (11): the Persian king.

2 The king consents; Nehemiah's tour of inspection

The sorry state of Jerusalem is a direct
consequence of Artaxerxes' decree that
building should cease (Ezra 4:7-23).
Nehemiah therefore takes his life in his
hands in championing a city which has
been represented to the king as a
hot-bed of rebellion. Even by letting his
grief show in the king's presence he
places himself in grave danger. But
Nehemiah's concern for his people
outweighs self-interest. God answers his
prayer, and Artaxerxes grants his
request.
  On arrival in Jerusalem he mentions
his plans to no one until he has made a
secret personal inspection of the city.
Verse 6: Nehemiah returned after 12

years as governor (5:14), but the term
agreed on here was probably shorter.
Sanballat, Tobiah (19): see also 4:1-9;
6:1-18; 13:4-9. 'Geshem' (Gashmu, 6:6):
tribal chief of Kedar in north Arabia.

3—6
THE BUILDING OF THE WALLS

3 A list of the builders

People of all sorts join together in the
work of rebuilding. The list mentions
priests and perfumers, goldsmiths and
merchants, rulers, even women. Some
undertook a double section. Nehemiah,
astute as always, sets the people to work
on sections near their own homes, for
which they naturally have a special
concern. The leaders named are citizens
of long standing; neither Ezra nor the
men of his party are mentioned.

4 Enemy opposition

The people have a will to work, and a
dynamic leader. Nonetheless they have
to face first ridicule, then terrorism from
powerful opponents. Nehemiah's reply is
prayer and faith, plus practical action:
'we prayed . . . and set a guard' (9);
'Remember the Lord . . . and fight' (14).
Verse 2: the walls had been burned, and
fire made the local limestone disintegrate.
Verses 4-5: Old Testament prayers like this
one fall short of Christ's standards. But the
motive behind them is not personal
vengeance, but concern for God's honour
which is at stake when his people are
under attack.

5 Internal troubles

While Nehemiah has been buying back
Hebrew slaves and loaning money and

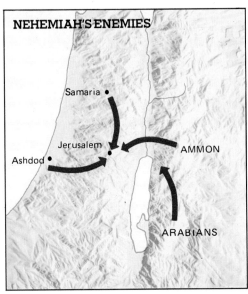

NEHEMIAH'S ENEMIES

Samaria

Jerusalem

Ashdod

AMMON

ARABIANS

food to the poor (even providing his own support as governor), rich Jews have been exacting interest from their fellow countrymen, contrary to the law (Exodus 22:25) and selling them as slaves to foreigners. Nehemiah takes firm action to set this right.

6 The wall is finished

The opposition realize that their only chance of stopping the work is to get rid of Nehemiah. Their first move is to try and persuade him to leave Jerusalem for talks (2). When that fails they try blackmail (5-7) and intimidation (10). Nehemiah's replies (3, 8, 11) are superb. He will allow nothing to deflect him from his God-given task. And in under two months the walls are finished – such a fantastic achievement that even Israel's enemies are forced to acknowledge God's hand in it.

7:1-73a
LIST OF THOSE WHO RETURNED WITH ZERUBBABEL

Verses 6-73: see also the practically identical list in Ezra 2. It refers to the first,

and main, party of Jews to return home in 538 following Cyrus' decree.

7:73b—8:18
EZRA READS THE LAW TO THE PEOPLE

The request comes from the people (8:1). Ezra reads and the Levites explain, possibly also translating for some who knew no Hebrew. When they learn the full measure of God's standards the people are overwhelmed with grief at the extent of their failures (just as King Josiah had been, long before; 2 Kings 22).

In the course of study, they rediscover the original instructions for the Feast of Tabernacles. And for the first time since Joshua's day they make leafy shelters to live in, as a reminder of the time of desert-wandering.

9:1-37
THE PEOPLE'S CONFESSION AND EZRA'S PRAYER

The nation's repentance is genuine. Wrongs are righted and the people turn to God in confession and worship. Ezra's prayer – the prelude to renewal of the covenant – recalls God's loving and faithful dealings with his rebellious people from the time of Abraham to his own day.

9:38—10:39
THE COVENANT IS RENEWED

Nehemiah the governor, priests, Levites and leaders sign the renewed covenant-agreement on behalf of the nation. It is ratified with a curse (on those who break it) and an oath (of loyalty to God). The people pledge specifically to keep the law's requirements on marriage, the sabbath, and taxes, tithes and offerings for the upkeep of the temple services, priests and Levites.

11—12:26
LISTS OF RESIDENTS

11:3-19: probably a list of those already

The massive wall of the south-east corner of the temple area may contain masonry going back to the time of Zerubbabel.

living in Jerusalem (it is substantially the same as 1 Chronicles 9:2-17). The number was increased by a 10 per cent levy on the villages around.

Verses 25-36: a list of occupied villages.

12:1-9: the priests and Levites who returned with Zerubbabel.

11:23: see 1 Chronicles 25.

12:9: there were two choirs who sang or chanted in reply to one another.

A gateway of the old city of Jerusalem today.

12:27-47
THE DEDICATION OF THE WALLS

Two processions, each led by a choir, make their way in opposite directions along the broad top of the wall, meeting in the temple area for the concluding thanksgiving and sacrifices. It is an occasion of tumultuous joy.

13
ABUSES AND REFORMS

Verses 1-3 seem more closely linked with 4-9 than with 12:44. In 433 Nehemiah went back to the court of King Artaxerxes. On his return he finds that various abuses have arisen in his absence. The high priest, of all people, has given Nehemiah's old enemy, Tobiah (who is not even an Israelite), quarters in rooms attached to the temple. The income for the Levites has not been forthcoming. Sabbath laws are being flagrantly broken. And yet again (see Ezra 9-10) the Israelites have contracted marriages with foreign women. Nehemiah adopts strong measures to deal with the abuses, and the offenders.

The achievements of Ezra and Nehemiah in the crucial years following the return of their decimated nation from exile are notable. Without the teaching of the law, without the invincible faith and fearless action of these two leaders, it is doubtful if a distinctive Jewish religion and community – with all that means for the world through the birth and death of Christ – could have survived. To this end their strong line on mixed marriage was essential. The objection to foreign women was not on the grounds of race, but because of their debased religions. (The Old Testament does not condemn inter-racial marriage if both partners worship the God of Israel.) History had taught them that the admixture of paganism, with its easy standards and its appeal to the lowest in human nature, could quickly bring the Jewish faith to the brink of extinction.

Esther tells the story of a plot to exterminate the entire Jewish nation in the days of the Persian king, Ahasuerus (Xerxes), and how it was thwarted. It also explains the origin of the Jewish Feast of Purim. Estimates of the book vary – largely on account of the seeming improbability of the events. Some regard it as pure fiction. Others see it as a historical novel. Others again think that the knowledge we have of Persian affairs in the 5th century BC gives good grounds for treating Esther as history.

The writer is unknown, but his nationalism and accurate knowledge of Persian ways make it likely that he was a Jew who lived in Persia before the empire fell to Greece.

Although the book does not mention God by name, it speaks plainly of his overruling in the affairs of men, and his unfailing care for his people. Had Haman's plot succeeded there would have been no Nehemiah and, far more important, no Christ.

Queen Vashti (9): Herodotus says Amestris was Ahasuerus' queen. It may be she succeeded both Vashti and Esther. The king may have had more than one wife, but there would have been only one queen.
He sent letters (22): Darius had set up an excellent fast-courier postal service which operated throughout the empire.

2 Esther becomes queen; Mordecai saves the king's life

The years of the disastrous Greek war – the battles of Thermopylae and Salamis – intervene between chapters 1 and 2. Four years pass before the king is able to get round to choosing a new queen. Among the beautiful girls rounded up to be taken to the capital for twelve months' beauty treatment, sampled by the king, and then for the most part forgotten, is a young Jewish girl, Esther, Mordecai's cousin. When her turn comes, she delights the king and he makes her his queen.
Verses 5-6: Mordecai would have been nearly 120 if he personally had been taken

1 Ahasuerus dethrones his queen

Ahasuerus reigned over an empire stretching from the Indus to northern Sudan (see map, page 305). His winter capital (unbearably hot in summer) was Susa, a city in Elam, 150 miles east of Babylon. The Greek historian Herodotus describes him as a cruel, capricious, sensual man – which fits well with his character in this book. In 483 he gives a huge feast, the climax to a six-month display of his wealth and power. But his queen (we are not told why) refuses to play along with his wish to make her part of the exhibition. And on the advice of his astrologers the king deposes her.

A queen and her attendants; an ancient relief.

captive in 597. It probably means that his
family was among the captives.
Hadassah/Esther (7): some make much
of the fact that the names 'Esther' and
'Mordecai' are similar to those of the
Babylonian gods 'Ishtar' and 'Marduk'. But
this is not surprising if both were names
given to them in captivity, as this verse says
Esther's was.
Tebeth (16): December/January 479.
Verse 23: this record in the court diary later
proves important (6:1-2).

3 Haman's promotion and plot against the Jews

We are not told why Mordecai refused to
make obeisance. He must have
considered that Haman's demand
went beyond court courtesy. To have
complied would have involved idolatry.
In his unreasoning fury Haman plans
the destruction of an entire race.
Superstition insists he must choose a
'lucky day'. And fortunately for the Jews it
was eleven months off. The king's assent
is easily won by accusing the Jews of
rebellion and promising a £3,000,000
rake-off. (Haman plans to raise the
money by plundering Jewish goods
and confiscating their lands.)

4 Esther hears the news

Esther is the only one of her people with
access to the king, and she has not been
summoned to him for a month. The only
way open is the dangerous step of going
to him unbidden. Anxiously she agrees to
take the risk.
Verses 14-16: although God is not
mentioned, Mordecai's faith is plain. The
fast would involve prayer.

*A Persian gold armlet, decorated with griffins,
from the Treasure of the Oxus.*

5 Esther gives a dinner-party

The king permits an audience. But Esther
proceeds cannily. She invites the king and
his favourite to dinner. In the mellow
after-dinner atmosphere she gives a
second invitation. Haman – suspecting
nothing, knowing nothing of Esther's
relationship to Mordecai – is greatly
flattered. He goes home and builds a
gallows topping the city wall, on which he
intends to hang his enemy.

7 Haman's villainy unmasked

After dinner on the second evening Esther makes her request. Haman is dumbfounded. And his action in throwing himself at Esther's feet as she reclines on her couch only succeeds in adding attempted rape to the charges against him. In the supreme irony of things, he ends his life on the gallows he himself had made.

They covered Haman's face (8): i.e. in token of the death sentence.

8 Mordecai becomes grand vizier; a new edict

There still remains the problem of Haman's edict. Since it was issued in the king's name and under his seal it cannot be revoked (8). But in answer to Esther's further plea the king authorizes a second decree permitting the Jews to defend themselves against attack.

Verse 11: the Jews were allowed to treat their enemies exactly as they were to have been treated themselves (see 3:13).

9 Jewish vengeance; the Feast of Purim

When the appointed day arrives, the Jews rid themselves of their enemies, including Haman's ten sons; but they take no plunder. There can be no excuse for Esther's vindictive request. She shows herself to be a child of her age. The bodies of Haman's sons are hanged to make their fate public knowledge.

In commemoration of the nation's deliverance, the 14th and 15th Adar become annual feast days, preceded by a fast on the 13th. To this day the Jews celebrate Purim, reading the book of Esther aloud, and remembering many more recent miracles of deliverance.

6 The king honours Mordecai

A sleepless night and the reading of the court diary give events a new twist. To his mortification Haman finds himself heaping on his enemy honours he had thought were intended for himself. His superstitious advisers see in this the beginning of his downfall.

10 Conclusion

The author closes with a final historical note, attesting the good use Mordecai made of his power.

POETRY AND WISDOM LITERATURE

Introduction

DEREK KIDNER

POETRY

The word 'poetry' may suggest to us a highly specialized branch of literary art, produced by the few for the few. But this would be a misleading term for any part of the Old Testament. A closer modern equivalent would be the measured oratory of, for instance, a Winston Churchill –

We shall fight on the beaches,
We shall fight on the landing-grounds,
We shall fight in the fields and in the
    streets

– in which reiteration (or other devices) and rhythm join to make a passage doubly memorable and impressive.

Reiteration was a favourite Canaanite technique, and is also a mark of some of the earliest biblical poetry:

Spoil of dyed stuffs for Sisera,
Spoil of dyed stuffs embroidered,
Two pieces of dyed work embroidered
    for my neck as spoil.   (Judges 5:30)

The rhythm, though tighter than this in the original, is a flexible matter of stresses, or beats, not of fixed numbers of syllables. Most often there will be three stresses to a line, matched by another three in the following line which pairs with it to form a couplet. But this pattern may be varied by an occasional longer or shorter couplet, or by a triplet, in the same passage; or again the predominating rhythm may be of couplets in which a three-beat line is

answered by another of two beats:

How are the mighty fállen
in the mídst of the báttle!

This last rhythm, with its touch of fading or drooping, is often used for taunts or laments (as in the book of Lamentations), and this has suggested the name *Qinah* (lament) for it, although its use is not confined to such themes.

What is almost the hallmark of biblical poetry, in contrast to our own, is parallelism: the echoing of the thought of one line of verse in a second line which is its partner:

Has he said, and will he not do it?
Or has he spoken, and will he not fulfil
    it?   (Numbers 23:19)

There are many varieties of this, from virtual repetition to amplification or antithesis. It has a dignity and spaciousness which allows time for the thought to make its effect on the hearer, and often also the opportunity to present more than one facet of a matter:

For my thoughts are not your thoughts,
neither are your ways my ways, says the
    Lord.   (Isaiah 55:8)

Bishop Lowth, whose lectures on Hebrew poetry in 1741 first introduced the name 'parallelism' for this poetic style, pointed out that this structure, based as it is on meaning, survives translation into the prose of any language with remarkably little loss, unlike the poetry that relies on complex metre or a special vocabulary.

There are, of course, such points of style in Old Testament verse, and occasionally such devices as assonance, rhyme, refrains, word-plays and acrostics; but they are secondary. The essence of this poetry is that it has great matters to convey forcibly to people of all kinds. It is therefore unselfconscious, and remarkably free from artificialities of language.

For this reason, poetry is not segregated into a few poetical books, but breaks out in various contexts at moments of special importance. The examples quoted above are drawn from books we might call histories (but the Jews called them the 'Former Prophets' and 'the Law') and from prophecy. In fact nearly all prophetic utterances are in this form, and are rightly set out as lines of poetry in recent translations of the Bible.

Three books of the Old Testament, however, were given a more elaborate system of accents than the rest by the Jewish grammarians, to mark them out as distinctively poetic. These were Job, Psalms and Proverbs. To our ears, a better candidate than Proverbs would have been the Song of Solomon; its pure lyric poetry a third example of Hebrew poetry to stand beside the rich eloquence of Job and the singable verse of the Psalms. On Job, more will be said under the heading of Wisdom, below; but purely as poetry it has been hailed as one of the masterpieces of world literature, for the wealth and energy of its language and the power of its thought. In the Psalms, poetry is put to work, to be 'the way to heaven's door' in worship or in teaching, furnishing inspired words for public festivals and royal occasions, and for the individual who might come to confess his sins, or plead for healing, or rejoice over some deliverance or revelation. The Song of Solomon, by contrast, scarcely gives the name of God a mention, but responds rapturously to his creation and to its crowning glory, the gift of love between man and woman. Its presence in the Bible is the most graceful of tokens that God's world is not properly divisible into secular and sacred, and that holiness cannot be indifferent to beauty.

WISDOM LITERATURE

Wisdom, in the Old Testament, is the voice of reflection and experience, rather than of bare command or preaching. We are persuaded, even teased, into seeing the connection between God's order in the world and his orders to men, and the absurdity of going against the grain of his creation.

It takes many forms. A vivid comparison, perhaps expanded into a parable or an allegory, is a favourite device; the Hebrew word for it, *mashal,* does duty for any of these, and equally for a proverb or a taunt. A riddle or an enigmatic saying is another means of pricking a person into thought. At a deeper level there will be searching reflection on the way God governs the world, and on the ends for which men live.

Like poetry, Wisdom is not confined to the books which we group under this name (in the Old Testament, Proverbs, Job, Ecclesiastes), for proverbs and pointed sayings are part of every culture, and Israel's was no exception. In the narratives we have, for instance, Jotham's fable of the trees, Samson's riddle, and various proverbs; while in the Psalms and prophetic oracles the teaching style of the Wise makes itself clearly heard from time to time (e.g. Psalm 1; Isaiah 28:23ff.; Jeremiah 17:5ff.; Hosea 14:9). We are confirmed in identifying this as a distinct ingredient in Scripture by the fact that Israel itself heard it as a third voice alongside Law and Prophecy. There was even a proverb to this effect: 'The law shall not perish from the priest, nor counsel from the wise, nor the word from the prophet' (Jeremiah 18:18).

Of all reputations for wisdom, Solomon's is pre-eminent; and it rests not only on his own brilliance but on his patronage of learning and the arts. The Queen of

Sheba was but one of a stream of visitors who poured into Israel to hear him and put him to the test. The names and places of 1 Kings 4:30-33 give a glimpse of an intellectual world that briefly found its capital in Jerusalem; and this openness to foreign enquirers finds some reflection in the authorship of Proverbs 30 and 31:1-9, which are apparently the work of non-Israelite converts.

Israel's Wisdom literature, then, never professed to have developed in an intellectual vacuum. Just how rich was the surrounding culture is becoming clear as the wisdom of Egypt and Mesopotamia comes increasingly to light. Some of their fables, popular sayings and precepts have been preserved, and they are largely concerned with the common stuff of life that occupies the biblical proverbs: teachability, sobriety, wise speech, kindness, trust in divine help, magnanimity, friendship. There is a certain amount of mere worldly wisdom here, but much, too, that is sound and high-principled, although the biblical material moves at a consistently higher level of informed faith. Another class of literature from these countries wrestles with the problems of suffering and the meaning of existence, arguing the points at considerable length in skilfully constructed poetic monologues and dialogues.

The fact that questions of this depth were being debated in writing, not only in the time of Solomon but for a thousand years before him, and that the Israel of his day was anything but a cultural backwater, should dispose of the idea (still current in some circles) that Israel's stock of wisdom consisted at this time of short popular sayings, which supposedly developed by degrees into longer and more religious units, and only in the latest period into the connected discourses of Proverbs 1-9 of the probings of Job and Ecclesiastes. The dating of these calls for better criteria than a scheme of religious evolution.

But while it is illuminating to see how high a level of discussion existed from these early times, the Old Testament treatment of these themes remains distinctive. In the book of Job, God is recognizably the faithful, righteous Lord whose ways, while they are past finding out, are to be trusted to the end. Job does not have to conclude, like one of the Babylonian sufferers, that what is evil on earth may be counted good in heaven; nor is there any question of placating God with gifts; still less of throwing in one's hand and renouncing him. And in Ecclesiastes the apparent pessimism of the book has only a surface resemblance to the deep-dyed cynicism of the Babylonian Dialogue between Master and Servant, where nothing has meaning or value, and only caprice remains. Ecclesiastes does indeed reduce everything the world offers to a mere breath, but this is done precisely because man was made for something bigger than time and space: the fear of God, whose assessment of every deed and 'every secret thing' as good or evil invests the whole of life with meaning (Ecclesiastes 12:13-14).

That expression, the fear of God, to which Ecclesiastes moves as its conclusion, is the starting-point of Proverbs (1:7) and the pivot of all the Wisdom literature (see Job 28:28; Psalm 111:10; Proverbs 9:10). Secular philosophy tends to measure everything by man, and comes to doubt whether wisdom is to be found at all. But the Old Testament with this motto turns the world the right way up, with God at its head, his wisdom the creative and ordering principle that runs through every part; and man, disciplined and taught by that wisdom, finding life and fulfilment in his perfect will.

The book of Job stands alone amongst the books of the Old Testament. It forms a part of the 'Wisdom' material (Proverbs, Ecclesiastes; see 'Poetry and Wisdom Literature', page 316), but in form and theme it is unique. No one knows who wrote it, or just when it was written, but the story is set in the days of the patriarchs. Job is a wealthy and influential sheikh – wealthy in terms of flocks and herds rather than cash. Part of the year he is a man of the city; for the rest, on the move with his cattle. He belongs to the days before the priesthood and organized religion or to a region where these things were not needed. He reminds us very much of Abraham: a man of the east.

A prose prologue introduces the great debate between Job and his friends which the author records in magnificent poetry. The subject is as old as the hills and as modern as the space-age. If God is just and good, why does he let innocent people suffer? (Why the casual victims of war and terrorism? Why the child dying of cancer?) As a man Job is *really* good: about the best any man could every hope to be. Yet calamity overwhelms him. Loss of possessions and family is followed by grim, prolonged physical suffering that shakes his faith to the depths.

As they tussle with the problem, both Job and his friends are hampered by ignorance of the larger issue, the challenge of Satan related in the prologue. They have no assurance of a future life. For them death is the end. So justice must be seen to be done in this life. According to the orthodox theology of the day – the position championed by the three friends – prosperity was God's reward for good living, calamity his judgement on the sin of the individual. Generally speaking this held good. But

the friends reduced a general truth to a rigid, invariable rule. If Job suffers, then he must be a wicked man. But Job knows this is untrue. So the argument goes back and forth, neither side shifting position, until they reach complete impasse, at which point God himself intervenes. He does not answer Job's questions. But, seeing God, Job is satisfied. If his friends' theology had been too narrow, his own concept of God had been too small.

The book leaves much unsettled. It is only in the New Testament that we approach an answer to the problem. As we look at Christ on the cross we see the suffering of the only really innocent Man. And we see a God who cares so much for us he is prepared to shoulder the whole burden of human sin and suffering. Yet the book of Job is not out-dated. Even today, suffering men and women find that this book speaks to their need as no other book in the Bible.

1–2
PROLOGUE

1:1-5: Job is introduced (see introduction).

1:6-12: in the court of heaven Satan accuses Job of serving God for what he can get out of it. God allows him to test this out – a measure of his confidence in Job – but Job himself is to be spared.

1:13-22: in the space of a single day Job loses everything – possessions, servants, family – but his confidence in God remains unshaken (compare verse 21 with Paul's words in Philippians 4:11-12).

2:1-6: Satan has lost the first round. Now he says Job is only really concerned for his own skin. So God allows a further test, stopping short only at Job's life.

2:7-13: Job's body breaks out in running sores. The great man becomes an outcast. His wife fails him. The three friends who remain loyal sit in silence, appalled at what has happened. But still Job holds fast to God.

Uz (1:1): a town to the east of Palestine – in Edomite territory, or possibly in the Hauran, south of Damascus.

Sons of God/heavenly beings (1:6): angels of God's court in heaven. Satan is among them, under God's authority.

Sabeans (1:15): nomads of south-west Arabia; 'Chaldeans' (17): nomads from south Mesopotamia, Abraham's homeland.

Job's friends (2:11): wise men from towns in Arab and Edomite territory, a region renowned for its sages.

3 – 14
THE FIRST ROUND IN THE DEBATE

3 Job's first speech: the bitterness of life

Job's suffering makes him wish he had never been born. He longs to find peace and release in death.

Verse 8: Job refers to magicians who can make a day 'unlucky'. Leviathan may be the monster supposed to have been imprisoned by God at creation. In chapter 41 Leviathan is the crocodile.

Verse 24: sighs and groans are his daily diet.

4 – 5 Eliphaz' first speech

Job has often helped others in trouble; now he should be prepared to swallow his own medicine. God destroys the guilty, not the innocent (4:7). No one is blameless before him (17). Trouble is an inevitable part of life (5:7). The best course is to turn to God (8), accept his reproof (17), and wait to be restored to favour.

There is much in what Eliphaz says,

but his diagnosis happens to be wrong in Job's case.

5:4: cases were tried and contracts made at the town gate; it was the hub of public life.

6 – 7 Job's reply

It is nauseating advice (6:6-7) to tell a man at the end of his tether to be patient (11-12). Job wants only to cease to be. His friends have failed to show sympathy when he needed it most (14ff.). He has done nothing to deserve suffering (30). Life is a succession of pain-filled days and sleepless nights (7:3-6).

7:11-21: Job turns to God and pours out his heart to him – his fear, his longing for death. Why won't God leave him alone? If sin is the trouble, why won't he forgive?

6:18-19: the caravans of traders crossing the desert come looking for water, and not finding it move on to die of thirst.

7:5: Job's sores breed maggots.

8 Bildad's first speech

Eliphaz had begun gently. Bildad takes a firmer line as Job's words grow wilder. God is just. He rewards the good and punishes the wicked. Bildad's words are salt to an open wound (4).

Papyrus (11): the reed which grew in the Egyptian marshes and from which paper was made. See pages 88 and 100.

9 – 10 Job's reply

Job believes as Bildad does in the justice of God. But his own case will not square with his belief. God has condemned an innocent man. How can anyone call him to account? Good, bad – it is all one (9:22). Disaster strikes both. Why (10:2)? The Creator has turned Destroyer (8). Will he allow no respite before life is over (20-22)?

Rahab (9:13): the legendary monster of chaos.

The story of Job is set in patriarchal times, his wealth measured in sheep and cattle; here Bedouin gather in the sheep market at Beersheba.

9:16-19: in his bitterness Job sees God as an unjust judge. Like many a man before and since, Job's basic problem was to get a hearing at all (19), and even if he got as far as the court he could not be sure of a fair hearing and impartial administration of the law.

11 Zophar's first speech

Zophar's words are harshest of all. Does Job think himself innocent? God is letting him down lightly (6). Job must put away his sin (13-14); then God will restore him.

12—14 Job's reply

Job is stung to sarcasm. His friends are not the only ones who can work things out. God is all-wise, all-powerful. If he turns the norms of wisdom and justice upside-down, what can anyone do about it (12:7-22)? Job's experience gives the lie to the arguments of his friends (13:1-4). He will put his case to God direct, and God will acquit him (18). What are the charges against him (23)? Life is short and there is no waking a man from the sleep of death (14:1-12). Job cries to God to hide him away in the land of the dead until his anger is past, and then to restore him (13-17). But despair floods back – what hope is there (19)?

15—21
THE SECOND ROUND

15 Eliphaz' second speech

The debate grows more heated. Job has needled his friends, and they make no allowances for the stress he is under. It never crosses their minds he may really be innocent. They go on doggedly defending their position and trying to bludgeon Job into submission.

Job is a self-opinionated old windbag (2)! All he has said – his wild accusations against God; his attempts to justify himself – merely serve to prove his guilt (6). Job is wrong in saying that the wicked get off scot-free. Their fate is a terrible one (17-35).

16 – 17 Job's reply

It is cold comfort his friends have to give. How easy for them to talk, when it is Job who bears the pain. (Like many since, their silent sympathy, 2:13, helped more than their well-meaning words.) God has worn him out with suffering and the cruelty of his fellow men. The pictures Job paints (16: 9, 12-14) convey his intense, unbearable agony – a tortured body and a mind tormented at the thought that God could do all this to him. Even now he cannot believe God is unjust: there must be one who will plead his cause in heaven (19; see 1 John 2:1). If his case rests till he is dead, what hope is there (17:13-16)?
17:3: Job speaks to God.

18 Bildad's second speech

Bildad bitterly resents Job's angry rejection of their advice. He replies by painting a terrible picture of the fate of the wicked, meant to put Job in his place. But Job is innocent, and Bildad's tirade irrelevant.

19 Job's reply

Job's friends have become his tormentors, levelling false accusations and offering no answer to his desperate questions. He is shut in on himself (8), despairing (10), utterly alone (13-16). He has become an object of loathing to those he loves most (17). Even pity is denied him (21-22).

Yet even in his darkest moments, faith and hope still well up inside him. He is certain of vindication. One day God himself will take up his case and clear him – and he will be there to see it (25-27). Then those who have maligned him will find themselves answerable to God.

20 Zophar's second (and last) speech

Zophar takes up Bildad's theme: the fate of the wicked. Their prosperity is short-lived, their punishment certain.

Transition from wealth to poverty can be swift for desert-dwellers, dependent on occasional rains for pasture and on the health of their flocks.

We hear no more from him after this: either he has nothing further to add, or a section of the third round of speeches has been lost. It is possible that 27:7-23, which sounds so strange coming from Job, belongs in fact to Zophar.

21 Job's reply

Zophar's theology is all very well, but it flies in the face of experience. The condition of Job, the good man, is pitiful (5). Yet more often than not, evil men flourish, live happily and die peacefully (7-18). The friends will argue that God's vengeance falls on their children (19). But what kind of justice is that? Their so-called comfort is nothing but a pack of empty lies.

22 – 31
THE THIRD ROUND

22 Eliphaz speaks for the third and last time

It is still the same stubborn line of argument. Job is in the wrong – Eliphaz even lists out his sins (5-9)! Job had thought he could hide the fact from God (14). Let him return to God, put away his sin, and all will be well again.

Ophir (24): so famous for the export of gold (see 2 Chronicles 8:18) that 'Ophir' and 'fine gold' became synonymous (see Good News Bible). The location is unknown.

23 – 24 Job's reply

If only he could find God and put his case to him. But God is not to be found, and his ways are inexplicable.

Chapter 24: look what goes on in the world. Life is neither fair nor just. God delays judgement, and those who trample the helpless underfoot seem to get away with it.

Remove landmarks/boundary stones (24:2): i.e. seize lands. The landmark was a stone sometimes inscribed with the landowner's title-deeds and boundaries.

Take in pledge (24:3, 9): take as security for credit, or seize in payment of debt.

Job and the other Wisdom literature challenged an inadequate orthodoxy and too narrow a view of the world. This 7th-century BC Babylonian plan of the world shows it surrounded by ocean, with Babylon on the Euphrates, mountains to the north of Assyria and swamps to the south.

25 Bildad speaks for the third and last time

If the speech is complete as it stands, Job's friends have exhausted their argument. They have nothing more to say. Bildad merely reiterates the obvious truth that no man is 100 per cent perfect in God's sight. This does not help Job. What point is there in godly living if God's punishment falls equally on good and bad?

26—31 Job's last reply

Chapter 26: in the created universe we catch a glimpse of God's dynamic power. But who can think to comprehend that power in all its fullness?

Chapter 27: his friends want him to deny his integrity, but Job will not perjure himself. Verses 7-23 sound strange coming from Job. This has previously been the argument his friends have put forward. Either Job's thinking has changed, or this passage really belongs to one of the others (perhaps Zophar's missing third speech).

Chapter 28: Job's mind turns again (see 26:14) to the question of wisdom. This is the heart of his problem: how to understand the inscrutable ways of God. But no miner can uncover a vein of wisdom; all the wealth in the world will not buy it. Only God knows where to find it. And man becomes wise through reverence for God and by rejecting evil.

Chapter 29: Job looks back on the golden days of God's favour – past enjoyment of home, of success in business, of universal respect.

Chapter 30: 'But now': he returns to the bitter present, which has made him the butt of all, an outcast, incessantly gnawed by pain.

Chapter 31: all this has befallen a man who has avoided immorality, even in his thinking (1); who has played fair with his employees (13); been generous in relieving need (16); never become obsessed with money (24) or turned idolater (26-27); turned no one from his door (32); harboured no secret sins (33); never kept quiet for fear of what others might think or how they might react (34). Job is prepared to swear to all

'Mines where copper is smelted' is no doubt a contemporary reference. In the mountains near the port of Eilat, 'King Solomon's Mines' are being worked again today.

Reflection in old age: an orthodox Jew.

this before God. How many of us could honestly do the same?

Abaddon (26:6; 28:22, some versions): another word for 'Sheol', the shadowy land of the dead.

Rahab (26:12): see on 9:13.

Ophir (28:16): see on 22:24.

32—37
ELIHU'S TIRADE

Chapter 32: Elihu is the original angry young man. His elders are lost for words, but he is simply bursting with indignation at Job's attitude, dying to have his say.

Chapter 33: Job has declared himself the innocent victim of God (9-11); but God will not answer his charge (13). Elihu says God speaks to man through warning dreams (15) and through suffering (19) – in order to save, not destroy him (30).

Chapter 34: Job has said God is in the wrong (5-6), and there is nothing to be gained by making him our delight (9).

But God is the judge of all men: supreme, just, impartial (10-30). Job has added to his other sins resentment and rebellion against God (36-37).

Chapter 35: Elihu (wrongly; see 2 Samuel 11:27; 12:13) sees good and bad conduct as a matter between men (8): God remains high above, untouched by either. People cry out to him in their need (9). But they are concerned for their own skins, not for him (10-12). This is why he does not answer (13).

Chapter 36: God is almighty, all-wise (5). He is a Teacher who uses suffering to open men's ears to listen and learn where they have gone wrong (8-10). Job should not be longing for death (20), but learning his lesson (22).

Chapter 37: God is great. He commands the thunder and lightning, rain and snow. He spreads out the clouds and the shining skies. Man is as nothing beside God's awesome splendour, his unassailable holiness. Men are right to fear him (24). He pays no attention to people (like Job!) who grow too big for their boots.

38—42:6
JOB FINDS SATISFACTION IN GOD'S ANSWER

God breaks in just when Elihu has finished his list of excellent reasons why Job cannot expect an answer! God *is* almighty, far and away above humanity. But he is also near. He hears, and he cares. Job had imagined himself putting his case to God, asking his questions. But imagination is not reality. It is God, not Job, who asks the questions now. And through the succession of searching questions Job finds his opinion of himself shrinking, his concept of God expanding. His mental image of God had been altogether too small. The God who confronts him is God on a different scale altogether.

Chapters 38 and 39: where was Job when God made the world, light and darkness, wind and rain, the constellations in their courses? What does Job know about

Sunset over the Galilee hills. Job had to bow before the wonder of God's majesty in creation to see himself and his own misfortunes in perspective. Only then did God restore to him his family and possessions and flocks.

the creatures of the wild – the lion, the goat, the wild ass and ox, the ostrich, the horse, the eagle? Did he make them? Can he feed them, tame them – *as God can*?

Chapters 40 and 41: is Job God's equal, that he calls him to book, and questions his justice? (Job's wild words had brought him dangerously near the sin of the first man.) Look at just two of my creatures, says God – Behemoth (the hippopotamus) and Leviathan (the crocodile). Look at their strength (40:16; 41:27); their sheer untameability (40:24; 41:1-2). Man is utterly powerless to control them. What folly then to claim equality with God who made them!

42:1-6 contains Job's reaction, the climax of the book. Job now realizes he had been dabbling in things beyond his understanding, totally out of his depth. Before, he had gone by hearsay; now he has seen God for himself, as he longed to do. There is now no question of putting his case; seeing God is enough. His questions remain unanswered, but he is satisfied. It is unthinkable that this God could ever let him down or act inconsistently. He can trust, where he does not understand. Now he can accept what comes. Self-righteousness melts away.

Job regrets the bitter things he has said. As he looks at God and worships, he sees himself and his problem in perspective.

42:7-17
EPILOGUE

Verses 1-6 are the high point in the story. This final passage in prose merely rounds things off. Job has been vindicated, and this must be visibly demonstrated. (There is no promise of a fairy-tale ending to every case of suffering.)

God has taken Job to task for his reaction to suffering, but his integrity is beyond question. Job's good name is as clear as his conscience. It is the three friends who have been wrong. Job's was an honest search for truth. They would not allow for truth being bigger than their understanding of it – and so they were guilty of misrepresenting God. They must obtain Job's forgiveness before God will forgive them.

Significantly, it is at the point when Job has accepted his suffering and forgiven his friends, that God reverses his fortunes. Friends, prosperity, family are all restored to him, with a long life in which to enjoy them.

The psalms express the whole range of human feeling and experience, from dark depression to exuberant joy. They are rooted in particular circumstances, yet they are timeless, and so among the best-loved, most-read, parts of the Bible. In our modern age we are stirred by the same emotions, puzzled over the same fundamental problems of life, cry out in need, or worship, to the same God, as the psalmists of old. We find it easy to identify with them. And we find their sheer, dogged faith, the depth of their love for God, both a tonic and a rebuke.

Psalms, the Old Testament hymnal, is a collection of five books: 1-41, 42-72, 73-89, 90-106, 107-150. At the end of each section (e.g. 41:13) the break is marked by a 'doxology' (a formal ascription of praise to God), Psalm 150 forming a doxology to the whole collection. Within the five books the psalms are often grouped, according to common themes, a common purpose, or a common author/collector. Most of the psalms are prefaced by a title or heading (these are omitted in New English Bible, Jerusalem Bible; given in notes in Good News Bible) which is later than the psalm itself but preserves very ancient Jewish tradition. Some name the author or collector, and relate to specific events in history (for a list of those linked with David's life-story, see page 247). Seventy-three psalms bear David's name – some, no doubt, dedicated to him as king; some collected by him; and a good many, surely, his own composition. (1 Samuel 16:17-23 and 1 Chronicles 25:1-8 are not the only indications that the king was a gifted poet and musician.) Many other titles concern the musicians, instruments, musical settings, or indicate the type of psalm ('Maskil', 'Miktam'), although the meaning of many of the terms used can now only be guessed at.

There have been many attempts to classify the psalms, and they can be grouped in a number of ways, for example by theme. There are psalms which plead with God and psalms which praise him; appeals for forgiveness, or the destruction of enemies; prayers for the king, or for the nation; 'wisdom' psalms (see page 317) and psalms which probe life's problem-areas; and psalms (such as 119) which celebrate the greatness of God's law. Many psalms are a blend of several of these common themes. All are part of the religious life of Israel.

Perhaps one of the most helpful ways of grouping the psalms is by the main literary types:

■ Hymns, in praise of God's character and deeds (e.g. Psalms 8; 19; 29).
■ Community laments, arising out of some national disaster (44; 74).
■ Royal psalms, originating in some special occasion in the life of the reigning king (2; 18; 20; 45).
■ Individual laments (3; 7; 13; 25; 51).
■ Individual thanksgivings (30; 32; 34).

It is very difficult to date individual psalms, or to discover just how and when they were collected and compiled, though the process began with David, if not before, and continued into the days after the exile. Manuscripts found at Qumran have shown that the whole collection as we have it must have been finalized some time before the Maccabean period (2nd century BC).

The words of C. S. Lewis underline one further important point:

'The psalms are poems, and poems intended to be sung: not doctrinal treatises, nor even sermons... They must be read as

*poems if they are to be understood…
Otherwise we shall miss what is in them
and think we see what is not.'*

So, before turning to the psalms
themselves, it is important to read the
outline explaining the conventions of
Hebrew poetry, page 316.

BOOK 1

PSALM 1 The blessing which results from the study and practice of God's law

Verses 1-3 depict the happy man, who
resolutely turns his back on evil and sets
his heart and mind on God's law. 4-6, in
terrible contrast, picture the present life
and future fate of the wicked.
Verse 3: compare the picture here with
Jeremiah 17:7-8.
Verse 4: see the picture of winnowing,
page 91.

PSALM 2 Rebel man – sovereign God

Verses 1-3: the world-rulers enter into a
futile conspiracy. 4-6 depict the power of
God and his chosen man (primarily the
king, ultimately the Christ, see note).
7-9: God delegates authority. 10-12: the
psalm ends on a note of solemn warning.
Zion (6): the citadel of Jerusalem.

PSALM 3 A cry to God in time of danger

(The title refers the psalm to the specific
time of Absalom's rebellion against his
father, King David, 2 Samuel 15.)
Verses 1-2 outline the situation. 3-6: in
God, the God who answers, is security
and freedom from fear. 7-8: the psalmist
calls on God to save him.

*A tree planted beside water was a vivid picture in
a dry country such as Israel. The roots of this tree
go down into the waters of the Lake of Galilee.*

PSALM 4 A prayer for the night

Trust in God sets mind and body at rest.

Verse 1: past answers to prayer give grounds for present confidence. 2-5: a reprimand is followed by command. 6-8 describe the joy and peace which nothing can shake.

PSALM 5 A prayer in the morning

Beset by men who lie and flatter while they plot his downfall (6, 8-10), the psalmist appeals to the God who loathes every semblance of evil (1-5), the Defence and Rewarder of the good (11-12). This is the God he will worship and serve (7).

PSALM 6 A cry of anguish

Sick at heart (disturbed in mind, ill in body), the psalmist pleads with God for his life (1-7), and is assured of God's answer (8-10).

Sheol (5, some versions): the shadowy world of the dead. Although the psalmists thought in terms of some kind of continued existence beyond the grave it was largely negative. Death cut a man off from all he could experience of God during his life. His tongue was still; he could no longer sing God's praises.

PSALM 7 A prayer for protection and the just judgement of God

The psalmist casts himself on God, knowing his cause is just (1-5). He calls on God to clear his name, to support the right and break the wicked (6-11). He describes the terrible fate awaiting those who refuse to repent (12-16) and closes on a note of thanksgiving.

Christ in the Psalms

The primary meaning of the psalms is always to be sought first of all in their immediate, historical context. But this does not exhaust their significance. No one can read the psalms without becoming aware that certain psalms and individual verses have a deeper, future significance beyond the simple meaning of the words. The Messiah is not mentioned by name, but his figure is foreshadowed, as later generations of Jews came to realize. And the New Testament writers are quick to apply these verses to Jesus as the prophesied Messiah.

■ Some psalms, particularly the 'royal psalms' (of which 2, 72, 110 are the most striking) picture an ideal divine king/priest/judge never fully realized in any actual king of Israel. Only the Messiah combines these roles in the endless, universal reign of peace and justice envisaged by the psalmists.

■ Other psalms depict human suffering in terms which seem far-fetched in relation to ordinary experience, but which proved an extraordinarily accurate description of the actual sufferings of Christ. Under God's inspiration, the psalmists chose words and pictures which were to take on a significance they can hardly have dreamed of. Psalm 22,

the psalm Jesus quoted as he hung on the cross (verse 1, Matthew 27:46), is the most amazing example. Compare verse 16 with John 20:25; verse 18 with Mark 15:24. (See also Psalm 69:21 and Matthew 27:34, 48).

■ There are also many other verses in the psalms which New Testament writers apply to Jesus as the Christ:
Psalm 2:7, 'You are my son': Acts 13:33
Psalm 8:6, 'everything under his feet': Hebrews 2:6-10
Psalm 16:10, 'not give me up to Sheol..': Acts 2:27; 13:35
Psalm 22:8, 'let him deliver him': Matthew 27:43
Psalm 40:7-8, 'I delight to do your will': Hebrews 10:7
Psalm 41:9, 'my close friend...has lifted his heel against me': John 13:18
Psalm 45:6, 'your throne endures for ever': Hebrews 1:8
Psalm 69:9, 'zeal for your house has consumed me': John 2:17
Psalm 110:4, 'a priest for ever after the order of Melchizedek': Hebrews 7:17
Psalm 118:22, 'the stone which the builders rejected..': Matthew 21:42
Psalm 118:26, 'blessed is he who comes in the name of the Lord': Matthew 21:9

The sun setting behind the cedars of Lebanon. God's creative power was seen to be expressed in the glory of the sun and stars and closer at hand in the wonders of nature.

PSALM **8** God – and man

Verses 2-4: as he contemplates the great expanse of the universe the psalmist is overwhelmed by a sense of man's littleness. He marvels that God not only bothers about man, but has set him over all other creatures (5-8). The psalm ends, as it began, with a refrain of praise to God (1,9).
Verses 4-6: see also Hebrews 2:6-9 and Genesis 1:28.

PSALM **9** A song of praise

One of a number of 'acrostic' psalms, in which the first letter of each verse follows the order of the 22-letter Hebrew alphabet. Only the first 11 letters (with one omission) are used here, and the acrostic seems to continue (imperfectly) in Psalm 10.

Verses 3-8 give the reason for the outburst of praise. God has executed justice and upheld the right. He is an unassailable fortress (9-10). Praise him (11)! Trouble is by no means over (13), but past experience gives ground for fresh hope (15-20). 'Thy kingdom come'!

PSALM **10** A prayer to God to defend the helpless

Verses 1-11: times are bad. Evil men defy God and disregard his laws and get away

with it. The poor are their helpless victims. 12-18: the psalmist calls on God to act, confident that he will break oppression and defend those who have no one but himself to turn to.

PSALM **11** A declaration of faith

No matter what the danger, the man who trusts in God has no need to panic (1-3). He knows God is still sovereign: the champion of justice, the Judge of evil (4-7).

PSALM **12** A prayer for God's help

Surrounded by men whose word cannot be trusted (1-4), the psalmist puts his faith in the utterly dependable promises of God.

PSALM **13** From despair to hope

In his misery it seems to the psalmist that God has forgotten him. How much longer must he bear it? Will only death bring an end to it (1-4)? No! All his past experience assures him he will again have cause to thank God for his goodness (5-6).

PSALM **14** The folly of godless man

Society is corrupt: the bias to sin universal (1-3). In wilful blindness men pit themselves against a God who not only exists but punishes and avenges every aggres-

sive act against his people (4-7).
Verses 1-3: Paul uses these verses to support his case that no human being is sinless when measured by God's standards (Romans 3).
Jacob...Israel (7): the psalmist calls the nation by the two names of its founder. The wily Jacob was given the new name 'Israel' after his momentous encounter with God at Peniel (Genesis 32:28).

PSALM **15** Testimonial of the man of God

What does God require of the individual who seeks his company? He expects right conduct, right speaking (2-3a), right relationships with others (3b-4), and a right use of wealth (5). See also Psalm 24.
Hurt (4): i.e. who keeps his word whatever the cost.
Verse 5: one of the Jewish laws, see Leviticus 25:36-37. It was not a total ban on lending at interest, but applied to fellow Israelites.

PSALM **16** The way of faith

The man who sets his heart on God and puts his life in God's hands (1-6) finds joy and security for the present and need not worry about what lies ahead (7-11).
Verse 6: the boundary lines of the plot of land a man inherited.
Verse 10: the psalmist is probably thinking of premature or sudden death. Paul, applying the words to Christ, sees their deeper significance (Acts 13:35-37).

PSALM **17** Appeal to God from a clear conscience

This psalm raises two problems which occur in a number of other psalms: self-justification and vengeance. See page 339.
Apple (8): i.e. the pupil; the part of the eye a man instinctively protects.

PSALM **18** Praise to God for deliverance

This is a revised version of David's victory song (2 Samuel 22). The outburst of love and praise (1-3), and the cataclysmic terms in which he describes God's rescue (7-19), give some idea of his previous desperation. He owes his life, his triumphs, his throne, everything to God (28-50).
Sheol (5): see on Psalm 6.
Verses 20-24: for the problem of self-justification see page 339.

PSALM **19** God's wonderful creation; his perfect law

God's universe describes his glory in speech without words (1-4). The psalmist's thought leaps straight from the sun, with its all-pervading, searching rays, to the law of God – pure and clean, bringing joy and wisdom, instruction and enlightenment to man's heart (4b-11); and to his own need of protection and cleansing from sin (12-14).

Terracotta head of a Babylonian demon, 6th or 7th century BC.

PSALM **20** Prayer for victory for the king

A national prayer; the king himself speaks in verse 6.

PSALM **21** Thanksgiving for the king

Verses 1-7 rejoice in all God's goodness.

Verses 8-12 look to the future. With God's help the king will put down all his enemies. King and people join to praise him (13).

PSALM **22** Suffering and salvation

It was the opening words of this psalm that Jesus used to express his anguish on the cross (Matthew 27:46). And the terms the psalmist chose to describe his own agony of mind and body became an extraordinarily precise description of the last hours of the Messiah (see page 329). The psalmist only *felt* himself deserted by God (confidence returns, verse 22), but the separation Jesus experienced was real – the crushing, suffocating weight of human sin which shut him out from the Father's sight.

Despair at God's silence (1-2) and his own situation (6-8, 12-18) alternates with hope – hope that springs out of every recollection of God's past dealings with him (3-5, 9-11). The final prayer (19-21) brings new inward assurance, expressed in open praise (22-31). If, at the deepest level, the early verses of Psalm 22 speak of Christ's suffering, surely the closing verses speak of the world-wide deliverance he made possible.

Bulls from Bashan (12): Bashan, north of Gilead on the east of the Jordan, was famous cattle country.

PSALM **23** Sheep and Shepherd

This best-known, best-loved of all psalms pictures God, the Good Shepherd (see also John 10). He provides all that his people need. He leads them through life. He secures them from all harm (1-4). Verse 5 introduces a second picture: God, the perfect host, feasting his people with good things.

His name's sake (3): i.e. because this is his nature. God's love and care are wholly in keeping with his character.

A shepherd leads his sheep to find green pastures.

'Even though I walk through a valley dark as death I fear no evil...'; rocky valleys in the hills of Samaria.

PSALM **24** Worship

This psalm is a processional hymn, possibly written for that great occasion in David's life when the ark was first carried into Jerusalem (2 Samuel 6:12-15).

The whole world and everything in it is God's. Who then is worthy to stand in his presence (1-3)? The answer (4, and see Psalm 15) would lead to despair if God were not 'the God of Jacob' (6) – the twisted character God took up and made the founder of Israel. Verses 7-10: the ark is at the gates of the city: open the doors for God himself to enter!

PSALM **25** Prayer of a troubled man

An acrostic psalm (see on Psalm 9). The psalmist is harassed by the incessant attack of his enemies, and disquieted in his own conscience (1-3, 16-21). Deeply aware of his need, he turns to God for his help and leading, asking to experience again his love and forgiveness (4-15). What more reassuring verse for any of God's children than verse 10?

PSALM **26** Prayer of a good man

The psalmist is not claiming perfection (see page 339) but a consistent life of trust and obedience to God. Compare this self-portrait with the first part of Psalm 1.

PSALM **27** Trust and commitment to God

The man whose priorities are right (4,8) has nothing to fear (1-3, 5-6). He knows where to turn in trouble (7-12) and his hope is well founded (13-14).

PSALM **28** Prayer—and its answer

Danger leads to a cry for help, and a plea for the punishment of those evil men who are the source of the trouble (1-5). Prayer turns to praise at the assurance that God has heard and answered (6-9).

The cataracts and 'mighty waters' of the upper reaches of the Jordan provided vivid imagery for the psalmists' poetry.

PSALM **29** The thunder of God

In the torrent of rain, the ear-splitting thunderclaps, the blaze of lightning, the roaring wind that sets the great forests in motion, the psalmist hears God's voice. For God made and orders them all (3-10). Let the hosts of heaven sing his glory (1-2)–and may he bless his people on earth (11).

The style of this psalm is very similar to ancient Canaanite poetry.

Sirion (6): 9,000 ft/3,000 m Mt Hermon, on the Israel/Lebanon border.
Kadesh (8): a place in the desert south of Beersheba.

PSALM **30** Thanksgiving for a new lease of life

(The events in 1 Chronicles 21 may possibly provide the background to this psalm.) The dark days when life was in danger are past (2-3, 6-10). Easy times bred self-reliance (6). But this experience has put life into perspective (5) and shown the psalmist his own helplessness (7-10). Now that the danger is behind him, he gladly and openly acknowledges his debt of gratitude to God (11-12).

PSALM **31** Trial and trust

Verses 1-8: the psalmist turns to God for refuge (1-5); trust deepens as he recalls God's past dealings with him (6-8), 9-13: his mind returns to the painful present. 14-24: from his own trouble he turns to God again, with such renewed trust in his goodness and love that he is able to give encouragement to others (23-24).

Verse 5: with his dying breath Jesus echoed these words (Luke 23:46).

PSALM **32** Confession and the joy of God's forgiveness

Guilt suppressed becomes an intolerable burden (3-4). Confession and forgiveness

bring a joyous lightness of heart (1-2, 5).
Out of his own experience the psalmist
encourages others to pray to God with
confidence. (In verses 8-9 God himself
speaks).

PSALM **33** Everybody sing!

Tune up the instruments. Sing aloud in
praise of God's character (4-5) and his
great power (6-7). Stand in awe of him
(8-9). Praise his sovereign rule in the
affairs of men – his unfailing care for all
who honour him (10-19). Sing a song of
trust in him (21-22).

A new song (3): to surpass the best of the
old. Every fresh experience of God calls
forth new praise. John, in his vision, heard
a new song in heaven (Revelation 5:9-10;
14:3).

PSALM **34** God's care for his people

An acrostic poem (see on Psalm 9). The
title seems to refer to the incident in
1 Samuel 21:10 – 22:1, although the king's
name there is Achish.

A man with such a story to tell of
God's faithfulness cannot help sharing it.
He owes it to God and his fellow
believers (1-10). In the psalmist's
experience, the man who honours God
finds life (11-14). His misfortunes may be
many, but God brings him through them
all (19-22).

PSALM **35** A prayer to God to uphold the right

(For the ethical problems raised by the
psalm see page 339). Confident that
right is on his side (he states his case in
7, 11-16, 19-25), the psalmist calls on God
to pay back his enemies in their own
coin (1-6, 17, 26) and clear his good
name. Then he will praise God and tell
others of his righteousness (9-10, 18, 28).

PSALM **36** The unfailing love of God

Verses 1-4 portray a man dedicated to his
own evil ways. 5-10 contrast the character

Elamite musicians, with harps and double pipes.

of God – loving, faithful, good; the source
of life and light and all the good that
man enjoys. 11-12: a personal prayer.

PSALM **37** Good and evil

An acrostic poem (see on Psalm 9) full
of the proverbial sayings that the
wisdom writers loved (see 'Poetry and
Wisdom Literature', page 316).

Wherever one looks, people are
flagrantly disobeying God's law, and
getting away with it. Don't be tempted to
envy them, says the psalmist. Things are
not what they seem (1-2, 7b-9). The
wicked are in a far from enviable
position. Their time will soon be up, but
blessing and security await God's
people (the message drummed home by
the proverbial sayings of 10-40, which
paint the contrast between the wicked
and the good). Go on doing good; be
patient; and trust God to act (3-7a).

PSALM **38** In great distress: a prayer for forgiveness

Sin has resulted in physical sickness (3,
5, 7), as well as mental anguish (2, 4,

6, 8). Friends and family stand aloof (11), and the opposition have the chance they have been waiting for (12, 16). The psalmist admits his sin, with bitter regret, and cries to God for help (21-22).

PSALM **39** Man's 'little life'

The psalmist struggles to contain his thoughts, for fear of dishonouring God, but they burst out (1-3). He feels death at his shoulder; life as insubstantial as a puff of wind (5-6). And he cries out to God to reassure (4) and forgive him (8), and to remove his troubles (10-13).

PSALM **40** Praise and prayer from a full heart

The psalmist has openly declared God's marvellous dealings with him (9-10). He looks back with deep thankfulness (1-3), and spells out for others the things he has learnt about God (4-8). But his troubles are not yet over (11-17). He is still conscious of his need. And he appeals afresh to God for his help. (Verses 13-17 are repeated in Psalm 70.)

PSALM **41** 'Prayer of a sick and lonely man'

Verses 1-3 state a general truth. Happy the man who helps those in need; when trouble hits *him* he finds that God is at hand to help. 4-12 outline the psalmist's own case: his illness, his isolation, his reliance on God. Verse 13 is a formal stanza of praise to God, added to mark the end of the first book of psalms.

dispirited, he contrasts past joys (when he led the pilgrim throng to the sanctuary, 42:4) with the unhappy present. He is filled with longing for God's presence (42:2; 43:3-4). And, black as things are, faith and hope still break through (42:5, 11; 43:5).

Verse 6: the River Jordan rises near the foot of Mt Hermon on Israel's northern border. 'Mount Mizar' remains unidentified.

This picture echoes the psalmist's thirst for God, which he compares to the longing of a hind for running streams.

BOOK 2

PSALMS **42** and **43** Longing for God

These two psalms share the same theme and the same refrain (42:5, 11; 43:5), and probably began as a single poem.

The psalmist is in exile in the north (42:6), surrounded by godless men who mock his faith (42:3, 10; 43:1-2). Deeply

PSALM **44** National lament

This psalm is prompted by a disastrous defeat. Israel is bewildered. After all the stories of God's amazing actions in their early history (1-3), and their complete reliance on him (4-8, 17-18), now this defeat! God had deserted them (9-12). They are disgraced (13-16), and cannot understand why (17-22). Verses 23-26 are a real cry from the heart for God's help.

The switch to 'me' and 'my' in 4, 6, 15 may indicate a single voice (that of the king or high priest) leading the public prayer.

Verse 19: 'the place where jackals live', i.e. the desert.

Verse 22: Paul quotes these words, describing the experience of Christians (Romans 8:36).

PSALM **45** A royal wedding song

The actual occasion may have been the wedding of King Ahab of Israel to Jezebel, princess of Tyre (12, and see on 8 below). If so, the king's reign soon changed for the worse (1 Kings 16:29-33).

Verses 1-9: the poet's eloquent praise of the king's majesty and godly rule. 10-15: a word to the bride in all her finery. Verses 16 and 17 are addressed to the king.

Palace ivory (8): a further possible link with Ahab. Archaeologists have discovered beautiful carved ivories in his palace at Samaria, see page 271.

Ophir (9): see on 1 Kings 9:28.

Tyre (12): important sea-port and city-state; modern Sour in Lebanon.

PSALM **46** 'A mighty fortress is our God'

This psalm – the one on which Luther based his famous hymn – may have been written following Sennacherib's attack on Jerusalem (2 Chronicles 32), some natural disaster, or in anticipation of the events heralding Messiah's coming. Verses 4-5 have a parallel in Revelation 22:1-5, where the ideal is perfectly realized. The psalmist glories in God's presence with his people (1, 4-5, 7, 11), and his real and unassailable protection.

PSALM **47** Shout and sing!

A psalm acclaiming God as Israel's King and Lord of the world. Let everyone rejoice and sing his praises.

PSALM **48** Zion, glorious city of God

An outburst of relief and joy at the city's reprieve from invasion (perhaps Sennacherib's, see 2 Chronicles 32).

North Zaphon (2): the psalmist may have used this phrase because the north was the traditional seat of the gods.

Verse 7: New English Bible, 'like the ships of Tarshish when an east wind wrecks them'. For 'ships of Tarshish', see on 1 Kings 10:22.

Mount Zion, lit here by the setting sun, was one of the hills on which Jerusalem was built. It came to stand for the city and its temple worship, and expressed the longing of the pilgrim and worshipper for his spiritual home.

PSALM **49** Meditation on life and death

A typical piece of 'wisdom' on life's inequalities. At the end of the line death waits for the materialist – not even he can buy himself off. The 'moral' is similar to that of Jesus' parable of the rich man (Luke 12:16-21).

Generally speaking the psalmists have no clear concept of life after death, and verse 15 is therefore often taken as a reference to premature death. But this undermines the reasoning, which re-quires an ironing out of this life's inequalities beyond the grave.

PSALM **50** God calls man to account

In verses 1-4 the summons comes. 7-15: God speaks in warning to his loyal people. It is not enough to go through the ritual motions. It is the thankful heart, not just the token thank-offering, that counts. 16-21: there are serious charges against those who mouth God's commands, yet disobey them; who take up with crooks but are prepared to ruin a member of their own family, leaving God out of account.

PSALM **51** Plea for forgiveness

The title links this psalm with Nathan's confrontation with David following his adultery with Bathsheba and the death of Uriah (2 Samuel 12). But verses 18-19 seem to be later, belonging to the time after Jerusalem fell to the Babylonians.

The psalm itself is profoundly moving. It lets us see right into the soul of a man who has loved God yet fallen into grievous sin. He has been made to see himself through God's eyes, and he is heartbroken. He makes no excuse, simply accepts God's judgement and admits his guilt. All he can do now – knowing God's love and mercy – is ask forgiveness and the chance of a fresh start.

Verse 5: the meaning is not that conception or childbirth are sinful in themselves, but that sin is ingrained from the very first moment of existence.

Hyssop (7): the herb used in the purifica-tion ritual described in Numbers 19.

Bloodguilt (14): this certainly fits David's case. He arranged for Uriah's death in order to cover up his own sin (2 Samuel 11).

PSALM **52** The doom of the wicked

Verses 1-4 describe man's guilt; verse 5 God's certain reprisal. 8 and 9 are a personal expression of trust and thanksgiving. The occasion of the psalm, according to the title, is Doeg's betrayal of David (1 Samuel 22).

PSALM **53**

A revised version of Psalm 14, see page 330.

PSALM **54** Cry for help

According to the title, this is David's appeal to God after the Ziphites betrayed his position to Saul (1 Samuel 23:19ff.).

PSALM **55** Prayer of a man in trouble

The title attributes the psalm to David. The content fits in well with the time of Absalom's rebellion (2 Samuel 15-17),

The people of Israel looked to God as all-powerful against the forces of evil. This relief from Assyria, showing the head of a demon, illustrates the fears of other contemporary peoples.

when Ahithophel, David's most trusted adviser, defaulted.

On top of all his other trouble (1-4, 9-11), a friend and fellow believer's treachery is the last straw (12-14, 20-21). The psalmist is full of conflicting emotions: fear and longing to opt out of the whole situation (4-8); and the desire to see his enemies worsted (9, 15). But trust eventually wins (16-18, 22)–for friends may be faithless, but not God.

PSALM 56 'In God I put my trust'

The psalmist has plenty to worry him and shake his nerve (1-2, 5-6). But he knows the answer to fear (3-4, 10-11). And he can safely and thankfully (12-13) leave God to deal with his enemies (7-9).

The title refers to the incident described in 1 Samuel 21:10-15.

PSALM 57 Prayer from among ferocious enemies

Circumstances may be black (4, 6), but the man who fills his mind with God can sing his praise, come what may (1-3, 5, 7-11). Traditionally the prayer belongs to the time when David was in hiding

Self-justification, Cursing and Vengeance in the Psalms

Christians reading the psalms are bound to come across two special problem areas. One is the self-justification of the psalmists. The other is their tendency to call down and spell out the most terrible vengeance. We cannot simply discard the offending passages. They are part of God's word, alongside passages no one would question. Nor will it do to excuse the psalmists on the grounds that they did not possess the teaching of Christ. Because they did possess the law. They knew as well as we do that no man is perfect by God's standards; and they were taught to behave in a loving way to others (Leviticus 19:17-18), even their enemies (Exodus 23:4-5). The law did not license retaliation, it set limits to it (an eye for an eye, *and no more*).

■ **Self-justification.** Two comments may help. First, the psalmist is claiming comparative, not absolute righteousness (i.e. in comparison with other people, not measured by God's standards). 'A good man may sin and yet be a good man.' There is all the difference in the world between those who endeavour to do right and those who deliberately set aside the common laws of God and society. David, in particular, was well aware of his shortcomings before God (see Psalms 51 and 19:11-13). Deep repentance features alongside self-justification in the psalms.

Second, the psalmist is very often picturing himself as 'the indignant plaintiff' putting his case before God the Judge. And, however much we dislike his self-righteous tone, from this point of view he is unquestionably 'in the right'.

■ **Cursing and vengeance.** Before we rush to condemn these passages as utterly 'un-christian', there are a few points worth bearing in mind.

The first concerns God's holiness. In emphasizing God's love we tend today to be over-sentimental about rank evil. But the psalmists knew God as One 'whose eyes are too pure to look upon evil', who cannot countenance wrongdoing. And this is what motivates their call for vengeance on the wicked. God's own character–his good name–demands it.

Second, the psalmists are realistic in recognizing that right *cannot* triumph without the actual overthrow of evil and punishment of wrong. We pray 'Thy kingdom come'. But we are often horrified when the psalmists spell out what this means–perhaps because we are less in love with good, less opposed to evil than they were; or because many of us have never known real persecution for our faith; or because we value life more than right.

However, if the psalmists are guilty of actually gloating over the fate of the wicked, if personal vindictiveness creeps in under the cloak of concern for God's good name, we are right to condemn it–and beware. We can ourselves so easily be guilty of the same thing. But in the psalmist's case the wrong thinking (if wrong thinking there is) never carries over into wrong action. There is no question of him taking the law into his own hands; no Inquisition. Vengeance is always seen as God's province, and his alone.

from Saul (1 Samuel 22:1; 24), but Paul and Silas also knew the truth of it (Acts 16:19-25).

PSALM **58** 'There is a God who judges'

The psalmist calls down God's terrible judgement on corrupt and evil men in power. See page 339.

Gods (1, some versions): a sarcastic reference to the rulers and judges.
Cobra (4): 'deaf' because it does not respond to the snake-charmer.
Verse 8a: in popular belief, slugs and snails left slimy trails because they melted as they moved.

PSALM **59** Prayer for protection and punishment

The title links the psalm to the incident in 1 Samuel 19:11-17, echoed in the refrain 'Each evening they come back...' (6, 14). The psalmist addresses his very personal prayer (1-4, 9-10, 16-17) to the Lord of all the nations (5, 8, 13).
Jacob (13): i.e. the nation of Israel.

PSALM **60** The nation in defeat

The title associates the psalm with the campaign recorded in 2 Samuel 8, when the faith of verse 12 and God's word in verse 8 were realized in eventual victory.
Verses 6-8: God's power over Israel – Shechem, in the heart of the country, between Mts Ebal and Gerizim; Succoth, a city east of the Jordan; Gilead, Israelite land east of the Jordan; Manasseh, Ephraim, Judah, the 'big three' of the twelve tribes – and over Israel's traditional enemies – the Moabites, east of the Dead Sea; Edomites, to the south-east; and Philistines, on the Mediterranean coast.

PSALM **61** Prayer of a burdened king

Precarious on his throne (2, 6-7), the

'O God, thou art my God, I seek thee early with a heart that thirsts for thee' (Psalm 63).

king craves the safety and security only God can give (1-4).

on Israel every nation will sing his praise.

PSALM 62 A psalm of longing and trust

Humbly, trustingly, the psalmist commits his cause to God. Man is bent on destruction (3-4), but what *is* he (9-10)? Power belongs to God, who wields it with love and justice (11-12).

PSALM 63 The thirsting heart

Having tasted the full joy and satisfaction of God's presence (2-8), who can bear to lose it (1)?

Verses 9-10: in sharp contrast to the rest of the psalm. See note on vengeance, page 339.

PSALM 64 Prayer for protection

In verses 1-6 the psalmist pictures his trouble. In 7-9 he expresses his certainty that God will punish all who plot and scheme and slander. The punishment will fit the offence exactly (compare verse 7 with verses 3-4).

PSALM 65 Hymn of thanksgiving

All praise to God who hears and forgives (1-3), who blesses, satisfies and saves (4-5). Praise to God the Creator and Controller of the natural world (6-8). Praise to God who gives the harvest and makes the whole earth ring with joy (9-13)

PSALM 66 Praise and worship: national and individual

Praise God for national deliverance, from the earliest days (5-7) until now (8-12). And thank him for his love and care for every individual (13-20).

PSALM 67 Harvest

At the sight of God's blessing poured out

PSALM 68 Israel's song of triumph

A battle-march cum processional hymn, sung as the ark was carried into Jerusalem (2 Samuel 6), or at the ceremony commemorating that event (see the allusions in verses 1, 7, 17-18, 24-25). The psalm paints a series of vivid pictures of God's victorious power.

Verses 1-6, a tribute to God; 7-10, God leads the nation through the desert; 11-14, the conquest of the land; 15-18, God chooses Mt Zion in Jerusalem to be his home; 19-23, salvation to Israel – death to the enemy; 24-27, the procession; 28-31, may God make a show of his strength to subdue the nations; 32-35, let everyone sing the power and majesty of Israel's God!

Verses 14-15, 22: 'Bashan' is the Golan Heights area, north-east of the Sea of Galilee. In the wide sense the region stretched as far as Mt Hermon, which may be the mountain referred to here. 'Zalmon' is probably another of the mountains in this region.

PSALM 69 Prayer of a man overwhelmed by suffering

A psalm often quoted in the New Testament (John 2:17; 15:25; Romans 15:3). The psalmist's picture in verses 2, 14-15 could be taken for an actual description of Jeremiah's case (Jeremiah 38:6). Verse 35 seems to pinpoint a time following the wholesale destruction of Judean cities, but before the fall of Jerusalem itself.

The psalmist is in desperate trouble, through no fault of his own. His suffering is borne for God's sake (1-12). He prays that God, in his love, will rescue him (13-18). The guilt of his tormentors is clear (19-21): may they be punished for all they have done (22-28). May God set him free to praise him; let the whole earth ring with praise at the restoration of God's people (29-36).

PSALM **70** An urgent call for help

These verses also appear at the end of Psalm 40.

PSALM **71** A prayer in old age

At the end of a long and troubled life (9, 20) there is still no let-up (4, 10-11). But trouble has schooled the psalmist in trust (6-7). Nothing can make him despair. As long as God is with him (9, 12, 18), the future is full of hope (14-16, 19-24).

PSALM **72** Prayer for the king

This last psalm in Book 2 is a fitting one for Solomon's reign (see title) – Israel's golden age of peace, prosperity and power. But it also looks beyond it to the perfect ideal: an endless reign (5) over the entire world (8, 11); a rule of God-like justice and righteousness (7, 12-14); a time of unequalled fruitfulness (16).
The River (8): Euphrates.
Tarshish, Sheba (10): meaning 'the remotest outposts of empire'. Sheba may be a region in Arabia. Tarshish is probably Tartessus in Spain.
Like Lebanon (16): for a small country Lebanon produces an amazing abundance and variety of fruit and vegetables.

BOOK 3

PSALM **73** This unjust world

How is it that those who flout God's laws prosper, and trouble falls on those who least deserve it (3b-14)? It is enough to make a good man envious and bitter (3, 21), and tempt him to say things better left unsaid (15). Only as he turns to God does he learn to see beyond appearances (16, 17). In reality, God's people have everything that matters (1, 23-26, 28). The wicked – for all their wealth – are destined for destruction (17-20, 27).

PSALM **74** Lament for the destruction of the temple

God has turned against his people (1-2). The temple has been desecrated and destroyed (3-8). How long will the anti-God enemy remain master (9-11)? The psalmist thinks of the power of his God (12-17) and pleads with him to keep his promise to Israel (19-20) and sweep the blasphemous enemy away (18, 22-23).
Verses 13-15: a description of the deliverance from Egypt, pictured first as a dragon, then as Leviathan, the crocodile of the Nile.

PSALM **75** God is Judge

Israel rejoices in God's sovereign justice. He alone has power to judge all men.
Verses 2-5: God is speaking as Good News Bible makes plain.
Verse 5: a picture of arrogant power.

PSALM **76** A song of deliverance

Israel marvels at the terrible glory of the God who overthrows all the might of the enemy.
Salem, Zion (2): Jerusalem.

PSALM **77** Past and present

The psalmist calls to mind all God's great deeds on behalf of his people (11-20). But now he seems no longer to care for them (5-10), and there is no comfort in the present troubles (1-4).
Verses 2-6: the trouble which sets the psalmist thinking may be a personal, or a national, crisis.

PSALM **78** Lessons from Israel's history

For a long time Ephraim was the most powerful of the twelve tribes. Joshua was an Ephraimite, and the tribe had great prestige under the judges (Judges 8:2; 12). But with David's accession Judah took the lead. The psalmist thinks over the reasons for Ephraim's rejection, and finds them in Israel's history.

God gave Israel the law to remind them

A bedouin squats in the market-place at Beersheba, demonstrating the present-day equivalent of the ancient 'pipes'.

of him (5-8). But Ephraim disobeyed (9-11). They forgot what had happened in Egypt and the desert – the miracles (13-16, 23-29, 44-53), the rebellions and the punishments (17-22, 30-43). They forgot the pattern that repeated itself after the conquest of the land (54-66). And God chose Judah instead – a city of Judah (Jerusalem) as capital and a man of Judah (David) to be king (67-72).

Verse 9: this seems to be a reference to the defeat of Saul and Israel on Mt Gilboa (1 Samuel 31:1).

Zoan (12): an ancient capital of Egypt.

Verses 13-16: see Exodus 14 and 17.

Verses 24-31: see Exodus 16; Numbers 11.

Verses 44-51: see Exodus 7-12.

Ham (51): one of Noah's three sons, ancestor of the Egyptian people.

Shiloh (60): for a long time the principal sanctuary in Israel – presumably destroyed when the ark was captured by the Philistines (1 Samuel 4).

PSALM **79** Jerusalem in ruins

A lament for the destruction and bloodshed of the fall of Jerusalem (1-4; the city fell to Babylon in 587 BC, see 2 Kings 25:8ff). The people call on God to forgive and help them (5, 8-10a, 11), and to destroy the pagan enemy (6-7, 10b, 12).

PSALM **80** A prayer for the restoration of Israel

The time may be after the exile of the northern kingdom of Israel (2 Kings 17) but before the fall of Jerusalem (2 Kings 25). (The psalmist mentions two northern tribes, and Benjamin, but not Judah in the south.)

Israel is pictured as a great vine planted by God (8-16), stretching out to the mountains and cedars of Lebanon in the north (10), west to the Mediterranean and east to the River Euphrates (11).

Walls (12): i.e. the walls enclosing and protecting the vineyard ('fences round it,' Good News Bible).

PSALM **81** God's message at harvest

Verses 1-5: the people are summoned to celebrate the Feast of Tabernacles. God reminds his people of all he has done for them (6-7) and all he longs to give (10, 14-16). Yet in obstinate disobedience they refuse him and choose trouble (8-9, 11-13).

Unknown voice (5): a puzzling statement, unless it refers back to the time before Moses' day (see Exodus 6:3).

Verse 6: a description of Israel's slave-labour in Egypt.

Meribah (7): see Exodus 17:1-7.

PSALM **82** The justice of God

There is corruption and injustice in the

law-courts: God calls the judges to account.
The gods (1): probably meaning those men who exercise God's right of judgement over others.

PSALM **83** Prayer for help

The nation is in grave danger from an alliance of all the old enemies, plus powerful Assyria (2-8). The people call on God's aid, remembering past victories (9-18).

Descendants of Lot (8): Lot fathered Moab and Ammon (see Genesis 19:36-38).
Verses 9-12: see Judges 4 and 5. Oreb and Zeeb, Zebah and Zalmunna, were Midianite princes put to death by Gideon (Judges 7 and 8).

PSALM **84** A pilgrim's song

He comes with a heart singing for joy at the prospect of worshipping God in his temple. The happiest people in the world – it seems to him – are those who can be there always (4, 10).
Baca (6): possibly an actual valley the pilgrim passes on his way to Jerusalem. But New English Bible 'the thirsty valley' gives the sense.

PSALM **85** Thanksgiving and a prayer

Praise for God's forgiveness in the past (1-3) and prayer for restoration in the present (4-7). All he knows and has experienced of God's love and faithfulness fills the psalmist with optimism (8-13). What God has yet to give will far exceed his past goodness.

PSALM **86** Prayer of a man in trouble

Because he knows God – and all his love and goodness (5, 7, 13, 15) and power (8-10) – he can be confident in putting his case (1-4, 6-7, 14), and trust God for the answer.
Poor and needy (1): a 'bankrupt', not financially, but before God.

PSALM **87** Zion; city of God, mother of nations

A prophecy of the holy city's glorious future: a capital whose citizenship includes even former enemies (4). The Old Testament sees this largely in

When the psalmists cry out for judgement on their enemies it is not without cause. Their language is mild compared to the atrocities they suffered at the hands of invading Assyrians and Babylonians. This relief of an Assyrian soldier holding the decapitated head of his enemy is from Tainat, N. Syria, 7th century BC.

material and geographical terms, the New in spiritual (Revelation 21:1–22:5).

Rahab (4): a poetic synonym for Egypt.

PSALM **88** Cry of a desperate man

This is the darkest of all the psalms. Here is a man who feels life ebbing away (3-9a), and he has no hope beyond death (10-12). There is no one to turn to but God, who is crushing him with trouble (7-8, 13-18). He is in the grip of the blackest depression. Yet faith lives on – how else can one account for his persistent cry to God?

Sheol, the Pit, Abaddon (3, 4, 11): all meaning the shadow-land of the dead as Good News Bible and New International Version make plain.

PSALM **89** A hymn and prayer

The psalmist sings the story of God's faithful love to Israel; his covenant and promise to the line of David (1-37). But now, in a very different present, God is angry with his people; the covenant is broken. Where is his 'steadfast love of old' (38-51)?

Rahab (10): see on Psalm 87.

Tabor and Hermon (12): Tabor, the rounded hump of mountain near Nazareth from which Deborah and Barak swept down to victory (Judges 4 – 5); Hermon, the 9,000 ft/3,000 m peak on the border with Lebanon.

Verse 52: the 'doxology' (see Introduction) added to mark the end of Book 3.

BOOK 4

PSALM **90** A short life and a hard one

The title links this psalm with Moses, who must often have felt like this in the long years of desert wandering. Ecclesiastes also shares the psalmist's mood.

The everlasting God (1-4) – and man,

as transient as a blade of grass (5-6). His span of life is short, yet even this must be worked out under God's judgement (7-10). The psalmist appeals to God's pity as he begs for the return of joy and gladness (13-17).

PSALM **91** Trust God and rest secure

In this psalm the voice of encouragement (1-13) and the voice of God (14-16) speak to the man of faith. Under God's protection nothing can touch him – neither man nor beast, by day or by night; not war, nor disease. (This is not to say his life will be all roses, or verse 15 would have no meaning.)

Verses 11-12: the devil quoted these verses to tempt Jesus (Luke 4:9-12). But Christ had no need to test the truth of God's word, neither had he come into the world to take the soft option.

PSALM **92** 'A song for the sabbath'

A joyous thanksgiving in music and song for all that God has done (5-9); his goodness to each individual, and to all his people (10-15).

PSALM **93** 'The Lord reigns'

– eternal, almighty; his laws and his holiness unchanging.

PSALM **94** God's justice

The starting-point is the wicked – how fully they deserve God's judgement; their stupid lack of understanding (1-11). But as he thinks of God, though the thought of vengeance is never far away, the psalmist moves on to all the help and love and blessing God pours out upon his afflicted people (12-22).

Psalms 95-100 are a group of psalms written in exultant praise of the God who reigns over all his creation.

PSALM **95**

Let us praise and worship God our

Maker (1-7a), remembering that he expects obedience (7b-11).
Verse 8: see Exodus 17:1-7.

PSALM 96

A song of God's salvation, of his greatness and his glory. A song of universal joy at his coming in judgement.

PSALM 97

In praise of God – supreme, triumphant; the Saviour and delight of all who hate evil.

PSALM 98

A song to God the Victor. He comes to rule his kingdom. Let the whole world go wild with joy.

PSALM 99

God the King, the Holy One, is on his throne; God who forgives and disciplines his people, from the least to the greatest.

PSALM 100

'The Lord is God'; 'the Lord is good'. Let the whole earth sing and be glad.
His gates, his courts (4): i.e. the temple.

PSALM 101 The king's manifesto

The king pledges himself to root out evil from private and public life and to reward integrity.
House (2): household and court.
Verse 8: most probably a reference to his daily administration of justice in Jerusalem.

PSALM 102 The cry of man on the rack

Verses 1-11 describe his suffering: ill in body, sick at heart, taunted by enemies, cast off by God. His life is slipping away (11), but God is not subject to time (24,

The psalmists used nature imagery. Beyond the breakers, the long 'hump' of Mt Carmel juts into the Mediterranean.

27). He is Sovereign for ever (12). Surely he will pity his city and free his people (13-22). Surely he will answer the psalmist's prayer (23-28).

PSALM **103** The love and mercy of God

A psalm of humble, heartfelt gratitude to God for all his goodness, but above all for his mercy and his unchanging, unchangeable love. What he has done for one (1-5), he does for all (6-18): so let everyone, everywhere praise him.

PSALM **104** To God the great Creator

The psalmist marvels at the grandeur and the detail, the perfection and completeness of God's work in creation (1-24 – verse 24 sums it all up). Earth and sea (25-26), with everything in them, are his work, and depend entirely upon him (27-30). The train of thought leads into a song of praise (31-35).

Badgers/conies (18): probably the Syrian rock hyrax, a shy little animal about the size of a rabbit, which lives among the rocks.

Leviathan (26): usually the crocodile (see Job 41), but here used more generally of large sea-creatures.

PSALM **105** Praise to God for his covenant with Israel

The call to praise (1-11) is followed by a history of how God chose Israel and gave them the land (12-45): the patriarchs (12-15); Joseph's story (16-23; Genesis 37-46); the deliverance from Egypt (23-38; Exodus 1-12); God's provision in the desert (39-42; Exodus 16-17) and the possession of Canaan (43-45).

PSALM **106** Israel's disobedience

The psalm begins with praise (1-5), but from verse 6 on becomes a confession of the nation's sin, from the very beginning to the psalmist's own day.

Verse 7: the first instance of rebellion, see Exodus 14:10ff.

Craving (14): for the good food of Egypt. God gave them meat but punished them with a plague (Numbers 11).

Verses 16-18: see Numbers 16.

A calf at Horeb (19): Horeb=Mt Sinai. While Moses was in the mountain receiving God's instructions, the people made a golden bull-calf idol to worship after Egyptian custom (Exodus 32).

Land of Ham (22): Egypt; see on Psalm 78.

Baal of Peor (28): the people turned to idol worship and laid themselves open to God's judgement (Numbers 25).

Meribah (32): see Numbers 20:2-13.

Did not destroy but intermarried (34-35): Judges 1 and 2 summarize this part of Israel's history. From that time on (40-46) the story became a repetitive pattern of rebellion against God, followed by enemy occupation, followed by repentance, followed by freedom, followed by further rejection of God.

Verse 48: the 'doxology' which closes the fourth book of psalms.

BOOK 5

PSALM **107** In praise of God the Redeemer

A single theme (man is beset by troubles of his own choosing or making, but God rescues him from them all) is spelt out in four word-pictures (the traveller, 4-9; the captive, 10-16; the sick man, 17-22; the sailor, 23-32). Circumstances differ for each individual, but all share the same experience: as they cry out to God in their need, he hears and answers. All have equal cause to praise him. Verses 33-43 describe God's unchanging love in dealing with his people.

PSALM **108** A hymn to God

The psalm combines extracts from Psalm 57:7-11, and Psalm 60:5-12.

Verses 7-13: see on Psalm 60.

PSALM **109** A cry for vengeance; a call for help

People the psalmist has loved and treated well have returned evil for good. They have no excuse for the attack which has reduced him to a shadow (1-4; 22-25). His bitterness is understandable, but the tirade of 6-20 seems to overstep the mark. See page 339.

PSALM **110** 'King and priest for ever'

This psalm speaks of the ideal, fully realized only in Christ, as the New Testament writers make plain (Matthew 22:41-46; Luke 22:69; Hebrews 5:8-10; 10:12-13). See 'Christ in the Psalms', page 329.

Melchizedek (4): the mysterious priest-king to whom Abraham gave a tenth of his possessions (see Genesis 14:17-20).

PSALM **111** In praise of God

This psalm is identical in form with Psalm 112. Both consist of 22 phrases each beginning with a successive letter of the Hebrew alphabet.

The psalmist rejoices in God's greatness; his faithfulness and justice; his integrity and trustworthiness; his provision and his redemption. Respect for God is the true starting-point of all human wisdom.

PSALM **112** Happy the man who respects and obeys God

For the form, see on Psalm 111 above.

The man who obeys God and cares for his fellow men is sure of reward. He can withstand life's knocks, secure and unafraid.

Verses 2-3: the psalmist describes the reward in material terms because in his day there was no clear concept of the after-life. What he says is generally (but not invariably) true. God's people have their full share of trouble, but are given resources to meet it (7-8).

Psalms 113-118 are a group of psalms linked traditionally with the Jewish feasts of Tabernacles (Harvest) and Passover. In Jewish homes Psalms 113 and 114 are sung before the Passover meal; Psalms 115-118 after it (see Matthew 26:30).

PSALM **113** Our incomparable God

He is above and beyond his creation, yet closely concerned for the humblest of his people.

Ash heap/dunghill (7): the rubbish dump, the place for outcasts (see Job 2:8; Good News Bible, 'misery').

PSALM **114** Passover hymn: God present with his people

The nation recalls God's marvels on their behalf at the time of the exodus.

Verses 3, 5: the reference is to the crossing of the Red Sea (see on Exodus 14) and the later crossing of Jordan (Joshua 3). **Verse 8:** see Exodus 17:1-6.

PSALM **115** The living God: lifeless idols

A psalm which gives an indication of the way many psalms must have been sung – with a single voice leading and the congregation joining in the response (9-11, etc.).

House of Aaron (12): 'priests', Good News Bible. **Verse 17:** meaning that praise is for the living; death stills all tongues.

PSALM **116** Hymn of thanks

A psalm for the individual as he comes to make his thank-offering in the temple. God has heard his prayer and brought him through dark days. Now he pours out his heart in gratitude.

Cup of salvation (13): this is vivid picture-language. God gave him back his life; now he offers it up to God in thanks.

PSALM **117** Call to praise

One version of the ancient harp was the 'nevel', reconstructed here in the Music Museum at Haifa, Israel. Another was the 'kinnor' (see page 238).

PSALM **118** A hymn for the Feast of Tabernacles

The hymn was sung in procession by king, priests and people. As they approach the temple, the king recalls God's victory for his people (1-18). Verses 19-27: the procession, carrying branches, moves from the gateway to the altar.

Verse 22: the despised nation of Israel has become the great power. By Jesus' day Israel, in turn, had forfeited their privileged position (Matthew 21:42-43).

PSALM **119** In praise of the word of God

This is the longest psalm of all – and the

most formal and elaborate in concept. There are 22 eight-verse sections. Each section begins with a successive letter of the Hebrew alphabet, and each verse within the section begins with the same letter. Within this stylized pattern the psalmist makes a series of individual, though not isolated or disconnected, statements about the 'law' (God's teaching) and the individual – interspersed with frequent prayers. He uses ten different words to describe it: God's law, his testimonies (instruction), precepts, statutes, commandments, ordinances (decrees), word, ways (paths), promises and judgements (rulings). And one or other of these descriptions occurs in all but a very few verses. He seems to have taken the same delight in the discipline set by this complex poetic form, as he did in the study of the law itself. In the psalm we see how eagerly and persistently he applies himself to the task of understanding the law. He learns it by heart. He longs for more. Nothing is allowed to deflect him from it. God's word rules his life and conduct, gives him hope and peace, leads him into life. His confidence in it is unbounded, and to see it broken genuinely distresses him. We possess far more of God's word than the psalmist did. But his love and regard for it often puts us to shame.

Psalms 120-134 (the 'Songs of Ascents') are a collection of songs thought to have been sung by pilgrims on their way to Jerusalem to celebrate the three great annual feasts. In many of them the thought and imagery focusses on the holy city.

PSALM 120 The whiplash of wagging tongues

The psalms are full of references to the sins of the tongue – lies, scandal, slander, hypocrisy. The man of God may suffer as much from what people say as from what they do.

Verse 5: a poetic way of saying he is living among barbarians!

PSALM 121 God, the Guardian

The man who trusts God knows where to turn in trouble. With God to guard him he can come to no harm.

The hills/mountains (1): perhaps those on which Jerusalem stands.

PSALM 122 Jerusalem, city of God

The pilgrim prays for the peace of the city, the centre of worship and seat of government for the whole nation.

PSALM 123 Plea for mercy

PSALM 124 God, the Rescuer

Without God's help the nation could not have survived the onslaught of their enemies. The credit is his alone. (How many times this has been true in Israel's history!)

PSALM 125 Secure in God

Those who trust in God enjoy complete security. But let the wicked be warned.

PSALM 126 Laughter and tears

A psalm often associated with the return from exile and the hardships that followed. Verses 1-3 express the people's exuberant joy at God's blessing; verses 4-6 the need to experience this yet again (or a prayer for the restoration of the nation as a whole).

Verse 4: for most of the year the river-beds in the southern desert (Negev) are dry, but when the rain comes the water rushes down them in torrents.

PSALM 127 The futility of human effort without God

Verse 5: disputes and business deals were settled at the city gate. Here the grown-up sons support their father in maintaining the family's interests.

PSALM **128** Blessings of the man who respects and obeys God

The psalmist's picture describes everything the man of his own day asked of life. But see also on Psalm 112:2-3.

Verse 3: the vine and the olive are symbols of peace and plenty—the fullness of God's blessing.

PSALM **129** A prayer for the downfall of all who have crushed God's people

Verses 5-8: see page 339.

PSALM **130** Praying, waiting, hoping for God's redemption

PSALM **131** A psalm of simple trust

PSALM **132** In commemoration of the day the ark was brought to Jerusalem

Verses 1-10: see 2 Samuel 6:12-15; 11-12: God's promise of a royal dynasty (see 2 Samuel 7:11-16); 13-18: Jerusalem is chosen as the religious centre of Israel.

Ephrathah (6): Bethlehem, David's birth-place.

Jaar/Jearim (6): an abbreviation for Kiriath-jearim, where the ark was kept for 20 years following its return by the Philistines.

PSALM **133** The family-unity of God's people

Verse 2: at the high point in his consecration ceremony the high priest was anointed with oil (Exodus 29:7).

Verse 3: the dew is seen as a symbol of blessing. Mt Hermon has an exceptionally heavy dewfall, which meant greater fertility there than elsewhere in the days before piped water and mechanical sprinklers.

PSALM **134** A psalm for those on nightwatch in the temple

PSALM **135** Hymn of praise for public worship

This psalm echoes many earlier ones. God is to be praised for choosing Israel (1-4), for his greatness (5-7, 15-18) and his mighty works (8-14). Let priests and people sing his praise (19-21).

Sihon . . . Og (11): see Numbers 21.

PSALM **136** The 'Great Praise' (Hallel)

The description of God's great works in creation (4-9) and history (10-24) alternate with the people's refrain to God's unchanging, timeless love.

The streams and hills of Galilee are mirrored in the delight of the psalmists in the beauty of the countryside around, expressing the renewal and refreshment God gives to those who trust in him.

Verse 13: see Exodus 14.
Verses 19-20: see Numbers 21.

PSALM **137** Lament of the exiles in Babylon

The old joyful songs stick in the exiles' throats at the memory of the terrible destruction of their city and temple. Instead they cry out for the punishment of the barbarian invaders.

Edomites (7): descendants of Esau and therefore closely related to Israel, but centuries-old hostility divided the two. The Edomites gloated at the news of Jerusalem's ruin (Obadiah 8-14).

Verse 9: see the note on cursing and vengeance in the Psalms, page 339. The Israelites had no doubt witnessed just such atrocities committed in Jerusalem by the Babylonian army (8).

PSALM **138** A song of thanks

God has answered prayer. Once again he has shown his faithful love. He is great and high, yet he cares for insignificant men and women. The psalmist has a continuing story to tell of God's protective care for individuals.

PSALM **139** The God who is there

The psalm is concerned with God's all-knowingness and 'everywhere-present-ness', not in an abstract, but in a highly personal way. God is all-knowing: he knows *me* through and through, even my thoughts. He has known me from before the day I was born (1-6, 13-16). God is present everywhere: wherever *I* go, he is there. He is always with me (7-12, 18b). I will align myself with him in the fight against evil. Let him search out and deal with all that is wrong in me (19-24).

PSALM **140** Prayer for help

The psalmist is in real trouble from the plotting of violent men, and from their venomous tongues. He prays that God will guard him (1-8) and punish them (9-11), in the confident knowledge that God is for the right and implacably opposed to evil (12-13).

Verses 9-11: see the note on cursing and vengeance in the Psalms, page 339.

PSALM **141** A prayer for right reactions

The pull of evil is a force to be reckoned with. The psalmist asks that God will keep him from the very things he condemns in others, in thought and word and action.

PSALM **142** Prayer of a man alone and in trouble

The title links this psalm with the time when David was on the run and in hiding from Saul (1 Samuel 23:19ff.). He cries to the One who knows all about him: the Lord, his refuge.

PSALM **143** Prayer for God's help

The psalmist has reached the end of the line: no more reserve or resources (3-4). But in a desperate situation one refuge remains: God himself (5-12). 'O Lord . . . teach me . . . deliver me . . . lead me . . . bring me out of trouble'.

PSALM **144** A song for the God of victory

What is man that the great God should spare him so much as a passing thought (1-4)? Yet time and again God comes to the rescue (5-11). The song closes with a prayer for peace and prosperity for the future generation (12-15).

Psalms 145-150 are a group of psalms in praise of God, probably intended for public worship. They are used by Jews today in daily prayer. Psalms 146-150 each begin and end with an Alleluia – 'O praise the Lord'!

Musicians in Egypt, with disks of perfume to 'drip' down their cheeks; from the Tomb of Nebamun, Thebes, about 1400 BC.

PSALM **145** 'Great is the Lord'

An acrostic (see on Psalm 9). One letter, missing from the Hebrew text, has been taken into the English versions from the Greek Septuagint as 13b.

Praise is poured out to God for his greatness and power (1-7, 10-13a), and for his character: loving, forgiving, good and faithful, just and kind, satisfying the needs of his creation (8-9, 13b-21).

PSALM **146** Praise from the individual

The focus is on God, the hope and help of his people, utterly dependable, caring for all in need.

PSALM **147** Praise from the nation

God commands the universe (4), the seasons (8), the nations (14), the elements (16-18), with a power that puts him utterly above and beyond mankind. Yet his heart goes out to individuals; all who are hurt and unhappy (2-3). He takes pleasure in those who love and respect him (11). And he gives his people his word to live by (19). Praise the Lord!

PSALM **148** Universal praise

Everything that is owes praise to the Creator: the angels in heaven; sun moon and stars; nature; the deep; every creature on earth and all mankind.

Waters above the skies (4): i.e. the rain.

Horn (14): symbol of power. New English Bible 'he has exalted his people in the pride of power' gives the sense.

PSALM **149** The song of God's faithful people

His people rejoice in the victory God has given, and exult at the judgement of the opposing nations.

A new song (1): see on Psalm 33.

Double-edged swords (6): in the New Testament the double-edged sword is a metaphor for the word of God (Hebrews 4:12; Revelation 1:16).

Vengeance (6b-9): see page 339. Victory for the downtrodden 'must' entail defeat for the forces of oppression.

PSALM **150** Choral symphony of praise

This is the grand climax and finale to the whole collection of Psalms. Every instrument in the orchestra, everything with life and breath in the whole creation, joins in a mighty crashing paean of praise to God.

Proverbs

Proverbs is a book of wise sayings: not simply an anthology, but an oriental textbook, schooling young men in wise and right living by the repetition of wise thoughts. It is wisdom distilled into short, sharp phrases, dramatic contrasts, and unforgettable scenes from life. It sets out what is right and what is wrong (not just a slick formula for success), because 'wisdom' in Proverbs is based on reverence for God and obedience to his laws. The 'fear of the Lord' is the essence of all true human wisdom. This is the starting-point. Proverbs applies the principles of God's teaching to the whole of life, to relationships, home, work, justice, decisions, attitudes, reactions, everything we do and say, and even think. God has taught what is best for us. Experience proves it.

The book divides into eight main sections: a general introduction on wisdom (chapters 1–9); six collections of sayings (10:1–31:9); and an acrostic poem on the perfect wife (31:10-31). For details see below.

It is now fairly generally agreed that in content the proverbs belong to the days of Israel's first kings, although editing continued for some centuries. King Hezekiah, who organized some of the editorial work (25:1), reigned 250 years after Solomon. The book as we have it was finalized, at the latest, by Ben Sira's time (180 BC).

The precise part Solomon played in all this is not known. His name appears in the title, and he is the author/compiler of the two longest collections (10:1–22:16 and chapters 25-29). Solomon was a man of outstanding wisdom (see 1 Kings 3; 4:29-34) and his court became an international centre for the exchange of learning. 1 Kings 4:32-34 tells us that Solomon 'spoke three thousand proverbs; and his songs were a thousand and five.

He spoke of plants…he spoke also of animals, and of birds, and of reptiles, and of fish. Men of all nations came to hear the wisdom of Solomon, sent by all the kings of the earth, who had heard of his wisdom'. Through marriage with pharaoh's daughter, Solomon had close links with Egypt, and perhaps knew the *Teaching of Amenemope* which is so closely paralleled in Proverbs 22:17–23:14, as well as other collections of wise sayings. He and his wise men culled the wisdom of the east, but they incorporated nothing that was not in line with God's standards. See 'Poetry and Wisdom Literature', introduction, page 316.

From chapter 10 on, Proverbs is best digested a few sayings at a time. It may also be a help to study them under themes (see page 358). This way we can weigh one saying against another, and get an idea of the general teaching on a particular topic. It is important to bear in mind that proverbs are by nature *generalizations.* They state what is *generally,* not *invariably,* true. The writers do not deny that there are exceptions. But exceptions are not within the scope of proverbial sayings. For instance, Proverbs states that those who live by God's standards will prosper in the world. This is generally the truth. But it is not an unqualified 'promise'. Job, and above all the life of Jesus, show the other side of the coin.

1:1-7
INTRODUCTION

Proverbs opens with a statement of its purpose (2-6) and basis (7). It is aimed especially at the young and uninstructed – but no one is too old or too wise to learn.

Verse 1: best taken as the title to the whole book, not just the first section. Solomon's own proverbs begin at 10:1.

Fear of the Lord (7): an important recurring phrase in Proverbs (see page 359). It describes a wholesome awe and respect (Good News Bible, 'reverence') for God which expresses itself in obedience, reliance on God and deliberate avoidance of evil (3:7).

1:8 – 9:18
LESSONS ON WISDOM

The teacher addresses his pupils as a wise father would his son. The young

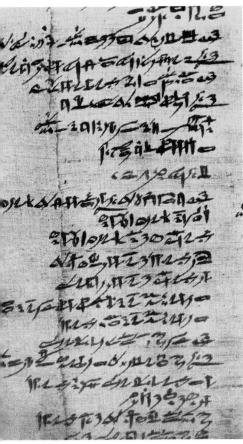

Proverbs is paralleled in contemporary cultures by other collections of wisdom. 'The Wisdom of Amenemope', on this papyrus from Thebes, Egypt, dates from about 1,000 BC.

man has a vital choice to make: between the right course and the wrong one; between wisdom and folly; between going God's way through life and going his own. The teacher describes the two alternatives, and shows where each leads. The theme of every lesson is the same: 'Get wisdom'. Repetition is still a good teaching method!

Chapter 1

Resist the blandishments of violent men (10-19). Listen instead to the voice of wisdom (20-33). All who disregard her call will live to regret it.

Verse 12: the pit of death, 'Sheol' – the place of the dead.

Wisdom (20): the teacher pictures wisdom as a great lady. She competes for Everyman's attention with another woman – Folly – who is no lady at all (see chapter 9). See note on Wisdom under themes, page 358.

Chapter 2

Wisdom is to be found through knowing God. It is hard-won, but worth every effort (1-10). It is a safeguard against wrong company, both male (12-15) and female (16-19). It sets our feet on the right path (20).

Chapter 3

Take wise teaching to heart; stay humble; trust God (1-12). Wisdom offers the things that money can't buy: peace, happiness, security (13-26). Wisdom was at work in creation. It continues to be worked out in the do's and don'ts of everyday life and relationships (27-35).

Chapter 4

The teacher passes on his own father's instruction. Wisdom is the thing to go for: it leads to life. Steer clear of wrongdoing and the company of wrongdoers.

The 'harlot at the window', depicted in this ivory carving from the Palace at Nimrud, Assyria, was a design often used by the Near Eastern craftsmen.

Chapter 5

Be wise when it comes to women. Don't fall for a cheap line, especially from a married woman. She is quite literally a *femme fatale.* Find your pleasure in your own wife: see that you stay in love with her.

Chapter 6

This chapter gives some timely warnings. Beware of accepting unlimited liability for anyone (1-5). Beware of idleness (6-11). Beware the fate of a 'bad lot' (12-19). Keep God's commands. They will save you from the schemes of seductive women.

Six things...seven (16): see on 30:15.
Flirting eyes (25): some things, it seems don't change! And long before Solomon's time women wore eye make-up to aid nature.
Verse 27: the Jerusalem Bible translates 'can a man hug fire to his breast...'

Chapter 7

The teacher describes a young man falling for a married woman's shameless seduction. To judge by the number of warnings in Proverbs this was common enough. Even Solomon, with all his wisdom, was as weak as any at this point – and in the end his foreign wives led him into idolatry (1 Kings 11:1-13).

Chapter 8

In marked contrast to the sly woman of chapter 7, slipping out at dusk to catch her man, Wisdom makes an open appeal to all as they go about their daily business. She is straight and true, the·

The sluggard takes his ease: in this case on a full-size bed under a sun-shade in the middle of a field of water-melons!

value of her instruction beyond any earthly fortune (6-21). She stands at the head of God's creation, the very first of all created things (22-31).

Chapter 9

All the teacher's previous lessons are crystallized in this vivid picture of Wisdom (1-6) and Folly (13-18). Each invites man – empty-headed, wayward man – to a feast. Wisdom sets life before him. On Folly's menu there is only death.

10–22:16
PROVERBS OF SOLOMON

The young man has been faced with the choice and urged to choose wisdom. Now the instruction begins; practical instruction that ranges over every aspect of life. In this first collection, the sayings get their punch from contrast. The second line, or half, of each saying is the antithesis of the first. Each proverb is complete in itself, though some are linked by words or themes into series. They reveal sound psychology and accurate observation of life. They demonstrate the outworking of wisdom and folly in the practical business of living. For the teaching in 10:1–31:9, see under themes, pages 358-9.

15:11: even the realms of the dead (Sheol and Abaddon) are open to God.

17:8: the man is confident his bribe will work, but the practice is wrong (see verse 23).

Proverbs was concerned with the ordinary affairs of daily living.

Important themes in Proverbs 10—31

■ **Wisdom and folly – the wise man and the fool**

This is the main strand of the whole book, the subject of the first nine chapters (see pages 354-357). The sayings point the contrast between wisdom – living by God's standards, keeping to what is right, and folly – man wilfully going his own way. Wisdom leads to life and all that is good; folly is a mere half-life that ends in death. The verses listed below detail the wise course of action in many different circum-stances. They outline the wise man's character, in contrast to the life and character of the 'fool', who shuts his mind to God and reason.

10:8, 13-14, 23; 12:1, 15-16, 23; 13:14-16, 20; 14:1, 3, 7-8, 15-18, 24, 33; 15:5, 7, 14, 20-21; 16:16, 21-23; 17:10, 12, 16, 24, 28; 18:2, 6-7, 15; 19:25, 29; 21:22; 22:3; 23:9; 24:3-7, 13-14; 26:1, 3-12; 27:12, 22; 28:26; 29:8-9, 11.

■ **The righteous and the wicked**

The individual's response to life's alternatives determines which of these two groups he joins. The wise man, on Proverb's definition of wisdom, will be righteous. The gullible fool is always teetering on the edge of wrongdoing. It is more than likely he will end up among the wicked. The proverbs below describe life the righteous life – the life of integrity – and the blessing it brings to the individual and the community. God loves and protects the righteous. The wicked are subject to his wrath. If they flourish, it is only for a short time. They are heading straight for death and destruction.

10:3, 6-7, 11, 20-21, 24-25, 27-32; 11:3-11, 17-21, 23, 28, 30-31; 12:2-3, 5-7, 10, 12-13, 21, 26, 28; 13:5-6, 9, 21-22, 25; 14:9, 11, 14, 19, 32; 15:6, 8-9, 26, 28-29; 16:8, 12-13; 17:13, 15; 18:5; 20:7; 21:3, 7-8, 10, 12, 18, 26-27; 24:15-16; 25:26; 28:1, 12, 28; 29:2, 6-7, 16, 27.

■ **Words and the tongue**

Proverbs places tremendous stress on the power of words and speech, for good and for ill. What we say, and how we react to what others say – advice, or rebuke, or gossip, or tempting suggestions – betrays what we are (see Matthew 12:34-37). The tongue is an incalculable force: it takes a wise person to master it (see also James 3). The proverbs below are full of sound advice and timely warning.

10:18-21, 31-32; 11:9, 11-14; 12:6, 14, 17-19, 22; 13:2-3; 14:5, 25; 15:1-2, 4, 23; 16:1, 23-24, 27-28; 17:4, 7, 27; 18:4, 6, 13, 20-21; 19:5, 9; 20:19; 21:6, 23; 22:10; 25:11, 15, 23, 27; 26:20-28; 27:2; 28:23; 29:20.

■ **The family**

Fads and fashions change, but the basic structure of family life, its joys and sorrows, remains constant. There are still unfaithful husbands, and wives who bicker and nag their husbands out of existence. There are still children from good homes who go off the rails. Proverbs' wise advice on the things that make for a happy and stable home-life, and the things that undermine it, is as sound today as ever.

Parents and children

10:1; 13:1, 24; 17:21, 25; 19:13, 18, 27; 20:11; 22:6, 15; 23:13-16, 19-28; 28:7, 24; 29:15, 17; 30:11, 17.

Wives

12:4; 18:22; 19:13-14; 21:9, 19; 25:24; 31:10-31. (The main advice to husbands comes in the earlier section, e.g. chapter 5.)

■ **Laziness and hard work**

Proverbs contains a good many sketches of the lazy man, too idle to begin a job, too slack to see it through, yawning his way through life until it is too late, and poverty and hunger are on him. There is nothing to commend slackness, but 'in all toil there is profit'.

10:4-5, 26; 12:11, 24, 27; 13:4; 14:23; 15:19; 18:9; 19:15, 24; 20:4, 13; 21:25; 22:13; 24:30-34; 26:13-16; 28:19.

SOME SECONDARY THEMES

■ **Rich and poor; poverty and wealth**
10:15; 11:4, 24-25; 13:7-8, 11; 14:20-21,
31; 18:11, 23; 19:4, 7, 17; 21:13, 17;
22:1-2, 7, 16, 22-23; 23:4-5; 28:3, 6,
11, 20, 22; 30:8-9.

■ **The world of business and affairs; plans
and decisions**
11:1, 15, 26; 15:22; 16:3, 9-11, 33; 17:8,
18, 23; 18:16; 19:21; 20:10, 14, 16, 18,
23; 21:14; 22:26-27; 27:23-27; 28:8.

■ **The proud and the humble**
11:2; 12:9; 15:25; 16:18-19; 18:12; 21:4,
24; 22:4; 29:23.

■ **Friends**
17:9, 17; 18:24; 19:4, 6; 27:6, 10;
and neighbours
25:8-10, 17-18; 26:18-19; 27:10, 14;
29:5.

■ **Masters and servants**
11:29; 14:35; 17:2; 29:19-21; 30:10,
22-23.

■ **Kings and rulers**
16:13-15; 19:12; 20:2; 23:1-3; 24:21;
25:1-7; 28:15-16; 29:12, 14; 31:4-5.

■ **Hopes and fears; joys and sorrows**
12:25; 13:12-19; 14:10, 13; 15:13, 30;
17:22; 18:14; 25:20; 27:9.

■ **Anger**
14:17, 29-30; 15:18; 16:14, 32; 19:11-12,
19; 20:2; 22:24-25; 29:22.

■ **The 'fear of the Lord'**
(although the phrase does not occur
all that often, this is no secondary
theme; as the basis of all wisdom, it
is absolutely fundamental to the
whole book): 10:27; 14:26-27;
15:16-33; 16:6; 19:23; 22:4; 23:17;
24:21. See also in the earlier section,
e.g. 1:7; 3:7.

18:18: in Old Testament times it was common practice to discover God's will by casting lots.

20:10: Leviticus 19:35 condemns the giving of short weight, and the prophets also denounce all such cheating in business.

22:17 — 24:34
TWO COLLECTIONS OF SAYINGS OF WISE MEN

It seems likely that in this section Proverbs makes creative use of material from abroad (see introduction, page 354 and 'Poetry and Wisdom Literature'), in addition to material from Israel's own 'wise men'. The sayings in this section are more connected than in the previous one. They begin with 'things to avoid' (22:22-29). Then come the hazards of social climbing (23:1-8); father and son – discipline and advice (23:12-28); a portrait of a drunkard (23:29-35); teaching on wisdom and folly (24:1-14), and right living (24:15-22). The group of additional sayings (24:23-34) focusses on justice and hard work, with a sketch of the lazy man in verses 30-34. See also under themes, pages 358-9.

Thirty sayings (22:20): the Hebrew has several possible meanings, but it seems to imply a book of sayings which consists of (roughly) 30 paragraphs or chapters.

Ancient landmark (22:28): 'old boundary stone'.

Narrow well (23:27): i.e. one it would be difficult to get out of; 'deadly trap', Good News Bible.

25—29
MORE OF SOLOMON'S PROVERBS (HEZEKIAH'S COLLECTION)

Under King Hezekiah Israel returned to the old neglected patterns of worship. He repaired the temple and resumed the sacrifices, restoring the temple music along the lines laid down by David (2 Chronicles 29). What is more likely than that he should then have turned his attention to the classic wisdom of Solomon? At any rate, it was his men who published this collection of Solomon's proverbs. There is more grouping here than in 10:1 – 22:16, and the proverbs rely more on comparison than contrast for effect. For the teaching, see under themes, pages 358-9.

Weaving material for the market was one of the duties of the good wife. These lengths of cloth are laid out in the traditional bedouin market at Beersheba.

25:6-7: Jesus uses the same theme in Luke 14:7-10, but he broadens it to cover a whole attitude to life.

26:4-5: these two verses are probably meant to be complementary, not contradictory. It is usually pointless to argue with a fool, but there are times when his false reason must be shown up for what it is.

26:8: what could be more nonsensical than fixing a stone to a sling or catapult so that it can't come out?

30
SAYINGS OF AGUR

Both Agur and Lemuel (31:1) are non-Israelites. 'Massa' was an Arab tribe descended from Abraham's son Ishmael. The east was famous for its wisdom, right down to Christ's own day (see Matthew 2:1). Agur is a man whose close observation of life and nature have taught him humility.

Three...four (15): a device indicating that the list is not exhaustive. See also 18, 21, 29 and 6:16.

Verse 19: he finds four sources of wonder: how the eagle can soar; how the snake can move without legs; how the ship can ride the waves; and the mysterious attraction which draws a man to a woman.

31:1-9
SAYINGS OF KING LEMUEL

See under chapter 30 above. Lemuel outlines his mother's teaching. We seem to catch a tone of mild reproach in verse 2.

Son of my vows (2): 'the answer to my prayers', Good News Bible.

31:10-31
THE PERFECT WIFE

Proverbs paints a remarkable picture of the power of woman, for good and for ill. It closes with this lovely acrostic poem (see on Psalm 9) about the ideal wife:

responsible, capable, hardworking and completely trusted. Not only do her husband, family and household depend on her provision and foresight for their physical needs; they owe her their well-being at a much deeper level (11, 12, 26). Her influence extends beyond this immediate circle to society at large (20). And she finds ample scope for all her gifts in the wider spheres of buying and selling and business transactions (16, 18, 24). Where does her secret lie? In that same 'fear of the Lord' in which all true wisdom has its roots.

A girl working at the loom, a picture of the care and industry of the ideal wife in Proverbs 31.

Ecclesiastes

Ecclesiastes is a piece of 'wisdom literature' (see 'Poetry and Wisdom Literature', introduction, page 316), a popular form of writing in Near Eastern countries in Old Testament times. It is not a familiar form today, and can seem disjointed to us, with its apparently disconnected thoughts and sayings and observations on life. But the theme of Ecclesiastes is singularly 'modern': it is shared by any number of 20th-century novels and plays.

The book simply observes life around and draws the logical conclusions. This is life 'under the sun', life as man sees it. The author imposes no preconceptions. Life as man lives it, without God, is futile, meaningless, purposeless, empty. It is a bleak picture. Nature and history go round in circles: there is nothing new. Add up the profit and loss of human life and you are better off dead. Life is unfair; work is pointless; pleasure fails to satisfy; good living and wise thinking are rendered futile by death. 'Be realistic', says the book. 'If life without God is the whole story, see it for what it is. Don't pretend. Don't bury your head in the sand. This is the truth about life'.

But this is not – like so many modern writings – just cynicism and despair. God never intended man to leave him out of the picture. God can inject joy into every aspect of living: from food and work to home and marriage (2:24-26; 3:10-15; 5:18-20; 9:7-10). He intended man to find ultimate satisfaction not in life but in him. The wise man dies like the fool, it is true, but wisdom is still good and right (2:13). And God will judge the just and the wicked (3:17). Enjoy life, not as an Epicurean ('eat, drink, for tomorrow we die'), but as a man of God, because you depend on him for life and for enjoyment (3:13; 5:19). An empty, futile existence is not inevitable: remember God while you are still young (12:1); respect him and keep his commandments (12:13).

'Ecclesiastes' is the Greek translation of 'Qoheleth' ('the Teacher', 'Preacher', 'Speaker', 'Philosopher'), a word which seems to indicate the author's official title rather than his name. It could be a pseudonym for Solomon, who was 'son of David, king in Jerusalem' (1:1, 12) and the embodiment of wisdom. What man was better qualified to pronounce on life, having tasted it to the full – power, fame, riches, women, all that any man could wish for – and tested out what life was like both under God and without him?

Chapter 1

The author states his theme: the emptiness and futility of life. Men come and go. The cycles of nature and history are constantly repeating themselves. There is nothing new. Even the search for wisdom – man's highest goal – is futile, for 'the more a man knows, the more he has to suffer'.

Verses 1, 12: see introduction.

Under the sun (3, 9, 14, except Good News Bible): a recurring phrase in Ecclesiastes. It indicates 'the world, seen simply from a human standpoint'.

Chapter 2

What is man to do with his days (3)? If he lives for pleasure – all that wealth and status can afford – life is still empty (10-11). Wisdom is far better than folly, but in the end death makes fools of us all. The things we work for must be left behind for others to enjoy. This is the futility of life 'under the sun'. For there is no joy or satisfaction in life apart from God (24-26).

Chapter 3

There is a time for everything in life (1-9). God has made it so. Man understands time, but he cannot comprehend the whole of God's work (11). So he learns to stand in awe of God. There is injustice and corruption in life (16ff.), but God has set a time for just judgement, although all men must die.

Youth and old age in Jerusalem today.

Chapter 4

Such are the oppressions in life that man is better dead; better still never to have been born (1-3). Men wear themselves out with work, trying to outdo one another, never stopping to ask what it's all for (4-8).

From this point in the book the thoughts and observations are more frequently interspersed with advice and teaching, in the proverbial manner adopted by the 'wise'. Wisdom may look foolish in the world's eyes (1:17, 18; 2:14-17) but 'Qoheleth' clearly still believes in it and intends men to live by it (see 12:9-11).

A three-strand cord (12): three are even better than two. A rope made of three strands is hard to break.

Chapter 5

Sound advice on promises made to God (1-7) and attitudes to money (10-12).

Another of life's evils (13-17) is the business crash. The way to live is to enjoy work, and to enjoy prosperity if it comes, for these are God's gifts. Enjoyment is the antidote to gloom about the passing of the years (20).

Verses 8-9: the meaning is not clear. New English Bible translates verse 9, 'The best thing for a country is a king whose own lands are well tilled'.

Chapter 6

What value is long life to a man, without the chance to enjoy all he has worked for (1-6)? Better be still-born or miscarried (3). The man who is ruled by his appetite and desires will never be satisfied (7-9).

Chapter 7

The wise man takes account of death as well as life (2). His outlook on life is serious (1-6). He knows how to enjoy good times and learn from bad ones (14). 'Qoheleth' observes another of life's anomalies (15). There are good men who die young, and wicked men who grow old in their wickedness. Everything is brought to the test of wisdom (23), but life will not add up. Man as God made him was all right; his troubles are all of his own making (29).

Verse 18: the advice is to avoid extremes. Verses 16-17 sould like the cynical tones of worldly wisdom. God would never say we were overdoing real goodness, or advise a little wickedness!

Verse 28: he has found only one man in a thousand worth the name, and not one woman!

Chapter 8

Faith cannot resolve the problem of evil: good men getting what the bad deserve; wicked men admired and having a cushy time. The man of God can only assert

The centuries come and go, village life changes little.

A fisherman is depicted in this relief from Assyria.

young rejoice in their youth, always mindful of God who calls us all to account. Don't wait till old age. Don't wait till life has become futile and empty and there is nothing ahead but death. Fear God – hold him in awe – and obey him.

12:2-6: verse 2 depicts life drawing to an end, the darkness of death closing in. Verses 3-5 are a series of pictures of old age, when strength fails, teeth are few, sight grows dim. Moffatt translates verse 5: 'When old age fears a height, and even a walk has it terrors, when his hair is almond white, and he drags his limbs along, as the spirit flags and fades'. The 'silver chain . . .' (6): metaphors of death.

Verses 9-14: the author's (or editor's) postscript. He has spoken the truth about life, shown it up for what it is without God. His constructive advice is scattered through the book. Now he pinpoints the one thing on which man's life turns: his attitude to God. There is a judgement, when good and evil will be sorted out. Man must live in the light of it. The 'fear of the Lord' (as Proverbs makes so plain) is where true wisdom – and real life – begins.

what he knows is true, though all the evidence is against it (12). Enjoyment is the best thing in life, says 'Qoheleth' (15). Yet he applies his own energy to wisdom, even though God has concealed from man the answer to life's mysteries (16-17).

Chapter 9

One fate – death – comes to all men, good and bad alike (with this one difference, that the good are in God's hands, 1). There is no knowing how long any man has (11-12). So work hard and enjoy life while it lasts, for death cuts men off from all the world has to offer (7-10). Wisdom may not pay, yet it is still worth more than power (13-18).

Chapter 10

A collection of proverbs on wisdom and folly, wise sayings and practical advice, continued in chapter 11.

Chapters 11 and 12

Practical advice leads straight in to the author's conclusions. If life is long, rejoice in it. Rejoice in the light before the dark night of death begins. Let the

'Life under the sun' is not so different today in traditional areas of the Middle East from what it was in the time of Ecclesiastes. Donkey-riders on a desert track pass a cultivated valley.

he Song of Solomon

This 'song of songs' is a series of lyric poems on the theme of love between man and woman. The setting is pastoral: the poems are full of images from the countryside. The time, appropriately, is spring. They are full of the passion and delight of human love.

The poems defy complete analysis and, partly for this reason, have been subject to all kinds of interpretation. Jews and Christians alike have seen them as allegories – of God's love for Israel; of Christ's love for his bride the Church. But the poems themselves give no direct warrant for this. Some see the poems as a drama with two characters: bride and royal bridegroom; some say three: Solomon, the girl, and her shepherd lover. There is, however, no evidence apart from the Song that this kind of literature existed in Israel. Others regard the poems as a series of songs sung during the week-long wedding-feast, as in Syria today, with the bride and groom crowned king and queen.

Whatever the form, the poems as they stand celebrate the beauty and wonder of human love. There is a frank and open delight in physical attraction, which underlines the fact that God intends man to enjoy physical love within the laws he has given.

The notes below provide only a general outline of the Song. All the modern translations provide headings to show who is speaking.

the women of Jerusalem (probably the court or harem). The bride and bridegroom then converse (9-17).

Solomon's Song of Songs (1): the title may imply that Solomon wrote it, or that it was written for, or about, him. He was as renowned in love (1 Kings 11:1-3) as he was in wisdom. But he can hardly be taken as the ideal of single-minded devotion! Nor does the country-shepherd image suit him, unless the language is pure literary-pastoral convention. Hence the appeal of the three-character interpretation of the Song, in which Solomon attempts to win the heart of the girl, who remains true to her shepherd lover.

Kedar (5): a nomadic Arab tribe. Bedouin tents are made of black goatskin.

Pharaoh's chariots (9): Solomon ran a thriving import-export trade in the horses and chariots for which Egypt was famous (1 Kings 10:26-29).

Verses 12-13: 'nard': spikenard, a perfumed ointment. Those women who could afford such luxuries wore sachets of fragrant myrrh, suspended from the neck, beneath their dresses; or on their cheeks, as in the picture on page 353.

Verse 14: a red cosmetic dye was made from henna. 'Engedi': a beautiful freshwater 'oasis' close to the barren shores of the Dead Sea.

Chapter 1

The Song begins (2-8) with a dialogue between the bride, a country girl, and

Chapter 2

The bride's thoughts are filled with the sweetness and longing of love. The bridegroom calls to her in the idyllic

A bride dressed in the traditional finery of the Yemenite Jews.

beauty of springtime (10ff.). It is all in a country setting. Only verse 7 contains any hint of the court.

Verse 7: see also 3:5; 8:4. The significance of this refrain seems to be that love must be allowed to grow naturally, in its own time. It is not to be forced or given an artificial stimulus.

The foxes (15): jackals. If they damage the blossom there will be no fruit.

Chapter 3

In a dream sequence the bride describes the desolate feelings separation brings, and the joy of reunion. Verses 6-11 describe the grand procession of King Solomon.

Wood from Lebanon (9): the famous cedar, imported for building the temple and palaces.

Chapter 4

The bridegroom glories in the beauty of his bride. The imagery is oriental, but love the world over shares the same delighted appreciation of the human form.

A flock of goats (1): their silky black coats gleam in the sun as they ripple over the hillside.

Verses 2-4: her teeth are white and even; her cheeks full and rosy; her neck like a tower hung with trophies.

Senir, Hermon (8): the 9,000 ft/3,000m mountain on the Israel-Lebanon border.

Verse 16: the voice of the bride inviting the bridegroom to enjoy his 'garden'–herself.

Chapter 5

The bride dreams again (2-8). This time the bridegroom comes and she is too slow in letting him in. And again joy turns to desolation. In reply to the women (9) she describes what he looks like. He is as 'altogether desirable' to her as she is to him.

Myrrh . . . (5): she is perfumed as a bride on her wedding night.

Chapter 6

The women question; the bride replies – and the bridegroom again describes the beauty of his one and only love. Not all the queens and concubines can rival her.

The Song of Solomon is full of imagery drawn from nature – as in this lovely scene from Galilee.

Tirzah (4): a beautiful city, the early capital of the northern kingdom of Israel.

Verse 12: New English Bible translates, 'I did not know myself; she made me feel more than a prince reigning over the myriads of his people'.

Shulam (13): if 'Shulam' is a place, its location is not known. There are no grounds for linking the girl here with Abishag the Shunammite (1 Kings 1:3-4), as some have done.

Chapter 7

Again the bridegroom marvels at the physical beauty of his bride. He cannot tear his eyes away. Every detail is perfection. The bride loves him utterly, without reserve (10-13), in all the glory of the springtime.

Carmel (5): the mountain of Elijah's contest with the prophets of Baal, which today makes an impressive backcloth to the port of Haifa.

Mandrakes (13): a plant considered from very early days to have aphrodisiac powers.

Chapter 8

The bride longs to display her affection openly. At verse 5 the scene changes, and the two are together at last. There is

The gazelle, swift on the mountains, provides a ready image for the poet.

nothing that can destroy true love.

Verses 8-9: the girl's brothers debate how to preserve her honour. This she declares she has kept (10).

Verses 11-12: the 'vineyard' is probably a poetic allusion to Solomon's harem and all its attendants. Let him keep it! The bride's love and person is her own to give: it is not for sale.

Introduction

ALEC MOTYER

The people of Israel had become a nation. They had been redeemed from slavery in Egypt. They had been given the law. They were committed to a life of obedience to God, and a religion which constantly reminded them of their dependence on God's forgiveness and mercy.

But they were constantly falling down on their calling and their promises. With idol-worship, civil war, immorality, complacency, the nation needed to be recalled again and again to the whole point of their existence.

The call to obedience

The prophets were men raised up by God to do just this – to call the people back to God and his way. Slackness had grown into forgetfulness. God's holy law for life had ceased to be an effective force moulding individuals and society.

Sometimes the fault was more a reversal of right priorities. The sacrifices were intended to make provision for lapses into disobedience. But there were periods in Old Testament history when they were seen as substitutes for the life of obedience – ritual techniques for keeping God happy.

When the nation's religion was corrupted into this sort of non-moral ritualism, the prophets raised their protest. This explains a whole series of verses in which the prophets at first sight seem to deny the divine authority behind the sacrifices (Isaiah 1:11ff.;

Jeremiah 7:21ff.; Hosea 6:6; Amos 5:25; Micah 6:6-8).

Their intention is rather to recall the people from false priorities; to insist on God's primary requirement that his people should obey his commands and live out his standards.

Distinguishing false from true

Our world today is full of conflicting voices, all claiming to be authoritative pronouncements. Religious opinion varies so widely that quite often there is headlong collision between different views, all of which are put forward in the name of God. How can we tell where the truth lies?

What the prophets said in a similar situation was that what accords with Scripture can be taken as God's truth. In Deuteronomy 13 the false prophet is one who calls people away after 'other gods' and speaks 'rebellion against the Lord your God, who brought you out of the land of Egypt...to make you leave the way in which the Lord your God commanded you to walk'.

In other words, the truth about God spoken by Moses stands as a test of the truth of people's opinions. This passage specifically mentions the command-ments of the Lord: does a prophet subscribe to the old morality of Mt Sinai, or is he preaching a new morality?

We can see this test at work in Jeremiah 23:9-22. Both in his personal life (verses 9-15) and in his public ministry (verses 16-22), the false prophet subscribes to another morality and encourages his hearers to do likewise. Consequently, Jeremiah infers, this man cannot have 'stood in the council of the Lord' (verses 18, 22).

The prophet's call

The true prophet claimed the privilege of being in the Lord's 'council', a word which conveys the idea both of consultation (see 1 Kings 22:19-22) and of close companionship with God.

It is this experience of being brought into close fellowship with God and learning his mind 'in council' that lies behind the three words describing the prophet. All three appear in 1 Chronicles 29:29.

The word translated 'prophet' signifies 'called (by God)', with the consequent task of proclaiming the message of God to men. God's call is not an invitation but an appointment. For instance, the Lord 'took' Amos (7:15) in order to make him a prophet 'to my people'.

The two other Hebrew words are both translated 'seer', meaning 'one who sees'. These words point to the fact that by God's inspiration the prophets have an altogether unique ability to 'see': both into the affairs of men and into the mind of God.

The three words are used synonymously throughout the Old Testament (though 1 Samuel 9:9 points back to a time when some distinction was observed in usage). Taken together, they show the two sides of the prophetic experience. 'Seer' refers to the change God makes in the man he 'takes' for this task (see 2 Peter 1:21). 'Prophet' indicates God's revelation of his mind and will to and through that man (see 2 Timothy 3:16).

'Thus says the Lord'

The prophets, then, were essentially men whom God chose to bring close to himself. The prophet's calling was not hereditary, like the priest's. And God chose his men from many different walks of life. Some,

like Jeremiah and Jonah, were very reluctant recruits, especially when they learnt what God wanted them to do.

But out of their fellowship with God (see 1 Kings 17:1) the prophets came with his message for their contemporaries, and for us too (see Acts 7:38). Sometimes they emphasized their message by means of dramatic action (e.g. Jeremiah 19; Ezekiel 4; see 2 Kings 13:14-19). But mostly their messages were presented in carefully constructed spoken discourses which bear all the marks of premeditation and preparation.

The prophets are very reticent about how they received these messages. We are often told no more than that 'the word of the Lord came' (e.g. Jeremiah 47:1; Ezekiel 17:1; Zechariah 8:1). 'Came' translates the Hebrew verb 'to be', meaning that 'the word of the Lord became a living, present reality', which tells us the content but not the nature of the experience.

However, there is no doubt that the prophets intended their claim to be taken seriously. 'Thus says the Lord' meant precisely what it said. They received from the Lord the very 'words' (note the plural, Jeremiah 1:9; Ezekiel 2:7; 3:4) which they spoke.

We can offer no logical description of their experience. We must simply observe the facts. On the one hand they themselves claimed to speak words which God gave to them; on the other hand they were clearly not impersonal 'tape recorders' of an external 'message'. On the contrary, they were great and colourful personalities.

From the far more remarkable personality of the Lord Jesus – Son of God, Son of man – we can only conclude that when man is wholly at one with God then true humanity, full individual personality comes to perfection. So, in the case of the prophets, God brought them into such close intimacy of fellowship with himself, such harmony of mind and will, such consecration of life (and all by means of the characteristic experiences of salvation) that they both grew to full maturity themselves and by his unique inspiration became the mouthpieces of God (see Exodus 4:15-16; 6:28–7:1).

The present and the future

A glance at the accompanying chart will show that these remarkable men were rooted in history. They were deliberately placed by God at crisis-points.

Amos spoke at a time when financial affluence and religious formalism combined to produce a high-tide of social decadence and permissiveness (see Amos 3:15–4:1; 4:4-5; 2:6-8).

Hosea addressed an era in which established social forms were dissolving before men's eyes.

Isaiah, according to God's estimate of the situation, preached to a people who by rejecting his message would have passed the point of no-return and condemned themselves out of hand (Isaiah 6:9ff.).

Jeremiah belongs in the thick of the final agonies of Jerusalem, and Ezekiel in the first traumatic experiences of exile.

They spoke in the name of the God who is neither an observer nor an occasional visitor but always the active Ruler of

The walls of Jerusalem: the prophets saw themselves as watchmen, warning the nation of coming disaster.

human history. Inevitably, therefore, the prophets not only explained the past (Amos 4:6ff.) and exposed the tendency of the present (Isaiah 5:11-13) but declared above all what God was about to do.

To predict what was about to happen was to them an essential consequence of their fellowship with the Lord of history (e.g. Amos 3:7). When in his presence they felt obliged to ask the vital question 'How long?' (Isaiah 6:11) and to wait to hear the answer. But when they proclaimed that answer it was not in order to satisfy men's curiosity about the future; it was to use their certainty about what was to come as a lever to bring people to repentance here and now.

The characteristic prophetic use of prediction is seen in the words of John the Baptist, the last and most privileged of the prophets. He did not say, 'Repent, in order that the kingdom of God may come,' but, 'Repent, for the kingdom of heaven is at hand' (Matthew 3:2). The sure facts of the future call for a present moral realignment, a getting right with God (see Isaiah 2:5, 10, 22; 3:1ff.; 31:6-7; etc.).

The message of the prophets

God rules in history, he calls men and women to repentance. These are two of the prophets' themes. With three others they constitute the core of their teaching.

■ **The Lord as Ruler of all history.** The prophets took this so seriously that they were prepared to risk depicting the mighty empires of their day as 'tools' in the hand of God (Isaiah 10:5-15). This constitutes a problem for Habakkuk (1:5-11, 12-17): how could the holy God use unholy, corrupt instruments? The only answer the Bible offers is to re-affirm God's sovereign control of the world, a control so intricately exercised that sinners act responsibly according to the dictates and pressures of their own natures, but over all the just and holy Ruler presides, governs and guides (see 2 Kings 19:25, 28; Ezekiel 38:3-4, 10-11, 16; 39:2-3).

■ **The primary need to be right with God.** Since it is God who determines the outcome of every situation, the important thing is not to have the best and strongest human allies (see Isaiah 30:1-2; Hosea 5:13) but to side with God, to get right with him (see Isaiah 30:15). God is always at work to bring his people back to himself (Amos 4:6-11); and the prophet summons men and women to personal readiness to meet with God (Amos 4:12).

■ **The moral foundation of religion and society.** We have already mentioned Jeremiah's rejection of a religion without morality (Jeremiah 7:1-15). The prophets as a whole insist that to be right with God men and women must live in obedience to his standards and commands, and that this produces a sound society. Once people are alienated from God they cannot maintain right relationships with each other (compare Amos 2:7-8 with 9-12).

■ **A blend of judgement and hope.** Time and again, as we hear the prophets analyse the situation in which they live, we see that God's judgement is inevitable. The whole landscape is filled with threatening clouds of gathering wrath, and yet, suddenly, surprisingly, a bright shaft of hope pierces through (Isaiah 6:13; 28:5; 29:5; 31:5; Amos 9:11ff.; etc.). This blending of darkness and light, judgement and hope is more than a fact of the prophetic message: it is a necessity, for they spoke in the name of Yahweh, the Lord, the God-who-saves-his-people-and-judges-his-enemies, the God of the exodus (see 'The Names of God', page 157).

■ **The messianic kingdom.** We use this heading as a general description of the bright future state God has in store for his people. It is seen as the setting up of the perfect covenant relationship (Isaiah 54:10; Jeremiah 31:31-34; Ezekiel 37:26-27), and in many other ways also. But it is chiefly described as centring upon some great coming Person. He is:

The new 'David'	Ezekiel 37:24
The 'branch' of David's line (or, to stress his divine ancestry) the 'branch of the Lord'	Isaiah 11:1; Jeremiah 23:5-6; 33:14-16; Zechariah 3:8; 6:12; Isaiah 4:2
Immanuel, 'God with us'	Isaiah 7:14
The 'mighty God' occupying David's throne	Isaiah 9:6-7
The servant, dying for his people's sins	Isaiah 53
The anointed Conqueror of his people's foes	Isaiah 63:1-6
The Lord himself coming in the wake of the appointed forerunner	Malachi 3:1
Born in Bethlehem, born of a virgin	Micah 5:2; Isaiah 7:14

It is the crowning glory of the Old Testament prophets that God permitted and enabled them to see this radiance afar off. It sets the seal on their prophecies as God's word to men, that all was so perfectly fulfilled in the Lord Jesus. And what greater incentive could we have to get to know the writings of these men than Jesus' own statement that without them we cannot understand him, but that with them we can both know him (Luke 24:27, 32) and preach him to the world (Luke 24:44-48)?

THE PROPHETS IN THEIR SETTING

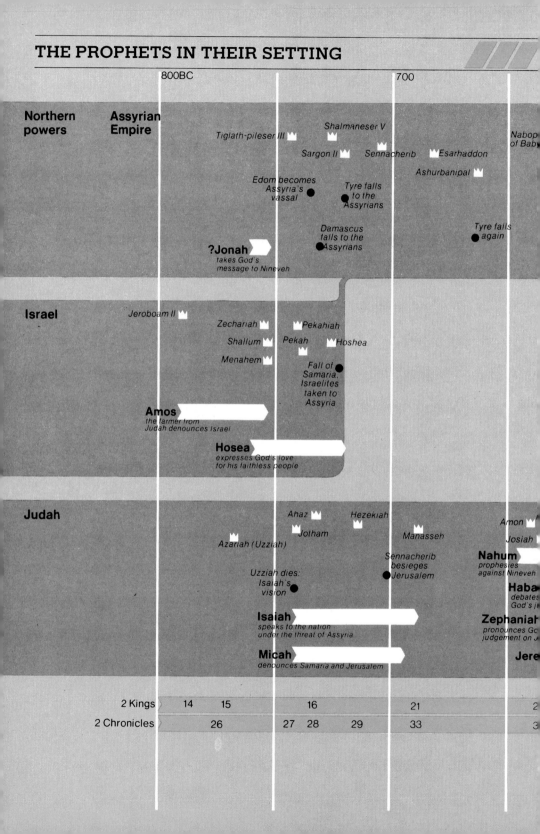

800BC

700

Northern powers — **Assyrian Empire**

Tiglath-pileser III

Shalmaneser V

Sargon II   Sennacherib   Esarhaddon

Ashurbanipal

Nabop of Baby

Edom becomes Assyria's vassal

Tyre falls to the Assyrians

Damascus falls to the Assyrians

Tyre falls again

?Jonah
takes God's message to Nineveh

Israel

Jeroboam II

Zechariah

Shallum   Pekah   Hoshea

Menahem

Pekahiah

Fall of Samaria, Israelites taken to Assyria

Amos
the farmer from Judah denounces Israel

Hosea
expresses God's love for his faithless people

Judah

Ahaz   Hezekiah

Jotham

Azariah (Uzziah)

Manasseh

Amon

Josiah

Uzziah dies: Isaiah's vision

Sennacherib besieges Jerusalem

Nahum
prophesies against Nineveh

Isaiah
speaks to the nation under the threat of Assyria

Haba
debates God's ju

Micah
denounces Samaria and Jerusalem

Zephaniah
pronounces Go judgement on J

Jere

2 Kings	14	15		16			21		2
2 Chronicles		26		27	28	29	33		3

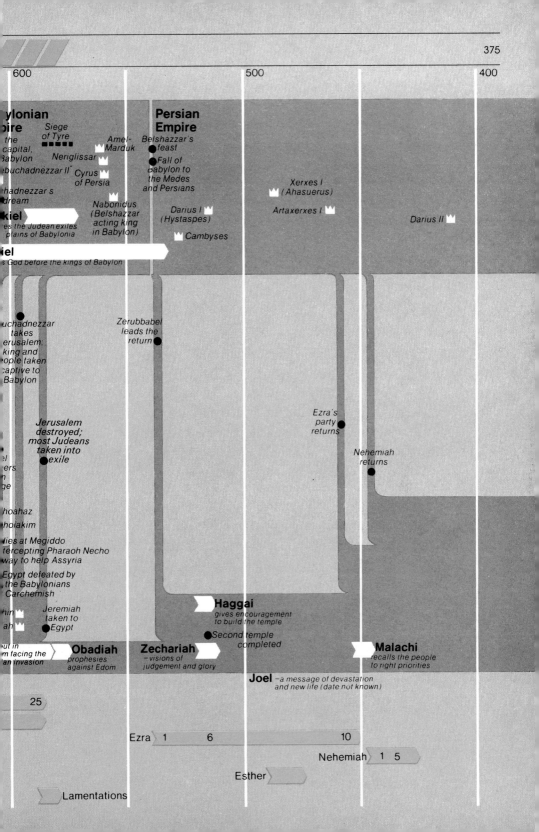

600

500

400

**bylonian
pire**

*the
capital,
Babylon*

*Siege
of Tyre*

Neriglissar

*Amel-
Marduk*

buchadnezzar II

*Cyrus
of Persia*

*hadnezzar's
dream*

*Nabonidus
(Belshazzar
acting king
in Babylon)*

kiel

*es the Judean exiles
plains of Babylonia*

iel

s God before the kings of Babylon

**Persian
Empire**

*Belshazzar's
feast*

*Fall of
Babylon to
the Medes
and Persians*

*Darius I
(Hystaspes)*

Cambyses

*Xerxes I
(Ahasuerus)*

Artaxerxes I

Darius II

*uchadnezzar
takes
erusalem;
king and
ople taken
captive to
Babylon*

*Zerubbabel
leads the
return*

*Jerusalem
destroyed;
most Judeans
taken into
exile*

*Ezra's
party
returns*

*Nehemiah
returns*

*el
ers
n
ge*

hoahaz

holakim

*ies at Megiddo
tercepting Pharaoh Necho
way to help Assyria*

*Egypt defeated by
the Babylonians
Carchemish*

hin

ah

*Jeremiah
taken to
Egypt*

Haggai
*gives encouragement
to build the temple*

*Second temple
completed*

*ut in
m facing the
an invasion*

Obadiah
*prophesies
against Edom*

Zechariah
*– visions of
judgement and glory*

Malachi
*recalls the people
to right priorities*

Joel *–a message of devastation
and new life (date not known)*

25

Ezra 1 6 10

Nehemiah 1 5

Esther

Lamentations

Isaiah

The prophets

Isaiah stands at the head of 'The Prophets', the third great section of the Old Testament. Sixteen prophets are named, and we have 17 books of their visions and prophecies (the odd one out being Lamentations: known in the Greek versions as the 'Lamentations of Jeremiah'). The four 'major' prophets are Isaiah, Jeremiah, Ezekiel and Daniel; the twelve 'minor' prophets, Hosea, Joel, Amos, Obadiah, Jonah, Micah, Nahum, Habakkuk, Zephaniah, Haggai, Zechariah, Malachi.

The books of the prophets belong to the time of the nation's decline, the exile and the return to their homeland. They span, altogether, a period of 250-300 years. Most of them address their messages primarily to the southern kingdom of Judah – Isaiah, Joel and Micah before Jerusalem fell to Babylon in 587 BC; Jeremiah, Habakkuk and Zephaniah at the time of the fall and during the exile; Haggai, Zechariah and Malachi at the time of the return, 538 BC and after. Of the others, Hosea and Amos had a special mission to Israel (the northern kingdom which fell to Assyria in 722 BC); Jonah and Nahum to the Assyrian capital, Nineveh; Daniel in Babylon; Ezekiel to the Jewish exiles in Babylon; and Obadiah to Edom, Israel's longstanding enemy.

God sent these prophets on a daunting and sometimes dangerous mission. They were for the most part despatched at the eleventh hour, to try to halt the people's headlong rush to destruction; to warn them of judgement; to call them back to God in repentance – and after the great crash came, to comfort the survivors with the assurance of God's continuing love and purpose for them. To a man, the prophets went out in the burning conviction that they had a message from God. Some braved death to make it known.

The book of Isaiah

Isaiah's place at the head of the prophetic books is well deserved. There is nothing to equal his tremendous vision of God and the glory in store for God's people until we reach John's book of Revelation, at the end of the New Testament. Other prophets came before him historically, but there was none greater.

Isaiah lived in Jerusalem in the 8th century BC. (For the historical background see 'The Threat of Assyria', page 395.) In chapter 6 he describes his call from God in the year of King Uzziah's death (about 740 BC). He prophesied for over 40 years, through the reigns of Jotham (a godly man like his father), Ahaz (one of Judah's worst kings) and Hezekiah. He may have lived on into the dark days of the evil King Manasseh. He knew from the outset that his words would fall on deaf ears, but he did have one great triumph. When Sennacherib's Assyrian army was hammering at the gates of Jerusalem in Hezekiah's reign (701 BC) the king took Isaiah's advice and the city was saved (chapters 36-37).

The initial vision of God in all his glory in the temple (chapter 6) coloured Isaiah's whole mission. He had seen God as the 'Holy One of Israel' and he never forgot it. He had seen human sin for the appalling thing it is, and he never forgot that either. And he had been forgiven and taken into God's service. Throughout his life, he preached God's righteousness, warned of the judgement on sin, and comforted his people with the knowledge of God's love, his longing to forgive, and all the glories in store for those who remained faithful to him.

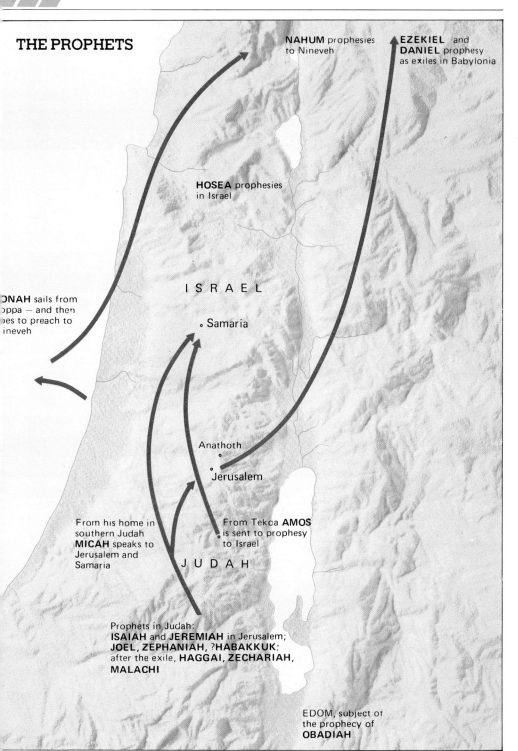

THE PROPHETS

NAHUM prophesies to Nineveh

EZEKIEL and **DANIEL** prophesy as exiles in Babylonia

HOSEA prophesies in Israel

I S R A E L

Samaria

ONAH sails from
oppa — and then
es to preach to
ineveh

Anathoth

Jerusalem

From his home in
southern Judah
MICAH speaks to
Jerusalem and
Samaria

From Tekca **AMOS**
is sent to prophesy
to Israel

J U D A H

Prophets in Judah:
ISAIAH and **JEREMIAH** in Jerusalem;
JOEL, ZEPHANIAH, ?HABAKKUK;
after the exile, **HAGGAI, ZECHARIAH,
MALACHI**

EDOM, subject of
the prophecy of
OBADIAH

In the book of Isaiah we have a collection of visions and prophecies belonging to various periods of the prophet's life. It is not always easy to follow – partly because we are unfamiliar with the language and ways of prophets and visionaries; partly because we do not know the principles which determined the present arrangement of material. In places there is clearly a time-sequence. Other parts seem to be arranged according to subject. Also, because Isaiah was a visionary, his thoughts range freely over the whole scale of time. One minute he is describing God's judgement on the Jerusalem he knows (the Assyrians about to pounce); the next it is God's universal judgement on evil – the end of the world as we know it; the beginning of a reign of perfect peace and justice. What he sees happening in his own time is the outworking of principles which are eternal and universal. And he moves in a flash from the particular to the universal and back again.

We do not know how the book was eventually put together. No doubt Isaiah himself wrote down at least some of his prophecies (see 30:8, and the use of the first person in chapters 6 and 8). Over the past century there has been a great deal of discussion over the differences between chapters 1-39 and 40-66. These have led many scholars to argue for more than one author – even allowing for the fact that the book was always written on a single scroll, and that the New Testament (which quotes Isaiah more than any other Old Testament book) assumes a single author. Some of the theories on authorship, in the past at least, have been open to criticism on the grounds that they have grown out of a basic presupposition that prediction in the prophets can simply be discounted. On this view, the 8th-century Isaiah could not have predicted with such accuracy events which took place long after his death (notably the fall of Babylon to Cyrus the Persian, 44:28ff.). But this runs counter to one of the main themes of Isaiah 40-48: that God demonstrates that he and he alone is God by announcing in advance the events which he as Lord of history will bring about. However, this by no means accounts for all the arguments about authorship. The debate continues.

1–5
GOD'S MESSAGE FOR JUDAH AND JERUSALEM

1 The sordid corruption of Judah

Although Jerusalem was not finally destroyed until 587 BC, by Isaiah's time the nation has already virtually reached the point of no return. They have rejected God. And God is sickened by their moral degradation, social injustice and religious hypocrisy. Yet he still offers forgiveness (18). Swift and terrible judgement will fall on all who persist in refusing.

The vision (1): Isaiah describes what God enables him to see in his mind's eye; 'messages which God revealed', Good News Bible. 'Amoz' is not the same as the prophet Amos.

Holy One/God of Israel (4): Isaiah's special title for God. It is used only twice in other parts of the Bible.

Verses 7-9: the Assyrians have overrun Judah. The northern kingdom of Israel has already fallen. Only Jerusalem (the 'daughter of Zion') remains. Genesis 19 describes the destruction of Sodom and Gomorrah, two utterly corrupt cities at the southern end of the Dead Sea.

New moon (13): the first day of each new month was a holy day.

Scarlet, red as crimson (18): both fast colours; only God could 'wash' these out.

Oaks (29): the sacred groves where Canaanite rites took place; symbols of the nation's idolatry.

'Though your sins are like scarlet' – wool, dipped in scarlet dye, is hung up to dry, at Hebron.

2—4
God's coming day: peace and judgement

In these chapters Isaiah looks far ahead to the time when Jerusalem will become the city of God for people of all nations (2:1-5). But before that God will execute fierce judgement on all the wickedness and pride which pollute his people (2:6–4:1). For evil has no place in the renewed city; only the few who are faithful to God will survive to enjoy it (4:2-6). The theme is developed in chapters 11–12.

Verse 2: 'mountain where the temple stands'.

2:6: the practice of magic (forbidden in Leviticus 19:31) and foreign alliances both led to idolatry.

2:13-16: symbols of pride. Solomon used the famous Lebanese cedarwood for his temple. The ships of Tarshish were great ocean-going vessels, the pride of the fleet.

The vineyard (3:14): symbol of the nation, see chapter 5.

Baldness (3:24): heads were shaved as a sign of mourning or degradation.

4:1: so many men have been killed in battle that the women offer to provide their own keep (unheard of in those days), if only the man will marry them.

The branch/plant (4:2): new growth shooting from the old roots (see 11:1); the community is to be reborn.

4:5: cloud and fire – the symbols of God's presence when they journeyed through the desert (Exodus 13:21).

5 The song of the vineyard

The Jewish nation is the vineyard of God. He has done everything necessary to ensure a heavy yield. But the vintage is bitter; so God will abandon the vineyard (but not for ever, see chapter 27). Jesus uses the same picture in Matthew 21:33-41.

In the land of Judah the vast estates built up at the expense of the poor (8) will become waste land. Ten acres of vines will yield only 22 litres; the harvest will be only a tenth of the seed sown (10). Again the prophet denounces pride.

luxury, drunkenness, injustice. God will give the signal for the enemy invasion (26ff.) – Assyria first and then Babylon – to destroy them.

Sheol (14, some versions): the shadowy world of the dead

6
ISAIAH'S VISION OF GOD AND CALL TO SERVICE

For the effect this had on his mission, see page 376. Isaiah had many visions, some so terrible, some so wonderful, he could hardly put them into words: but none to equal this. The knowledge that he had seen God with his own eyes, experienced his forgiveness and been sent out in God's service would sustain him all his life. And he would need it: for God sent him to a nation deaf and blind to his entreaties (9-10); a nation that would be destroyed and taken captive (11-12). Yet there was hope: the germ of a new nation would survive (13).

Verses 9-10: we trip up here, as elsewhere, over the Hebrew idiom which expresses result as if it were purpose. God did not intend to stop people repenting. He sent Isaiah out with the express purpose of saving people from judgement. But when they heard him they shut their ears and refused to act.

7—12
PRESENT AND FUTURE

7 The threat from the north: God warns King Ahaz

The date is about 735 BC. The new king, Ahaz, defied God (2 Kings 16), and in consequence his kingdom came under attack from all quarters. When he refused to join the Israel/Syria alliance against Assyria, they attacked Judah. It is at this point that Isaiah goes to him with God's message (3-9). In the crisis, Ahaz turned to Assyria, not God, for help. But Assyria would soon become a razor (20) in God's hand, to shave his rebel people of their pride and strength.

House of David (2): the royal household.

Syria and Ephraim (2 and 5ff.): Syria (strictly speaking at this date, Aram) was ruled from Damascus. As predicted, the kingdom was crushed by Assyria in 732. 'Ephraim' is the northern kingdom of Israel, which also fell to Assyria, 734-722 BC.

Shearjashub (3): the name means 'a remnant shall return'. The names of both Isaiah's sons stood as a constant reminder of his teaching – see chapter 8 and on 10:20.

Fuller's Field (3): the fuller ('clothmaker', Good News Bible) needed to be near water for his job of cleaning and whitening cloth.

Verses 14-16: the sign seems to have both present and future significance. 1. In the few years it takes for a child conceived now to reach an age when he can choose for himself, Israel and Damascus will cease to be a threat. 2. There will one day be born a child who will truly be 'Immanuel', 'God with us' (see Matthew 1:23).

Curds/milk and honey (15, 22): these symbols of natural plenty, here stand for a waste land where cattle and bees afford the only remaining food supply.

8 Isaiah's own family becomes a sign

God has any number of ways of getting his message across. This time, the fact that Damascus and Samaria are riding for a fall is embodied in the name of Isaiah's baby son. (Maher-shalal-hashbaz means 'Quick loot, fast plunder'.) When Assyria has dealt with the rebels she will sweep on into Judah, till Jerusalem itself is surrounded (see chapters 36–37).

The prophetess (3): Isaiah's wife.

Shiloah (6): probably an aqueduct outside Jerusalem. Hezekiah's Siloam tunnel (see page 301) had not yet been constructed.

The River (7): Euphrates.

9:1-7 The prince of peace

Isaiah sweeps his listeners far into the future with this glorious vision. Zebulun and Naphtali in Galilee were the first of the tribes to be crushed by Assyria. They will be first to see the light, to taste the joy, to be set free by the prince of peace. Nazareth, in Galilee, was the home of Jesus; Cana in Galilee the place where his public ministry began with the very first miracle.

The way of the sea (1): the main highway between Egypt and Syria passed through Galilee.

Day of Midian's defeat (4): Gideon's great victory against the Midianites, Judges 7.

9:8 – 10:4 God warns Israel of what is coming

Isaiah switches abruptly to the present. Israel (the breakaway northern kingdom) stands condemned for their arrogance and rebellion, injustice and oppression. They have already had a taste of judgement, but learnt nothing from it. Therefore God will not spare them.

(The Assyrians took many Israelites captive in 734, but Samaria held out till 722. Israel had turned a deaf ear to the warnings of Amos and the appeals of Hosea (Isaiah's contemporary), the two prophets God had specially sent them.)

The prophecy is written in four stanzas, each ending with the same refrain (12, 17, 21, 10:4).

10:5-34 God sends Assyria against his people

God makes use of a proud and cruel nation to punish his people. But Assyria's excessive ferocity is not excused: it will be punished. Even at the height of judgement God never loses sight of his purpose to save. A remnant – pathetically few – of his people will survive to trust and serve him.

Verse 9: a list of cities and city-states

conquered by Assyria – all Syrian except for Samaria.

Not one/not a (14): a vivid way of expressing the total absence of any resistance.

The remnant (20): this is one of the key themes in Isaiah. It goes back to the day God called him into service (6:13), and runs as a thread of hope through the darkest messages of judgement. This same faithful remnant, those who have survived, is to realize all the glorious promises for the future.

Verse 26: see Judges 7 and Exodus 14.

Verses 28ff.: Gibeah, just north of Jerusalem was Saul's capital; Anathoth, a few miles east, the home of Jeremiah. Isaiah pictures an attack on Jerusalem from the north, the usual route of invading armies from countries to the north or east. Sennacherib actually approached from Lachish, to the south-west.

11—12 The perfect king: the perfect kingdom

The theme of earlier passages (2:2-4; 4:2-6; 9:1-7) is developed more fully here. The coming king will be from David's family ('Jesse', 1, was David's father). He will possess the Spirit of God himself: just, righteous, faithful, like God. His will be an international kingdom, free of enmity and evil, utterly transformed. There will be a great gathering in of all God's people, and the song of God's salvation will be on everyone's lips. Isaiah pictures it all in physical terms. But what he sees is a radical change. This is a new, God-centred earth (see 65:17ff. and Revelation 21).

13—23
GOD WARNS THE NATIONS OF JUDGEMENT

These chapters bring together a collection of prophecies against foreign nations given at various times. God's concern is not limited to Israel. The world was his

then; it is his now, and his people should realize that.

13—14: 23 Babylon

See also chapters 46-47. In Isaiah's day Babylon was struggling for independence from Assyria. Here he steps forward 100 years to see Babylon at the height of her power – and to look beyond, to the day when Babylon in turn would be brought down. In 539 Babylon fell to the Medes and Persians led by Cyrus. Xerxes destroyed the city in 478, and it was finally abandoned in the 4th century BC. In the New Testament, Babylon is universalized, as the city of rebel man, implacably opposed to God (Revelation 17; it also serves as a cover-word for Rome).

Ophir (13:12): see on 1 Kings 9:28.

13:21-22: a list of repulsive creatures.

King of Babylon (14:4): the taunt-song is addressed, not to a particular king, but to the dynasty, representing the whole kingdom.

14:13: the very same thoughts which brought God's judgement on Babylon's predecessor, Babel (Genesis 11:1-9).

14:24-27 Assyria

Assyria's fate is also sealed (see on 10:5-34). Ultimately Babylon will break the power of Assyria. But before that there will be a signal defeat in God's own land (25; see chapters 36-37).

14:28-32 Philistia

The date is probably 716 BC. Assyria is in trouble, and the Philistines (old enemies of Israel, occupying the coastal plain) try to persuade Judah to join them in rebellion. But the Assyrians are far from finished (29, 31); and the Philistines are doomed. God's people must learn to trust in him.

15—16 Moab

The Moabites were descendants of

Abraham's nephew, Lot. They occupied the plateau land east of the Dead Sea. It was from Moab that Ruth came. At times the Moabites were on good terms wih the Israelites, but they had no share in Israel's faith. Isaiah is stirred to sympathy at the spectacle of Moab's suffering (15:5), now only three short years away (16:14). Moab sends to Jerusalem for help, and God urges his people to take the fugitives in (16:1-5).

The cities of Moab fell to Assyria in successive campaigns. They were to fall again to Nebuchadnezzar of Babylon.

15:1-9: these are all towns in Moab. 'Nebo' is the mountain from which Moses viewed the promised land; 'Zoar' a town at the southern end of the Dead Sea, spared in the overthrow of Sodom. The 'valley of willows/poplars' is probably the boundary between Moab and Edom to the south.

Baldness (15:2): see on 3:24.

Sela (16:1): 'the rock', the fortress in Jordan where Petra now stands.

16:3-5: these verses may be Moab's plea to Judah or God's word to his people.

Vineyards of Sibmah (16:8ff.): a region famous for its wine – here a symbol of national prosperity.

16:14: a person bound by contract works no more than the time contracted for; so, 'three years, and barely that'.

17 Damascus

A prophecy from Isaiah's early days – see on chapter 7. In response to King Ahaz' appeal for help against the Syria/Israel alliance, the Assyrians launched a series of raids in which Damascus was plundered and King Rezin met his death. This prophecy also attacks Israel for siding

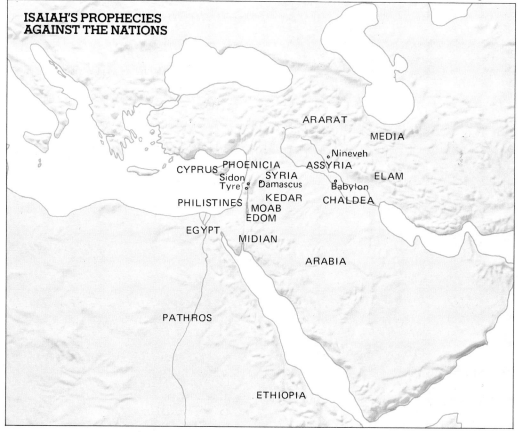

ISAIAH'S PROPHECIES AGAINST THE NATIONS

with Syria against their own brother-nation of Judah.

Asherah symbols (8): Canaanite cult-images and altars.

Hivites, Amorites (9): tribes destroyed by the Israelites in the conquest of Canaan.

18 Ethiopia/Cush

This is modern Sudan (as in Good News Bible). In Isaiah's day Egypt was ruled by a Sudanese dynasty. The Assyrian threat brings envoys from afar. But God will deal with the invader on the very eve of victory (5-6 – see 37:36ff.). And the far-off nation will send gifts in grateful homage to God (7; see 2 Chronicles 32:23).

19 Egypt

Isaiah foretells the disintegration of Egypt: internal strife, followed by conquest, a ruined economy and breakdown of leadership (1-15). Egypt was defeated by Assyria when Sennacherib's army beseiged Jerusalem (701 BC). Further defeats culminated in the sack of Thebes in 663 BC when the Assyrians pillaged centuries of temple treasures. But God uses the sword for surgery, not anarchy. Verses 16-24 reveal his ultimate purpose, the conversion of Egypt. 'That day' (i.e. the day of God's judgement – both temporal and final – a frequent phrase throughout Isaiah) is the day of God's final intervention in judgement and salvation on a worldwide scale. That day, the New Testament tells us, is the day of Christ's return.

The comparison of God's people to a vineyard is a recurring theme of the prophets – see too the picture illustrating John 15 in Part 3.

After Jerusalem fell in 587 there were numerous influential colonies of Jews in Egypt and in Assyria. A copy of the Jewish temple was even constructed at Leontopolis in Egypt about 170 BC. But all that was only a pale shadow of what Isaiah envisages here.

Zoan (11) ... Memphis (13): respectively the current and ancient capitals of Egypt. Zoan (Tanis) was in the delta region; Memphis just south of it on the Nile.

City of the sun (18): Heliopolis = On; centre of Egyptian sun-worship.

20 Egypt and Sudan

'The year' (1) is 711 BC, when the Assyrians crushed the Philistine rebellion at Ashdod. The support expected from Egypt had not materialized. God instructs Isaiah to play the role of a slave (2) to illustrate the coming captivity of Egypt and warn his people to place no reliance on help from that quarter. In 701 BC (see on chapter 19 above) Egypt was defeated by Assyria.

Naked (2): i.e. wearing only a loin-cloth.

21 Babylon; Dumah (Edom); Arabia

The 'desert by the sea' (1) is Babylon (9). See on chapters 13-14. The downfall of Babylon will be good news to the captives from Israel (10). Even so, Isaiah is appalled by what he foresees. There is temporary respite for Edom (Dumah, 11-12)—but judgement was to follow (see 34:5). Not even the remote tribes of Arabia (13-16) will escape the long arm of Assyria. This prophecy became reality when Sargon attacked Arabia in 715 BC.

Verse 16: 'Kedar', a powerful Bedouin tribe; 'servant/contract', see on 16:14.

22 Jerusalem, the 'valley of vision'

Jerusalem was Isaiah's base, the place where he had his visions. The city is surrounded by valleys and mountains, and he may have had a particular spot in mind. Despite the reprieve in Hezekiah's day (chapters 36-37), Isaiah foresees the future destruction of Jerusalem. (Nebuchadnezzar II of Babylon eventually took the city after a terrible siege in 587 BC. The walls were broken down and the temple destroyed.) The people's reaction in the face of disaster is a mixture of frenzied activity and sheer escapism (8-13). Verses 15ff. relate to Isaiah's own day. Shebna, a high official in Hezekiah's court (36:3) is to be demoted, and Eliakim promoted. But he will find himself unable to cope with his hangers-on, and his authority will be short-lived.

The lintel of a tomb, found at Siloam in Jerusalem, with the name of a royal steward, possibly Shebna; the tomb was among others belonging to people of high rank, and the inscription is one of the longest in ancient Hebrew so far discovered.

Elam ... Kir (6): outposts of the Assyrian Empire which no doubt supplied conscripts to the army.

House/palace of the forest (8): 'arsenal', Good News Bible; see 1 Kings 7:2; 10:17.

Verses 9, 11: it was vital to any city to ensure its water supply in the event of siege. See 2 Chronicles 32 for the Siloam tunnel, Hezekiah's solution to the problem.

23 Tyre

For centuries Tyre (modern Sour in Lebanon) dominated the sea-trade in the eastern Mediterranean. Her colonies, of which Cyprus was the nearest, were widespread. And her merchantmen ventured as far afield as the Indian Ocean and the English Channel. A major tradeline was Egyptian grain (3). Tyre was a city corrupted by its own wealth and success, and Isaiah warns of the approaching end. He spoke truly. In 722 the city fell to Sargon of Assyria. In 701 the

ruler of Tyre fled to Cyprus as
Sennacherib approached. As Assyria
declined, Tyre regained her power, only
to lose it again to the Babylonians.

Tarshish (6): probably 'Tartessus' in Spain.

Chaldeans/Babylonians (13): Chaldea
was part of south Babylonia, but when
Chaldean kings came to power in Babylon
the term was used of the Babylonian
kingdom as a whole.

Seventy years (15): probably a round
figure, meaning a lifetime.

A horseman and an archer, from Tell Halaf, north-east Syria, called Gozan in the Bible. Here Sargon of Assyria settled Israelite captives after 722 BC.

24–27
GOD'S FINAL JUDGEMENT AND VICTORY

From the particular – God's judgement
on specific nations – we move to the
universal – his judgement on the whole
world and everyone in it. Life will not go
on for ever just as it is. There will come
a point when God will step in and end the
world as we know it; when the earth will
rock on its foundations. Isaiah was in no
doubt about it. Neither was Jesus (see
Matthew 24). But God's purpose is not
just to condemn. One chapter (24) on
judgement is followed by three (25-27) on
his glorious salvation.

A song of joy in God, who makes the
weak and helpless his concern (25:1-5),
leads into a description of the joys
awaiting God's people on the far side of
judgement (25:6-12). Chapter 26 breaks
into song again. Its theme is trust. In life
there is waiting (8ff.), suffering and
failure (16-18). But God holds fast his
own, even through death (19). The song
of the vineyard in 27:2-13 contrasts with
chapter 5. The day will come when God's
purpose for his people will be fulfilled.
The present punishment is intended as a
corrective. The exile will end. In the final
harvest all God's people will be brought
home.

That day (24:21, etc.): see on chapter 19
above.

Moab (25:10): the current enemy of God's people stands for all such enemies.

Dew (26:19): a picture of God's power to revive the dead.

Leviathan (27:1): the dragon/serpent figure from pagan mythology. God's judgement extends to the superhuman realm (see 24:21). The same figure is used in Revelation 12:9 to depict Satan.

Asherah (27:9): see on 17:8 above.

27:10-11: refers to the oppressors, whose suffering will be far greater than that of God's people.

28–31
MORE WARNINGS TO GOD'S REBELLIOUS PEOPLE

28 Woe to Samaria and Judah's leaders

Attention is turned once again to the sins of Isaiah's own day. Verses 1-6, addressed to Israel, belong to the time before Samaria fell. The pleasure-loving, luxury-loving city is ripe for the plucking – and Assyria's hand is out-stretched to take it. Yet a core, 'remnant' (see on 10:20 above) will remain.

The leaders come under special attack (7ff.). Religious leaders and rulers alike have not led but misled the people. They are so cocksure, they think they can dictate terms to death itself. They will discover how wrong they are (18). Real security rests with God.

Verses 9-13: J. B. Phillips translates 10, 13: 'The-law-is-the-law-is-the-law, The-rule-is-the-rule-is-the-rule'. Isaiah's hearers are deliberately making nonsense of God's message; 9-10 may be their sneering reply to the prophet. To those who treat God's words as gibberish, Isaiah says that God will deliver his next message in Assyrian!

Verse 21: refers to David's victories; see 1 Chronicles 14:8-17.

Verses 23-29: a parable, meaning there is

method in the 'madness' of God's present actions, just as the farmer has good reason for the way he works.

29 Woe to Jerusalem

'Ariel' stands for Mt Zion/Jerusalem (8). The city will be besieged (3) and then reprieved (5ff. and see 37:36). God's word to his people has become a closed book, because they pay him only lip-service (11-16). But the day is coming (17ff.) when those who are deaf and blind to his message will hear and see, when God's people will once again fear and obey him.

Verse 17: a picture of things suddenly reversed: the forests become fields and fields forests. The same thought continues in the verses that follow.

Humble, needy (19): people loyal to God, not simply the victims of social injustice (see Matthew 5:3, 5).

30–31 Woe to the rebels who rely on Egypt

Judah is in league with Egypt and thinks herself secure against Assyria (28:15), despite all Isaiah's earlier warnings. But when it comes to the crunch Egypt will sit tight (7) while the Assyrians invade Judah (chapters 36-37). It is God – the One they would not trust (9-12) – who will save them in the end (27-33; 31:5-9; 37:36). He calls on them yet again to turn to him (31:6).

Zoan (30:4): see on 19:11.

30:6: the gifts are carried through the Negev desert to Egypt.

Rahab (30:7): a poetic synonym for Egypt.

30:33: the oppressor will be utterly destroyed. 'Topheth' ('a burning place') is in the valley of Hinnom, just outside Jerusalem, where in Israel's darkest days children were sacrificed to the pagan god Molech. The valley later supplied the name for hell, 'Gehenna'.

32—35

THE GLORIOUS FUTURE—AND THE DARK DAYS PRECEDING IT

32 The future king; peace by a hard road

Isaiah sees far into the future (1-8), returns to his own day at verse 9, and at verse 15 looks forward again to a time of lasting peace, justice and righteousness brought about by the working of God's Holy Spirit in his people. But before the king comes, present evil must be swept away, and people shaken out of their complacency. They will lose all that they now enjoy–until God steps in once again (15).

Verse 9: the cossetted women of Jerusalem typify the society of Isaiah's day.
Verse 19: the meaning is not clear; 'forest' and 'city' may refer to enemies.

33 When God intervenes

This is a chapter with many changes of speaker and mood. Isaiah does not name the destroyer (1). His description (7-9) can apply to many times beside his own. Only those who live by their faith in God remain unshaken in circumstances like these (2-6; 15-16). God never deserts his own; the city defended by him is unassailable (17-24). His presence guarantees stability, prosperity, security (20-21).

34 Judgement on the nations

God will one day avenge the wrong done to his people (8; see also chapter 24). Edom–the enemy par excellence–is singled out as an example. The destruction is total: the whole land rendered uninhabitable for man.

Bozrah (6): at various times Edom's capital city.

35 Salvation for God's people

This chapter stands in striking contrast to the horror of 34. Destruction gives way to re-creation. God is coming to bring his people home by a safe highway. At the sight of him everything is changed. The dry and lifeless desert, bursting for joy, becomes a paradise of flowing streams, great trees and the glowing colours of flowers.

36—39

CONTEMPORARY EVENTS: CRISES IN HEZEKIAH'S REIGN

See on 2 Kings 18–20, an almost identical account apart from Hezekiah's poem (38:9-20). See also 2 Chronicles 32. Hezekiah's illness and the embassy from Babylon probably preceded the siege (about 705-702 BC). The events may have been reversed here to provide a lead-in to the following chapters, which are focussed on Babylon as the world power she later became. 'Peace in my time' was Hezekiah's reaction to the terrible prediction of conquest and captivity (39:5-8). Isaiah could draw no comfort from the thought.

Sennacherib's terrifying invasions are pictured in his palace reliefs; this one shows his captives being decapitated.

40—48

ON THE BRINK OF FREEDOM

Up to this point Isaiah has been largely taken up with the threat from Assyria. Now that particular crisis is behind him. He is given a new vision for a new situation. Jerusalem has been saved from Assyria, but the city *will* fall to Babylon and the captive people will be taken into exile. This will not be the end of the nation, though it will seem like it. In due course Babylon itself will be overthrown by Cyrus the Persian, and he will return the exiles to their homeland. All this God reveals to the prophet, so that he may comfort and encourage the people, reassuring them for the bitter times ahead. So clear is all this in Isaiah's mind that from now on he leaves current events behind. In 40–48 he stands with the captives in Babylon at the end of their long exile.

40 A message of comfort: God's forgiveness and his infinite power

There is comfort for God's people: he is coming as he promised (1-11; see chapter 35). Israel's God is God the Creator: incomparable, eternal. He never stops caring for his people (12-31).

Double (2): not twice as much, but an equal measure; paid in full.

Verses 3-5: these verses sum up the mission of John the Baptist, see Luke 3:1-6.

Verse 11: Jesus took up this picture, describing himself as the good shepherd, see John 10:11.

41 'Fear not... I will help you'

God's tone is stern as he brings the nations to book (1). But with his own people he is infinitely loving and tender (8ff.). He is at hand to help. They have nothing to fear.

From the east (2)...from the north (25): 44:28 names the new conqueror, Cyrus the Persian (from Israel the route was north, then east).

Verses 21-24: the pagan gods–who are no gods–cannot predict things to come. Only God, the one true God, can do that.

42 A light for the nations

A new theme begins to unfold, alongside the forecast of Babylon's downfall: God's plan to open the eyes of the whole world

A highway in the desert... grass withering and fading; a track in the desert of Judah.

God promised to open rivers in the desert for the poor whose tongues were parched with thirst. In a dry land water was vital, and a ready symbol of blessing, life and prosperity. This boy is enjoying the water from the ancient spring at Jericho.

and bring salvation to all mankind. This was, from the very beginning, the intended role of Israel (Genesis 22:18). So, to begin with, the servant of God in Isaiah's series of 'songs' is the nation (or faithful remnant) of Israel. But Israel failed to be God's true servant in the way he intended (19-25). And so, in the series of portraits which follow (49:1-13; 50:4-9; 52:13–53:12; 61:1-4), the realization gradually dawns that God's purpose will ultimately be fulfilled not through the nation but through one who will be his true servant. The New Testament writers are in no doubt that the servant Isaiah foresaw – who would save men by suffering on their behalf – was Jesus Christ (Matthew 12:15-21). They have Christ's own authority for saying so (Luke 4:16-21).

43 God's unfailing love and care

By their constant disobedience, God's people have forfeited all right to his care (22-24) – yet he forgives (25). In all their sufferings he is beside them (2). He will set them free again, simply because he loves them (4ff.).

Fugitives in hiding from Assyrian troops; Isaiah's words about people being pursued and trapped – and about God's presence with them – were not just picture-language.

The superstition and fear involved in idol-worship is expressed by this colossal statue, which stands about 15 ft/5 m high.

Verses 16-17: this refers to the exodus from Egypt.

44–45 No God but God; the forecast of Israel's return

These chapters continue the themes that run through the whole section: Israel as God's servant, the object of his love (44:1-5); God as Lord of history, the only Person able to draw back the veil on the future (44:6ff.); the lifeless no-gods that men worship; God's promise that he will set his people free. 44:26–45:13 take us a stage further. The general promise becomes specific. In the reign of Cyrus, Jerusalem and its temple will be rebuilt (see on Ezra 1:1-4ff.).

Cyrus (44:28): many find it hard to believe Isaiah could actually have named the king so far in advance. But God can reveal what no man could possibly predict (41:21-24,

26-27; 42:9; 43:12-13; 44:6-8; 45:18-21).
45:22-25: God's love reaches beyond
Israel to the world. The New Testament
applies verse 23 directly to Christ; see
Philippians 2:10-11.

46–47 The downfall of Babylon

See also chapters 13–14 above. The
indictment of pagan gods reaches its
climax in the passive submission of the
Babylonian gods Bel and Nebo. These
dumb idols burden the backs of their
worshippers. The real God is One who
carries his people's burdens, who has
power not only to speak but to act.
Chapter 47 (like 14:4-21) is a taunt-song.
Babylon will be shown as little mercy as
she has shown others.
47:1: 'Virgin daughter', the city of Babylon;
'Chaldeans', see on 23:13.

48 God's patient love for faithless Israel

The history of Israel is one long tale of
hypocrisy, rebellion, scepticism, idolatry.
She has fully deserved all she has
suffered. God always purposed peace for
his people (18), but there could be 'no
peace for the wicked'. Now the moment
of liberation has come: he says 'Go
forth'.
Verse 16: there is a change of speaker
here; the voice may be the prophet's or
that of the servant/Messiah, as in 49:1,
etc.

49–55
THE SERVANT OF GOD AND THE REDEMPTION OF HIS PEOPLE

These chapters give us a series of
portraits of God's servant and his
mission (see on chapter 42 above) in the
course of God's message to his people.
The context generally indicates when
the term 'servant' refers to Israel, and
when it refers to that individual
representative of the true Israel who was
yet to come.

49–50 A word to put new heart into Israel

God's servant has a mission to Israel –
and beyond Israel to the world (49:6).
Comfort, compassion and restoration
are the keynotes of 49:14–50:3. 50:4ff.
returns to God's servant, and for the first
time we glimpse his suffering and
rejection (see chapter 53). But nothing
can deflect him from his purpose.
50:1: God did not divorce his unfaithful
'wife', Israel; he brought her lovingly home
(see Hosea 3:1; Hosea was declaring his
message to Israel at the same time as
Isaiah proclaimed God's word in Judah.)

51–52:12 Israel released and restored

God urges his people to draw comfort
from past history, and to look forward to
a greater exodus yet. It is time to shake
off grief and lethargy. There is good
news. God is about to escort his people
home.
Rahab (51:9): see on 30:7.

52:13–53:12 God's servant suffers for his people

The scene shifts from the joyous
home-coming to the lonely figure who
paid the price of it. He bore the whole
burden of sin which estranged humanity
from God, and it cost him his life. Isaiah,
eight centuries before Christ, clearly
foresaw him. He knew why he must come
and what he would do. He saw the
Saviour giving his life for mankind. He
saw God raise him high in exaltation.
(Compare 53:5-9 with Matthew 27:11-13,
26-31, 41-43, 57-60. Compare 53:4-6, 10-12
with Romans 5:6-9, 18-19; 1 Peter 2:21-24;
Philippians 2:5-11).

54–55 The expanding kingdom; salvation for all nations

God pledges himself in tender, unswerv-
ing, enduring love to his people. In peace
and security the foundations of a new

and dazzling city are laid (54:11ff.; and compare Revelation 21:18ff.). The gates stand wide in welcome to men of every nation who respond to God's invitation (55:1-7).

The vision in the later chapters of Isaiah (as earlier, at 2:2-4; 4:2-6; 9:2-7; 11–12; 25; 35) goes far beyond the events of the actual return from exile. The restoration of Israel which took place then, merges into a vision of the final glorious day when sin and sorrow will be no more, and the whole Israel of God (see Romans 9–11; Galatians 3) will be for ever at home with the Lord (Revelation 21).

56 — 66
ISRAEL'S SHAME AND ISRAEL'S GLORY

Isaiah turns back from Babylon and the exile to the land of Israel. In these final chapters scenes of sin and failure mingle with scenes of future glory.

56:1-8 Welcome for the outcasts

There is nothing exclusive about the love of God. There is a place among his people for all who will follow and obey him (1-8), even the most despised.

56:9—59:21 God's accusations against Israel

59:1-2 gets right to the heart of the matter: sin cuts men off from God. Israel has been guilty of many sins – the charges are quite specific. Spiritual and secular

Water in the Negev desert; water and green vegetation in the desert were a vivid symbol of new life and national restoration.

leaders alike have gone soft and failed in their jobs (56:9-12). The nation has gone running after pagan gods, joining in sexual rites and child-sacrifice (57:4-13; see 2 Chronicles 33:1-9). Their religious observance is a hollow mockery: the people love neither God nor their fellow men (58). Society is rotten to the core, riddled with lies, dishonesty, injustice, malice and violence (59:1-13). It has no time for truth and justice, or for the individual who upholds them (59:14-15). All these things stand in stark contrast to all that God, in his amazing love, wants for his people (57:14-19; 58:6-14; 59:20-21).

Beds (57:2, some versions**):** i.e. their graves.

57:5-8: the pagan rites involved prostitution. Idolatrous Israel, unfaithful to God, is pictured as a prostitute.

Molech (57:9): see on 30:33.

Public square (59:14): the 'lawcourt' of the day, where cases were heard and justice was dispensed.

59:21: compare this with the new covenant described in Jeremiah 31:31-34.

60—62 The nation's glory

In the unbridgeable gap between the shame of Israel and her glory stands the figure of God the Avenger and Redeemer (59:16-21). Chapter 60 pictures the incredible transformation. Isaiah sees the return to God's favour in very 'earthly' terms: fabulous wealth, power, influence. But it is very different from the earth we know (17-22); and the New Testament translates Isaiah's concept into spiritual and universal terms (see on chapters 54—55 above).

Although unnamed, the voice in 61:1-4 is that of the servant (see Luke 4:16-21). In 61:5-9 God's people become the nation of priests he always intended them to be (Exodus 19:6; and see 1 Peter 2:9), breaking into a song of praise (10-11). The day is coming (62) when God will be able to rejoice and delight in his people: a day to long for, pray for, prepare for.

60:6-7: 'Ephah', a Midianite tribe; 'Kedar' and 'Nebaioth', Arabian tribes. Their wealth lay in their camels, sheep and goats.

Double portion (61:7): here Isaiah has in mind the share of the firstborn son.

63:1-6 A vision of the Avenger

See also 59:16ff. Edom (which means red) and its capital, Bozrah, represents all the enemies of God's people. This is an appalling picture; but until the enemy is defeated, God's people cannot be set free (see Revelation 19:11-16).

63:7—64:12 Prayer for God's people

The recollection of all God's past goodness and faithfulness (63:7-14) leads into an impassioned appeal for his response to the crying need of his people.

65—66 God's answer: new heavens and a new earth

God will answer the prayer for his people in a way which exceeds their wildest dreams. But the answer will be two-edged: for those who align themselves against him, total destruction, the sweeping away of every vestige of evil; for his faithful ones, life, joy, peace beyond imagining, in a heaven and earth made new. So the final prophecies of Isaiah highlight the contrasting destinies of men, in a sharp play of light and darkness. God cannot overlook evil. Those who go their own sinful way (65:1-7, 11-14), who refuse to listen to God (66:3-4), will be punished. But God has a place reserved in his new world for men of humble faith: not only for faithful Israel, but for people of all nations (66:18-23).

65:8: the bunch is poor, but it contains some good grapes which are not to be wasted.

Fortune, Destiny (65:11): pagan gods of fate, Gad and Meni, to whom sacrificial offerings were made.

65:25: see 11:6-9.

66:19: Isaiah pictures men streaming in from distant lands – from Spain (Tarshish) in the far west, from Africa (Put, Lud) to the south, from the far north, Anatolia (Tubal) and across from Greece (Javan).

Country people return from the harvest to their village in the hills of Judea.

Sculpture in bas-relief representing Ashurbanipal, King of Assyria, from Nineveh.

The Threat of Assyria

ALAN MILLARD

For 200 years, from about 850 to 650 BC, the kingdoms of Syria and Palestine were overshadowed by Assyria. Her kings had reached the Mediterranean in the days of Israel's Judges, but pressure from Aramaean tribes then establishing themselves throughout Syria stopped them keeping control so far afield.

In 853 BC Shalmaneser III led Assyria against a coalition including Ben-hadad of Syria and Ahab of Israel, although he gained no clear victory until 841 BC. Ahab brought Israel into direct conflict with Assyria, who now looked upon her as a tributary state. Jehu's embassy is shown on Shalmaneser's Black Obelisk, bringing valuable gifts (see page 275).

Assyrian activity gave Israel some relief from oppression by Damascus. Although the usurper Hazael briefly reimposed this yoke (see 2 Kings 8:12; 12:17ff.), it was broken by an Assyrian campaign about 800 BC when Jehoash paid tribute; and Israel rapidly expanded. Jeroboam II and then Uzziah of Judah seem to have become the principal monarchs of southern Syria and Palestine while Assyria's fortunes varied.

However, in 745 BC Tiglath-pileser III (see page 277) began to restore Assyria's imperial state. Menahem of Israel paid tribute, but anti-Assyrian elements replaced his son by their nominee Pekah, only to see him displaced in due course by the Assyrian-approved Hoshea. It was Hoshea's defection that resulted in the Assyrian capture of Samaria in 722 BC and the deportation of its people.

The policy of exile had always been employed by powerful kings, and was an ever-present threat to smaller nations. Assyrian kings did not apply it indiscriminately; it was a final weapon against obstinately rebellious states. Where a vassal and people were loyal they lived undisturbed, even helped by Assyria when enemies attacked. It is in this light that Assyria's relations with Israel and Judah should be seen.

Pekah's anti-Assyrian stance pushed Ahaz of Judah into Assyria's arms for protection, and so Hezekiah's independent policies brought harsh retribution from Sennacherib (701 BC, see page 280). Thereafter, Manasseh remained loyal to Assyria, following an enforced visit to Babylon (2 Chronicles 33:11), and enjoyed a long reign (about 687-642 BC). Josiah profited from Assyrian complacency to strengthen Judah, but he lost his life trying to hinder Egyptian troops going to help the last Assyrian king (609 BC; 2 Kings 23:29).

It was to these situations that the prophets Amos, Hosea, Micah and Isaiah spoke. They showed that God's people could not escape the consequences of faithlessness in human affairs, any more than the other nations they quoted as examples. They showed, too, that God's people could not escape the consequences of disloyalty to their alliance with God. He could use other nations to chasten them in furthering his purpose.

Jeremiah

Jeremiah appears on the scene about 100 years after Isaiah. He was born into a priestly family at Anathoth (Anata), a few miles north of Jerusalem, about 640 BC, and was called to be God's prophet in 627. 2 Kings 22-25 and 2 Chronicles 34-36 provide the historical background to Jeremiah's prophecies.

The power of Assyria was already crumbling when he began to declare God's message to Judah. For 40 years – through the reigns of Judah's last five kings – Jeremiah warned of coming disaster and appealed in vain to the nation to turn back to God. With the death of godly King Josiah in 609 religious and political affairs worsened. Judah was caught in the crossfire between the contending world powers: Babylon to the north, and a resurgent Egypt to the south. Babylon emerged supreme, to become the instrument of God's judgement on his godless people. In 587 the army of Nebuchadnezzar of Babylon broke into Jerusalem, destroyed the city and took the people captive into exile. Jeremiah was offered a comfortable life at court, but chose instead to remain in Judah. When Gedaliah (the governor appointed by Nebuchadnezzar) was murdered, the people fled to Egypt, taking Jeremiah with them. As far as we know he ended his days there, still declaring God's words to men who refused to listen.

Jeremiah was not the only prophet of his day. Among his contemporaries were Habakkuk and Zephaniah; Daniel, at the Babylonian court; and Ezekiel, among the exiles in Babylon. But he stands out, a lonely figure: isolated by a message from God which made him increasingly unpopular; branded a traitor for advocating submission to Babylon. He was imprisoned and often in danger of his life. Yet this sensitive, unselfconfident man never once compromised his message from God. He could not help but declare the terrible fate he saw in store for his nation. And he grieved over their stubborn refusal to take notice. The times were dark; his message sombre; yet to write him off as a born pessimist does him injustice. There is a strong streak of hope running through his prophecies. After the judgement, after the exile, God will restore the joy and prosperity of his people in their homeland.

Jeremiah's book (which grew from the scroll dictated to Baruch, chapter 36) is a glorious mixture of literary forms: prose and poetry, taunt and lament, acted parable, biography and history. He added bits to it at various times, and not all of them are dated. The material is not arranged in historical order, which makes some of it difficult to set against the right background. The key events of Jeremiah's lifetime are listed opposite, and dates are indicated in the text wherever possible.

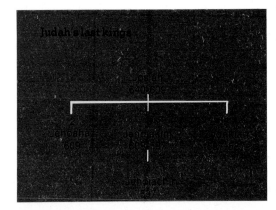

Judah's last kings

Josiah
640-609

Jehoahaz
609

Jehoiakim
609-

Jehoiachin

Jeremiah's birthplace, Anathoth, in the barren hills north of Jerusalem.

Major events of Jeremiah's lifetime

627 Jeremiah called to be God's prophet. Death of Ashurbanipal, last great king of Assyria.

621 Discovery of the book of the law. King Josiah's great reformation begins.

612 Nineveh, capital of Assyria, falls to Babylon.

609 The Egyptian army marches north to bolster collapsing Assyria. Josiah intercepts it at Megiddo and is killed. On his return from Assyria, Pharaoh Necho deposes the new king, Jehoahaz, placing Jehoiakim on the throne.

605 Egyptian forces routed at Carchemish by Nebuchadnezzar of Babylon.

604 Nebuchadnezzar subdues Syria, Judah and Philistine cities.

598 Alliance with Egypt brings the Babylonian forces down on Judah again.

597 King Jehoiakim dies. Jerusalem falls to Babylon after a two-month siege. The new king, Jehoiachin, is deported with others to Babylon. His uncle, Zedekiah, is put on the throne.

588 Under pressure from the pro-Egypt party, Zedekiah breaks faith with Babylon. Jerusalem under siege for 18 months.

587 The Babylonian army breaks into Jerusalem. The people are deported; the city plundered and burned. Three months later, governor Gedaliah is murdered. Jeremiah is taken to Egypt.

1—25
GOD SPEAKS TO JUDAH AND JERUSALEM

1 Jeremiah's call to be God's prophet

The date is 627 BC. Jeremiah is a young man, probably in his early twenties, and as reluctant to become God's spokesman as Moses before him (Exodus 3:10–4:17). But about one thing he had no doubt. His message was a word from God himself. 'The word of the Lord came to me' runs as a refrain right through the book, from first to last. In this lay his certainty, and his compulsion.

Verses 1-3: see introduction.

Almond...watching (11-12): there is a play on words in the Hebrew. The almond is the first tree to blossom in spring. God's actions follow his words equally swiftly.

Verse 13: the forces of Babylon are like a cauldron about to pour its scalding contents on Judah. In this period of Jewish history trouble always came from the north: the powerful armies of Assyria first; then, in Jeremiah's day, the Babylonians.

2–3:10 God charges his people with unfaithfulness

The heathen nations are at least loyal to their idols (10-11). Not so the people of the living God. Their offence is set before them in a series of vivid pictures. They prefer their own polluted water to God's fresh spring (13). They would sooner turn to Egypt and Assyria for help than to God (18). The vine of Israel has gone wild (21). Like a wife turned common prostitute, the nation has run after foreign gods (20, 23-25, 33; 3:1-10).

Baal (2:8): the Canaanite god.

Cyprus...Kedar (2:10): from west to east (Kedar is in Arabia): the whole pagan world.

2:13: compare Jesus' words: John 4:13-15; 7:37.

Memphis...Tahpanhes (2:16): cities of Egypt–Memphis near Cairo; Tahpanhes a frontier town in the eastern Nile Delta, on the route to Palestine.

Strangers (2:25, some versions): pagan gods.

3:1: such a thing was unlawful; see Deuteronomy 24:1-4.

3:6-10: 'Israel' here refers to the northern kingdom whose people had been carried into exile a century before, in 722 BC (verse 8). King Josiah's religious reforms (beginning in 621 BC), far-reaching though they were, did not change the heart of the nation.

3:11–4:4 'Return, O Israel, says the Lord'

Even now God will save his people if they repent. He will bring them back from exile a united nation (18) whose worship is a living reality, not a mere ritual (16; 4:4; and compare 31:31-34).

The ark/covenant box (16): in which the law was kept in the inner sanctuary of the temple. It is no longer needed when God's law is written on every heart.

Shameful gods (24): a euphemism for 'Baal'.

4:4: all Jewish boy babies were circumcised when they were eight days old, as a sign that they had entered into covenant relationship with God (Genesis 17:1-14). But no external mark can make a man God's child without an accompanying 'circumcision' of heart, mind and will.

4:5-31 Approaching disaster

Destruction and devastation are about to fall on Judah. Jeremiah is given a preview of the nation's collapse before the Babylonian army which fills him with unspeakable horror (19-31).

Verse 11: the scorching desert wind is a symbol of destruction.

Dan (15): the northernmost town in the land; first in the path of the invader.

Verse 23: God is unmaking the earth; see Genesis 1:2.

Verse 30: a picture of Jerusalem (the 'daughter of Zion'), unrepentant still; still seeking foreign aid.

A pagan altar at Byblos, Lebanon.

5 National corruption

God searches in vain for a vestige
of truth and justice among his people.
The nation is steeped in idolatry; happy
with a rotten society; untroubled by
conscience. God and his prophets alike
are disregarded. It is false prophecy the
people want to hear. God has no option
but to punish.

6 Declaration of war

All God's warnings have fallen on deaf
ears. His call to men to walk 'the good
way' (16) has met with flat refusal. So
God has rejected his people (30) and
turned them over to the invading
armies. Even Jerusalem will be besieged.
Tekoa, Beth-haccherem (1): two hills
south of Jerusalem.
Shepherds (3): a picture of the enemy
encampments.
Noon (4): it was not usual to attack in the
heat of the day.

Sheba (20): in Arabia; famous for the
incense it exported.

7 – 8:3 In the temple

The people had a superstitious faith in
the temple. They thought Jerusalem
could not fall because of the temple; but
they were wrong. God knows the
difference between religious ritual and
real religion (10). He sees all that goes
on (9). Jerusalem is no more sacrosanct
than Shiloh, the sanctuary the Philistines
destroyed (see on 1 Samuel 4). Security
and well-being rest on obedience to God
(23).
Verse 11: Jesus quoted these words of the
temple in his day (Matthew 21:13).
Ephraim (15): the leading tribe of the
breakaway northern kingdom.
Queen of heaven (18): the fertility goddess
Ashtoreth/Astarte/Ishtar, whose worship
involved sexual immorality.
Verse 22: Jeremiah is not denying that the
system of sacrifices was instituted at

God's command (see Leviticus 1-7). But the people were substituting sacrifice for obedience. Jeremiah is urging them to get their priorities right. As Samuel said long before, 'to obey is better than sacrifice' (1 Samuel 15:22).

Topheth (31): see on Isaiah 30:33.

8: 4-17 A false sense of security

The people refuse to repent, and the men of religion aid and abet them with their smooth words. The scribes (professional interpreters of God's law), the wise men who applied God's laws to the practical matters of life, prophets and priests, are all alike motivated by self-interest.

8:18 — 9:26 Lament for the coming destruction

Jeremiah shares God's own deep grief at his people's sin and its tragic consequences. Society is sick (9:3-6, 8): sick as a direct result of the nation abandoning God and his laws and going their own way (12-14). So inevitable has judgement become (15-16) that the professional mourners can already be called in (17).

Balm/medicine (8:22): Gilead was famous for its healing ointment from very early times (Genesis 37:25).

Wormwood (9:15, some versions**):** a bitter-tasting plant, and so a symbol for sorrow.

9:25-26: despite the outward mark of his covenant (see on 4:4), God's people have made themselves like the pagan nations around. And like them they will be punished. See chapters 46-51.

10 The living God – and idols made by men

The idols man creates – no matter how elaborate – are lifeless, powerless, motionless, speechless. Not so the God of Israel. This was one of Isaiah's great themes: Isaiah 40:18-20; 44:9-20.

Tarshish . . . Uphaz (9): Tarshish, Tartessus in far-away Spain; Uphaz may be Ophir (as New English Bible), famous for its gold.

Gather up your belongings (17): get ready to flee.

Shepherds (21): 'leaders', Good News Bible.

Verses 23-25: Jeremiah's prayer on his people's behalf.

11: 1-17 The broken covenant

The terms of God's covenant-agreement with his people, made at Sinai after the exodus (see Deuteronomy 5ff.), are still in force. By persistent disobedience to God's law, and by idol-worship, Judah has broken that agreement and come under the curse (see Deuteronomy 11:26-28; 27).

This chapter seems to belong to the period of reaction following Josiah's reforms (2 Kings 23).

11:18 — 12:17 The plot against Jeremiah's life

Jeremiah's message aroused such intense anger that the men of Anathoth, his home-town, were prepared to kill him (18-23). The discovery leads Jeremiah to question God about the way evil men get on in the world (12:1-4). He is neither the first, nor the last, to puzzle over this (see Psalm 73; Habakkuk 1:12-13). In answer, God tells him there is worse to come (5-6)! Nonetheless, he *will* punish (7-13), and afterwards restore (14-17).

Jungle by the Jordan (12:5): the Jordan runs below sea-level from the Sea of Galilee to the Dead Sea; and in Old Testament times the river was bordered by dense, steamy thickets which were the haunt of wild animals.

House, inheritance (7), vineyard (10): metaphors for the nation.

13 The loin-cloth: a dramatic parable

God makes use of every teaching method in the book to get his message across. The prophets often act out their message (see chapters 18, 19, 32). Actions often speak louder than words, and stick in the mind. Jeremiah got no joy from announcing God's vengeance (17), though he had earlier cried out for it (11:20).

Verse 4: the Euphrates represents the captivity and exile of the nation. It is some 350 miles from Jerusalem.

King and queen mother (18): almost certainly Jehoiachin and Nehushta (see 2 Kings 24:8-16).

14 — 15 The drought; Jeremiah's prayer

There is severe and prolonged drought (14:1-6). The people once again appeal to God (7-9). But God will not listen (10-12). Neither will he listen to Jeremiah's pleas that they have been duped by the lies of false prophets (13ff.). Yet Jeremiah goes on praying for them (13-22) though God is deaf and the people reward him with hatred (15:10). His self-pity (15:15-18) is understandable. Its cure lies in turning away from himself to God, in renewed confidence.

Sword, famine, pestilence (14:12): 'war, starvation, disease', all regarded, from earliest times, as punishments from God. The three together imply full-scale judgement (see also 16:4; 24:10; Ezekiel 14:21; Revelation 6:8; 18:8).

Your glorious throne (21): the temple.

Moses and Samuel (15:1): both interceded successfully for the nation (Exodus 32; 1 Samuel 12:19-25).

15:4: under Manasseh the nation reached an all-time low; see 2 Kings 21; 2 Chronicles 33.

16 Jeremiah forbidden to marry

By remaining single, in a society where this was almost unheard of, Jeremiah becomes a living symbol of God's message. Very soon there will be the most terrible famine and slaughter in Jerusalem. This is no time, no place, to raise a family. As God removes his peace and his love from them (5) the people will at last know him as the Almighty

Looking south from the walls of the present city of old Jerusalem, with the Valley of Kidron.

(21). Yet he still has a future for them (14-15).

Verses 6-7: customs connected with mourning, some of them pagan (see Leviticus 19:27-28).

17 God and the human heart; the sabbath

Judah's sin is indelible (1). Yet God still sets the alternatives before them (5-8; see Psalm 1). If only the people will listen (24) judgement can be averted.

Disregard for the day of rest which God instituted (19-27; see Exodus 20:8-11) is symptomatic of the nation's general disobedience.

Verse 1: an iron stylus was used to incise inscriptions on rock or stone. The nation's sin is just as permanently engraved on her hard heart.

Asherah (2): see on Isaiah 17:8.
Verses 14-18: this is Jeremiah's prayer.

18 The potter and the clay; more plots against the prophet

Another dramatic parable (see on chapter 13). Like the human potter, God has the unquestionable right to remould the spoilt nation. We can never simply assume that things will always be the way they are (7-10).

In verses 18-23 Jeremiah is so touched on the raw by those who spurn his God-given message that he comes out with a really vengeful prayer (very different from his reaction in 13:17).

Sirion (14, some versions): Mt Hermon, usually capped with snow all year round.
East wind (17): 'trouble', see on 4:11.

19:1-13 The shattered jug

Again, an acted parable: God will break the city and people as surely and as irreparably as the jug the prophet shatters before their eyes.

Hinnom (2), Topheth (11): see on Isaiah 30:33.

A potter's wheel in action at Hebron.

19:14—20:18 Jeremiah in the stocks

Jeremiah goes straight from the Hinnom Valley to the temple; and there his message lands him in trouble. With hands and feet made fast in the wooden stocks he pours out his heart to God. Jeremiah was not a thick-skinned man; it hurt to be hated and ridiculed (20:7-8). Yet he was continually driven by an inner compulsion to make God's word known (9). His role as prophet put him under tremendous pressure. And his mood fluctuates between confident faith (11, 13) and utter misery (14-18).

21 King Zedekiah's enquiry

The date is about 589, when Judah was involved in her final struggle with Babylon. Zedekiah turns to the prophet, hoping for a word of comfort. But none is forthcoming. The only hope lies in surrender.

22 A warning for King Jehoiakim

This prophecy is earlier than chapter 21. Jehoiakim reigned from 609 to 597 – the year Jerusalem first surrendered to Babylon, and 18-year-old Jehoiachin (Coniah, 24) was taken into exile with the first batch of captives. Verses 13ff. contrast Jehoiakim – who sees his kingship in terms of cedarwood palaces – with his godly father, Josiah.

The dead (king) (10): probably King Josiah, killed at Megiddo.
The exile (10), Shallum (11): King Jehoahaz, taken to Egypt by Pharaoh Necho on his return from Assyria in 609.
Lebanon, Bashan, Abarim/Moab (20); mountain ranges to the north, north-east and east of Judah.

23 Against the leaders and false prophets

The government (1-8) and religious leaders (9ff.) alike receive a stinging rebuke. Misrule, and the lies pronounced in God's name, will not go unpunished. God will set on the throne a king of his own choice (5-8). With such a message

The Dung Gate of old Jerusalem.

the pick of the bunch of God's people. (Ezekiel was among these first captives, and Daniel had been taken to Babylon earlier still.) And God is shaping a future for them. For those who remain in Judah there is no future but destruction. Yet through Jeremiah God still perseveres with his 'bad figs'.

25 Prediction of Nebuchad-nezzar's invasion and the exile

The year is 605 (1), when Nebuchad-nezzar routed the Egyptians at Carchemish. For 23 years Jeremiah has been repeating God's message, and still the people remain unmoved. Now he tells them that the city will fall and they will serve the Babylonians for 70 years in exile. The judgement of God will also fall on the pagan nations who so richly deserve it, and on Babylon itself (12-38).
Verse 13: for Jeremiah's prophecies against the pagan nations, see chapters 46–51.

A basket of figs.

against the men of religion (9-40), it is not surprising that Jeremiah encountered bitter hatred from the priests and prophets – as Jesus himself did (26:11; compare Matthew 21:45-46; 26:66).
Branch (5): 'descendant'; see on Isaiah 4:2; 11:1.
Adulterers/unfaithful (10): those who played God false by turning to pagan gods whose worship involved sexual rites and prostitution.
Burden (33): message.

24 The two baskets of figs

The date is some time after 597 (verse 1; 'Jeconiah' is Jehoiachin). The exiles are

26—45
JEREMIAH'S LIFE AND TIMES

26 Jehoiakim's reign: Jeremiah's life in danger

The date is 609 or after; the situation has links with chapter 7. It was one of those times when it is dangerous to declare the plain truth of God (15), and Jeremiah's straight speaking almost cost him his life. The priests and prophets wanted him dead (11), but the name of God still counted for something among the rulers and people (16). Uriah (20ff.; known only from this passage) was less fortunate.

Shiloh (6): see on chapter 7.
Verse 18: see Micah 3:12. The prophet's words are remembered a century later (Micah was Isaiah's contemporary).

27—28 Zedekiah's reign: the yoke of Babylon; Hananiah's false prophecy

It is 597: the Babylonians have taken the first captives from Jerusalem and placed Zedekiah on the throne. But already there is subversion. Jeremiah walks the streets of the city wearing a wooden yoke in token of submission to Babylon. Only by servitude can Judah (27:12-15) and the nations (27:3-11) escape destruction. It was not a popular message, and provoked a head-on clash with the false prophets. Hananiah flatly contradicted Jeremiah; broke the yoke (28:1-5, 10), and told the people what they wanted to hear. But time proved the truth of Jeremiah's words (28:15-17; and compare 27:19-22 with 52:17-23).

29 Jeremiah's letter to the exiles

The exiles to whom Jeremiah wrote were the captives deported with King Jehoiachin, among them Ezekiel. The false prophets predicted a swift return. Jeremiah advises the exiles to settle down and live a normal life: the exile will last 70 years. Then they will return. But even from Babylon his enemies stir up trouble for him (24ff.).

30—31 The promise of a new covenant

The message of hope comes at the nation's darkest hour. When it looked like total extinction, God promised his people a future. They would be saved (30:10ff.) and restored (18ff.). The exiles would return rejoicing to their homeland (31:7ff.). And a new covenant would replace the old one made at Sinai, which they had broken. This time God will remake them from within, giving them the power to do his will (31:31-34; and compare Romans 8:1-4; 2 Corinthians 5:17). Like Isaiah before him, Jeremiah here telescopes future events. He is talking, in the short-term, of the actual return from exile; in the long-term he looks forward to the new covenant brought in by Christ himself (see Hebrews 8ff.).

Ramah, Rachel (31:15): Rachel, mother of Joseph and Benjamin, died at Ramah near Bethlehem. Jeremiah pictures her weeping for her exiled sons. Matthew 2:18 sees this as a prophecy of the grief caused by Herod's slaughter of the young children.

32 Jeremiah buys land

It was 588/7, when Jerusalem was under siege, and Jeremiah's home town, Anathoth, under enemy occupation. Hanamel must have been an opportunist to try to sell land then! But Jeremiah's purchase spoke louder than words: 'God has a future for Judah.' And everyone in the city must have heard about it. Jeremiah acted under orders from God; only afterwards does he admit his puzzlement (25). In answer God outlines his immediate, and his ultimate purpose for the nation.

Verse 8: land was a family heritage; it never came up for sale on the open market. See Leviticus 25:25.
Baruch (12): Jeremiah's secretary; see 36:4ff.
Verse 35: see on Isaiah 30:33.

33 God's unbreakable promise

The theme is still future restoration.

Where God has destroyed, he will rebuild (6ff.). Joy and prosperity will return (10-11), and an ideal king will rule (14-16). It will happen as surely as night follows day (20).

Verse 21: see 2 Samuel 7 and Numbers 25.

Two families (24): judging by verse 26, this means the family of Jacob (the nation) and the family of David (the kings). But New International Version translates 'two kingdoms'.

34 The Jewish slaves

The date is still 588/7. After receiving God's message (1-7), King Zedekiah issues an order to free all slaves, hoping that this will win God's favour (see Deuteronomy 15:12ff.). But their owners quickly go back on it. And God condemns them as law-breakers.

Verses 4-5: see 39:7. There is no record of Zedekiah's death.

Beneath Jerusalem, even today, are ancient cisterns designed to conserve every drop of water. In Jeremiah's time (see 2:13) they were mostly round, carved out of the rock. This one is below the Ecce Homo Convent in Jerusalem.

Verses 18-19: the ceremony invoked a similar fate on whoever broke the covenant. See Genesis 15.

Withdrawn/stopped its attack (21): there was a temporary let-up while Nebuchadnezzar dealt with pharaoh's army (37:5).

35 The Rechabites

Chapters 35—36 take us back ten years to the earlier siege of Jerusalem. The Rechabites were bedouin descendants of Jehonadab, who took God's part against the Baal-worshippers in 2 Kings 10:15-23. Fear of the invading army brings them to the city (11), where their obedience to a pledge made 200 years before puts the people of God to shame.

36 King Jehoiakim burns Jeremiah's scroll

This is one of the most vivid and dramatic chapters in the whole Bible. The year is 605/4. Jeremiah is banned from the temple (5; no doubt to prevent him repeating what he said earlier, chapter 26). But the word of God cannot be stifled. The message is written; the prophet bides his time; and then within a single day it is read aloud in the hearing of the people, the rulers, and the king himself. Jehoiakim may burn the scroll, but not even he has power to destroy the message, or prevent its fulfilment. Patiently, Jeremiah and Baruch write the words again.

Verse 30: within three months of Jehoiakim's death his son was deported to Babylon.

37—38 Jeremiah's imprisonment

Zedekiah is king; the year, 588 (5). Jeremiah's counsel to surrender (38:2) lands him in his deepest trouble yet. He is flung into prison as a subversive influence and a traitor. Only through the

In prophesying invasion and ruin Jeremiah was accused of undermining the people's morale. But he was not being pessimistic for the sake of it. Only by facing up to reality could they avoid the catastrophe of destruction and exile.

Siege of a city; relief from the Palace of Ashurbanipal at Nineveh.

prompt action of a good friend, and the intervention of the king, is his life saved (37:20-21; 38:7-13). Zedekiah is anxious to know God's word (37:3, 17; 38:14), but lacks faith and courage to act on it. So Jeremiah's terrible vision (38:22-23) becomes reality (39:6-8). But even in the midst of judgement, God does not lose sight of individuals. Ebed-melech's life is saved (39:15-18).

39—40:6 Jerusalem falls; Jeremiah's choice

See also chapter 52; 2 Kings 25; 2 Chronicles 36. God's warnings finally give way to judgement (39:1-10) and Jeremiah is the only man to have any say in his own future (39:12; 40:1-5). Offered a place of honour at the Babylonian court, he chooses instead to throw in his lot with the have-nots, left behind in the land of Judah.

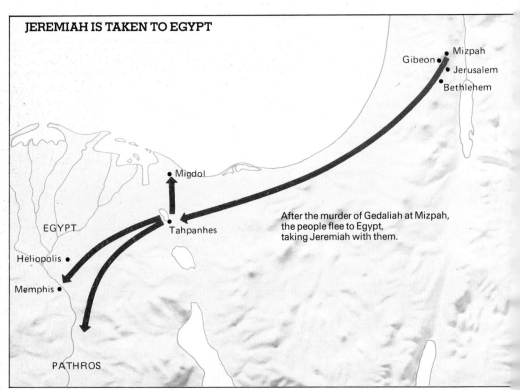

JEREMIAH IS TAKEN TO EGYPT

Mizpah
Gibeon
Jerusalem
Bethlehem

Migdol

EGYPT
Tahpanhes

Heliopolis

Memphis

After the murder of Gedaliah at Mizpah, the people flee to Egypt, taking Jeremiah with them.

PATHROS

Riblah (39:5): Nebuchadnezzar's base was a town to the south of Hama in Syria.
Gedaliah (39:14): son of the man who earlier saved Jeremiah's life (26:24).
Mizpah (40:6): a town a few miles north of Jerusalem; a place of national assembly from Samuel's time.

40:7—41:18 Assassination of the governor, Gedaliah

Gedaliah made a good start as governor. Those who had fled before the army returned and they gathered in a good harvest, after the hungry days of occupation. But after three months he was murdered, and the people, fearing reprisals, made ready to escape to Egypt.
41:9: see 1 Kings 15:16ff.

42—43:7 Escape to Egypt

For all their declared willingness to obey God's word, when the message came telling them to stay put, they disobeyed. Egypt seemed safer. They took Jeremiah and Baruch with them. And as God had predicted (15-18) in due course the long arm of Nebuchadnezzar, king of Babylon, reached down into Egypt (568 BC). According to Josephus, there were Jews among the captives he took back with him.
43:3: Baruch had obviously already warned them against going to Egypt.
Tahpanhes (43:7): see on 2:16.

43:8—44:30 In Egypt: Jeremiah's last appeal

Jeremiah enacts his last recorded parable (43:8ff.). But despite all that has happened, the people still refuse to listen. They will go back to worshipping the 'queen of heaven' (see on 7:18), and all will be well again! We hear no more of

Jeremiah after this. Tradition has it he was stoned to death in Egypt.
The pavement (43:9): archaeologists have uncovered a large area of brick paving on the site.
Heliopolis (43:13): see on Isaiah 19:18.

45 Baruch

This short chapter relates to the writing of the scroll in 605 (chapter 36). Baruch shared something of the prophet's distress. God promises him life in the coming slaughter (as he promised Ebed-melech, 39:15-18). That is enough.

46—51
PROPHECIES AGAINST THE NATIONS

See 25:13. Jeremiah, like Isaiah before him, sees God controlling the history of the world, not just one corner of it. God deals with evil wherever it occurs. These chapters contain some of the most magnificent poetry in the book.

Events in Jeremiah 41 took place at the 'large pool of Gibeon'. Excavations there have revealed this huge pit, with stairs down to a tunnel leading to a well.

46:1-26 Egypt

Verses 1-12 describe the defeat at
Carchemish 'in 605. Verses 13-26 forecast
Nebuchadnezzar's invasion of Egypt
(which took place in 568). Isaiah and
Ezekiel also prophesied against Egypt:
Isaiah 19–20; Ezekiel 29–32.

Verse 9: these are the mercenaries: from
Sudan (Ethiopia) and Libya (Put).

Balm/medicine (11): see on 8:22.

Apis (15): the Egyptian sacred bull. God
has overthrown the gods of Egypt.

46: 27-28 Comfort for Israel

47 Philistia

See also Isaiah 14:28-32. Pharaoh Necho
controlled Gaza at the time of his march
north in 609, but the city often changed
hands. Calamity is predicted from the
Babylonians in the north. Nebuchadnezzar must have overrun the Philistine
cities when he quelled Judah in 587.
Other prophecies: Ezekiel 25:15ff.;
Amos 1:6-8; Zephaniah 2:4-7; Zechariah
9:5-7.

Gaza, Ashkelon (1, 5): Philistine cities.

Caphtor (4): Crete, the island from which
the Philistines originally came.

*Oppression and exile have been the fate of the ordinary people of the Middle
East repeatedly down the centuries. Jeremiah saw only too clearly the suffering
and tragedy defeat and exile would bring.*

Anakim (5, some versions**):** people of giant height who had some connection with the Philistines (Joshua 11:22). But this may not be the right word here.

Dibon (22): the capital.
Horn (25): an image of power, strength, might.
Kir-heres (31): original capital of Moab; present-day Kerak in Jordan.
Verse 37: a picture of mourning.

48 Moab

See on Isaiah 15–16. Moab, Ammon and Edom seem to have joined forces with Judah in rebelling against Nebuchad-nezzar (27:1-3). Presumably he dealt with them when he dealt with Judah. Other prophecies: Ezekiel 25:8-11; Amos 2:1-3; Zephaniah 2:8-11.
Nebo (1): the city, not the mountain.
Chemosh (7, 13): chief Moabite god. Bethel was the sanctuary set up in the northern kingdom of Israel to rival Jerusalem.
Arnon (20): the river which was once Moab's northern boundary.

49: 1-6 Ammon

See on Moab above; also Ezekiel 25:1-7. Ammon is condemned for seizing Israelite land, but will later be restored.
Milcom (1): the Ammonite god.
Rabbah (2): the capital; modern Amman, capital of Jordan.

49: 7-22 Edom

Other prophecies: Isaiah 21:11-12; Obadiah (who seems to have borrowed some

JEREMIAH'S PROPHECIES AGAINST THE NATIONS

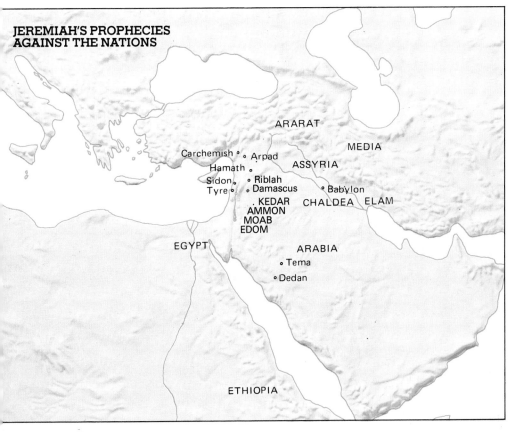

passages from Jeremiah). Edom's judgement will be total: see on Isaiah 34.
Verse 18: see Genesis 19.
Jungle by the Jordan (19): see on 12:5.

49:23-27 Damascus

See also Isaiah 17.
Hamath, Arpad (23): Hama, in Syria; and a town just north of Aleppo.
Ben-hadad (27): the name or title of a number of Syrian kings.

49:28-33 Kedar

As predicted, Nebuchadnezzar routed these nomadic tribes in 599.
Hazor/Hazer (30): probably nomad settlements; not the city in northern Galilee.

49:34-39 Elam

Jeremiah spoke in 597. Within a year Elam, east of Babylon, was attacked by Nebuchadnezzar.

50—51 Babylon

See on Isaiah 13—14 and 46—47. Jeremiah's impressive prophecy was sent with the delegation that went to Babylon in the fourth year of Zedekiah's reign, six years before the fall of Jerusalem. It was given a public reading, then sunk in the Euphrates, as Babylon itself would sink before its conqueror (51:59-64). The Medes (51:11) would pour in on Babylon from the north like the sea. God's people are warned in advance to be out of harm's way when it happens. Cyrus, at the head of an army of Medes

and Persians, took Babylon in 539. Babylon was God's instrument to punish his people (as the Assyrians had been earlier), but God could not overlook its sinful pride. He cannot ignore evil; judgement must always come.
Bel, Merodach (Marduk) (50:2): the Babylonian gods.
50:21: there is a play on the names Merathaim and Pekod, two Babylonian tribes.
Vengeance for his temple (50:28; 51:11): Jeremiah wrote this prophecy before the temple was destroyed this note was probably added after the destruction in 587.
51:27: Ararat in eastern Turkey; Minni in north-west Iran; Ashkenaz, the Scythians, in the same area. All were subject to the Medes.
Her sea (51:36): Babylon's prosperity and security depended on its elaborate system of canals and lakes.
Seraiah (51:59): Baruch's brother (32:12).
The words of Jeremiah end here (64): Chapter 52 is an addition.

52
HISTORICAL APPENDIX

See on 2 Kings 24—25, which are almost identical with this chapter; and Jeremiah 39.
Verses 28-30: the captives were deported in 597, 587 and 581.
Verse 31: with the accession of Nebuchadnezzar's son (562-560), things improved for Jehoiachin, a token of new hope for the nation.

Exile to Babylon

ALAN MILLARD

At about the time Jeremiah began to prophesy, the Assyrian Empire crumbled. Nabopolassar, Chaldean governor of southern Babylonia, took control of Babylon (626 BC) and gradually ousted the Assyrian garrisons from other towns. Then, allied to an army of Medes and Scythians from the Persian hills, he attacked Assyria, finally sacking Nineveh in 612 BC (see Nahum). The last vestige of Assyrian power was destroyed two years later, and the forces of the Egyptian Pharaoh Necho routed at Carchemish in 605 BC (see Jeremiah 25, page 404).

Thus the Chaldeans became masters of the 'Fertile Crescent', although the northern provinces of the Assyrian Empire fell under Median rule. The famous Nebuchadnezzar became king in 605 BC. His first 20 years saw much fighting as he subdued rebellious provinces, Judah among them.

After Carchemish, he retained Jehoiakim (the Egyptian nominee) as king in Jerusalem, exacting an oath of loyalty, and taking hostages (Daniel 1:1). The Judean disregarded his oath and linked his country to Egypt again. In righteous fury, Nebuchadnezzar brought his forces to besiege Jerusalem, whose king refused to surrender, despite Jeremiah's pleas.

The king died. His son, Jehoiachin, reigned a month or two until the city fell and he was taken into exile in Babylon (597 BC). There, according to ration-lists found in the ruins, he and his family were supplied from the royal stores. The throne of Judah was given to Zedekiah, yet he failed to learn the lesson, falling prey to Egypt's lures as his predecessors had done.

Judah's fate was inevitable. Babylonian forces attacked again, took Jerusalem and sacked it (587/6 BC). Large numbers of surviving citizens were settled in Babylonia, and the territory of Judah was placed under a governor.

The exiles seem to have been moved to Babylonia itself, living in various towns and villages as well as in the capital city. They were free to establish themselves as part of the community, so far as can be discovered, to maintain their own traditions and to practise their own religion as they wanted. No doubt the new surroundings and the refurbished splendour of ancient Babylon (justifying Nebuchadnezzar's boast, 'Is not this great Babylon, which I have built';

A bull in glazed tile from the walls of Babylon.

Daniel 4:30) awed the men of Judah. Some may have felt that Marduk of Babylon and his host of attendant gods was superior to the God of Israel. Others certainly found a profitable way of life in their new surroundings. Others longed to return to the promised land (see Psalm 137).

The impress of Babylonian culture can be seen in the figures of Ezekiel's visions and in the stories of Daniel. It was an amalgam of native concepts and foreign. In the streets and workshops of the city, exiles and visitors from Egypt, Syria and Palestine rubbed shoulders with others from Cilicia and Caria and Ionia, all speaking a common language, Aramaic.

Yet the empire of the Chaldean kings was not to last. As Isaiah, Jeremiah and Daniel foresaw, the hill-men of the east and north would overcome it. The picture, vague in Isaiah and Jeremiah, is clear in Daniel. Media grew ever more powerful after ridding herself of Scythian rule. By 585 BC the Median yoke extended half-way across Anatolia. And Media was clearly a rival to Babylon when, in 550 BC, her vassal, Cyrus the Persian, seized the throne.

In Babylon, Belshazzar governed while his father Nabonidus lived in northern Arabia. The king returned only to see his realm fall to Cyrus in 539 BC. The new king's policies were generally peaceable, and he liberally allowed Jews to return and restore Jerusalem's temple as he restored many other shrines.

Lamentations

We do not know who wrote these laments – although the Greek versions name Jeremiah. They are anonymous in the Hebrew text. And they differ in style and content from Jeremiah's prophecies. But the author must at least have been a contemporary of the prophet. The first four poems were obviously written by an eye-witness to the destruction of Jerusalem by Nebuchadnezzar's Babylonian army in 587 BC.

To the people of Judah, the fall of the city meant more than the loss of their beautiful and almost unassailable capital. It was more than just the destruction of a nation's capital city: because Jerusalem was in a very special sense God's city. His temple was there. This was where he chose to live with his people. And when Jerusalem was burned, the temple destroyed, the people deported, they knew that God had given them up to the enemy. It could not have happened otherwise. So these laments express the poet's grief, not simply over the suffering and humiliation of his people, but over something deeper and far worse, that God had rejected his people because of their sin.

The first four poems have the rhythm of the dirge, and they are written as acrostics. In 1, 2 and 4, each of the 22 verses begins with a new letter of the Hebrew alphabet. In 3, there are three verses to each letter. The fifth poem (chapter 5) also has 22 verses, but is neither a dirge nor an acrostic.

The poems are still read aloud in Jewish synagogues in mid-July to mark the anniversary of the destruction of the temple in 587, and remembering the later destruction in AD 70.

Chapter 1 The first lament
Jerusalem is alone, deserted, mourning; the people gone; the temple defiled and destroyed. God has judged and punished her for the enormity of her sin. Now, at last, she cries out to him.

Chapter 2 The second lament
The poet sees again the outpouring of God's anger: the starving children; the slaughter; the ruin of city and sanctuary. He hears again the taunts of old enemies, gloating over the fate of Jerusalem. Let her call out to God to look, and pity.

Chapter 3 The third lament
We see the agony of the nation focussed in the experience of a single individual. In the darkness, crushed and battered to the point where all hope dies (18), faith still rekindles at the thought of God in all his love and mercy (19-33). When he is all but lost, there comes the knowledge that God is near (54ff.). But he cannot forgive the bitter provocation of his enemies (59-66).

Chapter 4 The fourth lament
The city's former glory – and the horrors of siege. The cries of starving children; wizened faces; shrivelled bodies; never to be forgotten. The sins of the people, the prophets and the priests, have brought the city low. And Edom – the old arch-enemy – gloats, not knowing that her punishment is yet to come (21-22).

Chapter 5 The fifth lament – a prayer
The poet vividly depicts defeat: the loss of freedom, loss of land, loss of respect; rape and cruelty; forced labour; near-starvation. And all because of sin. He prays to God for restoration.

An old woman, veiled in black, in the old city of Jerusalem.

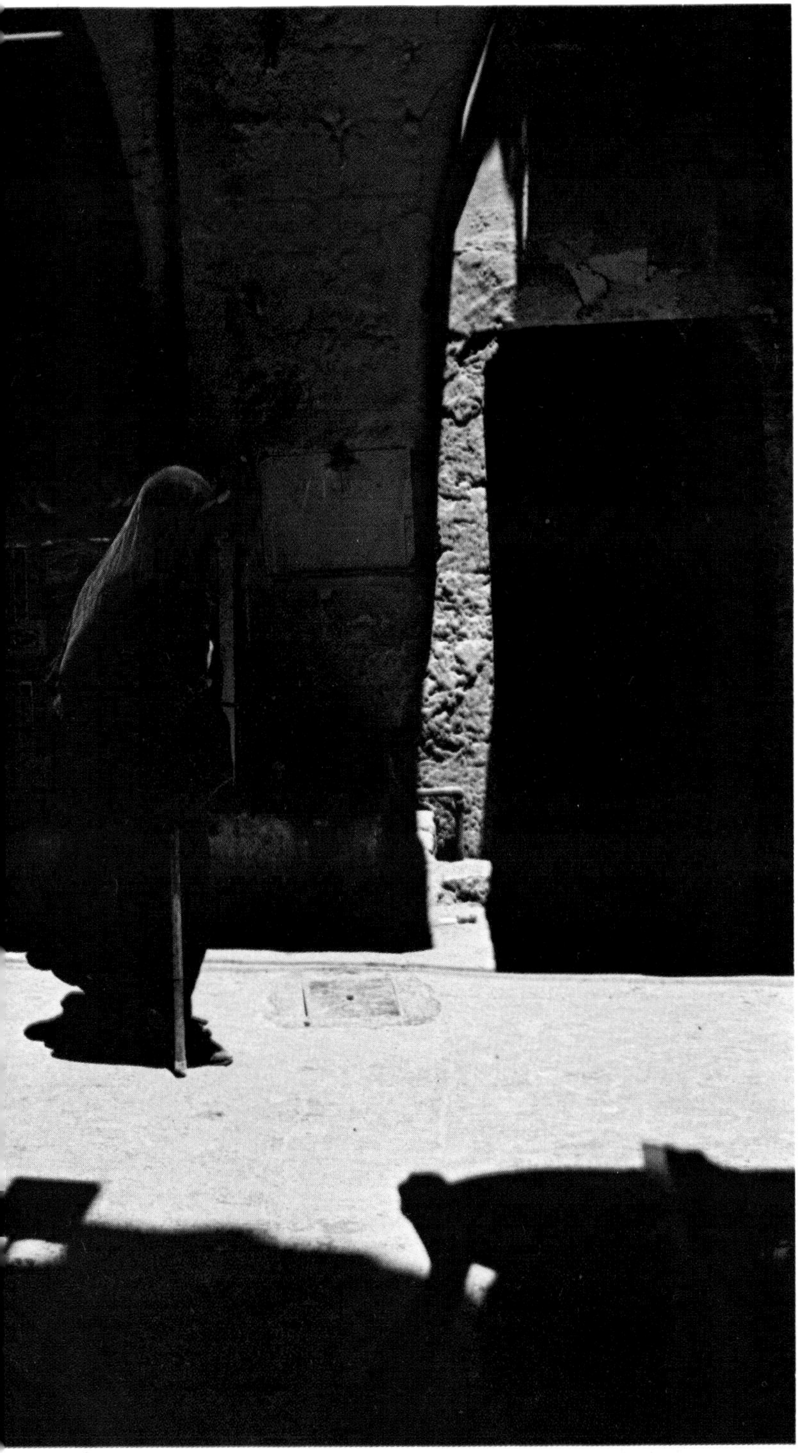

Ezekiel

In 597 BC King Jehoiachin surrendered Jerusalem to the Babylonian army, and was taken into exile. With him went 10,000 men – statesmen, soldiers, craftsmen (2 Kings 24:14). And among them was Jeremiah's younger contemporary, Ezekiel, then in his mid-twenties. Ezekiel was in training as a priest, looking forward to service in the temple like his father before him. Exile in the plains of Babylonia, far from Jerusalem, meant the end of all his hopes.

But five years later, when he was 30 (the age at which he would probably have taken up his duties as a priest – Numbers 4:3; and see on 1:1), God called him into service as a prophet. The call was accompanied by a vision of God which coloured his entire ministry (just as Isaiah's had done nearly 150 years earlier). He saw God in all his awesome majesty, above and beyond the world of men, all-seeing, all-knowing. It was a vision of fire and glory. And against this dazzling brilliance Ezekiel saw his people's sin in all its blackness. He saw the inevitability of judgement. And for six years this was his message. Only after the city and temple of Jerusalem were destroyed in 587 did he really begin to stress God's intention to 'resurrect' (chapter 37) and restore Israel, and to look forward to the time when the ideal would be realized: to the new temple in which God's people would offer him perfect worship (chapters 40ff.).

As he declared God's message to the exiles, a great weight of responsibility rested on Ezekiel. He saw himself as a 'look-out', who must give warning of danger or be held accountable. One of his most characteristic themes is that of individual responsibility before God. Ezekiel was an extraordinary man, a visionary, imaginative, by training a man who appreciated and understood ritual

and symbol. He was passionate, dedicated, utterly obedient to God. The most hardened onlooker could not fail to be impressed as Ezekiel acted out his sobering messages.

The book – written entirely in the first person, apart from the note in 1:2-3 – is in keeping with the man. The prophecies are meticulously ordered and dated, even to the day of the month. Message and language are consistent (often repetitive) throughout the book. Characteristic themes and phrases run right through. And although some scholars have questioned the authorship and background of Ezekiel, the various arguments tend to cancel one another out. Ezekiel's message is very close to that of Jeremiah (another prophet given to acted parables), whom he may have heard as a young man in Jerusalem. But although he writes for the most part in 'cold' prose, Ezekiel is more flamboyantly visual than the other prophets. With him, prophecy merges into 'apocalyptic' (see Revelation). The Bible book closest in spirit to Ezekiel is Revelation, which borrows many of his images.

For many Christians Ezekiel is a closed book, apart from a few familiar passages (the watchman; the valley of dry bones; the vision of the temple). It is easy to give up at the first chapter – the vision of flashing lights and peculiar creatures and wheels with eyes. But this is our loss. Because in our materialistic, man-centred world, we need Ezekiel's vision of the almighty God. We need to see sin as God sees it. We need to be reminded of our own accountability. We need to know that God is God – before we learn it the hard way, as Israel did, through judgement. Reading the Old Testament also helps us to understand the New. We need to be acquainted with Ezekiel in order to understand Revelation.

1—3
EZEKIEL'S CALL AND VISION OF GOD

Ezekiel is a book of visions and symbolic actions – beginning with this great vision of God. As Ezekiel gazed out over the plain, he saw what looked like an approaching storm: thunder, lightning, black clouds. Then he made out the figures of four cherubim (see 10:15), angelic creatures, standing wing-tip to wing-tip, forming a hollow square. At the centre, fire glowed; and above, under the blue vault of the heavens, was the Lord of glory in human form, seated on a throne, encircled by a dazzling rainbow.

Winged creatures like those of Ezekiel's vision were also used to decorate the supporting column of the palace gateway, Nineveh.

Beside each four-faced cherub was a terrifying, whirling wheel, moving like a castor and full of eyes. Who could look on this and live?

The Almighty, the God of Israel was present in all his power in the far-flung lands of Babylon. He came to make Ezekiel his messenger to the exiles, the watchman sent to warn the remnant of God's rebel people (2:1-7; 3:16-21). And the words of God, though they were hard, were satisfying (2:8–3:3). It became Ezekiel's life-mission to let God's people know that he is the Lord. They would learn it first through the terrors of judgement (7:4). Afterwards they would see his power to restore and renew (36:8-11).

Thirtieth year (1:1): most probably Ezekiel's own age. If, as seems likely, this was the age at which a priest took up his duties, it would have been a year of special significance for the prophet. But to become eligible at last for his life's work as a priest, when in exile, hundreds of miles away from Jerusalem and its temple, must have been a bitter experience.

Chebar (1:1): usually identified as the great canal which ran from the Euphrates north of Babylon, close to the city of Nippur.

Verses 2-3: a note added to explain Ezekiel's opening sentence. The date was 593 BC (see introduction).

Living creatures (5): cherubim (10:15), the figures which spread their wings over the mercy-seat above the ark of the covenant (Exodus 25:18ff.). As the son of a priest, Ezekiel may have been familiar with the figures of cherubim which decorated Solomon's temple. Similar winged, sphinx-like creatures frequently appear in Babylonian art.

Verse 26: although it was normally reckoned that no one could see God and live, there were some who shared Ezekiel's privilege and described what they saw – see Exodus 24:9-11; Isaiah 6; Daniel 7; Revelation 4.

Son of man/mortal man (2.1): Ezekiel is addressed in this way throughout the book. It simply means 'human being'. This is the term Jesus most often used to describe himself.

Briers and thorns . . . scorpions (2:6): a vivid picture of the hostile reception.

2:10: normally a scroll had writing on only one side; perhaps the implication is that there was no room left for Ezekiel to add anything of his own.

3:7: the call of Isaiah, and of Jeremiah, was equally daunting: see Isaiah 6:9-12; Jeremiah 1:17-19.

3:25-27: the meaning seems to be that Ezekiel would be dumb except on the occasions when God had a message for him to give. But some take this as a self-imposed, ritual dumbness, rather than an actual loss of speech. Either way, it gave added force to the utterances he did make. The dumbness lasted until news reached him of the fall of Jerusalem (24:27).

4—24
ISRAEL'S SIN: GOD'S JUDGEMENT

4—5 Ezekiel enacts the siege and destruction of Jerusalem

The 'props' for the drama were ready to hand: a large sun-dried brick on which Ezekiel drew an outline of the city; and the metal plate on which they baked their flat loaves of bread. The people watched, and got the message. They watched with growing horror as Ezekiel weighed out his meagre measure of mixed grain and eked out his water ration. They saw the prophet wasting away, as the population of Jerusalem would do under siege. They watched him shave his head, sharing Jerusalem's disgrace. They saw him burn the hair and toss it away, till only a tiny handful – representing the exiles themselves – remained. It was a telling lesson.

4:5-6: the Greek version has 190 days; from the fall of Samaria in 722 BC to the return of the exiles in 538 is 184 years. From the fall of Jerusalem in 587 to 538 is 49 years. 40 may represent a generation, rather than being an exact figure.

4:9: under siege no one is fussy about the ingredients they use to make bread.

Twenty shekels (10): about 8 ozs/230 gms.

Sixth part of a hin (11): about a pint/0.6 litre.

Unclean (13ff.): using dung for fuel defiled the food, according to Jewish regulations. It was hard for Ezekiel, a man trained to maintain ritual cleanness, to do as God instructed. Compare Peter's reaction in Acts 10:9-16.

Winged creatures carved in ivory, to decorate a piece of furniture.

An Egyptian model of bread-making. Ezekiel's bread-making was part of an elaborate object-lesson to convey his message.

may be actual practices, or the description may be symbolic. Either way the meaning is plain. There has been a total departure from the true religion of Israel. In the temple of God an image of the Canaanite goddess Asherah/Astarte (the 'image of jealousy', 3) has been set up, as in the days of King Manasseh. The nation's leaders are secretly practising animal worship (8:7-13). The women are mourning the Sumerian god Tammuz, who was supposed to die with the old year and rise again with the spring. Men turn their backs on God to worship the sun (8:16-18).

Contrary to popular belief (8:12), God both sees and judges (9:9-10). Only those who grieve for the loss of the true faith will be spared (9:4-6).

Chapter 10: following the terrible slaughter which made Ezekiel cry aloud for his people (9:8), he sees again the vision of the cherubim, the glory, the whirling wheels, that he first saw on the plains of Babylon (chapter 1). What greater contrast imaginable than this sight of God in all his glory – and the loathsome scenes of idolatry in his temple (chapter 8). Because of all this the glory of God will finally depart from Jerusalem.

But first Ezekiel sees two men he recognizes, rulers who are advocating resistance to Babylon, despite the insistence of God's prophets that this would prove fatal (11:1-4). Ezekiel pronounces God's judgement, and as he speaks, to his alarm, Pelatiah falls dead (11:5-13) in confirmation of God's word. But God is not making a 'full end' (13). The future lies with the exiles. And on this note, and with this message (25), the vision ends.

6—7 Against the land of Israel: the end has come

The acted message is reinforced by the spoken word. The people's flagrant idolatry is about to bring destruction upon them – judgement from which there is no escape. Then they will know that the Lord is God indeed. Terrible, total calamity is befalling the land.

From the desert to Riblah (6:14): from south to north. Riblah, on the River Orontes, is near Israel's northern boundary (New International Version, following most Hebrew manuscripts, reads 'Diblah').

The seller grieve (7:12): because he has been forced to sell the land which was his heritage.

7:18: shaven heads were a sign of disgrace as well as of mourning.

8— 11 Ezekiel's vision of Jerusalem – its guilt and its punishment

September 592. Ezekiel is transported in vision (or, as John would have said, 'In the Spirit') to Jerusalem, and set down beside the temple (8:1-4). What he sees

Jaazaniah (8:11): his father was King Josiah's secretary of state; his brother Ahikam, Jeremiah's friend. Not the same man as in 11:1.

The branch . . . (8:17): possibly a reference to some pagan practice.

A mark (9:4): Jeremiah, Baruch and the

foreigner, Ebed-melech, were among those 'marked' to be spared (Jeremiah 40:4; 45; 39:15ff.). In Revelation God's men are marked (14:1), and so are those who sell out to the forces of evil (13:16). The 'mark' here is the last letter of the Hebrew alphabet, *taw*, written as a cross in the oldest script.

11:3: a difficult verse, most likely meaning that this was not the moment for peace-time building. The cauldron protects the meat from the flames (Good News Bible).

A new spirit (11:19): compare Jeremiah 31:33-34; Ezekiel 36:26.

12 Ezekiel plays the part of an exile

Although most people refuse to listen, the prophet continues to make God's word known (1-3). As he put together the bare necessities, ready for flight, and as he broke through the mud-brick wall at night, Ezekiel was playing the part, not just of any exile, but of King Zedekiah ('the prince', 10). Compare 12-13 with Jeremiah 52:7-11. Ezekiel's prophecy proved accurate to the last detail. It was as God said it would be, and within a very short space of time (21-28).

13 False prophets

The work of Jeremiah and Ezekiel was constantly undermined by false prophets, who told people what they wanted to hear, and claimed God's authority for their message of false hope. They were like plaster, concealing the crumbling structure of the nation, but unable to stop it falling (10-16); for what God says will happen, always happens. Among them were prophetesses, practising magic and holding helpless individuals in thrall (17ff.).

Souls (18, some versions): 'lives' – the whole person; the idea of disembodied spirits was completely alien to Jewish thinking.

14 Idolatry and its consequences

God claims a unique place in the hearts of his people. Those who deny him his rightful place, worshipping other 'gods' alongside, are destined for destruction. The majority regard the few godly men among them as an insurance against disaster. But at this point in time not even a Noah or a Job could save anyone but himself.

Daniel/Danel (14): probably an otherwise unknown Jewish patriarch, and not Ezekiel's contemporary in exile. The name of the biblical Daniel is spelt differently. There is also a hero of this name in an ancient Canaanite epic.

Verse 21: these judgements represent the worst fears of ancient peoples (see on Jeremiah 14:12).

15 The parable of the vine

The vine was a popular symbol for Israel. There is by this time no question of it bearing fruit, and as wood the vine is useless. Israel is already partially destroyed (4): there is nothing for it now but total destruction (6-8).

16 The unfaithful wife: an allegory

God took Israel up when she was nothing – an abandoned waif – and lavished his love on her, making her into a great and glorious nation. She owed him everything. But prosperity turned her head and, like a wife turned prostitute, she played fast and loose with foreign nations. She 'courted' them and worshipped their gods, with all the hideous practices that involved (20-29). God was forgotten; the covenant (like the marriage-vow) broken. He must punish Israel (35-43): but he will also restore (53, 60).

Amorite . . . Hittite (3): the reference is to moral, not literal, parentage. Israel had become as decadent as the nations she destroyed at the conquest of Canaan.

Verse 4: these were the midwife's duties.

Spread my coat (8): with this symbolic gesture he claimed her in marriage. See Ruth 3:9. God sealed the contract with the Sinai covenant.

Verse 38: adultery was punishable by death.

Verse 46: 'Samaria': capital of the northern kingdom; destroyed in 722. 'Sodom': the city at the southern end of the Dead Sea, wiped out for its gross immorality (Genesis 19).

17 The eagles and the vine

The first eagle is Nebuchadnezzar of Babylon, who took King Jehoiachin captive (3, 4; see introduction). The seed he plants (5, 13) is Zedekiah. But Zedekiah soon turned to Egypt (the second eagle) for help (7, 15), bringing the Babylonians back to destroy Jerusalem. In 587, within three or four years, the prediction of 17-21 came true (see Jeremiah 52). But God will take a

'cutting' from the line of Israel's kings (the cedar) which will take root (22-24).

Verse 8: it seems best to take this as stressing the fact that Zedekiah was well off under Nebuchadnezzar (as in 5).

18 Each individual accountable to God

Contrary to popular belief (2), God is not so unjust as to punish one generation for the sins of another (20). He holds every man answerable for his own sins. It gives God no pleasure to sign the death warrant for any man (23). His concern, always, is that men should turn away from evil and live (30-32). And he makes his standards plain (5-9; 14-17).

Soul (4): 'life' – see on 13:18 above.

Verse 20: Ezekiel is redressing the

Ezekiel shared the life of a refugee settlement, acting out his prophecies to a people in exile.

balance, not denying the basic principle that in life children do suffer the consequences of their parents' wrong-doing (Exodus 20:5).

19 A lament for Israel's rulers

The poem is written in the familiar dirge-rhythm. The lioness is Judah; the kings her cubs. The first (3) is Jehoahaz, carried off to Egypt by Pharaoh Necho in 609. The second (5) is Jehoiachin (see introduction). Now, thanks to Zedekiah's rebellion, both the nation and its line of kings will be destroyed (10-14).

20:1-44 A history of the nation's rebellion

July/August 591. Ezekiel turns from allegory to historical fact. From the time in Egypt and the wilderness right down to his own day, Israel's history has been a weary repetition of idolatry and rebellion against God. All along, God held back from making an end of the nation. But now he will cut off the rebels (38). His own, he will restore (40-44).

I gave them…(25-26): these difficult verses seem best understood in the light of Romans 1:24, etc. God 'gave them up' to the evil things they wanted.

Bamah (29): high place. There is a play on words in this verse.

Verse 37: Jerusalem Bible translates: 'I mean to make you pass under my crook and I will bring a few of you back.'

20:45—21:32 Fire and sword

God's judgement will sweep across the land from south to north like a forest fire (20:45-48). The sword of God is drawn against Israel. It is in the hands of the king of Babylon (21:19), who will destroy the capital cities of both Ammon and Judah (21:20). (Five years after Jerusalem fell, Nebuchadnezzar attacked Ammon.)

Negeb (20:46, some versions): today this region is arid desert, but Palestine as a whole was more wooded in Old Testament times.

Rabbah (21:20): Amman, present capital of Jordan.

Until he comes…(21:27): see Genesis 49:10. There is one coming to whom the kingship rightly belongs.

22 The charges against Jerusalem

God's people are guilty – guilty of bloodshed, oppression, extortion, bribery, and sexual sin; they have made a mockery of their religion (6-12). When God tests them by fire, no trace of genuine metal will be found (17-22). Every section of society shares the guilt: rulers, priests, prophets and common people alike (23-31).

Unclean and clean (26): see on Leviticus 11.

Verse 28: see 13:8-16.

23 Parable of the two sisters, Oholah and Oholibah

Oholah is Samaria, capital of the northern kingdom of Israel. Oholibah is Jerusalem. Both sisters have behaved like common whores. Their appetite for their lovers (the pagan gods) is insatiable; their behaviour utterly disgusting. They have run, in turn, after Egypt and Assyria. Now Judah, outdoing her sister, is running after Babylon. Jerusalem will share Samaria's fate – shame and destruction at the hands of her latest lover. Her punishment is fully deserved (45).

Verse 10: the Assyrians destroyed Samaria in 722 BC.

Verse 23: Pekod, Shoa and Koa were probably tribes on the eastern borders of the Babylonian Empire. The Babylonians and Chaldeans were not separate peoples.

24 Jerusalem besieged; Ezekiel's wife dies

The date is the same as in 2 Kings 25:1; Jeremiah 52:4 – usually thought to be 15 January 588 BC. Jerusalem is like a rusty cooking-pot, set on the fire to burn. The behaviour of the people has polluted the city. The very same day that the siege is laid, Ezekiel's much-loved wife is suddenly taken from him. But God forbids him the customary forms of mourning. Ezekiel's personal loss is part of a grief beyond expression. Men will eat their hearts out for the fate of Jerusalem, though they go about dry-eyed, like the prophet. And when news of the city's fall reaches them, Ezekiel will at last be able to speak freely (27; see 3:26-27); the judgement will be over.

Verse 17: the mourning customs of the day: noisy lamentation; bared head sprinkled with dust and ashes; bared feet; veiled face; and the funeral meal provided for the mourners.

Slaves dumping earth: an Assyrian relief.

25—32
PROPHECIES AGAINST FOREIGN NATIONS

Although the prophets concentrated mainly on Israel/Judah, all of them were very conscious that God was Lord of the whole world. There is no nation beyond the reach of his judgement; and what he condemns and punishes in his own people, he condemns and punishes in other nations too. This collection of prophecies effectively marks the break in Ezekiel's ministry before, and his ministry after, the fall of Jerusalem in 587 BC.

25 Ammon, Moab, Edom, Philistia

For other prophecies, see on Jeremiah 47—49. These four nations were Israel's

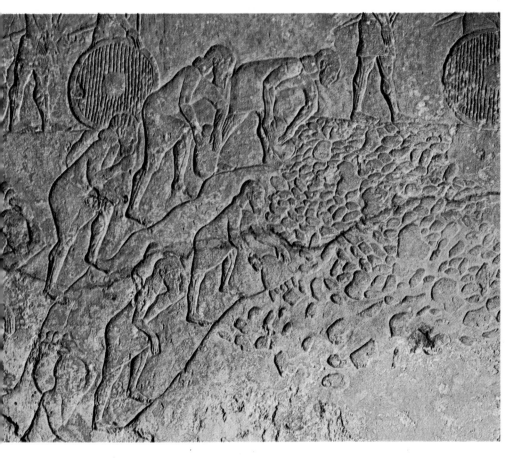

closest neighbours, and her oldest enemies. All took a vengeful delight in Israel's downfall, for which God will punish them. Shortly after this, Ammon, Moab and Edom were overrun by Nabataean tribesmen. The Philistines disappeared from history after Maccabean times.

26—28:19 Tyre

See on Isaiah 23. The date of Ezekiel's prophecy is probably the end of the 11th year – February 586 – assuming that Ezekiel learnt of the fall of Jerusalem that year, rather than the following one (see on 33:21). The forecast of chapter 26 proved all too true. Tyre did not laugh long over Jerusalem's fate. Within a few months Nebuchadnezzar's army was at her own gates, and for 13 years she was under siege.

Tyre was a tempting prey. The city lay at the foot of the Lebanese mountains and possessed the finest natural harbour in the eastern Mediterranean. It was in fact a double harbour, as the main city was built on an offshore island (26:5). As a centre of trade and commerce Tyre was fabulously wealthy, and her own glassware and purple dye were world famous. Ezekiel fittingly pictures the city as a great trading vessel (chapter 27) laden with the choicest of cargoes, and commanding human skills and resources from far and wide. News of her wreck will put the world into mourning. Chapter 28 is a lament for the king of Tyre, whose pride has proved his downfall.

Senir (27:5): Mt Hermon.

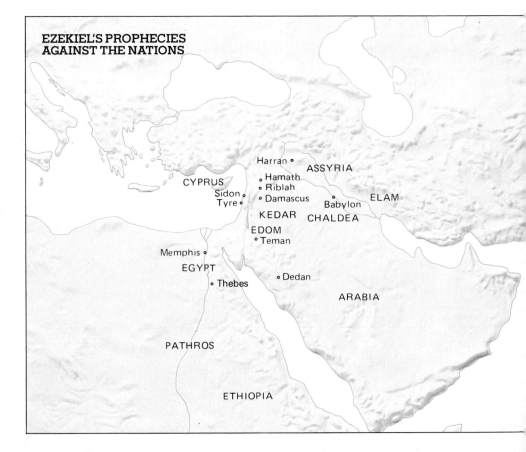

EZEKIEL'S PROPHECIES AGAINST THE NATIONS

CYPRUS

Sidon
Tyre

Harran
Hamath
Riblah
Damascus
KEDAR

ASSYRIA

Babylon
CHALDEA

ELAM

EDOM
Teman

Memphis

EGYPT

Thebes

Dedan

ARABIA

PATHROS

ETHIOPIA

Gebal (27:9): Byblos, now Jubail, in Lebanon.
Daniel (28:3): see on 14:14.
28:12ff.: much of the imagery is drawn from Genesis 2-3.

28:20-26 Sidon

Another famous Old Testament sea-port, Sidon is in Lebanon, 20 miles north of Tyre. Today both Tyre (Sour) and Sidon are small fishing-ports. The charge against Sidon is, again, contempt for God's people (24). Sidon, like Tyre, fell to Nebuchadnezzar. Verses 25-26 are a message of hope for Israel.

29-32 Egypt

A collection of seven prophecies, all (except the one beginning at 30:1) carefully dated.

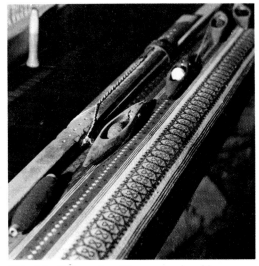

This rich silk brocade, still woven on hand-looms in the old city of Damascus, evokes the wealth and luxury of ancient Tyre.

■ 29:1-16, January 587. By his insufferable pride in placing himself among the gods, Pharaoh has exposed his whole land to God's anger. But he will learn who is God!

■ 29:17-21, New Year's day, 571 (the latest prophecy in the book). The long and costly siege of Tyre ended about 574. Ezekiel declares that Egypt will be Babylon's next prey.

■ 30:1-19, undated. Ezekiel depicts the judgement Nebuchadnezzar will execute on Egypt and her allies. God will put an end to Egypt's wealth (10-12) and her 'gods' (13ff.).

■ 30:20-26, April 587. Pharaoh Hophra's army had made a half-hearted attempt to relieve besieged Jerusalem, but had been defeated. His power will be yet further broken.

■ 31:1-18, June 587. Egypt is likened to a great cedar tree (2-9). Because of its overbearing pride the tree will be felled (10-14). Egypt will be removed to the place of the dead (15ff.).

■ 32:1-16, March 585 (after the news of Jerusalem's fall had reached the exiles). A lament for Pharaoh.

■ 32:17-32 (? March) 585. Egypt will join the other fallen nations: Assyria, Elam, Meshech, Tubal, Edom, Sidon. They are consigned to a great burial-chamber full of graves.

Pharaoh/king of Egypt (29:2): the particular pharaoh is Hophra. All the pharaohs were worshipped as gods. So also was the Nile crocodile (verse 3).

Migdol to Aswan (29:10): i.e. from north to south – the whole land. Migdol was a city on the Nile delta.

Pathros (29:14): upper (i.e. southern) Egypt.

30:5: Egypt's allies.

Assyria (31:3, many versions): Good News Bible, 'You are like a cedar in Lebanon', and Jerusalem Bible make better sense.

32:22-30: 'Assyria', the great power in Isaiah's day, overthrown by Babylon. 'Elam', a nation east of Babylon. 'Meshech and Tubal', little-known nations on Assyria's northern frontier. 'Princes of the north', presumably city-states north of Palestine.

33—48
ISRAEL RESTORED

33:1-20 The watchman
These verses reiterate the teaching of two earlier passages, 3:17-21; 18:5-29.

33:21-33 The exiles hear that Jerusalem has fallen
The news did not take Ezekiel by surprise. God had already given him back his speech, as promised (24:27), by the time the messenger arrived. Some texts have 'eleventh year' for 'twelfth' in verse 21, in which case the news takes the more likely time of six months to reach them. Those left behind in Judah, far from repenting, were busy annexing other people's property. And in Babylonia the exiles who seemed to lap up Ezekiel's words came simply for entertainment. They neither believed them nor acted on them: a depressing state of affairs after all that had happened!

34 God denounces the leaders and people of Israel
Both 'shepherds' (1-10) and 'sheep' (17-22) come in for condemnation. They have greedily, cruelly, selfishly exploited those committed to their care. But God will be a true shepherd, bringing his scattered flock back to good pasture in their homeland (11-16; and see Luke 15:4-7). He will appoint a good shepherd – a new David – to care for them (23-24; and see John 10:11), and the flock will dwell secure.

35 Prophecy against Edom
Edom is marked out for destruction, because of her callous reaction to Israel's downfall. She not only gloated, but planned to make capital out of it by seizing the land (10; the two nations are Israel and Judah). See 25:12-14 above. Other prophecies against Edom: Isaiah 21:34; Jeremiah 49:7-22; Obadiah.

36 The return to the homeland
God tells the desolate land it will soon be inhabited. His people are coming home. Israel's defeat has made men despise the God of Israel as powerless. Their return will vindicate his honour. The nations will know, and God's people will know, that he is the Lord. Those who returned from exile were truly and permanently cured of idolatry (25). But the total transformation of a 'new heart' is realized only 'in Christ' (2 Corinthians 5:17). Ezekiel was thinking of something far more complex than a heart transplant: the heart, in Jewish thought, stood for the whole personality, the essential man.

37 The vision in the valley of dry bones
After ten years in exile, and with Jerusalem destroyed, the people have given up hope. Not all Ezekiel's promises of restoration can raise a spark in his hearers. The nation is dead. But God can take even skeletons and make them into a living army. Ezekiel plays his part by making God's word known, but it is the Spirit of God who gives life. Israel will be remade and live again. The two warring kingdoms will become one nation under one king – a new David. And here (21-28) the promise to the exiles merges into the full blessing of the future golden age. The return is only a foretaste of all God has in store for his people.

Into one (17): 'hold the two sticks end to end in your hand so that they look like one stick', Good News Bible.

David (24): the ideal, messianic king, who will rule for ever in peace and righteousness.

38—39 The prophecy against Gog
Magog, Meshech, Tubal (2) and Gomer (6) were all sons of Japheth (Noah's son). They gave their names to Indo-European peoples living in the

Phoenician figure of a shepherd.

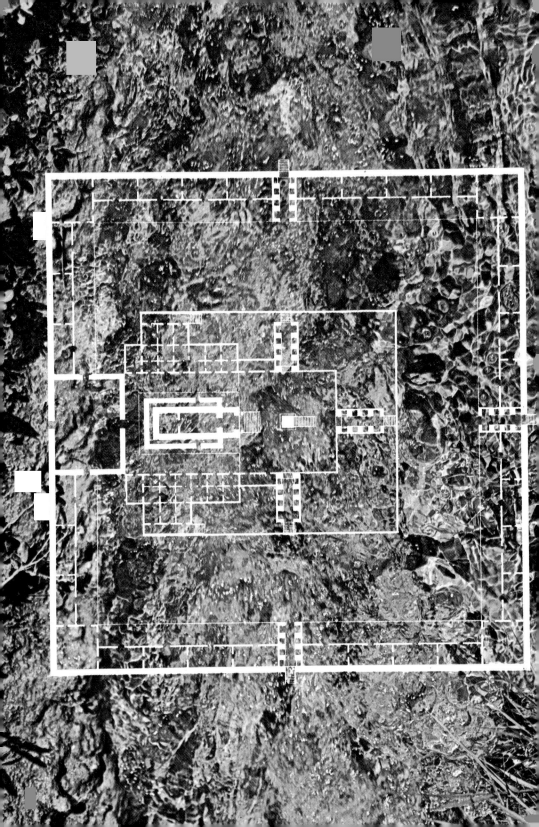

Black Sea/Caucasus region, on the northern fringe of the then-known world. Ezekiel pictures an invasion of these barbaric hordes from the north, led by the unidentified Gog, who may personify the cosmic forces of evil. Allied with armies from far and near (Persia, Sudan and north Africa, 5) he will wage war on the Lord's people. And God will demonstrate his power in the sight of all by taking on all the forces of evil singlehanded, and destroying them once and for all. 'Gog' is responsible for the plan, but the Lord's hand is always in control.

Chapter 39 repeats and enlarges on 38. So vast is Gog's army that the weapons provide Israel with seven years' fuel supply. And the carnage is so great it takes seven months to clean up the land. (For the Jews, the number seven symbolized perfection and complete-ness.) The judgement of God is a terrible thing, and Ezekiel conjures it up in horrifying pictures. The fact that these chapters immediately precede Ezekiel's vision of the new temple in which God dwells among his people, gives added point to John's choice of Gog and Magog to represent all who oppose God in the last great battle instigated by Satan at the end of time (Revelation 20:8).

40–48 The vision of the temple

These chapters were written some years after the rest (except for 29:17-21), in 573 BC. Although, for the most part, they make rather dull reading, they are in a very real sense, the climax to the whole book. Ezekiel began with a vision of God in the plains of Babylon. It ends with a vision of God returning in glory to a new temple – God in the midst of his people once again, never to depart.

For all the detail, Ezekiel's description

is no mere blueprint for the second temple. It was not the old Jerusalem, but a structure *like* a city that he saw (40:2). It is true that the new temple follows much the same layout as Solomon's temple, and is all set out for the sacrifices (40:38ff.). But when God returns in all his glory it is to live for ever in a temple and among a priesthood and people cleansed from evil (chapter 43). Everything is perfect. This is the ideal. Yet it is not as far-reaching as the vision in Revelation. It is still envisaged in earthly terms: there is still a temple and sacrifices; the people of God are synonymous with Israel (44:6ff.); the laws continue, so does death, so does the need for a sin-offering (44:15-27). Again there is the subtle blending and telescoping of near and distant future which is characteristic of the prophets. The laws, the offerings, the feasts of Exodus and Leviticus are reinstated (chapters 45 and 46). Yet suddenly, in chapter 47, we are given something gloriously new. Out of God's temple flows a great life-giving river bordered by trees whose fruit is for food and whose leaves are for healing (see Revelation 22:1-2). The new tribal boundaries with which the book concludes (47:13ff.) are stylized, rather than geographically feasible. And at the very end the city is named. It is not now Jerusalem, but 'The Lord is there' (compare Revelation 21:22ff.).

Long cubit (40:5): about 21 in/520 mm; so the measuring-rod was nearly 3 metres.

Sons of Zadok (40:46): Zadok, who replaced Abiathar (1 Kings 2:26-27, 35), was the first high priest to officiate in the temple.

43:3: see chapter 10 and chapter 1.

47:9-10: the salt water of the Dead Sea is made fresh. The 'Great Sea' is the Mediterranean.

Ezekiel's vision of the temple was a detailed reconstruction of the temple area in Jerusalem. But suddenly through it flowed a trickle which became a stream – which became the river of life.

Daniel

Daniel was a Judean exile at the court of Babylon. He was taken there as a boy a few years earlier than Ezekiel and the first main batch of exiles. He belonged to a noble (possibly royal) family and was exceptionally able and intelligent. Strictly speaking, Daniel was a statesman rather than a prophet, but his book rightly belongs among the prophetic writings. The first six chapters relate to historical events in Babylon over a period of 70 years. The remaining chapters, written in the first person, record a series of visions of future events. Two languages are used: 2:4–7:28 is in Aramaic, the international language; the rest in Hebrew. Right at the beginning of Israel's history God had his man – Joseph – at the Egyptian court. Now again, at this great crisis-point, God placed Daniel in a position of influence at the political centre of the Babylonian Empire, for the whole period of the exile.

To help explain a number of historical difficulties in Daniel (see in the text below), many think that the book as we have it was written in the 2nd century BC by an unknown author who used Daniel's name to give his work added authority. But the book of Daniel was widely accepted as Scripture in that same century, and the Jewish authorities were scrupulously careful about examining writings before they were given official approval. So either they had no objection

to the real author adopting the name of the 6th-century prophet; or they were themselves taken in by one of their own contemporaries. There is the added problem that although these men lived only 400 years after the events recorded in Daniel, they failed to spot (or at least failed to challenge) the book's historical inaccuracies. At the heart of the issue is the question of prediction, since Daniel alludes to events long after his own day. If the possibility of genuine prediction in prophecy is allowed, the book can be taken as it stands, as the record of the life and visions of Daniel himself. Only if it is denied is one bound to conclude that the book cannot be earlier than the 2nd century BC.

1–6
DANIEL AT THE BABYLONIAN COURT

1 Daniel and his friends win a place at Nebuchadnezzar's court
Daniel arrived in Babylon in 605 (see below). Good looks and natural ability ensured a place for him and his friends among those selected for special training. But the Babylonians did not observe Jewish rules on clean and unclean food (Leviticus 11), nor did they drain away the blood when they slaughtered animals (Leviticus 17:10ff.). Young as they were, Daniel and his friends were determined not to compromise their religion. So their only course was to restrict themselves to a vegetarian diet – and they thrived on it. What is more, they graduated from the king's school with honours!
The third year...(1): the date is 605. After defeating Egypt at Carchemish, Nebuchadnezzar attacked Jerusalem. Daniel and others were taken hostage for the good behaviour of King Jehoiakim, who had been placed on the throne by the Egyptian

MEDIA

Babylon

BABYLONIA
(CHALDAEA)   PERSIA

Jerusalem

pharaoh. Daniel uses the Babylonian reckoning for Jehoiakim's reign, beginning the year following the accession year. So 'the third year' here is the same as the fourth year (Jeremiah 25:1; 46:2) in Palestinian reckoning.

Shinar (2, some versions**):** the old name for Babylonia.

Verse 7: the endings of the Hebrew names (-el, -iah) link them with the name of Israel's God. At least one of the new names (Belteshazzar) is linked to that of a Babylonian god (see 4:8).

First year of King Cyrus (21): the year of the decree repatriating the exiles (Ezra 1:1-4).

2 Nebuchadnezzar's dream

Daniel had only just graduated when he was faced with this test. Nebuchadnezzar had either genuinely forgotten his dream, or he was deliberately making things difficult. It is clear from this chapter that Daniel's faith went much deeper than mere observance of the law. With his own life and the lives of many others at stake, he turns in complete trust to God. Astrology and divination, at which the Babylonians excelled, are not for him.

The image stands for four world empires: Babylonian (with Nebuchadnezzar as head), Medo-Persian, Greek and Roman. In the days of the Roman Empire, God would begin to carve out a new, everlasting, kingdom which would become universal. See further in chapters 7ff. (Those who think in terms of a 2nd-century writer looking back on events cannot include the Roman Empire, and are forced to make separate Median and Persian Empires. In point of historical fact, although there were Median kings, there was never a dominant Median Empire).

Chaldeans (2): in its general sense the term simply means 'Babylonian'; later it was used in a restricted sense of a class of wise men. Daniel uses the word in both ways. New International Version translates, 'astrologers'; Good News Bible, 'wizards'.

Verse 4: the Aramaic section starts here,

'Is not this Babylon the great which I have built ... ?' asked Nebuchadnezzar. This cuneiform tablet celebrating Nebuchadnezzar's achievements was found at Babylon.

and ends at 7:28. We do not know if the original used both languages.

3 The golden image and the fiery furnace

The years pass and Nebuchadnezzar, forgetting he once acknowledged Daniel's God as supreme, sets up his 90 ft/27 m idol, demanding that all his people worship it. But Daniel's companions will not compromise. They know God is *able* to deliver them from a terrible death; they do not know if he *will* (17). But come what may, they will not deny him (18). In the event, the flames killed those who flung them in, and burned through their own bonds; but they came out with not so much as a

Gangs of slaves landing a colossal statue from a raft on the River Tigris; from the decoration of Sennacherib's palace.

against himself, he does not turn to Daniel straight away (6-8). It is clear from Daniel's dismay that he does not wish the king ill. But the king's pride in his achievements (and archaeology shows they really *were* something to be proud of) overrides Daniel's wise advice. He is stricken with a rare mania, believing himself to be an animal. (Other cases are known, where patients have exhibited precisely the same symptoms: roaming out of doors, and living on a diet of grass and water.) Yet God is at work in the depths of his now humble mind, and as he worships the one true God his reason returns.

One would hardly expect to find open reference to such a seemingly shameful illness in contemporary official records. But events of the later years of Nebuchadnezzar are not known from ancient texts.

Verses 3 and 34-35: the echoes from Psalms and Isaiah may reflect Daniel's influence on the king.

Seven times (16): the length of time here as elsewhere in Daniel is unspecified. It was a definite, limited period of time fixed by God. (But 'seven years', Good News Bible, is also possible).

smell of burning about them. And a god-like figure walked through the fire with them. Again the king is compelled to worship.

Satrap (2): one of a number of Old Persian words which occur in Daniel. There is no reason why Daniel should not have used them; they were known before his day, and he lived on into the period of Persian supremacy. Or it may be that this Aramaic section (see on 2:4) is a later, or updated, translation.

Lyre, trigon/zither, harp (5): these are all Greek words. The instruments themselves are Mesopotamian, but Greek cultural influences had spread across this part of the world before Nebuchadnezzar's time. Greek colonies were widespread, and Greek mercenaries served in many armies.

Furnace (6): a kiln (probably for baking bricks) with an open top and an open door at the side through which the king could see the men.

4 The king's madness

Nebuchadnezzar himself authenticates this extraordinary story (1-18, 34-37). Perhaps sensing that this dream is

5 Belshazzar's feast

Strictly speaking, Nabonidus (556-539 BC) was the last king of Babylon. But he retired to Arabia early in his reign, leaving his son Belshazzar acting king in Babylon (hence the fact that Daniel could be made only 'third ruler', 16).

The date is 539, 23 years after Nebuchadnezzar's death. The great feast at the palace is going with a swing, when a mysterious hand begins to write on the wall. Three words are written. They are weights, or units of money: 'a mina, a mina, a shekel and a half-shekel' (see the chart in Part One). Daniel, now an old man, is summoned to interpret; and he goes to the root meanings of the words: 'number', 'weigh', 'divide' (see Good

Musicians; an Assyrian relief.

Gold drinking vessels of the time: these are Persian, from the Treasure of the Oxus.

News Bible). The king's days were indeed numbered. That very night Cyrus the Persian took the impregnable city of Babylon, so the ancient historians tell us, by diverting the course of the River Euphrates and entering along the dry river-bed, while the Babylonians were at a feast of their gods.

Father (2): i.e. ancestor, predecessor. The word often has this sense in the Old Testament.

The queen (10): as Belshazzar's wives were there already, this may have been Nebuchadnezzar's widow ('queen mother' Good News Bible).

Darius the Mede (31): no other historical record so far found mentions anyone of this name, or places any ruler between Nabonidus/Belshazzar and Cyrus. Darius has been variously identified, but none of the suggestions is completely satisfactory. This does not mean we can write Darius off as a fictional character. Since Cyrus was so well known the author could hardly have hoped to get away with such an invention.

6 Daniel in the lion's den

All his life Daniel has been a man of God. He is now in his eighties, and his enemies still cannot fault him. They can only attack him through his religion (4-5). Daniel could have stopped praying for a month, or he could have prayed in secret. But he is no more ready to compromise now than he was as a boy. So his enemies have him. The king's hands are tied by his own decree, but God's hand is not. Daniel was as safe from harm in the lion-pit as his friends had been in the furnace.

Verses 8, 15: see Esther 1:19; 8:8.

The den/pit (16): most probably an enclosure with an open top around which was a spectator's gallery. There was also a small entrance at the side, which Darius sealed up (17).

7–12
THE RECORD OF DANIEL'S VISIONS

7 The four beasts

Like chapter 2 this is a pictorial representation of history. Again there are four successive empires, and then the kingdom of God is established. The winged lion is Babylon; and verse 4 has Nebuchadnezzar particularly in mind. Verse 6 depicts the Greek Empire of Alexander the Great, on his death divided among his four generals. Seleucus founded a dynasty in Syria. Ptolemy founded a dynasty in Egypt. The other two kingdoms were Greece and Asia Minor. The 'ten horns' (7, 24) equate with the toes of the image in chapter 2, though the precise identification has been much debated. Verses 9-12 picture God's judgement of the world empires. In 13-14 God gives total dominion to 'one like a son of man', Jesus' favourite title for himself. The kingdom inaugurated at Christ's first coming will be finally realized when he returns (see Matthew 26:64). Opposing God's people in different guises throughout history is the 'little horn' (8, 20-21), until God finally removes its power. It is from this chapter that Revelation 13 draws its imagery.

A time, two times, and half a time (25): often taken to mean 3½ years; but see on 4:16. Evil is given its head, but for a strictly limited time.

8 The ram and the he-goat

The vision focusses on the second and third empires. The two-horned ram which symbolizes Medo-Persia will be superseded by the swift-footed goat – Alexander's Greek Empire. Alexander himself is the 'great horn'. The 'four horns' are the kingdoms into which his empire was divided (see on chapter 7). The little horn, in this chapter, refers to Antiochus IV, who ruled Syria 175-164 BC. Verses 9-14 vividly depict the atrocities of his reign (see on chapter 11), which resulted in the Maccabean revolt. 1 Maccabees 1–6 (the Apocrypha/Deuterocanonical books) recounts this period of Jewish history.

Susa (2): east of Babylon; one of the four capitals of Persia.

Prince (11, 25): God himself. In attempting to wipe out the Jewish religion Antiochus was directly challenging the God of Israel.

Verse 14: i.e. 2,300 days (see Genesis 1; though Good News Bible gives 1,150 days). Antiochus first meddled in Jewish affairs in 171; he died in 164.

Gabriel (16): this is the first time God's messenger-angel is named. It was Gabriel who appeared to Zacharias, father of John the Baptist, and again to Mary before the birth of Jesus.

The end (17): this usually refers to the winding-up of history, and God's final judgement. But verse 26 relates the vision to the distant future, and 19 to the period when the suffering will be over. The Bible writers often seem to step clear of time, and view contemporary and future events as one aspect of the total, final events of 'the end'.

9 The seventy weeks; Daniel's prayer

The date is 538. Babylon has virtually ruled Judah since the Battle of Carchemish in 605. The 70 years' captivity spoken of by Jeremiah is almost up. Daniel pleads with God for the return of his people to their homeland. He is completely one with his people, sharing the blame for sin (5ff.), and his request rests solely on God's mercy (18). He saw the answer to his prayer that same year, but Israel's troubles were not over. God now shows Daniel something of what lies ahead.

Verses 24-27 are very difficult, and numerous interpretations have been suggested. God has ordained a period of 70 x 7 ('seventy weeks of years') in which the salvation of his people will be completed (24). For the Jews, the number seven itself symbolized completeness, perfection. And it may be best to take the numbers symbolically. But the period of time between the decree to rebuild and restore Jerusalem and the beginning of Jesus' ministry (25) comes very close to the 7+62 weeks=483 days, standing for the same number of years – the total reached if we take the figures literally (though there is more than one possible starting-point, and even the end-date is not absolutely fixed). Verse 26 seems to point to the death and rejection of Christ and the destruction of the temple which followed in AD 70 – with a wider reference at the end. But the subject of verse 27 is not at all clear. 'He' is taken by some to be the Messiah, by others to be the destroying prince of the previous verse.

10 – 11:1 Vision and conflict

After a long fast, Daniel receives an awe-inspiring vision of a glorious figure: very like John's vision of Christ in Revelation 1:12-16. He is given insight into the continual battle raging in the spiritual realm between those protecting God's people and those bent on their destruction (see Ephesians 6:12). Michael is the special guardian angel of the Jewish people (12:1). The 'princes' in this chapter are patron angels of the various nations.

11:2-45 The struggle for power

This chapter claims to set out the course of future history in detail. And from our vantage-point in time we can look back

Babylonian boundary-stone with the emblems of many different gods (the origin of the signs of the zodiac).

on its amazingly accurate fulfilment in the history of the Greek Empire. There are to be three more Persian kings (2; Cambyses, Gaumata and Darius I), followed by a fourth (Xerxes). Xerxes invaded Greece but was defeated at Salamis in 480 BC. The power then passed to Greece (3-4; see on chapter 7). Verse 5 refers to Egypt (the 'king of the south') and to Ptolemy's one-time general, Seleucus, who became 'king of the north'–the powerful kingdom of Syria and the east. Fifty years later (6) the daughter of Ptolemy II married Antiochus II of Syria. But she was divorced and murdered, and her brother avenged her by attacking Syria (7). Verses 9-13 reflect the struggles between the two powers at the end of the 3rd century BC. The Jews then joined forces with Antiochus III of Syria to defeat Egypt (14-15). They gained their freedom from Egypt (16), and Antiochus made a marriage alliance with Ptolemy V (17). Antiochus invaded Asia Minor and Greece but was defeated by the Romans at Magnesia in 190 BC (18-19).

The 'exactor of tribute' (20) was his son Seleucus IV, who was shortly succeeded by his brother Antiochus IV, the persecutor of the Jews. Verses 21-24 aptly portray his character and policies. Through the treachery of Ptolemy's own men, Antiochus briefly gained control of Egypt in 173. On his return he attacked Jerusalem and slaughtered 80,000 Jews (25-28). The next time he attacked Egypt he was thwarted by the Roman fleet (29-30). He turned on Jerusalem again and desecrated the temple (31). He was aided and abetted by some Jews, but others refused to compromise their faith, though they died for it (32-33). Judas Maccabaeus instigated a successful revolt, so helping the faithful (34).

Verses 36-45 do not describe actual events at the end of Antiochus' life. They may refer to the end of Syrian domination, at the hands of Rome, the new king from the north. Or they may anticipate events at the end of time (see on 8:17), which the sufferings of God's people under Antiochus foreshadow. This then leads in to chapter 12.

12 Deliverance

Daniel is the first Old Testament book to speak explicitly of resurrection, though he is thinking only of the Jewish nation ('your people'). When that day comes, and all the terrible troubles are past, those who have shown themselves wise by their faithful obedience to God will rise to shine like stars for ever. All evil will be done away. But as for times, those are in God's hand. Not even Daniel understands this (6-8)–so a cautious approach to these matters may still be the wisest course!

Hosea

Hosea was one of Isaiah's contemporaries, a prophet of God in the 8th century BC. But Hosea, unlike Isaiah, was a northerner. His message was for Israel, the northern kingdom, although he occasionally refers to Judah. And Israel in his day was in a mess. Hosea became a prophet at the end of the reign of the nation's last powerful king, Jeroboam II. He prophesied for the next 40 years, until just before Samaria fell to Assyria in 722 BC. And during that time the country went rapidly down hill. Rejection of God and the wholesale adoption of pagan religious practices brought about a moral and political landslide. 2 Kings 14:23–17:41 gives the history of the period. But the fact that after Jeroboam's death Israel had six kings in just over 20 years, and four of them assassinated their predecessors, gives some idea of the state of the country.

What Israel's idolatry meant to God – how he continued to love and long for his people's return to him – Hosea learnt through bitter personal experience, as his own wife betrayed and deserted him. His message comes straight from the heart. And this is what makes the book unique.

1–2:1 Hosea's wife and children

God instructs Hosea to marry Gomer, a woman God knows will prove unfaithful. (This seems to be the only tenable interpretation of verse 2.) Three children are born, and each is given a name which speaks God's message to Israel (compare Isaiah 8). Through the prophet, God is giving his people a last opportunity to repent before judgement breaks on the land (2 Kings 17:13-14). Yet even though they refuse, his loving purpose is not thwarted (1:10–2:1).

Jezreel (4): the site of many bloody battles; here the reference is to the slaughter recounted in 2 Kings 10.

2:2-23 Unfaithful Israel; God's steadfast love

Hosea's voice, pleading with his unfaithful wife through his children, becomes one with the voice of God addressing Israel. The people are worshipping Baal, the Canaanite fertility god, thinking he is the one who gives good crops and plentiful harvests; when all the time it is God. Israel will be taught by punishment, and afterwards become God's dearly loved bride again (19-20).

Achor/Trouble Valley (15): near Jericho; the place where Achan sinned and was punished (Joshua 7).

My Baal (16): a substitute word must be used because 'baal', which was the everyday word for 'lord/master/husband' was also the name of the Canaanite god.

Jezreel (22): the word means 'God sows'.

3 Probation

Gomer, now seemingly the slave of another man, is bought back and put on probation. Again Hosea's action, and his continuing love, provide an object-lesson. For a while, Israel too will be deprived of the things she counted on – her king and her religious emblems – but in time she will turn back to God.

Raisin-cakes (1): offered to pagan gods.

Verse 4: sacrifice and ephod (part of the priest's regalia) belonged to the legitimate religion; pillar and teraphim (household gods) were part of the pagan admixture.

4 Idolatry in Israel

From now on there is no further mention of Hosea's family. But the experience is there – and it colours the rest of the book. Real faith in God issues in obedience to his standards. The prostitution of Israel's religion led to literal prostitution (11-14). Paganism brought in its wake sexual degradation (13-14) and the breakdown of law and order in society (1-2). It still does. The priests – who failed to make God's laws known, and feathered their own nests into the bargain (4-10) – and the men of Israel (14) are responsible for what has happened. And God holds them accountable.

Beth-aven (15): 'house of evil', a derisory name for Bethel, one of the religious centres in the northern kingdom.
Ephraim (17): Israel. Ephraim was the leading tribe.

5:1-14 Judgement

A generation has grown up to whom God is a stranger (7). The alarm is sounded on Judah's borders, for Judah shares the sin to which Israel has become addicted (8-12). Not even the great king of Assyria (13; Tiglath-pileser III – see 2 Kings 16:5ff.) can save them from God's judgement.
Mizpah, Tabor, Shittim (1-2): places where there were shrines for Baal worship.

5:15 – 6:6 A change of heart

Suffering turns the people to God again. But there is no deep change. Their 'love' evaporates as quickly as dew in the hot sun. It is lasting love and real knowledge of him that God looks for.

6:7 – 7:16 Catalogue of evil

Priests have turned butcher. At the heart of the nation's religion, at Shechem, there is intrigue and murder (6:7-10). At court it is the same. Kings fall at the hands of hot-heads and conspirators (7:6-7; see introduction). Israel turns to foreign peoples (8-9), foreign powers (11), foreign gods (16): but never to the Lord.

Oven (7:4): they baked their flat loaves on saucer-shaped 'hot-plates' placed upside down over the embers. The loaf (8) must be turned over to cook both sides.

8 God is forgotten

Israel will be caught up in the whirlwind of God's judgement. They have made gods, made up laws, set up kings to suit themselves: as if God and his laws did not exist. But neither idols nor allies will avail when the God they have forgotten strikes.
Bull-calf (5): Israel's first king set up two images at shrines in his own land to rival Jerusalem as religious centres (1 Kings 12:28). The calf had a long association with pagan cults in Egypt and in Canaan.

9 A terrible destiny for Israel

It was probably at the height of the festival to mark the grape-harvest that Hosea spoke out (1-5). The people may call him a fool, but he knows he is God's watchman, and he will not hold his tongue (7-8). Israel will become a slave-nation to Assyria, as she once was to Egypt (3, 6). Sin has become habitual, ingrained, to the point where God finally withdraws his love (12, 15).
Gibeah (9): see Judges 19.
Baal-peor (10): see Numbers 25.
Gilgal (15): the place where Saul was acclaimed king (1 Samuel 11:14-15). The people's eagerness to have a king had in it the seeds of danger. Some of the later kings would usurp God's place as the true Leader of his people.

10 Under the yoke

Outwardly, affluent Israel made a great show of religion (1), but inwardly the people moved further and further away from God. The calf-image at Bethel had become the nation's only 'king' (3-5), a king marked for destruction (6-8). Now they are reaping what they have long sown (13). Yet they could still sow an altogether different crop (12).

Shalman (14): probably a reference to the recent invasion of Gilead by Salamanu of Moab.

11 The Father's love

This chapter lets us see right into the infinitely loving heart of God. All down the long years of history, from Egypt on, and despite all he has done for them, Israel has rejected God's love (1-4). The nation deserves no mercy (5-7). Yet God still shrinks from destroying them (8-9). He is torn between love and justice, neither of which can be denied. This is the pain he took to himself in the cross of Christ.

Admah and Zeboiim (8): two cities to the south of the Dead Sea, presumably destroyed with Sodom and Gomorrah (Genesis 19).

12 Lessons from history

This is not an easy chapter to follow. Israel needs to be reminded of scheming Jacob (3-6, 12), and how he learnt to lean on God – and forget her proud independence and reliance on foreign powers. The people deride the prophets of their own day. They need the reminder that it was through a prophet (Moses, 13) that God brought the nation into being.

Verses 3-4, 12: incidents recounted in Genesis 25:21-26; 32:22-32; and 29.

A nation reaps what it sows. God will restore prosperity to the land if his people will return to him. Threshing out the harvest in the hills of Judea.

13 The east wind of God's judgement

Israel may turn to Baal and other idols, but there is in fact no God but God (what was true then is still true now). Men may forget him, or discount him, but he exists: and he has power to carry out all that he has warned of.

East wind (15): the scorching wind from the desert which dries and shrivels everything in its path.

14 'Return, O Israel'

After the fierce tones of chapter 13, this last chapter is full of love and pleading. The way is open. There is no need to pass through the fire of judgement. Men have only to give God their loyalty (2-3) to find his love and forgiveness, and embark on a new, transformed life (4-7). This is the truly wise course (9).

Hosea makes the way so plain. It is more than sad to realize that his contemporaries ignored it all – until the Assyrians swept down and destroyed their splendid capital, Samaria; took the remaining Israelites into exile; and repeopled their land with foreigners. When God gives warning of judgement, he is not playing with words. How many of the practices he condemned in Israel do we see all around us in our own society? How long do we expect his patience to last?

Joel

We know nothing at all about this prophet, apart from his father's name (1:1). And the prophecy contains few clues to the date when it was written. Joel is obviously familiar with themes which also occur in Isaiah, Amos and Ezekiel – particularly the 'day of the Lord', when God will finally judge the world and his own people. We may guess at dates – and guesses range from the 8th century BC to the 4th century BC and later – but the book itself is timeless.

1 The disastrous plague of locusts

Even in our own century Jerusalem has been stripped of all vegetation by a plague of locusts like the one Joel describes so vividly. The swarm of several million insects is carried into Palestine by the desert wind from Arabia. The locust grows rapidly from larva to winged adult (4), and at every stage its appetite is insatiable. It is worse than an invading army: when it moves on there is no green or growing thing left (6-12). There is nothing to offer to God (9, 13), or so little that the people are using all they have to ward off starvation. For Joel, the locust swarm is an object-lesson, a warning of the terror of God's approaching judgement day (15). He calls for a national day of prayer (14).

2:1-27 The coming day of the Lord; repentance and restoration

The locust-army becomes a picture of the invading army of God on the day of his judgement: the sky black with insects (2); the 'scorched earth' in their wake (3); their inexorable, totally irresistible,

onward march (4-9). This is what God's judgement will be like. Who can bear it (11)? But no one need endure God's judgement. He is still calling all men to repent (12). Joel calls the whole nation to turn to God and plead for mercy (13-17). And in response God promises to restore in profusion all that the locusts have robbed them of. He will rid the land of his great army (25), which is now identified with all his enemies ('the northerner', 20: see on Ezekiel 38–39; it is very unlikely that the locusts actually came from the north).

2:28 – 3:21 The outpouring of God's Spirit; judgement on the nations

Joel foresaw a day when God's Spirit would be poured out, not just on priests and prophets, but on ordinary people, regardless of sex, age, or class. He little dreamt that God spoke not just of Israel, but of all nations (Acts 2). Equally, God's judgement awaits men of all nations who refuse his call, including Israel (32). But all who call out to him, and whom he calls, will escape.

The nations will be punished for all they have inflicted on God's people (3:2-8). Multitudes will be gathered to God's judgement. There He will decide their destiny (14). All evil will be done away on that momentous, earth-shaking day. God will make his home in a city and among a people at last made holy; and the whole land will share in this abundant blessing (16-18).

Tyre, Sidon, Philistia (3:4): see on Ezekiel 25-28. Artaxerxes III sold the Sidonians as slaves in 345 BC, and in 332 Alexander the Great sold the people of Tyre and the Philistine city of Gaza into slavery.

Sabaeans (8): famous Arabian traders.
3:10: Joel reverses Isaiah's famous words (Isaiah 2:4).

Valley of Jehoshaphat (12): probably a symbolic name; it means 'the Lord judges'–hence Good News Bible, 'Valley of Judgement'.

A plague of locusts.

Amos

Amos was a layman, a shepherd and dresser of fig-trees. His home was in Tekoa, about 12 miles south of Jerusalem, on the edge of the Judean desert. But God sent him as his prophet to the northern kingdom of Israel. His base was the religious centre of Bethel, where Jeroboam I had set up a calf-image when the nation had first split into two rival kingdoms. Amos lived in the reign of Jeroboam II (793-753), Israel's Indian summer of prosperity and influence. But beneath the affluence the nation was rotten. Amos was sent to denounce the social and religious corruption, and warn of God's impending judgement. But the people turned a deaf ear, as they did to his contemporary, Hosea. And the king's chaplain told him to get back to Judah (7:10ff.)! Thirty years after Jeroboam's death the Assyrians destroyed Samaria and took the people into exile. Israel ceased to exist. But the prophet has a word for any nation in Israel's condition. Put his descriptions in 20th-century dress and they still strike home.

1—2:5 The indictment of Israel's neighbours

Syria, Philistia, Tyre, Edom, Ammon, Moab and Judah are each condemned in turn. Their offences are many (the formula 'For three . . . for four' indicates an indefinite number). They stand condemned for their crimes against humanity. Only Judah is judged against the full standard of God's law. The Syrians are guilty of wanton cruelty (running studded threshing-sledges over the bodies of their captives, 3); the Philistines of selling their fellow men. Tyre and Edom have transgressed the laws of kinship. Ammon's atrocities have been committed simply to gain more land. By desecrating a corpse Moab has violated one of the most universal of all ancient unwritten laws. God will punish each and every one.

Hazael, Ben-hadad (1:4): kings of Syria. Hazael seized the throne in Elisha's time and founded a dynasty.

Kir (5): the place the Syrians originally came from.

Gaza, Ashdod, Ashkelon, Ekron (6-8): four of the five Philistine cities.

His brother (11): Edom and Israel were descendants of two brothers, Esau and Jacob.

A traditional threshing-sledge made of studded wooden boards. They are shown in use in the picture on page 289.

Rabbah (14): the Ammonite capital; modern Amman, capital of Jordan.

2:6-16 Israel's crimes

The other prophets make it plain that Israel's basic sin was in turning away from God to worship idols. But Amos emphasizes the moral and social decline which resulted. They have grown hard and callous in their dealings with others; young and old make use of temple prostitutes; and they have gagged God's spokesmen. None will escape God's punishment.

Verse 8: the law humanely ordered that garments taken in pledge be returned by nightfall (Exodus 22:26-27).

Amorite (9): here an umbrella term for the original inhabitants of Canaan.

Nazirites (11): men consecrated to God by a special vow which involved renouncing wine.

Cart/wagon (13): more likely the threshing-sledge (as in the Jerusalem Bible).

3 Punishment

Israel has broken the covenant-agreement with God and must suffer punishment. It is simple cause and effect (like the other instances given in verses 3-6). God has spoken; he will act. Of beautiful Samaria, with its great stone houses and exquisite ivory panels, only a trace will be left; just enough to show that the city once existed. And God will demolish the trappings of debased religion at Bethel (verse 14).

4 God's warnings

The luxury-loving women of Samaria ('cows of Bashan'), living it up at the expense of the poor, will be led away with hooks. (The Assyrians actually did this to their captives.) While they crushed their fellow men, the people still kept up the religious façade (4-5). But 'insurance policy' religion is a mockery of the real thing (see James 1:26-27). By famine and drought, blight

Amos protested against the 'houses of ivory' being built by the affluent, the 'great houses' of those who oppressed the poor. Many ivories of the period have been found. This one is from the decoration of a palace in Assyria. Some of the ivories were brought back by the Assyrians from campaigns in the west.

and disease God warned them where they were heading – all to no avail.

5 'Seek me and live'

The lament (1-3) is quickly followed by an appeal. God calls on his people to save their lives by seeking him. And this means, not yet more sacrifices at the nation's corrupt sanctuaries (5, 21-23, 25-26), but reformed living – a return to God's standards of justice and right conduct in public as well as private life. Otherwise the 'day of the Lord' (18ff.), the day on which they expect to enter into God's blessing and see their enemies destroyed, will be a terrible day of condemnation for God's people.

The gate (10): 'court'; the city gate was the place for business transactions and the administration of justice.

Joseph (15): Ephraim and Manasseh (descended from Joseph's two sons) were leading tribes in the northern kingdom.

Verse 25: the meaning seems to be 'Was it 'only' sacrifice and offerings you brought to me...? Was it not also right living and obedience?'
Sakkuth, Kaiwan (26): Assyrian gods associated with the planet Saturn.

6 Exile

Affluence and comfortable living (then as now) insulate men from the real issues, and breed false security. Self-sufficiency and pride have been man's downfall from first to last (e.g. Genesis 11:1-9; Ezekiel 28).
Calneh, Hamath (2): two towns in Syria; Hamath is modern Hama.
Lo-debar, Karnaim (13): towns east of the Jordan, which Israel took from the Syrians.
Arabah (14): the dry valley running south from the Dead Sea to the Gulf of Aqaba.

7 The plumb-line

Twice Amos prevails on God to stay his hand; but judgement cannot be delayed for ever. Israel does not begin to measure up against the straight line of God's standards.

God's man and 'official religion' meet head-on in the confrontation between Amos and Amaziah (10-17). The prophet has God's authority for his message and will not be silenced. Amaziah will die in exile. The invading army will abuse his wife, kill his children and seize his land.
The Lord repented/relented (3, 6): i.e. he mercifully changed his mind (this does not imply that his original intention was wrong).
Sycamore (14): a kind of fig-tree; not the tree we call sycamore.

8 Israel ripe for ruin

Men like to think their 'little' sins too small for God to notice. But he sees everything: greed and sharp practice; short weight and sub-standard goods. And the poor, who always come off worst, are his special concern.
Ephah...shekel (5): this was a double cheat; the trader reduced the size of the measure for the grain (ephah) *and* increased the weight of the silver paid for it (shekel).
Ashimah (14, some versions**):** a Syrian goddess worshipped in Israel. Dan, in the far north, was the town where Jeroboam I erected his second calf-image.

9 Evil destroyed; the faithful remnant restored

For the nation as a whole judgement will be inescapable. God will deal with them like any foreign nation (7a). But for the faithful few the future holds unimagined blessing (11-15).
Caphtor (7): Crete, where the Philistines originally came from.

Israel would be 'sieved', said Amos. A woman sieves grain at Sychar.

Obadiah

A prophecy of Edom's downfall (for other prophecies against Edom, see Isaiah 34:5-15; Jeremiah 49:7-22; Ezekiel 25:12-14; 35:1-15; Amos 1:11-12). Edom occupied the mountainous region south-east of the Dead Sea. The capital, Sela (now Petra), was perched high on a plateau above a sheer rock cliff approached by a narrow gorge. It was virtually impregnable. From mountain strongholds like this the Edomites launched their raids on Palestine. As Esau's descendants they were in fact kin to Israel, but there was never any love lost between the two. The final outrage – and the occasion of Obadiah's prophecy – was their invasion of Judah while Jerusalem was being sacked by the Babylonians in 587 BC.

Obadiah denounces Edom's pride. The Edomites thought their strongholds invincible, but they would be utterly destroyed. In the 5th century BC Arabs took Edom, and in the 3rd century the region was overrun by the Nabataeans (who built the rock-city of Petra in present-day Jordan). Some Edomites settled in southern Judah. Herod the Great, ruler of the Jews at the time of Jesus' birth, was one of their descendants. After AD 70 the Edomites entirely disappeared from history. In contrast to dispossessed Edom, Obadiah foretells the return of Israel to possess a greatly extended land including former Edomite territory.

Teman (9): an important town in Edom, home of Job's friend Eliphaz; Mt Esau is Mt Seir.

Verse 19: 'Negeb', the southern desert; 'Shephelah', the hill-country behind the western coastal plain; 'Ephraim and Samaria', the northern kingdom of Israel; 'Gilead', east of the Jordan.

Verse 20: 'Halah', in Mesopotamia; 'Zarephath', modern Sarafand in Lebanon.

The narrow gorge into the rock fortress of Petra, the Nabataean capital of what was formerly Edom.

Jonah

2 Kings 14:25 is the only other mention of this prophet, and that would place him in the mid-8th century BC. Nineveh, capital of powerful Assyria (Israel's enemy) and subject of this book, was destroyed by the Babylonians in 612 BC. If Jonah did not write the story himself, it was probably written after this date (see 3:3). Whether we take the book as 'history with a moral' or as parable (and the Bible contains many parables, though none as long as this), there is no doubt about the main message. God's concern extends beyond Israel to the whole world. Jesus focussed attention on two further points: the parallel with the three days between his own death and resurrection; and the ready repentance of the Ninevites in contrast to his hearers (Matthew 12:40; Luke 11:32).

1 Jonah runs away

4:2 tells us why. Jonah was not afraid to go to Nineveh (verse 12 shows plenty of courage!). But he knew God: he knew that if the Ninevites changed their ways God would forgive them. And Jonah wanted this cruel threatening enemy nation destroyed. So in deliberate disobedience he sets out in the opposite direction. By trying to save his life, the heathen sailors display more humanity than the man of God (13).

A great fish (17): although sperm whales and large sharks capable of swallowing a man are not unknown in the eastern Mediterranean, this incident is clearly intended to be seen as a miracle. It is one of the many things God 'appoints' in the story (see 1:4; 4:6-8). Argument over this must not be allowed to blind us to the whole point of the story.

2 Jonah's prayer

This psalm records Jonah's cry to God when he was at death's door ('the belly of Sheol', 2). At last he comes to his senses, remembering his 'true loyalty' (8). And God, who has already saved him from death, gives him a 'second life'.

3 Nineveh's response

Given a second chance, Jonah leaps to obey. And his message produces a remarkable effect. The whole city, from the greatest to the least, repents. And God spares them.

Three days' journey (3): this applies to the district of Nineveh as distinct from the city: 'Greater London', so to speak.

God repented (10): see on Amos 7:3.

4 A hard lesson for Jonah

Jonah wanted God to confine his love and mercy to Israel. Let the heathen get their deserts. Far from being delighted that his message provoked such a fantastic response, he was furious. And it wasn't simply that he didn't want to look a fool. There was no spark of compassion for the people of Nineveh in Jonah's heart. And so God used a plant (the shady castor-oil plant) to make him feel something of his own pity for men and women: 'Should I not pity Nineveh?'

Verse 11: the city could well have housed this number of people. The inner wall formed a circuit of 7¾ miles/12 kilometres. Not knowing their 'right hand from their left' expresses their utter ignorance of God and his laws.

Micah was one of the 8th-century BC prophets, contemporary with Amos and Hosea (in the northern kingdom of Israel) and Isaiah (in Jerusalem). He was a countryman, from a town in south-west Judah, on the Philistine border. His message is for Samaria and Jerusalem, capital cities of the two kingdoms. And from a comparison with Amos it is clear that Judah had become infected with the same sins that beset Israel. So Micah, too, denounces rulers, priests and prophets; deplores the money-grubbing exploitation of the helpless; dishonesty in business; sham religion. God's judgement will fall on Samaria and Jerusalem; only after that will there be restoration. But Micah also sees a glorious future, when Jerusalem will become the religious centre of the world, and Bethlehem give birth to a greater David who will rule over all God's people.

1 The two cities

God is pictured coming down from heaven, treading upon the mountains, to destroy Samaria for her persistent idolatry. The gangrene has spread into Judah, and God's judgement is at the gates of Jerusalem. Micah pictures the approach of the invading army, coming from the coastal plain through the hills of Judah to Jerusalem (10ff., where the place-names frequently conceal a play on words). The parents in Judah will mourn for their exiled children. In 722 BC the Assyrians destroyed Samaria. In 701 they besieged Jerusalem, and the city escaped by a miracle (see 2 Kings 18:9–19:37). Micah most probably lived through both.

Dry mountains and luxuriant growth provided the prophets with pictures of spiritual barrenness and restoration.

Verse 1: Jotham (750-732) and Hezekiah (729-687) were good kings; Ahaz (735-716) was one of the worst, introducing terrible heathen practices, including child-sacrifice. (Overlapping dates indicate periods of co-regency.)

2—3 Exploitation; misrule; a perverted priesthood

The men with power and influence are all of them on the make, and they are not fussy about the means. So property is seized and families made destitute; and the preacher is told this is none of his business. (2:12-13 moves abruptly to the future, picturing God at the head of the remnant of his people.) The ordinary people are just so many animals to the rulers (3:1-3). Every man has his price: judge and priest and prophet alike (3:11).

4 Future greatness

Micah is full of contrasts. Verses 1-8 sweep us on to a new Jerusalem, from which God's word goes out to all men, and to which the nations flock, in an era of peace and plenty. Verses 9-10 return us to the condemned city, to a nation in exile, to God's judgement: not on his people alone, but on all the nations around (11-13).

Verses 1-3: almost identical with Isaiah 2:2-4.

Babylon (10): the enemy in Micah's day was Assyria, but like Isaiah he looks 100 years ahead to the power which would destroy Jerusalem.

5 The King from Bethlehem

In the midst of the Assyrian siege, Micah speaks of a deliverer – *the* ultimate deliverer – who would come, like David of old, from Bethlehem (see Matthew 2:1-6). Historical perspectives blur, as so often in the prophets, and current events melt into those of the near and far distant future. In the messianic peace,

even the Assyrian will be overcome. But Judah too will be purified 'in that day' (10ff.). All that she has relied on in place of God will be destroyed: armies, defences, witchcraft and false gods.

Ephrathah (2): the district around Bethlehem.

Seven . . . eight (5): idiomatic, for 'an indefinite number': no matter how many leaders are needed they will be forthcoming.

Nimrod (6): Assyria (see Genesis 10:8-12).

6 What God requires of his people

Verse 8 gives us the essence of true worship. God accepts no substitute. Though men may try to buy him off with all kinds of impressive gifts, he sees and will punish their sharp practice, their violence and deceit.

Verse 5: see Numbers 22-24.

Shittim to Gilgal (5): i.e. at the crossing of the Jordan (Joshua 3-4).

My first-born . . . (7): the sacrifice of the firstborn crept into Israel with other pagan practices in the dark days of the nation's last kings.

Verse 11: see on Amos 8:5.

Omri . . . Ahab (16): two kings of Israel notorious for introducing Baal-worship.

7 Darkness and light

Micah watches the breakdown of society in his country. The rot which began at government level has permeated the whole nation. And now all human relationships are crumbling. Friendship and family count for nothing. The human scene is black. But with God there is still light. He may still be relied on. His promise will not fail. He will build again. He will deliver again. In his compassionate love he will forgive again.

Watchmen (4): the prophets (Good News Bible) were posted as watchmen to warn of coming judgement (see Ezekiel 3:17-21).

The subject of Nahum, like that of the earlier book of Jonah, is Nineveh, the great capital city of Assyria. But whereas Jonah records the city's reprieve, Nahum predicts its destruction. The date is somewhere between the fall of Thebes to the Assyrians in 663 BC (3:8-10), and the fall of Nineveh to the Babylonians and Medes in 612 BC. Nahum seems to have been a Judean, but apart from this we know nothing about him, except that he was capable of writing the most graphic poetry in the whole of the Old Testament.

1 Vengeance on God's enemies; comfort for his people

Nahum starts, not with Nineveh, but with God: his power, his anger, his goodness. The days of Assyria, whose armies had destroyed Israel and threatened Jerusalem itself less than a century before, are now numbered.

An overwhelming flood (8): impregnable Nineveh eventually fell when floodwaters breached her walls, making way for the attacking army.

One/a man (11): perhaps Sennacherib, the Assyrian king who took Lachish and then laid siege to Jerusalem in 701 BC (see Isaiah 36-37).

2 The assault on Nineveh

Once, God had used the armies of Assyria to punish his people. Now the forces attacking Nineveh are his instruments. Blood and thunder; plunder and desolation; the den of the Assyrian lion is no more. Nahum pictures the final assault in all its horror.

Mantelet (5, some versions): a siege-engine armed with battering-ram.

Verse 6: see on 1:8.

3 Destruction

Nahum pictures the city as a prostitute, enticing the nations into submission. Now she will receive a prostitute's punishment (5-6). She will share the terrible fate she inflicted on the Egyptian city of Thebes (No-Amon). (At Thebes, city of Amun, state-god of Egypt, the treasures of centuries had been accumulated. The Assyrians took the city with fire and slaughter and plundered all its wealth.) Though the nation is as great as a swarm of locusts (see picture, page 443) they will vanish like a swarm that has flown. For all its might, Nineveh fell quickly into ruin, leaving no trace but a mound which is known today as Tell Kuyunjik, 'the mound of many sheep'.

Ethiopia/Cush (9): present-day Sudan, which supplied a dynasty of Egyptian kings. 'Put' may be Libya or possibly Somalia.

A siege-engine with battering-ram is shown being used by the Assyrians in this relief at Nimrud.

Habakkuk

The prophet Habakkuk is battling with much the same problem as Job and the writer of Psalm 73: the fact that while God's people suffer, the wicked go free. Current events faced him with this problem in a particularly acute form. God had announced that he would use the Babylonians – a far more wicked nation – to punish his own people. So Habakkuk, the man of faith, questions God.

The book belongs to the latter part of the 7th century BC, when Jeremiah was prophesying in Jerusalem. Some would place it before, some just after, the fall of the Assyrian Empire (Nineveh was taken by the Babylonians in 612 BC) and the defeat of Egypt at Carchemish in 605. Babylon is on the march, but so far Judah has escaped. In 597 BC, not long after this, Jerusalem fell into enemy hands, and the city was destroyed in 587.

1 The prophet's dilemma

In response to Habakkuk's first question (2-4), God presents him with an even greater stumbling-block (5-11). How can God, who is just and good, who hates evil, send against his people a nation that he openly admits makes a god of its own might? Will he let Babylon ('the Chaldeans', 6) fish the sea of humanity for ever (17)?

2 God's answer

The answer is no. When the final scores are added up, only the man who trusts God and remains loyal to him will live. God will punish all man's arrogant pride. Woe betide those who greedily grab what belongs to others; who for selfish ends justify the cruellest means; who climb to power on the backs of others; who destroy and dehumanize; who give their worship to man-made idols. The lives of all such men are forfeit whatever their nationality.

3 The triumph of faith – Habakkuk's prayer

The musical form of this prayer has led some to believe that Habakkuk was a Levite, attached to the temple. Its focus is on God himself; God approaching from the mountains of the southern desert (Teman is in Edom; Paran part of Sinai); God wrapped about with thunder and lightning in the storm of his wrath; God setting the world trembling with a glance. Habakkuk sees the inevitability, the fury of judgement. Yet though it means the loss of every good thing in life, God is still to be trusted. The prophet will wait for the day when God deals with the invader (16). He will rejoice in God, though life is stripped of all that gives natural joy and satisfaction.

A watchtower in the hills north of Jerusalem.

Zephaniah

Zephaniah prophesied in King Josiah's reign (640-609 BC), about the time Jeremiah's ministry began. From his stern words, it seems he spoke before Josiah launched his great programme of reform in 621, following the discovery of the law-book in the temple. The two previous kings, Manasseh and Amon had brought the religion and morality of the nation to an all-time low. Zephaniah himself seems to have been of royal blood, tracing his ancestry back to Hezekiah, who was king in Isaiah's day, 70 years or so before.

1 The great and terrible day of judgement

In popular thinking the 'day of the Lord' would bring untold blessing to all God's people, and destruction to their enemies. Amos, years before this, had warned that on that day all evil would be punished, making it a black day for many in Israel. Zephaniah spells out the same message, in detail, to Judah. The day is close at hand when all who are guilty of idolatry (4-6), violence, fraud (9), all who sit by in idle indifference (12), will be set apart for destruction (this is the meaning of verse 7). And their cry will be heard in every quarter of the city of Jerusalem (10-11).

Baal (4): the Canaanite god of fertility whose worship involved sexual licence and prostitution.

Milcom (5): the national god of the Ammonites.

Wine left on its dregs (12): a picture drawn from wine-making; one of the secrets in making wine is not to let it settle.

2 Judgement on the nations

The only hope for God's people is to seek him, and begin living by his standards. If they do not, they will share the fate of the nations around: Philistia (4-7) to the west; Moab and Ammon (8-11) to the east; Ethiopia (12) to the south; Assyria (13-15) to the north.

Gaza, Ashkelon, Ashdod, Ekron (4): the four remaining Philistine city-states.

Kerethites (5): the Philistines, who originally came from Crete.

Sodom, Gomorrah (9): cities at the southern end of the Dead Sea, destroyed by God for their wickedness (Genesis 19).

Ethiopians/Cushites (12): Sudanese; at this time the ruling dynasty in Egypt.

Nineveh (13): capital of Assyria; see on Nahum, particularly chapter 3.

3 Jerusalem condemned; a remnant saved

The city (1-7) is clearly Jerusalem. Beginning with rebellion against God, and the corruption of religion, the rot spreads into every sector of society. In the end, God has no alternative but to wipe the city out – but not completely. Zephaniah has already spoken of 'a remnant' (2:7, 9). Now he enlarges on God's purpose for the humble, faithful few who will survive when all human pride and self-sufficiency is done away. There is cause for great rejoicing. God is in the midst of his people: he will pour out his love on them. He will change and make them into those who are 'pure of heart' (9, 13). With exultant song they will be brought home and restored to favour. All the nations of the world have their share in this (9).

aggai

The last three books of the Old Testament take us on past the exile to the time when the Jews were repatriated, the time of Ezra and Nehemiah. Haggai delivered his 'word from the Lord' in 520 BC, Zechariah in 520-518. When the first party of exiles returned to their homeland under the leadership of Zerubbabel (grandson of King Jehoiachin) in 538, they made an enthusiastic start on rebuilding the temple which had been destroyed by the Babylonians in 587. But opposition and apathy very soon brought the work to a standstill (Ezra 4:4-5). For years nothing was done, until Haggai and Zechariah began to stir things up (Ezra 5:1-2). Thanks to them, by 516 the temple was completed. Haggai's little book is one of the gems of the Old Testament. It has permanent relevance, because its basic concern is not with the rebuilding of the temple but with priorities.

Four times Haggai comes to the people with a message from God (1:2-15; 2:1-9; 2:10-19; 2:20-23). 1:2-15: life is hard, with food and clothing in short supply, and prices soaring. Why? Because the people have their priorities wrong. Every man is wrapped up in his own selfish concerns. God is neglected. And so the very things man works for evade him.

For all the good things of life are God's to give or withhold. Haggai's words strike home to the nation's conscience. Within three weeks, work on the temple is resumed.

2:1-9: Solomon's fabulous temple had been demolished 70 years before. Few of those now building would have seen it – but all had heard of it. And the glory had lost nothing in the telling. The new temple seems a feeble thing in comparison. But let the builders take heart. The present building is just a foretaste of the splendour and glory of the end-time, the era of peace and prosperity to which the prophets all looked forward.

2:10-19: work on the temple has been resumed, but this in itself will not make the workmen 'holy' (right with God). It is rottenness, not soundness that is contagious (Haggai makes his point from the ritual law). Their previous neglect of God brought all kinds of unpleasant consequences. But from the day they begin to put first things first, God will bless every aspect of life.

2:20-23: a word for Zerubbabel. It is to Zerubbabel the heir to David's throne, rather than to Zerubbabel the individual, that these messianic promises are made. He stands in the line from David to Christ.

Zechariah

Zechariah came from a family of priests, and with Haggai was closely involved in the rebuilding of the temple following the return from exile (see on Haggai, and Ezra 5–6 for the historical background). Like Daniel and Ezekiel he was a visionary. And his book at one and the same time distils the wisdom of many of the earlier prophets, and brings the events of the far future into sharp focus. It contains detailed references to the Messiah which are clearly fulfilled in the life of Christ. There is a marked break (some would say a change of author – someone writing much later) between the visions of the first eight chapters and the spoken messages of chapters 9–14.

1:1-17 The four riders

In point of time, verses 1-6 slot in between Haggai 2:9 and 10; the vision of verses 7-17, two months after Haggai's last recorded message. Zechariah is probably a young man (his grandfather, Iddo, returned with the exiles less than 20 years before: Nehemiah 12:4). Verses 2-6 retell past history, warning the present generation not to behave as their fathers had done. Zechariah's first vision (7-17) is of four horsemen patrolling the world on God's behalf, like the mounted patrols which 'policed' the Persian Empire. (The significance of the colours, if any, is now lost.) The message is one of comfort and encouragement for God's people. Jerusalem will be rebuilt; prosperity will return.

1:18-21 The four horns

The second vision is a vivid picture of the destruction of the hostile powers which had ground the nation down. ('Four' indicates completeness – the four quarters of the earth.)

2 The measuring-line

The man may be Zechariah's projection of his own image, measuring up the city for rebuilding. The walls had been destroyed in 587. They were not rebuilt until Nehemiah's day (445, 75 years after this prophecy). But God pledges himself to protect Jerusalem. He calls to the remaining exiles to return.

A rider in the desert: in his first vision Zechariah saw four horsemen sent by God to patrol the earth.

The land of the north (6): Babylonia; in point of fact, east, but the invading armies of Assyria and Babylonia all entered Palestine from the north.

3 The investiture of the high priest

The taints of exile, when strict observance of dietary and other laws was impossible, are removed. And Joshua – high priest and partner with the ruler Zerubbabel in the exiles' return – is fittingly robed for office. God promises to send the long foretold Messiah, the Branch (8, and see Isaiah 11) from the family of David; the all-seeing, all-knowing 'stone' (the seven facets are literally seven eyes). He will usher in a day of universal peace and prosperity (this is the meaning of the vine and fig-tree idiom, 10).

4 The lamp and the olive-trees

Both these images are taken up in Revelation (1:12, 20; 11). The seven-branched lampstand stood in the tabernacle and temple (see picture, page 179). Here it may represent God's people or their worship, supported and 'fed' by the royal and priestly leaders, Zerubbabel and Joshua (the two olive-trees). From small beginnings (the start already made on the temple) great things will be accomplished, through the power of God's Spirit. Zerubbabel will lay the last stone in the temple building, as he had laid the first.

5 Sin removed

In ancient thinking a curse possessed destructive power. This is the concept behind the picture of the scroll. The woman in the great measure, or barrel, is sin personified; perhaps particularly the sin of idolatry, since she is removed to Babylon (Shinar is the old name) where a temple is built for her.

6 The four chariots

This last vision is like the first (1:7-17). God is keeping watch over the whole world. He is actively in control. His 'patrol' has power to execute judgement (this time there are chariots, not just reporting horsemen). In verses 9-14 the crowning of Joshua prefigures the dual role of the Messiah, as priest and king.

7 The question of fasts

The fast in the fifth month (July/August) commemorated the fall of Jerusalem in 587. The fast in the seventh month was in memory of the murdered governor, Gedaliah (2 Kings 25:25). Now that the temple was being rebuilt, need the fasts continue? In reply, God questions *them* about the spirit in which the fasts were kept, and reminds them of the standards they refused to keep before the exile (8-14). They still apply.

8 Hope burns bright

God promises a glorious future for his people and for Jerusalem. His purpose is wholly good. Judgement is past. God will return to make his home in the city. His people will enjoy peace and plenty. Right will prevail. And men and women of every nation will flock to Jerusalem seeking God. At the time of the prophecy only a few had returned from exile; the building was scarcely begun. But it was a foretaste of the wonderful days to come.

Verse 19: the two additional fasts were probably to mark the beginning of Nebuchadnezzar's siege of Jerusalem (the tenth month) and the breaching of the walls 18 months later (the fourth month). In answer to the question in 7:3, Zechariah replies that God wants all these fasts to be turned into feasts. The future for God's people is one of rejoicing.

9 — 11 Israel and the nations

For the break at this point, see introduction. Chapter 9 pictures the joyous arrival of the Messiah, riding an ass (not a war-horse), inaugurating a rule of peace (9-10; see Matthew 21:5). Before him Israel's old enemies will fall (1-8). There will be no more oppression. The Philistines (5-7) will be absorbed into Israel, as the Jebusites (from whom David captured the city of Jerusalem) had been long before. The Jewish captives will be released, and Israel's military power will equal even that of rising Greece. God is his people's protection and salvation.

Chapter 10 condemns the careless leaders of God's people. He is full of pity for the straying flock. Every one will be brought home.

In chapter 11 the prophet becomes shepherd to God's flock – but the people prefer exploitation to genuine care. They get what they want (15-16). The covenant with God is broken and the nation divided.

9:1-7: many relate this to Alexander's advance after defeating the Persians in 333 BC.

10:2: in the absence of any real spiritual lead, the people are dabbling in magic. The old household gods (teraphim) were used in divination.

11:1-3: the 'clearance' in preparation for the returning Israelites. In Old Testament times the thickets fringing the Jordan were the haunt of lions.

Thirty shekels/pieces of silver (11:12): the prophet sarcastically calls it a 'lordly price' – this was the price of a slave (Exodus 21:32; and see Matthew 26:15; 27:3-5).

12 — 14 Israel's future

Chapter 12 pictures God strengthening his people for a great battle against the nations (1-9). But in the midst of triumph there is national mourning – the people weep as the pagans wept for their dying vegetation-god (11). The phrase 'him whom they have pierced' inevitably makes us think of Christ. But if Zephaniah is speaking of the Messiah, this national Jewish remorse for the One they crucified is yet to come.

13:1 takes our thoughts to Christ again. Verses 2-9 describe the 'refining' of God's people; the removal of everything that offends God. 'The prophets' are false prophets; the 'wounds' are self-inflicted – part of the religious frenzy of the old prophets of Baal (1 Kings 18:28).

Chapter 14 pictures the last battle and the age to come. God himself will appear, ushering in perpetual day. The idea of life-giving water flowing from Jerusalem echoes Ezekiel 47. The whole earth will become God's kingdom. Those who set themselves against God will be destroyed. All who survive will worship him. Everything will be sacred. But the world is still not perfect. The possibility of disobedience and punishment remains. It is not yet the new Jerusalem of Revelation.

Malachi

The name means 'My messenger', which may have been the prophet's actual name or a pseudonym. From the conditions reflected in the book it is usually dated around 460-430 BC – either just before Nehemiah became governor of Jerusalem, or during his absence later on. This is about 80 years after Haggai and Zechariah spurred the people on to rebuild the temple. And since then disillusionment had set in. Times were hard, and the promised prosperity had not been realized. The people tended to feel that the prophets had been shooting them a line; that God was a bit of a let-down. This showed in an increasingly casual attitude to worship and the standards God had set. Malachi's message about God's claims on his people was needed. It still is.

1 The very best for God

Malachi's starting-point is God's love. His people, struggling with economic hardship and persistent sniping from the opposition (see e.g. Nehemiah 1:3; 4), cannot see much evidence of it. In answer they are told to look at their brother-nation, Edom – overrun like themselves by Babylon, but not restored (see on Obadiah). Israel enjoys a unique Father-son relationship with God. He is in a special sense their Lord. But their attitude over the sacrificial offerings shows their contempt for him. The left-overs are good enough for God, although they know the rules (Leviticus 22; Deuteronomy 15, 17). They dishonour and belittle his greatness. It would be better to close the temple and stop the sacrifices altogether (10).

Love...hate (2-3): the Hebrew idiom is over-strong in English. It means, not literal love/hate, but the special choice of one and not the other.

Verse 11: God is receiving more acceptable worship from the Gentiles – a statement intended to shock Malachi's Jewish hearers.

2:1-9 God's charges against the priests

The task God committed to his ministers, the Levites, was to teach the truth, and by their own lives to set an example (6). But instead of turning people away from wrong, they have actively misled them.

2:10-16 Marriage and divorce

See on Ezra 9–10 and Nehemiah 13. When God and his laws are respected, so are our fellow men. Indifference towards God is soon reflected in callousness towards one another. The Jews were marrying pagan women (11), which was forbidden (on religious, not racial, grounds). What is more, the older men were cruelly discarding their ageing wives for these attractive young foreigners – a situation not without parallel! And family life, as always, suffered. God cares about these things. He requires faithfulness from his people: faithfulness to himself and faithfulness in human relationships.

2:17 – 3:18 Justice; and giving

God's people can always look around and see godless men and women flourishing. It seems unfair (2:17; 3:13-15). But in the final winding-up of things there will be absolute justice (3:1-5). The Lord is coming, first to purify, and then to judge. And a messenger will be sent on ahead to prepare the way (see on 4:5).

God does not change; nor do his people (6, New English Bible). They have been fickle from first to last. God gives them all they have, yet they rob him even of his legal dues. (The tithe was a sort of income tax to provide for the upkeep of the temple and the 'salaries' of the ministers.) Anything we give to God is only a small return on all we owe him. When we hold back from giving, through self-interest, we deprive ourselves of all the good things God would otherwise give us.

Verses 16-18 warm the heart. There are still some who encourage one another in the love of the Lord; and he knows and honours them.

4 The Day of the Lord
The day is coming when God will even things out once and for all. For some (the wicked) the fierce brilliance of that day will burn like fire. But those who honour God will rejoice in its healing rays.

Verses 4-5 serve as postscript, not just to Malachi but to the Old Testament as a whole. They look back to the laws given at Sinai (Horeb), and these must always be kept in mind. They look forward to a new age, to the reconciling work of Christ and the end of all things. With Malachi the voice of Old Testament prophecy falls silent. Four hundred years later, God sent one last prophet, John the Baptist (the promised 'Elijah'), to herald the coming Messiah (Matthew 17:10-13).

Sun (2): Malachi draws his picture (but not his theology) from the winged disk which represented the sun-god in Persian and Egyptian art.

Like a flower among thorns, the prophets' predictions of a glorious future stand out from the warnings of judgement and disaster.

The Apocrypha: Deuterocanonical Books

DAVID CLINES

Christians everywhere agree that the Old Testament belongs in the Christian Bible. But they differ over the question of which books belong in the Old Testament. No one doubts that the 39 books of the Hebrew Scriptures are the core of the Old Testament. The question concerns only the status of about 15 books, called Apocrypha by Protestants and Deuterocanonical books by Roman Catholics. ('Deuterocanonical' means that they have a lower status then the 39 Hebrew books. Catholics reserve the term 'Apocrypha' for the books Protestants call the 'Pseudepigrapha' – works of similar character and date to the Apocrypha which have never been considered by anyone to be part of Scripture.) All Catholic Bibles contain the Deuterocanonical books, usually distributed among the historical, prophetic and wisdom books of the Old Testament. Most copies of Protestant versions do not contain the Apocryphal books, but when they do, they are printed together as a group between the Old and New Testaments.

The origin of the difference

The oldest manuscripts of the Christian Bible contain the apocryphal or Deuterocanonical books (or most of them). But the church father Jerome (died AD 420), a great biblical scholar, argued that books that were not to be found in the Hebrew Bible should not be regarded as having the same authority as those which the Jews themselves recognized as sacred scripture. Jerome thought the apocryphal books were valuable for reading in church, however. His reason for calling them 'apocryphal' (Greek for 'hidden') was apparently because the important book of Second Esdras (Fourth Esdras in Catholic reckoning) contained 'hidden' mysteries and knowledge disclosed by God to Ezra the seer.

Nevertheless, for most practical purposes the church regarded all the Old Testament books alike until the Reformation. Then Luther, in his Bible of 1534, extracted the apocryphal books from their usual places in the Old Testament and had them printed at the end of the Old Testament under the heading:

'Apocrypha: these are books which are not held equal to the Sacred Scriptures and yet are useful and good for reading.'

This became the norm for Protestant versions of the Bible, though gradually the practice developed of omitting the apocryphal books altogether. In recent years, however, increasing contacts between Protestant and Catholic Christians have led to a renewed interest in the apocryphal books, both for their historical value in helping to fill the time-gap between the Old and New Testaments and for their spiritual value as heirs of the Old Testament faith.

The Deuterocanonical books

The Deuterocanonical books of Roman Catholic Bibles are only about one-sixth of the length of the Old Testament. They consist of 7 books:

Tobit (Tobias)
Judith
The Book of Wisdom
Ecclesiasticus
The First Book of Maccabees
The Second Book of Maccabees
Baruch

These 7 contain all the Protestant Apocrypha except First and Second Esdras and the Prayer of Manasseh (which are not included in Roman Catholic Bibles). The additions to Esther are included in Esther; the Letter of

Jeremiah often in Baruch; and the Song of the Three Children, Susanna, and Bel and the Dragon form part of Daniel.

The books of the Apocrypha form a very varied collection of Jewish literature from the period between about 300 BC and AD 100. The majority of the books were written in Hebrew, but in many cases the original Hebrew has disappeared since the Jews themselves eventually refused to recognize these writings as inspired. Most of the books have survived only through their use in Greek and other versions by the early Christian church.

Historical books

1 Esdras (the Greek form of the name Ezra) is largely identical with our canonical Ezra, though it begins the story with the events of 2 Chronicles 35 (Josiah's Passover celebrations) and ends with the story of Ezra's reading of the law (Nehemiah 8). Its major addition to the biblical account is the 'debate of the three young men' (1 Esdras 3-4) which purports to explain how Zerubbabel gained permission from the Persian king to rebuild the temple.

1 Maccabees is a much more valuable book, since it is our chief source for the history of the Maccabean revolt against foreign and Jewish purveyors of Greek culture. Apart from his obvious desire to eulogize the family of the Maccabees, the author has no axe to grind, and provides us with an essentially reliable as well as graphic history of the years between 175 and 134 BC.

2 Maccabees covers much the same ground as 1 Maccabees, but is less reliable. It is written from a distinctly Pharisaic point of view, and tends to lay greater weight upon moralizing and doctrinal observations than upon historical accuracy.

'Religious fiction'

Tobit is a charming tale of domestic piety. It was so popular among early Christians that it was translated from Hebrew into Greek, Latin, Armenian, Syriac and Ethiopic. The story tells how Tobias, a righteous but afflicted Jew, is healed of his blindness and his son Tobit is saved from an unpleasant death. It has many folk-tale motifs, and is plainly not a historical work.

Judith contains the tale of an altogether more daunting heroine, who used her charm to lure the invading Assyrian general Holofernes to his death by decapitation. This rather horrific story not without its lighter moments contains some gross historical blunders, but these would not have detracted from its purpose of stiffening the resolve of Jewish freedom fighters in Maccabean times.

The additions to **Esther** are popular expansions of the biblical story, partly designed to introduce some religion into that apparently secular book, which does not even mention the name of God.

The additions to **Daniel** are partly legends about Daniel the sage and God-fearer (**Susanna, Bel and the Dragon**), and partly liturgical texts: **The Song of the Three Children** contains a historical prayer attributed to Daniel's companion Azariah, and a doxology (the *Benedicite* of Christian worship) attributed to the three in the fiery furnace.

'Wisdom'

'Wisdom' literature is represented in the Apocrypha principally by Ecclesiasticus and the Wisdom of Solomon. **Ecclesiasticus,** composed by Joshua (or Jesus) ben Sira (Sirach) about 180 BC, offers advice on practical and godly living in the spirit of the Proverbs. Chapter 44 contains the memorable lines beginning, 'Let us now praise famous men.' A great favourite in the early Christian centuries (James 1:19, for example, probably alludes to Ecclesiasticus 5:11), the book, earlier known as the Wisdom of Jesus ben Sira, became entitled the 'church-book' (Ecclesiasticus).

The Wisdom of Solomon, a 1st-century BC composition, more indebted to Greek ethics and rhetoric than any other Jewish wisdom book, pays homage in its title to the traditional founder of wisdom literature without seriously claiming to be written by Solomon.

Baruch, likewise ascribed in honorific manner to an Old Testament notable, contains a prayer of confession, a poem in praise of wisdom, and songs of comfort. Its appendage, the **Letter of Jeremiah,** is an attack on idolatry cast in the form of a letter to the exiles (compare Jeremiah 29); and the **Prayer of Manasseh** is a free composition based on 2 Chronicles 33:13, 19.

Apocalyptic

Only one example of this fourth category is included in the Apocrypha: **2 Esdras.** Written probably in the 1st century AD, 2 Esdras comprises some Christian chapters 'predicting' the rejection of the Jews in favour of the church, and a Jewish book of visions of the future ascribed to Ezra.

The Apocrypha today

What is the Christian today to make of the Apocrypha? The theological problem of its authority remains. Here we must acknowledge the fact that Christians have never been in complete agreement over the precise limits of the Old Testament, though they are at one in affirming its authority and inspiration. Some would argue that the Bible which Jesus and the apostles held as authoritative was the Hebrew Bible of 39 books, which did not include the apocryphal books. Even those who regard the Apocrypha as Scripture would admit that its authority is secondary to, and derived from (or dependent on), that of the 39 books.

But even though Christians may not give the Apocrypha the same standing as the books of the Hebrew Old Testament, they will find within it passages of deep piety and thoughtful spirituality.

In *Grace Abounding,* John Bunyan recounts how, searching for the verse, 'Look at the generations of old, and see, did ever any trust in God and were confounded', he was at first daunted to find it came from the Apocrypha (Ecclesiasticus 2:10). But he came to realize that 'as this sentence was the sum and substance of many of the promises, it was my duty to take the comfort of it, and I bless God for that word, for it was of God to me'. Those who read the Apocrypha devotionally will handle it best for they will discriminate, as they do when they read any religious literature, between what conforms and what does not conform to the essentials of the Christian faith.

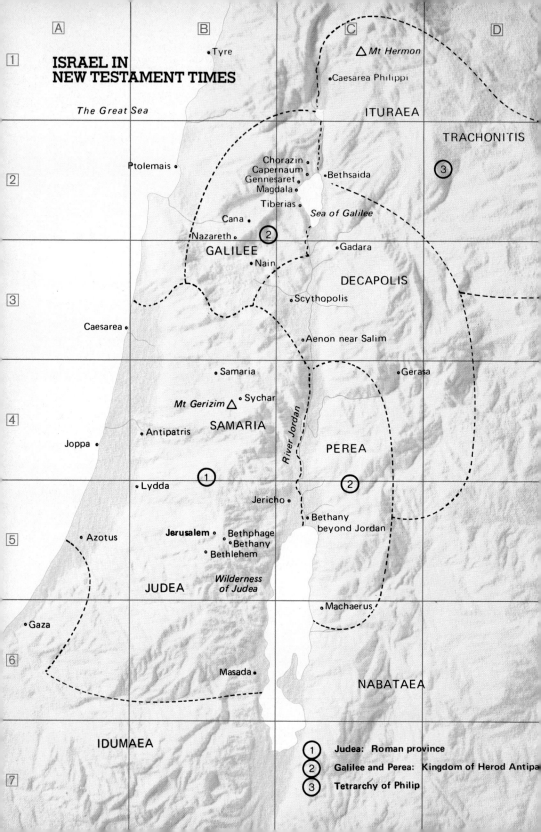

ISRAEL IN NEW TESTAMENT TIMES

	A	B	C	D
1				

The Great Sea

• Tyre

△ Mt Hermon

• Caesarea Philippi

ITURAEA

TRACHONITIS

③

• Ptolemais

Chorazin
Capernaum
Gennesaret   • Bethsaida
Magdala

Tiberias

Sea of Galilee

Cana

Nazareth   ②

GALILEE

• Gadara

• Nain

DECAPOLIS

• Scythopolis

Caesarea •

• Aenon near Salim

• Samaria   • Gerasa

Mt Gerizim △ • Sychar

SAMARIA

River Jordan

Antipatris

PEREA

Joppa •

① Lydda

② ②

Jericho •

Jerusalem • Bethphage
• Bethany
• Bethlehem

• Bethany
beyond Jordan

JUDEA *Wilderness
of Judea*

• Azotus

• Machaerus

• Gaza

NABATAEA

Masada •

IDUMAEA

① **Judea: Roman province**

② **Galilee and Perea: Kingdom of Herod Antipa**

③ **Tetrarchy of Philip**

3

NEW TESTAMENT HISTORY AT A GLANCE

Many New Testament dates. especially for the letters. are very approximate

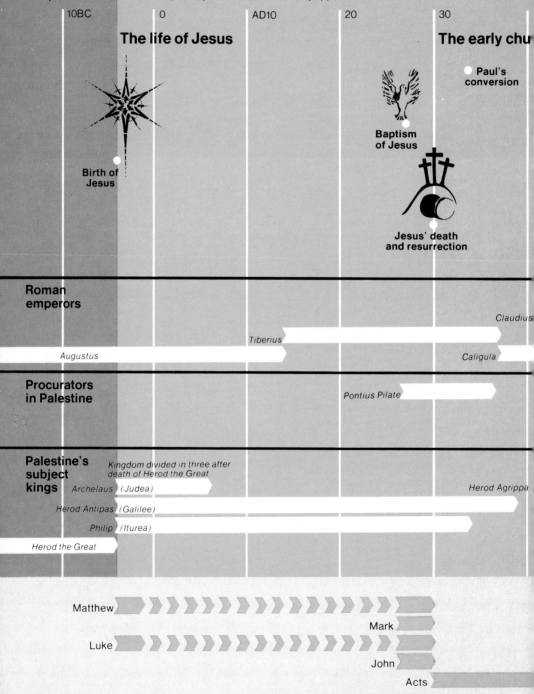

	10BC		0		AD10		20		30

The life of Jesus

The early chu

Birth of Jesus

Baptism of Jesus

Paul's conversion

Jesus' death and resurrection

Roman emperors

Augustus

Tiberius

Caligula

Claudius

Procurators in Palestine

Pontius Pilate

Palestine's subject kings

Kingdom divided in three after death of Herod the Great

Archelaus (Judea)

Herod Antipas (Galilee)

Philip (Iturea)

Herod the Great

Herod Agrippa

Matthew

Mark

Luke

John

Acts

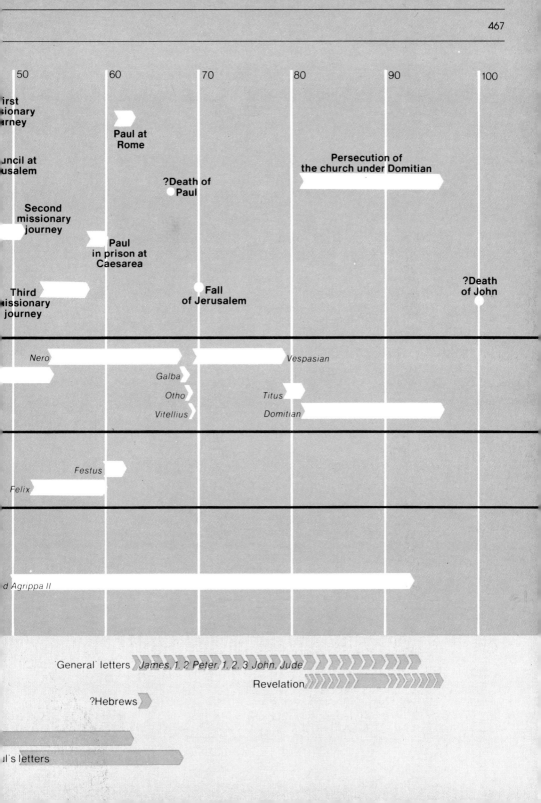

| | 50 | 60 | 70 | 80 | 90 | 100 |

**First
missionary
journey**

**Paul at
Rome**

**Council at
Jerusalem**

**Persecution of
the church under Domitian**

**?Death of
Paul**

**Second
missionary
journey**

**Paul
in prison at
Caesarea**

**Third
missionary
journey**

**Fall
of Jerusalem**

**?Death
of John**

Nero   *Vespasian*

Galba

Otho   *Titus*

Vitellius   *Domitian*

Festus

Felix

...d Agrippa II

'General' letters *James, 1, 2 Peter, 1, 2, 3 John, Jude*

Revelation

?Hebrews

...ul's letters

The Gospels and Jesus Christ
HOWARD MARSHALL

Virtually all we know about the earthly life of Jesus is to be found in the four Gospels contained in the New Testament. The life of a travelling preacher in an obscure corner of the Roman Empire was not likely to find its way into the writings of Roman historians, who had (as they thought) more important things to occupy their attention. Tacitus refers very briefly to Jesus, and then only by way of explanation of the name of the 'Christians' who were put to death by Nero.

Even Jewish historians offer us little more. The standard history of the Jews was written by Josephus towards the end of the 1st century, and he does refer to Jesus at one point in his narrative as a miracle-worker who was the Messiah; he was put to death by Pilate but later reappeared to his disciples. The passage may have been tampered with by later Christian scribes (for would Josephus have called Jesus the Messiah?), but is probably genuine in essentials.

Other Jewish traditions about Jesus have been preserved in the writings of the rabbis. They tell us that he practised magic, beguiled the people, and said that he had not come to destroy the law or add to it. He was hanged on the eve of Passover for heresy and misleading the people, and had five disciples who healed the sick. This gives some idea of how Jesus would have been regarded by people who shared the outlook of the Sanhedrin, the Jewish council that condemned him to death.

More recent discoveries do not alter the picture. The Dead Sea Scrolls, the library of a Jewish sect living just before and during the time of Jesus, shed light on the thought-world of ancient Palestine, but they make not the slightest reference to Jesus. What is recorded of the members of the sect and their enemies in no way affects the historicity of Jesus.

A more promising source of information lies in various 'gospels' which were not included in the New Testament. Such works have long been known, but in recent years interest has been rekindled by the discovery of the 'Gospel of Thomas' at Nag-Hammadi in Egypt. This work contains a set of sayings ascribed to Jesus. They have obviously been worked over by radical Christians, but it is possible that here and there in this and other similar documents fragments of genuine tradition about Jesus may be preserved. However, the fact that the early church excluded them all from the canon of Scripture is some indication that the hunt is not likely to be very successful.

This means that for all practical purposes our knowledge of Jesus must come from the New Testament alone. Within the New Testament itself the field narrows down to the Gospels. The letters of Paul and the other apostolic writers make very little reference to the life of Jesus as such – though this is not because they did not attach great importance to his ministry as a historical fact, or were not strongly influenced by what he had taught.

The Gospel records

It is, then, to the Gospels that we must turn for the written record of the life and teaching of Jesus. The Gospels were not composed until at least 30 years after the death of Jesus. During this period the material for them was preserved and handed down both by word of mouth and by written records that no longer survive.

The tradition would have been handed down carefully. The Jewish rabbis were extremely careful to hand down oral material accurately, and we may presume that the Christians did the same. The Gospel material was originally taught in Aramaic, the language spoken by Jesus, and in a poetic form which was easy to memorize.

People remember what they want to remember. This does not mean that Jesus' hearers conveniently forgot what they found disturbing and unpalatable. On the contrary, there is much in the Gospels that must have been challenging and difficult, and yet it has been faithfully preserved. The story of Jesus was remembered and retold because it was relevant to the life of the church. For example, the first Christians had to argue with the Jews, so it was essential to remember how Jesus had debated with them. Faced with decisions on ethical issues such as marriage and divorce, they needed his teaching as their authority on such matters. So it is good, when we read a passage in the Gospels, to ask what significance it had for the early church. The story of Jesus was not preserved out of an academic interest in history for its own sake, but because of its practical relevance for the first Christians. It was not 'pure' but 'applied' history.

People also tend to remember and pass on stories and teaching in a certain pattern. Stories of healing miracles, for example, describe in turn the condition of the sufferer, the way in which the cure was effected, and the results it produced. Many stories about Jesus describe a situation in which he was placed, or a question which was put to him, and culminate in the essential point: an authoritative saying of Jesus on the topic at issue.

The article on 'The Gospels and Modern Criticism', page 530, shows how these factors have been used to try to explain the actual composition of the Gospels. The clearest example is John's Gospel. For the author has to some extent interpreted the story of Jesus to show its significance for his readers. He has offered a kind of commentary on the ministry of Jesus in which it is hard to distinguish between the original 'text' and its 'interpretation'.

The important point, however, is that there really is a 'text' which he is explaining for us; he is not commenting on something that never existed. Behind the Gospel stands the figure of John the apostle, just as apostolic testimony is the basis of the other Gospels. It is also being increasingly recognized by scholars that it is one and the same Jesus who is described in all four Gospels. Whereas the critics of a former era argued that the Gospel of John had little or no basis in history, it is now seen that all four Gospels build on historical tradition, each preserving different aspects of it.

The purpose of the Gospel writers

John's Gospel raises the question of the relation of the Gospels to history. Did what is described in the Gospels really happen? We have already indicated that the Gospels rest on reliable tradition, handed down with care in the church. At the same time we must bear in mind that the Gospels are concerned to present the Christian significance of Jesus. Their basic purpose is to preach the gospel in order to convert the unbeliever and to build up the believer in his faith.

This means that they are not simply historical reports, as for example the biography of some famous soldier might be. The writers were not biographers, giving a detailed historical account of Jesus' life with everything in proper chronological order. We have only to compare the order of events in Mark 4-5 with Matthew 13; 8; 9 to see this fact plainly.

Or again, the Gospels record very little of some aspects of Jesus' life: scarcely anything is mentioned before he reached the age of 30; and even the account of his ministry is incomplete. There is by no means enough incident to fill the whole time it lasted. We have no right to blame the Gospel writers for not doing something they never intended.

But this does not mean they were unconcerned about history. The Gospels are not invention. In the preface to his Gospel (Luke 1:1-4), Luke lays particular stress on the fact that he was making use of authentic eye-witness testimony. History certainly mattered for him, and there is no reason to think that the other writers thought differently.

What, then, were they trying to do? They were preaching the gospel, the good news. They were presenting Jesus as the Christ, the Son of God (Mark 1:1). They wrote in order that their readers might believe in him and so have eternal life (John 20:31). They therefore portrayed Jesus as his followers saw him. To them he was no ordinary man, not even a unique prophet. He was the Lord whom God had raised from the dead and who was now alive and active in heaven. They knew no other Jesus than this. They might have thought differently about him before the resurrection (see Luke 24:19-24), and even the resurrection did not compel everybody who heard about it to believe. But they had come to believe in Jesus as a result of the total impact which he had made upon them, and so they could not present him in any other way.

So the history in the Gospels is history as seen by Christians. A non-Christian would see it differently; he would claim, for instance, that the resurrection could not have happened. It might be interesting to have an account of Jesus written from that point of view, but none has come down to us. What we have are the Gospels, written by Christian believers, written to persuade men to believe, but none the less historical for that.

Four portraits of Jesus

Each of the Gospel writers presents Jesus to us in his own characteristic way. The greatness of this person could not have been captured in one picture. So we have four portraits, each bringing out its own distinctive facets of the character of Jesus.

Matthew concentrates on the relationship of Jesus to the Jewish faith. He shows how Jesus came to fulfil the Old Testament, but at the same time to judge the Jews for their unfaithfulness to their religion. No other Gospel denounces so forcibly the hypocritical outlook of the Pharisees. The Jews are called to see Jesus as the promised Messiah, the Son of David; and judgement is pronounced upon them for their failure to respond to him. Matthew portrays Jesus very much as a teacher. He has given us systematic accounts of Jesus' teaching for the church's inner life and evangelistic mission.

Mark emphasizes action rather than teaching. He stresses how Jesus taught his disciples that the Son of man must suffer and be rejected, and that they must be prepared to tread the same path. Those who tried to understand Jesus other than as a crucified Saviour would misunderstand him. The Jews expected a Messiah who would be a political leader and a figure of glory. They found it hard to recognize Jesus as the Messiah because he chose the path of humble service and suffering. Only at his second coming would he appear as the King in his glory.

The Gospel of Luke stresses the blessings of salvation brought by Jesus. It emphasizes the signs of the coming of the Messiah, prophesied in the Old Testament, and seen in Jesus' healing of the sick and preaching of the gospel to the poor and needy. Luke especially brings out the grace of God revealed in

Jerusalem in New Testament Times

This reconstruction is at the Bible Museum, Amsterdam. Excavation of the ancient city of Jerusalem continues, and it is hoped to discover with more certainty the exact extent of the city. Much of the detail in a reconstruction of this sort is of course a matter of guesswork, but the main sites of importance in the New Testament are as follows:

1 **Herod's Temple**
2 **Kidron Valley**
3 **Mount of Olives**
4 **Garden of Gethsemane**
5 **Fort Antonia** (Pilate's residence)
6 **Pool of Bethesda**
7 **Pool of Siloam**
8 **Hinnom Valley**
9 **Herod's Palace**
10 **Golgotha** ('Place of a Skull', traditional site of the crucifixion)
11 **'Gordon's Calvary'**
12 **City of David**
13 **Western (Wailing) Wall**

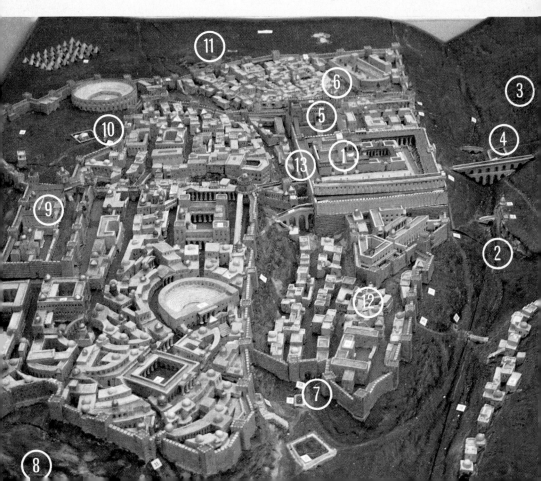

Jesus and bestowed upon those who seemed least worthy of it, sinful women and rapacious tax-collectors; for this is precisely what grace means, that men and women can do nothing to deserve it.

Finally, the Gospel of John reveals Jesus as the One sent by God the Father into the world to be its Saviour. As the Son, he has his Father's authority, living in close communion with him. John goes deepest into the things God has revealed and brings out the eternal significance of the 'God-become-man'.

An outline of the life of Jesus

Behind these four accounts stands a figure who is recognizably the same in all of them. Jesus was the son of the virgin Mary, born at Bethlehem shortly before the death of Herod the Great (4 BC). He spent his early life in Nazareth where he worked as the village carpenter. When John the Baptist began to preach beside the River Jordan (about AD 27), Jesus came and was baptized by him. He immediately received the gift of the Spirit, commissioning him for his work. In the strength of the Spirit he withstood Satan's inducements to divert him from his calling. He then commenced a ministry of preaching and healing, mainly in Galilee. This was preceded by a period in Judea (John 1–3) and included visits to Jerusalem. It concluded with a journey to Jerusalem which culminated in his arrest and death at Passover time (about AD 30).

Jesus' message was concerned with the good news of the rule (or kingdom) of God. In the Old Testament the prophets looked forward to a future era when God would act in power and set up his rule over Israel. This hope was associated with the coming of a king (or Messiah; Greek, 'Christ') who would belong to the kingly line of David. In the time of Jesus, the people had come to expect a warrior-king to deliver them from their Roman overlords.

Jesus taught that this hoped-for era was already dawning. He looked forward to the future consummation of God's rule, with himself as King. But the coming of God's rule was to be seen not in military victories but in Jesus' mighty works of healing and his preaching of salvation. God was already acting in the ministry of Jesus.

This good news demanded a response from men. Jesus called them to repent of their sin; he offered forgiveness to the penitent; and he summoned men to become his disciples. To accept the good news of the rule of God meant accepting Jesus as Master. Out of the many who responded, Jesus appointed twelve men to be the leaders of the new people of God who were to replace the old Israel which rejected the message of God, and to be associated with his missionary work.

Jesus taught his disciples a new way of life. It is summed up in the Sermon on the Mount (Matthew 5–7). Jesus took over the Old Testament commandments to love God and one's neighbour and filled them with new life and vigour.

Jesus taught with such self-confident authority that men asked who he thought he was. Some people dismissed him as mad. Others were prepared to see him as Messiah, but when he showed no inclination to lead them to war against Rome they turned away from him. This was probably why Jesus did not claim the title of Messiah openly. He preferred to speak of himself cryptically as the 'Son of man', a phrase which he took from Daniel 7:13 and filled with new content. For him it meant a figure who would one day be invested with power and glory by God (Mark 14:62), but who was for the time being humble and unknown (Matthew 8:20) and destined for suffering and death (Mark 8:31).

After his disciples had realized who he was, he began to teach them that he must die, although they were slow to take it in. Jesus saw himself fulfilling the role of the Servant of the Lord who suffers humiliation and death (Isaiah 52:13–53:12). He laid down his life as a ransom for men to save them from death

(Mark 10:45; John 10:11). Only to his closest disciples did he reveal that he was the Son of God in a unique, intimate manner. And he shared with them his privilege of addressing God in prayer by the name of 'Abba', 'Father' (Matthew 6:9; 11:25-27; Mark 14:36).

Throughout his ministry Jesus was involved in conflict with the religious authorities, mainly because of his scorching criticisms of their man-made traditions which diverted men from the real purposes of God's law. He attacked the hypocrisy which substituted tradition for the law of Moses. His messianic claims spurred the Jewish leaders on to arrest him. They feared he might be the centre of a popular uprising against Rome which would lead to grim reprisals and the loss of their own positions (John 11:47-53). So when Jesus came to Jerusalem and flung down the gauntlet by his attitude to the temple, they took steps to arrest him with the connivance of one of his followers.

Meanwhile Jesus held a last meal with his disciples. He filled a familiar table ritual with new content by using the bread and wine as symbols: his body was about to be broken in death on their behalf, and his blood about to be shed sacrificially, to ratify God's new covenant with men and to bring in his kingdom. After the meal, he went out to pray – and to meet his enemies. He was put through a trial which appears to have broken the appropriate legal rules. When the witnesses failed to produce sufficient evidence to condemn him, he was forced to make what his judges regarded as the blasphemous statement (to Christians it was the simple truth) that he was the Messiah. He was condemned to death. The Jews handed him over to the Roman governor as a political rebel against Rome, and although the governor was privately convinced of his innocence he allowed him to be put to death by the Roman punishment of crucifixion.

From the third day after his death, however, many of his disciples claimed that his tomb was empty and that he had himself appeared to them. God had raised him from the dead. The appearances took place over a period of 40 days, at the end of which time Jesus gave his final command to his disciples to be his witnesses throughout the world, and ascended from their presence as a symbol of his return to be with God and as a promise of his second coming to them at the end of the world.

That is the gospel story in brief. There is no other Jesus. The attempts of sceptical scholars to peel off the Christian interpretation and leave behind an ordinary, human person as the real 'historical' Jesus have proved fruitless.

It leaves with us the picture of a person about whom men must make up their minds. Throughout the Gospels Jesus appears as more than a man. His message, his deeds, and his person force the reader to decision.

Matthew

Each of the four Gospels has its own special emphasis. Matthew, writing for his fellow Jews, concentrates on Jesus as the long-awaited Messiah – the Christ predicted in the Old Testament (see 'The Religious Background of the New Testament', page 494). Many Jews were expecting a political leader who would free them from Roman domination. So Matthew is careful to record what Jesus said about his kingdom – the kingdom of heaven. He gives us a great deal of Jesus' teaching, which he collects together into five main sections. These alternate with sections of narrative in the Gospel, and include the famous 'Sermon on the Mount'. Matthew's Gospel, more than any other, is the link between the Old Testament and the New, the old Israel and the new world-wide church of God's people.

The writer

The Gospel does not name its author, but from earliest times it has been attributed to Matthew, the apostle and one-time tax collector. Little is known of him. And beyond the fact that it belongs to the period between AD 50 and AD 100 no one knows for certain when or where the Gospel was written. Much of Matthew's material is almost identical with Mark's – and Mark's source of information was Peter. Scholars today mostly believe that Matthew drew on Mark – not vice-versa; see 'The Gospels and Modern Criticism', page 530.

1—2
JESUS, THE MESSIAH, IS BORN

1:1-17 Christ's family line
See also Luke 3:23-38. The two lists are in reverse order and give a different set of names from David onwards (only Zerubbabel and Shealtiel appear in both). Matthew is showing Jesus as Messiah, descended from the royal line of David.

STORIES AND EVENTS FOUND ONLY IN MATTHEW

Parables
The tares/weeds
Hidden treasure
The pearl
The net
The hard-hearted servant
The workers in the vineyard
The two sons
The marriage of the king's son
The ten 'bridesmaids'
The talents

Miracles
The two blind men
The dumb man who was possessed
The coin in the fish's mouth

Incidents
Joseph's dream
The visit of the wise men
The escape to Egypt
Herod's massacre
Pilate's wife's dream
The death of Judas (also in Acts)
The 'saints' resurrected in Jerusalem
The bribing of the guard
The great commission

Some of Jesus' **teaching** is found only in Matthew, including his wonderful invitation to 'Come to me'.

He may be listing the heirs to the throne, while Luke lists Joseph's particular line. Matthew's list is stylized and abbreviated to fit his pattern: 14 names from Abraham to David; 14 from David to Jechoniah; 14 from Jechoniah to Jesus. This pattern of '14s' may have been suggested by the fact that the Hebrew letters in the name 'David' add up to that number. (The letters of the alphabet also served as numbers.)

Son/descendant of David (1): King David was promised an unfailing succession. But Israel ceased to be a monarchy at the time of the exile. And the promise came to be understood as referring to the Messiah.

Verses 3-6: it was unusual to list women. And if God's love and purposes had been limited to decent people of a particular race none of these would have been included. Tamar had children by her father-in-law, Judah (Genesis 38); Rahab was a Jericho prostitute (Joshua 2); Ruth a foreign Moabite woman (Ruth 1-4); and Uriah's wife was Bathsheba, with whom David committed adultery (2 Samuel 11).

Verse 11: 'father', like 'son' (verse 1), can be used in a wider sense. Josiah was Jechoniah's grandfather.

1:18-25 Mary and Joseph

Luke's fuller account of the birth focusses

The lights of Bethlehem seen from the fields surrounding the hill-top town. See too the picture on page 516.

Nazareth lies over 1200ft/400m up among the hills of Galilee.

on Mary; Matthew's on Joseph. It takes little imagination to appreciate the very human dilemma. But Mary's pregnancy had a supernatural beginning. Matthew recalls Isaiah's words, giving them a significance the prophet could not have dreamt of. 'Jesus' means 'the saviour'; 'Emmanuel', God with us, in the world of men. (See also 'The Virgin Birth', page 515.)

Verse 18: unlike modern engagement, this pledge was legally binding and could be broken only by divorce.

Verse 25: the implication is that after the birth Mary and Joseph lived a normal married life (see also 13:55-56).

2 The arrival of the wise men; the massacre; escape to Egypt

The wisdom of these men lay in the stars and their meanings. They were astrologers. And they had no doubt what the new star meant – the birth of the promised king in Judah. Tradition, not the Gospels, says the Magi were three kings and that the presents they gave the baby had special significance – gold for a king; incense for God; myrrh for mortal man.

The news was not so welcome at the palace. Herod was king of the Jews (this is Herod the Great, who reigned 40-4 BC). He wanted no rivals. The massacre is in keeping with other cruelties mentioned in historical records. The little family escape to Egypt, as Jacob's family had done long before when famine struck.

Verse 6: Matthew part-quotes, part-interprets Micah's words.

The house (11): some time has passed; the cave where the animals were stabled was only temporary shelter.

Rachel (18): mother-figure of Israel; Jacob's much-loved wife who died in child-birth at Ramah on the way to Bethlehem.

Archelaus (22): inherited one third of

Herod's kingdom, but his repressive measures soon led the Romans to depose him and take control of Judea. See 'The Herod Family', page 540.

3—4
JESUS' BAPTISM AND TEMPTATION

3 The preaching of John the Baptist; Jesus' baptism

See also Mark 1:2-11; Luke 3:2-22. Luke 1 tells the story of John's birth. John's compelling preaching – calling men to make ready for the Messiah – draws the crowds out to the desert to hear him. Peter's brother, Andrew, was one of those baptized by John, following genuine repentance for past wrong-doing. The 'washing' of baptism symbolized a radical cleaning up of a man's life – wiping the slate clean of all previous wrong – in preparation for the coming rule of God. This was not necessary in Jesus' case. He was baptized, not in order to be forgiven, but to identify himself completely with men. When he stepped into the Jordan, it was as if he was asking to take on the responsibility for human sin. He was accepting his destiny with all that that involved. God's words (17), combining Psalm 2:7 and Isaiah 42:1, proclaim Jesus as his Son, the Messiah, and the Servant who would suffer for his people.

Verse 4: see note under Mark 1:1-8.

Pharisees and Sadducees (7): see 'The Religious Background of the New Testament', page 494.

4 The temptation; the call of the first disciples; Jesus begins to teach

See also Mark 1:12-13; Luke 4:1-13. In the temptations that follow his 40-day fast, Jesus faces up to all he will have to go through in his ministry. He now has power – power to feed the hungry, heal the sick, raise the dead. How will he use it? To satisfy his own needs? To try God out? To compel a following? When it comes to it, will he use his power to save himself,

or will he trust himself entirely to God and tread the path to the cross? Jesus replies to Satan's test questions in words from Deuteronomy (8:3; 6:16; 6:13) – key passages from Israel's 40 years in the desert, when God tested their obedience to him (Deuteronomy 8:2).

After John's arrest, Jesus travels north, making the lakeside town of Capernaum his base. Here he calls his first disciples and begins his public ministry.

Decapolis (25): 'Ten Towns', Good News Bible; ten free Greek cities south-east of Galilee.

5—7
THE SERMON ON THE MOUNT: STANDARDS OF DISCIPLESHIP

See also Luke 6:20-49. The 'sermon' is the first and longest of the five sections in which Matthew gathers together the Lord's teaching. Jesus shows his followers how people ought to live – not simply according to a set of rules but by an inner revolution of attitude and outlook. The glorious thing is that having

Jesus' first disciples were fishermen, called from mending their nets. These fishermen are in the harbour at Acco, on Israel's Mediterranean coast.

set a seemingly impossible standard, he went on to give men the power to live up to it.

5:1-16 Where true happiness lies

Jesus turns ordinary human ideas about happiness upside down. Contrary to general opinion, it is not the go-getters, the tough ones, those who bend the rules, who are the real successes. The truly happy ones are those who recognize the spiritual poverty (verse 3) of self-reliance and learn to depend wholly on God. Everything else follows from this. The people who can be certain of a future are the humble, the forgiving, the pure, those who set their hearts on what is right, who try to heal the rifts. And here and now, these are the ones who put the seasoning into life, who stop the rot, who light up the way. By what they do and say and how they react, they show men something of what God himself is like.

5:17-48 The old law and the new

Nothing can ever supersede or do away with the law God gave through Moses.

'You are like light for the whole world', Jesus said. 'A city built on a hill cannot be hidden'. This is Tsefat in northern Galilee.

But the law is a minimum standard. It can only deal with actions, not with the thoughts that give rise to them. Jesus takes five examples to show what the principles expressed in the law involve at the personal level. Sin begins in the mind and will. That is where it must be rooted out. The standards of the new society – God's kingdom – are way above the standards of the law-courts.

The five case-studies: murder (21-26; Exodus 20:13); adultery (27-32; Exodus 20:14); oaths (33-37; Numbers 30:2 – and see Matthew 23:16-22); retaliation (38-42; Exodus 21:24); loving others (43-48; Leviticus 19:18; see also Luke 10:29-37).

The law and the prophets (17): i.e. all the Old Testament precepts. There were three divisions in the Jewish Bible – the Law (Genesis to Deuteronomy); the Prophets (Former: Joshua, Judges, Samuel, Kings; and Latter: all the prophets except Daniel); and the Writings (the rest of our Old Testament).

Verse 22: the progression is difficult to understand, unless 'fool' should be 'apostate' – meaning that any man who calls another an outcast of God is in danger of being cast out himself.

Verse 23: a sacrifice offered by an individual was of no value if he had not put right an offence committed against a fellow man.

Verses 31-32: in Moses' day a wife could be dismissed at whim. His law gave her some security. Jesus goes back to the fundamental meaning and purpose of marriage. The bond made when the two become 'one flesh' is indissoluble. Divorce is unthinkable, except where one of the partners has broken the bond already. See 19:3-9.

6:1-18 Warnings against a mere parade of religion

Motives, thoughts, intentions, what goes on deep inside, are what matter in religion, too. God gives no prizes for an outward show of piety. So Jesus tells us to give and pray and fast without

The hills and valleys of Galilee, where Jesus lived and taught.

drawing attention to ourselves – and God will reward us. Our prayer is to be simple, trusting. We are to come as children to our Father, eager to please, conscious of our failings. (Luke 11:2-4 also records the Lord's Prayer.)

6:19-34 Singlemindedness

Men can choose what to set their hearts on. They can go all out for money and material things, or for God and spiritual things. But not for both. Everyone must decide his own priorities. Those who put God first can rest assured he knows all their needs and will not fail to supply them. They can be free from worry.

Verses 22-23: the eyes were thought of as windows, letting light into the body.

7 Instructions and warnings

Do not be harshly critical (1-5); do be discriminating (6). Never give up praying (7-11). Always treat others as you would like them to treat you (12). Make sure you are on the right road to eternal life (13-14), there are plenty of people out to mislead (15-20). And many more are self-deceived (21-23). Words are not enough, the only safe course is to act on what we hear Christ say (24-27).

At the end of the teaching, it is the note of authority that most impresses the listeners. They have heard no one before like this man.

8—9:34
HEALING AND TEACHING

8:1-17 Miracles of healing

Verses 1-4: the leper. To the Jew lepers were unclean, untouchable. Jesus could have healed the man with a look, or a word – instead he reached out and touched him. (For the leprosy regulations, see Leviticus 13-14: the term 'leprosy' in the Bible covers a number of skin diseases, hence Good News Bible, 'dreaded skin-disease'.)

Verses 5-13: the centurion's boy. Jesus' mission is to Israel, but nowhere among his own people has he found faith to equal that of the Roman officer who recognized authority when he saw it.

Verses 14-17: Jesus cures physical, spiritual and psychological ills at Capernaum.

8:18-27 Storm and calm

Son of man (20): a phrase Jesus often uses to describe himself. It emphasizes his humanity (Psalm 8:4), yet points beyond it (Daniel 7:13-14).

Verses 21-22: the disciple wants to wait till after his father's funeral before joining Jesus. This need not mean that his father is dead. 'I must first bury my father' is a colloquial way of saying, 'I will follow you sometime – when my father is dead and I am free to go'. Jesus' reply stresses the urgency of his work. It calls for a response now.

Verses 23-27: see also Mark 4:36-41, with some differences of detail.

The Lake of Galilee, scene of so much of the teaching and so many of the healings of Jesus. The view is from the fishing harbour at Tiberias looking towards Magdala and the north-eastern corner of the lake.

8:28—9:8 Further healings

Verses 28-34: two men possessed by demons. In their accounts, Mark and Luke focus on just one of the men, 'Legion' or 'Mob' (Mark 5:1-17; Luke 8:26-37). Here Matthew tells how Jesus restored both men to sanity. But the residents of Gadara – a town six miles from the lake – were so scared that they sent Jesus away.

9:1-8: the man with paralysis. Jesus uses the physical healing as proof that the spiritual cure, the man's forgiveness, is equally real.

His own town (9:1): Capernaum – see 4:13.

9:9-17 Matthew's call; questions about fasting

In Mark (2:13-17) and Luke (5:27-32) the tax collector is called Levi, and they make it clear that the feast is held at his house. 'Matthew' may have been Levi's 'Christian' name, as 'Peter' was Simon's. Jesus' presence in such company scandalizes the religious Pharisees. John's followers are also puzzled. Why does Jesus feast whereas John fasted? Luke (5:36-37) gives Jesus' answer most clearly. His radically new teaching cannot be squeezed into the mould of the old legalism. It must find new forms of expression – or else the old will be destroyed and the new spoilt. Luke 5:39 is a perceptive comment on human nature – the conservatism which mistrusts anything new.

9:18-34 More healings

Verses 18-26: Jairus' daughter; the woman with a haemorrhage (see on Mark 5: 21-43; Luke 8:40-56).

Verses 27-31: two blind men. The reason for secrecy (30) is not explained. Presumably Jesus is anxious to avoid his miracles giving people the wrong ideas about his mission.

Verses 32-34: the dumb man who was possessed.

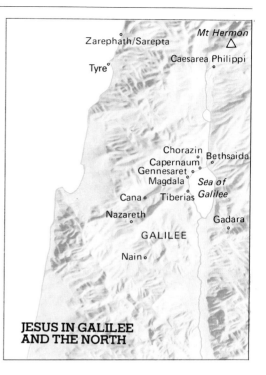

JESUS IN GALILEE AND THE NORTH

Verse 23: musicians were often hired to play dirges at a house where someone had died.

9:35—10:42
JESUS' CHARGE TO THE TWELVE

The second teaching section. See also Mark 6:7-13; Luke 9:1-6, and other parallel passages. The choice and training of the Twelve was a vital part of Jesus' mission. The task of spreading the good news about eternal life would rest with them after his death. Now he sends them out for the first time, with power to heal. He gives them their instructions (some only temporary – see Luke 22:35-36) and warns them of the kind of reception they are likely to get, both now and in the future. They are to expect hardship; trust in God's care; and fear no one.

The tax collector (10:3): it seems Matthew could never forget he was once a social outcast.

Verse 23: Jesus said that even he did not know when his second coming would be. The reference here may be to his triumphant return from death at the resurrection.

Beelzebul (25): see 12:22-24.

The housetop (27): a favourite place for gossip and discussion.

Verse 28: only God, not Satan, has this power.

Verses 34-35: the division is a 'result' of Jesus' teaching. The Bible often expresses consequences as if they were deliberate intention.

Verse 39: 'whoever finds'–i.e. the man who denies his faith to save his skin.

11–12
THE CLAIMS OF JESUS

This is one of Matthew's narrative sections–but it contains a good deal of teaching.

11:1-19 Messengers from John the Baptist

John–imprisoned by Antipas, younger son of Herod the Great, and ruler of Galilee and Perea–is puzzled by reports of Jesus. He expected the Messiah to come in judgement. Jesus' reply reminds him of the other aspect of Messiah's work (predicted in Isaiah 35:5-6; 61:1), which he is fulfilling. John is the last and greatest of the Old Testament prophets– the latter-day Elijah predicted by Malachi (4:5). Jesus thinks no less of him for his doubts. But the humblest Christian enjoys far greater privileges (11).

Verse 12: it is difficult in retrospect to see exactly what Jesus meant. He may be referring to Zealot militants, from whom he disassociated himself; or to the fact that the kingdom opens its gates to those who are desperate, not just drifters (see Luke 16:16).

Verses 16-17: like sulky children, Jesus' contemporaries refuse to 'play weddings' with him, or to 'play funerals' with John. They will listen neither to good news–nor to warnings.

11:20-30 'Come to me'

Most of Jesus' miracles took place in the small area at the north of the sea of Galilee–around Capernaum, Chorazin and Bethsaida. They evoked so little response from the people that God's judgement on

Jesus used familiar pictures in his stories. Then as now the workers and their pay-packets was a popular subject. The field on the left is in Galilee, the orchard on the right on the edge of the Plain of Sharon near the foothills of Samaria.

their stubborn disbelief was inevitable. Tyre and Sidon – the prosperous, godless sea-ports denounced by the prophets (e.g. Isaiah 23) – even Sodom, that byword for evil (Genesis 19), could not have seen what they had seen and remained unmoved.

It was the ordinary folk who received Jesus – and he was glad. To all who are worn down by burdens he offers relief. Those who enter his service will find him no crushing task-master.

12:1-14 The Lord of the sabbath

See on Mark 2:23–3:6.

12:15-37 Hope of the nations? Or devil's emissary?

The Pharisees see Jesus as the devil's agent (24), despite the transparent goodness of his work (22-23). If they were right, Satan would be set on a suicide course (25-29) – as are all who, like the Pharisees, call good evil. They are stubbornly denying the Holy Spirit's work, and making their own forgiveness impossible (31-32).

12:38-50 'Give us a sign'

After all Jesus' miracles of healing, the lawyers and Pharisees have the effrontery to demand a spectacular sign. Only one such sign will be given – Jesus' resurrection from the dead – the incontrovertible proof that he is who he claims to be.

Verses 43-45: the story is a warning to those who have repented as a result of what they have seen and heard. Unless they take the further step of whole-hearted commitment, they are in grave danger.

Verse 40: by Jewish reckoning any part of the 24 hours which make up day and night could count as the whole. So Friday afternoon to Sunday morning is spoken of as three days and nights.

Verse 42: the Queen of Sheba (1 Kings 10:1-10).

Verse 49: presumably younger children of Mary and Joseph (see on 1:25). It is usually thought that Joseph was dead by this time.

13:1-52
PARABLES ABOUT GOD'S KINGDOM

The third teaching section. Jesus made many of his points by means of parables – stories that could be taken at two levels, the superficial or the more perceptive.

They were a means of sorting out his followers; discovering who had come just because of the miracles, and who really wanted to understand his teaching. The former were happy to listen to stories; the latter were prepared to look for the deeper meaning and ask him to explain. There was so much misunderstanding – even among the disciples – about the nature of his kingdom that he needed to straighten them out one point at a time.

Verses 1-9: the seed and the soils (explained in 18-23) pictures the varied response his message will bring.

Verses 24-30: the wheat and the weeds (explained in 36-43) is concerned with the mixture of good and bad in this life, to be sorted out at the judgement.

Verses 31-33: the mustard-seed, and the yeast. From small beginnings, quietly and unnoticed, the kingdom will make great growth.

Verses 44-45: the treasure, and the pearl. So valuable is the kingdom, it is worth giving all we have to make sure of it.

Verses 47-50: the fisherman's net. This describes the sorting out of good and bad at the end of time.

The Kingdom of God and the Kingdom of Heaven

DAVID FIELD

The two expressions 'kingdom of God' and 'kingdom of heaven' represent exactly the same idea. To a devout Jew the word 'God' was far too sacred to be used lightly or frequently. Matthew, writing primarily for Jewish readers, therefore normally speaks about the 'kingdom of heaven', whereas Mark and Luke prefer the alternative 'kingdom of God', as an easier expression for non-Jews to understand.

It is surprising to find that neither expression is used at all in the Old Testament. And even in the New Testament the phrases seldom occur after the three Gospels. This highlights the important part the theme of the kingdom played in the teaching of Jesus himself. We are told that it was right at the heart of his gospel message (Mark 1:15), and when the disciples were sent out on their first missions it was the message of 'the kingdom' that they were to proclaim (Luke 9:2; 10:9-11).

The meaning of 'kingdom'
Jesus never defined exactly what he meant by the kingdom of God. But in answering the charge of rebellion before Pontius Pilate he was careful to disown all claims to temporal, territorial dominion. 'My kingdom', he said, 'is not of this world' (John 18:36). Some modern versions translate 'kingdom' in this verse as 'kingship' or 'kingly authority'. The kingdom of God, in the Bible, normally means God's active reign in the world. Sometimes Jesus could talk about 'entering' the kingdom (e.g. Mark 10:23), much as we might speak of entering a country, but the idea behind the word he used is far more often that of 'rule' than of 'realm'. Perhaps the Lord's Prayer comes closest to an exact definition when it equates the coming of God's kingdom with the doing of his will. Where God's will is done with perfect submission, there, according to the New Testament, is his kingdom revealed.

Although the Old Testament authors did not write about the 'kingdom of God' as such, they eagerly anticipated the great Day when he would display his glory (Isaiah 24:23) in such a dramatic way that all men would acknowledge his rule (Zechariah 14:9). This keen sense of anticipation, both a cosmic hope and a longing for the liberation of the land, persisted well into Jesus' time. (Joseph of

13:53 — 14:12
NAZARETH REJECTS JESUS; THE DEATH OF JOHN THE BAPTIST
See on Mark 6:1-6 and 14-29.

14:13 — 17:27
TEACHING AND MIRACLES IN GALILEE AND THE NORTH

14:13-36 5,000 people fed; Jesus walks on the water
See on Mark 6:30-56. See also Luke 9:10b-17; John 6:1-21.

15:1-20 The Pharisees and the question of tradition
See also Mark 7:1-23. From the first, Jesus' teaching on religion (6:1-18) brought him into conflict with the Pharisees. For them 'tradition' (the oral teaching of the rabbis which supplemented and interpreted Scripture) was binding. But Jesus never hesitated to denounce tradition wherever it watered down or undermined scriptural principles. Their ruling on vows is a case in point. Exemption from his duty to maintain his parents was allowed a man if he dedicated the money to God.

Arimathaea, Mark tells us, was one man who was 'looking for the kingdom of God'.) So when John the Baptist announced 'the kingdom of heaven is at hand' (Matthew 3:2), he was immediately surrounded by crowds of excited people who had come to witness the long-expected display of God's ruling power in history.

God's kingdom – present and future
Jesus' first preaching was apparently couched in very similar terms to John's, but according to Mark he prefaced his announcement of the kingdom's imminence with the words 'The time is fulfilled' (Mark 1:15). This declaration of fulfilment strikes a note which sounds right through the Gospels, that in Jesus the kingdom of God has become a living reality. His miracles, and especially his exorcisms, testify to the fact that God's sovereign rule is breaking in upon man (Matthew 12:28). His preaching, with its unique note of authority, is evidence of the kingdom's arrival (Mark 1:27; Matthew 11:5). Because 'the kingdom of God is in the midst of you', he tells his disciples (Luke 17:21), the kingdom's blessings – forgiveness, salvation and eternal life – are theirs to enjoy, not only for the future but in the present. For centuries the prophets had forecast a time when God's kingly power would be displayed on earth; now, in the person and ministry of Jesus, that time had come.

If Jesus taught that the kingdom had actually arrived in his own person, it is equally clear that he looked to the future for a final demonstration of God's ruling power. His disciples must *pray* 'Thy kingdom come' and watch alertly to see 'the kingdom of God come with power' (Mark 9:1; Matthew 25:1). The miracles they saw him perform – and performed themselves, in his strength – were a mighty token of the kingdom's presence, but the battle with Satan still raged and the result, though not in doubt, awaited the final showdown (Matthew 25:41). Forecasts of a great future consummation intertwine, therefore, with clear evidence of the kingdom's present arrival, and it is obvious from the 'parables of the kingdom' in Matthew 13 that Jesus intended his disciples to grasp both truths. The seed is sown and grows before the climax of harvest is reached.

The demands of the kingdom
Whether present or future, God's kingly rule demands man's obedient submission. Men are not called upon to build or establish the kingdom for themselves, but only to seek for it and enter it (Matthew 6:33; Mark 9:47). Its ethical standards are exacting – far above those of the scribes and Pharisees (Matthew 5:20) – and they call not only for theoretical knowledge but for practical expression (Mark 12:34). In short, entry into the kingdom requires the unquestioning obedience of a child (Mark 10:15) and makes absolute demands on the disciple's loyalty and devotion. Yet submission to God's rule is in man's very best interests, because his kingdom, like hidden treasure or a pearl of great price, is the one thing of supreme value in life, for which any sacrifice is worth while (Matthew 13:44-46).

That way he could still enjoy the proceeds himself. It is not clean hands (2) but a clean heart (18) that matters.

15:21-39 The Canaanite woman; further healings; 4,000 fed

Tyre and Sidon (21) lay outside Jewish territory. Jesus could not refuse a request made with such tenacious faith.

Verses 29-39: the differences of detail between this passage and 14:13-21, and the fact that Mark also records both miracles, make it unlikely that this is a second account of the same event, despite the basic similarity.

The dogs (26): an abusive term for Gentiles. Jesus is testing the woman out, leading her to faith.

Magadan (39): the location is not known.

16:1-12 Jesus warns against the teaching of the Pharisees and Sadducees

See also Mark 8:11-21. The Pharisees had demanded a sign once before (12:38ff.). Now the Sadducees, the ultra-conservatives, join them. Jesus' answer is still the same.

16:13-28 Peter's great declaration: Jesus predicts his death

Simon speaks for all the apostles in asserting his belief that Jesus is the Messiah. And Jesus sees in him the man of rock (Peter) he will become after the shattering experience of denial and forgiveness (26:69-75). It is Peter the natural spokesman who will be responsible, more than any other, for the formation of the church at Pentecost (Acts 2–5).

Jesus went to the synagogue on the sabbath and taught there. This ancient synagogue is at Tsefat, Israel.

Verses 21-28: Jesus begins to prepare his disciples for the suffering that lies ahead. But the recent promise has gone to Peter's head. The rock becomes an obstacle. God's spokesman turns devil's advocate.

Verse 19: the authority given to Peter is given equally to the others (see 18:18). The idea of the keys echoes Isaiah 22:22. God is not bound by whatever Peter may say. But anything done by the disciple in accordance with Christ's will is to have permanent validity.

Verse 28: see on 10:23.

17 The transfiguration and what follows

See on Mark 9:2-32; Luke 9:28-45.

Verses 24-27: as Son of God, the one on whose behalf the tax is levied, Jesus is exempt. But as Man, identified with us, he pays it.

18
LIFE IN GOD'S COMMUNITY

This is Matthew's fourth teaching section. God's kingdom operates by totally different standards from the world's. Status-seeking is out (1-4). So is the policy of 'the weakest to the wall'. On the contrary, the spiritually weak are the special responsibility of the strong (5-14). In the new community wrongdoing matters; every effort must be made to set the defaulter right (15-20). Unlimited forgiveness is expected from those whom God has forgiven (21-35).

Verses 8-9: see on Mark 9:44-45.

Verses 24, 28: 'millions' and 'a few pounds' (New English Bible): the point being the immeasurable extent of our 'debt' to God, compared to anything we may have to forgive our fellow men.

19—20
THE JOURNEY TO JERUSALEM

19:1-15 Marriage and divorce
See also 5:31-32; Mark 10:2-12; Luke 16:18.

The rabbis disagreed about divorce. Some allowed it for anything that displeased the husband; others only for unfaithfulness. Jesus goes back to God's purpose for man and woman at the very beginning. That is the ideal. Moses, dealing with a situation that fell far short of the ideal, placed a restriction on divorce. Jesus says that unfaithfulness is the only legitimate reason for it.

19:16—20:16 Eternal life; the disadvantage of wealth; rewards

19:16-30: see also Mark 10:17-31; Luke 18:18-30. Jesus' first answer is the one any Jewish teacher would have given. And the man – a ruler in the synagogue – could claim he had kept the commandments. But Jesus pinpoints the root of

Jesus' denunciation of the religious leaders was scathing: those who led 'little ones' astray were fit only to have a mill-stone tied round their necks and be cast into the sea. These mill-stones are in the Agricultural Museum at Jerusalem.

this man's trouble. His commandment-keeping is not wholehearted. His possessions mean too much to him. Because of them he is failing to love God and his neighbour without reserve. So Jesus tells him to sell up. It is better to possess nothing than to love things more than God.

20:1-16: this story, illustrating Jesus' words in 19:30, comes only in Matthew. He is not talking about pay structures, or saying that all will be equal in heaven. The point is that many who expect to be made much of will be in for a rude shock in God's kingdom. God will honour some very unexpected people. Eternal life is for all who will receive it: 'good' and 'bad', young and old. The remarkable thing is the landowner's (God's) generosity – not his unfairness.

19:24: there have been various 'explanations' of the 'needle's eye'. But it seems that Jesus is being deliberately humorous in suggesting the impossible – a camel going through the eye of a literal needle.

19:25: they were surprised because they thought riches were a reward for goodness – an index of a person's spiritual state.

'Whited sepulchres' was Jesus' scathing term for the hypocritical religious leaders: whitewashed outside, but full of rottenness inside.

19:28: the apostles have a special place in the new kingdom. Only Matthew records these words.

19:29: those who follow Christ will be repaid many times over, here and now – but 'with persecutions' (see Mark).

20:2: New English Bible gives the meaning, 'the usual day's wage'. The denarius was a Roman silver coin.

20:3-6: the times are 9 a.m. (the third hour), 12 noon, 3 p.m. and 5 p.m. – an hour before sunset, which was when the men were paid for the day's work.

Model of a synagogue in the time of Jesus.

20:17-34 Jesus again predicts his death; status in God's kingdom; two blind men healed

See also Mark 10:32-52; Luke 18:31-43. Jesus' patience is amazing. Over and over again he explains that the kingdom is for the humble. There is to be no lording it. Yet even when he speaks of his death the disciples are taken up with their own status. The place at the top is reserved for the disciple who – like his master – is prepared to live for others and if need be to die for them.

Sons of Zebedee (20): i.e. James and John.

The cup (22): i.e. the cup of suffering. James was the first of the loyal apostles to meet a violent death (Acts 12:2).

Verses 29-34: Mark and Luke mention only one blind man – perhaps because Peter, who probably supplied the information, knew one of them personally (Bartimaeus – see Mark).

21—25
JESUS IN JERUSALEM

It was spring, and people from far and near were crowding into Jerusalem for Passover, the great feast commemorating the nation's liberation from Egypt. Not all could find lodgings in the city itself. Jesus and his friends stayed at nearby Bethany, where Martha, Mary and Lazarus had their home. Each day they walked the two miles into Jerusalem, over the shoulder of the Mount of Olives and down through the thick groves of trees.

21:1-11 His triumphant arrival

See on Luke 19:28-44. See also Mark 11: 1-10. Characteristically, Matthew quotes the prophecy from Zechariah 9:9.

21:12-17 The purging of the temple

See also on John 2:13-25. The dealers operated in the outer court of the temple, the Court of the Gentiles. Jews from abroad were not allowed to use their own currency to pay the annual temple dues. And the money-changers fixed a high rate of exchange. (The annual revenue from the temple tax is estimated at £75,000: the moneychangers' annual profit at £9,000.) Poor people, who could only afford the cheapest sacrifice (two pigeons), were charged extortionate prices. The priests turned a blind eye to all this. Yet their indignation knows no bounds at the 'irreverence' of Jesus.

He actually healed people in the temple courts and let the children chant the earlier tributes of the crowds!

21:18-22 The fig-tree

See also Mark 11:12-14, 20-24. A healthy fig-tree bears fruit for ten months of the year. Since the tree was in leaf, there should have been green figs. Mark makes it clear that it was the following day when the disciples found the tree withered. Jesus uses the incident as an object lesson: faith can move insurmountable obstacles. It also indicates the fate of the spiritually barren nation of Israel.

21:23-46 The priests question Jesus' authority

The question is natural, in the light of

A street in the Old City of Jerusalem.

what has happened (12-17). Jesus makes no direct answer, but it is clear that he and John derive their authority from the same source. In the three parables that follow his critics find themselves under fire.

Verses 28-32: the two sons. The first represents the religious leaders, with their mock obedience; the second the social outcasts, who have made a genuine response to John and to Jesus.

Verses 33-41: the vineyard (the nation of Israel whose owner is God – Isaiah 5:1-7). The men to whom God has entrusted spiritual leadership have abused the prophets and are about to kill his Son.

Verses 42-43: see Psalm 118:22-23. Jesus transfers the picture from Israel to himself – cast aside, crucified, by the nation, but reinstated by God.

22:1-14 The parable of the wedding-guests

Jesus illustrates what he has just said (21:43). The day will come when God no longer invites those who repeatedly refuse him. The invitation will go to others. Verses 11-13 are a warning to the newcomers. Those who come must come on God's terms.

22:15-46 Test questions; the Pharisees plot against Jesus' life

See on Mark 12:13-44.

23 Jesus denounces the lawyers and Pharisees

Chapters 23–25 contain the fifth and last teaching section. The subject is judgement. Jesus launches into a scathing attack on Israel's legalistic, but much-respected religious leaders. The man who cared so deeply and had such patience with ordinary people – even the wicked, the weak-willed and the stupid – could not stomach the religious sham, the self-righteous pride, the hair-splitting

pedantry of the Pharisees and scribes. Proud and selfish hearts still lurk beneath such 'proper' exteriors. How he must hate to see Pharisaic hypocrisy in his own followers.

Verse 2: they are 'the authorized interpreters of Moses' Law', Good News Bible.

Verse 10: 'teacher' gives the sense. The same Greek word is used today of a 'professor'.

Verse 15: 'twice as fit for hell' gives the sense. New converts are often more fervent than those brought up in the faith.

Mint, dill, cummin (23): common garden herbs.

Verse 27: tombs were specially white-washed for Passover to prevent people inadvertently touching them and becoming ceremonially defiled.

Verse 35: this may be Zechariah son of Jehoiada, as there is no record of the prophet Zechariah being murdered. Genesis 4:8; 2 Chronicles 24:20-21.

Verses 38-39: Jesus may be predicting the destruction of the city. Verse 39 refers to his return in glory and judgement.

24–25 The fall of Jerusalem and Jesus' return in judgement

24:1-44: questions and answers. See also Mark 13; Luke 21 and 17:23ff. Jesus is answering questions about when the temple will be destroyed and what indications there will be that the age is coming to an end. Jerusalem and the temple were actually to be destroyed by the Romans in AD 70. The disciples seem to think of the end closely following. And Jesus does not clearly separate them – both are part of the total judgement of God (although more than 1900 years already separate the two events). The disciples are not to be misled – there will be many wars and natural disasters, persecutions and false Messiahs (4-13, 23-27). These are not signs of the end. There will be time for world-wide preaching of the gospel (14). And when the end does come, it will be totally unexpected (36-44). But there will be clear warning signs of the destruction of

Jerusalem (15-22, 32-35).

24:45–25:46: parables of judgement. Jesus uses stories to drive home the points of the previous chapter.

24:45-51: the good and bad servants. Because his return will be unexpected, Jesus' followers must always be ready.

25:1-12: the wise and foolish girls. The same lesson, but stressing that one day time will run out, and preparedness is an individual thing. It cannot be borrowed from someone else.

25:14-30: the 'talents'. The talent was a large amount of money – not a coin. Each man is entrusted with a capital sum in line with his business ability, and he is expected to trade with it. Our future depends on how we use what we have been given in this life.

25:31-46: the sheep and the goats. At the judgement God takes account of how we have treated others in this life. In the parable, the 'goats' are punished for failing to do what they should have done.

24:15: Daniel 11:31. An alternative rendering, in line with Luke's paraphrase is 'so when you see the abominable sign spoken of by the prophet Daniel (let the reader understand)'. This could be a reference to the emperor's image on the ensign carried by the Roman soldiers.

24:21: over 1,000,000 people lost their lives in the fall of Jerusalem, and Herod's magnificent cream stone and gold temple was razed to the ground.

24:28: the picture seems to be of the 'eagles' of the Roman army converging on the 'corpse' of the city.

24:29-31: symbolic language used of Christ's return. In the light of verse 36, 'immediately' cannot be taken literally. Jesus is again telescoping the two 'comings in judgement'.

24:34: a reference to the destruction of

the temple within the lifetime of his hearers. It took place about 40 years after Jesus' prediction.

26–27
THE FINAL CLASH: JESUS' TRIAL AND CRUCIFIXION

26:1-5 Jesus forewarns his disciples; the Jewish leaders plot his death

26:6-13 A woman anoints Jesus
See on Mark 14:3-9.

26:14-29 Judas turns traitor; the Last Supper
See also Mark 14:12-25; Luke 22:7-38; John 13–14.

On the first evening of the festival,

Jesus' words about the coming destruction of Jerusalem were dramatically fulfilled in AD 70. Jerusalem was destroyed, its temple plundered. On the Titus Arch in Rome is this relief of the seven-branched candlestick and other temple plunder being carried away by the victorious Romans.

Jesus and his close friends meet as a family to eat the Passover meal together. At the exodus each Jewish household sacrificed a lamb or kid and daubed the blood over the door to ensure their safety as death struck the firstborn of every Egyptian family. Now the Lamb of God (John 1:29) is about to offer himself, to secure life for the whole world. The old Passover is transformed into the Lord's Supper. At the exodus, the nation of Israel was born. By Christ's sacrifice, the church is born, a people drawn from all the nations. The Passover looked back. The Lord's Supper is also a reminder for us today of a past event. It looks forward, too, to the joyous day when Christ will come and make his home with his people, in a new world which has no place for sin or death or pain.

26:30-56 The garden of Gethsemane; Jesus is arrested

See also Mark 14:26-52; Luke 22:39-53. It is Luke who depicts most vividly the agony of Christ's prayer in the garden. So intense was Jesus' last plea that – God willing – he might be spared the terrible suffering about to begin, that his sweat

Man, boy and donkeys in an arched street in the Old City of Jerusalem.

The Passover and the Last Supper

The Passover meal followed a fairly standard pattern in every Jewish household. First comes the opening prayer – the blessing of the cup (the first of four cups of wine passed round during the ceremony). Then each person takes herbs and dips them in salt water (see Matthew 26:23). The head of the family takes one of the three flat cakes of unleavened bread, breaks it and puts some aside. Then, in response to a question from the youngest member of the

family, the story of the first Passover is recounted and Psalms 113, 114 sung. The second cup (see Luke 22:17) is filled and passed round.

Before the meal itself, all wash their hands (probably the point at which Jesus washed the disciples' feet, John 13:4-12), grace is said and bread broken. Bitter herb dipped in sauce is distributed (this was when Jesus gave the sop to Judas, John 13:26). The climax of the ritual is the festive meal of roast lamb.

fell like great drops of blood. What was it he shrank from? Surely not simply physical suffering. We can never know just what he faced during that lonely hour. But the prospect which filled him with such horror was God's judgement on *our* sin – the penalty which would have been ours had Christ not paid it for us (1 Peter 2:24).

The moment passes, and as the mob comes out to arrest him he is once more utterly in command. He expresses only love for the traitor. When Peter draws his sword (John 18:10), Jesus heals the injured man (see Luke 22:51). No man can ever have been so completely in control of such a situation. He had come to fulfil the scriptures. He knew it must be so – even when everyone deserted him.

26:57-68 Trial before the high priest

See on Mark 14:53-65.

26:69-75 Peter denies all knowledge of Jesus

See on Luke 22:54-65.

27:1-26 Judas commits suicide; Jesus before Pilate

Only Matthew records Judas' remorse. He flings back the money – but a clear conscience is not so easily bought. (Acts 1:16-20 has a slightly different version of the story.) For the trial before Pilate, see on Luke 23:1-25.

27:27-56 Mockery and crucifixion

See on Mark 15:16-41.

27:57-66 Jesus' burial; a guard is set

See on Mark 15:42-47. Matthew is the only one to mention the guard; see also 28:11ff.

28

THE RESURRECTION

See on Luke 24 and 'The Accounts of the Resurrection', page 529.

Verses 1-10: the women hear the news and see the Lord. Verses 11-15: the guards are bribed to lie. The penalty for falling asleep on duty was death. But perhaps Pilate could also be squared with a bribe. Verses 16-20: Jesus' last command. This most Jewish of all the Gospels closes with a word from the Lord that throws the kingdom open to people of every nation.

It was after this that Jesus instituted the Lord's Supper, breaking the bread laid aside earlier and passing round the third cup of wine, the 'cup of blessing'. (The words 'this is...' in Matthew 26:26, 28, must mean 'this represents...' since he was himself there, giving the disciples the bread and wine.) The ritual concludes with the singing of the remaining 'Hallel' (or Hallelujah) psalms (115 – 118) and the 'Great Hallel', Psalm 136. These psalms are probably the 'hymn' Matthew mentions (26:30). Then the final cup of wine is drunk.

The setting of the Lord's Supper at the heart of the Passover meal explains its meaning. Jesus is thinking of himself as the Passover lamb, offered up for the deliverance of his people. The wine speaks of his death, and of the new covenant it ratifies, reconciling God and man. Until he comes again, we are to remember the significance of what he has done for us.

The Religious Background of the New Testament

RICHARD FRANCE

Jesus was a Jew. The Christian church began its life in Palestine, and its first members were Jews. So the most important element in the religious background to the New Testament is the Jewish religion itself.

JEWISH RELIGION

The last of the Old Testament prophets lived 400 years or more before John the Baptist appeared. Since that time the Jewish religion had not stood still. The classical religion of the Old Testament had evolved (some might say, degenerated) into Judaism.

Some important institutions in Judaism
■ **The temple.** The simple temple built by the Jews who returned to Jerusalem after the exile had been replaced by a magnificent structure commissioned by Herod the Great (40-4 BC). It was begun in 19 BC; it was still not complete in the time of Jesus (John 2:20), and was not finished until AD 64 – six years before it was destroyed by the Romans! It was this imposing complex of buildings in huge cream-coloured stones, marble and gold, which evoked the admiration of Jesus' disciples (Mark 13:1). Here the age-old ritual of sacrifice and worship continued, with its elaborate establishment of priests and temple servants, though all under the watchful eye of the Roman garrison in the fortress of Antonia, which overlooked its courts (Acts 21:31ff.). Here too, in the Court of the Gentiles (beyond which no Gentile dare venture, on pain of death – Acts 21:28-29 and picture page 567; Ephesians 2:14), was the thriving market in sacrificial animals and sacred money for the temple offerings which was the object of Jesus' anger. And here in the shaded porticos men would gather to listen to any teacher who cared to set up his stand.

■ **The synagogue.** There was only one temple, but each community had its synagogue. Here there was no sacrificial ritual. It was the local centre for worship and study of the law. On the sabbath day the community would meet, men and women seated apart, to listen to the reading and exposition of the set passages from the Law and the Prophets

(Luke 4:16ff.), and to join in the set liturgical prayers. But the synagogue was more than a place of worship. It was the local school, the community centre, and the centre of local government. Its elders were the civil authorities of the community, the magistrates and guardians of public morals.

■ **The law and the traditions.** Israel had always had a law, since the days of Moses. But from the time of Ezra (5th century BC; following the exile in Babylon which the prophets saw as a direct result of the nation's disobedience to the law) greater emphasis had been placed on the study of the law, until the Jews had become 'the people of the book'. This intensive study had resulted in an increasing body of 'traditions', which came to be regarded as no less binding than the law itself. *Scribes,* professional students and exponents of the law and traditions, were needed to prescribe exact regulations for every occasion. There were, for example, 39 types of action prohibited on the sabbath: reaping and threshing were forbidden – this included plucking ears of corn and rubbing the grain out in the hands (Luke 6:1-2); a 'sabbath day's journey' (Acts 1:12; about two-thirds of a mile) was the maximum travel permitted. Sadly, in their meticulous care over details of tradition the scribes sometimes forgot the more fundamental concerns of the law itself (Mark 7:1-13; 3:4-5; Matthew 23:23).

Parties, sects, and movements in Judaism
■ **The Pharisees.** These were the religious purists – a party which grew from the 2nd century 'Hasidim' (God's loyal ones) and concentrated on control of religious, rather than political, affairs. Their supreme concern and delight was to keep the law (including, of course, the traditions) in every exact detail. (Most scribes belonged to the Pharisee party.) Judged by this standard, they were model Jews (Philippians 3:5-6). To this end, they kept themselves as far as possible apart from other men: they could not eat with a non-Pharisee in case the food had not been tithed (i.e. one tenth given to God).

Inevitably, perhaps, this policy of separation led to disdain for all lesser mortals, a 'holier-than-thou' attitude which has made their name a term of reproach today. This arrogance, combined with a dry legalism which put exact ritual observance before love and mercy, led them into conflict with Jesus. He did not dispute their orthodoxy, but the proud and unloving way in which they upheld it. The influence of the Pharisees was out of all proportion to their numbers, which were seldom large. It was the Pharisees who laid down the lines along which Judaism developed after the destruction of Jerusalem in AD 70. They ensured a continued emphasis on individual piety and strict ethical standards, as well as their better-known rigid legalism. They were respected, if not loved, by other Jews.

■ **The Sadducees.** The Sadducees were the other main party at the time of Jesus, though they were already declining in influence. They were drawn largely from the rich land-owning class who in earlier days, by shrewd manipulation of political advantage, had secured a dominant position. They still controlled a roughly equal proportion of the seats in the Sanhedrin (the Jewish supreme council) with the Pharisees (Acts 23:6-10). Many of the chief priests were Sadducees, or worked closely with them. Their religious position was conservative, to the extent of refusing to accept any revelation beyond the Five Books of Moses (Genesis to Deuteronomy). They thus rejected more recent religious ideas, such as the belief in immortality, resurrection, angels and demons, which were fostered by the Pharisees (Mark 12:18; Acts 23:8). As an aristocratic minority, they enjoyed little popular support.

■ **The Essenes.** This rather shadowy 'party' has come dramatically to light with the discovery of the Dead Sea Scrolls since 1947. These scrolls are from the library of the *Qumran Community*, a monastic sect living in isolation in the barren desert near the shores of the Dead Sea. Although this sect cannot firmly be identified as Essenes, it was certainly very similar. The sect was founded by the otherwise unknown 'Teacher of Righteousness', probably about 165 BC, and survived until AD 68, when it was destroyed in the Jewish revolt. They regarded themselves as the true people of God, and all others, including the Jewish leaders at Jerusalem, as his enemies. They were the 'Sons of Light', and they lived for the day when in the final battle against the 'Sons of Darkness' they would be given the victory and dominion which was their due.

Meanwhile they kept themselves to themselves, occupied in the diligent study of the

The ruins of Qumran, the 'monastery' of an ascetic community near the Dead Sea. The Dead Sea Scrolls, their library, were hidden in caves (out of the picture on the right, see page 69) because of the threat of Roman invasion, and dramatically rediscovered in 1947.

scriptures, bound by a strict monastic discipline, loving one another and hating all those outside. They produced elaborate biblical commentaries, applying every phrase of the Old Testament passages to their own situation and expectations. They looked forward to the coming of two Messiahs, of Aaron (priestly) and of Israel (royal) – or possibly one Messiah combining both roles. The importance of the Qumran documents is not so much for the sect in itself, but that they give evidence of an ascetic, apocalyptic strain in Judaism, far removed from the Jerusalem establishment, which may well have been much more widespread than this single isolated group. If before 1947 we were tempted to think of Pharisees and Sadducees as constituting 'the Jews', we must now recognize that the situation was not so simple.

■ **The Zealots.** While Pharisees and Sadducees tried to make the best of Roman rule, and the men of Qumran dreamed of the mighty intervention of God to deliver them, many Jews sought salvation more actively. The Zealots, as they later came to be called, were the freedom fighters, the revolutionaries of the Jewish people. It was they who eventually sparked off the great rebellion which led to the Roman destruction of Jerusalem in AD 70. By the time of Jesus abortive revolts had already occurred (Acts 5:36-37; and ➤➤

possibly Barabbas), and the people were ripe for revolutionary propaganda. Intensely patriotic, the Zealots founded their appeal on the belief that subjection to Rome was treason to God, the true King of Israel. At least one of the apostles was a former Zealot.

■ **The apocalyptic movement.** In this atmosphere the type of literature known as the 'apocalypse' (revelation) flourished. Many apocalypses were written in Palestine from the 2nd century BC onwards. They are marked by a strong dualism: good and evil, God and Satan, light and darkness, are irreconcilably opposed and on a collision course. The present world-order is under the control of the forces of evil, but the final battle is about to be fought, and then the tables will be turned. God will crush all opposition, destroy all evil for ever, and create a new blessed order, in which his faithful people will be released from their oppression and reign in glory.

Herod's Temple

A reconstruction at the Bible Museum, Amsterdam; the style and decoration are of course guessed. See too the article on page 253.

1 Porticos
2 Court of the Gentiles
3 'Wall of Partition' (forbidding entry to non-Jews; see picture on page 567)
4 ?Beautiful Gate
5 Court of the Women
6 Court of Israel
7 Court of the Priests
8 Altar
9 Bronze laver
10 The Holy Place (with Holy of Holies)

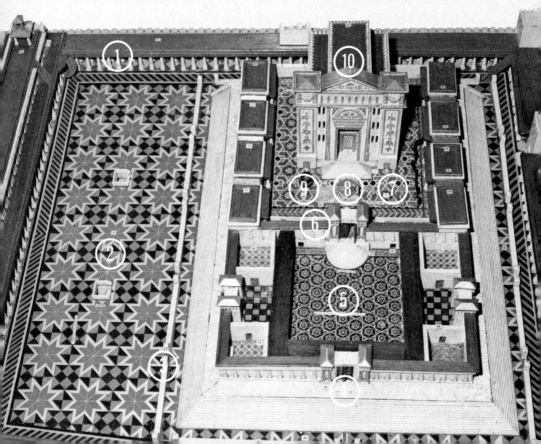

This message is conveyed in often extra-ordinary visions, with symbolic numbers, and a careful calculation of dates and times, usually in cryptic form. It is a message of hope for a people near despair, a triumphant appeal to the sovereignty of the one true God, the God of Israel. The New Testament book of Revelation is in many ways a typical apocalypse (though written from a Christian standpoint), except that its author uses his own name, whereas Jewish apocalyptists attributed their visions to such famous Old Testament figures as Enoch, Moses, Elijah, or Ezra. Another important difference is that Jewish apocalyptists wrote past history as if it were prophecy, whereas Revelation concentrates on the future.

■ **Messianic hopes.** The extravagant visions of the apocalypses were only one among the many hopes currently cherished by the Jews. Many messianic figures from the Old Testament had taken firm root in popular expectation: the prophet like Moses (Deuteronomy 18:15-19); the returning Elijah (Malachi 4:5-6); but above all the Son of David, a great king and warrior, whose mission it would be to bring victory, peace, and glory to Israel. Some saw a place for the Gentiles in this hope, others were exclusively nationalistic. Some thought of spiritual restoration, most of victory over the Romans. To utter the word 'Messiah' (Greek, 'Christ') would inevitably stir up hopes of political independence, so it is no wonder that Jesus was cautious in letting others call him 'Christ'. He came to a people who, if they were not agreed quite *what* they were hoping for, were united in eagerly 'looking for the consolation of Israel' (Luke 2:25). But none expected it to come by way of a cross.

■ **'The Dispersion'.** So far we have thought only of the Jews in Palestine. But the Christian church soon spread outside Palestine, and there, too, its first contacts were with Jews. At least since the exile in the 6th century BC Jews had begun to scatter around the world of the Middle East and the eastern Mediterranean, so that by the 1st century AD there were a million Jews in Egypt alone. In Alexandria Jews made up a considerable part of the population, and in most of the main cities a Jewish colony, with its own synagogue (or at least a place for prayer, Acts 16:13), was to be found. These are the Jews of the Dispersion (Greek, *Diaspora*), sometimes referred to, a little inaccurately, as the Hellenistic Jews.

'Hellenism', the wave of Greek culture and ideas which had rolled over the Mediterranean world and far beyond with the conquests of Alexander the Great, was still the dominant strand in the culture of the Roman Empire, and these dispersed Jews, away from the more conservative atmosphere of Palestine, adapted more readily to the Greek way of life. Not that they abandoned their distinctive religion and culture, and ceased to be Jews; but they were more willing to learn from and enter into dialogue with Greek ideas. Many of the later Jewish writings, particularly those from Alexandria (e.g. the Wisdom of Solomon, or the writings of Philo) are deeply influenced by Greek philosophy. Apollos, the learned Jew from Alexandria (Acts 18:24), no doubt belonged to this school, before his gradual conversion to Christ.

■ **Proselytes.** The Jews are often unjustly charged with a rigid exclusivism. In fact, particularly among the Dispersion, they recognized their mission to the Gentiles, and there was a sincere attempt to win converts. To accept the Jewish religion was no light matter for a Gentile. He must accept circumcision and baptism, and agree to keep the whole law of Moses, including such ritual prescriptions as the sabbath and the laws about unclean food. He must in fact renounce his own nationality. There were a considerable number who took this drastic step, and it is to them that the term 'proselyte' applies.

Many more were attracted by the monotheistic faith and the strict morality of Judaism in contrast with the decadent polytheism of Rome. They were prepared to identify themselves with the faith and ideals of the Jews, but stopped short of the proselyte's full commitment. These fellow-travellers, many of them rich and influential officials, are known in the New Testament as 'those who fear God' or 'the devout' (Acts 13:26, 43, 50; 17:4).

■ **The Samaritans.** The Samaritans were descendants of the surviving Israelites of the northern kingdom who intermarried with the newly imported alien population after the fall of Samaria in 722 BC. They never effectively made common cause with Judah, and in the time of Nehemiah the rift was clearly irreparable. The building of the Samaritan temple on Mt Gerizim, overlooking Shechem (John 4:20), set the seal on the Jewish rejection of this heretical sect. It was the Jewish king Hyrcanus who destroyed the Samaritan temple in 128 BC. Yet the Samaritans worshipped God, as the Jews did. Their authority was the Five Books of Moses (Genesis to Deuteronomy); but not the rest of the Old Testament), hardly altered from the Jewish version. Like many of the Jews, they awaited ➤➤

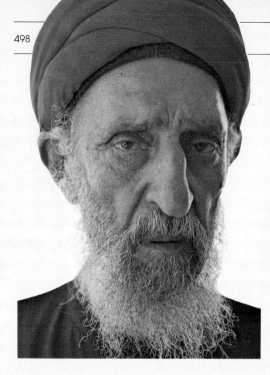

The Samaritan High Priest is leader of the small community of Samaritans surviving today.

the coming of a prophet like Moses. Jewish hatred and disdain for the Samaritans sprang more from historical and racial considerations than from any fundamental difference of religion.

GREEK AND ROMAN RELIGION

The old classical religion of the Greeks, with its pantheon of gods and goddesses who loved, quarrelled and fought like men and women, had become effectively fused with the similar polytheism of Rome. It was preserved and officially fostered as part of Greek and Roman culture. Most Greeks and Romans would still give a formal assent to the old beliefs, and take part in the rituals, but the heart had gone out of them.

Further east in the Empire these gods were associated with local deities, sometimes producing absurd results, such as the identification of the earthy fertility-goddess of Ephesus with the severely chaste Artemis of the Greeks (Roman Diana; Acts 19:24ff.). The Lycaonian worship of Zeus and Hermes (Roman Jupiter and Mercury; Acts 14:11ff.) was probably a similar dignifying of a local cult with the classical Greek names.

It was from the East that new religious ideas came. One such was the worship of the emperor. This was not officially encouraged

by the Roman emperors until Domitian (AD 81-96) insisted on being addressed as 'Lord and God'. But it was freely practised in the East by their grateful (or flattering) subjects throughout the New Testament period. Even before the birth of Christ, Herod the Great had renamed the city of Samaria 'Sebaste', in honour of Augustus (Greek, *Sebastos,* 'The one to be worshipped'), and built in it a temple of Augustus.

Those who wanted a more personal and emotional faith gravitated to the mystery religions. The Greek mysteries – those of Eleusis, or the Orphic cult – had long been known in the West, but the spread of the Empire brought to light similar cults from Egypt (Isis and Osiris/Serapis), Persia (Mithras), and elsewhere in the East. Although these religions differed in detail, they shared the element of personal commitment by initiation into what amounted to a secret society, whose rites were never divulged to an outsider. The rites often centred on a mythology of the death and resurrection of the god (Persephone, Orpheus, Osiris, and the rest), which was re-enacted in a drama in which all participated. They inspired a spirit of warm, personal devotion, far removed from the cold intellectualism of the official state religion.

Also from the East came the fascination of astrology (still very much with us today), divination, magic, demon-worship, and other occult practices, all trying to bring a reality and a practical efficacy into religion.

About the time the New Testament letters were being written there began to develop a number of sects which later (in the 2nd century) came under the general heading of 'Gnosticism'. They varied considerably in detail, but shared the basic belief that 'matter' was evil and spirit was good. It followed that God could not have created the world out of matter, nor could his Son have become incarnate in it. So they envisaged a whole range of subordinate beings between God and the world. Humanity shares in the evil of the material world, but they also (or some of them) contain a divine spark which can be set free and thus redeemed. In order to be redeemed they need to have knowledge (Greek *gnosis*) of their heavenly origin. These views were expressed in fantastic myths and made known to initiates in sects like those of the mystery religions.

The world was, as Paul put it, '*very* religious' (Acts 17:22). People wanted a faith worth following, not an empty mythology. It was a world searching for God, eagerly trying every avenue which might lead to a real, practical, satisfying religion.

Matthew is formal and stately. Mark is bustling with life; full of action. Matthew collects Jesus' sayings. Mark concentrates on the marvellous things Jesus did, and the places he went to.

This is the shortest of the Gospels, and probably the first to be written (AD 65-70 or even earlier). There is a strong early tradition that John Mark wrote it in Rome, setting down Jesus' story as he had heard it direct from the apostle Peter. This would certainly account for the Gospel's extraordinary vividness. And Mark often explains Jewish customs, so he obviously had non-Jewish readers in mind.

He tells the story roughly in the order things happened – moving swiftly through from Jesus' baptism to the critical events of the cross and resurrection. Within this framework the material tends to be grouped by subject. Only four paragraphs in these 16 chapters are unique to Mark. All the rest appears again in either Matthew or Luke, or both. Yet to lose Mark would be to lose something beyond price. In Mark we see Jesus in action. And as we watch, the things he does convince us that he is the Son of God himself.

The writer

The name 'John Mark' occurs often in Acts and the epistles ('John' the Jewish name, 'Mark' the Latin). His mother had a house in Jerusalem where the early church met (Acts 12:12). And he was cousin to Paul's companion, Barnabas. Mark blotted his copybook with Paul by going home half-way through the first missionary tour. But Barnabas gave him a second chance, and he later won the love and respect of Paul and of Peter. He was a real comfort to Paul in prison (Colossians 4). And Peter, whose companion he became, loved him as his own son (1 Peter 5:13).

1:1-13
THE GOOD NEWS OF JESUS

1:1-8 John the Baptist
See also Matthew 3:1-12; Luke 3:2-22, and map. Mark passes over Jesus' birth. For him the good news begins with John, the voice Isaiah had predicted, crying out from the desert, urging the nation to make ready for God's coming. The rest of his account will show that Jesus is the Messiah – the one whose coming John announced – and Son of God.

Verses 2-3: Mark, like Matthew, combines Old Testament references: Exodus 23:20; Malachi 3:1; Isaiah 40:3.

Verse 8: water is a symbol. It can only clean the outside. The Holy Spirit can clean heart and mind and will.

The prophet from the desert: the 'wilderness' or desert-country around Jericho and south of Jerusalem is rough and uninviting. Scarcely anything grows: it is empty of human habitation, occupied only by wild animals. No doubt the very loneliness of the place, and the freedom from distraction, made it the ideal training-ground for John. Paul, too, was prepared for his mission during a time in the desert. There seems to be something in the stark simplicity of desert life which puts men – some men at least – in close touch with God. In the harsh sunlight there is only black or white, no shades of grey. It afforded John no other luxuries – only the simplest of food and rough clothing. His camel-hair tunic and leather belt may have been worn in conscious imitation of Elijah (see 2 Kings 1:8 and the prophecy in Malachi 4:5). He was certainly recognized instantly as a prophet. He not only looked the part, he possessed the prophet's cast-iron assurance that he had a God-given message to proclaim. The people flocked from far and wide to hear him, probably gathering beside the Jordan

The Jordan river, where John baptized, winds from the Lake of Galilee, well below sea level, down through the semi-tropical rift-valley to the Dead Sea.

near Jericho, close to the place where Joshua had crossed into the promised land so many centuries before.

1:9-13 Jesus' baptism and temptation

See on Matthew 3-4; Luke 3:21; 4:1-13. Mark gives only a brief résumé.

1:14—9:50
JESUS IN GALILEE

The Roman province of Galilee, under Herod's jurisdiction, lay to the west of the Sea of Galilee. We tend to think of it as a remote country district. But in Christ's day the region was prosperous and densely populated, criss-crossed by Roman military roads and ancient trade routes – north, south, east and west. The fresh-water Lake of Galilee – 13 miles/ 21 km long, 7 miles/11 km wide, sunk in the deep trough of the Jordan rift valley over 600 feet/180 metres below sea-level – is the focal point in Jesus' travels. It divided Herod's territory from that of his half-brother Philip, to the east. Most of the apostles came from the towns around the lake-shore which enjoyed a sub-tropical climate. Capernaum was Jesus' base. Tiberias, 10 miles/16 km away, was a spa town famous for its hot baths. Many of the sick people Jesus healed must have come to the area for the mineral waters at Tiberias. On the hill behind the town was Herod's splendid summer palace. The lake is ringed round with hills – brown and barren on the east; in those days green, fertile, wooded on the west. Over the tops, and funnelling down through them, races the wind that can whip the lake into a sudden fury of storm. North, the snow-capped summit of Mt Hermon dominates the skyline – the mount of the transfiguration. In Jesus' day palms, olives, figs and vines grew on the hillsides round the lake. And the little towns and villages on its western shore were thriving centres of industry – fish pickled for export; boat-building; dye-works; potteries. John the Baptist lived an ascetic life in the desert. By contrast, Jesus chose to be in the thick of things, in Galilee, one of the busiest, most cosmopolitan regions of Palestine.

1:14-20 Jesus calls his first disciples

John's voice is silenced. Jesus travels north again, and begins his own public proclamation of God's good news. By the Lake of Galilee he calls his first disciples – all of them fishermen. (John 1:35-42 fills in the background.)

1:21-45 Jesus begins to teach and heal

From now on Capernaum is Jesus' headquarters. His teaching in the synagogue and his handling of the possessed man both convey an extra-ordinary *authority*.

Again and again, as in the case of the leper here, Mark stresses Jesus' insistence on *secrecy*. The people were expecting the Messiah to be a political leader. News of Jesus' amazing powers, which marked him out as the Messiah, could easily have sparked off a rising against the Roman occupation. It was imperative the miracles should be accompanied by teaching to explain the kind of 'kingdom' Jesus had come to inaugurate, and the Messiah's real mission.

Verse 32: at sunset the sabbath was over, and restrictions on movement no longer applied.

Verse 44: see Leviticus 14:1-32. In the Bible, the term 'leprosy' covers a variety of skin diseases.

At Capernaum the local Roman centurion had contributed to the building of the synagogue. The ruins of the Capernaum synagogue pictured here (probably built two or three centuries later) show a combination of Roman style and traditional Jewish symbols.

2:1-12 The paralytic walks

It is easy enough simply to tell a man his sins are forgiven. But by healing him Jesus visibly demonstrates his power in both physical and spiritual realms. When he says the word, something really happens.

Verse 4: the house would have an outside staircase leading to a flat roof, giving extra living-space. The roof would be made of tiles or lath and plaster – not difficult to break through.

Verse 11: ordinary people slept on the floor on a mat or bedding which could be rolled up in the daytime.

2:13-22 Levi (Matthew) becomes a disciple; the question of fasting

See on Matthew 9:9-17; Luke 5:27-39.

Scribes, Pharisees (16): see page 494.

Fishing in the Lake of Galilee

GEORGE CANSDALE

Situated towards the northern end of the rift valley, the Lake of Galilee is the world's lowest fresh-water lake, with a surface some 680 feet/207 m below sea level, and a maximum depth of 150 feet/45 m. Roughly 13 x 7 miles/20 x 11 km, it has an area of 90 square miles. For some periods Israel had control over the whole lake and it is strange that the Old Testament mentions it only three times, in each case as marking a boundary.

Although the importance of fishing is shown by the number of technical Hebrew words used by many writers it is only in the New Testament that Chinnereth, or Gennesereth, is pictured as a rich fishing lake. It is the scene of much of the Gospel narrative, with Christ's ministry based on towns around the north of the lake. At least seven of the disciples were fishermen from the lake, which partly accounts for the

emphasis on fishing. Bethsaida, one of the cities that rejected Christ, and the home of Peter, Andrew and Philip, means a 'place of nets' or 'fishery'.

Except for two fish introduced since then, which are still caught only in small numbers, the lake fish today are those that Peter and his comrades knew. Although there are some 25 native species, only a few are important. The best known is the Cichlid, *Tilapia*, known generally as 'St Peter's fish'. It is likely that this was the principal catch in biblical times. There is no way of knowing how many were caught but today, using intensive methods under scientific control, the annual yield of *Tilapia* is about 300 tons, and of other kinds some 1,000 tons. Of this total, lake sardines *(Acanthobrama terrae sanctae)* make up 800 tons, all taken by a sophisticated modern method of night fishing.

Higher up the Jordan Valley, and about 900 feet/275 m above Chinnereth, is the former Lake Huleh, referred to as the 'waters of Merom' in Joshua 11:5. At that time it was an open lake but centuries of silting, resulting from bad farming in the surrounding hills, gradually reduced it to a series of swamps and pools which continued to be a rich fishing-ground until the whole area was reclaimed for farming in the 1950s.

Although the Old Testament has little to say about fish and fishing, the prophetic books are rich in terms from which it is possible to learn something of the methods used. Hebrew *resheth* is a general word for net and the context in Ezekiel 32:3 suggests it was used as a cast net, thrown to take a particular shoal or fish. *Cherem* is a much larger net, perhaps similar to the seine net commonly used today (see under Greek *sagene* below). Hebrew *makmor* and *mikmar* are also large nets in Isaiah 19:8 and in Habakkuk 1:15-16 variously translated 'net', 'drag', 'seine', 'trawl' in the different Bible versions. This same net was also set in the desert to catch the Arabian Oryx.

The Greek terms in the Gospels are mostly used literally. *Diktuon* could well be a general word for net: e.g. Matthew 4:20, '(Peter and Andrew) left their nets and followed him'. They had just been throwing their cast nets and it must be assumed that, as professional fishermen, they would own a set of the standard types. This general use is probably seen also in the references to washing and mending their nets. Today this work is made much easier and lighter by the universal use of artificial drip-dry filaments. It also seems that *diktuon* could have a more specific meaning, as what is today called a gill net.

The net which Peter and Andrew were casting is mentioned only in this incident. The word is Greek *amphiblestron* and is usually taken as equivalent to the cast net still used in some tropical countries, especially in shallow waters and coastal lagoons. It is circular, with small weights set at regular intervals around the perimeter, and is thrown with a spinning motion to fall spread and flat on the water. The weights sink quickly to the bottom and as the cord attached to the centre is pulled the perimeter is drawn in, entangling in the mesh any fish that have been covered. It is still sometimes cast on the Lake of Galilee simply to demonstrate the ancient method.

Greek *sagene* occurs only once, in Matthew 13:47, where the kingdom of heaven is compared to a drag net. This is now generally thought to be a seine, which can be several hundred yards long. Such a net catches all sorts and sizes of fish, which are then sorted into edible and inedible in the way the parable describes.

2:23 – 3:6 The purpose of the sabbath; opposition

See also Matthew 12:1-14; Luke 6:1-11. Jewish interpretation of the fourth commandment (Exodus 20:8-11; 34:21) had hedged it about with so many petty rules and restrictions that its primary purpose was lost. The day of rest was intended for man's physical and spiritual good, not to deny him food and help. It is a day for doing good – and not only in an emergency.

2:25-26: see 1 Samuel 21:1-6. The loaves David took were those the priests placed each week on the altar.

Herodians (3:6): supporters of Herod Antipas, see page 540. They collaborated with the Romans, and were therefore normally abhorrent to the scrupulous Pharisees.

3:7-19 The Twelve

Crowds flock to Jesus from the south (Judea, Jerusalem, Idumaea); from the east across the Jordan; and from Tyre and Sidon, the coastal towns in the north-west. See map.

Jesus chose an inner circle of 12 disciples who became founder-members of the new kingdom – the counterparts of Jacob's 12 sons, who gave their names to the tribes of Israel. Three – Peter, James and John – were specially close to him. Four of the Twelve, all from Galilee, were partners in a fishing business (Peter and his brother Andrew; James and his brother John). One (Matthew/Levi, who may have been the brother of James son of Alphaeus) was a tax collector, serving the Romans. Simon, at the other end of the scale, belonged to an extremist guerila group (the Zealots) working to overthrow the occupation. We know little of the others. The full list also appears in Matthew 10:2-4 and Luke 6:12-16. The 'Thaddaeus' of Matthew and Mark seems to be the same as 'Judas son of James' (Luke, Acts 1:13). Bartholomew is often identified with the Nathanael of John 1. They were certainly a very mixed bunch of men.

The parable of the soils (or the sower) is illustrated in this scene from Galilee, with good soil, rocky ground, thorns, and wheat bearing grain.

Here on the east side of the Lake of Galilee the Gadarene swine rushed into the lake. In the distance is the place where Jesus fed the crowd of 5,000.

Verse 12: see on 1:21-45

3:20-35 Suspicion and accusation

See on Matthew 12:15-37 and 49.

4:1-34 Jesus teaches in parables

See on Matthew 13:1-52.
> Verses 1-25: the seed and the soils.
> Verses 26-29: the wheat and the weeds.
> Verses 30-32: the mustard-seed.

Verse 12: in Jewish idiom, result is often expressed as if it were intention. This verse refers to the 'consequence', not the 'purpose' of Christ's teaching. It is clear from verses 22-23 that the reason for wrapping up the meaning is to encourage the listener to search it out for himself.

4:35-41 Jesus calms the great storm

Sudden storms sometimes whip the Lake of Galilee into fury (see page 500). Jesus has power to control the elements.

5:1-20 Across the lake; the man possessed by demons

See also Matthew 8:28-34; Luke 8:26-39. The man is a pitiful sight – a fragmented personality at the mercy of a hundred conflicting impulses; totally incapable of a normal life. Is any greater contrast imaginable than the description of 2-5 and verse 15? Jesus had power not only over nature but also over human nature; and not only over human nature but over the spiritual forces of evil.

Region of the Gerasenes (1): the general area south-east of the lake. At only one point on the eastern bank is there a steep slope (13).

Decapolis (20): 'Ten Towns'; ten free Greek cities.

5:21-43 Jairus' daughter restored to life; the woman with the haemorrhage

See also Matthew 9:18-26; Luke 8:40-56.

The woman tries not to advertise her presence, because the haemorrhage makes her polluted and untouchable to her fellow Jews. There is no magic about Jesus' clothes. He knows the difference between the casual contact of the crowd and someone reaching out in need. The incident must have encouraged Jairus. The fact that he came to Jesus shows that not all religious leaders were against him.

Verse 39: this was not just a coma – the child really was dead. Everyone knew it (40). Jesus' words describe death as God sees it – a sleep from which we wake to a new day.

6:1-13 In and around Nazareth; the Twelve sent out

Verses 1-6: in Jesus' home town it is not a case of 'local boy makes good' but 'who does this jumped-up carpenter think he is?' It was not in line with Jesus' purpose to make a display of his powers in order to convince sceptics (see Matthew 4:6-7).

Verses 7-13: see on Matthew 9:35-10:42.

Verse 3: see on Matthew 12:49. James later became the leader of the church in Jerusalem (Acts 15:13). Judas wrote the Epistle of Jude.

Five loaves and two small fish. These fish from the Lake of Galilee are known as St Peter's Fish, as their large mouths, in which they carry their eggs, could hold a coin (see Matthew 17:27). The fish in the story of the feeding of the 5,000 may have been pickled rather than fresh.

6:14-29 Herod and John the Baptist

Guilt and superstition make Herod think Jesus is John come to life again. Herod had divorced his own wife to marry Herodias, wife of his half-brother Philip. John had denounced this as incest (Leviticus 18:16; 20:21), and been imprisoned for his pains. According to Josephus his prison was the fortress of Machaerus in the far south, east of the Dead Sea. But Herodias wanted to still the preacher's tongue permanently.

6:30-44 5,000 miraculously fed

See also Matthew 14:13-21; Luke 9:10b-17; John 6:5-14. John's death casts a shadow. Jesus is desperately tired and hard-pressed.

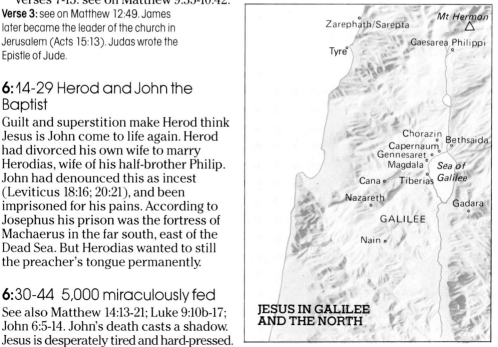

Zarephath/Sarepta
Mt Hermon △
Tyre
Caesarea Philippi
Chorazin
Capernaum   Bethsaida
Gennesaret
Magdala   Sea of
Cana   Tiberias   Galilee
Nazareth
Gadara
GALILEE
Nain

JESUS IN GALILEE AND THE NORTH

Yet instead of being annoyed or irritable with the pursuing crowds, his heart goes out to them.

Verse 37: needless to say they did not have this kind of money: the denarius 'silver coin' was a working man's wage for the day – this would be over six months' wages.

6:45-56 Jesus walks on the lake

It was some time between 3 a.m. and 6 a.m. Again it is the disciples' need that calls out Jesus' love. And again he demonstrates his supreme power over creation: he is Lord of wind and water.

Fringe/edge (56): the blue-tasselled border of his cloak. See page 90.

7:1-23 The Pharisees and their traditions

See on Matthew 15:1-20. Mark adds an explanatory note for non-Jewish readers (3-4). The Pharisees were concerned not with hygiene but with religious 'cleanness'. Man's real problem is not dirty hands but a polluted heart, which no amount of washing can clean. Jesus exposes their wrong thinking.

Sunrise over Mt Hermon, probable site of the transfiguration of Jesus.

7:24-37 The Greek woman's daughter; the deaf mute

Verses 24-30: see on Matthew 15:21-28.

Verses 31-37: the man's speech defect, as so often, was the result of his deafness. Saliva was popularly thought to have healing power.

8:1-21 4,000 fed; the demand for a sign; the 'yeast' of the Pharisees

Verses 1-9; see on Matthew 15:29-39. Dalmanutha is not known.

Verses 11-21: see on Matthew 16:1-12. The disciples lack spiritual discernment. They are so taken up with the bread-supply that they cannot see that Jesus is warning them against the ever-present danger of religious hypocrisy (see Luke 12:1) and materialism (the prime concern of the pro-Herod faction).

8:22-26 A blind man regains his sight

Jesus once again guards against publicity – see on 1:21-45.

8:27—9:1 'Who do men say I am?'; Jesus predicts his death

See on Matthew 16:13-28. Here and elsewhere Mark records in full incidents which show Peter's failings, but plays down the credit side – understandable if the information came from Peter himself. This episode is a pivotal point in the story. From now on, Jesus stresses the suffering which lies ahead.

Caesarea Philippi (27): 25 miles/40 km north of the Lake of Galilee. See map.
9:1: see on Matthew 10:23.

9:2-13 The disciples see Jesus transfigured

See also Matthew 17:1-13; Luke 9:28-36. The apostles are sure now that Jesus is the Messiah. This special glimpse of his glory, given to the inner three, must have been tremendously reassuring through all that lay ahead. Moses (Israel's great law-

Roman Soldiers in the New Testament

HAROLD ROWDON

Roman soldiers had many duties besides active service in military conquest. They policed the streets when there was danger of rioting – so there was always a force stationed in Jerusalem. This was heavily reinforced during the Jewish festivals, when huge crowds of excitable people filled the city to overflowing. Soldiers also stood guard on prisoners, acting as escort to those who were being moved. They were always present at the execution of criminals, both to prevent a last-minute rescue and to carry out the actual execution.

Centurions were officers in charge of 100 men. Usually they had risen from the ranks and were chosen for their courage and reliability. Several centurions are mentioned in the Gospels and Acts, two by name. All appear in a favourable light on account of their regard for the Jews, their fairmindedness and the positive response of some of them to Christ.

Jesus healed the servant of a centurion stationed at Capernaum (Matthew 8:5-13; Luke 7:1-10). The local Jewish leaders regarded him as a friend of the Jews – as well they might, since he had built a synagogue for them. The centurion in charge of the soldiers who crucified Jesus was so impressed by what he saw and heard that he concluded Jesus was both innocent and divine (Matthew 27:54; Mark 15:39, 44ff.; Luke 23:47). In Acts 10 we read of *Cornelius*, the God-fearing centurion who was converted through the preaching of Peter. Several unnamed centurions were involved in the arrest and imprisonment of Paul (Acts 21:31ff.; 22:25; 23:17, 23; 24:23). *Julius* was the centurion in charge of Paul and other prisoners sent to Rome (Acts 27:1). He treated Paul kindly (verse 3), though he paid more attention to the captain and the owner of the ship than to Paul's advice (verses 9-11).

Six 'centuries' of men formed a cohort, which was commanded by a tribune (Acts 21:31). *Claudius Lysias* was the tribune in charge of the force keeping order in the outer courts of the temple when the Jews rioted and Paul was arrested (Acts 21:26ff.; 23:17ff.). Cohorts were often named. The *Italian Cohort* (Acts 10:1) was probably recruited in Italy. The *Augustan Cohort* was named in honour of Augustus, first emperor of Rome.

Ten cohorts formed a legion which was commanded by a legate. On paper, at least, its strength was 6,000 men.

A Roman soldier: a relief at the Damascus Museum.

giver) and Elijah (the first great prophet) converse with Jesus about his coming death (Luke 9:31).

Verse 2: the mountain is believed to be 9,000 foot/2,700 m Mt Hermon as it is only 12 miles/19 km north-east of Caesarea Philippi. The tradition that it was Mt Tabor does not fit the geography so well. Peter wants to prolong the present moment. Perhaps Moses and Elijah will stay if they make shelters for them, like the tent (tabernacle) where God was present in the old days, before the temple was built. The glory of all he saw that day imprinted itself indelibly on Peter's memory (2 Peter 1:16-18).

Verse 13: 'Elijah', i.e. John the Baptist (see Matthew 17:13). Malachi (4:5) had predicted a reappearance of Elijah to announce the day of God's coming.

9:14-29 The epileptic boy
See also Matthew 17:14-19; Luke 9:37-42. The disciples fail because of their lack of faith (see Matthew 17:19-20). Yet Jesus will accept even a grain of faith in him (24). He does not wait to heal the child until the father's faith is greater.

9:30-50 Status and Christian responsibility
See on Matthew 18. No one who is preoccupied with selfish ambition can become a 'great' Christian. It has to be other people first, self last. Today we lay great stress on self-fulfilment and the full development of personality. Jesus puts this in perspective. It is better deliberately to limit that fulfilment, to handicap ourselves in this life (44-45) than miss God's kingdom altogether.

Verses 43-48: Jesus draws his terrible picture of hell from Jerusalem's permanently smouldering refuse-tip in the valley of Hinnom (Gehenna), and the dead bodies gradually eaten away by worms.

Verse 49: 'Salted with fire'—i.e. purified in the 'refinery' of suffering (see Good News Bible).

10
ON THE WAY TO JERUSALEM

10:1-12 Divorce
See on Matthew 19:1-15.

10:13-16 Jesus blesses the children
To enter God's kingdom we must all become, not childish, but childlike – receiving him with humble, loving trust (15).

10:17-31 The positive disadvantage of wealth
See on Matthew 19:16-30; Luke 18:18-30. This incident does not imply that all Christ's followers must become penniless. He is speaking to one man, not to all, and in this case the man's possessions kept him from becoming a disciple. Anything that takes first place – God's place – in our lives must go. So Jesus tells him, 'Go, sell' *and* 'Come, follow me'.

10:32-45 Jesus again predicts his death; the disciples bicker over their future status
See on Matthew 20:17-34.

10:46-52 Blind Bartimaeus
See also Matthew 20:29-34 (where there are two men); Luke 18:35-43. Only Mark tells us the beggar's name. As he afterwards joined the company of Jesus' followers, Peter presumably came to know him.

11 – 13
JESUS IN JERUSALEM

11:1-11 The triumphant entry
See introduction to Matthew 21; and see on Luke 19:28-44.

11:12-26 The fig-tree; the purging of the temple
See on Matthew 21:18-22 and 12-17.

11:27 — 12:12 The religious leaders question Jesus' authority; the parable of the vineyard

See on Matthew 21:23-46.

12:13-44 Test questions; Jesus in the temple

See also Matthew 22:15-46; Luke 20:19–21:4. Luke 20:19-20 gives the background to these questions.

Verses 13-17: there was little love lost between the strictly religious Pharisees and the opportunist Herodians. But they join forces to try to trap Jesus into a treasonable statement.

Verses 18-27: the blinkered Sadducees try to ridicule the idea of resurrection with an absurd case of Levirate marriage (see page 226). But the laugh is on them, because there *is* a resurrection – to a life where there is no sexual union or procreation because there is no death.

Verses 28-34: the third question is a genuine one. With 613 commandments to choose from, Jesus replies in the words of Israel's creed (the Shema; Deuteronomy 6:4-5) and Leviticus 19:18. If the Pharisees hoped for an unorthodox reply (Matthew 22:34-35) they were disappointed. The astonishing wisdom of Jesus silences his opponents – but *he*

has not finished with *them* (35-40).

In strong contrast to the self-advertisement of the men of religion comes the little incident in verses 41-44. What counts with God is not the size of the cheque, but the amount of love and self-sacrifice it represents.

13 Judgement on Jerusalem: Jesus speaks about his return

See on Matthew 24. See also Luke 21 and 17:22ff.

14 — 16
JESUS' DEATH AND RESURRECTION

14:1-11 The plot against his life; the costly flask of perfume; betrayal

See also Matthew 26:6-13; John 12:1-8. Jesus' public ministry is at an end. As the Passover festival approaches (see on Matthew 26) events move swiftly to a climax. Against a dark backcloth of hatred and treachery shines the story of one woman's love for the Lord (3-9). Perhaps intuitively sensing the tragedy ahead, Mary (see John 12:3) pours out the precious perfumed oil in a lavish, extravagant gesture of affection. (A working man earned one denarius/'silver coin' a day. This luxury import was

An alabaster flask, like Mary's, inscribed 'cinnamon'; Hellenistic, from Egypt.

worth nearly a year's wages.) John (12:1-8) places the event some days earlier and tells us the unpleasant truth about Judas' embezzlement of the funds. In Luke 7:36-50 the occasion is similar, but the woman concerned different.

14:12-25 The Last Supper

See on Matthew 26:14-29.

14:26-52 Gethsemane; Jesus is arrested

See on Matthew 26:30-56. There seems little point in the mention of the young man (51-62) unless this is Mark himself.

14:53 — 15:15 The Jewish trial; Peter denies Jesus; the Roman trial

Pilate

HAROLD ROWDON

In 1961 a stone slab was discovered at Caesarea bearing the name Pontius Pilatus. This is one of the few pieces of evidence outside the Bible for the life and work of this unhappy man. Tacitus, the Roman writer, does refer to the execution of Jesus by Pilate, and two Jewish writers, Josephus and Philo, relate several incidents. Apart from this, we have only the biblical evidence. In addition to the accounts given by the writers of the Gospels, there are brief references to him in Acts 3:13; 4:27; 13:28; 1 Timothy 6:13.

Pilate was evidently a middle-class Roman with military and administrative experience who in AD 26 was appointed to the office of procurator of Judea. As procurator (or governor) he possessed very wide powers, especially in military and financial matters. He appointed the high priest and controlled the temple funds.

Philo describes Pilate as a harsh, spiteful and brutal man. According to Josephus, in one of his historical works, Pilate antagonized the Jews almost as soon as he was appointed. He allowed the Roman troops to bring their regimental standards into Jerusalem. These contained representations of the emperor, and the Jews were furious because they felt that the holy city had been desecrated by these idolatrous symbols. Pilate bowed to the storm and ordered the removal of the standards.

On another occasion, according to Philo, the Jews took violent objection to some golden shields which Pilate had dedicated in his residence in Jerusalem. This time Pilate refused to remove them, but the Jews appealed to the Emperor Tiberius, who ordered them to be removed to Caesarea, Pilate's headquarters.

Josephus records an incident arising from Pilate's plan to use money from the temple treasury to finance the building of an aqueduct to bring water from a spring 25 miles away into Jerusalem. Mass protests were met by force, and many Jews died. This may be the incident referred to in Luke 13:1.

Each of the Gospels records the trial of Jesus before Pilate (Matthew 27:1-26; Mark 15:1-15; Luke 23:1-25; John 18:28 — 19:16). Mark records the basic story. Luke adds the sending of Jesus to Herod (23:6-12) and Pilate's triple assertion that Jesus was innocent (23:4, 14, 22). Matthew relates the dream and message of Pilate's wife (27:19), how Pilate disclaimed responsibility for Jesus' death (27:24f.), and his setting a guard on the tomb (27:62-66). John, who had been present at the trial, supplies even fuller details.

Pilate's final blunder was to seize a number of Samaritans who had assembled on Mt Gerizim as a result of a rumour that sacred vessels from the tabernacle were hidden there. Some of the ringleaders were executed. In response to a Samaritan protest, Vitellius, governor of Syria and Pilate's superior, ordered the ham-fisted procurator to answer to the emperor for his handling of the affair. The reigning emperor, Tiberius, died before Pilate reached Rome. We do not know the outcome of the affair, but Eusebius, the 4th-century Christian historian, recorded a report that Pilate had committed suicide.

Several unreliable traditions regarding Pilate's body are in existence. A number of *Acts of Pilate*, alleged records of Pilate's rule, appeared during the early Christian centuries. They are forgeries, intended to discredit Christianity.

Judas betrayed his master for thirty pieces of silver; the coins here are lit by an oil-lamp.

See on Luke 22:54-71.

The trials

The Jewish court which tried Jesus was the Sanhedrin, the supreme court at Jerusalem. Its 71 councillors came from influential families – elders, lawyers, Pharisees and Sadducees. The high priest for the year presided. The Sanhedrin had wide powers in civil and religious matters in Judea, but under Roman rule was not empowered to carry out the death sentence. So Jesus had also to appear before the Roman governor on a charge which would merit the death sentence under Roman law. Blasphemy was sufficient for the Jews. To be sure Pilate would ratify the sentence, the safest charge was treason. The Jewish trial was far from regular. It was held at night. There were no defence witnesses. The witnesses for the prosecution could not agree. And the death sentence, which should not have been pronounced till the day following the trial (the Jewish day ran from sunset to sunset), was immediate.

The sequence of events

1. The audience with Annas, father-in-law of high priest Caiaphas (John 18:12-14).
2. The late-night session at Caiaphas' house before the Sanhedrin (Matthew 26:57-68; Mark 15:53-65; Luke 22:54-65; John 18:24).
3. The early morning ratification of the sentence by the Sanhedrin (Matthew 27:1; Mark 15:1; Luke 22:66-71).
4. Jesus before Pilate (Matthew 27:2, 11-14; Mark 15:2-5; Luke 23:1-5; John 18:28-38).
5. Since Jesus is a Galilean, Pilate refers him to Herod (Luke 23:6-12).

The traditional site of the crucifixion, the 'Place of a Skull', is marked by the Church of the Holy Sepulchre. It was General Gordon in the last century who suggested that this rocky outcrop outside the walls of the Old City of Jerusalem bore a striking resemblance to a skull, and could be the place where Jesus died.

After the soldiers had mocked him with the crown of thorns Jesus was taken to be crucified. He died in utter loneliness, bearing the weight of human sin. And for three hours while he was on the cross there was darkness.

6. Jesus before Pilate again. He is scourged, sentenced and handed over to the soldiers (Matthew 27:15-26; Mark 15:6-15; Luke 23:13-25; John 18:29–19:16).

15: 16-41 Mockery and crucifixion

Jesus is now utterly alone. The Gospel writers play down the physical horror of the six hours (9 a.m.-3 p.m.) on the cross when Jesus touched a depth of suffering in body, mind and spirit beyond the stretch of our imagination. But the whole New Testament declares that his suffering was 'for us'. By his death he paid in full the penalty for our sin. He saved us from the death sentence, making possible the free gift of eternal life.

Seven times in those six hours (the last three in darkness) those who watched heard him speak.

Verse 21: Cyrene in north Africa had a strong Jewish colony. Alexander and Rufus evidently became Christians. This may be the same Rufus as the one mentioned in Romans 16:13.

Salome (40): Zebedee's wife; mother of James and John (Matthew 27:56).

15:42-47 Burial

Death by crucifixion was long drawn out. It often took two days or more. But Jesus was dead in six hours. Joseph saves him from the final indignity of a mass grave.

Preparation Day (42): i.e. the day before the sabbath, which began at 6 p.m.

16 The resurrection

See on Luke 24. For some unknown reason – most probably damage to very early copies of the Gospel – the best manuscripts we have of Mark end abruptly at 16:8. Verses 9-20 represent early attempts to round the Gospel off more satisfactorily.

The words from the cross

1. *'Father, forgive them; for they do not know what they are doing'* (Luke 23:34)
– a prayer for the Jewish people and the Roman soldiers.

2. *'I tell you the truth, today you will be with me in paradise'* (Luke 23:43)
– his word to the repentant thief, crucified beside him.

3. *'Woman, here is your son!' 'Here is your mother!'* (John 19:26-27)
– commending his mother to John's care.

4. *'My God, my God, why have you forsaken me?'* (Matthew 27:46; Mark 15:34)
– expressing in the words of Psalm 22:1 the agony of separation from God as the full weight of human sin pressed upon him.

5. *'I am thirsty'* (John 19:28).

6. *'It is finished'* (John 19:30).

7. *'Father, into your hands I commit my spirit!'* (Luke 23:46).

The body of Jesus was bound in linen cloths with spices and laid in a rock-cut tomb. This picture is of the Garden Tomb in Jerusalem.

Luke

Luke gives us the fullest life-story of Jesus we possess. The Gospel is part one of a two-part history of Christian beginnings – Luke/Acts. Both parts are dedicated to the same man, the Roman Theophilus, and both are written with the same purpose. The Gospel is carefully compiled from reliable, first-hand sources. Luke is not simply a biographer. His overriding concern is to get at the truth of what happened in Palestine in the critical years of Jesus' life-time. His Gospel shows Jesus as the Saviour of all men; his coming, a world-event. He lets us see Jesus the Man. And his selection of stories reflects his own warm interest in people, especially the sick and helpless, the poor, women, children, the social outcasts.

The writer

The Gospel does not mention the author's name, but all the evidence points to Luke the doctor, Paul's companion on his missionary journeys (see introduction to Acts). The precise way diseases are described in the Gospel fits in well with this. From the Gospel itself it is clear the writer is an educated man, with a wide vocabulary, and capable of marshalling and selecting material. He is an artist with words. And he is at home with both Greek and Jewish

backgrounds – although he writes for non-Jews, using Greek titles and quoting from the Greek version of the Old Testament. Archaeology has proved him an accurate historian. Luke worked with Mark and knew him well (Colossians 4:10, 14; Philemon 24), and the Gospel Mark wrote is one of his main sources.

1:1-4
PREFACE

The church very soon realized the need to get down in writing the stories of Jesus and his teaching which were circulating by word of mouth. Luke – perhaps having time on his hands, and opportunity to check on the facts during Paul's imprisonment at Caesarea – sets himself the task of compiling an acccurate record.

Theophilus (3): an otherwise unknown Roman, who had at least some interest in Christianity. 'Most excellent' may be his title as a high-ranking official: Good News Bible, 'Your Excellency'.

1:5—2:52
THE BIRTH AND CHILDHOOD OF JOHN AND JESUS

Only Matthew and Luke take their accounts as far back as Jesus' birth. The two accounts supplement one another. Luke's is fuller. Much of his information must surely have come from Mary herself.

1:5-25 The angel's message to Zechariah

God was in the events which led up to the

An inscription with the name of 'divine' Augustus Caesar, the Roman emperor who gave the decree for the census which took Joseph and Mary to Bethlehem.

birth of Christ. John's conception is in itself inexplicable on a purely human level (as with Isaac, Jacob, Samuel, Samson). Zechariah was in Jerusalem for his annual two-week spell of duty as a priest. This year came the honour of a lifetime. He was chosen to offer the incense alone in the temple. And at that moment God sends to tell him that the long years of prayer for a son are over. He will remove the stigma of childlessness – but more than that. As he answers the deep inner longing of this couple God at the same time fulfils far wider purposes – for the nation, and for the world. John will be the link between the Old Testament and the New. He will be the new Elijah (17; Malachi 4:5), herald of the long-promised, long-awaited Messiah.
Verse 15: compare Samson's dedication to God, Judges 13:4-5; and the Nazirite rules, Numbers 6.

1:26-38 The angel's message to Mary

Six months later the Messiah's birth is announced – this time to the young woman chosen to be his mother, and without the agency of a human father. Mary's quiet acceptance of a situation bound to cause scandal, and possibly the breaking of her marriage contract, shows something of the kind of woman through whom God chose to fulfil his purposes.

1:39-56 Mary visits Elizabeth

Having heard the news, Mary sets straight out on the four- or five-day journey south. It is a meeting of special joy and significance for the two women who have much to share. Their thoughts and feelings are crystallized in Elizabeth's benediction and Mary's hymn of praise. The hymn is full of the Old Testament phrases which Mary must have known and loved from childhood (see especially Hannah's song, 1 Samuel 2:1-10). Matthew 1:18-25 tells us what happened after Mary went home.

The Virgin Birth
JOHN SIMPSON

Both Matthew (1:18-25) and Luke (1:30-35) state that Jesus Christ was conceived by an action of the Holy Spirit without the intervention of a human father, and thus born of a virgin, Mary. We call this event the virgin birth – or, more accurately, the virginal conception – of Jesus.

In both Matthew and Luke the emphasis lies on the power and activity of the Holy Spirit in the birth of Jesus. It is this, not the absence of a human father, nor even the co-operation of the virgin mother, which is the important point. From his mother, Jesus was born as a man, but by the creative act of the Spirit his is a new humanity, the starting-point of a new race.

It is arguable that this would have been possible apart from a virgin birth, but the biblical evidence points to this miracle as the means which God employed in order to bring his Son into the world. We are not told anything about the physiology of the incarnation, but simply that it was through the activity of the Spirit that Mary became pregnant.

That is indeed all that can be said, since we are concerned here with the entry of the infinite God into his creation, and this is something that cannot be described, any more than the act of creation itself can be described. Nor can the virgin birth be rejected simply because it is a miracle. The supreme miracle is the incarnation itself, and if we can accept that miracle, there should be no difficulty about accepting the means by which God chose to effect it.

The virgin birth is seldom mentioned elsewhere in the New Testament. That is a warning to us not to get it out of proportion. The fact is stated, but Scripture nowhere makes the deity of Christ, nor his incarnation, nor his sinlessness stand or fall by the method of his birth. The prophecy of Isaiah 7:14 that a 'young woman' should conceive and bear a son called 'Immanuel' ('God with us') was seen to have a deeper meaning after the birth of Jesus (see Matthew 1:22-23). In Mark 6:3 the people of Nazareth call Jesus 'son of Mary', a phrase that may well have been an insult based on the rumour that Joseph was not his father. John 8:41 contains a similar slander. Some have found further references to the virgin birth in Galatians 4:4 where Paul says that God 'sent forth his Son, born of woman', and again when he spoke of Jesus as the 'second Adam', the first of the new race (1 Corinthians 15:45-47).

1:57-80 The birth of John

The child's strange name, Zechariah's sudden recovery of speech and the outburst of prophecy as his pent-up thoughts find voice, make a deep impression on the people around. They expect great things of John.

In the desert (80): other people at the time also withdrew, world-weary, from ordinary life and people. For instance the Essene community at Qumran flourished in John's day in the same area. John, by contrast, had a message for his nation. See also the note under Mark 1:1-8.

2:1-20 The birth of Jesus

Bethlehem – 6 miles/9 km south of Jerusalem, 70/110 south of Nazareth – had a long history. It was the home of Ruth and Boaz, birthplace of King David. But for Jesus there was no room; just an outhouse, a cradle shared with the animals. And the only ones to be told that the King of glory has come are some humble shepherds. 'He became poor' – Paul's phrase was the literal truth.

Bethlehem, set on a ridge in the mountains south of Jerusalem, is still surrounded by fields where 'shepherds watch their flocks'.

Verse 2: we know Quirinius governed Syria-Cilicia AD 6-9, but Luke's census is at least nine years earlier. It may be that Quirinius served an earlier term as governor; or possibly the name should read Saturninus. Luke has been proved such a reliable historian elsewhere that it is difficult to think he would make such a factual blunder.

Verse 7: the 'inn' may equally well be the guest-room of a house (see New English Bible and Matthew 2:11). The animals were probably stabled in a cave beneath the house.

Verse 14: 'peace to men on whom his favour rests'. God's peace does not come to people because they deserve it.

2:21-40 The presentation of Jesus in the temple; Simeon and Anna

Leviticus 12 gives the Jewish background. Forty days after Jesus' birth his parents present him to the priest in the temple. They are poor people who cannot afford to sacrifice a lamb. It is all routine procedure – until Simeon and Anna see the child, and recognize their Messiah.

Verse 39: Matthew 2 supplies the other events which took place before the family settled in Nazareth.

2:41-52 Jesus astonishes the teachers in the temple

When he was 12, a Jewish boy underwent preparation for adult status in the religious community. This visit to Jerusalem is therefore a special one for Jesus. Visitors flocked into Jerusalem for Passover (see page 492), travelling in large parties for safety. Jesus' parents had no reason to suspect he was missing till the evening halt. Next day they retraced their steps, and on the following morning found him in the temple. This is the first indication we have that Jesus realized his special relationship with God. The next 18 years are passed over in total silence.

Market scene at Bethlehem.

3—4:13
JOHN THE BAPTIST AND JESUS

3:1-20 The preaching of John
See also on Matthew 3; Mark 1:2-8. Luke's historical detail makes it possible to date John's ministry (and the beginning of Jesus' ministry a few months later) somewhere between AD 26 and 29. Verses 10-14 occur only in Luke. Genuine repentance shows itself in daily life – in kindness, generosity, honesty. The soldiers are told, 'No bullying; no blackmail; make do with your pay!' (New English Bible).
Verses 19-20: see on Mark 6:14-29.

3:21-22 Jesus' baptism
See on Matthew 3.

3:23-38 Jesus' family line
See on Matthew 1:1-17. Luke traces the line beyond Abraham to Adam, emphasizing Jesus' work for all mankind, as well as establishing his claim to be the Messiah descended from David.

4:1-13 The temptation
See on Matthew 4; Mark 1:9-13. Luke reverses the order of the second and third temptations. The real target of attack is Jesus' relationship as Son to his Father. Satan's attempts to undermine it and sow doubts are not so different from his methods in Genesis 3 – 'Did God say? ...' But this time he does not succeed.

4:14—9:50
TEACHING AND HEALING IN GALILEE
See note on Galilee, page 500.

4:14-30 In Nazareth
Luke chooses to start here, although this was not the first event in Jesus' ministry. Astonishment at Jesus' teaching quickly changes to hostility. And at the implication that because of their disbelief the

The people of Nazareth took Jesus to a nearby cliff 'to throw him headlong'.

gospel will be offered to non-Jews, the people are all set to lynch him. See also Matthew 13:53-58; Mark 6:1-6.

The synagogue (16-17): anyone might be invited to take part in the service of prayers, readings and sermon. The leader stood to pray and read from the scrolls, sat down to teach (20).
Verses 26-27: see 1 Kings 17:8-16; 2 Kings 5:1-14.

4:31-44 Capernaum
See on Mark 1:21-45.
Judea (44): the term is used here of Palestine generally, not the south in particular. Jesus went there later.

5:1-11 The catch of fish; Peter and his partners follow Jesus
Luke fills in detail omitted in Matthew (4:18-22) and Mark (1:16-20). The decision to follow Christ was based on more than casual contact.
Gennesaret (1): another name for Galilee.

5:12-16 Jesus heals a leper
See on Matthew 8:1-4.

5:17-26 The paralytic walks
See on Mark 2:1-12.
Pharisees (17): see page 494.

5:27-39 Levi (Matthew) becomes a disciple; questions about fasting
See on Matthew 9:9-17.

6:1-11 Controversy over the sabbath
See on Mark 2:23-3:6.

6:12-16 Jesus chooses the Twelve
See on Mark 3:7-19. Only Luke tells us of Jesus' night of prayer. He tells us more about Jesus as a man of prayer than any other Gospel writer.

6:17-49 Jesus teaches his disciples
This is most probably a shorter version of the sermon recorded in Matthew 5-7. Jesus must have taught these truths on many different occasions. Having chosen the Twelve, Jesus comes some distance down the mountainside to a level area. Here he sits down to teach, with the apostles, disciples and crowd gathered round him. His words are for his followers – those who realize their poverty in God's sight, who have an appetite for spiritual truth, who grieve at the evil they find in their own hearts. This is not a question of material poverty or riches.

Verses 20-23: a description of Jesus' disciples – men who seem pitiable now, but who have a great future.

Verses 24-26: the dreadful predicament of those who enjoy all life offers now, and fail to look beyond it. See on Matthew 5:1-16.

Verses 27-36: the command to treat others as God treats us – even in the face of injustice; even those who do us down. See on Matthew 5:17-48.

Verses 37-49: see on Matthew 7.

The village of Nain, where Jesus raised the widow's dead son.

7:1-10 The centurion's slave

See on Matthew 8:5-13, and 'Roman Soldiers in the New Testament', page 507.

7:11-17 Jesus brings the widow's son back to life

We have no other record of this incident. It is a further example of Luke's concern for the underprivileged. The widow's son is her only means of support. Once again Jesus shows himself Lord of life and death.

Nain (11): a village south of Nazareth. See map.

Verse 13: Luke is the only Gospel writer to refer to Jesus as 'the Lord', a term probably not much used during his lifetime.

7:18-35 Messengers from John the Baptist

See on Matthew 11:1-19.

Verse 35: 'God's wisdom, however, is shown to be true by all who accept it'. People turned to God in response to the preaching of both John and Jesus.

7:36-50 In the Pharisee's house

This is a different incident from the one recorded in the other Gospels. Simon shows Jesus no special courtesy. But a common prostitute, to whom he has opened up the possibility of forgiveness, pours out her gratitude in lavish love – not caring what anyone thinks. Her love does not *earn* forgiveness (47), it follows it.

8:1-21 'If you have ears…then hear'; Jesus teaches in parables

Verses 1-3: only Luke tells us the part the women played in Jesus' mission. Susanna is not mentioned again. Mary Magdalene stood watching at the crucifixion, and she and Joanna were at the tomb and saw the Lord on the resurrection morning. Their love, and that of many other women who

The New Testament Miracles

HOWARD MARSHALL

The Gospels contain stories of about 35 different occasions when Jesus performed various kinds of deeds that seemed miraculous to those who saw them. In addition there are several passages where we are told in quite general terms that Jesus performed miracles.

More than half of these stories about Jesus tell how he healed the sick of various diseases including fever, leprosy (probably not the modern disease of that name), dropsy, paralysis, blindness, deafness, and dumbness.

In other cases he cast demons out of people who were suffering from physical or mental disorders.

Three times we hear that he raised people from the dead.

The remaining stories show his power over things – to feed a large multitude with very little food, to walk on the water and still a storm, to curse a fig-tree so that it withered away, to change water into wine, and to catch enormous quantities of fish.

Modern objections to miracles
These stories testify to the tremendous impression which the work of Jesus made on those who saw it. Even if the stories were legendary (which they are not), we should still want to know what it was about Jesus that made people tell such stories about him. One thing is certain at the outset, that we cannot dismiss the miracles to try to have a non-miraculous Jesus. They are an integral and central part of the story. Why, then, do people try to dismiss them?

First, it is argued that science rules out the possibility of miracles. In fact, however, this argument is nothing more than the statement of a presupposition, namely that in a purely material universe nothing can happen that cannot be accounted for in terms of natural causes. But that is purely an assumption about the nature of the universe which cannot be proved to be true. At most it could be argued from it that normally miracles do not occur; but it is illegitimate to claim that therefore miracles can never occur. We ought at least to have open minds on the point.

Second, it is argued that we have no re-

»

liable historical evidence for miracles. We must have good evidence that the alleged miracle happened, and that it cannot be explained in a non-miraculous manner. Since we are dealing with something as unusual as a miracle, the evidence needs to be extremely strong, since (it is argued) it is more likely that the witnesses got it wrong than that a miracle actually happened.

The resurrection
If, however, only one miracle could be claimed as historical, this would be sufficient both to demonstrate that miracles are possible and to make further ones probable. Such an event is the resurrection. The evidence that reliable witnesses claimed to have seen Jesus alive after his death (1 Corinthians 15:3-8) is incontrovertible. The only explanation that makes sense of the evidence is that he was miraculously raised from the dead. If you want to disagree, then you must produce some convincing alternative explanation.

If the resurrection did take place, then it makes the fact of other miracles highly likely. For, first, it establishes the possibility of the miraculous taking place at all. It means that God can act in the natural order in an unusual manner. Second, the resurrection is God's 'Yes' to the life of Jesus – including Jesus' own claim to work miracles (Luke 7:21f.; 11:19).

This evidence is confirmed by the reliable historical tradition that Jesus did work miracles, which is found in the Gospels. To be sure, we cannot test and affirm on purely historical grounds the truth of every single miracle story. In some cases, what seemed miraculous to 1st-century people may be explicable in natural terms (e.g. in the psychological healing of a psychosomatic disease); in other cases there may not be enough evidence to confirm or disprove the Gospel story.

The purpose of the miracles
One important point often raised against the historicity of the New Testament miracles is that similar stories are told of other great men of the period. Hence it is likely that Christians, who shared the superstitions of their day, would invent similar stories about Jesus.

One could reply that if it was necessary for Jesus to be a miracle-worker in order to be seen to be 'the greatest' in 1st-century terms, then God could and would do mighty wonders through him. More important is the fact that the stories of Jesus display some important differences from those told about other men. The importance of Jesus' miracles lies not so much in the miraculous power which he displayed in them, as in the significance attached to them.

- In general they were effected by his simple word (Mark 1:27; 2:11) or touch (Mark 5:41) rather than by the use of magical devices.
- They did not bring glory to him, but were meant to bring glory to God (Luke 7:16).
- They testified to God's love for suffering humanity (Mark 1:41; 8:2).
- They fulfilled the Old Testament promises of the coming time of salvation when God would heal men's bodies as well as their souls (Luke 7:22; Isaiah 29:18-19; 35:5-6; 61:1).
- They were done in order to lead men to faith in the saving power of God at work in Jesus (Mark 9:23f.). They were not compelling signs of God's power: the Pharisees felt able to attribute them to the power of Satan (Mark 3:22). But to those with the eyes to see, they constituted the sign that God was at work in Jesus in fulfilment of his promises, and were meant to awaken and confirm faith in him.

All this applies to the miracles of Jesus himself. It also applies to the miracles in the early church. The early Christians displayed powers similar to those of Jesus. We hear of sick people being cured, the dead being raised, the miraculous release of prisoners and even the power to inflict physical judgement. These were signs that the same power of God which was at work in Jesus was still at work in his disciples, confirming their message of salvation, and also warning of the reality of God's judgement.

followed him from Galilee, never wavered. Mary is not the woman of 7:36ff., but there was a real battle in her heart before she became a disciple.

Verses 4-15: see on Matthew 13:1-52. See also Mark 4:1-20.

Verse 10: see on Mark 4:12.

Verse 19: see on Matthew 12:49.

8:22-39 The stormy crossing; the man possessed by demons

See on Mark 4:35-41; 5:1-20.

Verse 32: pork was forbidden food for Jews. But the country east of the lake was largely non-Jewish.

8:40-56 Jairus' daughter; the woman with a haemorrhage

See on Mark 5:21-43.

9:1-17 The Twelve sent out; Herod is puzzled; 5,000 fed

Verses 1-6: see on Matthew 9:35 – 10:42.

Verses 7-9: Luke seems to have a special source of information about Herod, perhaps through Joanna (8:3).

Verses 10-17: see also Matthew 14:13-21; Mark 6:30-44; John 6:1-14. This is yet another example of Jesus' power.

9:18-27 'Who do you say I am?'; Jesus speaks about his suffering

See the fuller version in Matthew 16: 13-28, and Mark 8:27 – 9:1. Luke abridges at this point.

9:28-36 Jesus is transfigured

See on Mark 9:2-13.

9:37-50 The epileptic boy; 'Who is the greatest?'

Verses 37-43: see on Mark 9:14-29. Verses 46-48: see on Matthew 18 and Mark 9:30-50.

9:51 — 19:27
ON THE MOVE TOWARDS JERUSALEM: TEACHING AND HEALING

In this section Luke groups incidents and teaching from various periods of Christ's ministry, on the general theme of discipleship. He may have had several journeys to Jerusalem in mind. Much of what is recorded in these chapters is unique to Luke.

9:51-56 The Samaritan village

Jesus' insistence on going to Jerusalem was red rag to a bull to the Samaritans (see page 497 and on 10:29ff.).

Verse 54: no wonder Jesus nicknamed these two brothers 'sons of thunder'!

9:57-62 No turning back

See on Matthew 8:18-22.

10:1-24 Jesus sends out the seventy

Compare this with Jesus' instructions to the Twelve (Matthew 10:5-15). See also Matthew 11:20-27. Those entrusted with God's good news are entitled to support from the people they go to. But they are not to look for luxury (the 'going from house to house', 7, is with a view to a better living). Time is too precious to waste on endless social formalities (4). There is work to be done, a message to be made known. And God himself will judge those who reject it. The seventy are overjoyed at their new power. But greater cause for joy is the certainty of eternal life (20).

Verses 13-17: for the places mentioned, see page 505. Tyre and Sidon: heathen cities denounced by the Old Testament prophets. 'Hades': the place of the dead – a metaphorical phrase, 'brought down to the depths' (New English Bible). **I saw Satan fall (18):** their ability to

A model of an Eastern inn.

exorcise evil spirits is a sign that Satan's power is broken. The preaching of the new age means that the power of evil is to be defeated at last. Jesus rejoices in this fulfilment of his ministry.

10:25-37 A test question; the good Samaritan

Only Luke tells this story. Jesus gives a textbook answer to the question. The lawyer, chagrined, in an attempt to save face asks another. Instead of answering directly, Jesus replies with a parable. There was a long history of hatred between Jew and Samaritan (see page 497). The Samaritans were regarded as scum–untouchables. Yet Jesus shows this one carrying out the law whereas the injured man's fellow Jews–even the religious leaders–fail. A real 'neighbour' is one who gives help wherever it is needed, even to someone who yesterday, so to speak, kicked him in the teeth.

Verse 30: the road which winds its way down from Jerusalem to Jericho (dropping 3,300 feet/1,000 m in 17 miles/27 km) passes through lonely, desolate, rocky terrain–ideal brigand country.

10:38-42 Martha and Mary

The two sisters and their brother Lazarus lived at Bethany, near Jerusalem. Martha gets into a state slaving to prepare an elaborate meal. She would have done better to keep the menu simple and leave time to listen to Jesus.

11:1-13 Jesus teaches his disciples how to pray

Matthew (6:9-13) gives the longer form of the Lord's Prayer. Jesus is not supplying just a form of words. His prayer provides us with a pattern. It teaches us to come to God simply, talking to him as we would

On the desert road going steeply down from Jerusalem to Jericho it is easy to imagine the robbers of Jesus' story.

our own father, both sharing his concerns and confidently telling him of our own needs. And we are not to be discouraged if time goes by and we see no answer. Persistence will in the end win over even the most reluctant friend – and there is no reluctance to answer on God's part. See also Matthew 7:7-11.

Verse 7: a poor family slept all together on thin mattresses on a raised section of the one all-purpose room.

Verses 11-12: fish and serpents look alike, so do eggs and rolled-up scorpions.

11:14-36 Opposition; Jesus slates his contemporaries

Verses 14-23: see on Matthew 12:15-37.
Verses 24-26: see on Matthew 12:43-45.
Verses 29-32: see on Matthew 12:38-42.
Verses 34-36: see on Matthew 6:22-23.
Only Luke includes 27-28.

Verse 24: dry, desert places were thought to be the natural home of evil spirits.

11:37-54 Jesus' rebuke infuriates the Pharisees

Verses 37-41: see on Matthew 15:1-20.
Verses 42-52: see on Matthew 23.

12 — 13:9 Warning and reassurance; be ready

A collection of Jesus' teaching about the future, and the way future events should affect life here and now. The consequences of following a short-sighted materialist philosophy will in the end prove disastrous. Much of this section is paralleled in Matthew.

Verses 1-12: see on Matthew 10:26ff.
Verses 13-21: the parable of the rich fool – unique to Luke.
Verses 22-34: see on Matthew 6:9-34.
Verses 35-48: see on Matthew 24:42-51.
13:1-9: Roman troops had slaughtered some Galilean pilgrims in the temple at Passover. People assumed that the victims of the two disasters must have

been specially wicked – but that was not true. The whole nation is ripe for judgement and will meet an equally horrible fate if present opportunities for a change of heart are let slip.

Verse 10: see on Matthew 12:15-37.

Verse 35: 'be ready for action'; for freedom of movement at work the long tunic was drawn up through a belt.

Verses 49-50: the good news of the gospel will run through the earth like fire. But first Jesus must plumb the depths of suffering.

13:10-17 The woman with arthritis

Only Luke records this story. It is one of numerous clashes with the Pharisees over healing on the sabbath. See also Mark 3:1-6.

Verse 16: Satan bears ultimate responsibility for bringing suffering into the world along with sin.

13:18-21 Pictures of what God's kingdom is like

See on Matthew 13, and 'The Kingdom of God and the Kingdom of Heaven', page 484.

13:22-35 The narrow door

Verses 22-30: speculation over how many will be saved is futile. The important thing is for each individual to make sure of his own place. It is not enough merely to recognize Christ. He requires response – and there is a time limit.

Verses 31-35: Jesus is not bothered by Herod's threats. He knows what lies ahead, and grieves at the fate of the city that will destroy him.

14:1-24 Jesus dines out; two parables

Verses 1-6: another sabbath healing – see 13:10-17; Mark 3:1-6. Human life is cheap, livestock precious!

Verses 7-11: guests were carefully seated according to rank and status (as at a formal banquet today), but everyone wants a seat at the top table. Jesus is commending a genuinely humble spirit, not false modesty.

Verses 12-14: real generosity does not look for returns.

Verses 15-24: the story illustrates how people react to the invitation God makes through Jesus. Many reply with a snub. It is not really a case of 'I *cannot* come', but 'I *will* not come'. The 'reasons' are no more than excuses.

Dropsy (2): fluid collecting in parts of the body and causing swelling and pain.

14:25-35 Counting the cost of discipleship

The guests in the story had their priorities wrong. Jesus' claim must take precedence over all others. No one can follow him unless he is prepared for all that this means. Too many people start to build in fine style and then run out of funds (28-29).

Verse 26: Jesus teaches us to love even our enemies. He is not telling us to hate our family! He means we must love him more than anyone or anything else (33). The black-and-white contrast was a figure of speech.

15 The lost sheep; the lost coin; the drop-out son

These three stories contrast strongly with the severity of chapter 14. God cares for those who have gone wrong in life. He is always ready to forgive any who turn to him. The men of religion (1-2), like the elder son in the story, show neither love nor pity for those who fail to meet their standards. But God rejoices at their rescue.

Verse 8: the silver coins were probably the woman's dowry, worn round her neck or on her headdress.

16 The dishonest manager; the danger of being taken up with money

Verses 1-13: Jesus commends the manager's astuteness, not his dishonesty. He knows how to make money work for him.

Verses 16-17: compare Matthew 11:12-13. The emphasis here is different.

Verse 18: see on Matthew 19:1-15.

Verses 19-31: the rich man and Lazarus. Jesus uses popular picture language (Abraham's bosom; the great chasm, etc.). But the story makes it clear that if we will not respond to the message God has already clearly given in the Bible, we

Jesus' story of the shepherd searching for his lost sheep evokes a timeless picture.

Model of rich man's house at the time of Jesus.

of how we could handle wealth of a different kind. Is God, or money, our master?

17:1-10 Forgiveness; faith; duty

17:11-19 The ten lepers

The men are sent to the priests in order to be declared fit to return to normal society. By going, they demonstrate their faith in Jesus' word. All are cured, but only one takes the trouble to say thank you.

Samaritan (16): see page 497.

17:20-37 Teaching about Jesus' return

See on Matthew 24. No amount of calculation can fix the time (20-21) or place (37) of Christ's return in judgement. The world will be caught unprepared, as it was by the flood.

18:1-14 More about prayer

Two parables which appear only in Luke. Like all Jesus' parables, these are stories from life.

Verses 1-8: God is no unjust judge. If a woman could persist with her plea against such odds, surely we can pray on if the answer does not come at once.

Verses 9-14: the Pharisee 'prays' simply to give himself a pat on the back. It is the tax collector, who can find nothing

will not respond at all. No amount of miracle-working would make any difference. Our future is determined by our present response, or lack of it.

Verse 9: New English Bible gives a plausible rendering of a difficult verse. Friends bought by money 'cannot' get us to heaven. But the way we use our money now may affect our eternal destiny. It is a test

A shepherd leads his flock across barren country in the hills of Judea, seeking fresh pastures.

in himself to be proud of, whom God hears.

18:15-17 Jesus and the children
See also Matthew 19:13-15; and on Mark 10:13-16. To the disciples, the children were a nuisance. But Jesus loved them. Verse 17 makes the same point as the story of the Pharisee and the tax collector. Admission to God's kingdom is never denied to those who come in humble trust.

18:18-34 The rich ruler's question; Jesus again predicts his death
See on Matthew 19:16-30; 20:17-19; see also Mark 10:17-34.

18:35—19:10 At Jericho: the blind beggar; Zacchaeus
18:35-43: see on Mark 10:46-52. 19:1-10: Zacchaeus, like Matthew, was a social outcast because of his job. He made himself a fat living by fleecing his own people of money to pay the Roman taxes. But when Jesus chose to stay at his home, Zacchaeus became a new man.

19:11-27 The parable of the pounds
This story is similar to the parable of the talents in Matthew. Verse 11 is the key. Herod's son, Archelaus, did just what the nobleman in Jesus' story did – went to Rome to be given his title to the kingdom of Judea. (He was followed by a delegation of Jews opposed to his rule.) Jesus is no despot, like Herod, but he too is about to leave his people for a time. In his absence they must faithfully carry out the work given them to do. For he will return with authority to judge every man.
The pound/gold coin (13): the Greek mina. See the chart on page 108.

A model of the Fort of Antonia – where the Roman garrison was stationed at the time of Jesus' trial – in the Ecce Homo Convent.

19:28 — 21:38
JESUS IN JERUSALEM

19:28-48 The triumphant ride into the city; Jesus in the temple
See also Matthew 21:1-17; Mark 11:1-19. Jesus rode in on an ass (Zechariah 9:9), not a war-horse. He came on a peace mission. But Jerusalem would have none of it, choosing instead the violent course which led to total destruction at the hands of the Romans in AD 70.
Bethphage and Bethany (29): villages east of the Mount of Olives, two miles from Jerusalem.
Verse 38: Luke paraphrases for his non-Jewish readers.
Verse 45: see on Matthew 21:12-17. Luke, like Matthew, compresses the events; compare Mark 11:11 and 15ff.

20:1-18 On whose authority…? The parable of the vineyard
See on Matthew 21:23-46. See also Mark 11:27–12:12.

20:19—21:4 Jesus' enemies set traps

See on Mark 12:13-44. See also Matthew 22:15-46.

21:5-38 Jesus talks about the destruction of the temple and the end of the world

See on Matthew 24. See also Mark 13.
    Verses 8-11: signs of the end.
    Verses 12-19: suffering and witness of the disciples.
    Verses 20-24: the fall of Jerusalem: phase 1 of the end.
    Verses 25-28: cosmic upheaval and Jesus' return: phase 2 of the end.
    Verses 29-33: the certainty of these events. 'All' (32) must refer to the warning signs, including the fall of Jerusalem. All the indications are that Christ's coming is near: yet God still delays, giving time for the good news to be made known throughout the world. The fig-tree is the first to come into leaf in Palestine. See page 97.
    Verses 34-36: the need to be ready.

22—24
JESUS' LAST HOURS: THE CROSS AND RESURRECTION

22:1-38 Judas turns traitor; the Last Supper

See on Matthew 26:14-29. See also Mark 14:12-25; John 13—14.
Verse 10: it was usually the woman's job to carry water, so this man would have been conspicuous.

22:39-53 On the Mount of Olives; the arrest

See on Matthew 26:30-56. See also Mark 14:26-52.

22:54-65 Peter denies Christ; the mockery of the soldiers

Only Peter and one other disciple had the courage to keep within sight of Jesus.

But with nothing to do but wait, courage oozes away and fear takes control. Three times Peter says what he swore he would never say (22:33; Mark 14:29-31). Even Peter, leader of the disciples, denies him. Afterwards one look from Jesus is enough to break the big fisherman's heart.

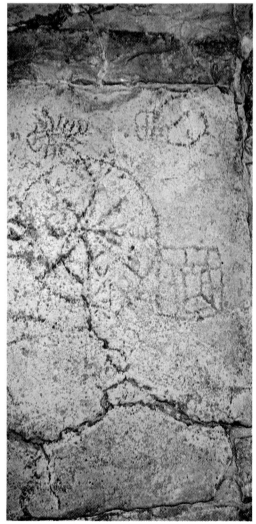

Jesus was taken to the Fort of Antonia to be tried. There, on the 'Pavement', he was mocked and ridiculed. The actual Pavement was discovered earlier this century below the Ecce Homo Convent built on the site. These stones are scratched with the games the Roman soldiers played.

22:66–23:12 Jesus before the Sanhedrin; before Pilate; before Herod

See also on Mark 14:53–15:15. Blasphemy is a capital charge under Jewish law. But the accusation and charge is rephrased for Pilate in order to get Jesus convicted of treason. The Roman governor is not interested in offences against Jewish religious law.

Herod was in Jerusalem for the Passover. If Pilate was attempting to pass the buck by sending his prisoner to Herod, it did not work. It is strange that the exchange over Jesus should have brought these two old enemies together.

Verse 3: the answer is non-committal. What Jesus would mean by the title, and what Pilate would understand, are two very different things. See the fuller record in John 18:33-38.

The Herod family tomb in Jerusalem, like that of Jesus, was rock-cut and sealed with a great circular stone.

23:13-31 Sentenced to death

Although acquitted by both Herod and Pilate, Jesus is condemned to death – because Pilate dare not risk another unfavourable report reaching the emperor (John 19:12). So a convicted murderer is freed, and an innocent man scourged and crucified.

23:32-49 On the cross; the two criminals; Jesus' last words

See on Mark 15:16-41. Only Luke tells us that one of the mocking robbers repented and was forgiven.

Verse 45: the curtain divided the sanctuary from the body of the temple. Only once a year could the high priest pass through and intercede for the people (Hebrews 9:7). Now no intermediary is needed – all may have access to God (Hebrews 10:19-22).

23:50-56 Joseph sees to the burial

See on Mark 15:42-47.

24 Christ is risen!

In the stillness of that Easter morning the extraordinary news gradually broke, the light dawned. The tomb was empty. Jesus was alive! The details given in the four accounts of what took place on that momentous morning are difficult to harmonize. The fact that it happened is clear, and has stood up to the most searching examination. Like reports of any major event, it is difficult to piece together the information of a number of independent witnesses. A rough sequence of events is set out in the article 'The Accounts of the Resurrection', page 529.

No matter what the variation in detail, the main facts are absolutely clear. As day broke on that Sunday morning, Jesus' followers were shadow-men. When Jesus died the group became a body with the heart wrenched out. They were terribly afraid. They were without hope. They did not expect a sequel to the story. Peter, the natural leader, was crushed beyond bearing by the knowledge that he had denied Christ. The two on the Emmaus road were typical of the rest.

Yet within twelve hours everything is changed. Not only is the tomb empty – Jesus himself has been seen on at least five different occasions, by more than 16 of his followers. And it really was Jesus, not a ghost. They recognized him. They saw the crucifixion scars. And he ate with them. Peter is a new man. Despondency and mourning are things of the past. Fear is gone and in its place, indescribable joy. On the concrete certainty of the resurrection rests the whole of subsequent Christian history. Nothing else can account for the facts.

Verses 50-52: Luke compresses events. As he makes clear in Acts, his sequel, the ascension took place 40 days later.

The Accounts of the Resurrection

DAVID WHEATON

A superficial reading of the accounts of the resurrection in the four Gospels may suggest that there are many points of disagreement among them. Closer examination reveals a remarkable degree of unanimity, and suggests that in fact the apparent discrepancies provide evidence that although the Gospel writers obtained their information from different sources in the early Church, all four had the same basic tale to tell. Anyone who has heard evidence from different witnesses to an accident knows how in that situation people with different interests, backgrounds and emotional make-up tend to notice and remember different elements in a composite picture.

The main witnesses who first saw the empty tomb were a group of women who had recently been under severe emotional strain. Immediately after the momentous discovery they would appear to have scattered in order to take the news to different people. So it is not surprising that the accounts vary in detail. It would indeed be more surprising, and the evidence would in a sense be less valuable, if they did not. The variation suggests that the writers collected their evidence from more than one source, which makes the over-all agreement of the four accounts all the more impressive. The events in the records can be set out more or less as follows:

The Bible evidence
■ A group of women go to the tomb early on the first day of the week to embalm the body of Jesus (Matthew 28:1; Mark 16:1-2; Luke 24:1, 10; John 20:1a).

■ They discover that the stone has been rolled back (Matthew 28:2-4; Mark 16:3-4; Luke 24:2; John 20:1b).

■ The body of Jesus is no longer in the tomb; instead they see an angel who explains the situation and gives them a message (Matthew 28:5-7; Mark 16:5-7; Luke 24:3-7).

■ The women run back to Jerusalem to tell the other disciples, and are greeted in the main with disbelief (Matthew 28:8; Luke 24:8-11, 22-23; John 20:2).

■ Peter and the 'other disciple whom Jesus loved' go to the tomb and find it empty; they then return home (John 20:3-10; see Luke 24:24).

■ Mary Magdalene follows them back to the tomb, and remains there after they have left. Jesus then makes his first appearance to her (John 20:11-18; Matthew 28:9; Matthew names Mary Magdalene and 'the other Mary').

■ On that same day he appears to Peter (Luke 24:34; 1 Corinthians 15:5), to the two going to Emmaus (Luke 24:13-32; see Mark 16:12-13), and then to the rest of the disciples apart from Thomas back in Jerusalem (John 20:19-23; Luke 24:36-43; Mark 16:14). Other appearances, outside the scope of this article, are recorded in the four Gospels, Acts 1 and 1 Corinthians 15. What emerges from all the accounts is a remarkable consistency on two points – that Jesus could now reveal himself and disappear at will and that he only showed himself to his followers. **»»**

Apparent discrepancies

■ **Which women went to the tomb?**
Apparently Mary Magdalene, Mary the
mother of James, Salome, Joanna, and 'the
other women from Galilee' (Luke 23:55).
John singles out Mary Magdalene for mention
(20:1) presumably because it was she who
brought information back to Peter and the other
disciples: she herself implies in 20:2 that there
were others with her – we do not know. So the
writers could each be mentioning by name
those of the party whose behaviour made an
impact on those from whom the writers gained
their information.
■ **When was the stone rolled back?** Mark
16:3-4 and Luke 24:2 imply that it had been
rolled back before they arrived on the spot.
Then Matthew 28:2-4 could have happened
before their arrival, and as a result the guards
went off back to the city (in 28:11-15 the
guards have presumably already reached the
city and are busy spreading their tale by the
time the women are on their way back from
the tomb).
■ **How many angels were there?** When the
women arrive, the angel who descended to
roll back the stone (Matthew 28:2) has
moved inside the tomb and been joined by
another (Luke 24:4 – Mary Magdalene also
sees two, John 20:12). Matthew and Mark
may refer only to the one who acted as
spokesman, and therefore engaged the
attention of their informants, and the plural
in Luke 24:5 ('the men said') may refer
loosely to the fact that while one spoke the
other corroborated.

■ **What did the angels say?** Again, the
accounts can be put together to help us see
the full picture:
> Do not be afraid: we know why you
> have come.
> Jesus is not here because he has risen.
> Look at the empty tomb.
> Tell his disciples; he is going to meet
> you in Galilee.
> Remember how he foretold all this.
■ **Who was the first to see Jesus?** Mark 16:9
says he first showed himself to Mary
Magdalene, and this agrees with John's story.
Luke has nothing to conflict with this. In
Matthew 28:9 Jesus appears to Mary
Magdalene (the key figure) and 'the other
Mary'. It seems likely that this is the first
appearance, and natural that when the story
went round Mary Magdalene was named
and the other Mary forgotten (just as the
other Gospel writers mention Bartimaeus,
but not the other blind man; and Legion, but
not the other demoniac – and only Matthew
in each case mentions the pair).

It has been pointed out that Matthew and
Mark both record appearances of Jesus to
the disciples in Galilee, and Luke and John in
Jerusalem. In fact, of course, John 21 takes us
back to Galilee, and Mark in his postscript
refers to the Jerusalem appearances. In the
case of Matthew and Luke, it accords with
the purpose and structure of the writers for
Luke to conclude his Gospel where he
began – in Jerusalem – and for Matthew to
conclude with the King's final proclamation
on a mountain (28:16-20).

The Gospels and Modern Criticism

LEON MORRIS

The Gospels are not biographies, though they contain much biographical information. They are books written by convinced Christians to commend and explain their faith to others (see Luke 1:3-4; John 20:31). They are quite unlike any other type of ancient literature. This means that they cannot be approached in quite the same way as other documents. We must bear in mind, first and foremost, that they are documents of faith; and second that they convey historical information.

The New Testament scholar comes to the Gospels with such questions as these: What purpose were these writings meant to serve? How accurate is the history recorded in them? What can we learn about their method of composition and what light does this throw on their authors' intention and achievement?

Some scholars consider it possible that writers seeking to commend their faith may not be very interested in historical accuracy. They have sometimes concluded that there is very little history in the Gospels at all. They feel that theology is all-important to the Gospel writers, and that they never intended their history to be taken seriously.

Others think that this approach is too subjective. A more objective approach finds good evidence that the Gospel writers do take their facts with the utmost seriousness; Luke, for example, claims to have made a careful examination of the evidence before writing his Gospel (Luke 1:1-3).

Textual criticism

The scholar's first task is to establish the text. Textual criticism, as this is called, is a patient study of the manuscripts, the versions (that is, translations into languages other than the original), the quotations in early writings, the lectionaries used in worship and anything else that can help establish the text.

Behind all this is the fact that it is a trying process to copy out by hand a book as long as a Gospel, and mistakes are liable to creep in. But a careful comparison of the manuscripts, and a study of the methods of scribes, helps the textual critic to distinguish between early and later readings, and so to establish the text.

With thousands of manuscripts involved, textual criticism is an arduous business. But those engaged in it are agreed that the text of the New Testament is in surprisingly good shape (much better than the text of most of the classics). Although we may be uncertain of the original reading here and there, this rarely affects anything important. None of the basic Christian doctrines is in any doubt. And we may now be confident that we have the text of the New Testament substantially as it was written.

Source criticism

Having established the text, critics go on to observe that there are important similarities between the first three Gospels, over against the fourth. Matthew, Mark and Luke all describe a ministry of Jesus in Galilee, with a journey to Jerusalem at the end, at which time he is arrested and crucified. The passion story, with its sequel, the resurrection, occupies a large proportion of each account. But apart from this and the stories of Jesus' birth in Matthew and Luke there is not much that can be confidently located in Judea. John, on the other hand, speaks of a longer ministry (this is clear from his references to Passover feasts; there would be a year between successive feasts), and he describes many incidents which took place in Judea.

The resemblances between the first three Gospels led to their being given the name 'Synoptic Gospels': they can be set side by side and studied together. When this is done, however, differences as well as resemblances come to light, and the problem of the relationship between these Gospels (the 'Synoptic problem') has teased scholars for generations.

At one time it was commonly held that Matthew wrote first and that Mark has abbreviated him. A few still hold this view. But most scholars these days are impressed with the greater freshness of Mark, and by the fact that Mark's order seems always to be followed by either Matthew or Luke. They also point out that, although Mark is the shortest of all the Gospels, it is usually longer than Matthew in the narratives they have in common, which does not look like abbreviation. There is also very little indeed in Mark that is not contained in Matthew or Luke, so why should this Gospel have been written after the others? For these reasons it is now commonly held (though it has not **»** been proved beyond doubt) that Mark was written first and that both Matthew and Luke made use of our second Gospel.

There is also a certain amount of material common to Matthew and Luke but absent from Mark. This is usually thought to represent another source, which has not survived, denoted by the symbol Q. Most see Q as a collection of sayings, with little narrative material. Many scholars think of it as a single document. Others point out that the amount of resemblance in the sections common to Matthew and Luke varies greatly. Sometimes the two are almost word for word (e.g. Matthew 3:7-10=Luke 3:7-9), but in other places there are considerable differences (e.g. the Beatitudes). They therefore think in terms of several documents (see Luke 1:1), and use Q to denote the shared material in general, without committing themselves to any particular theory of documents.

Other material appears in only one Gospel, and clearly each of the Gospel writers had sources of his own. Symbols used for these are M for material that occurs only in Matthew, and L for material only in Luke. It has been suggested that in the case of Luke this is particularly important. Luke has his material from Mark in blocks, sometimes with long stretches in between. Some scholars hold that he first combined L and Q into a Gospel which has been called 'Proto-Luke'. Later he came across Mark's Gospel and incorporated a good deal of it to make up our present third Gospel. This view of Gospel origins takes the Lukan material very seriously and sees Proto-Luke as quite old and reliable.

Form criticism

That is about as far as source criticism has been taken, perhaps as far as it can go. In recent times attempts have been made to get behind the written sources to the time when the tradition was transmitted by word of mouth. The form critics pay attention to the form of the units which make up the Gospels and identify miracle stories, 'pronouncement stories' (i.e. stories leading up to some memorable saying) and so on. They point out that these units must have been passed on orally for many years.

Why were these particular stories preserved, out of the vast amount of material originally available? The answer, according to the form critics, is that they met the needs of the early Christians; it was the requirements of preaching that determined what would be preserved. Many form critics are rather radical and think that the preachers manufactured stories when they did not have suitable ones, under the belief that the Spirit of God was inspiring them to say what Jesus would have said in the circumstances confronting them. Usually they feel that the Gospels tell us more about the faith of the early church than they do about the teaching of Jesus. This is a highly subjective judgement, and form critics have often been criticized for propounding bold hypotheses on very little actual evidence.

Redaction criticism

The redaction critics take up where the form critics leave off, concentrating on the editorial framework which links together the various units of the Gospel story. Redaction critics find these links highly important, for they help us to see the evangelists' purpose as they wove the stories into their complete accounts. Thus the critics conclude that Matthew was interested in the church and provided a manual for teachers; that Mark used the 'messianic secret' to show that Jesus' true nature was not known until it was revealed by the cross and associated events; and that Luke was the theologian of 'salvation history'.

It is not easy to compare the fourth Gospel with the Synoptists and some feel that the Jesus of John's Gospel is so different from the Jesus of the other Gospels that we must reject one or the other. But Jesus must have been so great a figure that no one evangelist could be expected to capture his whole personality. It has been suggested that the Synoptists reflect the public teaching of Jesus; whereas John reflects Jesus' informal teaching of his disciples and his disputes with his enemies. The two portraits are not irreconcilable.

Probably no other documents in any language have been subjected to such detailed critical examination as the Gospels. The most minute details of vocabulary and syntax have been critically weighed for their bearing on the larger questions. That this searching examination has disclosed difficulties need not surprise us. It could scarcely have been otherwise. But in the judgement of many competent scholars the difficulties are by no means insuperable. They should certainly not deter us as we approach the Gospels. It requires no intellectual compromise, even today, for the greatest of scholars to read these books humbly and find the Saviour there.

See further 'The Gospels and Jesus Christ', page 468.

John's Gospel is strikingly different from the other three. It was the last to be written – probably about AD 90 – and seems to assume that the readers already know the facts about Jesus' life. John supplements the other accounts, and concentrates on interpreting and bringing out the meaning of what took place. He selects from Jesus' many miracles certain 'signs' which show most clearly who he was. Everything he writes is subordinated to the main aim of bringing the reader to faith (20:30-31). He records mainly what Jesus said – especially about himself – in a style very different from Matthew, the other Gospel which concentrates on Jesus' sayings. There are no parables in John. Most of the events recorded take place in and around Jerusalem at the various festivals. And it may well be that Jesus adopted a different teaching method for the nation's capital city and theological centre. The keynote of John's Gospel is Jesus as Messiah and Son of God.

The author

The author (who may, like Paul, have used a secretary) refers to himself simply as 'the disciple whom Jesus loved' (21:20, 24). He is one of the Twelve, and one of those closest to Jesus and also to Peter. These facts – and the fact that this Gospel makes no mention of the apostle John and describes the Baptist simply as 'John', make it likely that he is himself John, son of Zebedee, brother of James, and business partner of Peter and Andrew. The early church certainly thought so – and taught that the aged apostle wrote or dictated this 'spiritual' Gospel from Ephesus in

present-day Turkey. John may have been Jesus' cousin (his mother, Salome, being Mary's sister: Matthew 27:56; Mark 15:40; John 19:25).

The Capernaum fishing business must have been a flourishing one, as the household had hired servants, and a house in Jerusalem. If the 'other disciple' of 18:15-16 is John it may have been through the business that John was acquainted with the high priest (John 18:15-16). He may also be the unnamed disciple of John the Baptist referred to in John 1:35, 40.

John and James (nicknamed by Jesus 'sons of thunder') with Peter were the leaders of the Twelve disciples and later

Nathanael was meditating under a fig-tree – a place of deep shade out of the fierce heat of the sun.

of the Jerusalem church. They were the inner circle of three who were allowed to see Jesus transfigured, who saw him restore Jairus' daughter to life, and who were near him in the garden of Gethsemane. Jesus committed his own mother to John's care as they stood near the cross. It was not given to many to know Jesus as closely as John did.

1:1-18
PROLOGUE

John begins his Gospel with a tremendous statement about Jesus Christ: on these truths his whole case rests. In him (the Word) God speaks to man. He is the most perfect and complete expression of the Person of God we can ever know. He is far and away above all humanity – God's executive in creation. When God spoke (see Genesis 1), his Word brought life itself into existence. And it was this Supreme Being who became man – the man we know as Jesus Christ. His life shone out – and still shines – against the darkness of a world which failed to recognize him. But to individuals who give him their allegiance he makes available all God's loving forgiveness (grace, 16). And he makes a new, transformed life possible (12).

John (6): John the Baptist (see on Luke 1, Matthew 3, Mark 1), the herald sent by God to tell people of the coming Christ and prepare for his arrival.

Verse 14: John may be thinking especially of the transfiguration – the time when he and Peter and James saw something of Jesus' supernatural splendour (Matthew 17:1-8).

1:19 — 2:12
EARLY DAYS

1:19-34 John the Baptist identifies Jesus as Messiah

John's dramatic preaching attracted much attention. But he directs it away

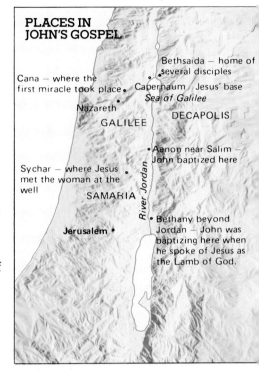

PLACES IN JOHN'S GOSPEL

Bethsaida — home of several disciples

Cana — where the first miracle took place

Capernaum Jesus' base

Sea of Galilee

Nazareth

GALILEE

DECAPOLIS

Aenon near Salim — John baptized here

Sychar — where Jesus met the woman at the well

SAMARIA

River Jordan

Bethany beyond Jordan — John was baptizing here when he spoke of Jesus as the Lamb of God.

Jerusalem

from himself. He is not Messiah. Nor will he admit to being the predicted second Elijah (Malachi 4:5; in contrast, Jesus leaves us in no doubt that this prediction was realized in John, Matthew 17:10-13). Nor is he the prophet like Moses (Deuteronomy 18:15). As soon as God has shown him the Messiah (32-34) he directs men to Jesus.

Pharisees (24): see page 494.

The Lamb of God (29): a phrase from the Old Testament sacrifices (Leviticus 4:32-35; see also Isaiah 53:4-12). Sin puts every individual under sentence of death – separation from God. But in Old Testament times God accepted the death of an animal as substitute for the death of a person. Further sin meant repeated sacrifices. Jesus was to die to give his life once and for all, sacrificed like a lamb for human sin throughout the ages.

1:35-51 Jesus' first followers

See also on 'The Twelve', Mark 3:7-19. At John's words, two of his followers leave him for Jesus – Andrew, the fisherman (see also 6:8-9; 12:22) and an unnamed follower, possibly the apostle John. The news is too good not to share; so first Andrew brings Peter, and then Philip (see also 6:5; 12:21; 14:8) brings the intellectual Nathanael.

Verse 39: John uses the Roman (and modern) method of reckoning the hours, the time is 10 a.m.; but most modern versions give 4 p.m.

Verse 42: 'Cephas' and 'Peter' both mean 'the rock-man'.

Verse 48: Nathanael was following the Jewish custom of meditating on the scriptures under his fig-tree. It seems likely, from Jesus' words in verse 51, that he was thinking about Jacob's dream of a stairway between heaven and earth (Genesis 28:12). Jesus is himself a 'ladder' giving man access to God.

The Son of man (51): Jesus' favourite description of himself. The title was one applied to the Messiah (Daniel 7:13-14).

2:1-12 Jesus at the wedding

Jesus' first miracle has a homely setting. The wedding festivities lasted several days, and when the wine ran out the bridegroom (who footed the bill) must have been highly embarrassed. This is the first of seven 'signs' selected by John. All have a purpose – they actively support the claims Jesus made, and are intended to lead to faith. Here the new wine of the Gospel is contrasted with the water of the old faith (see verse 6). Jesus had come to bring something really new.

Cana (1): Nathanael's home town (21:2); a few miles north-east of Nazareth.

Cana-in-Galilee, scene of the wedding where Jesus turned the water into wine.

A large water-pot at the Rockefeller Museum, Jerusalem.

Verse 4: no one, not even his mother, has the right to put pressure on Jesus. But his reply is not as harsh as some translations make it sound. New English Bible 'Your concern, mother, is not mine' is better.
Verse 6: the water-pots were there for the ritual washing of hands and utensils.

2:13–3:36
JESUS' PUBLIC MINISTRY BEGINS: JERUSALEM

2:13-25 Jesus ejects the traders from the temple

See on Matthew 21:12-17. John places this at the beginning of Jesus' ministry, the other Gospels at the end. Jesus may, of course, have turned the traders out of

the temple on more than one occasion. But it seems more likely that John overrules strict chronology for more important considerations. The incident illustrates the dishonesty, hypocrisy and prejudice at the heart of Israel's religious life. It makes us see that a head-on clash between Jesus and the religious authorities is inevitable.
Passover (13): see on Matthew 26:14-29.
Verses 20-21: the temple was in a special sense the place of God's presence – the closest people could come to God himself. With the coming of Jesus that changed: he could accurately describe himself as the Temple of God. For the temple of Jesus' day, see page 496.

3:1-21 The interview with Nicodemus

Nicodemus comes secretly; later he comes out openly on the side of Christ (7:50-51; 19:39). Men need an entirely new spiritual re-birth in order to enter God's kingdom. The new age Jesus was announcing was not to be bound by the old cycle of physical birth and death. It was to be a radical new beginning, a new quality of life – eternal life.

Verses 16-21 may be Jesus' words or John's comment. They contain the heart of the Gospel message. Jesus comes to save – but the consequence of his coming, for those who refuse him, is judgement.
Verse 14: see Numbers 21:4-9; Jesus is referring to his crucifixion.

3:22-36 John the Baptist steps down

For a while Jesus' ministry overlaps with John's, and Jesus draws the bigger crowds. John's reaction, in a situation which goes very much against the human grain, is absolutely right. He allows no trace of bitterness or jealousy to sour his gladness at Jesus' God-given success.

Verses 31-36 may be the Baptist's words or the apostle's comment.

Verse 24: see Mark 6:17-29. The writer here as elsewhere assumes that his readers know the basic facts.

4:1-42
SAMARIA: THE WOMAN AT THE WELL

Jesus chooses the short route from Jerusalem to Galilee which takes him through Samaria – normally avoided by Jews, for over 700 years of religious and racial prejudice separated the Jew from the Samaritan (see page 497). Add to this the Jewish prayer, 'Blessed art thou O Lord . . .who hast not made me a woman' and one can understand the Samaritan woman's surprise (9) when Jesus talks to her. Tired and thirsty though he is, he can never ignore human need. As the conversation develops he makes it clear that the woman's need is spiritual rather than physical (7-15), moral rather than 'theological' (16-26). As a result of this seemingly insignificant encounter, many others believe – some through the woman's testimony, more through Jesus' own words.

Verse 20: for the Samaritan, Mt Gerizim was the centre of worship; for the Jew, Jerusalem. Jesus says that the place is unimportant. What matters is that worship should be genuine and spiritual.

4:43-54
GALILEE: HEALING OF THE OFFICIAL'S SON

This is the second of the signs recorded by John (see on 2:1-12 above). Jesus never performed miracles simply to impress. They were intended, as here (verse 53), to lead to faith. John's purpose in recording them is precisely the same.

Verse 44: Jesus was speaking about Nazareth (Mark 6:1-6). John may be giving the words a wider reference, to lack of response in Judea.

Women at a well in the hills of Judea.

5
JERUSALEM AGAIN

5:1-18 Trouble over healing on the sabbath

This is the third sign (see above). Jesus clashed with the religious authorities a number of times over healing on the sabbath (Mark 3:1-6; Luke 13:10-17; 14:1-6; John 9). It was not the general principle of the sabbath that he disagreed with (he regularly attended the synagogue) but the petty restrictions imposed by the religious authorities, which often worked *against* God's purpose in giving people a weekly day of rest. Here the Jews attack him on two counts – sabbath-breaking and blasphemy – because he puts his own work on the same level as

The Pool of Bethesda – where Jesus healed the sick man – with its five 'porches', has been discovered deep below the level of present-day Jerusalem.

God's (17). God's activity in the world did not finish with the creation.

5:19-47 The claims of Jesus

The Jews were right. Jesus *was* making himself God's equal (18) – though this did not mean setting himself up as an independent authority (19). In this passage alone he claims to have:

- knowledge of God's plan (20)
- God's authorization for all he says and does (19, 30)
- power to give eternal life (21, 24, 40)
- the right and authority to judge all men, living and dead (25-29).

A man who makes these claims must be 'mad, bad, or God'. What support can he give them?

- the word God spoke at his baptism (37)
- the testimonial given by John the Baptist (33-35)
- the evidence of his own miracles (36)
- the words of Old Testament Scripture (39).

6
GALILEE

6:1-21 Food for 5,000; Jesus walks on the lake

See on Mark 6:30-56. See also Matthew 14:13-36; Luke 9:10b-17. These are the fourth and fifth signs. The events stand out clearly in John's mind. He remembers which disciples replied to Jesus' question; he recalls the lad; he remembers how far they had rowed from shore when they saw Jesus.

6:22-59 The crowd tracks Jesus down; Christ, the bread of life

The crowd is all in favour of a Messiah who can provide free meals for the asking (26, 34). No one can live without food. But life is more than physical existence (27). Jesus comes to provide bread for the spiritually starving. He is the giver *and* the gift itself. He is the bread of the new life; the one on whom we depend entirely for existence. And the bread we feed on – the source of life for us – is his death (51). Because sin has placed us under God's sentence of death, we live only because of Christ's death on our behalf. We know life only as we make his death and all it means our own. The forgiveness his death has brought is the meat and drink of Christian living. Each one of us must receive it for himself (52-58). The Lord's Supper proclaims this same fact in visual terms (Matthew 26:26-28).

Manna (31): see Exodus 16 and Deuteronomy 8:3.

6:60-71 Reaction

Those who put a crudely literal interpretation on Jesus' words were disgusted. The law forbade the drinking of blood. Meat had to be specially butchered to meet the law's requirements. Yet had they bothered to think back to the reason for the rule they would have understood. Leviticus 17:11 says, 'it is the blood that makes atonement, by reason of the life.' Jesus is saying, 'I am atoning for your sin; avail yourselves of my sacrifice.' The crowd turn away – they do not want this sort of Messiah. But the Twelve remain, in growing faith.

7 – 10:21
TO JERUSALEM FOR THE FEAST OF TABERNACLES

7:1-13 Danger

Last time Jesus visited Jerusalem there

The hills across the Lake of Galilee glow with the reflection of the setting sun.

The Herod Family

E. M. BLAIKLOCK

When the Romans organized the East in 63 BC, Pompey appointed a priest named Hyrcanus to rule Galilee, Samaria, Judea and Peraea. Hyrcanus had an astute vizier, an Idumaean named Antipater, who knew how to use his power shrewdly for his family's advantage. He secured his two sons, Phasael and Herod, in key governorships, and when Antipater was murdered in 43 BC, the two young men succeeded jointly to the viziership in Hyrcanus' court.

Phasael was soon a victim of a Parthian raid which followed the assassination of Julius Caesar, who had intended pacifying their frontier. Herod escaped to Rome, and so impressed Octavian (the future Augustus) that he received a mandate to recover Palestine, which he did between 39 and 36 BC. He successfully carried on a pro-Roman administration for 34 years, marked by the building of the Roman port and base at Caesarea, and the building of a temple to Augustus at Samaria.

Simultaneously, he conciliated the Jews, who hated him for his Edomite blood, by building the great temple at Jerusalem. He was a superb diplomatist. He divided the opposition by suppressing the old aristocracy –yet married Mariamne, one of their number, and set up a nobility of officials. He stimulated loyalty to his house by founding a pro-Herod Jewish party, the 'Herodians'; established a bureaucracy modelled on that of the Ptolemies in Egypt; and secured his power by a mercenary army and a system of strongholds (one of which was Masada). The price he paid for his dangerous living was tension within his own family, murder, and ultimately paranoia. This was the Herod who was king when Jesus was born. Herod's jealousy of this 'rival king' and ruthless slaughter of the children at Bethlehem is in keeping with what we know of his character.

Herod's will divided the kingdom which he had ruled so long, so dexterously, and so ruthlessly. Archelaus, son of the Samaritan woman Malthace, took over Judea and Idumaea, by far the choicest share. Herod Antipas, son of the same mother, received Galilee and Peraea. And Philip, son of a Jewess named Cleopatra, took Ituraea, Trachonitis, and the associated territories in the north-east. Archelaus, who inherited his father's vices without his ability, bloodily quelled disorders which broke out in Jerusalem. The result was a wider uprising, which required the strong intervention of Varus, governor of Syria. Archelaus' stupid rule continued till AD 6, when Jewish protest secured his banishment. Judea was placed under the control of a procurator (a governor responsible to the Roman authorities). Herod Antipater (Antipas), on the other hand, equalled his father's long reign. The Herodian flair for diplomacy bolstered his puppet rule while Tiberius was emperor. But Antipas misread the mad Caligula. He sought a royal title, was deposed and exiled, an ordeal loyally shared by the notorious Herodias. It was Antipas who imprisoned and executed John the Baptist. He also had a brief meeting with Jesus, when Pilate referred the prisoner to Herod during the trial.

Herod Agrippa I, the grandson of the first Herod, was brought up at Rome, managed Caligula better, and so succeeded to Philip's tetrarchy when Philip, the best of the three brothers, died. When Antipas was exiled, Galilee and Peraea were added, and in AD 41, Agrippa received from the Emperor Claudius the whole of his grandfather's domains. This is the Herod who appears in Acts 12. He died of a grave intestinal disorder in AD 44 at the age of 34, and Palestine came wholly under Roman rule.

Agrippa left a teenage son who was set up by Claudius as the king of Chalcis in AD 48. In AD 53, the domains of Philip the tetrarch and Lysanias were added by Claudius to this realm, together with an area on the western side of Galilee, including the new town of Tiberias. The appointment carried the title of king, so in AD 53 Agrippa became Agrippa II, last of the Herodian line. He appears only in the brilliantly told story of Acts 25, where, as the procurator Festus' guest, he heard the defence of Paul.

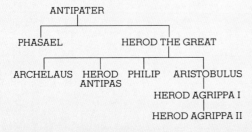

was trouble, ending in a plot against his life (chapter 5). This time he avoids publicity.

Tabernacles/Shelters (2): September/ October – the 8-day Jewish harvest festival, commemorating the nation's desert wanderings. See 'Feasts and Festivals', page 181.

Not going (8): some manuscripts add 'yet', showing that Jesus did not intend to mislead. He waited for the opportune moment and then seized it.

7:14-52 Jesus' message gets a mixed reception

As opposition mounts, individuals take sides. Jesus' teaching (40) and his miracles (31) convince some. Others raise difficulties (27, 41-42). But no one who genuinely wants to do God's will is left in doubt (17). Jesus draws his imagery from the ceremony appointed for each day of the festival, when water from the Pool of Siloam was offered to God. Jesus is a bubbling spring, reviving and transforming the thirsty human heart.

Dispersion (35, some versions): the Jewish communities abroad.

Verse 42: they cannot have heard the story of Jesus' birth. The Old Testament reference is Micah 5:2.

7:53 – 8:11 The woman guilty of adultery

Although this story is quite genuine, it is unlikely that it originally belonged here (some manuscripts place it at the end of John's Gospel, others insert it after Luke 21:38). The lawyers were trying to trap Jesus. They intended to push him either into contradicting the Mosaic law, or into falling foul of the Roman authorities, who did not allow Jews to carry out a death sentence. But Jesus did neither – nor did he condemn, or condone, the woman's conduct. He gave her a second chance.

8:12-59 Jesus, the light of the world

Jesus again uses one of the ceremonies of the feast to explain his own mission. At dusk they lit four great golden candelabra to symbolize the pillar of fire by which God guided his people through the desert by night (Exodus 13:21). Jesus lights the way through life for all who follow him. He strengthens his claim to be, in a unique sense, God's Son (see also on 5:19-47).

Verses 12-30: unlike the rest of us, he knows where he comes from and where he is going. He knows the future. The Jewish people have their origin and ancestry in this world, but not Jesus.

Verses 31-47: other men are held in the grip of sin. Jesus is free, and has the power to free others.

Verses 48-59: Jesus asserts his control over death and the eternal destinies of men. Only God has these powers.

9 The blind man sees; the sighted shut their eyes

Jesus really is the light of the world. This sixth sign makes that plain. It also gives us some insight into the problem of human suffering.

■ Although there is a direct connection between human suffering and man's sin, the individual is not necessarily suffering because of his own or his parents' sin (3).

■ There are times when God allows suffering for a purpose. And he brings good out of it, for the individual himself and all he comes into contact with. Here the man's blindness leads to an encounter with Jesus. His eyes were opened and he saw (7). His mind was opened and he believed (35-37). By contrast, the sighted men allow prejudice and pride to blind them to the truth (40-41). Confronted by a miracle, all they can see is a broken rule (16). Their minds are closed. They will not listen to the simple logic of the man in the street (30-34).

Verse 6: Jesus uses the methods of popular medicine (saliva was thought to have healing properties). But the method is not the important thing. What counts is the man's faith, demonstrated by his ready obedience (7).

Sent (7): because the water was channelled from another source.

Verse 22: anyone who followed Christ faced excommunication.

10:1-21 Jesus, the good shepherd

This passage follows straight on from chapter 9. The shepherd was a familiar figure in Palestine. He spent much of his life with his flock. His own sheep knew and responded to his voice. He led (not drove) them to fresh grazing, and guarded them from wild animals by lying across the entrance to the sheepfold at night, so becoming its 'door'. In the Old Testament God is often called the shepherd of Israel. And his chosen leaders are also the nation's 'shepherds'. Now Jesus chooses to describe himself as the *true* shepherd. The phrase sums up so much: the close, personal relationship between himself and each of his followers; the absolute security we have in him; his leadership and guidance; his constant company; his unfailing care; his sacrificial love.

Verse 16: Jesus' concern goes out beyond the Jewish nation to the waiting world. Jew and non-Jew, slave and free man, man and woman, all are one flock (see Galatians 3:28).

10:22-42
JERUSALEM: THE FEAST OF DEDICATION

This eight-day feast – the festival of lights – took place in December. It commemorated the great Jewish victory under the Maccabees and the rededication of the desecrated temple.

The Jews remain in suspense because they will not believe (24-26). They are ready to stone Jesus as a man making

himself out to be God (33). But they have it back to front. Jesus is not man made God, but God made man (30).

11
LAZARUS RETURNS FROM THE DEAD; JESUS, THE RESURRECTION AND THE LIFE

This is the seventh sign. Lazarus' death is permitted for the same reason as the man's blindness (4 and 9:3). Time and again we see how Jesus' miracles back up the claims he made. No wonder he so often referred his critics to the work he was doing. He claims he can give men new, spiritual life. What clearer assurance that this is so than Lazarus' return from the dead after four days in the grave? So we too can take him at his word. Neither the disciples nor the two sisters could understand Jesus' behaviour, but the result for all of them was renewed trust in him (15, 27, 42). The event is decisive – for faith and life on the one hand (45); for hatred and death on the other (53).

Thomas (16): see also 20:24-29.

Verse 50: the high priest's words took on a significance he never dreamed of.

12
FINAL DAYS OF PUBLIC TEACHING IN JERUSALEM

12:1-8 Mary's precious flask of perfume
See on Mark 14:1-11.

12:9-11 The plot to kill Lazarus

12:12-19 Jesus rides in triumph into Jerusalem
See on Luke 19:28-48 and introduction to Matthew 21. See also Mark 11:1-11.

A shepherd leads his sheep, as the sun sets behind the hills of Galilee.

Branches of palm (13): the symbol of victory.

12:20-36a The Greeks search Jesus out

The arrival of the Greek converts brings Jesus face to face with his destiny. The time has come for him to buy life for mankind with his own death. Verses 20-36 and 44-50 record his last public statement. It is full of paradox: life through death; glory through the ignominy of the cross; the world judged in the execution of judgement.

Verse 25: Jesus is not advocating a death-wish. But love for him and concern for eternal things must far outweigh all selfish, material concerns.

12:36b-50 Jesus steps out of the limelight

Verses 36b-43: at the end of Jesus' public ministry and despite all his miracles the Jews remained unconvinced. And many of those who did believe were too afraid to say so openly.

Verses 44-50: it matters how each of us reacts to Christ. Because he comes on God's authority, it is all-important whether we believe in him or not.

Verse 40: God never hardens the heart of someone willing to respond. But in the end, if we choose to be blind and persistently reject his truth, he lets us become immune to it.

13 — 17:26
JESUS' LAST WORDS TO THE TWELVE

13:1-20 Jesus washes the disciples' feet

The occasion is the Last Supper (see on Matthew 26:14-29). The disciples have been arguing over who is greatest (Luke

A reconstruction of Jerusalem, with Herod's temple on the right, the Roman quarter (with amphitheatre) inside the wall to the centre and left.

22:24). Jesus gives them the answer in this simple action. The Master, conscious of who he is and in his love for men, has willingly made himself their slave (Luke 22:27). His followers must do the same.

13:21-30 Judas, the traitor

Judas has already volunteered to help the priests make a secret arrest (Luke 22:3-6). Now the moment has come. The rest of the disciples have no idea of what is afoot. But Jesus knows. 'It was night' – quite literally. But light and darkness acquire a special meaning in this Gospel (1:4-9). These were Jesus' darkest hours, but nothing could extinguish the light of his life (1:5). Judas, by contrast, stepped from the light into darkness so intense it destroyed him (3:19-20; Matthew 27:3-5).

Verse 23: most probably John himself; see introduction.

13:31-38 The command to love one another; Jesus predicts Peter's fall

The prospect of death on the cross, cut off from his Father by the colossal burden of the world's sin, appalled Jesus (Luke 22:42-44). Yet because of all it would achieve, he could describe it in terms of triumph and glory. It was his love for others that took him there. And it is love of this same calibre he looks for in his followers.

14 Jesus reassures his disciples; 'I am the way, and the truth, and the life'

The disciples are worried and upset by the talk of betrayal and the thought of Jesus leaving them. Jesus himself is concerned at the effect his death will have on them all. And so he tries to get them to understand why it has to happen.

His death means his return to the

Jesus taught in the porches of the temple area in Jerusalem.

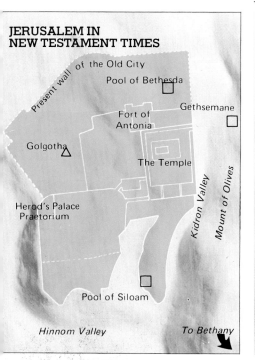

JERUSALEM IN NEW TESTAMENT TIMES

Present wall of the Old City

Pool of Bethesda

Gethsemane

Fort of Antonia

Golgotha

The Temple

Kidron Valley

Mount of Olives

Herod's Palace Praetorium

Pool of Siloam

Hinnom Valley

To Bethany

The village of Bethany near Jerusalem, where Jesus could withdraw to enjoy the hospitality of friends.

A vine with the main 'stock', branches growing from it, bunches of grapes on the fruitful branches, and the unfruitful branches cut off to be burnt.

Father (12, 28). He is making the approach-road for men and women to come to God (6). He is going to get a permanent home ready for his disciples, and in due course he will come for them (2-3). Meanwhile his return to God will be to their good: it will bring new power in action, new certainty in prayer (12, 14). Best of all, the Holy Spirit will come to be with them always and everywhere (not limited by a physical body as Jesus had been). He will teach and counsel and bring to mind all that Jesus has said (16-17, 26). And Jesus' own unshakable peace will be theirs (27).

For their part, the disciples must continue to love and trust him (1). And the way to show their love is to do all that he says (15, 21, 23).

15 – 16 Jesus, the true vine; opposition; the promise of the Holy Spirit

The conversation continues as they make their way to Gethsemane (14:31). There is not much time left.

15:1-17: in the Old Testament, Israel is the vine – so often failing to yield fruit (see Galatians 5:22-23). But Jesus was the true vine, the fulfilment of God's purpose where Israel had failed. Those who believe in him are branches. Every branch of a vine grows directly from the main 'stock'. When they are cut back, branches which have borne fruit are pruned to within an inch or two of the stock. They then 'abide' in the stock for most of the year as it grows round them. Then the branches grow out rapidly to bear fruit again. Branches which have not borne fruit at all are cut right back, and are fit only for burning.

15:18 – 16:4a: those who belong to Christ will inevitably encounter the hatred of self-centred humanity, just as Christ himself did. They will even be hounded by men who (like Paul) consider themselves to be doing God a service.

16:4b-15: Jesus' going means the coming of the Holy Spirit to convict men of the truth and lead them into deeper understanding of it.

16:16-33: at Christ's death there will be grief, but only for a little. With the resurrection will come lasting joy.
16:25, 29: figuratively speaking.

17 Jesus' prayer; for himself and for his followers

Jesus has accomplished all he set out to do during his lifetime. He has passed God's message on. He has made God known. Now there remains only death, and beyond it the glory he renounced to become man. But his followers will be left bereft in a hostile world. So he prays that God will protect them; that their lives may be shaped by the truth of God's word; that they may display such unity among themselves that the world will be shaken out of its disbelief; and that they may, in the end, go to be with him and see his glory for themselves.
Verse 12: the reference is to Judas.

18–21
TRIAL, DEATH AND RESURRECTION

18:1-12 Betrayal and arrest

See on Matthew 26:30-56. See also Mark 14:26-52; Luke 22:39-53. John omits Jesus' prayer in the garden. But he tells us the name of the slave, and that the swordsman was Peter.
Verse 1: see map, page 545.

18:13–19:16 Jesus before Annas and Caiaphas; Peter's denial; Jesus before Pilate

See on Mark 14:53–15:15; Luke 22: 54–23:31. See also Matthew 26:57–27:26. The detail John fills in shows his close knowledge of what happened – the cold night; the charcoal fire (18:18); the blow to the prisoner (18:22); Jewish religious scruples over entering the Roman's house at such a time (18:28); the exchanges

between Jesus and Pilate, and Pilate and the Jews; the terrible national apostasy as God's people declare they have no king but Caesar.
The Pavement (19:13): see page 527.
19:14: unlike the other Gospel writers, John probably uses Roman time, counting as we do from midnight (though some versions give 'noon'). Unless, as some believe, John dates the Passover one day later than the other Gospel writers (see Mark 14:12), the reference here is to the preparation for the sabbath of Passover week (19:31).

19:17-37 The crucifixion

See on Mark 15:16-41; Luke 23:32-49. See also Matthew 27:27-56. Again John

Across the Kidron ravine from the city of Jerusalem is the Garden of Gethsemane, the twisted forms of the ancient olive-trees recalling Jesus' agony.

shows his vivid recollection of events – the details of the inscription (20-22); the seamless tunic (23-24); the moment when Jesus entrusted his mother to John's care (26-27); the incontrovertible evidence of Jesus' death (34).

Verse 31: Jewish law said that the bodies of criminals must not be left hanging after sunset (Deuteronomy 21:23).

Verse 34: John is implying more than that Jesus was without question dead. As a Jew, he could not help seeing special significance in the flow of blood (for sacrifice) and water (for cleansing). The blood atones for man's sin, the water gives him a clean, new start. Jesus' death brings us forgiveness and new life.

19:38-42 Burial

See on Mark 15:42-47. See also Matthew 27:57-66; Luke 23:50-56. The death of

Jesus prepared a breakfast by the lake for the fishermen. They were wearied by a night's fishing and now astonished at the catch he had given them.

Jesus brings two secret disciples out into the open. Only John mentions the part played by Nicodemus (see 3:1-15).

20 The resurrection; Jesus appears to the disciples in Jerusalem

See on Luke 24. See also Matthew 28; Mark 16. John gives his own personal account of what happened – what he heard and saw for himself, and what he learnt from Mary Magdalene. Thomas the realist's momentous declaration of faith – 'My Lord and my God!' – is the climax of the whole Gospel. John's purpose in writing is to bring men to just such assured and clear-cut belief in Jesus (31).

Verse 7: John sees the grave-clothes and head-cloth lying undisturbed, still in place. But now an empty space separates the head-cloth from the rest. No one could steal a body and leave the grave-clothes like that. Jesus' body can only have passed through them. So John took note, and believed.

21 Jesus appears again in Galilee; the author's final word

Only John tells us how Jesus came to the seven of them as they were fishing, just as in the old days. John was there. He remembers how many fish they caught, and their surprise and relief at finding the net intact. He remembers how Jesus gave Peter the chance to cancel out his three-fold denial with the three-times-repeated question 'Do you love me?'; how he restored Peter to his old place as leader, and gave him the task of caring for his people. He remembers Peter's question about his own destiny – and sets the record straight.

And having remembered it all, he closes his Gospel with an affirmation of the truth of what he has written.

Verse 18: a prediction of Peter's death – stretched out on a cross, like his Master.

The book of Acts covers a period of some 30 years, from the birth of the church on the Day of Pentecost to the close of Paul's imprisonment at Rome. It describes the spread of Christianity around the northern Mediterranean – through present-day Syria, Turkey and Greece, to the heart of the Roman Empire. The 'acts' related are mainly those of the apostles Peter and Paul, though the book might well be called 'the acts of the Holy Spirit'. It is under his direction that the new-born church bursts through the national frontiers of Israel to become an international, world-wide movement.

Who wrote it?

All the evidence, from earliest times, points to Paul's 'dear friend Luke, the doctor'. He wrote Acts as a sequel to his earlier volume, the third Gospel. Luke is the only non-Jewish writer in the New Testament. He came from Antioch, or possibly Philippi. Although we have few facts about his life, his writings prove him a fine and reliable historian. We know, from the way he changes from 'they' to 'we' in Acts (16:10; 20:5; 27:1), that he was present at many of the events he describes. He was with Paul at Philippi. He made the fateful journey with him to Jerusalem, stuck by him during the two years at Caesarea, and shared the voyage and shipwreck on the way to Rome. He had plenty of opportunity to obtain his other information first-hand – from Paul and Barnabas and others in the church at Antioch; from James, the Lord's brother, among others at Jerusalem; and from Philip and his daughters at Caesarea. And we know from Luke 1:1-4 just how concerned he was to get at the facts.

Time-chart

There are not enough fixed points to be exact, but the dates below are accurate within a year or two either way.

AD 30	The founding of the church in Jerusalem (Acts 1—2)	48-51	Second missionary journey (Acts 15:36—18:22)
32/35	Paul's conversion (Acts 9)	50	Paul reaches Corinth (Acts 18)
34/37	Paul's first visit to Jerusalem (Acts 9:26ff.)	53	Third missionary journey begins (Acts 18:23)
		54-57	Paul's stay in Ephesus (Acts 19)
45 or 46	Famine relief sent to Jerusalem from Antioch (Acts 11:27ff.) Death of James	57-58	Paul in Greece (Acts 20)
		58 (June)	Paul reaches Jerusalem (Acts 21)
		58-60	Imprisonment at Caesarea (Acts 24—26)
46 or 47	First missionary journey (Acts 13—14)	60-61	Appeal to Caesar and voyage to Rome (Acts 27)
48	Apostolic Council at Jerusalem (Acts 15)	61-63	Imprisonment in Rome (Acts 28:30)

Why did he write?

It was in order to give the Roman Theophilus an accurate record of the true facts about Christianity (Luke 1:1-4). There were plenty of strange and distorted rumours flying about. This explains Luke's emphasis on the spread of the gospel to the Gentiles, who, unlike many Jews, were eager to hear (28:28). He is also concerned to account for the disturbances which so often followed the preaching. In every place the troubles are fomented either by Jewish jealousy, or vested interest. Time and again he relates how the Roman authorities cleared the Christians of all charges of subversion and sometimes protected them from the fury of the mob.

When was Acts written?

Most probably at the close of Paul's two-year imprisonment in Rome, in the early or mid-sixties. There is no hint of Nero's persecutions, or the Jewish revolt (AD 66-70), or Paul's death (about AD 67). On the contrary, the book ends on an optimistic note. It must have been written after the Gospel, which some date later than AD 70. But the evidence points to a date about AD 60, which makes 63 or thereabouts a likely date for Acts.

1—8:1a
THE BIRTH OF THE CHURCH: JERUSALEM

1:1-14 Introduction; the 40 days from resurrection to ascension

Luke's 'first book' (his Gospel) is an account of all that Jesus 'began to do and teach' during his life on earth. Acts continues the story of his work after the ascension, by the power of the Holy Spirit in the lives of the apostles. It shows how the promise in verse 8 was fulfilled: in Jerusalem (2:1–8:1a), Judea and Samaria (8:1b–11:18) and way beyond (11:19 to the end).

A cloud (9): all that human eyes could see of the glory of God's presence (compare also Exodus 40:34 and Luke 9:34-35).

Sabbath day's journey (12): the law limited travel on the sabbath to 2,000 cubits – about two thirds of a mile/1 km.

Mary...and his brothers (14): this is the last time Jesus' mother is mentioned in the New Testament, and the first time his brothers are associated with the disciples. We know at least one of them – James – had seen the risen Jesus (1 Corinthians 15:7).

1:15-26 A twelfth apostle

As far as we know, this is the last time the apostles use the time-honoured method of casting lots. It is not just a 'lucky dip' – the decision is made after much prayer. The twelfth man had to have been with Christ throughout his earthly ministry, and to have seen him after the resurrection.

The Mount of Olives, scene of the ascension of Jesus.

2:1-13 Pentecost: the coming of the Holy Spirit

With the coming of the Holy Spirit – made unmistakably evident by inward transformation and signs that all can see and hear – the waiting is over. The apostles and disciples become the new church, full of life and power, as different from their former fearful selves as can be imagined.

Pentecost (1): the old Jewish festival of firstfruits, which took place at the beginning of the wheat harvest. It was 50 days after the Passover, the time of Jesus' crucifixion.

Each heard in his own language (6): the audience of Jews and converts were from many countries, though all would speak either Greek or one of the Aramaic dialects. Normally the apostles' difficult Galilean speech would have been hard to follow. Now, to their astonishment, everyone in this mixed audience heard his own language being spoken. The curse of Babel (Genesis 11) is dramatically reversed.

2:14-47 Peter's sermon and what follows

The sermon evokes an immediate response. Baptism is followed by a new, joyous sense of community. And spiritual unity finds practical expression in readiness to share money and possessions.

The third hour (15): 9 a.m., and on that day there was fasting till mid-morning.

3—4:31 Healing of the lame man; Peter and John taken into custody

Healing and teaching, as in Jesus'

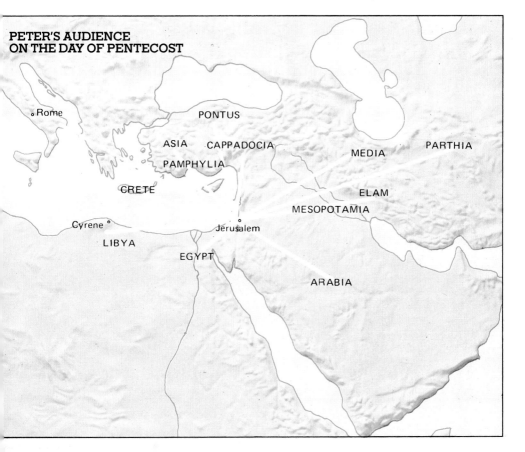

PETER'S AUDIENCE ON THE DAY OF PENTECOST

Rome

PONTUS

ASIA   CAPPADOCIA

MEDIA   PARTHIA

PAMPHYLIA

CRETE

ELAM

MESOPOTAMIA

Cyrene

Jerusalem

LIBYA

EGYPT

ARABIA

ministry, go together, both made possible by the power of the Spirit of God. It is the teaching, centring as always on the risen Christ, which annoys the Sadducees – naturally enough, as they denied the possibility of resurrection. Paul, in his turn, divided the Pharisees and Sadducees over the very same question (23:6). The resurrection was the core of the Christian message from the very earliest days. Everywhere the apostles spoke about Jesus and the resurrection – so much so that the Athenians thought Paul was talking about *two* new deities (see on 17:18).

The ninth hour (3:1): 3 p.m. Prayer times were early morning, afternoon (as here) and sunset. The first two coincided with the morning and evening sacrifices.

Annas...Caiaphas (4:6): Annas was senior ex-high priest, his son-in-law, Caiaphas, ruling high priest (AD 18-36). **He is the stone (11):** a quotation from Psalm 118:22. **Verse 13:** 'ordinary men of no education'; 'untrained laymen', New English Bible.

4:32–5:11 Ananias and Sapphira

The pooling of property was quite voluntary, but some were prompted less by real generosity than by a desire to impress. In lying to the church, Ananias and Sapphira were practising deceit against God himself. The terrible consequences served as an example to the whole church.

Barnabas (4:36): later chapters show how aptly he was named. A leader in the church at Antioch, he and Paul were sent out

Looking across from the temple area in Jerusalem toward the Mt of Olives, from which Jesus left his disciples. The arches are in the position of the porticos which surrounded the temple courtyard in New Testament times. There the disciples met in 'Solomon's Porch'.

together as missionaries. Paul benefited from Barnabas' encouragement – so too did his young cousin, John Mark.

5:12-42 The apostles before the council

It was like the days of Jesus in Galilee all over again, so many were being healed by the apostles. No wonder the Jewish authorities grew jealous of their enormous influence. But threats, imprisonment, even the lash are no weapons with which to resist the power of God.

Solomon's Porch (12): it was common practice for groups to meet for teaching and discussion in the courts of public buildings, and for disciples to listen to their teachers in the courts of the temple. The Christians met in Solomon's porch (see picture on page 545) – but knowing the authorities' hostility towards them, the bystanders kept their distance.

This man's blood (28): the apostles openly held the council responsible for Jesus' death, and they fear reprisals.

Hanging him on a tree (30): the upright of the cross was a fixture, and might well be a sawn-off tree-trunk. See also Deuteronomy 21:22-23.

Gamaliel (34): leader of the Pharisees; Paul's teacher. His is wise advice.

The Nazareth Decree

This remarkable inscription most probably dates from the first century AD. It was sent to a French collector from Nazareth in 1878. Was it the rumour that Jesus of Nazareth had risen from the dead that made the decree necessary?

❝ ORDINANCE OF CAESAR. It is my pleasure that graves and tombs remain undisturbed in perpetuity for those who have made them for the cult of their ancestors, or children, or members of their house. If, however, any man lay information that another has either demolished them, or has in any other way extracted the buried, or has maliciously transferred them to other places in order to wrong them, or has displaced the sealing or other stones, against such a one I order that a trial be instituted, as in respect of the gods, so in regard to the cult of mortals. For it shall be much more obligatory to honour the buried. Let it be absolutely forbidden for anyone to disturb them. In the case of contravention I desire that the offender be sentenced to capital punishment on charge of violation of sepulture. **❞**

---

6 Seven assistants appointed; Stephen arouses opposition

Complaints come from the Greek-speaking, non-Palestinian Jews of unfairness in the daily share-out. The apostles' answer is to let them choose seven of their own number – men of spiritual calibre – to oversee these practical matters. At least two left a permanent mark on the young church: Stephen, a powerful preacher, the first martyr, and Philip the evangelist.

The charge against Stephen is blasphemy – the very same charge that was brought against Jesus. Stephen seems to have been among the first to foresee the inevitable break with Jewish worship which the new teaching entailed.

The synagogue of the Freedmen (9): probably attended by freedmen from the places mentioned.

7—8:1a Stephen's defence and death

The defence takes the form of a review of the nation's history. The court knows the facts, but the interpretation is revolutionary. And the sting lies in the tail (51-53). Israel of old rejected the prophets from Joseph and Moses onwards. The present generation has rejected the

Messiah himself. Verses 44-50 are Stephen's answer to the charges about the destruction of the temple. A permanent building to 'house' God was never more than second-best.

Handed down by angels (53): Galatians 3:19 and Hebrews 2:2 also connect angels with the giving of the law, but there is no mention of this in the Old Testament.

The witnesses…Saul (58): the prosecuting witnesses, by law, had to cast the first stones – though in other respects this particular affair was little more than a lynching. The 'young man' Saul was probably in his thirties. He appears here for the first time. As the apostle Paul (the Roman version of his name) he is the central figure in the later chapters of Acts. Here he shares the responsibility for Stephen's death. ('Consenting' may mean that as a member of the Sanhedrin he cast his vote against Stephen.) But the scene at Stephen's death burnt into Saul's mind (22:20), and must have played its part in preparing him for the encounter on the Damascus road.

Early Christian Preaching

MICHAEL GREEN

The truly amazing thing about early Christian preaching is that it did not proclaim religious duties or moral standards, or even a reforming programme, but a person: one Jesus who was crucified and whom the Christians knew to be alive. They devoted their energies to understanding him better (from studying the Old Testament) and making him real to people who had never met him. Common belief and varied presentation are the keynotes of their achievement. Above all it is crucial to recognize that both the content and the dynamic of their preaching was the Risen One, whom many of them had known and followed for several years while he had been a carpenter and rabbi.

It has been shown that the early Christians had a broadly uniform pattern for preaching Jesus Christ. It ran something like this:

'The ancient prophecies have been fulfilled and the new age has been inaugurated by the coming of Christ. He was born of David's family, died according to the scriptures in order to deliver us from the present evil age. He was buried, rose again the third day as scripture foretold, and is now exalted at God's right hand as Son of God and Lord of the living and the dead. He has given his Holy Spirit to his followers as an assurance of his Lordship and as a foretaste of his return to be the Judge and Saviour of men at the Last Day.'

This pattern of teaching was already developed from an early date. This can be seen in the pieces of early preaching, or hymns, or creeds, incorporated into the Letters. For instance, Philippians 2:4-11 is very early, possibly coming from the Aramaic-speaking church; yet it is as doctrinally advanced as anything in the New Testament. Other fragmentary statements of belief from very early days have been preserved in such passages as 1 Corinthians 15:3-4; Romans 1:3-4 and 1 Timothy 3:16.

Slight variations in emphasis may also be detected. When speaking mainly to Jews, the deliverance Christ gives from the broken law of God is stressed. Forgiveness, justification, cleansing are the important things. When the readers are predominantly pagan in background, stress is laid on the deliverance Christ gives from the demonic powers of which men of the ancient world were so acutely aware.

So to the Jews Jesus was shown as Christ, the messianic Deliverer, the climax of the Old Testament revelation. To non-Jews, to the pagan world, he was presented as Lord and conqueror of all the forces of evil.

When preaching to the pagan world, without the background of the Old Testament revelation of God, the early missionaries also had to start further back in their teaching. Acts gives us two examples, one of preaching to unsophisticated people (14:15-17), the other the approach to the

8:1b—11:18
PERSECUTION: THE GOSPEL SPREADS TO JUDEA AND SAMARIA

8:1b-25 The response among the Samaritans

The persecution following Stephen's death led to the first broadening of the church's outreach. The attack seems to have concentrated on Stephen's fellow Hellenists (Greek-speaking Jews), leaving the apostles free to remain in Jerusalem.

Wherever the scattered believers went they preached the good news – in Philip's case with such marked success that two of the apostles came down to see what was happening.

Verse 10: Simon saw himself as the sole agent of the supreme God.

That they might receive the Holy Spirit (15-17): every believer has the Spirit of God – see Romans 8:9; 1 Corinthians 12:13. But the visible sign of the coming of the Spirit – given when the apostles officially recognized that these members

cultured (17:22-31). In both cases the Christians seek to establish the fact that there is one God, discredit idolatry and through the light of natural revelation (God the Creator and Sustainer) to prepare the way for the special revelation of God contained in Christ. This way of proceeding had been used by Jews in the previous century or so, when seeking to commend the ethical monotheism of Israel to an immoral and idolatrous but wistful pagan world. It formed a useful introduction to the specifically Christian proclamation, and it remained the staple approach for centuries.

Whether preaching to Jews or Gentiles, the early Christians emphasized not only what God had done for men through Christ, but what he offers (new life by the Holy Spirit, forgiveness of sins) and what he requires (repentance, faith and commitment). This commitment involved three strands which must be held onto together: baptism, faith and reception of the Holy Spirit. These three make a person a Christian.

Acts makes a point of the depth at which this early preaching was carried on. Words are used which indicate that the Christians acted like heralds, like teachers, like debaters. They discussed this good news, argued it, gave testimony to it, and showed how it fitted in with the Old Testament scriptures. It was the task of no single category of Christians; women chattered it at the laundry, philosophers argued it at the street corner, prisoners told their fellows. Men of every background and culture demonstrated its power by their transformed lives (see 1 Corinthians 6:9-11) and their willing acceptance of suffering and death (e.g. Acts 20:22-24).

It was these qualities which commended

the new message, with the power of the Spirit in their social and personal lives which backed up their claims. There was also an intellectual characteristic which contributed largely to their success. They discovered how to interpret Jesus in varying ways to meet varying needs – they were not rigorously hidebound. Neither were they 'syncretists': they did not say that other religious insights were equally true and could be merged with the new faith. Christianity, like Judaism, would have nothing to do with the syncretism of the pagan world. But Christians succeeded, as Judaism never did, in giving great flexibility to the expression of their faith while retaining the main common pattern and content which we have seen.

For instance, Jesus' preaching of 'the kingdom of God' might be meaningful in a Jewish constituency but could be politically inflammable elsewhere. So the early preachers preferred to use Jesus' other expressions 'eternal life' or 'salvation'.

Again, 'Son of man' was a peculiar form of address with highly apocalyptic associations understood in some circles in Judaism but meaningless elsewhere. Words which rang a bell with pagans – such as 'Son of God' or 'Lord' – were used instead by these versatile early preachers.

When engaged in interpreting the person of their Master, they used the language and thought-forms familiar to those they sought to reach. Their aim was to make crystal clear the unique saving work of the divine, crucified and risen Jesus who was both the Lord they served and the message they proclaimed.

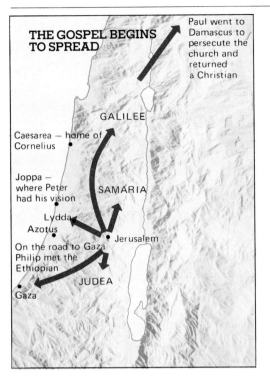

THE GOSPEL BEGINS TO SPREAD

Paul went to Damascus to persecute the church and returned a Christian

GALILEE

Caesarea — home of Cornelius

Joppa — where Peter had his vision

SAMARIA

Lydda
Azotus

On the road to Gaza Philip met the Ethiopian

Jerusalem

JUDEA

Gaza

of the despised enemy nation had become God's children – underlines the special significance of the Samaritans being welcomed into the church.

8:26-40 Philip and the Ethiopian treasurer

At the height of Philip's flourishing Samaritan campaign God calls him away to meet the need of an individual.

An Ethiopian (27): the man, a Jewish convert, was treasurer not of present-day Ethiopia, but of the old kingdom in northern Sudan.

Candace (27): the title of the queen mother who ruled the country on behalf of her son. The king himself, deified as the child of the sun-god, was considered too holy for such secular functions.

Scripture (32): Isaiah 53:7-8. The quotation is from the Greek (Septuagint) text which differs slightly from the Hebrew (Massoretic) text on which our Old Testament is based.

Caesarea (40): Philip seems to have settled at this sea-port and brought up a family. See 21:8-9.

9:1-31 The Damascus road: Saul's conversion

Saul's conversion marks a turning-point in the history of the early church. The story is told three times in Acts, once, here, by Luke, and twice by Paul – 22:5-16; 26:12-18. Never has any conversion meant a more complete about-face and radical change of thinking. The encounter with Christ was followed by three sightless days: Saul was identified with Jesus in his death and three days in the grave, and identified with him too in baptism and newness of life. By the time Ananias reached him, Saul the persecutor had become 'Brother Saul' – a man to be hunted down, in his turn, by those whose cause he once led. With his

The 'Street called Straight' in Damascus is still a main artery of the old covered market.

conversion, the church for a while had peace.

The Way (2): the church was known by this name before the people of Antioch invented the new name 'Christian' (11:26).

Tarsus (11): a university city with a population of half a million; meeting-place of East and West, Greek and Oriental. See map, page 558.

9:32-43 Peter at Lydda and Joppa: Tabitha raised from the dead

With peace at last, Peter is free to visit the Christian groups. He settles for a time at Joppa (the port from which Jonah, another reluctant missionary to the Gentiles, embarked). His host's job is the 'unclean' one of tanning – perhaps an indication that Peter is already to some extent emancipated from his religious taboos. But a far more radical challenge is to follow.

10 Peter and Cornelius

Up to this point the gospel has been preached only to Jews, converts to Judaism (proselytes) and Samaritans (who observed the law of Moses). Now God steps in to make it plain that the message is for all men (34-35). He prepares Cornelius, and he prepares Peter. Three times the vision and message come – apparently instructing Peter to break the Jewish food-laws (see Leviticus 11). But when the men from Cornelius arrive, he is quick to realize the far deeper, human implications of his dream (28). A second Pentecost – the coming of the Holy Spirit on the Gentiles – follows his teaching. No one could then deny baptism to those who had received such an obvious mark of God's favour.

Cornelius, a centurion (1): one of those who formed the back-bone of the Roman army. The centurions stationed in Palestine appear in a very favourable light in the New Testament. Cornelius was an

adherent to Jewish faith and worship, but not a circumcised convert. (See article page 507).

Peter's trance (9-16): it was midday when Peter fell into his waking dream – and Cornelius' men were already nearing Joppa. Peter's hunger, and perhaps the leather awning overhead, shape the images of a vision which God uses to convey his message.

11:1-18 The apostles approve Peter's action

This repetition of the events at Caesarea underlines their significance. The criticism Peter faces from a particularly narrow faction of Jewish Christians in Jerusalem is to dog every stage of Paul's missionary work. The admission of Gentiles to full membership of the church, without circumcision, is the most controversial question of the apostles' generation. But Luke makes it clear that the apostles and leaders had a full report from Peter and fully approved his action – the hand of God was so evident in it all.

11:19 – 16:5
ANTIOCH AND THE MISSIONARY EFFORT: ADVANCE INTO PRESENT-DAY SYRIA AND TURKEY

11:19-30 Antioch: the first Gentile church

At about the same time as the events in Caesarea, things are moving in the north, at Antioch, third largest city in the world (after Rome and Alexandria), busy commercial centre and capital of the Roman province of Syria. The warm response of the Greeks to the Christian message brings Barnabas back from Jerusalem. He in turn tracks Saul down at his home city of Tarsus. And the stage is set for the next great advance, described from chapter 13 onwards.

A severe famine...in the days of Claudius

The first stop for Paul and his companions on their first mission was Salamis in Cyprus. Here they confronted the power of the contemporary Roman civilization.

PAUL'S FIRST MISSIONARY TOUR

(28): Claudius was emperor AD 41-54. The famine hit Palestine about AD 46.

12 Death of James; imprisonment of Peter

While Paul and Barnabas are in Jerusalem, handing over Antioch's donation for the famine relief, Herod (posing as a champion of the law) instigates a new wave of persecution. James, one of the three apostles closest to Jesus, dies. But God has other plans for Peter. Even a maximum security prison presents no problems to God.

King Herod (1): Herod Agrippa 1, grandson of Herod the Great (Luke 1:5). The kingdom was given him by his friend, the Emperor Caligula, and extended by Claudius. His sudden death (23) in AD 44 is also described by the Jewish historian Josephus. See further page 540.

Unleavened Bread (3): the seven-day feast immediately following Passover, and regarded as part of that festival (4).

Four squads of soldiers (4): one squad of four soldiers for each watch of the night, two with Peter, two at the door.

13 – 14 Barnabas and Saul sent out: the first missionary journey

The church, directed by the Holy Spirit, selects its best men for pioneer work.

The tour begins with **Cyprus** (13:4-12: Barnabas' native island) where they encounter Elymas, the magician, and make a notable convert, the proconsul Sergius Paulus. Saul adopts the Roman version of his name, Paul, and becomes the natural leader of the company.

At **Perga** (13:13) John Mark returns home – for what Paul considers insufficient reason (15:37ff.).

Pisidian Antioch (13:14-52): Paul's first reported sermon; opposition from the Jews.

Iconium (14:1-6): a mixed reception followed by attempted stoning.

Lystra (14:6-20): the cripple healed; Paul and Barnabas acclaimed as gods.

Pisidian Antioch was a Roman city in a commanding position overlooking a wide area of what is now central Turkey. Paul followed his usual tactics of making for the main regional centres. Pictured here is the aqueduct built to bring water to the city, of which little remains today.

Derbe (14:20-21): a good reception after Paul's narrow escape from death by stoning at Lystra. This does not deter him from a follow-up visit there and to each of the other towns on his way to the coast.

15:1-35 The Council at Jerusalem

Ten years or more have passed since the apostles approved the admission of Cornelius' Gentile household to the church (chapters 10-11), and opposition

The New Testament and History

E. M. BLAIKLOCK

The New Testament tells a story that was to change the course of all subsequent history. The four Gospels, describing the active years of Jesus, are set in various levels of society in Rome's most turbulent province, highlighting the imperial administration and clearly indicating the situation which led, in AD 66, to Rome's most awful provincial war.

The Acts of the Apostles picks up the theme. It is a narrative written by an educated Greek, a major historian in his own right, and shows the triumphant spread of the movement which was to change the world.

That movement was shaped by one who can justly be called the first European – the educated rabbi Paul, who was thoroughly at home with Greek literature and philosophic thought (as the Areopagus address demonstrates), and who was also a Roman citizen, supremely conscious, as his plan of evangelism demonstrates, of the worth, the power, and the significance of the Empire and the Roman Peace.

Test Luke on detail, as archaeology has demonstrated he can be tested, and he emerges a man of meticulous accuracy. Read him at length, and see Ephesus and Corinth come to life. Pick single words – 'proconsuls', for example, the *plural,* in the Ephesus riot story – and see a small fact of history accounted for....

Paul's letters, in the full stream of ancient correspondence, are just as historically illuminating. Corinth, vicious, cosmopolitan, pseudo-philosophical, polyglot, disordered, argumentative, controversy-ridden, comes to life in the letter to its turbulent church, into which the restless spirit and urban vice of the place had infiltrated.

Or turn to the poetry of Revelation – the last New Testament book – a riot of symbolism, which this age above all should richly appreciate. Here is Rome as seen nowhere else – through the eyes of a bitter provincial foe – Rome, tyrannous, drunk with blood, madly persecuting ... and doomed.

Anyone who knows the New Testament in its context, and against its background, has an open window into the mind, the society, the problems, the spirit of the 1st century. Its brewing storms – the vast Jewish revolt, for example – are visible. Its fumbling administration in the East, which set the stage for disaster, is clear to view. Its experimentation with puppet kings, its repressive legislation, its patches of anachronistic city-rule, its frontier life (as for example at Lystra), its philosophic divisions, its collaborating groups, the obvious symptoms of coming catastrophe – the New Testament reveals them all.

As a collection of historical documents, the New Testament is unique.

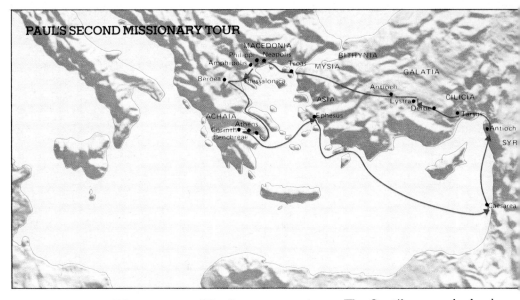

has hardened. When reports of Paul's successes amongst the Gentiles reach the 'salvation by faith *and* circumcision party', they see the red light and openly oppose his teaching. On such a vital matter an authoritative decision by the apostles and elders is essential to avoid a complete split. Peter's reminder of the earlier events, and the account given by Paul and Barnabas of God's work among the Gentiles, carry the day. The final summing-up and verdict given by James, the Lord's brother and leader of the Jerusalem church, finds general acceptance. The Gentiles are asked only to accommodate the Jewish Christians in certain social matters, so that the church may meet together as one.

15:36 – 16:5 Paul and Barnabas separate; the second missionary journey begins; churches in present-day Turkey revisited

The dispute over Mark results in two missionary journeys instead of one. Barnabas' special gift of encouragement no doubt helped his young nephew to make the grade and win Paul's approval later (2 Timothy 4:11).

Silas (Silvanus) (15:40): representative of the Jerusalem church (15:22). Like Paul, he was a Roman citizen. He travelled with the apostle as far as Beroea (17:14) and rejoined him at Corinth. Silas was associated with Paul in the writing (from Corinth) of 1 and 2 Thessalonians; also with Peter in the writing of his first letter.

Timothy (16:3): the decision to circumcise Timothy was taken in order to regularize his position as a Jew, not in order to secure his salvation. Paul had a special

Philippi was another Roman city and regional centre; near the ruins of the ancient town are river banks, where the 'God-fearers', met. See too the pictures on pages 36 and 609.

affection for his loyal, though timid, companion and successor. He came to regard him almost as his own son.

16:6 – 19:41
PAUL TAKES THE GOSPEL TO EUROPE

16:6-40 At Philippi

At Troas, close to ancient Troy, Luke joins the party for the first time, and Paul receives his call to cross to Europe. It is tempting to think that Luke himself was the man in Paul's dream.

The church at Philippi is born from a bunch of oddly assorted converts – a business woman and her household, a slave-girl and a gaoler. But the Philippian Christians brought Paul much joy down the years by their loving, faithful support and unfailing concern for him (Philippians 1:3ff.; 4:10ff.; 2 Corinthians 8). When Paul moves on, Luke the doctor remains behind. Philippi was a medical centre. See also on Philippians.

A place of prayer (13): small groups of Jews would often meet for prayer. A minimum of ten men was required to constitute a synagogue proper. The riverside at Philippi was a quiet place near the town.

Thyatira (14): a church was later formed in Lydia's home town (see Revelation 2:18ff.)

Rutted by chariot wheels, the Via Egnatia is the road Paul and his companions trod on their journey from Philippi to Thessalonica.

The Agora, or forum, at Athens. The acropolis, surmounted by the Parthenon temple, rises behind. To the right is Mars Hill. There the council of the Areopagites used to meet, before whom Paul was called to explain his new teaching. In his time they probably met in a 'stoa', a colonnaded building as reconstructed on the left of the picture.

17:1-15 Thessalonica and Beroea

Thessalonica (1-9): the response to Paul in this sea-port and capital city of Macedonia was no mere flash in the pan (see 1 Thessalonians 1:2-10; 2 Thessalonians 1:3-4). The Jews were 'jealous' because here as elsewhere Paul won over the 'devout Greeks', those already attracted to Judaism – the very people they themselves hoped to win as converts.

Beroea (10-15): the Jewish group here were notable for their open-minded study of the scriptures.

17:16-34 Paul at Athens

The apostle Paul was a strategist. He campaigned in the great cities of the Roman world. He selected centres on trade-routes, sea-ports, places where there was much coming and going. From these centres the message would run like fire far and wide. He started with present-day Turkey, moved on to Greece and then set his sights on Rome, and beyond that, on Spain. So he came from Beroea to Athens, a city with 1,000 years of history, glorying in past greatness; Athens, the founder of democracy, home of Aeschylus, Sophocles, Euripides, Thucydides, Plato, Socrates; the greatest university of the world, centre of philosophy, literature, science and art – but hard ground for the gospel.

The Epicureans (18): materialists whose

The Holy Spirit in Acts

G. W. GROGAN

The Acts of the Apostles is a book in which the Holy Spirit is especially prominent. Indeed his activity dominates it. The book might well be called 'The acts of the risen Christ by the Holy Spirit through the apostles'.

A divine Person

It is quite clear from the book that the Spirit is personal, for he did what only a person can be said to do. He spoke (1:16; 8:29; 10:19; etc.), and caused others to speak (2:4; 4:8; 31; etc.). He bore witness (5:32), sent out Christian workers (13:4), forbade certain courses of action (16:6-7) and appointed men to office in the church (20:28). He is associated with other persons (15:28) and is clearly believed to be equal with God (5:3, 9).

The agent of Christ

Acts 1:1 may imply that Jesus continued his work after the ascension through the Holy Spirit. He is the gift of the ascended Christ to his disciples (2:33) and is called 'the Spirit of Jesus' (16:7). He is also described as 'the promise of the Father' (1:4).

The creator of the church

The church as we know it today was created at Pentecost. Wind and fire (2:2-3) are Old Testament symbols of deity (see Exodus 19:18; 1 Kings 19:11-12). The gift of tongues (2:4-13) may have been deliberately chosen by God to symbolize the ultimate universality of the church, its presence among men of every language. The Spirit created a fellowship of love and unity (2:43-46) and he was promised to those who responded to the Christian message (2:38; see also 5:32).

The uniting force of the expanding church

Luke is vitally interested in the progress of the gospel and the consequent expansion of the church through the activity of the Spirit. The church at Pentecost was composed of *Jews* and *proselytes*, Gentiles who were committed to Judaism and so reckoned as if they were Jews (2:10). Jews hated Samaritans, who were of mixed race and schismatic religion, but in Acts 8:14-17 the Spirit came upon *Samaritan believers*. It is significant that this happened only after the (Jewish) apostles had laid their hands on them, in-dicating an attitude of love and fellowship on their part as well as the fact that 'salvation is from the Jews' (John 4:22). The barrier between Jew and Gentile was broken down in Acts 10:44-48 (see also 11:1-18) when the phenomena of Pentecost were repeated by the Spirit as Peter preached the gospel to *Gentiles.* It was through John the Baptist that the promise of the Spirit had first been given (Matthew 3:11-12; see Acts 1:5; 11:16), so Luke records how a group of *John's disciples* also received the Spirit (19:1-7). These passages reveal how the Spirit bound these divergent groups together and prevented division.

The power behind the church's witness

The Holy Spirit was given to the church to enable it to witness for Christ (1:8; compare 4:33). The church was directed by the Spirit when they sent Barnabas and Saul to evangelize the Gentiles (13:1-4), just as he had earlier guided Peter to preach the gospel to Cornelius and his friends (10:19ff.; compare also 8:29; 16:6-7). Filled with the Spirit they spoke with power (4:8, 31; 6:10) and undertook the various aspects of the new church's life and witness (6:3, 5; 11:22-24). The Holy Spirit gave people power to reveal Christ both by their lips and by their lives.

The life of the church

The Spirit of God is concerned with the inner life of the church in every place (9:31). It was the Spirit who appointed elders of the church as its guardians (20:28). The new age was to be one of prophecy (2:17-18), concerned with the instruction and upbuild-ing of the church itself (15:32) and prediction of things to come (11:28; 21:4). The church in council sought guidance and believed that this was given through the Holy Spirit (15:28).

So Acts occupies a unique position in the revelation of the person and role of the Holy Spirit. It records a fulfilment which is also a new beginning. The prophecies of the Old Testament and the promises of the Lord Jesus about the Holy Spirit find their fulfilment at Pentecost. The new age, the age of the Spirit, preached by Jesus, so evident in the Letters, had begun.

philosophy often amounted to little more than the pursuit of pleasure.

The Stoics (18): rationalists, propounding a philosophy of self-sufficiency and dogged endurance.

Foreign gods (18): so inseparably did Paul speak of Jesus and the resurrection ('anastasis') that the Athenians took these to be the names of two new-fangled deities. Several philosophical schools believed in the immortality of the soul, but the Greeks regarded the idea of 'bodily' resurrection as completely ludicrous (32).

The Areopagus (19): an ancient court of great prestige, possibly responsible for licensing public lecturers.

In him we live and move...(28): Paul quotes the Cretan poet Epimenides. According to legend, it was he who advised the Athenians to erect 'anonymous' altars.

18:1-17 Paul in Corinth

See on 1 Corinthians for background. Paul was there during Gallio's proconsulship, probably arriving in AD 50. Gallio's decision was an important one for the Christian faith (see article, page 573).

Aquila and Priscilla (2): tent-makers or leather-workers. They became staunch friends of Paul. Travel took them to Corinth, Ephesus and back to Rome. Everywhere this hospitable pair were a great support to the young churches.

Claudius' edict (2): issued about 49-50 against the Jews for 'constantly rioting at the instigation of Chrestus'. No doubt an allusion to disputes between Christian and non-Christian Jews in Rome.

18:18-28 Paul returns to Antioch; start of the third missionary journey; Apollos meets Aquila and Priscilla

Apollos (24): thanks to Aquila and Priscilla this eloquent Alexandrian became a man of great influence in the Corinthian church (see 1 Corinthians 1:12; 3:4ff.).

19 Paul at Ephesus

Ephesus was another great commercial centre, although its fine harbour was already beginning to silt up by Paul's day. Situated at the end of the Asiatic caravan-route, the city was a bridgehead between East and West. The tradition is that the apostle John made his home there. So

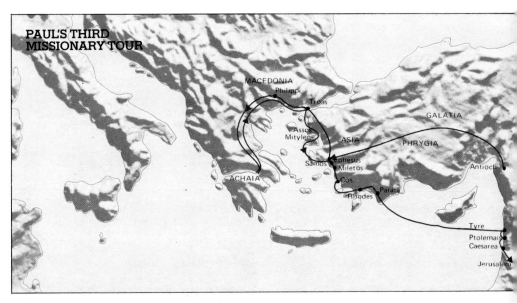

PAUL'S THIRD MISSIONARY TOUR

MACEDONIA
Philippi
Troas
Assos
Mitylene
ASIA
GALATIA
PHRYGIA
Samos
Ephesus
Miletus
Antioch
ACHAIA
Cos
Patara
Rhodes
Tyre
Ptolemais
Caesarea
Jerusalem

Extensive ruins of Ephesus from the time of Paul include the theatre where the crowds chanted 'Great is Diana of the Ephesians'. It was many years before the site of the actual temple to the goddess was found, some distance from the other ruins. Today the temple, one of the wonders of the ancient world, is no more than a great rectangular area littered with pillars. The nearby Museum of Ephesus contains two larger-than-life-size statues of the goddess. This one is a Roman version in white marble. For other pictures of Ephesus see pages 573, 605, 607, 646.

effective was Paul's ministry that it actually affected the takings of the silversmiths. Probably all seven churches mentioned in Revelation 1:11, as well as those at Colossae and Hierapolis, were also founded during this period.

Hall of Tyrannus (9): a lecture-hall which according to some manuscripts Paul used during siesta-time, from 11 a.m. to 4 p.m.

Magic ... books (19): such was the city's name for magical papyrus scrolls of spells that these were known in the Roman world as 'Ephesian letters'.

Artemis (Diana) (24): the cult adopted the name of the Greek goddess, but continued to worship the many-breasted mother-goddess figure of the ancient religion of Asia Minor. The temple was one of the seven wonders of the world, four times the size of the Parthenon. The 'sacred stone' (35) was a meteorite, supposed to resemble the goddess, and kept in the temple.

The theatre (29): an ideal place for the crowd to gather, since it could hold 25,000 people.

The Asiarchs (31, some versions): important officials specially responsible for maintaining order at religious functions.

The town clerk (35): the leading civic official, answerable to the Romans for such an illegal assembly.

Paul was constantly on the move, travelling considerable distances overland and frequently taking ship across the Mediterranean. One of the ports he used is Tyre, pictured here.

20—28
HOW PAUL EVENTUALLY REACHES ROME

20:1-16 Paul sets out for Jerusalem

2 Corinthians fills in some of the details for the period covered in 20:1-6. The apostle is preoccupied with the collection for the poverty-stricken Christians in Jerusalem (the men listed in verse 4 are delegates from the Gentile churches). His mission to the Gentiles has been much criticized by the Jews. This is his great gesture–a practical expression of the unity of Jew and Gentile in the church of Christ. It is supremely important to him–hence his determination to get to Jerusalem.

Before he left Ephesus, Paul wrote 1 Corinthians. From Macedonia (1) he wrote 2 Corinthians. From Corinth he wrote the letter to the Romans. It is likely he also visited present-day Albania and Yugoslavia ('Illyricum', Romans 15:19) at this time. Back in Philippi, Luke joins the party to Jerusalem.

Troas (7-12) provides an interesting glimpse of early church worship–the meeting on a Sunday evening for the Lord's Supper followed by a meal together (11); the length of time given to Paul's preaching (they had no New Testament); the private house, lit by torches; the effort to listen for so long, so late at night, which proved too much for the weary Eutychus.

20:17—21:14 Paul addresses the Ephesian elders; Miletus to Caesarea

This is the only address we have in Acts which was given to Christians–and the only recorded address by Paul which Luke actually heard him give. The apostle foresaw so clearly the troubles the church would face, from inside and out. Revelation 2:2 shows what notice the elders took of his warning.

Trials/hard times (20:19): there was serious trouble in Asia quite apart from the riot at Ephesus (see 2 Corinthians 1:8-11).

Philip…one of the seven (21:8): see Acts 6:5; 8:4-40.

Agabus (21:10): acted prophecy of this kind is familiar from the Old Testament (e.g. Ezekiel).

21:15—23:35 Paul in Jerusalem: the arrest

Garbled tales have reached the Jewish Christians in Jerusalem that Paul has been teaching *Jews* to abandon circumcision and the law. The troubles loom so large that the relief fund on which Paul set such store is not so much as mentioned by Luke.

The vow (21:23): compare Numbers 6: 13-21. By identifying with these men Paul openly shows his respect and conformity to the law.

Brought Greeks into the temple (21:28): anyone might go into the outer court, but notices in Greek and Latin forbade Gentiles, on pain of death, to enter the inner courts. See picture and page 496.

The barracks (21:34): the cohort was stationed in the fort Antonia. Two flights of steps led down from the fort to the outer court of the temple.

The Egyptian (21:38): leader of the 'dagger-men' who specialized in assassinating Romans and pro-Roman Jews. They murdered Ananias the high priest in AD 66.

Is it lawful…? (22:25): the Roman citizen had a right to a fair trial, and even if guilty he was spared the scourge. This horrible whip of several thongs armed with pieces

One of the inscriptions in Greek from Herod's Temple in Jerusalem forbidding non-Jews to enter the inner courts of the temple, on pain of instant death.

of lead or bone was a far more deadly instrument than the Philippian 'rods'.

Caesarea (23:23): headquarters of the administration of the Roman province of Judea. The size of the escort provided for Paul and his friends – heavy-armed infantry, cavalry, light-armed troops – is an indication of the restiveness in the province.

Felix (23:24): Pilate's successor; governor of Judea AD 52-59. His residence was the palace built by Herod the Great (35).

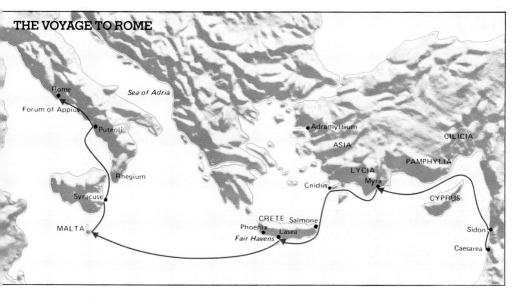

THE VOYAGE TO ROME

Rome
Sea of Adria
Forum of Appius
Puteoli
Adramyttium
CILICIA
ASIA
PAMPHYLIA
Rhegium
LYCIA
Cnidus
Myra
CYPRUS
Syracuse
MALTA
CRETE Salmone
Phoenix
Lasea
Sidon
Fair Havens
Caesarea

Paul spent two years in prison at Caesarea, the port built by the Romans as their administrative and communications base. Roman pillars can be seen there washed by the sea, and built into the later Crusader fortifications.

daughter of Herod (Acts 12:1), was his third wife. She was presumably the source of Felix' information about 'the Way'. Paul's talk of 'justice and self-control and future judgement' was too near the bone for this pair, especially as Felix was hoping for a fat bribe from his prisoner (26).

Before Festus (25:1-12). Festus was not governor for long: he died in AD 62. His attempt to curry favour with the Jews compelled Paul to appeal to Caesar. He had more hope of justice from Nero than from the Sanhedrin!

Before Agrippa (25:13–26:32). This is Agrippa II, son of the Herod of Acts 12:1, great-grandson of Herod the Great. Bernice, his sister and acting wife, went on to complete an inglorious career by becoming mistress to the emperors Titus and Vespasian. The mention of resurrection strikes the pagan Festus as completely crazy. Agrippa laughs it off – to avoid either losing face with Festus or annoying the Jews by denying the prophets.

Paul's conversion story in chapter 26 differs in emphasis from the account in chapter 22. The 'goads' are the pressures compelling Paul to a complete change of direction in life. Verses 16-18 summarize the Lord's words on the Damascus road, what Ananias said, and the message which came to Paul in the temple (22:17ff.).

24—26 In Caesarea: the defence before Felix, Festus and Agrippa

Paul spends two years in custody in Caesarea, probably AD 58-60. Three times he is called before the authorities, and the skill with which he conducts his case is some measure of the apostle's ability. So effectively does he answer the charges that his hearers are compelled to admit there is no case against him – no case, that is, apart from the theological question of the resurrection.

Before Felix (chapter 24). A violent but ineffective governor, Felix was eventually recalled (about AD 59) for mishandling riots in Caesarea. Drusilla, a Jewess,

27—28 Paul's journey to Rome: shipwreck and house-arrest

The voyage is made in three ships: a coaster from Caesarea to Myra; a cargo vessel (carrying grain on the regular run

Beyond what is called today St Paul's Bay in Malta, a sandy spit runs out into the sea. Everything here fits Luke's description of the shipwreck: while they were making for the bay to beach the ship, it struck the sand-bar and began to break up. The crew and passengers used timber from the ship to float ashore on the calmer water beyond.

Models from the Maritime Museum,
Haira, Israel

A Roman Corn Ship

from Alexandria to Rome) from Myra to Malta; and another from Malta to Puteoli in the Bay of Naples. Luke gives a superb account of the eventful passage, and a vivid impression of the outstanding courage and leadership of Paul under strain. So Paul reaches Rome at last, though hardly in the way he imagined.

After the Fast (27:9): the day of Atonement, September/October. These were dangerous months for sailing, which ceased for winter in mid-November.

Secure the boat (27:16): the dinghy had been towed behind – now they brought it on board.

Syrtis (27:17): quicksands and whirlpool off the North African coast.

Neither sun nor stars (27:20): without which they were unable to set a course or calculate their position.

The twin gods (28:11): Castor and Pollux, the sailors' patrons.

Two whole years (28:30): Paul made good use of his free custody. It is not known what happened after this time. Most probably he was released, went to Spain as planned, and then back east before further imprisonment and execution in about AD 67.

Outside Rome a stretch of the ancient Roman road the Via Appia is lined with monuments. Nearby are the Catacombs, where the Christians later met secretly to avoid persecution.

The Historical and Political Background of the New Testament

COLIN HEMER

The Persian Empire was overthrown by the spectacular conquests of Alexander the Great (336-323 BC). Alexander aimed to unite the cultures of Greece and the East, and from his time Greek influence spread in the eastern Mediterranean. After the conqueror's untimely death his enormous dominions were divided. His general Ptolemy took Egypt and also established control over Palestine. The country was of strategic importance to Ptolemy and his successors, but he allowed it a large measure of autonomy in religious affairs. Many Jews actually migrated to Alexandria, his new capital in Egypt, and their community received limited political rights in that brilliant and successful city.

Greek influence

The whole succeeding period is often called the Hellenistic age (*Hellen* = 'Greek'). The *Koine* ('common') dialect of Greek became an international language. The 'Dispersion' (expatriate) Jews particularly in Alexandria, adopted it, and a Greek translation of the Old Testament, the Septuagint, was made there, commissioned originally, it is said, by King Ptolemy II himself, and completed by the middle of the 2nd century BC.

The Hellenizing movement was also strong among the Jews, though the Hasidim ('pious'), and later the Pharisees, resisted Greek influences in the name of devotion to the Jewish law.

When the power of the Ptolemies declined, Palestine finally fell in 200 BC to Antiochus III ('the Great'), one of the Seleucids, the rival Macedonian dynasty of Syria. The Seleucids at first treated Jewish institutions with respect. But Antiochus made a fatal error. His ambitions in Asia Minor and Greece provoked a clash with the rising power of Rome. He was decisively beaten in 190 at Magnesia in western Asia Minor, and forced to surrender large territories and to pay punitive reparations. So Rome became a force in the East.

Antiochus IV Epiphanes ('god manifest') (175-164 BC) tried to restore the fortunes of his kingdom. He profited from intrigues among the Jewish factions to force upon the Jews a Greek culture and then a pagan altar and cult actually in the temple in Jerusalem.

This act provoked a violent response. The Jewish patriots found a leader in the priest Mattathias and then among his five sons. The family are known collectively as the Maccabees, from Judas Maccabaeus, the third son, who first assumed the leadership upon his father's death.

After a long struggle the brothers achieved religious freedom for their people and eventually established a virtually independent Jewish state, ruled by a succession of high priests of the Maccabean family. These rulers are known by the dynastic name Hasmoneans, and they later took the title of 'kings'. They cultivated good relations with Rome, conquered Samaria and Galilee to the north, and remained in power until 63 BC. In that year Pompey, the Roman commander in the East, intervened in a dynastic dispute, occupied Jerusalem, and added Palestine to the Roman province of Syria, newly organized from the former Seleucid dominions.

Rome: from Republic to Empire

The Roman state itself was deeply divided by social and party strife. It had become evident that its municipal institutions were hopelessly unequal to the government of its huge conquests. A series of Roman civil wars had repercussions throughout the East. Julius Caesar defeated Pompey and became dictator until murdered by republicans in 44 BC. His faction, now led by Antony and Octavian, overthrew the republicans under Brutus and Cassius at Philippi in Macedonia in 42. Antony and Octavian in their turn fought for supremacy, and Octavian won the decisive victory at Actium in western Greece in 31.

The new master of the Roman world was still a young man, the great-nephew and adopted son of the great Julius Caesar. In 27 the Roman Senate conferred upon him the title 'Augustus'. He was careful to disguise the extent of his power by a scrupulous appearance of legality. He claimed to have restored the Republic, but in fact founded what we must call the 'Empire', though in theory the idea of hereditary monarchy was abhorrent to the Romans. He and his immediate successors gave a new peace and prosperity throughout the Mediterranean world. He died in AD 14.　**»**

Among the New Testament writers only Luke ever names a Roman emperor. His references give us in outline a framework for the events of the Gospels and Acts. Jesus was born in the time of Augustus (Luke 2:1). The preaching of John the Baptist (Luke 3:1-2) and the ministry, death, resurrection and ascension of Jesus happened under Tiberius (AD 14-37). Paul's journeys occupied much of the reigns of Claudius (AD 41-54; mentioned in Acts 11:28 and 18:2) and Nero (54-68), the Caesar to whom Paul appealed. Paul reached Rome about AD 60.

The fullness of time

The times were ripe for the coming of Jesus and the spread of the gospel. Augustus had given his world respite from war. A great network of new roads united the civilized world, with its focus in Rome. Communications became easier than ever before. Latin and Greek became official languages, with Greek spoken everywhere in the East. It was already the language of the Septuagint translation of the Old Testament, and now was to become the natural vehicle of the new scriptures.

Among the Jews there was fervent expectation of the prophesied Messiah (see 'The Religious Background of the New Testament', page 494), and among the Gentiles a less articulate reaching after a personal 'salvation'. Meanwhile the communities of Dispersion Jews scattered in strategic centres throughout the Empire provided a ready-made audience for the future preaching of Paul and others.

Rulers of Palestine

The more immediate political background to the Gospels goes back to a dominant figure in Palestine before the Roman occupation, an unscrupulous, half-Jewish adventurer named Antipater. He and his son Herod courted the favour of successive Roman rulers, and Herod ('the Great') was made king of the Jews by them. He reigned 37-4 BC: Jesus was born just before he died (see Matthew 2; Luke 1:5).

At his death his kingdom was divided among three of his sons. Herod Archelaus, the ruler of Judea and Samaria (Matthew 2:22), was deposed in AD 6 and replaced by direct Roman rule under 'procurators', junior governors subject to the governors of Syria. Galilee and other territories continued for the most part to be ruled by the Herods. Herod Antipas, ruler of Galilee (4 BC-AD 39), was responsible for the death of John the Baptist (Matthew 14 and parallels). In the Acts we read of Herod Agrippa I (died AD 44; Acts 12), under whom all Palestine was again briefly united, and his son Herod Agrippa II (Acts 25—26). (See too the article on page 540.)

The best known of the procurators is Pilate (26-36), known from other sources as a tactless, violent offender of Jewish scruples (see too page 510). Paul later appeared before the procurators Felix and Festus (Acts 23—26).

Political tensions

Palestine was an occupied country, and a strong resistance movement emerged. Nationalists looked for a political Messiah who would liberate his people from the Romans. There were messianic pretenders, especially in turbulent Galilee. The Zealot party of extreme nationalists resisted payment of taxes to Rome.

Meanwhile the high priests and their Sadducee followers collaborated with the Romans. Annas and his family in particular had a vested interest in co-operating with the authorities to whom they owed their position. The Herods too were servile in their dependence on Rome. And the 'publicans' and their tools enriched themselves in the process of collecting taxes for the Romans.

There were evidently many who expected Jesus to fulfil the role of nationalist leader and who were alienated when he showed no intention of fitting in with their plans for him (see John 6:15, 66). But the tenseness of the whole political situation emerges in the manoeuvres at the time of his trial. Pilate was only impelled to action by the supposed political implication of the charge presented.

The gospel in the Roman world

The history of the times is too often viewed exclusively through the perspective of Roman imperial affairs. The Acts of the Apostles stands in its own right as a most important document of the neglected aspects of provincial life and administration. There we have vivid glimpses of provincial governors, client kings and Greek city magistrates. Asia Minor, the land where so much of the narrative is set, was the real centre of the Greek civilization of the period, and it became a strategic focus of Gentile Christianity. There Rome worked through the institutions of Greek civic life, while also accepting and finally authorizing as a bond of loyalty the ruler-cult congenial to the oriental mind. In many of the strategic cities there were wealthy Jewish communities, with privileges guaranteed by the Romans.

Paul of Tarsus was at once Jew, Greek and Roman, a man singularly fitted to communicate the gospel across racial and cultural barriers. We may trace his route along the great roads, and see him adapting his approach to the individual character of each audience. The record of Acts notes the various local institutions with minute correctness: the 'town clerk' at Ephesus, the 'politarchs' (Authorised Version 'rulers of the city') at Thessalonica, the court of 'Areopagus' or 'Mars' Hill' at Athens. The pride of Philippi in its status as a 'colony' of Roman citizens comes over clearly and with an ironic humour (Acts 16:12, 20-21, 37-39; compare Philippians 3:20, Revised Version). The confirmation of many details of this kind is preserved for us on stone in contemporary inscriptions from these cities.

The cosmopolitan Paul found in Roman institutions a protection and aid for the gospel. Judaism was a legally recognized and licensed religion, and in Jesus was the messianic fulfilment of Judaism. At Corinth this view faced a severe challenge. It was a test case and a potential legal precedent. Paul was accused before Gallio, the new Roman governor, of teaching a religion contrary to the law (Acts 18:13). Gallio, brother of the famous philosopher Seneca, the tutor of the future Emperor Nero, was not impressed. In his view the whole thing

was a matter of Jewish sectarian theology, in which he took no interest. But by dismissing the case he implicitly acknowledged that Paul's message was entitled to the same standing as other forms of Judaism. This event may probably be dated in 52: an inscription from Delphi in Greece mentions Gallio and gives a fixed point for the chronology of Paul's life.

Paul made full use of the advantages of being a Roman citizen, an unusual privilege at this period for a provincial Jew. At a time of increasing tension in Palestine he exercised his ultimate right of appeal to the emperor. He finally reached Rome as a prisoner, but apparently confident of gaining justice and a vindication of the gospel before the highest tribunal of Nero. The narrative of the Acts breaks off suddenly without telling us the outcome.

Crisis and persecution

The history of the following years was marked by events of far-reaching consequence. In 64 Nero made the Christians the scapegoats for the great fire which destroyed much of Rome. He killed a great number of them with every refinement of cruelty. This was, however, no part of a considered policy, but an irrational, and perhaps quite localized, outburst.

Meanwhile events were moving to a tragic climax in Palestine. The misdeeds of the later procurators and the defiance inspired by the Zealots culminated in a desperate rebellion and war against Rome (66-70). The Roman commander Vespasian was proclaimed emperor in 69 and left his son Titus to finish his campaign. In 70 Titus captured Jerusalem, utterly destroyed Herod's temple and laid waste the city.

The disaster was fraught with profound consequences for Jews and Christians alike. The two faiths became much more decisively separated. Judaism lost some of its privileges and Christianity was faced with new problems and the renewed peril of official persecution.

The relation of some of the later New Testament books to the fall of Jerusalem and the early persecutions is often debated. There are strong reasons for believing at least that Revelation belongs to the last years of the Emperor Domitian, Vespasian's younger son (81-96). Rome was not now a protector, but a mortal adversary. Domitian demanded as a test of loyalty the worship of himself as 'Lord' and 'God'. People were faced with a fundamental choice between Christ and Caesar.

This theatre at Ephesus was the scene of the demonstration against Paul and his companions described so dramatically in Acts 19.

Introduction
DONALD GUTHRIE

The letters make up about a third of the New Testament. Their contents are varied, but all are important because they represent what the apostles and their associates taught. They combine teaching about God and the Christian gospel with instruction on life and behaviour. They also give an insight into the problems of the early church and how they were met.

As letters they were written by real people because of real situations or needs. So it will help to trace the story which lies behind them. It will also help us to understand them to know the ideas which were held at the time. Then we can gather together some of the main themes of the letters.

Paul mentions that he is a prisoner, consist of Ephesians, Colossians, Philippians and Philemon. Some of his most profound teaching is included in these letters.
■ The 'pastoral letters', 1 and 2 Timothy and Titus, are concerned with practical matters of church leadership and organization.

The other letters are often grouped under the title of 'General Epistles'. They are addressed to a more general, less precisely defined, readership than Paul's letters. Exceptions are Hebrews, which really stands on its own, and 2 and 3 John, addressed to a specific individual or church.

THE LETTERS IN GROUPS
The obvious way to group the letters is by author, and this is in fact already done for us in the New Testament. There are thirteen letters under Paul's name, one anonymous letter (Hebrews), one by James, two by Peter, three by John and one by Jude.

Paul's letters fall naturally into four groups:

■ 1 and 2 Thessalonians are probably the earliest, and are particularly concerned about Christ's return.
■ Romans, Galatians and 1 and 2 Corinthians share a common emphasis on the gospel which Paul preached.
■ The 'captivity letters', in all of which

THE SETTING OF THE LETTERS
It is not always easy to reconstruct the historical setting of the letters. They were the products of the life of the early church, not written systematically. They supply much basic Christian teaching, but not in a formal way as theological or ethical treatises. The fact that the letters grew out of the life of the church in this way is also their strength: Christian teaching was dynamic, not stereotyped.

The book of Acts is our only other source of historical information about the early church. But Acts was selective. It did not claim to be a complete record of the events, so there are many gaps in our knowledge.

This creates a problem when it comes to trying to decide the setting of the letters. There are many issues about which we cannot be dogmatic. But the following possible reconstruction may help by showing in outline the story behind the letters.

The first letters

We can be certain of the rough dates of the first letters at least. **1 and 2 Thessalonians** were written during Paul's time at Corinth on his second missionary journey. An inscription at Delphi helps to fix this date at about AD 50-51.

After his remarkable conversion Paul had spent some years at Tarsus. He had had time to think over the implications of his new faith. He had also spent a year teaching at Antioch, and about two years in missionary work, when many churches were established in non-Jewish areas.

So Paul's first letters were from someone whose Christian thinking had already matured. They were also essentially practical, and did not call for the great assertions of Christian truths which are so characteristic of some of his later letters.

The 'gospel' letters

The next group may fairly confidently be placed during the third missionary tour, though there is a good case for assigning **Galatians** to the period between the first and second tours.

Paul had sailed from Corinth in Greece to Ephesus. He had spent some time there when he heard reports of difficulties in the church back at Corinth. He also received a letter from the church itself. **1 Corinthians** was his reply. Again this is essentially a practical letter which throws light on the many problems facing a newly established community in a pagan environment notorious for its immorality.

Paul's various contacts with the church at Corinth are not easy to unravel, though **2 Corinthians** provides some information. Paul may have visited Corinth after writing his first letter, and

have written another letter which has not been preserved. At any rate, it is plain that he was not too happy about the Corinthians' attitude to him. Then Titus was sent to Corinth, and gave Paul better news of the situation. So in 2 Corinthians Paul expresses his relief, his anxiety to restore good relations, and warns and encourages the church.

Shortly afterwards Paul visited Corinth again himself. While there he wrote his famous letter to the **Romans,** the nearest of all his letters to a theological treatise. In it he works out in some detail the great theme of righteousness by faith and shows the practical outcome of the doctrine.

It is not certain why he wrote in this way to the Romans. He expected to be visiting them soon, so may have wanted them to know the basics of his thinking. He may also have wanted to lay the foundation of further outreach to Spain.

But it was not to work out as Paul had planned. Soon afterwards he travelled to Jerusalem, where he was arrested. He was held captive for some time at Caesarea. Then he claimed his right to be tried before the emperor. He arrived in Rome – as a prisoner.

The prison letters

Tradition favours Rome as the place from which Paul wrote a number of his letters. However some believe these 'captivity letters' were written at Caesarea. There is also growing support for Ephesus as the place of origin of the letter to the Philippians, if not of the others too. If it was in Rome, this would agree with what is said in Acts: Paul was allowed considerable freedom during his imprisonment there. This would also agree well with the allusions in these letters to frequent communication between himself and his associates.

Ephesians and **Colossians** are close in content. The former seems to deal in general terms with a situation seen more specifically in the latter. A heresy was threatening the churches in the Lycus Valley east of Ephesus, and Paul writes his letter to Colossae there to strengthen the Christians and give them positive teaching about the person and work of Christ to help them resist the error. Many of the same themes are echoed in Ephesians, often in similar words, but applied more to the doctrine of the church. In spite of its title, this letter may well have been a circular letter sent round to many churches in the province of Asia.

The little letter to **Philemon** belongs to the same period. Paul writes tactfully, pleading for leniency towards a runaway slave. Many of Paul's associates mentioned in Colossians are also mentioned in Philemon.

Philippians deals with a different situation. Paul wants to thank the Christians at Philippi for the concern they have shown in sending him gifts. The main reason for writing is because he wanted to return to Philippi. He also wanted to prepare the way for Timothy's coming visit.

The remarkable feature of these 'captivity letters' is the depth of Christian understanding Paul shows in them. Perhaps it was a by-product of a period when physical freedom was denied him.

The pastoral letters

If Paul wrote these letters in his old age, he must have been released from his captivity in Rome. **1 and 2 Timothy** and **Titus** show something of his care and concern for the churches and their organization. Some have queried whether in fact Paul was the author of the letters as stated, partly because they require a period of further activity in Ephesus and Crete of which there is no hint in Acts.

Hebrews

The letter to the **Hebrews** seems to have originated in, or been addressed to, Rome, although it is impossible to be certain about this. The letter is not addressed to a specific church, but to a group of Christian Jews who, it is generally sup-

posed, were segregating themselves from the main church and were hankering after the glories of Judaism. The unnamed author shows the superiority of Christ to the old religion.

The general letters

It is difficult to be certain of the precise historical setting of the general letters.

1 Peter is the most specific, mentioning Christians in five provincial districts of Asia Minor who were threatened with persecution. The letter is intended to encourage those who are suffering for Christ's sake, and the basis of that encouragement is found in the sufferings of Christ himself.

2 Peter was presumably sent to the same general circle of readers. It warns against a particular heresy which encouraged immorality, and gives an idea of the influences which threatened the teaching and conduct of the early church.

1, 2 and 3 John are generally thought to be among the latest of the New Testament writings. They probably date from the last decade of the 1st century. According to tradition John lived in Asia Minor, so the background to the letters is probably the church life there. For instance 'Docetism', a heresy which regarded Christ as a heavenly being incapable of suffering, and so denied his incarnation, was beginning to take root and spread.

Of the remaining letters, **James** is almost wholly practical, concerned with encouragement and warning. There is some uncertainty about the setting of this letter, but there seems no reason to doubt that it reflects early conditions within the church. It could well belong to a period before the fall of Jerusalem in AD 70. It appears to come from the Jewish Christian section of the church. The brief letter of **Jude** is closely linked to 2 Peter since much of the material about the heresy occurs in both, often in similar language. Jude describes himself as James' brother. It is reasonable to suppose that both were brothers of Jesus.

THE BACKGROUND OF THE LETTERS

It seems clear, then, that all the letters belong to the second half of the 1st century, the formative period of early church development. They are therefore our main source of information on what the apostles taught.

To interpret them properly we need to understand their background. We have to know something of the thought and practice against which the letters were written for many of their ideas to be meaningful. The following paragraphs simply draw attention to the main areas, to indicate the methods by which light can be thrown on problems of interpretation.

The Old Testament

Although some letters make more direct use of the Old Testament than others, there is a basic assumption that Christianity is essentially a fulfilment of what the Jewish scriptures predicted. The writers therefore appeal to the Old Testament as their authority. Paul frequently uses it to support his arguments. Sometimes he strings quotations together as the rabbis did, with little consideration for the original context (for example in Romans 3), but more often he cites separate passages to lend authority to his argument.

Much of the imagery of the letters is drawn from Old Testament sources: for instance, the 'redemption' and 'priesthood' themes in 1 Peter and the allegory of Sarah and Isaac in Galatians. Many of the phrases in a letter such as James are echoes of Old Testament language. There can be no doubt that since the church took the Old Testament as their scriptures it played a dominant part in the thinking of those who wrote the New Testament letters. All these writers were Jews who had become Christians.

Hellenism

How far Greek thought influences the writers has long been a matter of debate. Certainly much of the earliest missionary activity took place in areas where Greek influence was very strong. When Paul dis-

Paul's letters played a key role in his relations with the churches. Recorded for posterity, they were to prove the basis of Christian teaching and practice for all time. This papyrus letter from the 1st century AD begins, 'Prokleios to his good friend Pekysis, greetings...'

cusses 'wisdom' it is not necessary to see this as evidence of Hellenistic influence. Even so, his Christian interpretation of wisdom cannot properly be understood except against the kind of debate common in his time. Similarly, his idea of 'fullness' must be understood against the Greek philosophical background.

The method of argument in Hebrews is in some respects similar to that of Philo of Alexandria (although there are even more striking differences). In 1 John some find echoes of Greek catchwords which have been taken up and used in a Christian sense. The ideas of light and life, for example, have parallels in contemporary thought.

Paganism

The New Testament church grew up in a pagan environment. Some of the problems discussed in the letters stem directly from this. The situation behind 1 Corinthians is a classic example of the practical difficulties which arose in the church as a result of the previous pagan back-

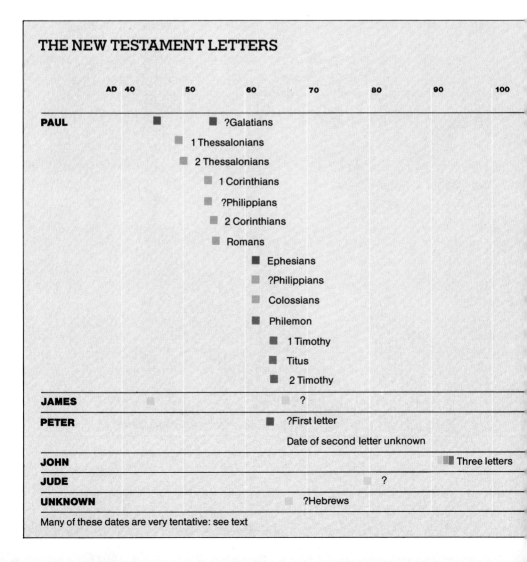

THE NEW TESTAMENT LETTERS

	AD 40	50	60	70	80	90	100
PAUL	■	■ ?Galatians					
		■ 1 Thessalonians					
	■ 2 Thessalonians						
		■ 1 Corinthians					
		■ ?Philippians					
		■ 2 Corinthians					
		■ Romans					
			■ Ephesians				
			■ ?Philippians				
			■ Colossians				
			■ Philemon				
			■ 1 Timothy				
			■ Titus				
			■ 2 Timothy				
JAMES	■		■ ?				
PETER			■ ?First letter				
			Date of second letter unknown				
JOHN							■ Three letters
JUDE				■ ?			
UNKNOWN				■ ?Hebrews			

Many of these dates are very tentative: see text

ground of the converts. Some Christians were taking legal action against each other before pagan judges, and Paul had to point out the incongruity of this. There was even a problem from the market-place: meat offered to idols was the only meat sold and this posed a dilemma for sensitive consciences.

The immorality of the Gentile world is vividly painted by Paul in the opening chapter of his letter to the Romans. When the developing church is set against its environment, the grace of

God – such a dominant theme in the New Testament letters – is most triumphantly seen.

Judaism

In the ancient world, before the rise of the Christian church, the most ethical form of religious teaching was undoubtedly Judaism. It was because they were dissatisfied with pagan religions that many of the more thoughtful Gentiles became proselytes, adherents of the Jewish faith.

From this growing group of interested

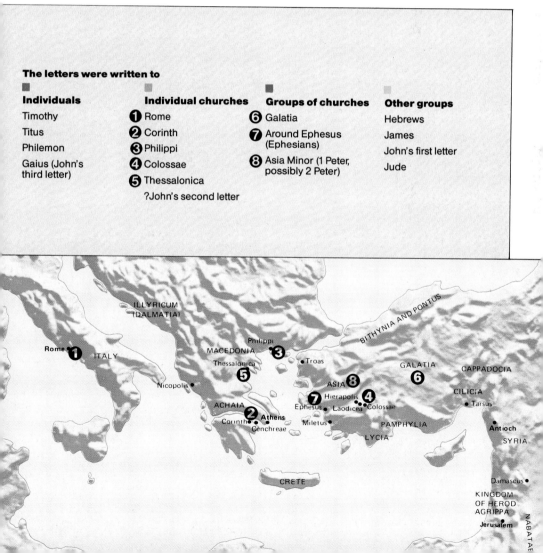

The letters were written to

Individuals
Timothy
Titus
Philemon
Gaius (John's third letter)

Individual churches
1 Rome
2 Corinth
3 Philippi
4 Colossae
5 Thessalonica
?John's second letter

Groups of churches
6 Galatia
7 Around Ephesus (Ephesians)
8 Asia Minor (1 Peter, possibly 2 Peter)

Other groups
Hebrews
James
John's first letter
Jude

Gentiles Paul won many converts on his missionary journeys. The letter to the Hebrews points out Christ's superiority to Judaism by showing that the old system of worship has its spiritual fulfilment in Christianity.

THE MAIN THEMES OF THE LETTERS

It is not possible to summarize here all the themes of such a varied collection of letters. In some letters important doctrines are carefully discussed. In others they are merely stated, and in yet others no more than implied. Nevertheless, in spite of the variety, there is a basic uniformity in the teaching – explicit or implicit – which runs through them all.

God

The letters teach that God is a holy God who expects holiness. He is himself the pattern for Christian behaviour. He is moreover sovereign. The Christians were in no doubt that he controls the world. But the most characteristic view is that which Jesus taught, echoed many times in the Epistles: that God is Father. The intensely personal view of God which the letter-writers all share springs from this conviction. God is both Creator and author of the new creation. Paul describes the cosmic reconciliation of the world to God through his action in sending Christ.

Christ

The early Christians expressed their view of Jesus in a variety of ways. This is reflected in the letters, and shows the impossibility of reducing the person of Christ to a single formula.

They use various titles to describe him. 'Jesus Christ' is used to show Jesus as the fulfilment of the promised Jewish Messiah (Christ). But the fuller title, 'Lord Jesus Christ', is also frequent, and shows that the Christians at once acknowledge his sovereignty.

The most characteristic passages of Paul's letters are those which show his exalted view of the person of Christ. He existed before the world was made. He set aside his riches to become poor for our sakes (2 Corinthians 8:9). He humbled himself to become a man in spite of his position of equality with God (Philippians 2:5-11). He was the exact 'image' of God (Colossians 1:15).

The other letters demonstrate a similar view of Christ. Hebrews shows him as fully God (chapter 1) and at the same time fully man (chapter 2), able to represent his people as their High Priest before God the Father. The letters of Peter and John show no essential difference. Through Christ God the Father brings salvation to men. He is the supreme expression of God's love.

Man and his salvation

The world is corrupt and evil. The completely new start, the new era brought in by Christ, is the only answer. The new creation, salvation, eternal life, this is the main theme of the Letters, expounded in them or simply reflected and expressed. Life in Christ demands a new morality, living not according to the old pagan ways but according to God's law of love, and this must be worked out not only in church life, in the new community, but in the world.

Paul, the traveller and Roman citizen, had still not been to Rome when this letter was written (about AD 57). He had made three prolonged and extensive journeys, pioneering the Christian message throughout the eastern provinces of the Empire and establishing churches. Now, probably in Corinth, about to take the relief fund to Jerusalem (see on Acts 20), Paul felt free at last to turn his eyes west – to Spain. And on the way he would fulfil the ambition of years and visit the Christians at Rome. He was not to know that three weary years would elapse between the letter and the visit, or that when he eventually entered Rome it would be as a prisoner (Acts 28).

The city and the church

Rome in Paul's day was the capital of an empire which stretched from Britain to Arabia. Wealthy and cosmopolitan, it was the diplomatic and trade centre of the then-known world. There was constant coming and going. The Roman Peace made travel safe; Roman roads made it relatively swift and easy. Visitors from Rome heard Peter's first sermon in Jerusalem on the Day of Pentecost. So it is not surprising that there was a large and flourishing Christian community there by the time Paul wrote. It was the usual mixture of Jews and Gentiles. There was no serious rift between the two sections, as there had been in the Galatian churches. But there was a tendency for each to criticize and look down on the other.

Some time earlier there had been trouble with the authorities. And although all was now quiet, the Christians were still suspect. Their Founder had, after all, faced a charge of treasonable activity against the emperor. And despite their efforts to live as loyal citizens of Rome, only a few years after this letter (in AD 64) Nero was able to make a scapegoat of the Christians, laying the blame on them when the city went up in flames. Tradition says that Paul – and Peter too – died in the ferocious persecution that followed.

The letter

Romans takes pride of place among the New Testament letters. In point of time, it follows the Thessalonian and Corinthian letters and Galatians, and precedes Colossians and Ephesians. Some of the themes of the earlier letters are taken up again in Romans, which is the fullest and most closely reasoned statement we have of the basic Christian truths. It is Paul's gospel manifesto. What impelled him to write this unique document we do not know. Perhaps he already sensed he was risking his life by going to Jerusalem, and felt he might never give his message to the Roman Christians in person.

The great theme of Romans is faith in Christ as the only ground of man's acceptance by God, who treats all men alike, Jew and Gentile. Paul pulls no punches in describing the state the world is in (1:18-32). Every one of us stands condemned by God's standards. Even the Jew, who has the unique privilege of knowing God's law, cannot keep it (2–3:20). But God offers us free pardon and new life. Jesus has served our sentence for us (chapter 5). We are free to make a fresh start – this time with all the power of God at our disposal (chapters 6–8). Why, then, when the Gentiles respond to God's offer of salvation, do the Jews reject it? It is because they see salvation in terms of works. But in the end they too will come in (chapters 9–11). God's forgiveness and love spur us on to live up to our new calling – to reshape our whole way of thinking and manner of life. God's 'good news' is not an end in itself. It is meant to transform human relationships – making it possible for Jews and Gentiles to treat one another as equals in the church – and to permeate every aspect of daily living (chapters 12–15).

The impact and influence of Romans is immeasurable. It has fired great men – Augustine, Luther, Bunyan, Wesley – and through them shaped the history of the church. But God has also touched the lives of countless individuals through this letter – ordinary men and women who have read and believed and acted on the apostle's teaching.

1:1-15
INTRODUCTION
The apostle's whole life-mission is captured in this first, typical, aside (1-6). Paul, Christ's slave and emissary, whose commission is to carry God's good news to the nations, writes to his fellow Christians in Rome. His 'grace' and 'peace' blend the traditional Greek and Jewish greetings into something uniquely Christian. Romans is the product of an intellectual, someone with a keen mind – but also a warm, human personality. That much is clear from verses 8-15. Paul is full of appreciation, longing to see and share with a group of Christians he has not yet met.

Saints (7): 'his own people' (Good News Bible), not a special, super-grade elite, but all who belong to Christ.

Barbarians/savage (14): New English Bible, 'non-Greek' – and therefore uncivilized!

1:16—8:39
THE CHRISTIAN GOSPEL

1:16-17 The gospel in a nutshell
Paul glories in his message: that God is able to save – and will save – anyone prepared to rely completely on him.

Verse 17: the first part means that salvation is a matter of faith, from beginning to end. The quotation from Habakkuk is open to more than one interpretation. Here the meaning is: 'the person who is put right with God through faith shall live'.

1:18—3:20 The old humanity
Why should anyone need to be 'put right with God'? Paul begins his thesis with a penetrating analysis of the human situation.

    The pagan world (1:18-32). Here mankind is caught in a downward spiral. Evidence of God is all around us, in the natural world that God has created. But we close our mind to the truth. Because of this our whole mental process becomes warped. We are determined to go our own way, and in the end – since we have been given real freedom of choice – God lets us. So we sink deeper and deeper into the morass of our own perverse and perverted behaviour.

Paul was not exaggerating the gross immorality and decadence of the Roman world. It is illustrated in contemporary writing – and in the remains of Pompeii. Soon after Paul wrote this letter, a violent eruption of the volcano Mt Vesuvius buried the city in lava. Like Sodom and Gomorrah in the Old Testament, it was utterly destroyed.

Wrong thinking (irrationality) and wrongdoing go hand in hand. The person who rejects reason (25) will not listen to conscience either (32).

Moralist and Jew (2 – 3:20). There were some high-principled individuals, even among pagans. And there were the Jews, who prided themselves in possessing and knowing God's law. Both would be quick to condemn the vices of the pagan world. But are they in any better position? Does the moralist actually live up to his high standards? Is his conscience clear? Does the Jew actually keep the law he is so proud of? If not, he is as morally bankrupt as the pagan. God judges with strict impartiality.

Paul can imagine the questions the hecklers will fling at him. He meets their points one by one.

■ Has the Jew any advantage, then? Yes, the fact that God has entrusted him with his revelation (3:1-2).

■ If the Jews have failed in their trust and will be judged, what about all God's promises to them? God still keeps his word (3:3-4).

■ It seems human sin serves a good end, then, by throwing God's goodness into relief. So why should it be punished? Why not go on sinning so that people can see God's goodness all the better? Because God is a just Judge – and the end does not justify the means (3:5-8).

■ Are the Jews any better off than other people? No. Everyone is in the grip of sin. And the law makes us accountable – it is powerless to put anyone in the right with God (3:9-20).

2:6-10: the point is God's impartiality, not that salvation can ever be earned, as 3:20 makes clear.

Circumcision (2:25): see on Genesis 17.

2:29: there is a play on words here. 'Jew' is derived from 'Judah', which means praise.

Justified (3:20): Paul often uses this legal term. It means acquittal or free pardon, being 'put right' (Good News Bible). See 4:25.

3:21—5:21 Acquittal

Free pardon on the ground of faith (3:21-31). Since God is just, the man who infringes his law must be punished. The whole human race stands under sentence of death unless the demands of justice can be met some other way. Jesus has provided that other way by standing in for us at the cost of his own life (chapter 5 explains how this was possible). God will now forgive and receive *anyone* who comes to him trusting in Jesus. This opens up a new life. It is the essence of the good news Paul was commissioned to preach, and the heart of the Christian message still.

The case of Abraham (chapter 4). Paul picks up on his statement in 3:21-22 that this same faith-principle is inherent in the Old Testament scriptures. If he can prove his point in the case of Abraham – father of the Jewish nation, and the prime example of an upright man – surely the Jewish objectors will be convinced. And he can. God accepted Abraham not because of his good life, but because of his faith (4:3; Genesis 15:6) – because against all the odds Abraham stuck to his conviction that God would do what he promised (21). The covenant-agreement, of which circumcision was the outward sign, came later (Genesis 17). So it is to those who share Abraham's faith, not simply his national identity, that God extends his friendship still.

Christ and Adam (chapter 5). The death and resurrection of Jesus has given us a new standing before God. We have life. We have peace. We have hope. We have the presence of the Holy Spirit. There is point and meaning now to the rough and tumble of life (1-5). But how can one man's death result in pardon for millions of others? The key lies in the solidarity of the human race. Sin, disobedience, began with one man (Adam) and spread to all his descendants. We all share the 'disease' and its inevitable consequence, death – being cut off from God. On the same principle, Jesus has made acquittal and life available to all. Adam was the head of the old humanity; Jesus is the head of the new, reborn humanity. We were 'in' Adam when he sinned. We are 'in Christ' when we put our trust in him.

Grace (5:2): another of Paul's favourite words. It means the (wholly undeserved) favour of God.

5:20: we all have an innate tendency to feel that laws were made to be broken. The fact that something is forbidden actually makes us want to do it more (see 7:8).

6—8 The new humanity

The old life and the new (chapter 6). God's forgiveness is 'big' enough to deal with any amount of human sin. Does that mean Christians have an insurance policy to go on as before? What an absurd idea! Becoming a Christian means identifying ourselves with Christ – becoming one with him – and so sharing in his death and resurrection. Baptism – going down into the water and coming up again – gives us a living picture of what has actually happened. There is as complete a break between the old life and the new as if we had actually died and been reborn. We were dead to God before; now we are alive to him (11). We have been given a new inclination to obey, with which to fight the old tug of sin (17). And we must act on it. Sin is not our master any longer. We are in the service of God. The result of serving sin is death (21), but the result of serving God is life – God's life at work in us, transforming us (22).

The law and its limitations (7 – 8:4). In order to counteract the widespread belief that men can 'work their passage' to heaven, Paul has said some harsh things about the law. Now he stops to set the record straight. For Jews like himself, who took the matter seriously, the law could be a real tyrant. Christ sets us free from the killing struggle to get right with God by keeping the law to the letter – but not free to do as we please.

There is nothing wrong with God's law in itself. It is wholly good. And the Christian, with the new power at his disposal (6, and 8:4) has the potential to keep it. The root of the trouble, as Paul shows from his own experience, is not the law but our own bias to sin (7:14). And conversion does not end the tension (22-23). Left to ourselves we are still helpless to obey. But we are not now left to ourselves. The law serves its purpose when it makes us despair of our own efforts. Only at this point are we ready to ask Christ to do for us what we cannot do for ourselves.

The Holy Spirit – and God's eternal purpose (8:5-39). The Holy Spirit of God is alive and actively at work in everyone who belongs to Christ (9). He helps us to keep God's law. It is his presence that convinces us we really are God's children (16). He is our foretaste (first instalment, 23) of glory to come – a living spring of hope within us. And he turns our inarticulate longings into prayer (26-27).

It is God's intention that every one of us should be like Christ (29). Like him in character now. Like him in glory eventually. In other words, God is recreating us 'in his own image' (Genesis 1:27). And every little circumstance of life is worked into this great overall purpose (28). Nothing can shake it. No one can ever make him write us off – we have Christ in heaven to plead our cause. And there is no power in heaven or earth that can cut us off from his love. So whatever life may bring, we can win through. These are the great certainties of the Christian life.

Sinful body (6:6, some versions): not the human body, but the 'sinful self'.

Verse 11: this is not a matter of playing games, pretending to be what we are not – but of being what we are. 'Dead to sin': in the sense that the score for the old life has been settled, not that we no longer feel its pull.

Flesh (7:5, etc.): Paul often uses this word, in distinction from the 'spirit'. He means 'self' – the old, sinful nature. Good

News Bible's human nature does not catch the full meaning.

Body of death (7:24): human nature, subject to the laws of sin and death.

Likeness of sinful man (8:3): Paul chooses his words with care. Jesus was a real man, but in one respect he was not identical to other men. He did not share the sinfulness that ordinarily goes with human nature.

8:10: 'your bodies are going to die'.

8:11: Christians are promised a resurrection like Christ's.

Abba, Father (8:15): the ordinary word a Hebrew-speaking child still uses for his 'daddy'.

Creation (19ff.): because man is part of nature, when he sinned he brought pain and death not only on himself but on the whole created world. So in the day man is transformed, the creation will share his transformation. There will be 'a new heaven and a new earth' (Revelation 21:1).

Predestined/already chosen (8:29): see the note on Election.

9—11
THE NATION OF ISRAEL

As Paul dwells on God's glorious provision for all who are 'in Christ', he is filled with distress for Israel, God's own specially chosen and privileged people. How could they refuse to believe in their own, promised Messiah? The Gentiles responded eagerly to the gospel – but not the Jews. And Paul would have sold his own soul to have had it otherwise.

How can he account for this strange anomaly? God has not broken his word (9:6). All along he exercised his sovereign right of choice (9:6-13). And we can hardly call him to task for it. The Maker has an indisputable right to do as he pleases with what he makes (9:14-21). It is only by virtue of his patience and mercy that even a remnant of stubborn, rebellious Israel survived his judgement (9:22-29). People of other nations, knowing their failure, welcomed God's offer of acceptance through faith. The Jews, thinking they could earn salvation by keeping the law, refused to consider it (9:30-33).

Paul himself once shared this misplaced zeal. Now he longs for the Jews to share his faith (10:1-4). God offers salvation – life – to men and women on only one condition: an open declaration of belief in the risen Christ as Lord (10:5-13; and see Philippians 2:11). It is the preacher's task to see that everyone hears about it. And Israel *has* heard, and understood – yet still refused to believe (10:14-21).

Is this the end for Israel, then (11:1)? No. The very fact that Paul and some of his fellow Jews had become Christians is living proof God has not given Israel up. The nation's blindness is partial and

Olives: Paul took his picture in Romans 11 from the practice of grafting new branches onto olive-trees.

temporary. And it has given the Gentiles their opportunity all the sooner. They owe the Jews a great debt; they should never disparage them. And in due course their own faith will lead to a great turning to God among the Jews. God's ways are beyond us, but his purpose is forgiveness through Christ for Jew and Gentile alike.

9:12-13: the quotations are from Genesis 25:23 and Malachi 1:2-3. Both refer to nations – Israel, descended from Jacob; Edom, descended from Esau – rather than individuals. See on Obadiah.

9:18, 22: see the note on Election.

Like Sodom…like Gomorrah (9:29): i.e. utterly obliterated. See Genesis 19:24ff.

10:6-10: in the style of a rabbi of his day, Paul gives a running commentary on Moses' words in Deuteronomy 30:11-14.

11:7: see the note on Election.

11:17: it was the ancient practice, when a cultivated olive failed to yield, to graft in a slip of wild olive to give the tree new vigour.

All Israel (11:26): the phrase means Israel as a whole, rather than every Jew without exception.

Mercy to all (11:32): without distinction, rather than without exception.

12 — 15:13
THE CHRISTIAN LIFE

Out of sheer love, and at great cost, God has saved our lives. What stronger motive could we have for turning them over to him from now on? This means complete mental re-orientation affecting our whole character, our motives and our behaviour (12:1-2).

12 Human relationships

This is where the transformation begins, as every individual takes his place in the new 'family' of Christ. His own stock goes down. His opinion of others goes up. And individual gifts are pooled for the good of the whole Christian community. We put ourselves at God's disposal, and we don't pull out when the going gets hard. Old attitudes change – not only towards fellow Christians but towards the outside world. Instead of giving tit-for-tat when we are wronged, we treat the enemy as if he were our best friend, and leave God to do the judging.

Burning coals (20): in Egypt people went through the ritual of carrying a pan of burning charcoal on their heads as a token of their penitence.

Election

In Romans 9 and 11 we have perhaps the most forthright treatment of this subject in the whole Bible. Paul's starting-point is that no one has any claim to God's mercy. He shows how God in his love has chosen certain individuals down the ages to play a special role in his purpose for the world (9:6-13). And he emphasizes the wideness of God's mercy (11:28-32). God the Creator has the right to choose, and we have no right at all to question his choice or doubt his justice.

If God selects some men for forgiveness, does he select others for destruction? Paul is much more cautious about this ('What if …?'). He contents himself with asserting God's right to do so – but at the same time stresses God's patience (9:22). He talks about God hardening men's hearts (9:18; and see 1:28), but in every instance these are people who have deliberately refused to listen to him. God never hardens someone's heart against his will.

Human beings are not helpless pawns in the hands of a capricious god. The Bible teaches God's election. It also teaches man's responsibility: his freedom to choose. It may be beyond our understanding how both can operate simultaneously (just as it is hard to understand how scientists can describe light in terms of both waves and particles – two ideas which seem mutually contradictory). God is outside time: we cannot imagine anything beyond our limited range of understanding. So we can only take God's word for it, and hold on to both God's sovereignty and man's freedom to choose – not try to find a compromise between them.

The Colosseum in Rome was built in AD 80. It took its name from the colossal statue of Nero that stood nearby. Here 45,000 spectators could watch fights between gladiators, even simulated naval battles. It was probably Nero, the cruel persecutor, who was emperor when Paul wrote that Christians should obey and respect the authorities, for authority is ordained by God.

13 The powers that be

God delegates his power to the authorities for the public good. Christians must therefore respect them. Taxes are to be paid, and laws observed. The Christian has a duty to meet all 'Caesar's' authorized demands. Only when these demands directly conflict with the commands of God is it right to say 'No' (Acts 5:29).

We must incur no debt, other than our permanent obligation to love – and not to wrong – our fellow men. The time we have left is short, and we must live accordingly (11-12 – Paul is alluding to Christ's return).

14 Freedom and responsibility

There are some matters of conscience over which Christians disagree. (Paul instances the eating of meat, 2-3 – see on 1 Corinthians 8 – and observance of Jewish feast-days, 5). We should not try to force agreement, and so create division. We ourselves may feel free to do things that would give a weaker Christian a bad conscience. That is no reason to despise him. We are answerable, not to one another, but to Christ. It is better to limit our own freedom than exercise it at a fellow Christian's expense.

14:2, 14: there was the problem that meat sold in the market had been sacrificed to pagan gods; and there were also the Jewish food-laws about 'clean' and 'unclean' animals and the method of slaughter. If Jewish Christians insisted on the letter of the law, and Gentile Christians stuck out for freedom, the two sections would never share a meal together.

15:1-13 The example of Christ

There is nothing Christian about pleasing ourselves. Good relations between Christians are far more important than 'my rights'. We must do all we can to promote real oneness, regardless of former background.

15:14— 16:27
EPILOGUE

15:14-33 Personal

In more than 20 years as apostle to the non-Jewish world, Paul has seen churches established all over the countries we now call Cyprus, Syria, Turkey and Greece. Now he has discharged his responsibilities. And once the Jerusalem trip (about which he has real misgivings) is over, he can look west.

Illyricum (19): present-day Yugoslavia.
Macedonia and Achaia (26): northern and southern Greece.

16 Greetings to friends

It is in one way surprising to find such a long list of friends in a church which Paul had never visited. (For this reason some believe this chapter originally belonged to a copy of Romans which was sent to Ephesus.) Yet all roads led to Rome, and many Christians from the eastern provinces must have passed through the capital at one time or another. It is obvious that despite his busy life Paul did not lose interest in people or lose touch with them.

His last word is one of warning against a set of troublemakers whose disruptive influence on the churches he knew all too well (17ff.). But, as always, at the close his thought returns to the wisdom and glory of the eternal God.

Phoebe (1): it was probably Phoebe – travelling from Cenchreae, the port of Corinth – who carried Paul's letter to Rome.
Priscilla and Aquila (3): a couple whose home was in Rome, but who travelled extensively in the course of their leather-working business. They did sterling Christian work at Corinth and Ephesus (Acts 18:2-3; 18-28).
Rufus (13): may be the son of Simon of Cyrene (Mark 15:21).
Verse 21: Timothy is well known in the letters. He was like a son to the ageing Paul. Jason may be Paul's host from Thessalonica (Acts 17:5-8).Sosipater may be Sopater from Beroea (Acts 20:4).
Tertius (22): the Christian who acted as Paul's secretary in writing this letter.
Erastus (23): this may be the same public official whose name has been found inscribed on a marble paving-block at Corinth, dating from this time.

1 Corinthians

Paul probably wrote this letter from Ephesus, about AD 54. Acts 18 recounts Paul's 18-month stay at Corinth on his second missionary journey – and describes the founding of the church.

The city

The old Greek city of Corinth was destroyed and rebuilt by the Romans. It stood in a strategic position to control trade across the narrow neck of land between Aegean and Adriatic. A thriving centre of commerce and a cosmopolitan city where Greeks, Latins, Syrians, Asiatics, Egyptians and Jews rubbed shoulders, it was an obvious target for Paul. Establish a church here, and the Christian message would quickly spread far and wide.

Yet in other ways it is hard to imagine a less likely place for Christianity to take root. The town was dominated by the temple of Aphrodite (goddess of love; what a contrast to 1 Corinthians 13!), built on the heights of the acropolis. Thousands of temple prostitutes, a large floating population, and the general racial hotch-potch, all contributed to Corinth's unsavoury name. The city was a by-word for excess and sexual licence. There was even a word for it: to 'Corinthianize'.

The church

The Christian church, like the city, was a racial and social mixture. There were a few Jews, but more Gentiles: some men of wealth and position, but most from the lower classes. Many were converts from a permissive pagan background. They had little to boast of – yet, in Greek fashion, they prided themselves in their intellectual prowess. They bandied about such slogans as 'Liberty' and 'Knowledge'. It was a group which had little cohesion.

The letter

Two factors lie behind the writing of 1 Corinthians.

First, Paul had received reports of the church which made him very uneasy (1:11; 5:1).

Second, a delegation arrived from Corinth, and (or with) a letter seeking his advice on various questions (7:1; 16:17).

In the letter, Paul takes up five of the matters reported to him:

- divisions in the church;
- a case of incest;
- court-cases between members;
- the abuse of Christian 'freedom';
- the general chaos reigning in church services, even in the Lord's Supper.

He also answers questions the Corinthians have written about:

- questions about marriage and single life;
- problems over food consecrated to idols and social functions held in the temples;
- whether or not women should be veiled, and their place in public meetings;
- the matter of spiritual gifts;
- the meaning of the resurrection of the dead.

His reply takes the lid off one of the early churches, and gives us a fascinating glimpse of the none too edifying contents.

1:1-9 Greeting and prayer

Opening and thanksgiving (1:4-9) are characteristic. Paul believes in encouragement. Only Galatians, of all the letters to churches, lacks this note of praise.

Sosthenes (1): possibly the synagogue leader mentioned in Acts 18:17. He may be acting as Paul's secretary.

1:10—4:21 Rival cliques

In a day before church buildings, when Christians met in houses or halls, and a large group might well have to split up, it is easy to see how divisions could arise.

Paul mentions three sects centred on rival 'leaders': Paul (their founder), Apollos and Cephas (Peter). A fourth sect, in their pride, claimed exclusive rights to the label 'Christian'.

Apollos (1:12) was a Jewish Christian from Alexandria (Egypt). When he arrived in Ephesus, Aquila and Priscilla took him home for fuller instruction (Acts 18:24ff.). He travelled to the province of Achaia (of which Corinth was capital), where he proved a powerful and eloquent teacher.

The mention of Peter (Cephas, 1:12) does not necessarily mean he visited Corinth. As leader of the twelve apostles it would be natural for him to have a following, particularly among Jewish Christians.

It is clear from these chapters that the groups were making invidious comparisons between Paul and the more eloquent Apollos. Paul, although a trained scholar, had had his troubles at Corinth (Acts 18:9-10; 1 Corinthians 2:3). God's message, not polished speech, was his main concern.

But the Corinthians were infected with something of the spirit of nearby Athens. They fancied themselves as thinkers and took pride in their supposed intellectual superiority. In fact, as Paul points out (3:1-4), their argumentative, judgemental attitude shows they are still bound by the world's way of thinking. They stand in need of teaching. They have to be reminded that human cleverness is a far cry from God's wisdom (1:18–2:16). It is not proud and clever people who appreciate the wisdom of God's plan of salvation through Christ's death on the cross, but those who are spiritually wise. This kind of wisdom, and with it true values and real judgement, is God's gift to man through his Holy Spirit. A man must become a fool in the world's eyes in order to be really wise (3:18).

So Paul and Apollos are not rivals but partners, sharing the work of building God's church (3:5-9). Once the basic foundation of faith in Christ is laid, every Christian is responsible for what he does with the new life he has been given. We must see to it that we build to last (3:10-17).

There should be no place for pride among Christians and no looking down on others. The greatest Christians regard themselves as no more than

Ideas from Greek philosophy constantly infiltrated into the Christian community, leading it away from the truth of Jesus Christ made man. This 2nd-century statue of a philosopher was found at Ephesus.

God's slaves. We are to follow their example (chapter 4).

Chloe's people (1:11): presumably members of Chloe's household.

Stephanas (1:16): a founder-member of the church at Corinth, and one of the delegation sent by the church to Paul at Ephesus (16:15ff.).

Jews and Greeks (1:22): national char-acteristics show through. The Jews always wanted miracles as concrete evidence. The Greeks saw salvation in terms of wisdom.

The Day (3:13): when Christ returns; the day of judgement.

The cross was offensive to the Jews, absurd to the Gentiles. A Roman execution is shown in this figure found at Halicarnassus.

5 Incest

In the name of their boasted 'liberty' the church is condoning incest. It is a case which would shock even the pagans in that notorious city. The old immorality – and worse – has gained a foothold and the whole church is endangered (as Paul had warned in a previous letter, 5:9).

His father's wife (5:1): 'his step-mother', Good News Bible.

Hand over to Satan (5:5): Paul is expressing God's judgement on the man for abusing his body through gross sexual immorality. Short-term discipline is to be exercised for long-term good. Such discipline would certainly include expulsion from the church.

Leaven (5:6-8): yeast – often (though not always) used as a picture of the corrupting power of evil. Bread for the Passover was made without leaven, as a reminder of the Israelites' hasty departure from Egypt. Christ has become our Passover sacrifice, says Paul; it is time we got rid of the old yeast of evil in our lives.

6:1-11 Lawsuits

Even Jews would not take cases before Gentile courts – not because the courts were corrupt, but because it would be an admission of Jewish inability to operate their own laws. Surely the Christian community – these 'wise' Corinthians – should be capable of settling internal disputes. Better to be wronged than drag one another to court.

God's people will judge the world (6:2): a development from Christ's teaching in Matthew 19:28. The angels are mentioned as the highest order in the created universe.

6:12-20 Freedom or licence?

The Corinthians claim they are free to do anything. 'No doubt', says Paul, 'but I for one will not let anything make free with me' (6:12). Sexual needs, they argue, are like hunger: they must be satisfied. The body is not important anyway. But this is wrong thinking, a carry-over of the old Greek ideas. For the Christian the body is part of the whole personality. Body *and* soul are the Lord's. You cannot sin with the body and keep the 'soul' untarnished: every individual is a unity.

7 Questions about marriage

The Corinthians have raised six questions about single and married life. Several reflect the Greek tendency to regard the physical side of existence as evil.

■ Are married couples to continue normal sexual relations after conversion? Yes (7:1-7).
■ Should single people marry? Paul prefers the single life – but only for those with the gift of self-control (8-9).
■ Is divorce between Christians permissible? No (10-11).
■ What about the unconverted husband or wife? The Christian is to stick to his pagan partner unless that partner wants a separation (12-16).
■ This question is not so clear. Most likely it is: 'Should engaged couples marry?' This must be a matter for personal decision, but in the very troubled times Paul sees ahead, single people will find it easier to work out their Christian priorities (25-38).
■ May widows remarry? Yes, but Paul qualifies this (39-40).

8 Food offered to idols: problems over social customs

It was hard in Corinth to make a clean break with paganism. Trade groups and clubs held their social functions at the temples. Most of the meat sold in the shops had first been offered to idols. Some Christians maintained that 'idols were nothing'. They were free to eat meat and attend club dinners. But others were worried. Freedom is right, says Paul. But no one should exercise personal freedom at the expense of another person's conscience.

9 Forgoing rights

Paul takes examples from his own life to push this lesson home. If anyone has rights, surely it is the apostle. Yet he has gladly given up his right to take a wife with him on his trips and expect the

The great Temple of Apollo at Corinth. The fact that meat on sale in the markets had been offered to idols in pagan temples was a real problem of conscience to the Corinthian Christians.

church to provide for her keep. There are more important things than rights. He willingly restricts his freedom to help him win people for Christ.

In a race ... (24-27): the Isthmian Games (second only to the Olympics) were held every three years at Corinth. Each competitor underwent 10 months' stiff training, hoping to be crowned with the victor's pine wreath. Paul was afriad, not of losing his salvation, but of forefeiting his 'crown'.

Paul, writing from Ephesus where this sculpture was found, compared the Christians to athletes: they compete for a fading wreath, Christians for a wreath that never fades.

10:1-13 A warning from history

It is easy to be over-confident, especially when life is smooth (10:12-13). The fate of many of the people of Israel during the wilderness wanderings stands as a solemn warning. (Hebrews 3:7ff. draws similar lessons from the same events.)

10:14 — 11:1 Paul's appeal and summary

Christians must choose between the Lord and idols (empty in themselves, but behind them, real demonic powers).

There can be no compromise. It is playing with fire to have any part in pagan sacrifices. As far as meat is concerned, the rule is unselfish concern for the good of others.

The cup of blessing/thanksgiving (10:16): the name given to the third cup in the Passover feast, over which a prayer of thanksgiving was said. This may well have been the cup with which Jesus instituted his memorial Supper – hence the thought here.

11:2-16 Women and the veil

No decent woman would appear unveiled in public at this time. The veil guaranteed safety and respect in the streets. But there were differences in Greek and Hebrew custom when it came to prayer. Greek women, as well as men, prayed bareheaded. Roman and Jewish men and women prayed with their heads covered. The church needed a ruling.

The ruling Paul gave rested on the relative roles of men and women in the created order. He was also concerned not to flout current social convention and so bring the Christians into disrepute. Men, because they are the 'head' of creation, are under no authority but Christ's. They were therefore to pray bareheaded. Women were to pray veiled, the veil being a token both of their acceptance of their husband's authority and of the current standards of decency.

Dishonours his head (4-5): i.e. 'disgraces Christ'. The veil was a token of submission to another person; he should submit only to Christ. *Dishonours her head:* i.e. 'disgraces her husband'. By discarding the veil she discarded her husband's authority, as if she were a prostitute.

Have her hair cut off (6): the punishment for a prostitute at that time.

The image and glory of God (7): Genesis 1:26-27 includes both sexes in God's 'image', but does not mention 'glory'.

Because of the angels (10): the angels, representatives of order, would not want to look on immorality, or even the appearance of it.

11:17-34 Disorder at the Lord's Supper

In the early days the Lord's Supper took place in the course of a communal meal. All brought what food they could, and it was shared together. Not so in Corinth. There they could not even wait for everyone to arrive before they began eating. And some got drunk while others went hungry. It is not surprising that Paul could not 'commend' them – it was a disgrace. He pulls them up short with a reminder of the circumstances in which the first Lord's Supper took place. Their offence is serious.

This is my body (24-25): this is the earliest record we have of Jesus' words.

In an unworthy manner (27-30): no Christian is ever 'worthy' to come into God's presence, but that is not the point here. Judgement has overtaken the Corinthians not for insufficient self-examination, but for stuffing themselves at the meal as if it had no connection with the Lord's death.

12 – 14 Spiritual gifts

In contemporary religions trances or strange, ecstatic speech showed a man's spiritual status. It was therefore not surprising that the Christian church at Corinth, to whom God gave a variety of gifts by his Holy Spirit, should have been specially taken up with the more spectacular ones, among which was the ability to speak in unknown 'tongues'.

Paul does not underestimate these gifts. He would have them all speak in tongues, he says (14:5); and he himself excels in this gift (14:18). But it does not top the list on his scale of values. Those seeking experiences for themselves needed to be reminded that the life of the church was more important. There are other gifts Christians should seek even more strenuously.

Christian unity does not imply uniformity. The gifts come from a single Source, and are given for the good of the whole church. Every individual has an indispensable part to play in the life of the one body. This should prevent a universal scramble for the same gifts. The important thing is not which gifts are most impressive, but which best serve to build up the church. This means that prophecy – a message from God which everyone can understand – is of more value than tongues.

Yet there are things more important still. Three qualities of life – faith, hope, love – will outlive all the gifts. And these are for everyone. Without them no one is anything. And Christian love outshines all. This is the best way of all; this is what we should really set our hearts on. Paul bursts into a great hymn on the theme (chapter 13), one of the most glorious passages in the whole Bible. And as he paints his picture of what love is, he consciously or unconsciously draws us a portrait of a person – Jesus himself. He is the living embodiment of this outgoing, long-suffering, self-giving, self-effacing love. Without it – without him – there would be no church.

14:26-33 provides a glimpse into an early-church service. Again Paul stresses the need for order. Paul forbids the women to disturb the service by talking (34-35). From verse 35 it seems that some were calling out questions and comments (they sat apart from the men). Their new liberty was not to be abused. But it is clear from 11:5 that he did not condemn the women to absolute silence: the gift of prophecy was exercised in public.

12:8: 'One man ... has the gift of wise speech, while another ... can put the deepest knowledge into words' (New English Bible).

Faith (12:9): not the faith we all need for salvation, but a special measure of faith.

Prophecy (12:10): 'the gift of speaking God's message', Good News Bible. *Tongues:* inspired speech to express the praise of God or other deeply-felt emotion; the person uttering it did not know its meaning, hence the need for interpretation.

15 The resurrection

This chapter is the classic Bible passage on the subject. Most of the Jews believed in the resurrection of the body (the same body that had died). To the Greeks it was the soul that was immortal. The very idea of resurrection seemed ridiculous to them (see Acts 17:32).

Paul declares that Christ's resurrection is of the first importance: it is no optional extra. On it the Christian faith stands or falls. What is more, it is a fact and a well-attested one. Most of those who saw the risen Lord are still alive (about 25 years after the event). Christ's resurrection implies resurrection for the Christian. But the body which is raised will be better than the body which is buried. The old was physical, the new will be spiritual and immortal – but still a body. It will as far outshine the old body as a full-grown plant outshines the shrivelled seed from which it grows.

Baptized on behalf of (or for) the dead (29): possibly by proxy for those who died unbaptized. But the meaning may be that people became baptized in order to be reunited with Christian friends and relatives who had died.

Wild beasts at Ephesus (32): one of the spectacles at the arena was to watch men fighting savage wild animals. But Paul is probably speaking metaphorically about what he went through there. Ephesus had a magnificent theatre (see page 573) but no arena as such.

16 Practical matters

Paul gives directions for collecting money for the poor at Jerusalem (the Gentile churches were contributing). He looks forward to an extended visit to Corinth. And he gives news and instructions about various individuals. The letter closes with greetings from the Asian churches (Ephesus was the provincial capital), especially from Aquila and Priscilla, the leatherworkers in whose house Paul lived during his stay in Corinth. The final greeting he writes himself (the rest presumably having been dictated to a secretary).

Macedonia (5): Philippi and Thessalonica were both in this province.

Apollos (12): is probably reluctant to return because of the split (3:4).

Paul speaks of fighting wild beasts (perhaps literally, perhaps metaphorically) among his various trials. This mosaic at Paphos, Cyprus, shows a man spearing a tiger.

2 Corinthians

An interval of not much more than a year separates Paul's two letters to Corinth. The second letter was probably written about AD 56, from a town in Macedonia (the Roman province in northern Greece whose capital was Philippi).

After 1 Corinthians was written, affairs seem to have come to a head, and Paul paid a swift unscheduled visit (his second; on his first visit to Corinth the church was founded) which proved unpleasant both for him and for the church (2:1). He promised to return (1:16). But instead, to avoid an even more painful visit (1:23), he returned to Asia (where he ran into grave danger, 1:8ff.) and wrote them a sharp letter which caused him a great deal of anguish (2:4). He could enjoy no peace of mind until he heard their reaction, so he left for Troas, on the coast, hoping for news. Although things were going well there, he could not bear to wait, and crossed the Aegean into Macedonia (2:12-13) where at last Titus reached him with the news that the letter had brought the Corinthians to their senses (7:6ff.). His relief knew no bounds.

Now, as he writes again, the worst is over. He looks forward to a third visit, which he hopes will be a happier one. So the final part of the letter is specifically intended to clear the air (13:10). (He did pay his visit, and wrote to the Romans during his stay at Corinth. So there was presumably a happy ending to the troubles.)

2 Corinthians is perhaps the most intensely personal of all Paul's letters. We feel for ourselves the weight of his burden of care for all the churches (11:28): the depth of his love for them and his anguished concern for their spiritual progress. We see in personal terms the cost of his missionary programme: hardship, suffering, deprivation, humiliation, almost beyond human endurance. And we see unshakable faith shining through it all, transforming every circumstance.

The personal nature of the letter makes it difficult to analyse. Paul's thought flows on, almost unbroken (apart from the break before chapter 8, when Paul turns to the matter of the relief fund for Jerusalem; and again before chapter 10, when he takes up the accusations made by his critics), and themes are often recurring. In the main, Paul writes in defence of his ministry and his God-given authority as an apostle.

1:1-7 Greeting and thanksgiving

Paul's associate in this letter is Timothy. His readers are the Christians at Corinth and the surrounding province of Achaia, which would include the groups at Athens and Cenchreae.

His prayer strikes a more personal note than usual. Instead of praise for the church, Paul thanks God for his special goodness during recent trials. His suffering has had two wholly good side-effects:

■ the experience of God's comfort in it all;
■ a new ability to help and comfort those in similar circumstances.

1:8—2:17 News and explanations

Facing death (1:8-14). The reason for Paul's prayer is now explained. While in the province of Asia (capital city, Ephesus) Paul ran into trouble so serious it seemed likely to cost him his life. At first sight this looks like a reference to the uproar at Ephesus recounted in Acts 19:23-41. But there Paul's life was not in danger. It is perhaps more likely he was either seriously ill, or in danger from mob-violence somewhere in Asia Minor.

Paul accounts for his changes of plan (1:15 – 2:11). In his first letter (1 Corinthians 16:5) Paul promised to come to Corinth via Macedonia. Later he decided to make two visits, on the way to and from Macedonia (1:16). In the event he has done neither, and the Corinthians have criticized him for shilly-shallying. But this is not the reason for the changes of plan. He took his decision because of the state of affairs in the church. Having had one head-on clash, he wanted to delay visiting them again until relations were happier. So he tried to sort things out by letter – a letter he feared would hurt them, and which cost him a great deal to write.

The trouble seems to have been personal antagonism to Paul on the part of one man (2:5-11; not the man guilty of incest, 1 Corinthians 5:1). Now that the church has dealt with him, Paul urges his forgiveness.

Paul's recent travels (2:12-17). After writing the letter, Paul could not rest. He went to Troas hoping to meet Titus on his way back from Corinth with news of the church's reaction. Not finding him there he crossed the Aegean Sea to Macedonia. The reason for the thanks-

The road leading down from Corinth to its port. Behind the ruins of the ancient city rises its fortified acropolis.

Listing some of the dangers he had undergone for the sake of the gospel, Paul mentions several shipwrecks. Many of the Mediterranean trading vessels carrying passengers would have been quite small, as they still are today. And with no power but the wind, travelling by ship could be hazardous, particularly out of season.

appointed ambassador of God himself, charged with his amazing message to mankind (3:4-6; 4:1ff.; 5:16–6:2); on the other, he is subjected to every kind of human weakness, persecution and suffering (4:7-12; 6:3-10). But the future, in all its glorious certainty, eclipses any suffering the present can hold (4:13–5:10). Weigh the cost of discipleship, incredible though it seems, against the 'eternal weight of glory' being made ready for the Christian and you have the true balance of things.

Letters of recommendation (3:1): in the early days, Christians moving to a new town often took with them such letters from the old church to the new. Paul has no need of such a letter – the very existence of the Corinthian church is sufficient testimony.

Moses' face (3:7ff.): when Moses came down from Mt Sinai with the tablets of the law, his face dazzled the Israelites, so close had he been to God. In order to overcome their fear he veiled his face (Exodus 34:29ff.).

Reflecting the glory (3:18): the 'glass' or 'mirror', being made of polished metal,

giving of verses 14-17 becomes clear in chapter 7. In Macedonia he met Titus, and the news from Corinth was good.

Verse 14: Paul takes this picture from the triumphal procession accorded to a victorious Roman general. He headed a parade through the streets of Rome, accompanied by incense-bearers and followed by his captives and the spoils of war.

3–6:10 Paul's ministry

Past, present and future interweave in these chapters. As for the past, the old covenant has been replaced by a new life-giving one (3:6-18). The present is an anomaly: on the one hand the apostle is

In Paul's day mirrors gave only a dim and imperfect image, for they were made of polished metal, like the bronze mirror pictured here.

gave only an imperfect reflection.

Clay pots (4:7): cheap pottery lamps (see verse 6), or, if Paul is picturing the Roman triumphal procession, earthenware pots deliberately chosen as a foil to the magnificent treasures inside.

The earthly tent (5:1): our physical body. Paul uses an ordinary Greek expression, which at the same time reminds us of the body's impermanence.

Found naked (5:3): 'without a body'; as a disembodied spirit.

6:11–7:1 The need for a clean break

Paul's feelings are deeply stirred (6:11-13). He longs for the Corinthians to match his own complete open-heartedness towards them.

The change of tone at 6:14 is abrupt – but there is no evidence that this section has been misplaced, as some argue. Paul's love for his churches always holds them to the highest standards. He has warned them before of the dangers of compromise with the pagan world (1 Corinthians 8:10). Now he stresses the utter incongruity of permanent relationships between Christians and heathen.

7:2-16 Paul's joy at the good news from Corinth

He had reached this point in the story at 2:13. Now he takes it up again. At last Titus is able to set Paul's mind at rest. The Corinthians' reaction to his letter is all he could have hoped. The result has been entirely good. The apostle's relief and joy are overwhelming. His faith in them has been completely vindicated.

Not on account of ... (12): a Jewish idiom meaning 'not so much on account of'.

8–9 Money matters

Now that confidence is restored, it is possible to raise the matter of the relief fund for the poor in Jerusalem. Titus had helped the Corinthians make a start, following Paul's instructions in his earlier letter (1 Corinthians 16). Now he

is to return and supervise the completion of the collection, accompanied by delegates from the Macedonian churches (8:18, 22) as a safeguard against any charge that Paul was embezzling the fund (8:20-21; 12:16-17).

The Jerusalem church seems to have been in financial trouble almost from the start, probably because the break with Judaism cut the convert off from his family and often cost him his job. Converts from Islam face the same problems today. Paul was quick to encourage the Gentile churches in Galatia, Macedonia and Corinth to help their Jewish fellow Christians. By doing so they would learn the duty and blessing of systematic Christian giving, and at the same time show their appreciation of what they owed the Jewish parent-church.

Practical instructions rub shoulders with spiritual principles in these chapters. Christian giving is a loving response to the self-giving of the Lord Jesus. Christians should need no urging to give cheerfully and generously. Those with more than they need will make up the incomes of those with too little, so that all have enough.

The churches of Macedonia (8:1): included Philippi (see Philippians 4:15ff.), Thessalonica and Beroea. Harsh treatment from the Romans and a succession of civil wars had impoverished the province, and the persecuted Christians must have been worse off than most.

10–12:13 Paul answers his critics

Paul now turns his attention to the hostile minority at Corinth who have challenged his authority and criticized his behaviour. This sounds very like a continuation of the old rival cliques of 1 Corinthians 1–4, particularly the pro-Jewish faction. They show the same conceit, the same old mistaken standards of judgement. They have attacked Paul on a number of counts:

■ He may be a brave letter-writer, but

meet him face to face and he's a coward (10:1, 9-11).
■ He is no speaker (10:10; 11:6).
■ He is a second-rate apostle (11:5; 12:11)–his insistence on earning his own living underlines this (11:7ff.).
Paul answers every charge, showing the hollowness of their standards of judgement.
■ When he comes, they will discover he is as ready to act as he is to write: but he would much rather use his authority to build up the church (10:1-11).
■ Their boasting counts for nothing: it is God's commendation which is all-important (10:12-18). Yet he can surpass them all in boasting, though he will make suffering and weakness his boast, and the vision and revelation God has given him (11:16–12:10).
■ Apostleship does not consist in oratory and lording it over the church (11:6, 13-15, 19-20). Paul is not lacking in any of the qualities of true apostleship (11:6; 12:12). As for earning his own living, he was concerned that no one should think him a sponger, and anxious not to burden them (11:7ff.).

King Aretas (11:32): Aretas IV ruled the Nabataean kingdom (stretching from the Euphrates to the Red Sea) from his capital, Petra, from 9 BC to AD 40. The Jews were behind the governor's action – see Acts 9:22-25.

Visions and revelations (12:1): we know of three early visions from Acts: on the Damascus road (9:4ff.); at the house of Judas (9:12); and in the temple at Jerusalem (22:17ff.).

A man in Christ (12:2-3): i.e. a Christian. Paul is speaking of himself. *Fourteen years ago:* AD 41-42, six or seven years after Paul's conversion, but before the great

Gentile missions. The *third heaven* ('highest heaven', Good News Bible) is a Jewish expression meaning to be actually in the presence of God. Paul is describing the most sublime experience imaginable.

A thorn in my flesh (12:7): this may be some physical illness (a painful eye disease, or malaria) or a reference to the unremitting opposition he encountered. Either way it was a constant source of pain and depression – Satan's work – yet the means God used to keep Paul humble and to demonstrate his power.

12:14–13:10 The coming visit

Paul looks forward to his third visit to Corinth. And the reason for the tone of these last chapters becomes clear. He is afraid he will find the same bickering splinter-groups, the same cockiness and general disorder that made him write the first letter. He is afraid his pride in them will take a knock, in the face of typical 'Corinthian' sins: sexual promiscuity, bitter quarrels and disorder (12:20-21). And so he calls them to put things right before he comes, so that he may not have to discipline the church severely.

Two or three witnesses (13:1): the procedure laid down under Jewish law (see Deuteronomy 19:15).

13:11-14 Conclusion

After last-minute instructions, and fare-well, Paul closes with the lovely words of 'the grace'.

A holy/brotherly kiss (12): a kiss on the cheek had become the customary Christian greeting, expressing a loving family relationship.

Galatians

Galatia was a huge Roman province extending almost from coast to coast through the mountain and plain of central Turkey. How much of it Paul evangelized we do not know. But Acts 13 and 14 record how he founded churches in the southern cities of Antioch, Iconium, Lystra (Timothy's home town) and Derbe on his first missionary journey. And we know of two follow-up visits made later on (Acts 16:6; 18:23).

Not long after Paul's first visit, other Jewish teachers arrived in Galatia. Whereas Paul had taught that repentance and faith were all that was needed in order to receive God's forgiveness and the gift of new life, these men insisted that non-Jewish converts must also be circumcised and observe the Jewish law – virtually become Jews – in order to be saved. (The same thing happened at Syrian Antioch, Acts 15:1.) When Paul heard this he was distraught (Galatians 4:20). He saw that it struck at the roots of the Christian message. Salvation – new life – is God's gift to all who believe. No man can earn it by living the perfect life God's standards demand. But these men were saying that faith is not enough; there are things we must do to merit salvation. And the Gentiles in Galatia were being taken in. It was a desperate situation, requiring the most strongly worded of all Paul's letters.

The date is probably about AD 47, shortly before the committee of enquiry met in Jerusalem to resolve this very issue (Acts 15). Paul raises many of the same points nine or ten years later, in the letter to the Romans, when less extreme circumstances allowed a more dispassionate consideration of the issues. But the letter to the Galatians stands out, none the less, as the great charter of Christian freedom.

1 The God-given gospel

We can sense Paul's urgency right from the start. The abrupt assertion of authority (1) and lack of any word of praise are most unlike him. He gets straight to the point (6) – and he does not mince his words. The matter is

Galatia was a large province in what is now central Turkey. It includes mountains, broad high plains and lakes. Paul and his companions probably passed Lake Egredir, pictured here, on their way from the coast to Pisidian Antioch on their first missionary journey.

serious. The whole fabric of the Christian gospel is threatened. As if this were not enough, the Jewish trouble-makers have tried to undermine confidence in Paul himself. They have accused him of currying favour (10). They have called him a bogus apostle, and he is forced to defend himself (1, 11ff.). In flat contradiction of the charges, Paul asserts his God-given commission and authority. The very gospel he preaches was revealed to him, not by man – not even the other apostles – but by God. This is the point of his brief autobiography (13-24).

Verses 4-5: Paul stresses the fact that the initiative was God's.

My former life . . . (13): see Acts 8:1; 9.

Arabia (17): probably the Nabataean kingdom whose capital was Petra in present-day Jordan. Acts 9:22-23 does not mention this. The 'three years' may have been one full year and part of two others. Paul does not say why he went. Perhaps after the dramatic about-turn of his conversion, he needed a time away on his own to reorientate his thinking.

Cephas (18, some versions**):** Peter. This seems to be the visit of Acts 9:26ff.

Syria and Cilicia (21): Antioch was in Syria, Tarsus (Paul's home town; Acts 9:30) in Cilicia – the south-east corner of the coast of modern Turkey.

2 The apostles sanction Paul's mission

Paul's next visit to Jerusalem seems to be the one mentioned in Acts 11:30. He took the opportunity to raise the matter of his own position with the other apostles. This attack of self-doubt seems rather out of character but Paul had, after all, been working very much on his own. And he was under attack (4). The apostles had no hesitation in approving his work among the Gentiles – God's hand was so clearly in it (7-9). But Peter later failed to practise what he preached, and had to be called to task over his inconsistency (11ff.). As Jews, Peter and Paul both knew that it was hopeless for any man to try to earn acceptance with God (15-16). Having once gained their freedom through faith in Christ, how could they put their heads back in the noose of the law? If good deeds had been enough to save a man, Christ need never have died.

From James (12): James did not share their view, see Acts 15:13-21.

Ate with the Gentiles (12): see on Romans 14:2, 14.

Verses 17-18: Paul is saying that the real sin lies not in breaking Jewish food-laws, but in turning back to the law for salvation.

Verses 19-20: see on Romans 6 – 7.

3 – 4 Slavery under the law

Anyone willing to exchange Christian freedom for the Jewish law is a fool. The

Paul wrote his letter to challenge the wrong teaching of 'Judaizers' in the church. Jewish influence was strong. Remains of synagogues have been found in 'Galatia'. This synagogue from the early centuries AD is at Baram in northern Israel.

A sundial inscribed with Greek symbols at Ephesus. Paul was concerned that the Galatians, delivered from being slaves of the 'elemental spirits of the universe', should not fall into the new bondage of observing 'days, months and years'.

Jews talk about making the Gentiles sons of Abraham through the rite of circumcision. But Gentile Christians are already Abraham's sons and heirs – because they share his faith (3:7, 29). God accepted Abraham centuries before the law was given through Moses. So how can the law win man free pardon (3:15-18)? The law operated as a temporary restraint until the promise made to Abraham was fulfilled in the coming of Christ (3:19-24). Now, by faith in him, we are all God's children – regardless of race or status or sex.

The Galatians had responded eagerly to Paul's preaching. What happened to make them change (4:12-20)? Can they really want to throw their freedom away (4:8-9)? Those under the law are like the son Abraham had by his slave-woman, Hagar. But Christians are free-born – heirs, like Isaac, to all God's promises.

Elemental/ruling spirits (4:3, 9): the forces that once controlled them; the pagan no-gods they once served.

Days . . . (4:10): Jewish feast-days.

I was ill (4:13): see on 2 Corinthians 12:7.

Mt Sinai (4:24): where the law was given to Moses.

5—6 Freedom in Christ

It is not circumcision that matters, but what it stands for. Paul is so incensed by those who have unsettled his young converts that he could wish they would go the whole hog and castrate themselves (5:12)! Christ has saved us to set us free – free, not to live permissive, self-indulgent lives, but to put ourselves at God's disposal. We harvest what we sow in life (6:7-9). When we live to please ourselves it shows in the way we behave (5:19-21). When we live to please God we harvest a life and character produced in us by the Holy Spirit (5:22-24). And there is no mistaking the two. Christ has dealt with the old life (24) and made us new. Now we have to act accordingly, letting his Spirit control our everyday life and transform our relationships (5:25–6:10).

At this point (6:11) Paul takes over from his secretary to pen the last lines himself. For him there is only one thing worth glorying in: the power of the cross of Christ to re-create and transform human lives.

The marks of Jesus (6:17): the scars Paul's Christian service has earned him (see 2 Corinthians 4:7-12; 6:4-10; 11:23-29); living proof, if proof is still needed, that he is Christ's true apostle.

A well in 'Galatia', or central Turkey.

Ephesians

Paul's letter to the Ephesians differs considerably from his other letters. There are none of the usual personal greetings, although Paul had spent some years in Ephesus and had many friends there (see on Acts 19). Nor does Ephesians deal with particular problems or news. Even the words 'at Ephesus' (1:1) are missing from some of the early manuscripts. So it seems likely that Ephesians began as a circular letter written to a group of churches in what is now western Turkey – of which Ephesus itself was the most important. John's 'seven churches' (Revelation 1:11) were in this general area, as was the church at Colossae.

The fact that Paul wrote from prison (probably in Rome in the early 60s) links this letter with Philippians, Colossians and Philemon – the other 'letters from prison'. Of the three, Ephesians is closest in thought to Colossians. Because of its general nature the letter provides few clues to the situation in the churches. But it is clear that the Gentile Christians predominated, and that they tended to look down on their Jewish fellow Christians. Paul had been specially commissioned to work among the Gentiles, but he held no brief for a divided church. And so his great theme in this letter is God's glorious plan to bring men of every nation and background together in Christ (1:10). As Christians, all are on equal terms. We are one. And we must see that we express that oneness in personal relationships and the way we behave.

1–3
GOD'S GREAT PLAN

1:1-14 The eternal purpose of God
Paul catches his breath in wonder at the very thought of it. God has poured out his love on us. From the very beginning he determined to share his spiritual riches and glory with us – 'in Christ' (the key phrase of Ephesians). Christ stands at the very heart of God's plan. As we believe in him, his death sets us free: we can be forgiven. We can also share his new, risen life. We are made one with him, part of him. And in him we too are caught up in God's great world-plan as we live to his glory.

Saints (1); grace and peace (2): see on Romans 1.

Mystery (9): 'secret plan'; no human mind could have guessed God's intention. Paul usually uses this word to mean the 'open secret' of the gospel.

1:15-23 Paul's prayer
It warms Paul's heart to hear of the faith and love of these Christians. He prays that they may have greater understanding, a surer grasp of their glorious destiny, and increased awareness of the power at their disposal. The power God exercised in raising Christ from the dead and setting him in supreme control of the universe is at work in us, too!

2:1-10 From death to life
Because of our sinful nature we could not have fellowship with God: and to be cut off from him means death. But Christ has taken our death himself. God in his goodness – through no effort of our own – has given us new life in Christ. He has made us part of his new creation, set us off on a new life with power to carry out what he intends.

Ruler of the spiritual powers (2): Satan, whose rebellious spirit is actively at work in the world of men.

2:11-22 Broken barriers

In the ancient world the Jew was separated from the Gentile by racial, religious, cultural and social barriers. (Non-Jews were, for example, forbidden on pain of death to enter the inner courts of the Temple in Jerusalem – see page 567.) If Christ could bring these two together, there was, and is, no human gulf too great for him to bridge. And he did. His death on the cross is the one means of peace with God for all men, without distinction. And all who belong to him have a common bond which is deeper and stronger than any of their former differences – of race or colour or status or sex or background. Jew and Gentile are one in Christ.

The circumcised (11): i.e. the Jews. See on Genesis 17.

Verse 12: the Gentile Christians have no cause to give themselves airs. Up till now they have been outsiders. The Jews, as God's people, were the only ones for whom there was hope.

3:1-13 Paul's mission to the Gentiles

Before Christ came, God's promises had been largely confined to the Jews. His purpose for the world at large had

This road at Ephesus is lined with the ruins of buildings. It was at Ephesus that Paul hired 'the hall of Tyrannus' and taught the gospel there. The harbour, silting up by Paul's time, formerly lay beyond the forum in the distance. The magnificent theatre is to the right.

remained a secret (4-6, 8-9). When Paul was commissioned to take the message of salvation to the Gentiles, a new phase in God's plan was opened up. As men of all nations are brought together in Christ they demonstrate God's power and wisdom, not just to the watching world (see John 17:21), but to the cosmic powers beyond and behind it (10). The scope of God's purpose is breathtaking. In the light of it, Paul could keep his own troubles in perspective – and so can we.

Verse 3: not necessarily a separate letter – Paul had just told them how God had revealed his 'secret plan' to him (1:9, etc.).

3:14-21 Paul prays again

Paul has prayed that the church might have understanding (1:15-23). Now he prays more urgently than ever that they may have love; that they may be strong; that Christ may make his home in their hearts; that God may fill them completely. He can do all this and more.

4–6
CHRISTIANS IN ACTION

4:1-16 Unity – in practice

Christian unity is a fact. We are bound together by a common faith, a common life, common loyalty, common purpose. We serve one Master. He is the head, we are the limbs of a single body (see also 1 Corinthians 12–13). But we are not identical in temperament, personality or gifts. We must constantly cement the bond by a loving, forbearing attitude to one another, and by using our different gifts for the common good. We have to grow up together until we are all Christ wants us to be – until we are really like him.

Verse 8: following his ascension Christ gave gifts to men (see verse 11).

4:17 – 5:20 The new life

Salvation is God's free gift, but it carries with it the obligation to live and behave from that point on as God wants (4:1). This means deliberately discarding the old, selfish way of life, shedding former habits – and letting the new life change our thinking and remould our pattern of behaviour. This calls for truth and honesty; no harboured grudges, no spite and bitterness – instead kindness and a new readiness to forgive. In a word, we are to copy God's character. All that we think and do and say must be able to stand his searchlight.

5:21 – 6:9 Christian relationships: family and household

If everyone subordinates his own interests (21), no one can lord it. The Christian wife gives her husband complete respect and loyalty. The Christian husband cares for his wife with

A seat reservation in the theatre at Miletus, just near Ephesus, read 'For Jews and God-fearers only'. The Christian message of 'All one in Christ' was a revolutionary doctrine.

Temple dedicated to the Roman Emperor Hadrian at Ephesus.

'Put on God's armour', wrote Paul to the Ephesians; a statuette of a Roman soldier.

unselfish, undemanding love. Each depends on the other, and both model themselves on Christ. Their relationship, in turn, reflects the relationship between Christ and the church. In the family, children owe their parents respect and obedience. Parents must exercise discipline – not behave like petty tyrants; Christian slaves (and, presumably, employees) serve their masters as willingly and well as they serve Christ. Christian masters (and employers) will not bludgeon or bully, knowing that they must answer to a Master themselves.

5:32: the close physical bond between husband and wife is an illustration of Christ's spiritual oneness with his church.

6:10-24 The armour of God

Paul does not pretend it will be easy to maintain these standards – to keep our feet in the Christian life. The fight is on. And we are up against powerful external forces. It is a spiritual struggle for which we need spiritual weapons. But we are not left helpless. The whole armoury of God is at our disposal – and with this defence we can stand.

Philippians

Philippi was a Roman colony, on the Egnatian Way – the great northern east-west highway. It was occupied by Italian settlers following Octavian's great battles, first against Brutus and Cassius, then against his former ally Antony. The colonists were proud of their special rights and privileges, and intensely loyal to Rome. In Philippi, as in the province of Macedonia as a whole, women enjoyed high status. They took active part in public and business life – a situation which is reflected in the church.

The church

The church was founded about AD 50, during Paul's second missionary journey (see Acts 16:12-40). When Paul, Silas and Timothy left, Luke, the doctor, stayed on. Philippi was a medical centre, and may possibly have been Luke's home town. He no doubt did much to put the group on its feet and continue the evangelistic outreach. The letter reveals a church taking its share of suffering (1:29), and in some danger of division (1:27; 2:2). There may have been some leaning to a doctrine of perfectionism (3:12-13). And the arrival of the Judaizers (see on 3:2ff.) introduced a new threat. But Paul loved this church and rejoiced over its progress.

The letter

Paul wrote from prison (1:12). If this was in Rome (Acts 28:16, 30-31), the date was about AD 61-63. But conditions are harsher than they appear in Acts; judgement is imminent, and there is a real possibility of death. Timothy, but not Luke (to judge by 2:20-21), is with him. It may therefore be that the imprisonment is an earlier one not recorded in Acts. A good case has been made out for Ephesus, which would make the date of writing about AD 54. We cannot be certain either way.

There are several reasons for writing. Paul wanted to explain why he was sending Epaphroditus back. He wanted to thank the Philippians for their gift. He had news for them. And what he had heard about them made him long to encourage and advise. Further news reached him while he was writing that made it imperative to add a word of warning (3:1b).

1:1-2 Opening greetings

The letter comes from Paul 'and Timothy' – the young man who was with Paul when the church was founded, and who would shortly be coming to Philippi again (2:19). The 'slaves of Christ Jesus' write to the 'saints': not an elite, but all the Christians, as men and women set apart for God's service. The 'bishops' (overseers) and 'deacons' (administrators) receive special mention.

1:3-11 Paul's prayer for the church

Paul's prayer is full of love, joy (a keynote of the whole letter) and thankfulness. He longs for them to enjoy progressively richer and deeper spiritual knowledge which will mould their lives to God's pattern.

The first day (5): see Acts 16:12-40.
My imprisonment (7): see introduction above.

1:12-26 Personal news

Paul speaks of the past (12), present (13-18) and future (19-26), weighing the alternatives of life and death.
What has happened to me (12): if Paul writes from Rome, this includes mob violence, injustice, plots, prison, shipwreck and long detention under constant guard.

The whole praetorian/palace guard (13): the crack imperial force from which Paul's warders were drawn.

Deliverance (19): if the judgement goes against him, death will deliver him into Christ's presence; if it goes for him, his captors will release him to serve the church.

To live is Christ…(21): possessing more and more of him, becoming more and more like him, until on his death the process is completed in one glorious moment.

1:27 – 2:18 A plea for a united stand

There is more than a hint of division in the church (see for example 4:2). Paul urges them all to pocket their pride, and to live and work and think as one. Anything less lets down the gospel and the Lord, whose life on earth is the supreme example of humility. It is because Jesus gave up all that was his by right – even his life – that God has given him the highest place of all. (2:5-11 is probably a quotation from an early hymn in praise of Christ).

2:5: 'The attitude you should have is the one that Christ Jesus had' (Good News Bible).

The form of God (6): the actual nature, not just the appearance (as also in verse 7).

Littered stones and a few standing pillars remain at Philippi, in Paul's time an important town and a Roman colony on the Via Egnatia. Ruins of a Byzantine church are in the distance. See too pictures on pages 36 and 560.

'I press towards the goal to win the prize…' Paul wrote; pictured here is a Roman racing-chariot.

Emptied himself (7): 'gave up all he had'; 'made himself nothing'. In becoming man the Lord stripped himself of his glory: he lived a life of humble obedience. But he cast off none of his essential deity.

Day of Christ (16): the day of his return.

A libation/offering (17): Paul's death adds only the finishing touch to the real offering, the faith and life of the church.

2:19-30 Paul commends his fellow workers

Verses 19-23: Timothy (see on 1:1-2).
Verses 25-30: Epaphroditus. The Philip-

pians had sent him to help Paul. In sending him home, Paul is anxious to make it clear he has not fallen down on his job. Far from it.

3 Warning and example

Paul had been rounding off his letter (3:1a), but fresh and alarming news compelled him to take up his pen again. He does not mind repeating former advice, as a safeguard (3:1b). They must beware of those 'dogs' the Judaizers – that group of Jewish Christians who followed Paul everywhere, insisting that Gentile converts must be circumcised and keep the law (despite the official edict of Acts 15:19ff.). They are in fact altering the whole basis of salvation, making it 'by faith *and*...', instead of 'by faith only': hence Paul's anger.

The true circumcision (3): the true Israel, the true people of God.

Profit...loss (7-8): God does not operate

a credit and debit account. The finest human achievement is garbage compared with the standard of life he demands, and provides for us, in Christ.

I press on...(12ff.): like the athlete or charioteer, who does not waste time looking back, but strains every nerve and concentrates every effort to cross the line or pass the post. Paul counters the idea that perfection can be reached here and now.

Their god is their stomach (19): i.e. appetite; whatever they want; revelling in things they should be ashamed of.

Our citizenship (20): they are to regard themselves as a colony of heaven. The Philippians, being intensely proud of their status as a Roman colony, would be quick to grasp all that that meant.

4 Advice and encouragement: grateful thanks

Verse 1: a general appeal. Verses 2-3: personal appeals. Euodia and Syntyche are two women who have quarrelled.

Verses 4-9: rejoice, rejoice. The advice comes from a man in prison, facing death; a man who had been stoned and beaten and hounded by the mob. Yet experiences which leave others sour and bitter leave Paul overflowing with joy! The secret is in verses 6-7: learning how to off-load all our cares on the One who cares for us (1 Peter 5:7). Nothing is beyond him. Having emptied our minds of worry, the next step is to fill them with the sort of things that will shape a truly Christian character (8).

Verses 10-20: the apostle's appreciation of the church's gifts. From the very first they have supported him (15), with a generosity that extends to all in need (2 Corinthians 8:1-5). At real cost they have given themselves and all they possess. No wonder Paul loves these Christians: a group of faithful, loyal, thoughtful, generous, outgoing men and women.

Caesar's household (21): Christian members of the Emperor's staff (the palace staff, if Paul is at Rome).

Paul wrote his letter as a 'slave' of Jesus Christ. These slave chains from Roman towns were found under water off the coast of Israel.

Colossians

Colossae was a small town in the beautiful Lycus Valley, about 100 miles east of Ephesus, near Denizli in modern Turkey. Its near neighbours were the more prosperous Laodicea (Colossians 4:16; see on Revelation 3:14ff.) and Hierapolis. There were Christian groups in all three towns.

The church

We have no record of how it began. But it was probably during Paul's three years in Ephesus (Acts 19) that two prominent men from Colossae – Epaphras and Philemon – became Christians. And they were active in spreading the Christian message in their home area (Colossians 1:6-7; 4:12-13; Philemon 1-2, 5).

The letter

Although Paul had never visited the group at Colossae, he had heard all about it from Epaphras. There was much to be thankful for, but some of the news was worrying. So he wrote to them from prison – probably in Rome, about AD 61. He had a ready-made opportunity to send the letter with Tychicus (who may well have carried the letter to the Ephesians at the same time) and Philemon's runaway slave Onesimus, whom he was sending home (see on Philemon).

The problem

The trouble at Colossae was 'syncretism' – that tendency to introduce ideas from other philosophies and religions on a level with Christian truth, which is also perhaps our greatest temptation today. It was understandable. There were Greeks and Jews in the Colossian church, as well as 'native' Phrygians. It was natural that they should cling to their own ideas and want to incorporate them into Christianity. It seemed harmless enough. But Paul knew that it struck at the heart of the Christian faith. By trying to retain circumcision, their food-laws and festivals (2:11, 16), the Jewish Christians brought the whole basis of man's acceptance with God into question (see on Galatians). The idea of angel intermediaries (2:18) was a direct challenge to the supremacy of Christ. And the introduction of asceticism and high-flown philosophy threw man back on himself and on human wisdom (2:18-23) – which had already been proved a failure. Although Paul does not deal with these issues point by point these are the thoughts that lie behind his letter. The Colossians needed to take fresh hold on Christ, on his complete supremacy and utter sufficiency. This is Paul's theme.

1:1-14 Opening greetings and prayer

It is characteristic of Paul to begin with thanksgiving. He has his Christian priorities – and his psychology! – right. But his warm-hearted praise is genuine, not just sugar to coat the pill of the lecture to follow. His loving care (and his prayer-list) extended beyond the churches he himself had brought into being, to groups of Christians he had never even met (2:1). It cheered him immensely to hear of their faith and love and hope. And he longed for God to give them fuller understanding and spiritual maturity.

1:15-23 Jesus Christ the Lord

Jesus is the living expression of God himself – active in the creation and holding together of all that exists. He was first, he is first – in existence, in power, in position. He has first place in God's new creation and his new people, the church. He brought it into being. He is its Head. Through his death it is possible for us to become God's friends – this is the good news of the gospel.

Firstborn (15): not first to be created, but the heir whose position is unique.

Thrones…(16): unseen beings and powers outside our visible world.

1:24 – 2:5 Paul's own task

The apostle's job is to make God's message known. The philosophers hint at secrets, at deep things known only to the initiated. This is God's open secret: Jesus Christ – at home in every Christian, preparing him for a glorious future. And Jesus really is a 'secret' worth knowing. This makes all Paul's efforts worthwhile.

What is lacking…(1:24): Paul is not implying that Christ's suffering was not enough for our salvation. But the church – Christians – cannot be perfected without suffering too.

2:6 – 3:4 Wrong teaching and right attitudes

False argument was filtering into the Colossian church from various quarters (see introduction above). It was misleading and dangerous. The Christian cannot afford to compromise either with philosophy or with legalism. Both of these are man-centred. Christianity is Christ-centred – or it is nothing at all. We have all we need in him. We do not need to invoke other spiritual powers or intermediaries (2:8, 23), because Christ is infinitely greater. No religious rite (2:11) can give us more than we already have. Old Testament practices are no more than a shadow of the reality – which is Christ (16ff.). He is our life. He is the One we must hold on to. We depend on him, not on ourselves, our spirituality, our asceticism.

2:12: see Romans 6.

Paul warned his readers against 'sham apostles'. Those bringing false teaching and writing letters purporting to have apostolic authority must have been a constant problem. Some of these writings, and stories of the life of Jesus embroidered with pious but fantastic inventions, have survived. These fragments of an unknown 'Gospel' date from the first half of the 2nd century.

Food and drink...(2:16): despite all that the Jews said, salvation does not depend on things like these.

Elemental/ruling spirits (2:20): Christians must throw off the old pagan superstitious idea that spirits control the world.

3:5—4:6 The old life and the new

Becoming a Christian means a definite break with the old selfish way of life. It means determination to let the new life which is in us govern all we think and say and do. It means a permanent resolve to become like Christ, to take on his character (3:10). His life–his love and forgiveness–is our model (3:12ff.). His word (3:16) shapes our thinking. The hallmark of the Christian life is prayer and thanksgiving to God, and outgoing unselfish love in all our human relationships. Our concern is no longer to get, but to give.

3:18—4:1: see on Ephesians 5 – 6, where Paul treats the same subject more fully.

4:7-18 Personal news

The reference to Tychicus and Onesimus links this letter with Ephesians (see 6:21-22) and Philemon. All three letters would seem to have been sent at the same time by the same messenger. (The letter from Laodicea, 16, may be Ephesians.) It is good to find Mark reinstated after the trouble he once caused between Paul and Barnabas (Acts 13:13; 15:36-40). Aristarchus, who though a Jew came from Greece, was another longstanding companion of Paul's and had been involved in the

Colossae lay at one side of the Lycus Valley, near Laodicea and Hierapolis. With the mountains, streams and fertile landscape, it was a likely breeding-ground for mystical, pantheist or 'Gnostic' ideas, which Paul wrote to oppose.

riot at Ephesus (Acts 19:29). Luke stayed with Paul to the end, but Demas defected (2 Timothy 4:10-11). Epaphras, the Colossian, has been mentioned already (1:7, and see introduction). Archippus may be Philemon's son (Philemon 2). Nympha, in Laodicea, is only one of those who opened their homes to the local Christian group long before there were church buildings. Aquila and Priscilla at Ephesus (1 Corinthians 16:19) and later at Rome (Romans 16:5), Philemon at Colossae and Gaius at Corinth (Romans 16:23) all did the same. The whole church is deeply in their debt.

1 and 2 Thessalonians

Thessalonica was a free city, capital of the Roman province of Macedonia (northern Greece). It was a prosperous port on the Aegean Sea, across the bay from Mt Olympus. It also stood on the Egnatian Way, the land trade-route from Dyrrachium on the Adriatic to Byzantium (Istanbul). Thessaloniki is today a flourishing modern city, centre of government for northern Greece, and second only to Athens.

The church

The church was founded about AD 50, after Paul (with Silas and Timothy) left Philippi on the second missionary journey. See Acts 17:1-9. Paul did not stay in Thessalonica long: three successive sabbaths preaching in the synagogue, followed by a short time based at Jason's house. Then the Jews stirred up trouble. Jason and the other Christians were hauled before the magistrates and bound over to keep the peace. For safety's sake the newly-formed church sent the missionaries away. But persecution continued, from Jews and others.

The letters

From Thessalonica, Paul and his party went to Beroea, then Paul continued alone to Athens. It seems Timothy joined him there (1 Thessalonians 3:1-2), but was almost immediately sent back to Thessalonica for news. Paul was acutely anxious to know what had become of the Christians. He was in Corinth by the time Timothy returned with good news. 1 Thessalonians, written at this point, is full of relief and joy. Paul answers questions that had arisen, and repeats his teaching on matters where the church was weak. The second letter followed a few months later, reinforcing the teaching and clearing up misunderstandings, particularly over Christ's return. These two letters are the earliest of Paul's surviving writings (with the possible exception of Galatians). They were written only 20 years after the crucifixion of Jesus.

1 Thessalonians

1:1 Opening greetings

Paul is the author of the letter. But he writes in association with Silvanus (=Silas, see on Acts 15:40) and Timothy, his companions on the mission to Thessalonica, and now in Corinth.

1:2-10 Paul thanks God for good news of the church

What happened at Thessalonica was the work of God. What else could account for the way this little group – persecuted, deprived of their teachers from the word go – stood firm? More than that, within months they have become an example of unwavering faith to the rest of Greece (7), spreading the good news far and wide by word and life. No wonder Paul has cause for thanks.

They themselves (9): the people of Macedonia, Achaia, etc.
Verses 9-10: the gospel in a nutshell. Paul had preached the character of God; Jesus, his Son, who died to deliver man from judgement; the resurrection; and the return of Christ from heaven. The promise of the Lord's return is specially precious to all who suffer. These letters are shot through with it.

2:1-16 Paul recalls his visit

It is clear that Paul's enemies have been pursuing a campaign of vilification. The apostle clears himself of their charges by reminding the Christians of what actually happened when he was with them. He did not come as an itinerant quack teacher peddling dubious wares, and out to deceive (3). Nor was he on the make, in any sense (5). He came to give, not get (8), willing to face more trouble while still smarting from the wounds of Philippi (2; see Acts 16:22ff.). He even refused financial support (9).

Each one of you (11): Paul counselled enquirers personally, individually.

Verses 15-16: nowhere does Paul speak so harshly of his own people. His tone is prophetic. There is a point of no return for those who implacably oppose God. Judgement is as certain as if it had come already (16b).

2:17 — 3:10 Subsequent events

Paul is as close to his converts as parent to child. No matter how far away, they are deep in his heart and thoughts. The knowledge that they are in trouble fills him with unbearable anxiety. Paul's happiness – his life, even – depends on their continuance and progress in the faith. So he longs to see them and hear from them. He is even prepared to face Athens alone, rather than do without news. So Timothy's welcome report brings the apostle an influx of joy, a new lease of life.

Satan hindered us (2:18): it is in his interest so to engineer circumstances that the missionary and his converts are kept apart.

We told you beforehand…(3:4): 1st-century Christians were taught from the outset to expect trouble and suffering.

3:11-13 Paul's prayer

Paul prays for reunion, and for love and holiness in the church.

4 — 5:22 Specific teaching

■ On sexual matters (4:1-8). Pagan standards of sexual behaviour fell far short of Jewish and Christian ones. The pull of the old ways was strong for the young converts.
■ On Christian love and right living (4:9-12). Even where love already exists there is always room for more. The

Greeks despised manual labour. And there were idlers in the church quite happy to sponge on the generosity of fellow Christians. But Paul worked with his hands and encouraged others to do the same. The prospect of Jesus' return was a great temptation to opt out of hum-drum daily work (see also 2 Thessalonians 3:11-12).
■ On the Lord's return (4:13 – 5:11). Two problems have arisen out of Paul's teaching on the subject.

1. Some had died in the months between Paul's departure and the writing of this letter. So will Christians who die before Christ comes lose out (13-18)? Far from it, says Paul. They will be raised first when Christ comes. And dead and living together will join in the Lord's triumph and enjoy his presence.

2. When will the Lord come (5:1-11)? No one knows. But he will come suddenly and unexpectedly – and we need to be ready.
■ On general matters (5:12-22). Time, or space, is running out. But Paul manages to pack seventeen practical and characteristic commands into these few verses.

Wrong his brother (4:6): the same principle applies before and after marriage – sexual promiscuity deprives a fellow man of what is rightly his.

Asleep (13)…fallen asleep (14): for the Christian, death is merely a sleep from which he awakes to the presence of Christ.

The breastplate (5:8): faith, love and the certainty of future salvation are the Christian's defences against all attack. Compare Ephesians 6:14ff.

5:23-28 Conclusion

Paul's prayer is comprehensive: for the whole man in every aspect ('spirit, soul, body'). Authority (the stern command to read the letter to the whole church) sits beside humility. The apostle, who never ceases to pray for his readers, knows how much he needs their prayers.

A holy/brotherly kiss (26): see on 2 Corinthians 13:12.

2 Thessalonians

1:1-2 Opening greetings

1:3-12 Praise and encouragement

Verses 3-4: the Thessalonians seem to have protested against the extravagant praise of Paul's first letter (chapter 1). He replies that it is only right to thank God for their growing faith and love, and their firm stand in face of persecution.

Verses 5-12: the universe is a moral universe; God is a just God. It is therefore certain that those who make his people suffer, and reject his truth, will themselves be eternally, irrevocably punished at his coming. This is a fact no Christian gloats over.

2:1-12 The events leading up to Christ's return

This passage is one of the most difficult in all Paul's letters; and even Peter found Paul hard to understand (2 Peter 3:16)! He alludes to teaching of which we have no surviving record, so that much which was clear to his first readers is now obscure. It is better, in some cases, to admit we do not know the meaning, than to speculate.

Some of the Thessalonian Christians thought the day of the Lord had already begun. But Paul has never said (or written, 2) so. Before this happens, he explains, there will be a great, final rebellion against God, headed by an individual utterly opposed to him. (Compare Revelation 13, and 1 John 2:18-25). At present there are forces at work restraining evil – but in the end these will be swept away. Victory will come only through Christ, at his coming.

Man of lawlessness (3): not Satan himself, but the leader of the anti-God forces, who sets himself up as God. ('Son of perdition' is Hebrew idiom, meaning 'the one who is doomed to destruction'.)

The one who holds it back (7): perhaps Paul personalizes the principle of law and government which holds evil in check; perhaps he means an angelic being. We really do not know.

Those who will perish (10): because they do not welcome the gospel. They turn their backs on the truth which offers salvation. In effect, like Satan, they say 'Evil be thou my Good' (12).

2:13 – 3:5 Thanksgiving and prayer

Paul turns, with tremendous contrast, to the Thessalonians. They responded gladly to the truth. And now all the glory of the Lord awaits them.

From the beginning (13): from eternity (see Ephesians 1:4).

The traditions (15, some versions): not customs, but the truth about Jesus and his teaching, faithfully handed down by the apostles: the same truth that we possess in written form in the New Testament.

Comfort (17, some versions): in the old sense of strengthen.

3:6-15 The need to work for a living

Paul stressed this in his first letter (4:11). But excitement about Christ's coming

Little remains of ancient Thessalonica today. As Thessaloniki, it is the second largest city in Greece. In later Roman times the Via Egnatia passed under the Arch of Galerius pictured here. The street is still called by the same name.

Paul had to tell the Thessalonians to get on with their daily living, and not to stop work in their expectation of the Lord's return.

seems to have made the situation worse, not better. So Paul speaks out in strong terms against those who idle their life away and sponge on others. They can find no warrant for this in his own behaviour.

3:16-18 Conclusion
The present is tough, the future will be tougher (2:3-12). But no matter what times may be like, no matter what may be going on around, the Christian has an inexhaustible, unfailing source of peace.

At verse 17 Paul takes over from his secretary. His own signature authenticates this letter (see 2:2). He added his personal signature to each of his letters in the same way.

1 and 2 Timothy

Timothy was the child of a mixed marriage – his mother being Jewish, his father Greek. His home was at Lystra in the Roman province of Galatia (not far from Konya in present-day Turkey). Paul came to Lystra on his first missionary journey, and it must have been then that Timothy was converted. He made such strides as a Christian that when Paul called again he decided to take Timothy with him on his travels. The local church leaders formally commissioned the young man and gave him their blessing. And from then on he became Paul's constant, loyal, trusted and greatly loved companion.

Timothy was not naturally brave, and he was often unwell. He needed a good deal of encouragement. But Paul's confidence was not misplaced. In the letters to the different churches he speaks most warmly of this 'son in the faith'. Timothy not only travelled with Paul and was associated with him in many of his letters, he frequently acted as Paul's envoy to the churches. Very early on he was left behind in Beroea to consolidate and follow up Paul's work there and at Thessalonica. He was sent to Corinth when Paul heard of the troubles in the church there – no easy assignment. And at the time Paul wrote to him he was in Ephesus, supervising the local Christian groups and responsible for choosing and training church leaders.

The letters

1 and 2 Timothy and Titus belong to the end of Paul's life. Paul was free when he wrote 1 Timothy and Titus, and had recently been engaged in further evangelism in Greece and what is now Turkey. This does not tally with anything we know from Acts, and it may be assumed that Paul was released from the imprison-

ment described in Acts 28, resumed his preaching for some time, and was then re-arrested and taken to Rome for trial. In 2 Timothy he is in prison and expecting to be executed.

In these 'pastoral letters' – the general title for the three letters – we have a directive from Paul on the way Timothy and Titus should handle the various problems they encountered in the oversight of the churches in their charge. Paul sets out the qualities to look for in appointing church leaders. He gives advice on personal conduct. And in the face of much false and misleading teaching he urges them to concentrate on essentials and not be side-tracked. The best way to counter wrong ideas is to teach the truth.

The early church had no doubt that these letters were genuinely written by Paul to the two men named. Modern scholars have questioned this on the grounds that they differ in language and content from Paul's other letters, and that they counter 2nd-century heresies. Some suggest they are the work of a later writer who incorporated some genuine Pauline material. This raises fresh problems, however, and there may be a simpler explanation.

We know that Paul often used a secretary, for instance, and if he was given a good deal of freedom this would make arguments based on vocabulary very uncertain (even with computer analysis!). The problem over content is that Paul tells Timothy and Titus things they must surely have known already. The reason may be that the instructions were meant to be read to the churches over which the two men ministered. Even the point about heresies is by no means certain. There is nothing in the letters that we can categorically say Paul could not have written.

1 Timothy

1 The trouble at Ephesus; Paul and Timothy

There had been a tremendous response to Paul's preaching in and around Ephesus (Acts 19). A great many Christian groups had sprung up almost overnight. And Paul was quick to realize how vulnerable they were to wrong teaching (Acts 20:29-30). Ten years later his fears had materialized. Apocryphal Jewish legends and family-trees (4) were being made the basis of strange teaching. This was a wrong approach to the Old Testament law, and Timothy must stop it spreading. The Christian message should result in faith and love and a clear conscience – not idle speculation. It has always seemed more exciting to argue over abstruse topics than to live the Christian life.

Paul had been a Christian for over 30 years. He had been on the road with the gospel message for 20. Yet he never forgot that he had once gone all out to destroy this sect (13; Acts 8:1-3; 9). He never ceased to be amazed that God should have taken a man like him into his service. Paul's directive is a good one: 'hold to your faith; obey your Christian conscience'.

Words of prophecy (18): the indication (given either to Paul, or at Timothy's commissioning) that God had chosen Timothy for this work.

Handed over to Satan (20): we do not know exactly what this means – but see on 1 Corinthians 5:5.

2 Prayer; the place of women

The first duty of the Christian church is prayer. It is in answer to prayer that God gives conditions in which Christians can lead peaceable lives and put all their

energy into making his good news known to the whole world (4).

The Christian message upgraded the status of women (see e.g. Galatians 3:28). But God did not intend them to take over. Men and women are equal in his sight, but their roles in life are not identical. So Paul's word to Christian women is to be conduct-conscious, not clothes-mad, and not to lord it over the men.

Verse 15: Paul could never have meant that women win eternal salvation through childbirth (compare verse 5)! The thought may follow on from verses 13-14 – i.e. though woman was the first to sin, it was through woman that the Saviour was born (Revised Standard Version margin). Or he means that women will be 'brought safely through' childbirth.

Head of a Roman woman, from the 2nd century AD.

3 Church leaders

It was Paul's practice to appoint several elders (the same thing as bishops, 1) to take charge of each church (Acts 14:23). These in turn were assisted by 'helpers' (deacons, 8). His list of qualifications for these leaders makes sound sense. They must be men (and women, 11, unless these are deacons' wives) who can control themselves and their families, who have proved to be stable Christians, and who have the respect of the outside world. Timothy was not a naturally forceful character. To have Paul's written authority was the next best thing to having the apostle with him (14ff.).

Mystery (9, some versions): God's revealed secret in Jesus Christ; the Christian faith is God-given, not man-made.

Verse 16: Paul seems to be quoting a Christian hymn.

4 False teachers – and true

The ultimate source of false teaching is the devil himself. It is promoted by men who are dead to conscience. They ban marriage and lay down rigid rules about diet – things God has designed for our good. They claim that their thinking is super-Christian. In fact it is sub-Christian. Timothy, as a true teacher, has to make this clear. And this does not stop at words. His whole life must bear out what he teaches others. So he has to let the truth mould his own life (6); he has to keep spiritually fit (7, 8). He has always to watch himself, and watch his teaching.

5 – 6:2 Dealing with people; widows; elders

To treat other people as we would our own family (1-2) is sound advice. There was no welfare state in Paul's day and the widow's lot was unenviable. The church was quick to realize and accept its responsibility to help (Acts 6:1). It soon had a sizeable problem, and not all of the cases were equally deserving. Paul's rule is that the church should reserve its help for those who are really destitute. It should take on to its books only older widows of good Christian character, and committed to Christian work. The younger ones should remarry. And wherever possible widows should be cared for by their own relatives. In the city where the goddess Diana was served by a host of prostitutes, the reputation of those who serve Christ must be beyond reproach.

Elders must be carefully chosen, treated with respect, and paid for their work.

As Christians, slaves are free men – but they are not to drag Christ's name in the mud by turning on their masters (see also on Ephesians 6:5ff.; Philemon).

5:9: not 'married only once', but 'faithful to her husband', New International Version.

5:22: 'lay hands on': i.e. commission for Christian service.

5:23: sound medical advice at the time; wine counteracted some of the harmful impurities in the water.

6:3-21 Real wealth; personal instructions

The subject of false teaching comes up

'I have finished the course, the victor's wreath awaits me' – Paul uses the vivid picture of the athlete's crown. This gold wreath was found at Pergamum.

yet again. The superior 'knowledge' (*gnosis,* 20) claimed by these men soon grew into the full-scale heresy of 'Gnosticism', whose initiates felt free to discard some of the cardinal Christian truths, including the fact that Christ was a real man.

Some see Christianity as a road to riches. And Christians *are* rich–though not in money. Not that money is wrong in itself. It can and should be put to good and generous use. It is the *craving* for money that leads to all kinds of evil. The 'man of God' (11) craves for a truly Christian character, and all his effort is directed to this end. He knows that Jesus will one day return in glory, and he lives in the light of that fact.

The root/source (10): more accurately, 'a root'.

2 Timothy

This is Paul's last and most moving letter. After a lifetime of service and suffering for Christ he is in prison again, and death is imminent. He is alone except for Luke, and longs to see Timothy again. Yet there is no hint of self-pity; there are no regrets. His last word is one of encouragement to all who follow after. He can face death without fear and without doubt. The race is over–ahead is his reward.

1 'I thank God'

Gratitude was the habit of Paul's Christian life. He had long since ceased to grumble about his own discomforts. Deep thankfulness fills his heart now as he thinks of Timothy. And he longs for this man of many fears, as well as real faith, to share his own confidence. The secret is simply to *know* Christ (12; and see Philippians 3:10). We have good news for the world–a gospel that brings life. We need neither apologize for it, nor try to improve on it.

Tears (4): shed when they parted.
That day (12): the day of the Lord's return; the day of judgement.
All…in Asia (15): false teaching took such a hold in Ephesus (see on 1 Timothy 1) that Christians rejected the very man to whom they owed their faith. It must have been a bitter moment for Paul.

2 On active service

It costs something to be a Christian–no man knew this better than Paul. Timothy will need single-minded determination not to get sucked in by the demands of life (4) or side-tracked by fruitless, divisive argument (16, 23). Not everyone who makes a good beginning stays the course. The way we live must demonstrate the truth of what we say. We are not to bicker and fight over words, but hold to the truth with gentleness and love.

Verses 11-13: Paul is probably quoting a hymn.
The resurrection (18): they 'spiritualized' the teaching and denied any future bodily resurrection.

3 Troubled times ahead

Paul warns that as the time for Christ's return draws near evil will intensify–even within the church (5-6). Those who are true to Christ will go through persecution–as Jesus himself predicted (John 15:20). Timothy must stand firm in the truths taught him from the scriptures. They contain all that is necessary for salvation and for right living.

Jannes and Jambres (8): in Jewish tradition, the names of Pharaoh's magicians (Exodus 7).
Verse 11: see Acts 13–14. Timothy would vividly recall these events since they took place near his home. Paul was stoned and left for dead at Lystra, Timothy's home town.

4 Final instructions

Paul may be put to death any time now. The prospect does not ruffle him. But he

Paul signed his own dictated letters, adding a greeting. This wooden pen-case containing reed-pens, with an ink-well half-filled with black ink, dates from the same period.

has a last charge for Timothy: to go on declaring God's message, come what may; though, sadly, this is not what men are itching to hear.

Personal news is left till last. Paul's fellow missionaries – Titus, Tychicus, Trophimus – are all away. One is ill, and one (Demas) has defected. At the first stage of his trial (16) Paul, like Jesus, stood alone. All his friends deserted him, and his enemies were not slow to make capital. Now winter is coming and he wants his books and papers, and his thick cloak. He has only Luke's presence, and the faithful Christians in Rome (21), to warm his heart – and the hope that Timothy and Mark will reach him in time.

Endure suffering (5): despite his fears, Timothy did just that (see Hebrews 13:23).

Books and parchments (13): possibly copies of Old Testament books, Paul's own notebooks, or personal papers.

Alexander (14): see 1 Timothy 1:20.

The lion's mouth (17): this may just be a manner of speaking; or it may refer to the lions in the arena, to Nero, or to the devil.

See introduction to 1 and 2 Timothy.

Titus is not mentioned in Acts, but it is clear from the letters that he was one of Paul's trusted inner circle. As a Greek he was made a test case on the visit to Jerusalem, to clarify the position of non-Jewish converts (Galatians 2:1-4). Later when, despite Timothy's work, trouble flared up in Corinth, Paul chose Titus as the man for the job. He not only sorted things out, but established really good relations with the church – no small tribute to his tact and strength of character (2 Corinthians 2; 7; 8; 12). Some years later again, when Paul wrote this letter, Titus had been left to consolidate the apostle's work in Crete. He faced a situation very similar to Timothy's at Ephesus (see 1 Timothy). The last mention of Titus is in 2 Timothy 4:10, when he was away (presumably still furthering the Christian cause) in Dalmatia (Yugoslavia).

Crete

Crete was probably one of the first places to hear the Christian gospel. There were Jews from Crete in the crowd that listened to Peter on the Day of Pentecost (Acts 2:11). But the message fell on rough ground. The Cretans were such habitual liars (1:12) that the Greeks coined a special verb for lying – 'to Cretize'. And it is plain from Paul's letter that even the Christians were an unruly, hot-headed, volatile bunch who needed firm handling.

1 Elders – and trouble-makers

It is the thought of the Cretans and their lies (12) that makes Paul dwell on the dependability of God's word. When he holds out the promise of eternal life, we can rely on it. He tells us the truth – we can pass it on with absolute confidence.

For the qualifications of church leaders (5-9) see on 1 Timothy 3.

False teachers have produced a situa-

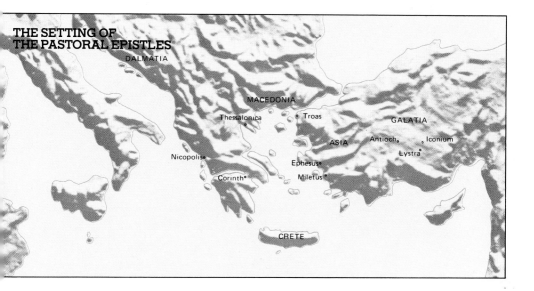

THE SETTING OF
THE PASTORAL EPISTLES
DALMATIA
MACEDONIA
Thessalonica   Troas
GALATIA
ASIA   Antioch   Iconium
Nicopolis   Lystra
Ephesus
Corinth   Miletus
CRETE

tion so bad it calls for a really strong line. Physical force is never justified, but there are times when forceful words certainly are. The worst heretics were Jewish – but there were others too (10, 14; and see on 1 Timothy 1).

Verse 12: a quotation from the poet Epimenides.

Verse 16: the acid test of faith is how we live. It is not enough simply to call ourselves Christians.

2 – 3:11 Christian conduct

By the way we behave we can discredit, or reinforce, the Christian message. Paul's instructions throw no flattering light on the Cretan temperament. They were a naturally belligerent, argumentative people, uncontrolled, resentful of authority and partial to the bottle! But the Christian life calls for discipline, obedience and respect for others – within the family and household, within the church, and in relation to the authorities. Jesus gave his life to buy us back from our old sinful ways and make us into people whose consuming passion is to do good (2:14). The Christian teacher must use his authority to insist on Christian standards – and he must set a good example. Doing good results *from* (not *in*) salvation (3:3-7).

Washing (3:5): a picture of the cleansing, renewing work of the Holy Spirit which is symbolized in Christian baptism.

Genealogies/lists of ancestors (3:9): see on 1 Timothy 1.

3:12-15 In closing

When his 'relief' arrives, Titus is to join Paul at Nicopolis on the west coast of Greece. Tychicus is another member of Paul's inner circle of partners in the gospel (Ephesians 6:21, etc.). Zenas and Apollos (see Acts 18:24-28) may have been the ones who brought Paul's letter to Titus.

Philemon

This is a private letter from Paul to Philemon, one of his converts and a good friend. Philemon was a man of some standing. A group of local Christians regularly met in his home at Colossae. One of his slaves, Onesimus, had stolen some money (18) and run away to the big city (probably Rome) where he could easily escape detection. There he somehow came into contact with the imprisoned apostle, and through him became a Christian. Paul loved this young man like a son, but he was Philemon's legal property. It was hard for Paul, and hard for Onesimus – who was liable to terrible punishment for what he had done – but he must go back and make amends. Paul could not keep him without Philemon's willing consent. So he wrote this 'covering note' for Onesimus. And Tychicus went with him for company and moral support, taking the latest news and a letter from Paul to the Colossian church (Colossians 4:7-9).

Paul's intention in writing is to ask Philemon to be lenient. A very different Onesimus is returning from the one who ran away. He is not just a slave now, but a brother-Christian. And Paul wants Philemon to welcome him as such. He could have insisted. He had the authority – and Philemon was deeply indebted to him. But instead his letter is loving and tactful, considerate and full of warm praise. He knows this man. He knows his faith and his Christian love. There is no need to make demands. Philemon will do all that he asks – and more.

Apphia (2): probably Philemon's wife. Archippus may be their son.

No use…(11): Paul plays on Onesimus' name, which means 'useful'.

Verses 15-16: it is not clear whether Paul has any thought of Onesimus being set free. But the ideas expressed here are radical enough to have a far-reaching effect. Slavery was such an integral part of the social structure of the day that to preach freedom would have been tantamount to revolution. Paul's brief was not to engage in political campaigning but preach a gospel capable of transforming human life from within.

Verses 18-19: Paul's 'IOU' recalls the Samaritan's good neighbourliness (Luke 10:35).

Epaphras, Mark…(23-24): see on Colossians 4.

Hebrews

Who wrote the letter?

The origin of Hebrews is something of a mystery. The oldest manuscripts are anonymous, and there are none of the conventional greetings with which a 1st-century letter usually began. In fact it is more a treatise than a letter. Even in the first few centuries AD no one knew for certain who the author was, though many people attributed it to Paul. Today this is considered very unlikely. Hebrews reflects neither Paul's style nor his thought. But having said that, we are no nearer to solving the puzzle. From the letter, we know that the author knew Timothy (13:23). He writes extremely polished Greek. And he is plainly an able teacher. He knows the Old Testament inside out. And the version he quotes is the Greek Septuagint – which means he is probably a Greek-speaking (Hellenistic) Jew, writing to fellow Greek-speaking Jews. He is a Christian who has thoroughly thought through the relation of his faith to Judaism.

To whom was it sent?

The title 'To the Hebrews' is very old, but may not be original. It is a fair inference from the letter – with its discussion of priests and sacrifice and its many Old Testament quotations – that it was written to a group of Jewish Christians. They were men of some intellectual ability. The group had been established a good many years (2:3; 13:7), and had a history of persecution. They should have been mature Christians by this time, capable of teaching others (5:11 – 6:2). Instead they are withdrawn and inward-looking. And they seem to have half a mind to turn back to Judaism. They need a forceful reminder that what they possess in Christ is far better.

When was it written?

The most likely date is the late 60s. If Jerusalem and the temple had already fallen to the Romans the author would have been almost bound to mention it when he referred to the priests and sacrifices. So it is fairly certain it was written before AD 70. If the letter was written to Rome (see on 13:24) and alludes to Nero's persecution this places it sometime between AD 64 and AD 70.

What is it about?

Hebrews was written for a group of Christian Jews wavering between Christianity and Judaism. It is in a sense the counterpart to Paul's letter to the Romans, this time directed to a Jewish audience and explaining Christ's relationship to all that had gone before in the religious history of Israel. So the writer compares and contrasts the person and the achievements of Jesus with the Old Testament priesthood and sacrificial system. He is not only incomparably greater and better than these, he is the ultimate realization of all they stand for. He is the perfect priest, offering the perfect sacrifice. He has finally removed the barrier of sin and given men access to God in a way the sacrificial system could never do. That was the copy: he is the original pattern. That was the shadow: he is the reality men have always been searching for. If we turn away from him – back to an inferior substitute, back to a proven failure – we lose everything.

1 Jesus Christ – the Son of God

The letter begins with a tremendous affirmation of the deity of Christ (1-4). Through Jesus, God has made his supreme and final revelation of himself to man. Jesus is the living embodiment of the character and majesty of God. He has dealt with the problem of human sin, once and for all. He is now at God's side, in the position of supreme power.

The angels – whom the Jews came near to worshipping – themselves worship Christ (6). They are spiritual beings, but no more than God's servants (14). The Son is far and away above them – as the scriptures prove.

The writer's use of the Old Testament. The quotations in Hebrews are from the Greek Septuagint version, which differs in some respects from our own Old Testament. And the writer is in any case more taken up with the meaning than with the precise words used. Comment and quotation are often merged, as was then quite customary. And if we look the references up, we find that the writer – like other New Testament writers – exercises a surprising freedom of interpretation. Some verses are filled with meaning far beyond their original context. See 'New Testament Quotations from the Old Testament'.

The quotations in this chapter are from Psalm 2:7; 2 Samuel 7:14; Psalm 97:7 or Deuteronomy 32:43; Psalm 104:4; Psalm 45:6-7; Psalm 102:25-27; Psalm 110:1.

2 Jesus Christ – the Son of man

If the message of the angels – that is the law of Moses, Acts 7:53 – proved true, how much more important is the Son's message of salvation (1-4).

We are not to underestimate Christ because he shared our human nature. God created man for a great destiny (7-8) – a destiny we can now realize, because Christ has suffered and died for all men (9-10). He became man to win forgiveness for us. He became man to help us.

Verses 6-8, 12, 13: the texts quoted are Psalm 8:4-6; Psalm 22:22; Isaiah 8:17-18.
Perfect (10): the idea is not moral improvement, but that through suffering Jesus was perfectly able to do the task God gave him. Only by this means could he make man's salvation possible.

Verse 17: this idea is more fully explained in chapter 5.

3 Jesus Christ – greater than Moses

Moses made Israel into a nation. He led them out of slavery in Egypt and through the desert. He gave them God's law and their forms of worship. No man was more revered by the Jews, and rightly so. But he could never be more than God's faithful servant. Jesus is God's Son (1-6).

The readers are in a very similar position to Israel at the time of the exodus. Both have seen God at work in an amazing way. But despite this the Israelites rebelled against God in the desert – and never entered the promised land (11). What happened to them can happen to us if we now turn our backs on God.

Verse 8: see Exodus 17:1-7; Numbers 20:1-13.

4:1-13 God's rest

The parallel is made more explicit. The 'rest' God spoke of was more than just a stable and secure life in the land he had promised. Through the psalmist (Psalm 95), hundreds of years after Joshua's day, God was still appealing to people to enter his rest. There is a spiritual counterpart to the promised land, and the passport to it is faith. We enter into God's eternal rest, his peace, as we trust him and take him at his word (3). Salvation is his gift, not a reward for our own hard work (10). And we cannot hope to conceal our real attitude from him.

4:14—5:10 Jesus – our great high priest

Aaron (5:4) was the first high priest of Israel appointed by God. He was the intermediary between a holy God and a sinful people, the go-between who represented each to the other. The Jewish religion – the system these Jewish

Christians were tempted to return to – still had its high priest. But in Christ we have a high priest who fulfils all the statutory requirements, and far more, because he has no need to atone for his own sins. He is the perfect high priest appointed by God as mediator for all time.

Melchizedek (5:6, 10): the king/priest of Salem to whom Abraham gave a tenth of his possessions (Genesis 14:18-20). Chapter 7 develops the thought of these verses.

5:8: not learning to obey, but learning the full cost and meaning of obedience through suffering.

5:9: see on 2:10.

Model of the sacrifice in the tabernacle, the sanctuary in the wilderness. See too the picture on page 166.

5:11—6:20 Warning – and encouragement

The writer breaks off to do some plain speaking. His readers have got stuck at the ABC of Christianity (5:11–6:3). Their lack of progress is bad enough in itself. But it is symptomatic of something much more serious. They are in danger of throwing the whole faith overboard. The situation calls for shock tactics. So the writer spells it out. If, despite all their Christian knowledge and experience, they deliberately reject Christ there is no hope for them. It is not that God refuses to forgive, but that they refuse the one available means of forgiveness. And their thinking is leading them in this direction, though they have not yet reached the point of no return.

But he is quick to comfort. He cannot believe they will go so far – or that God will allow it. Faith and perseverance will lead to the realization of all God has promised. The presence of Jesus in heaven guarantees that hope (6:19-20).

6:2: 'baptisms' – not the usual word for Christian baptism. The teaching may be on the difference between Christian baptism and Jewish ritual washings. 'Laying on of hands', at baptism and commissioning for special service, symbolized the empowering of the Holy Spirit.

7 A new high priest

6:20 brings us neatly back to the point made in 5:10 – this chapter carries it forward. Jesus has superseded the Levitical priesthood by becoming high priest for all time. This fact is anticipated in Psalm 110, where the Messiah is described as priest of a different order. The shadowy figure of Melchizedek (Genesis 14:18-20) reflects something of the nature of Christ's priesthood – the dual role of king *and* priest; the timelessness of it; its superiority to the old order. Levi in a sense acknowledged this by paying Melchizedek tithes through his ancestor Abraham! If the priesthood of Aaron and his fellow Levites had been good enough, no change would have been needed. Neither these men nor their work was perfect. Jesus is. They were not able to meet our needs. Jesus can and does.

8 A new covenant

The Old Testament is constantly pointing forward. David anticipated a new priesthood. Jeremiah (31:31-34) spoke of a new covenant – because the old agreement God had made with his people (Exodus 34:10-28; 20) had already broken down. The system of sacrifices instituted by Moses, and the tabernacle he had built, are only copies. In Jesus we have the original – the pattern – the reality. When Jesus offered up himself as the one final sacrifice (7:27) he arranged a new and better covenant between God and men – the one Jeremiah looked forward to. And the new supersedes the old.

9 — 10:18 Shadow and reality; the perfect sacrifice

The writer's thoughts are again back in the time of the exodus, when God made his covenant with Israel through Moses and gave them the pattern on which to construct the tabernacle. (The temple was later modelled on it – but it is not the temple he has in mind here.) Although God had chosen to live with his people, in a tent like their own, they had no right of access to him. The layout of the tabernacle and the whole system of animal sacrifice emphasized God's apartness and the people's sin. Only one man (the high priest) once a year (on the Day of Atonement) was allowed to enter the inner sanctuary (9:7). And the very repetition of the sacrifice made its ineffectiveness all too clear (9:25).

These things are the shadow. They point forward and prepare men for Christ, who is the reality. When Christ came, the whole system was reformed

(9:10). As perfect high priest he offered himself as the perfect sacrifice (9:14) – a single offering for sin, valid for all time. He has dealt with human sin once and for all, removing the stain completely – something the Old Testament animal sacrifices lacked the power to do (10:10-12). And his death brought the terms of his will (the new covenant) into effect (9:16ff.). We are forgiven. We can come to God. No further sacrifice is needed (10:9).

10:19-39 No turning back

The way is open. We can come right into God's presence – if only we will. Christ's death has made it possible (19-22).

If we reject that sacrifice there is no other. We condemn ourselves to God's judgement. He holds us accountable for our actions (26-31).

No one pretends the Christian life is easy (32ff.). It calls for courage and perseverance. But it is infinitely worth while. If we turn back, we are lost – eternally. If we hold on, and keep trusting, God will give us all he has promised.

Through the curtain (20): see Mark 15:38.

11 Faith

The faith under discussion here – following directly on from 10:38-39 – is not man's first unsteady step towards God. It is a life-long attitude of confident reliance on God's word. To have faith is to be certain – not of the here and now, the tangible things – but about things future, the unseen realities (1). The Old Testament abounds in examples of men who possessed a faith like this, and who lived and died accordingly. God has given us their record – he is proud to own them and be known as their God (16). They all looked forward to the time when God would fulfil his promises, but none of them lived to see it (13). Because God planned to include us too – to save and perfect every one of his people through Christ (39-40).

Abel demonstrated his faith – and was killed (Genesis 4). Enoch walked by faith – and lived (Genesis 5:21-24). Noah's faith saved his whole family (Genesis 6 – 8). Abraham's took him away from his settled life at home (Genesis 12:1-7) and made him an alien and refugee. Faith made him willing to offer up his only son, trusting that God would bring him back to life (Genesis 22). Isaac, Jacob and Joseph in turn all demonstrated their belief in God's promise (Genesis 27; 48; 50:24-25). Faith overcomes fear (23). It determined Moses' choice to leave court and throw in his lot with a nation of slaves (Exodus 2; 12; 14). Jericho was taken by faith, not superior force (Joshua 2 and 6). And so on through the Judges – Gideon (Judges 6 – 7); Barak (Judges 4); Samson (Judges 15 – 16); Jephthah (Judges 11 – 12) – through King David and the prophets. Daniel's faith saved him from the lions (33; Daniel 6). Elijah and Elisha brought the dead back to life (35; 1 Kings 17; 2 Kings 4). In answer to faith, God has given men remarkable triumphs and victories. But not always. Faith is demonstrated – equally – through those who have endured imprisonment, torture and death. Jeremiah was beaten and imprisoned (36; Jeremiah 38); Isaiah, it is said, was sawn in half (37); Zechariah was

New Testament Quotations from the Old Testament

RICHARD FRANCE

The sayings of Jesus alone contain over 40 actual quotations from the Old Testament, the letters of Paul nearly 100, and the total for the New Testament as a whole is something like 250. But these verbatim quotations are only the beginning. There are far more allusions which are so clear that no one could reasonably deny that they are intentional (about 70 in the sayings of Jesus, and up to a thousand in the whole New Testament), and these are no less significant than the word-for-word quotations. Beyond that point, scholars differ widely in what they will count as an intentional allusion.

The New Testament writers were so steeped in the Old Testament that its language came naturally to them. For instance, the Beatitudes (Matthew 5:3-10) contain no actual quotation of the Old Testament, but there are two obvious verbal allusions (verses 3-4 allude to Isaiah 61:1-3, and verse 5 to Psalm 37:11), and practically every phrase could be roughly paralleled in the Old Testament. Even more remarkably, the book of Revelation, which contains no formal quotation, is modelled throughout on Old Testament passages, particularly from the books of Daniel, Ezekiel, and Zechariah. Where you draw the line between intentional allusion and an unconscious use of Old Testament phraseology is very much a matter of taste.

Old Testament predictions

The New Testament writers had been brought up from childhood to know and love the Old Testament, then, to model their thoughts and lives on it, and its words would be a part of their normal vocabulary. So not all these quotations and allusions are necessarily the result of a set theological purpose. But in very many cases much more is at stake. The New Testament writers delight to point out how the predictions of the Old Testament prophets have been fulfilled in the life, death and resurrection of Jesus, and continue to be fulfilled in the growth of his church. Matthew includes in his Gospel a series of quotations heralded by such formulae as 'to fulfil what was spoken by the prophets' (Matthew 1:22-23; 2:5-6, 15, 17-18, 23, etc.).

Some passages seem to have been special favourites with the New Testament writers (e.g. Psalm 110:1, 4; Isaiah 53; Daniel 7:13-14). So some scholars have suggested that collections of 'testimonies' (prophetic oracles regarded as referring to Jesus) were circulat-

stoned (37; 2 Chronicles 24). And there were many more.

12 The incentive to go on

We are being watched by these great heroes of faith. They are crowding round the track to see us run. Let us strip off everything that hinders, and run the Christian race with all we have. Christ did not give up when the going got hard; neither must we. When we suffer, it is not because God does not care – but because he cares enough to discipline us for our own good. We must not be discouraged and give up.

We have come to God by a better way than the terrors of Sinai (18-21; Exodus 19) – through Christ himself. But we must not forget who God is. We do well to listen carefully to what he says (25) and take his warnings to heart (15-17), because our life depends on it. One day the world as we know it will cease to exist. We need to be sure we have put first things first.

Esau (16-17): see Genesis 25:29-34; 27:34-40.

13:1-17 Pleasing God

God is concerned with the whole of life – with how we use our homes; how we

---

ing in the early church, or at least that certain passages were generally recognized as fruitful sources for predictions of Jesus and his church, to which appeal could be made in preaching and debate.

Pictures of coming events
But no less common are the allusions to passages which in themselves were not predictive at all, but which the New Testament writers regard as 'fulfilled' in the coming of Christ. Jesus himself made many such allusions (see e.g. Matthew 12:3-6, 40-42; 13:13-14; Mark 7:6-7), but the method is most fully developed in the Letter to the Hebrews, where the whole ritual of the Mosaic Law is regarded as a prefiguring of Christ, the true high priest and the perfect, final sacrifice.

This principle is known as 'typology', by which Old Testament persons, institutions, or events are interpreted as 'types' of the coming decisive work of God in Christ. The aim of typology is to show how Jesus fulfils not only the explicit predictions of the Old Testament, but its whole fabric, to establish his coming as the final, complete embodiment of the pattern of God's saving work through the ages. It is used, particularly, to show that Jesus is himself the true Israel, and his church therefore now the people of God, in whom the hopes and destiny of Israel are coming to fulfilment.

Thus the main purpose of New Testament quotations of the Old Testament is to hammer home the conviction of the early Christians that in the coming of Jesus all is fulfilled; the 'last days' to which the Old

Testament looked forward have come, and God has visited his people.

Accuracy of quotation
A careful comparison of the New Testament quotations with the Old Testament originals will in many cases reveal differences of wording, usually insignificant, but sometimes quite striking. In a few cases the reason may be that the text of the Old Testament which has come down to us is incorrect at that point, and the New Testament preserves the true text. More often, the explanation lies in the different versions of the Old Testament available to the New Testament writers: sometimes they echo the Aramaic Targums, but in most cases they use the Septuagint, the Greek text, which often differs from the Hebrew.

In several cases, however, the explanation is that the New Testament writers were not reluctant to alter the wording themselves, in order to bring out the interpretation and the application of the passage as they saw it. The aim was not to alter the essential meaning, but to bring it out more clearly, if necessary by incorporating the interpretation in the wording of the quotation, just as a modern preacher will often paraphrase a biblical text to 'get the message across' to his hearers, and to show how it applies to their particular circumstances. The reason why they exercised a freedom in quotation from which we might shrink today was that they were convinced that the Old Testament was the word of God, supremely relevant to their situation, and they would spare no pains to bring this home to their readers.

respond to the need of others; with marriage; with our use of money. We grow strong as Christians, not by a code of religious observance, but by obeying God. Those who depend on the Jewish sacrifices cannot benefit from Christ's sacrifice. It is a straight choice – and the principle still holds good. Christ offers salvation to all, but there is an exclusiveness at the heart of Christianity which men have always found hard: one, and only one, sacrifice for sin; one, and only one, way of coming to God. He calls us to identify ourselves unashamedly with him (13).

13:18-25 Personal messages

The writer closes with a deeply moving prayer and blessing (20-21). He has intended his letter to be one of encouragement, not censure. He hopes to see the readers soon.

Verse 24: this may mean the letter was sent *to* Italy; equally it may mean *from* Italy.

A superior Greek pictured on a coin, and a stylish Roman lady. James criticized his readers for snobbery, paying more attention to the rich than the poor.

ames

James is the first of a group of letters addressed to Christians in general (see on 1:1), rather than to a particular church. It is an extremely practical letter about the Christian life. Christian freedom can be a heady thing to people previously bound by a strict legal code of conduct. If salvation is God's free gift, what does it matter how we live? There is no question in James' mind – it matters immensely. In fact we can tell whether someone's faith is real by how they behave. Genuine faith in Christ *always* spills over into the rest of life. It affects our basic attitude to ourselves, to other people, and to life in general. There should be no discrepancy between belief and action. James reminds us of the need for genuinely Christian standards and values in every area of life. It is so easy to let things slip; so easy for the world around to squeeze us into its own mould, to convince us that there are no absolutes, no black and white, only grey. The early Christians needed the letter of James – and so do we.

We know little or nothing of how the letter came to be written, or who it was sent to. We are not even sure who the author was. But the most likely candidate is the James who was Jesus' brother. He became a Christian when he saw the risen Jesus (1 Corinthians 15:7) and went on to become a leader in the church at Jerusalem (Acts 12:17; 15:13ff.; 21:18). The letter was written early, but the exact date is unknown.

1 Deeds not words

This somewhat staccato chapter mentions almost all the topics dealt with more fully later: testing (2, 12-15), endurance (3; 5:7-11), wisdom (5; 3:13-18), prayer (5-8; 4:2-3; 5:13-18), faith (6; 2:14-26), riches (9-11; 2:1-13; 5:1-6), the tongue (19, 26; 3:1-12; 4:11), Christianity in action (22-25; 2:14-26). The crisp, succinct style and some of the themes remind us of Proverbs in the Old Testament and the Sermon on the Mount in the New (Matthew 5–7).

James' comments in this chapter provide us with a fair idea of what a Christian should be like. He has a positive attitude to the difficulties of life, knowing their value. He does not blame God when things go wrong. He knows where to turn for help and guidance. His values are right. He has control of his tongue and his temper. He sets himself to discover God's standards and to live them out. He puts faith into practice – and it shows.

Twelve tribes in the dispersion (1): the Dispersion was a technical term for the Jews scattered abroad. Here the phrase symbolizes all God's people.

Verse 27: real religion shows itself in care for the needy and in an exemplary life. But James is not saying that these things are all God looks for.

2:1-13 Social distinctions

We all have a natural tendency to play up to social superiors and despise those below us on the social scale. But Christians must not make these distinctions. We are to treat everyone with equal respect – regardless of status, intellectual ability, race or colour. When we fail to do so we are breaking one of God's greatest commandments (8; Mark 12:28-31).

Law that gives freedom (12): the law of Christ, under which we are forgiven and set free from sin – something the law of Moses could not do.

2:14-26 Faith and actions

Faith that stops at words is not faith at all. Even the devil believes in God in that way, but it won't save him from God's judgement. Faith is proved – and develops – as we act on it. God accepted Abraham (Genesis 15:1-6; 22) and Rahab (Joshua 2) not because they *said* they believed him, but because they proved it by what they did. It is a good test.

Verse 24: only by taking this right out of context can James be made to contradict Paul (Romans 4). James is discussing the difference between real faith and mere words; he is not saying we can earn salvation.

3:1-12 The ambition to teach – and controlling our tongues

The man who wants to be a teacher in the church must first learn to control his tongue. A wrong word in public can have serious repercussions. James' terrible description is no exaggeration. Words can be so destructive – wrecking character, reputation, relationships, undoing years of good work. By one careless, venomous, inflammatory remark we can unleash forces we are powerless to stop. What is said can never be unsaid. If we can iron out the contradictions here, we have our whole personality under control.

Verse 6: 'it sets the whole course of his life on fire'.

3:13-18 True wisdom

Christian wisdom is a very different thing from being worldly-wise. The worldly-wise are full of selfish ambition, eager to get on, asserting their own rights. God reckons a man wise when he puts selfishness aside and shows disinterested concern for others. This kind of wisdom is seen in a man's personality and behaviour – not in mere intellectual ability.

4 – 5:6 God's way – or the world's?

Christians can sell out to the world – the hostile, unchristian, anti-God world – and not even realize it. It happens every time we let the things we want from life overpower our judgement and Christian principles. This is the stuff wars are made of. It happens when we try to use prayer to further our own ends. It happens when we set ourselves up as judges of other people. It happens when we plan our lives without reference to God. It happens when wealth and pleasure become an end in themselves and justice flies out of the window.

How can we avoid it? By prayer – the right kind of prayer. By continually resisting the things we know are wrong. By seeking God out; by seeing ourselves as we really are and submitting whole-heartedly to him. By realizing we can count on nothing in this life – not even tomorrow – and depending on him. 4:15 expresses our whole attitude to life – not just tacking an automatic 'God willing' on to our own plans.

There is a special danger in affluence (5:1-6; 2:6-7). It cocoons people in false security. They are so well-insulated that they cease to feel for those who are cold and hungry. And values become warped. This life is so pleasant they lose sight of eternity. But God sees it all – and judges. Compare this with Jesus' parable of the rich fool (Luke 12:16-21).

5:7-20 Patience and prayer

Job is our model of patient endurance of suffering, and its reward; Elijah our example of the power of prayer (1 Kings 17:1; 18:1, 4). The Christian life is God-centred. In trouble we pray; in joy we praise. Believing prayer is a force to be reckoned with. God heals the sick and forgives sin in response to it. It is the prayer, not the oil, that is important. And there is nothing more worth while than bringing a man back to Christ, who can cover all his sin. Heaven itself rejoices (Luke 15:7).

1 and 2 Peter

Peter met Jesus first of all through his brother Andrew (John 1:40-42). The two brothers came from the fishing-village of Bethsaida. But they were living at Capernaum, at the northern end of the Lake of Galilee, when Jesus called them to leave their fishing business and become his disciples. Peter quickly became the leader and spokesman of the group of twelve men who were with Jesus right through his ministry. He was one of the inner three who saw some of Jesus' greatest miracles and who were allowed to see him in his true glory (Mark 9; 2 Peter 1:16-18). But when Jesus stood trial, Peter, for all his fine words, denied all knowledge of him – a fact he never forgot. Knowing his remorse,

Jesus appeared to Peter before any of the other apostles after the resurrection. And he became the leader of the new-born church, as Jesus had predicted (Matthew 16:13-20) – the very first to preach the gospel (Acts 2). After a lifetime of preaching and teaching (accompanied in his travels by his wife), tradition has it that Peter was crucified head downwards in Rome during the Emperor Nero's terrible persecution which began in AD 64.

The letters

The first letter was sent to scattered

A wooden writing-tablet from about the time of the New Testament. Originally 6 leaves were hinged on cord. It was found in Egypt.

groups of Christians in the five Roman provinces which covered the greater part of modern Turkey, north of the Taurus mountains. Peter most probably wrote from Rome (see on 5:13), at the outbreak of Nero's persecutions. He had John Mark with him, and Paul's companion Silvanus (Silas) to help him write. Christians in other parts of the Empire would soon be suffering as they were in Rome. Peter's message is one of comfort, hope and encouragement to stand firm.

The second letter mentions neither place of writing nor destination. Scholars have very great doubts whether the letter is really Peter's. It certainly differs in language and subject from 1 Peter – and some scholars point out anachronisms and believe the writer 'borrowed' from Jude. It is possible that a disciple of Peter wrote in his name, incorporating his teaching, but there is no conclusive proof. Long-standing tradition, and the care taken by the early Councils to exclude documents they regarded as forgeries incline us to assume the letter is Peter's. He is facing death as he writes (1:14). The church is beset and confused by false teaching – about Christian behaviour, and about Christ's return. His theme, therefore, is true knowledge.

live as we should, modelling our behaviour on what we know of God's own character?

Dispersion (1:1, some versions): see on James 1:1. *Pontus...*: see map, page 579.
Verses 10ff.: the Old Testament prophets had a message for their own generation – but they also looked to the future, when Christ would come. The author of Hebrews writes in very much the same vein (11:39-40).

2—3 Instructions for living

■ Remember who you are (2:1-10) – God's own people, chosen to make known the wonderful things he has done and still does. We are all being built into the fabric of a living temple which rests on the work of Christ. The world sees God in the lives of his people, individually and collectively.

■ The world at large and the powers that be (2:11-17). The Christian will always be suspect because he is a 'foreigner' in the world – but he must ensure that the accusations are groundless. Civil authorities must be obeyed – even if Nero is emperor! (See also Mark 12:17; Romans 13:1-7.) Christians in Peter's day had to live down unsavoury rumours that they practised incest, held sexual orgies and even indulged in cannibalism.

■ Slaves (2:18-25). The emphasis all through this section is on accepting authority and giving respect and loyal service where it is due, no matter what the other person is like. If we suffer unjustly, we have Christ's example before us.

■ Wives and husbands (3:1-7). In every case Christians are to do what is right, not insist on their own rights. Love and respect – sheer quality of life – is the surest way to win over a non-Christian partner. Christian character is more important in a woman than the latest fashion. The Christian husband, for his part, will be considerate. Prayer withers in an atmosphere of friction.

1 Peter

1 Faith and hope

Christians can be glad, even in times of suffering. This is the way faith is tested and proved genuine. The dark days are short in comparison with the joy that lies ahead, when hope will be realized and we shall come into our promised inheritance. These are the realities nothing can change. One day soon we shall see the Lord we love and trust – and then what inexpressible joy and blessing. What greater impetus could there be to

■ In summary (3:8-22). Be at one. Be loving. Be humble. If suffering comes, let it be undeserved, let it be for doing good.

Living stone (2:4): a favourite New Testament metaphor for Christ (see Mark 12). The quotations are from Isaiah 28:16; Psalm 118:22; Isaiah 8:14-15.

Spiritual sacrifices (2:5): see, e.g., Romans 12:1; Hebrews 13:15-16.

Spirits in prison...(3:19-22): Peter seems to say that between his death and resurrection Jesus preached (or proclaimed his triumph) to the spirits of the disobedient men (or fallen angels – see 2 Peter 2:4-5; Genesis 6:1-8) of Noah's day. The flood-water which destroyed the world saved Noah and his family by floating the ark. Similarly, Peter sees the water of baptism as a symbol of rescue from death. Of course it was the ark, not the water, which really saved Noah. So it is the risen Christ, not baptism in itself, who saves those who trust him and are cleansed from sin.

4—5 When suffering comes

Peter anticipates a time of suffering and persecution for his readers. When it comes, they must be ready – level-headed, alert, prayerful and unfailingly loving to others. It should come as no surprise to Christians to suffer for Christ's sake. It is a cause for joy, not discouragement! Christ's suffering was the prelude to glory. So it is for the Christian. God always keeps his promises.

As a leader himself – and a witness of the crucifixion – Peter appeals for a real 'shepherd spirit' in all church leaders (5:1-4; and see John 10 and 21:15ff.). And the younger people must respect their authority. Every Christian needs to acquire a genuinely humble spirit, like Christ's. He also needs a stout heart to face formidable and unrelenting opposition (8-9). But God cares for us. He perfects our Christian character through the things we suffer. He is in control!

4:1-2: the reference may be to the Christian's identification with Christ in his

1st-century ornament from a necklace; Peter had to exhort his readers to avoid ostentatious dress.

Head of Nero, the Roman emperor behind the persecution which was the subject of Peter's letter.

death, and the freedom from sin – the new life – that follows.

To the dead…(4:6): i.e. Christians who are now dead. They suffered the judgement of death, like other men, but they will live.

Love covers…(4:8): a proverb also quoted in James 5:20.

Judgement (4:17): the thought may link with 4:6, see above.

5:5ff.: these verses echo the thought in James 4:6ff. The 'roar' is intended to frighten, but Satan no longer has the power to destroy the Christian.

Silvanus (12): Silas, companion to Paul on his second missionary journey (Acts 15:22, 32ff.), and his associate in writing to the Thessalonians.

Babylon (13): probably a code-name for Rome (see on Revelation 17).

Mark (13): see introduction to Mark's Gospel.

Peter wrote to Christians in what is now Turkey. He used vivid pictures of seedtime and harvest, flocks and shepherds, 'waterless springs and mists driven by a storm'.

2 Peter

1 Knowing God and his message

The purpose of our salvation is that we should become like Christ (4). And Christian growth depends on knowledge (2-3) – the kind of knowledge which gets translated into action (8). Peter shares Paul's determination to know Christ, and to put every effort into growing like him (see Philippians 3:10-16). Like James, he stresses the fact that real faith shows itself in the quality of life, in love and goodness (5:11; see James 1:26-27; 2:14-17).

The Christian message does not rest on myth and legend, but on the evidence of eye-witnesses (16). Peter actually saw Jesus in all his glory – transformed (see Mark 9:2-8). We have in addition the written testimony of the prophets – not simply human opinion, but a word from God himself.

Verse 14: Peter, facing death, recalls the Lord's words: John 21:18-19.

Verse 19: the scriptures light our path through life until the dawning day of Christ's return. Psalm 119:105; Revelation 22:16.

Verse 20: this may mean either 'it is not the interpretation that authenticates the prophet's message', or 'the true interpretation, like the message itself, is God-given'.

2 False teachers

The argument of this chapter is closely paralleled in Jude 4-16. To be forewarned is to be forearmed – so Peter warns his readers against the false teachers who have already disrupted other Christian groups. They are anti-authority. They respect no one. They teach self-gratification, and their dissolute lives deny the Lord and shame his church. They are out to exploit others for profit. And they are merchants of false hope, like a dried-up spring in the desert, or clouds that promise rain but blow over (17). Their punishment is certain. The Old Testament affords plenty of examples of God's punishment of wicked men, and his ability to rescue those who are his: the flood, and the saving of Noah (Genesis 6–8); the destruction of Sodom and Gomorrah, and the rescue of Lot (Genesis 19).

Angels (4, 10-11): see on Jude.

Balaam (15): it seems this true prophet turned traitor when the price was high enough (Numbers 31:16).

Verses 19-22: for all they had learned of Christ, their conduct makes it clear that their basic nature remained unchanged.

3 The certainty of Christ's return

There will always be men who scoff at the idea of Christ's return – the more so as time passes. But Peter and Paul are unanimous on the subject (15-16; see e.g. 1 Thessalonians 4:13–5:11; 2 Thessalonians 2). We have God's word that it *will* happen; a word of such power that it brought our whole world into being (5; Genesis 1:3). If God 'delays' it is out of mercy, not weakness. The certainty that Jesus will come, and that it could happen any day, is our strongest incentive to Christian living. We want to be ready. We want him to be pleased with what he finds – and we may have only today.

Second letter (1): the first may be 1 Peter, or some other letter now lost.

The fathers (4): either the Old Testament fathers, or the first Christians. *Fell asleep:* this is the way Jesus talked of death.

Verse 16: it is a comfort to know that Peter sometimes found Paul hard to understand! But he had a high regard for Paul's writings – placing them alongside the other scriptures. Romans 3 shows how people twisted Paul's words – they took his teaching on freedom, for example, as carte-blanche for licence.

1, 2 and 3 John

1 John

John's Gospel was written to bring men to faith. This letter, clearly by the same person, is intended to reassure Christians about their faith – to renew confidence shaken by false teaching. Both Gospel and letter belong to the close of the 1st century. The Christian faith was 50 or 60 years old by this time and had spread throughout the Roman Empire. John, living out his last years at Ephesus in modern Turkey – a strategic centre of the Christian church – was probably the only apostle still alive. There was pressure on many Christian groups to incorporate ideas from other philosophies as part of the faith.

John's letter was written to counter some early form of 'Gnosticism' being propounded by men who were once church members but had now withdrawn from the group. They liked to think of themselves as intellectuals – possessing a superior knowledge of God. They made a complete distinction between the spiritual (which was pure) and the material (which was evil). In practice this often led to immorality – because nothing the body did could tarnish the purity of the spirit. It also led to a denial of Christ's human nature – which was either 'make-believe' or only temporary. The Christ – being spirit – could not have died.

In this strong but tender appeal to his 'little children' in the faith, John makes it plain that these ideas cut the heart out of Christianity. If Christ did not become man and die for human sin there is no Christian faith. If any man sins deliberately and habitually he is not a Christian. God is light, and he calls men to walk in the light of his commands. He is love, and he requires his people to love one another.

1 God is light

John writes as one who knew Jesus, the life-giving Word of God (see John 1:1-5), personally. He knew that Jesus was both Son of God and real man: no apparition but a person you could see and touch.

Jesus, the 'light of the world' (John 8:12), shows us that God is light. By 'light', John means not just the blinding radiance of his presence, but truth, purity, moral perfection. No one who has access to him can live in 'the dark' – dealing in sin and evil and lies, qualities opposed to his very nature. This is not to say that Christians are perfect. The searchlight of God's presence shows us up. Friendship with him involves seeing ourselves as we really are, and constantly asking his forgiveness.

2 To know God is to obey him

We are not perfect, but that is our constant aim: to become, to behave just like Christ (6). And when we fail, he has provided the remedy (1-2). Being a Christian means obeying God; doing what is right; loving, not hating, our fellow men. This is the real test of any man's claim to know God. To know is to obey.

The early Christians were taught that an arch-enemy of Christ – the embodiment of evil – would come on the scene when the Lord's return was imminent (18; the actual word 'antichrist' occurs only in John's letters, but 2 Thessalonians 2 makes the same point). John sees the 'explosion' of false teachers – who deny that the man Jesus was the Messiah and Son of God – as a sign that the time is near.

Remaining in him (6, 28): see on John 15.
Children ... fathers ... young men

(12-14): the threefold address is probably used for emphasis. Forgiveness, knowledge of God and victory over evil are things all Christians possess.

The world (15): mankind organized for some end of their own without thought of God, or in open hostility to him. God, of course, loves the world of mankind (see John 3:16), despite its rebellion.

Anointing/pouring (27): John refers to the discernment the Holy Spirit gives to Christians. See also 4:4-6. He is talking about false teachers, not saying that Christians have no need of teaching.

3 Right living; true love

For the Christian – the child of God – sin is no longer inevitable. On the contrary, it is a denial of his new nature. Christ has really given us the freedom not to sin, and we are to live in the light of that fact. It is not possible for anyone born into God's family to go on breaking his law deliberately and habitually (the Greek John uses conveys the sense more clearly than some English translations: verses 6 and 9, in the light of 1:8–2:2). A man who behaves like this cannot be a Christian, no matter what he may say.

The Christian life-style can be summed up in the one word 'love'. The command to love one another rolls up into one all God's instructions about human relationships. But Christian love – Christ's love – is more than just words or feelings. It will inevitably touch our pockets and possessions – it may cost us life itself. We can measure the reality of our love for God by our determination to do as he says and love our fellow men. If our conscience is clear on this score, we can be confident that God will answer our prayers.

4 Distinguishing false from true; God is love

There is one basic test by which to judge any teacher – his recognition of Jesus Christ as man (emphasized here because this was the particular heresy of the day) and God. No one who denies this can possibly come with a message from God. The Holy Spirit enables Christians to recognize truth when they hear it.

God is love. In the death of Christ for human sin he has shown us what love is (10). And if we really share his life – his nature – that love must flow through us to all around. Genuine love for God is bound to show itself in action towards others. This is John's favourite theme. But love is not trite or sentimental, nor inconsistent with plain speaking (of which verse 20 is a sample!). Love and obedience are bound up together (21). If we love and obey God we need not dread the day of judgement (17-18).

Roman head, found at Antioch, 2nd century AD.

5 We can be sure

To know God is to love God. To love God is to obey God. To be his child is to love his children. Eternal life (the life of God), and the ability to defeat the anti-God forces of the world we live in, are ours as we believe in Jesus Christ as God's Messiah. God himself stands witness that Jesus is his Son. 'To believe is life, to disbelieve is death' (12). We can be sure of these things. We know he hears all we ask. We know he always answers.

The false teachers loved to talk about 'knowledge'. John makes his own list of things Christians know for a certainty. We know the gravity of sin. We know it is no longer the norm for Christians. We know we are absolutely secure in Christ. We know we belong to God in an alien world. We know that through the Son of God we know God himself, and real life.

Verses 6-8: the King James/Authorized Version incorporates words that do not form part of the original letter, but are a late addition. These are omitted in all modern versions.

Three witnesses (8): the Holy Spirit, the baptism of Christ and the death of Christ – of which Christian baptism and the Lord's Supper stand as permanent reminders.

Verse 16: John does not say what this deadly sin is. The New Testament knows only one 'unforgivable' sin – that which attributes the Holy Spirit's work to the devil, and persistently rejects the One who makes forgiveness possible (see Matthew 12:31-32; Hebrews 6:4-6; 10:26).

A clay statuette from Salamis, Cyprus, of a woman writing with a stylus on a folding tablet. It may go back to the 4th century BC.

2 John

There is little doubt that all three letters are the work of one author – traditionally the apostle John, since we know of no other apostle still alive at this time. As an apostle and senior elder of the church at Ephesus John's choice of the term 'Elder' is appropriate enough. The 'lady' is most probably a local church, rather than an individual. The 'children' would then be church members (as in 1 John); the lady's 'sister', John's own church.

Here again we have John's favourite theme: Jesus' command that those who follow him should love one another (5; John 15:12-17). To love others as Jesus loves us means keeping all God's commands. 'Love' which breaks any of the basic rules God has set to govern human relationships is not love at all. The love of Jesus is self-giving, not self-seeking.

For the Christian, love and truth go hand in hand. But he should content himself with what Christ taught. Only the false teachers are compelled to eliminate or elaborate (9-10). John is combatting the same sort of trouble here (7) as in his first letter (see page 640). There had been travelling evangelists and teachers from the very start of the Christian mission, usually responsible to one of the apostles. The time had come to tighten up and refuse hospitality to anyone whose teaching contradicted the fundamental truth about Jesus Christ. It was essential for survival.

3 John

See on 2 John above. This is a personal letter to an individual. **Gaius** was a common name, and it is not likely that this Gaius is the same as any of the others mentioned in the New Testament. If tradition is anything to go by, he may have been a leader of the church at Pergamum. What matters more, Gaius was a man who 'lived in (and therefore lived out) the truth'. His words, his deeds, his character were all of a piece. His life and conduct are in striking contrast to that of another local leader, **Diotrephes.** Gaius, a man of integrity, is doing all in his power to help his fellow Christians, especially the travelling evangelists and teachers who depended on Christian hospitality and support. Diotrephes is damaging John's own character, suppressing his letter, spreading lies, hugging his own position as leader and hindering missionary outreach. It seems the church has always had its petty dictators, men like Diotrephes who consider themselves indispensable. The third character in the letter, **Demetrius,** may have been John's messenger (there was no postal service!). This man's life speaks for itself. He richly deserves the high regard in which John holds him.

Jude

The author is Jude, the younger brother of Jesus and James, now an old man (the date is uncertain, but may be around AD 80). He was already thinking of writing, when alarming news of false teaching (see below) made him pen this short, vigorous letter with all speed. The letter is obviously Jewish – full of Old Testament references and allusions, and drawing its illustrations from at least two Jewish apocryphal writings (see below). Jude is dealing with a situation very like that dealt with in 2 Peter. And in fact the bulk of Jude's letter is paralleled in 2 Peter 2. The two are so similar that either one made use of the other, or both drew on an existing tract which countered false teaching.

Jude writes to a group of Christians threatened from within by men who have 'slipped in' and are now creating division by their false teaching. These men are characterized by arrogance and immorality, and their claim to superior knowledge. They are anti-authority. They are out for what they can get. And they are self-indulgent to a degree. They will argue black is white if it suits them.

But they are marked out for destruction – as Sodom and Gomorrah were for their sexual immorality and perversion (Genesis 19); as Cain was for murdering the brother whose life showed up his own (Genesis 4); as Balaam was for betraying his position as a prophet (Numbers 31:8, 16 – see on 2 Peter 2:15); and as Korah was for his rebellion against God-given authority (Numbers 16). The examples are carefully chosen. These are the very things of which these teachers are guilty.

Jude's intention is to stiffen the resistance to such teachers. The Christians are not defenceless, but they must make full use of their defences. They must build on 'the faith' – that definite body of truth they have been given. They must pray and use the power of the Holy Spirit. They must live in the light of Christ's coming again. There is no need to be afraid or despair, for God is indeed able to keep them from falling.

The angels (6): the statement about the 'sons of God' in Genesis 6:1-2 led to a belief in an earlier war in heaven between good and evil angels whose pride and ambition led to their downfall. It was an apt illustration for Jude's argument.

Verse 9: the story comes from the apocryphal *Assumption of Moses*. Michael was sent to bury Moses, but the devil challenged his right to the body, on the ground that Moses had murdered an Egyptian. Jude uses Michael's circumspect reply as a lesson to men to watch their words, and not to treat the devil lightly.

Verses 14-15: a quotation from the apocryphal *Book of Enoch*. Jude takes his illustrations from books he and his readers know and respect, as well as from the scriptures themselves.

Revelation

Revelation was written about AD 90-95, though some say earlier. The author is named as John. The style and language of Revelation is so different from John's Gospel that many have concluded this writer must be a different John. But we do not know of anyone apart from the apostle so well known that he could simply describe himself as 'John'. And tradition says that the apostle left Israel to make his home in Ephesus – capital city of the Roman province of Asia, in which the seven churches of Revelation 2–3 are located, and itself the recipient of one of the letters.

The book was written during a time of persecution. John's own exile on Patmos (1:9) probably entailed hard labour in the island's quarries. Some Christians had been killed (2:13) and others imprisoned for their faith. And there was worse to come (2:10), as worship of the Roman emperor became obligatory. The early Christians lived in eager expectation of Christ's return. But 60 years after his death this hope was still unrealized. It was only human for some to waver. So the letters to the churches, and the book as a whole, were needed to encourage them to stand firm. God is in control, no matter how things may look. Christ, not the emperor, is Lord of history. He has the key of destiny itself. And he *is* coming again to execute justice. There is a glorious, wonderful future for every faithful believer – and especially those who lay down their lives for Christ. This world and all that happens in it is in God's hands. His love and care for his people is unfailing.

John's message was conveyed in a form designed to inspire as well as instruct. The vivid symbols, only too clear to those who first heard his circular letter to the churches, would have meant little to the authorities (who were always ready to pounce with a charge of sedition). More important, they would be equally vivid to Christians of every age. Christians are still enduring the pressures of totalitarian regimes. The victory of Christ and his people is vitally relevant today, when the machine, or the state, so often takes the place of God.

In our own materialistic age it has been only too easy to miss the spirit of the book. On the one hand, instead of seeing it as something to catch the imagination, we reduce it to a timetable of events. On the other, reacting against the rational, we reduce it to fantasy and mysticism. But to understand Revelation we must see it both as a book of vision and imagination *and* as a book firmly rooted in history, proclaiming Christ as Lord of history. Today – perhaps more than ever – we need its eternal, timeless realities. And we need its perspective.

A few basic pointers to the interpretation of the book may help those coming fresh to it:

■ The first thing to establish about any Bible passage is what it meant to the original readers; to see it in the light of contemporary history.

■ Revelation belongs to a particular type of literature – apocalyptic (see note, page 651). It is poetic and visionary, expressing its meaning through symbols and imagery. To take this picture-language literally, or treat the book as a logical treatise or timetable, is to go against the whole spirit of it.

■ Revelation is rooted in the Old Testament. This is where we find the clues to the meaning of the various symbols – comparing scripture with scripture.

■ Obscure passages must always be understood in the light of passages that are clear – never the other way round.

■ This is a book of visions. The fact that John is not over-concerned about harmonizing details makes it clear that it is the main thrust of each picture which is important. We should treat visions as we do parables, looking first at the whole picture and trying to discover the main idea.

■ We are not necessarily meant to take John's visions as a sequence of events which follow on one after the other. The eastern mind is not so preoccupied with chronology as those in the west tend to be.

1
INTRODUCTION: JOHN'S VISION OF CHRIST

In more than one sense this book is 'the revelation of Jesus Christ' (1). He is John's source *and* his subject. Jesus draws back the veil on future events for John to make them known. There is nothing speculative about it. These are certainties, things that will take place 'soon'. The vision of Christ is at one and the same time for John's immediate audience – the seven churches in the Roman province of Asia (western Turkey; see map below) – and for Christians down the ages. No true Christian group is ever alone and abandoned. Jesus stands among his people (12-13,

The Seven Churches of Revelation

A messenger from John in exile in Patmos would have crossed to Ephesus and then taken a circular route. The seven churches are listed in the order he would have visited them.

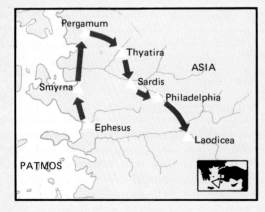

Ephesus
The leading city of the Roman province of Asia. Paul stayed there teaching for 2 years on his third missionary journey. His letter to the 'Ephesians' is addressed primarily to the church there. By tradition John spent his last days there. Extensive ruins have been excavated (see also pages 565, 573, 605, 607).

20): the living Christ in all his power and glory; the Master of life and death and human destiny.

Soon (1): we do not know God's timescale, and the prophets tend to foreshorten the future. The word serves to remind us to be ready.

Reads (aloud) (3): this was how the scriptures were made known in John's day.

Seven churches (4, 11): John makes great use of the number seven (seven seals, seven trumpets, seven bowls, etc.), which usually in this book stands for complete-ness, perfection. Here the number is also literal. Of the seven churches only Ephesus is well known (Acts 19). Acts 16:14 mentions Thyatira as Lydia's home town. The church at Laodicea is mentioned in Colossians 4:15-16. The rest

occur nowhere else in the New Testament.

Alpha and Omega (8): the first and last letters of the Greek alphabet.

Patmos (9): a small Greek island off the west coast of Turkey (see also introduction).

Lord's day (10): usually taken to mean Sunday.

Sword (16): see Hebrews 4:12. Jesus' words are double-edged. They can cut a man free, or administer judgement.

Hades (18): the place where the dead await resurrection and judgement.

Angels (20): some see this as a reference to pastors, some to guardian angels, some to the essential spirit of each church. Elsewhere in Revelation angels are always heavenly beings.

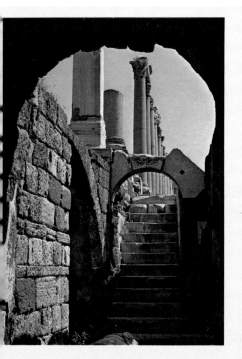

Smyrna
Modern Izmir, main city and port on the west coast of Turkey. The most important remains of Roman times is the Forum, pictured here. It was at Smyrna in about AD 155 that the aged bishop Polycarp refused to renounce Christ and was martyred.

Pergamum
The ruins of the ancient town lie on the acro-polis high above the modern town of Bergama. 'Satan's seat' may refer to the great Altar of Zeus which overlooked the town. Pergamum was also the base for the official cult of emperor-worship, and a centre of healing associated with the Temple of Asclepius. **»**

2—3
SPECIAL MESSAGES TO THE SEVEN CHURCHES

The letters are addressed to particular churches, but the message is for the whole church. It is worth noting that – with the exception of Smyrna and Philadelphia – the danger from within each church is more destructive than the danger from without. Jesus knows the strength and weakness of each one. The opening description reminds each church of some specially relevant aspect of his person and work.

2:1-7 Ephesus

See on Acts 19. The church at Ephesus was firmly established and possessed spiritual discrimination. There was sound teaching but an absence of the love – for Christ and one another – which had been their hallmark to begin with.

Nicolaitans (6): unknown outside this book. Their abhorrent behaviour sprang from false teaching (15), which had infiltrated the church at Pergamum.

Tree of life (7): the ban of Genesis 3: 22-24 is lifted for all who are faithful to Christ. Eternal life is his to give.

2:8-11 Smyrna

The little church at Smyrna was poverty-stricken – but rich in all that mattered. Jesus' word to them is all encouragement. He has set a definite limit to their suffer-

Thyatira
A commercial centre on the road east, now the small town Akhisar. Nothing remains of the city from ancient times. Reference to earthenware might reflect one of the town's industries. Another was purple dye. Lydia, who traded in these dyed stuffs and whom Paul met at Philippi (Acts 16:14), was from Thyatira, and may have returned home to help form the church here. Another woman was instrumental in leading church members away from their faith and into immorality; her evil influence earns her the code-name Jezebel in the letter, after her Old Testament counterpart.

Sardis
Formerly the capital of the ancient kingdom of Lydia. The king of Sardis, Croesus, had legendary wealth ('as rich as Croesus'). The Greeks then colonized the area. Pillars still remain of the great Greek temple there. The gymnasium has also been reconstructed; and the archaeologists were surprised to discover this early Jewish synagogue.

ing – and he holds out to them the gift of life beyond the grave.

Synagogue of Satan (9): those Jews who harass the church are not God's people. See John 8:39-44.

Second death (11): explained in 20:14-15.

2:12-17 Pergamum

At Pergamum the church had made a brave stand despite external pressure, but some members had become addicted to false teaching. As a result, old pagan practices were creeping in.

Satan's throne (13): Pergamum was the principal centre of emperor-worship in the region. An immense altar to Zeus dominated the town from its acropolis.

And people flocked to be healed at the Temple of Asclepius. One or all of these may be referred to.

Balaam, Balak (14): see Numbers 31: 16; 25.

Food offered to idols (14): see on 1 Corinthians 8.

Verse 17: *manna* (Exodus 16) – i.e. food which God supplies. The meaning of the *white stone* is unknown. The *name* stands for the whole character. In the ancient world, to know a man's name was to possess power over him.

2:18-29 Thyatira

This was another very mixed church. In many ways it was healthy. But within the

Philadelphia

A small town in the edge of a broad valley which made fertile farming country. Today the town of Alasehir derives its prosperity from the same source. 'A pillar in the temple of my God' may be a reference to the temple on the hill up behind the town.

Laodicea

A prosperous city near Hierapolis and Colossae in the Lycus Valley. The letter refers to several factors in the town's prosperity: fine wool and eye-salve were two of the city's products, and it was also a banking centre; see too page 650 for a picture explaining the reference to lukewarm water.

fellowship there was an influential woman advocating easy compromise with the immoral, idolatrous pagan world. And many fell in with her way of thinking. There were 'Christians' who plunged deep into evil – perhaps to demonstrate their moral superiority; perhaps because they drew a false (Greek) distinction between soul and body. Those who remain faithful are promised Christ's power and his presence (the morning star – see 22:16).

Jezebel (20): King Ahab's evil wife; see 1 Kings 21:25-26.

3:1-6 Sardis

For all its reputation, the church at Sardis was dying on its feet. It was not opposition this church had to overcome but apathy, indifference and self-satisfaction.

Verse 2: it is by his life that a man demonstrates the reality of his faith. A formula of words will not save him – see Matthew 7:21.

3:7-13 Philadelphia

This letter, like the letter to Smyrna, contains no word of blame. To judge by these letters, it is not the biggest, most impres-sive-looking churches, or those with most prestige, which are necessarily in best spiritual shape. Christ opens the door for effective work (8 and 1 Corinthians 16:9), not to those who are strong, but to those who are faithful.

Verse 9: see on 2:9.

3:14-22 Laodicea

The worst case of all seven is a church so self-satisfied as to be totally blind to its true condition. It is so far from what it should be that Jesus stands *outside,* knocking for admittance to the lives of individuals who call themselves Christians (20). This letter is full of local colour. Banking and the manufacture of black woollen clothing made Laodicea affluent (17-18). The town was proud of its medical school, and renowned for a special ointment for sore eyes (18). Laodicea's water-supply was channelled from hot springs some distance away, reaching the town tepid (16). The church was like its water – lukewarm. There was nothing to commend it.

Beginning (14): 'the origin' (Good News Bible) or 'prime source' (New English Bible).

4
JOHN'S VISION OF HEAVEN

The scene shifts, characteristically, from what is happening on earth to what is happening in heaven. John is constantly getting this life into perspective by turning to the eternal realities. So the picture of the struggling churches fades before this sublime vision of the throne: God in control of all that goes on. Everything speaks of his power and glory, his utter faithfulness (3, and see Genesis 9:12-17), and purity (the white garments, the shining, transparent 'sea').

The waters from the hot springs at Hierapolis flow over the cliffs, leaving mineral deposits which have built up into terraces and lime 'waterfalls'. Nearby, Laodicea had water channelled from other hot springs – which arrived 'lukewarm'.

The 'elders', who represent all his faithful people, join with the 'living creatures', who represent the whole creation, to honour him.

Seven spirits (5): the Holy Spirit. See on 1:4 for the meaning of seven.

Four living creatures (6): similar, but not identical, to Ezekiel's 'cherubim' (Ezekiel 1 and 10).

5—8:1
THE SEVEN SEALS

5 The sealed scroll

At this point John begins to see the things which must take place (4:1). The scroll contains the world's destiny, revealed to John in a series of pictures (6:1–8:1). Only Christ has the right to set these things in motion – not by virtue of his power (the Lion) but through his sacrificial death (the slain Lamb). Chapter 4 pictured God the Creator. This chapter pictures God the Redeemer. The response to both is universal praise and worship (4:8-11; 5:8-14, and see Philippians 2:8-11).

Seven horns, seven eyes (6): i.e. all-powerful, all-seeing.

6 The breaking of the seals

The breaking of the seals sets in train a series of disasters. On the heels of conquest (2) come slaughter, famine and disease (4-8) – the classic judgements of God so often predicted by the prophets (see on Jeremiah 14:12; Ezekiel 14:21; the riders come from Zechariah 1:8). But no matter what the disaster, God is in control. His love and care for his people never fails (9-11). Verses 12-17 picture the cataclysmic events which usher in God's great day of reckoning. In apocalyptic language John depicts the disintegration of the fixed and stable world we know. See also Matthew 24:29; Joel 2; Zephaniah 1.

Verse 2: not the same figure as in 19:11.

Verse 6: the price of basic essentials is so inflated that ordinary people must give their whole day's wage for bread.

7—8:1 The people of God; the seventh seal

The four winds may be the same as the four horsemen of chapter 6 (see Zechariah 6:5). If so, John sees the forces of destruction held back while God sets his mark of ownership on everyone who

Apocalyptic Literature

The period from 200 BC to AD 100 was one of the hardest in all Jewish history. The voice of the prophets had long since fallen silent. And instead of the golden age they foretold, the Jews had suffered defeat, occupation and violent religious persecution. It is not surprising that a number of writings emerged from this period of tension with common characteristics and the same preoccupation – a distinctive body of literature known as 'apocalyptic'.

The writers harked back to the vision and inspiration of the prophets. Their concern was the messianic kingdom – God's age, in contrast to the present evil age – and its cataclysmic coming. To authenticate their message, they wrote under the pseudonym of some great Old Testament figure. By taking the standpoint of someone in the dis-

tant past they were also able to 'predict' events up to their own time. Their theme was expressed in visions and revelations in the style of Daniel, making great use of symbolism and (often bizarre) imagery.

In form and style John's Revelation is clearly similar to this type of literature. His concern, too, was with eternal realities, the end of the world, new heavens and a new earth. Like the apocalyptists, John is steeped in the Old Testament and draws on the rich evocative imagery of the prophets. But there are vital differences. John did not survey the past. He had no need of pseudonym or pseudo-prediction to authenticate his message. He knew – as certainly as Isaiah, Jeremiah, Ezekiel and Daniel knew – that what he wrote was directly God-given, stamped with his authority (1:1-3; 22:6, 18-20).

belongs to him. The Christian is not promised a trouble-free life on earth. But he will come through it to the permanently trouble-free life of heaven (14-17). Solemn silence follows the breaking of the last seal. We are brought to the time of the end.

After this (1,9): indicates a new vision not time in relation to the events of chapter 6.

144,000 (4): this number has been much debated, but it seems best to take it symbolically, as the complete total of all God's people (12 x 12 x 1000), identical with the 'great multitude' (9). We take Israel to mean, not the nation, but God's people – Old Testament believers and New Testament Christians alike.

8:2 — 11:19
THE SEVEN TRUMPETS

8:2-13 The first four trumpets are blown

The trumpets follow the pattern of the seven seals, but the judgements are intensified. The prayers of God's people play a significant part in all this (5:8; 8:3-4). The trumpets sound a note of warning. The judgements, though severe, are not total. They are intended to bring men to their senses (9:20-21). In symbolic picture-language John describes four calamities affecting the natural world – earth, sea, water and the heavens. The 'woes' of the lone eagle imply that there is worse to come. The remaining judgements directly affect mankind.

9 The fifth and sixth trumpets

Demonic forces (monstrous locusts-cum-scorpions), servants of 'the Destroyer' (Apollyon/Abaddon, 11), are next unleashed. But God sets them a time-limit (five months is the approximate life-span of the real locust). Though human beings are their target they have no power to touch those who belong to God (4).

The 'locusts' torture; the angel army has power to kill – within limits. Yet even in the face of the most fearsome warnings people stubbornly refuse to change their ways (20-21). This is the world we live in: a world that resists God to the bitter end; a world that prefers to make its own 'gods', to choose its own standards of behaviour.

200 million (16): there were so many, John had to be told the number. He could not count them. God always has colossal powers at his disposal.

10 — 11:13 Interlude; the little scroll and the two witnesses

There is a break between the sixth and seventh trumpets, as there was between sixth and seventh seals. God delays his final judgement, but not for ever (6-7). The glorious angel brings John a message for the world – a message which is 'sweet' to him as a Christian (9; and see Jeremiah 15:16; Ezekiel 3:1-3). But he derives no joy from the bitter message he must make known to those who refuse God.

Chapter 11 is difficult. John draws his symbols from Ezekiel 40-41 (the measuring of the temple) and Zechariah 4 (the olive-trees). The measuring indicates God's protection and care for his people. The two olives represent the church, faithful to the death. (The Old Testament law required that evidence must be attested by at least two witnesses – Deuteronomy 19:15.) Warring against them are the anti-God forces of the Satanic 'beast', with power to kill and dishonour, but not destroy or prevent their triumph.

10:4: John is under orders about what he writes. Not all he sees is for public knowledge.

Forty-two months (11:2): equal to 1,260 days (3), and 'a time (1 year), times (2 years) and half a time (6 months)' (12:14). This may be derived from the length of Antiochus Epiphanes' tyranny in Jerusalem, or from Israel's 42 encampments in the desert. But the precise length of the trial is less important than the fact

that God has set a definite limit to it.
Sodom and Egypt (11:8): bywords for evil
and oppression. The final phrase suggests
Jerusalem, but it is more likely that the
'great city', here as later in the book,
stands for the city of rebel mankind.

11:14-19 The seventh trumpet

The seventh trumpet announces the
end. Jesus reigns: the world is his
kingdom. Praise God! The ark, once
hidden away in the most sacred and
inaccessible part of the temple, is now
visible to all (19). The way into God's
presence is wide open.

12 — 14
VISIONS CONNECTED WITH THE TROUBLES OF THE CHURCH

12 The woman and the dragon

John was writing for a persecuted
church, and these chapters are full of
encouragement to take heart. The
woman (1, and contrast 17:3ff.) stands for
God's chosen people, from whom first
the Messiah (5), and through him the
church (17), was born. The dragon bent
on destruction is Satan himself (9).
Verses 7-12 are a reminder that the
struggle Christians are caught up in is
part of a much greater conflict (Ephesians
6:11-12).

The main message is clear. Although
Satan is strong and powerful – his attack
fierce – his time is short. He has been
overpowered by Christ: he can be
overcome by Christians. He is destined
for destruction, the church for triumph.
God's people are at all times and
everywhere under his sovereign
protection.

13 The two beasts

The beast from the sea (an evil place in
Jewish thinking) is a composite creature
drawn from the four beasts which represent successive world empires in Daniel 7.
With its crowns and horns (sovereignty

and power) and its open defiance of
God, it stands for the authoritarian
anti-God state. It derives its power from
the evil one (2, 4) and it is seemingly
indestructible (3). It dupes the world,
but not the Christian (8).

The second beast – the pseudo-lamb
which speaks with Satan's voice (11) – is
state-sanctioned, state-dominated religion. 16:13; 19:20 identify it as the 'false
prophet'. It apes the real thing, and
misdirects people's worship. Refusal to
worship cost some their lives (15),
others their livelihood (17). For John, the
two beasts were the Roman Empire and
emperor-worship. But every age – our
own included – has its equivalents.
Forty-two months (5): see on 11:2.
The mark (17): indicating ownership, and
acceptance of the beast's authority. Men
bear either the 'mark' of the world or the
'seal' of God – and it shows (16; 7:3).

*Head of Domitian, the Roman emperor who
started the persecutions which formed the
background to the book of Revelation.*

The number (17-18): many have tried to identify an individual (e.g. Nero Caesar), since the letters of the alphabet doubled as numbers in ancient times. But the key may lie in the symbolism of the numbers, 6 being 'a human number', the number of mankind. No matter how many times repeated, it always falls short of 7, God's number. No matter how powerful the 'beast', it is not God.

14 The joy of the redeemed; the harvest

This chapter stands in dramatic contrast to chapters 12–13. In the world God's people can expect implacable hostility. In God's kingdom the tables are turned (compare 9-11 with 13:15-17). The world sets its face against God; God sets his face against evil. He offers men a gospel which is timeless (6); the greatest of world-powers is temporary (8). In the end there will be absolute justice. All that is good will be lovingly harvested; all that is evil, totally crushed (13-20).

Verses 3-4: see on 7:4. The Bible nowhere implies that sexual intercourse is in itself defiling, or that it is more godly to be celibate than married. Verse 4 must therefore refer to those who are faithful to God. The

prophets frequently use the same figurative language: idolatrous Israel is a 'prostitute', and 'adulteress'. The 'first-fruits' are that part of the world harvest which belongs to God.

Babylon (8): see on chapter 17.

One like a son of man/human being (14): since he is under orders (15) this must be an angel, not Christ himself.

1600 stadia (20): the *stadion* was about 202 yards – so 'three hundred kilometres long', Good News Bible. But *1600 stadia* is clearly another symbolic number – 4 (which stands for the earth) x 4 x 10 x 10 – the complete destruction of the wicked throughout the earth.

15 – 16
THE SEVEN LAST PLAGUES

The great disasters of human history are warnings of the final, total calamities which will overtake those who refuse to listen. The plagues John describes here vividly recall those which fell on Egypt at the time of the exodus. But first we see the joy and security of God's people. They are not subjected to the final terrors, which are specifically directed against evil (16:2, 9, 11). Again and again in Revelation heaven is seen as a place of song – not everlasting, lugubrious, dutiful hymn-singing, but spontaneous song. In heaven life is so good, people so utterly happy and carefree that they just cannot help singing. Praise, at last, comes naturally.

Song of Moses (15:3): the great rejoicing after the crossing of the Red Sea (Exodus 15). Both songs are songs of deliverance and freedom.

16:12: the Euphrates separated the civilized world from the barbarian hordes beyond.

Armageddon (16): the hill (mound) of Megiddo, the famous fortress on the edge of the plain of Jezreel which guarded the

Temple dedicated to the Roman Emperor Trajan at Pergamum, one of the seven churches addressed in Revelation.

pass through the Carmel range. The scene of so many battles, it came to stand for battle itself.

The great city…great Babylon (19): see on chapter 17.

17–20
GOD'S FINAL TRIUMPH

17–19:5 The fall of Babylon

So often and so vigorously did the Old Testament prophets denounce the literal Babylon (see references below) that it became a byword for human pride and vainglory. For John and his readers, Babylon, the luxury-loving prostitute, was Rome, city of the seven hills (see verse 9)–pampered, decadent Rome; Rome, where Christians were thrown to the lions and burnt alive as public entertainment; Rome, the cess-pit of the Empire. But every age has its 'Babylon', the personification of all the greed and luxury and pleasure which entice men away from God; the things that promise so much and give so little. And Babylon, the epitome of all that cheats, is doomed!

Chapter 18, describing Babylon's fall, echoes the spirit and language of all the great 'downfall' prophecies of the Old Testament. (Isaiah 13–14, 24; Jeremiah 50–51; Ezekiel 26–28.) It is one final, comprehensive pronouncement of doom on every power in every age that grows fat on evil and treats men as mere commodities to be bought and sold (13). God's people are tempted to come to terms with the world. But they are called to take an uncompromising stand (4). They will be vindicated. Justice will be done. It is so certain, it can even be said to have happened already. Babylon *has* fallen!

Was, now is not (17:8): at times evil powers rampage through human history; at times they go underground–but they always return.

Seven kings (17:10): these may be emperors, or empires.

Ten kings (17:12): sometimes taken to mean Roman emperors, but John is describing a future coalition.

19:2-3: this is not sheer vindictiveness, or gloating over the fate of others. God's people stake their lives on his truth and justice. They rejoice to see militant, unrepentant evil overthrown.

19:6-10 The wedding-feast of Christ and his bride, the church

John paints a lovely picture. The bride's wedding-dress has been woven out of all those truly Christian acts in which the Lord himself takes pleasure.

19:11-21 Christ victorious

Satan's two henchmen and their allies are now seized and destroyed–in a 'war' without weapons, armour, or battle, so great is the power of Christ.

A name (12): see on 2:17.

Armageddon, or 'Har-magedon', meant the hill or mound of Megiddo. The mound of the ancient city can be seen in this picture beyond the pass it guarded through the Carmel hills.

20 Evil eradicated; the overthrow of Satan; the last judgement

There has been a great deal of argument over the meaning of this chapter – which contains the Bible's only mention of a 'millennium'. But first the things that are clear.

John sees Satan under God's firm control (1-3). He sees the souls of the martyrs, not every Christian (and this is important for the persecuted early church), resurrected to reign with Christ 1,000 years (4-6). At the end of it the forces of evil muster to attack God's people, but are utterly destroyed – even Satan and his henchmen (7-10). There is a general resurrection, when everyone stands before God and each is judged on his own record. The verdict is life or death. And for those who live there will be no more death (11-15).

With regard to detail it pays to be cautious. The same rules of interpretation apply here as for the rest of the book (see page 645). To ask 'where' the reign takes place, and work out a time-table of events, is to miss the spirit of the book. The idea of an earthly millennium belongs to the Old Testament, not the New. Peter simply speaks of 'new heavens and a new earth'. John himself gives no location (elsewhere in Revelation thrones, 4, are in heaven). Nor does he mention timing, or the relation of all this to Christ's return.

1,000 years (2): other numbers in Revelation are symbolic figures. 1,000 years is long enough to show God's complete authority over Satan, and to far outweigh the earthly sufferings of the martyrs.

Gog and Magog (8): see on Ezekiel 38.

The city he loves (9): the community of God's people in contrast to the 'great city' of Babylon.

21—22:5
GOD'S NEW WORLD

With everything evil gone, and death destroyed, what is the new age like? What

John describes is a heaven-on-earth. The new life is one long unclouded wedding-day for all God's people – the happiest, most joyful time imaginable. And there is never anything to spoil it: no sorrow; no pain; no parting with loved-ones; no night, even. For God is always there. He is *near.* There is no sin, outside or in, to drag us down, to spoil the perfect relationship, or to fill us with shame. The cities of the world have their riches and beauty, but they are nothing to the glorious splendour, the shining radiance, of the city of God's people. There is peace there, too, and freedom and security. It is all infinitely precious, infinitely worthwhile.

12,000 stadia (21:16): 1,500 miles/2,400 kilometres. But this is not intended to be taken literally. It is 12 x 1000 (see on 7:4 and 14:20). On earth God's people seem few and scattered. But they are part of a vast community – a great heavenly city.

21:19-20: the list of jewels echoes those which were set into the high priest's breast-piece, to represent Israel (see picture, page 169).

22:2: fallen mankind were denied access to the 'tree of life' (Genesis 3:22-24). Now the edict is reversed. Redeemed mankind will never again abuse their freedom.

22:6-21
EPILOGUE

The final statements may be somewhat disjointed, but they lack nothing in vigour. John affirms the truth of what he has written. In the sternest terms of his day, he warns against tampering with it. His closing words are full of urgency. The things he has described will happen soon. Christ's coming is imminent. And men will then be fixed in their attitudes. It will not be possible to change. In the end, those who are not saved will be lost; those who do not enter into eternal life and the presence of God will be shut out for ever. So 'let him who is thirsty come'. Let him 'take the water of life' which is 'without price'.

4

This is a directory both to the Bible and to the material contained in this book. It is divided into sections: Key Themes, Prayers, the Miracles and Parables of Jesus, Nations, People, Places, Subjects and Events. First it gives main Bible references: it can be used to find where in the Bible events took place, or to follow up some of the Bible's main teaching, or to look up people and places. It also serves as a series of indexes to this Handbook. Pictures or articles can be looked up in the relevant section: for instance pictures and maps of Jerusalem throughout the book can be looked up under the 'Jerusalem' entry in the Gazetteer of places. Or those wanting sources of material on Arts and Crafts, or Ships, or the Calendar, can look them up in the Subjects list.

Key Themes of the Bible

Passages of the Bible on key ideas or themes, selected as examples as a starting-point for study.

ATONEMENT God and man made 'at one' by the 'covering' of man's sin before God: Leviticus 4; 16; Romans 3:25; 1 John 2:2; 4:10. See also under Reconciliation and Redemption.

CHURCH The people of God: John 1:12-13; 1 Corinthians 12:12-31; 2 Corinthians 6:16-18; Galatians 3:6-29; Ephesians 2:11-22; Colossians 1:15-20; 1 Peter 2:4-10.
Its foundation: Matthew 16:18-20; 28:16-20; John 10:7-18; Acts 1:6-8; 2.
Its mission and purpose: Matthew 28:19-20; John 17:18, 22ff.; Acts 1:8; 26:16-18; 2 Corinthians 5:18-21; Ephesians 3:7-13; 5:25-27; Philippians 1:5-11; 1 Peter 2:5, 9; Jude 24-25.
Unity: John 17; 1 Corinthians 1:10ff.; 11:17ff.; Galatians 1:6-9; 3:23-29; Ephesians 4; 1 Peter 3:8ff.
Leadership: Acts 6:1-6; 13:1-3; 14:21-23; 20:17-35; 1 Corinthians 12:4-30; 1 Thessalonians 5:12-13; 1 Timothy; Titus; Hebrews 13:17.
Gatherings: Acts 2:41-47; 11:19-26; 19:8-10; 20:7-12; 1 Corinthians 11:17-33; 14:26-39; Hebrews 10:23-25.
Discipline: Matthew 18:15-20; Acts 4:33 - 5:11; 1 Corinthians 5; 2 Corinthians 2:5-11; Galatians 6:1-3; 1 Timothy 5:17-22.
Message: see Gospel.

COVENANT A 'treaty' or 'agreement' setting out God's promises to man (see too special article pp.198-199, and pp.134, 164-165):
With Noah: Genesis 6:18; 9:9-17.
With Abraham: Genesis 15; 17.
With Israel: Exodus 19ff.; Deuteronomy 4ff.

With David: 2 Samuel 7; Psalms 89; 132.
The 'new covenant': Jeremiah 31:31-34; Matthew 26:26-28; 2 Corinthians 3; Galatians 4:21ff.; Hebrews 9:15ff.

CREATION AND PROVIDENCE Genesis 1 - 2; Job 38 - 42:6; Psalms 8; 33:6-22; 104; Isaiah 40:21-26; Matthew 6:25-33; Acts 14:15-18; Romans 1:18-23; 8:18-23; 13:1-7; Colossians 1:15-20; Hebrews 1:1-3. For the new creation, see Life; for the new heaven and earth, see Heaven.

DEATH The physical and spiritual consequence of man's sin—alienation from God: Genesis 2:17; Romans 5:12ff.; 6:23; Ephesians 2:1-5.
Victory over death: John 5:24; 8:51; 11:25; Romans 5:17ff.; 6; 8:6-11, 38-39; 1 Corinthians 15:26, 54-56; 1 John 3:14; Revelation 21:4.
The 'second death': Revelation 2:11; 20:6, 14; 21:8.

ELECTION God's choice; his right to single people out for blessing (see too note, p.586): Romans 9:18ff.
God's choice of individuals for a particular purpose or job: Genesis 12:1-2; Exodus 3; 1 Samuel 3; Isaiah 6; 45; 49; Jeremiah 1.
God's choice of a people: Deuteronomy 7:6ff.; Romans 8:28-30; 1 Corinthians 1:27ff.; Ephesians 1:4-12; 1 Peter 1:2; 2:9.

FAITH *Trust in God; belief in his promises:* Genesis 15:6; Psalm 37:3ff.; Proverbs 3:5-6; Jeremiah 17:7-8.
A way of life: Habakkuk 2:4; Hebrews 11; James 2.
Commitment to Jesus Christ, trusting him for salvation: John 1:12; 8:24; Acts 16:30-31;

Romans 1:16-17; 4; Galatians 3; Ephesians 2:8-9; 1 John 5:1-5.
The means of access to God's power: Matthew 17:20-21; Mark 9:23; James 5:13-18.

FLESH *Flesh and blood; mortal man:* Genesis 6:3, 12; Psalm 78:39; Job 19:26; 34: 15; Isaiah 40:5.
The sinful self: Romans 7:13-25; 8; Galatians 5:16-24.

FORGIVENESS God's loving mercy: Exodus 34:6-7; Psalm 51; Isaiah 55:6-7; 1 John 1:5-10.
The death of Christ as the basis of God's forgiveness: Matthew 26:26-28; John 1:29; Acts 5:31; 13:38; Ephesians 1:7; 1 John 2:2, 12.
Forgiving others: Matthew 6:14-15; 18:21-35; Ephesians 4:32; Colossians 3:13.

FREEDOM Isaiah 61:1; Luke 4:18; John 8:31-36; Romans 6:16-23; 8:2, 21; 2 Corinthians 3:17; Galatians 3:28; 5:1; 13; James 1:25; 2:12; 1 Peter 2:16.

FUTURE DESTINY The day is coming (Old Testament 'that day', the 'day of the Lord') when God will judge all men; when all his glorious promises to his people will be realized in a new heaven and earth (see also Heaven, Jesus Christ, return and Resurrection): Isaiah 2 - 4; 65:17-25, etc.; Daniel 12:1-3; Joel; Amos 5; Zephaniah; Matthew 24 - 25; Acts 1:6-11, 1 Corinthians 3:10-15; 1 Corinthians 15:20-28, 35-58; Revelation, especially 19 - 22.

GOD One God who has disclosed himself in three persons—Father, Son (Jesus Christ) and Holy Spirit: Deuteronomy 6:4; Genesis 1:1-2 and John 1:1-3; Judges 14:6, etc.; Isaiah 40:13; 45:18-22; 61:1; 63:10, etc.; Matthew 28:19; John 14:15-26; 2 Corinthians 13:14; Ephesians 2:18; 4:4-6; 2 Thessalonians 2:13-14; 1 Peter 1:1-2.
The 'otherness' of God: the eternal spirit; the creator: Genesis 1; Deuteronomy 33:26-27; 1 Kings 8:27; Job 38ff.; Psalms 8; 100; 104; Isaiah 40:12-28; 55:9; John 4:23-24; Romans 1:19-20; Revelation 1:8.
The power of God: Genesis 17:1; Exodus 32:11; Numbers 24:4; Job 40 - 42:2; Isaiah 9:6; 45 - 46; Daniel 3:17; Matthew 26:53; John 19:10-11; Acts 12; Revelation 19:1-16.
—his knowledge: Genesis 4:10; Job 28:20-27; Psalm 139:1-6; Daniel 2:17-23; Matthew 6:7-8; John 2:23-25; 4:25-29; Ephesians 1:3-12.
—his presence everywhere: Genesis 28:10-17; Psalm 139:7-12; Jeremiah 23:23-24; Acts 17:26-28.
The character of God—his holiness and righteousness: Exodus 20; Leviticus 11:44-45; Joshua 24:19-28; Psalms 7; 25:8-10; 99; Isaiah 1:12ff.; 6:1-5; John 17:25-26; Romans 1:18 - 3:26; Ephesians 4:17-24; Hebrews 12: 7-14; 1 Peter 1:13-16; 1 John 1:5-10.

— *his love and mercy:* Deuteronomy 7:6-13; Psalms, e.g., 23; 25; 36:5-12; 103; Isaiah 40:1-2, 27-31; 41:8-20; 43; Jeremiah 31:2-14; Hosea 6; 11; 14; John 3:16-17; 10:7-18; 13:1; 14:15-31; 15:9, 12ff.; Romans 8:35-38; Galatians 2:20; Ephesians 2:4-10; 1 John 3:1-3, 16; 4:7-21.

GOSPEL The 'good news' brought by Jesus: Mark 1:14-15; Luke 8:1; etc.

The gospel message: e.g. Matthew 4:17; John 1:11-13; 3:1-21, 31-36; Acts 2; 13; 17; Romans 1 - 8 (especially 1:16-17; 5:1; 6:23); 2 Corinthians 5:17ff.; Galatians 2:20; 4:4-7; Ephesians 1:3ff.; 1 John 1:1-4; 5:11-12. See also Kingdom, Life, Salvation.

GRACE God's love poured out on undeserving man (the Old Testament uses a number of different terms): Deuteronomy 7:6-9; Psalms 23:6; 25:6-10; 51:1; Jeremiah 31:2-3.

God's grace in salvation: Ephesians 2:4-9; Romans 3:19-24; 6:14.

The Christian's dependence on God's grace: 2 Corinthians 12:9; Ephesians 4:7; 1 Timothy 1:2; 1 Peter 5:5, 10; 2 Peter 3:18.

HEAVEN The dwelling-place of God, the perfect, unseen world (also sometimes simply a word for 'sky'): Deuteronomy 26:15; Nehemiah 9:6; Matthew 5:45; 6:9; Mark 13:32; 1 Peter 1:4.

The 'new heaven and earth': Isaiah 65:17ff.; 2 Peter 3:10-13; Revelation 21 - 22.

HELL 'Sheol', Old Testament place of the dead (=New Testament 'Hades'): Psalms 88:3-5; 139:8; Proverbs 9:18; Isaiah 5:14; 38:18; Amos 9:2. New Testament 'Gehenna', the fate of those finally cut off from God: Matthew 5:22, 29-30; 10:28; 23:33; 25:41; 2 Peter 2:4; Revelation 1:18; 20:13-15.

HOLINESS God's moral perfection; his separation from evil and distinctive character: Exodus 3:4-6; 15:11; 1 Chronicles 16:10; Isaiah 6:3-5; 10:20; Hosea 11:9; John 17:11; Revelation 4:8.

Expressed in Jesus: Acts 4:27, 30; John 1:14-18; 14:6ff.

In God's people: Exodus 19:6; Luke 1:74-75; 2 Corinthians 7:1; Ephesians 4:23-24; Colossians 3:12ff.; Hebrews 12:10-11; 1 Peter 1:15-16; 2:9.

HOLY SPIRIT One with God the Father and Jesus Christ, actively at work in the world of men, particularly in and through God's people.

His nature and person: Genesis 1:1-2; 2 Samuel 23:2-5; Psalm 139:7-12; Matthew 12:25-32; 28:19; John 14:15-17; 15:26-27; Acts 5:1-3; 20:28; Romans 8:9-11; 2 Corinthians 3:15-18; 13:14; Ephesians 4:29-31.

His work: Exodus 31:3; Judges 3:10; 14:6, etc.; Psalm 51:10-12; Isaiah 11:1-3; 32:14-18; 42:1-4; 63:10-14; Ezekiel 36:26-27; John 3:5-8; 14:25-26; 16:7-15; Acts 1:6-8; 2; 11:16-18; Romans 5:1-5; 8:1-27; 1 Corinthians 2:1-13; 12:3-13; 2 Corinthians 1:20-22; Galatians 5:16-25; 2 Peter 1:20-21.

HOPE Confident expectation: Romans 4:18; 5:1-5; 8:24-25; 12:12; 15:4; 1 Corinthians 13:13; 15:19ff.; Colossians 1:5, 27; 1 Peter 1:3ff.; Hebrews 11:1ff.

INCARNATION God become man: Matthew 1 - 2; Luke 1-2; John 1:1-18; Romans 8:3;

Philippians 2:6-11; Colossians 1:13-22; Hebrews 1 - 2; 4:14 - 5:10; 1 John 1 - 2:2.

JESUS CHRIST *Son of God — his own claims:* Matthew 26:59-64; 27:41-44; Mark 2:1-12; John 5:17-47; 6:25-51; 7:16-31; 8:54-59; 10:22-39; 14:8-11; 17:1-5, 20-24; 19:7. Also God's word: Matthew 17:1-8; Mark 1:9-11.

— *the opinion of his disciples and others:* Matthew 16:13-20; 27:50-54; Mark 1:21-27; 5:1-13; Luke 1:31-35; John 1:29-34, 43-51; 6:66-69; 11:23-27; 20:28; Acts 2:22-36; 7:54-60; 9:17-22; 10:34-43; Romans 1:1-4; Ephesians 1:20-23; Philippians 2:5-11; Colossians 1:15-20; Hebrews 1; 1 John 1:1-4; 2:22-25; 4:9-16.

— *for the evidence of his actions,* see Miracles of Jesus.

Son of man: a real human being (yet sinless — Luke 4:1-13; 23:39-41; John 8:46; 2 Corinthians 5:21; Hebrews 4:15; 1 Peter 2:22-23; 3:18): Galatians 4:4; Matthew 4:2; 21:18; Mark 1:41; 10:21; Luke 7:13; John 4:6; 11:33, 35, 38; 13:1; 15:13; Acts 2:22-23; Hebrews 2:14-18; 4:15; 1 John 4:2.

The significance of his death: Mark 8:31-33; Luke 24:13-27, 44-48; John 1:29; 3:14-15; 11:50-52; 12:24; Acts 2:22-42; 3:12-26; 10:34-43; Romans 5:6-21. 1 Corinthians 11:23-26; Philippians 2:5-11; Hebrews 10:5-14; 1 Peter 2:24. See also under Forgiveness and Redemption.

The promise of his return: Matthew 24; 26:64; John 14. Acts 1:11; 3:19-21; Philippians 3:20; Colossians 3:4; 1 Thessalonians 1:10; 4:13-5:11; 2 Thessalonians 1:5 - 2:12; 2 Peter 3:8-13. See also Messiah.

JOY Psalms 16:11; 30:5; 43:4; 51:12; 126:5-6; Ecclesiastes 2:26; Isaiah 61:7; Jeremiah 15:16; Luke 15:7; John 15:11; 16:22; Romans 14:17; 15:13; Galatians 5:22; Philippians 1:4; 1 Thessalonians 2:20; 3:9; Hebrews 12:2; James 1:2; 1 Peter 1:8; Jude 24.

JUDGEMENT See Future destiny

JUSTIFICATION A legal term: acquittal. The New Testament declares that God can acquit man of breaking his law because the penalty has been paid in the death of Jesus (see also Forgiveness): Exodus 23:7; Job 13:18; 25:4; Psalms 51:1ff.; 103:6; 143:2; Isaiah 50:8-9; 53:11; Luke 18:14; Acts 13:39; Romans 2:13; 3:4, 19-30; 4:2ff.; 5:1-10; 8:30-34; 1 Corinthians 6:11; Galatians 2:15-21; 3:6-14; Titus 3:7; James 2:14-26.

KINGDOM God's rule: the new age (see special article 'The Kingdom of God and the Kingdom of Heaven', pp.484-485): Psalms 103:19; 145:11-13; Daniel 2:44; 4:3; 7:13-14, 27; Matthew 3:2; 4:23; 5:3, 10, 19-20; 6:9-10; 33; 13:11, 19, 24-52; 16:19, 28; 18:1-4, 23ff.; 19:12, 14, 23ff.; 20:1ff., 21ff.; 21:43; 22:2ff.; 23:13; 24:14; 25:1ff., 34; 26:29; many similar references in Mark and Luke; John 3:3, 5; 18:36; Acts 14:22; 28:31; Romans 14:17; 1 Corinthians 4:20; Galatians 5:19-21; Colossians 1:13.

LAW God's instructions for right living.

Ritual and ceremonial law: Exodus 25 - 30; 34 - 40; Leviticus 1 - 9; 11 - 17; 22 - 25; Deuteronomy 14; 16; 18; 26.

Moral and social law: Exodus 20:1-17; 21 - 23; Leviticus 18 - 20; Deuteronomy 5:1-21;

10:12-21; 15; 19 - 25.

Delight in the law: Psalms 1; 19; 37:31; 40:8; 119; Proverbs 29:18.

Its permanent value: Matthew 5:17-20; 22:36-40; 23:23; Luke 10:25-28; Romans 3:31; 8:3-4.

The impossibility of meeting God's standards by human effort; the law's limitations: John 7:19; Acts 13:39; Romans 2:25-29; 3:19-21; 7:7-25; 8:3; Galatians 2:16; 3:21-24; Hebrews 7:18-19; James 2:8-12.

LIFE *Human life (creation):* Genesis 2:7, 9; Matthew 6:25, etc. etc.

God, the source of life; his life-giving laws and wisdom: Deuteronomy 30:15-20; Psalms 36:9; 133:3; Proverbs 8:35; 14:27; Jeremiah 21:8.

'Eternal' life (new creation): Matthew 7:14; 10:39; 16:25-26; 18:8-9, 19:16ff., 29; Luke 12:15; John 1:4; 3:15-16, 36; 4:14; 5:24; 6:27, 35, 40, 47-51; 10:10, 28; 11:25; 14:6; 17:3; 20:31; Romans 6:4ff., 22-23; 8:6; 2 Corinthians 4:10-12; 5:17ff.; Galatians 6:8; Ephesians 2:2ff.; 1 Timothy 6:12; 1 John 1:1-2; 3:14; 5:11-12; Revelation 22:1-2, 17.

LOVE 1 Corinthians 13; Galatians 5:22; 1 John 4:7 - 5:3.

The love of God; Christ's love: Deuteronomy 7:7-8; Proverbs 3:12; Isaiah 63:7-9; Jeremiah 31:3; Hosea 3:1; 14:4; John 3:16; 13:1; 15:9, 12-13; Romans 8:35-39; Galatians 2:20; Ephesians 2:4; 3:17-19; Hebrews 12:6; 1 John 3:1.

Man's love for God: Exodus 20:6; Deuteronomy 6:5; 11:1, 13, 22; Psalms 31:23; 116:1; 119:47-48; John 14:15, 21-24; Romans 8:28; 1 Corinthians 8:3; 1 Peter 1:8.

Loving others: Leviticus 19:18, 34; Matthew 5:43-46; John 13:34-35; 14:15, 21-24; 15:9-14; Galatians 5:13-14; Ephesians 4:2; 5:1-6; Philippians 2:2; Hebrews 10:24; 1 John 4:7 - 5:3.

Love between man and woman: Genesis 29:20; 2 Samuel 13:15; Proverbs 5:18-19; Song of Solomon; Ephesians 5:25ff.; Colossians 3:19.

MAN Created by God — with a mortal, yet moral and spiritual nature — to worship, obey and enjoy his friendship: Genesis 1 - 2; 17:1ff., etc.; Deuteronomy 5:28-33; 8; 2 Samuel 19:12-13; Psalms 8; 27; 66; 78:5-8; Isaiah 40:6-8; 43; Ecclesiastes 12:1-7; Micah 6:6-8; Luke 12:13-21; Romans 1:18-25; 8:18ff.; 1 Corinthians 15:45-50; 2 Corinthians 5:1-5; 6:16-18.

In rebellion against God: Genesis 3; Judges 2:11-23; Psalm 2:1-3; Daniel 9:3-19; Romans 1 - 3; 7:13-25. Hebrews 3:7-19; Revelation 1 - 7 - 18. See also Sin and evil. For man's re-creation in Christ and glorious destiny, see Future destiny, Life. Regeneration, Heaven, etc.

MEDIATOR The go-between, reconciling God and man (see also Reconciliation): Galatians 3:19-20; 1 Timothy 2:5; Hebrews 8:6; 9:15; 12:24.

MERCY Kindness; readiness to forgive (see also Grace): Exodus 34:6-7; Nehemiah 9:7, 31; Psalms 23:6; 25:6; 40:11; 51:1; 103:4, 8; Daniel 9:9; Jonah 4:2; Micah 6:8; Matthew 5:7; Luke 18:13; Romans 9:15; 12:1; Ephesians 2:4.

MESSIAH The Christ — God's chosen

deliverer: Deuteronomy 18:15ff.; Psalms 2; 45:6-7; 72; 110; Isaiah 9:2-7; 11; 42:1-9; 49:1-6; 52:13 - 53:12; 61:1-3; Jeremiah 23:5-6; 33:14-16; Ezekiel 34:22ff.; Daniel 7; Zechariah 9:9-10; Matthew 1:18, 22-23; 16:16, 20; 26:63; Mark 14:61-62; Luke 2:11, 26; John 4:25, 29; 7:26-27, 31, 41-42; 9:22; Acts 2:36; 3:20-21; 4:26-28; 18:28; 26:22-23.

PEACE Numbers 6:26; Psalms 4:8; 85:8-10; 119:165; Proverbs 3:17; Isaiah 9:6-7; 57:19-21; Jeremiah 6:14; 16:5; Ezekiel 34:25; Matthew 10:34; Luke 1:79; 2:14; 7:50; 19:38, 42; John 14:27; Acts 10:36; Romans 1:7; 5:1; 8:6; 14:19; Galatians 5:22; Ephesians 2:14-17; 4:3; 6:15; Philippians 4:7; Colossians 3:15; 2 Thessalonians 3:16; James 3:17-18.

PRAYER See Prayers of the Bible. *Jesus' teaching on prayer:* Matthew 6:5-15; 7:7-11; 26:41; Mark 12:38-40; 13:33; 14:38; Luke 11:1-13; 18:1-14.

RECONCILIATION *Between God and man:* Romans 5:6-11; 11:15; 2 Corinthians 5:18-20; Colossians 1:20-22.
Between men: Matthew 5:23-24; John 17:11, 20-23; 1 Corinthians 7:11; 12:12ff.; Galatians 3:28; Ephesians 2:11-22.

REDEMPTION Payment of a price to buy deliverance and freedom: Leviticus 25:25-55; Exodus 13:13; 21:30; 30:12; Numbers 18:15-16.
God's redemption of his people: Exodus 6:6; Deuteronomy 7:8; 21:8; 2 Samuel 4:9; Job 33:22-28; Psalms 103:4; 107:2; 130:8; Isaiah 50:2; 63:9; Hosea 13:14.
Christ as a ransom: Matthew 20:28; Romans 3:24; 8:23; 1 Corinthians 1:30; Galatians 3:13; Ephesians 1:7; 4:30; Colossians 1:14; Hebrews 9:12, 15; 1 Peter 1:18-19; Revelation 5:9; 14:3, 4.

REGENERATION Being re-born, re-created, made alive to God: Psalm 51:10; Jeremiah 24:7; 31:33-34; Ezekiel 11:19; 36:26; Matthew 19:28; John 1:12-13; 3:3ff.; Romans 8:9ff.; 2 Corinthians 5:17; Ephesians 2:5; Titus 3:5; 1 Peter 1:23; 1 John 2:29; 3:9; 4:7; 5:1, 4, 18.

REPENTANCE Turning from sin and self-centredness to God: 2 Kings 17:13; 23:25; 2 Chronicles 33:10ff.; Job 42:6; Psalms 51; 78:34; Isaiah 1:16-20; 55:6ff.; Jeremiah 3:12-14; Ezekiel 33:12ff.; Daniel 9:3-20; Hosea 14:1ff.; Joel 2:12-14; Matthew 3:2, 8; 11:20-21; Mark 1:4; Luke 5:32; 13:3, 5; 15:7, 10, 18-21; 24:47; Acts 2:38; 17:30; 20:21; 26:20; 2 Corinthians 7:10; Hebrews 12:17; 2 Peter 3:9; Revelation 2:5.

RESURRECTION Being raised from death to a new life (a bodily resurrection like Christ's): Job 19:25-27; Psalm 49:14-15; Isaiah 26:19; Ezekiel 37; Daniel 12:2; Matthew 22:30-32; Luke 14:14; 20:34-38; John 5:29; 6:39-40, 44, 54; 11:25; Acts 2:22-36; 4:33; 17:18, 32; 23:6-8; 24:15; Romans 1:4; 4:24-25; 6:5ff.; 1 Corinthians 15; Philippians 3:10-11; Colossians 2:12; 3:1-4; 1 Thessalonians 4:13ff.; Hebrews 11:35; 1 Peter 1:3; 3:21; 1 John 3:2; Revelation 20:4-6, 11-15.
Accounts of Jesus' resurrection: Matthew 28; Mark 16; Luke 24; John 20; 1 Corinthians 15:3-8.

REVELATION What God makes known to

man. The whole Bible is God's revelation; these references simply pinpoint some examples: Deuteronomy 29:29; 1 Samuel 3:7, 21; Isaiah 22:14; 40:5; Daniel 2:22, 28ff.; Amos 3:7; Luke 17:30; John 12:38; Romans 1:17-18; 2:5; 8:18; 16:25; 1 Corinthians 14:6, 26; 2 Corinthians 12:1, 7; Galatians 1:12; 3:23; Ephesians 1:9-10, 17; 3:3, 5; 1 Peter 1:5, 12-13; 5:1; Revelation 1:1.
Christ as the revelation of God: e.g. John 1:1-18; 14:7; Colossians 1:15ff.; Hebrews 1:1-3; 2 Peter 1:16ff.; 1 John 1:1ff.; Revelation 1:12-16.
God revealed in his creation: Job 38 - 40; Psalms 8; 19; 104; Romans 1.
God specially revealed in his power and glory: Exodus 24:9-11; 33:18 - 34:9; 1 Kings 19:9ff.; Isaiah 6; Ezekiel 1; 10; Daniel 7:9-14; Matthew 17:1-5 (Christ's transfiguration); Revelation 4.

RIGHTEOUSNESS The right action and justice which characterize God and which he requires of men. Genesis 15:6; 18:23ff.; Leviticus 19:15; Deuteronomy 4:8; Job 4:7; 36:7; Psalms 1:5-6; 11:7; 23:3; 34:19; 37:25; 97:6; 98:9; Proverbs 10:2; 11:4ff.; Isaiah 53:11; 64:6; Ezekiel 33:12-21; 33:12ff.; Habakkuk 1:4, 13; Matthew 5:6, 10, 20; 6:33; 9:13; 13:43; Luke 18:9; John 16:8-10; Romans 3:10-26; 4:3ff.; 5:17ff.; 6:13ff.; 10:3ff.; 2 Corinthians 5:21; 6:14; Ephesians 6:14; Philippians 1:11; Hebrews 12:11; James 5:16; 1 Peter 2:24; 2 Peter 3:13; 1 John 2:1; 3:7.

SACRIFICE *Old Testament sacrifice and offerings:* Genesis 4:2-4; 8:20; 22:1-14; Exodus 12 (the Passover); 29 - 30; Leviticus 1 - 9; 16 (the Atonement); 17; 1 Samuel 15:22; Psalms 50:5; 51:15-19; 107:22; Proverbs 15:8; Isaiah 43:23-24; Jeremiah 6:20; Hosea 3:4; Amos 4:4-5; 5:21-24.
In the New Testament: Matthew 9:13; 26:28; Luke 2:24; John 1:29; 6:51ff.; Romans 12:1; 1 Corinthians 10:14ff.; Ephesians 5:2; Philippians 2:17; 4:18; Hebrews 5:1-3; 7:27; 9:11-28; 10; 13:15-16; 1 Peter 2:5.

SALVATION God's rescue of man from sin and death to 'eternal' life, a new quality and dimension of existence. The theme of salvation—God as saviour—runs right through the Bible. It is the heart of the Christian message: Exodus 14:30; Numbers 10:9; Deuteronomy 33:29; Judges 2:16-18; 1 Samuel 15:23; 1 Chronicles 11:14; Job 22:29; Psalms 28:8-9; 34:6; 37:40; Isaiah 30:15; 43:11-13; 45:21-22; 59:1; Jeremiah 30:10-11; Hosea 13:4; Matthew 1:21; 10:22; 19:25; 27:42; Luke 2:11; 8:12; John 3:17; 10:9; Acts 2:21; 4:12; 16:30-31; Romans 5:9-10; 10:9-13; 1 Corinthians 3:15; Ephesians 2:8; 1 Timothy 1:15; 2:4; 4:10; Hebrews 7:25. Salvation is also described in a series of metaphors or pictures: God covers man's sin—see Atonement; he acquits—see Justification; he reconciles—see Reconciliation; he redeems—see Redemption; he gives new life—see Regeneration and Life. See also Gospel.

SANCTIFICATION Making holy, setting apart for God (see Holiness); having an increasingly Christ-like character: Exodus 31:12-15; Leviticus 22:9; Deuteronomy 5:12; Joshua 3:5; 1 Chronicles 15:14; Ezekiel

37:24-28; John 10:36; 15:1-17; 17:17-19; Romans 12:1ff.; 15:16; 1 Corinthians 1:2, 30; 6:11; 7:14; Ephesians 4:24; Philippians 1:9-11, 27; Colossians 1:10; 1 Thessalonians 3:11-13; 4:3-4; 5:23; 2 Thessalonians 2:13; 1 Timothy 4:5; Hebrews 10:10, 14, 29, 2 Peter 1:3-11; 1 John 3:2-3.

SIN AND EVIL Wrong-doing; disobedience; rebellion against God. *Its coming into the world:* Genesis 3; 2 Peter 2:4; Jude 5-7; Revelation 12:7-12.
Satan—the personification of evil—and his work: Genesis 3:1-6; Job 1 - 2; Matthew 4:1-11; 12:22-28; 16:23; Luke 13:16; 22:3-6, 31; John 8:43-47; Acts 26:15-18; 2 Corinthians 2:10-11; 11:14; 12:7; 1 Thessalonians 2:18; Hebrews 2:14; 1 Peter 5:8; 1 John 3:8-10; Revelation 2:13; 12:7-17.
The universality of sin, and its effect on man: Genesis 3:16-24; 4; Deuteronomy 9:6-24; Psalm 14; Isaiah 59:1ff.; Jeremiah 44; Ezekiel 36:22-32; Matthew 15:16-20; Romans 1:28-32; 5:12; 6:23; Galatians 5:19-21; Ephesians 2:1-3; James 1:12-15; 4:1-3, 17; 1 John 3:4.
God's victory; sin's ultimate destruction: Psalm 103; Romans 5:15-21; 1 Corinthians 15:54-57; 1 John 3:4-10; Revelation 20.

SPIRIT Mind, heart, will; spirit as distinct from, or opposed to 'flesh' (see above; see also Holy Spirit): 2 Kings 2:9; Job 32:18; Psalms 31:5; 34:18; 51:10; Isaiah 26:9; 31:3; Ezekiel 37:1-10 ('breath' and 'spirit' translate the same Hebrew word); Matthew 5:3; 26:41; John 3:6; 4:23-24; Romans 2:29; 8; 1 Corinthians 2:11ff.; Galatians 5:16-25; Ephesians 4:23.

TEMPTATION Trial, testing: Genesis 3; 22:1; Exodus 17:7; Deuteronomy 6:16; Psalm 95:9; Matthew 6:13; 22:35; 26:41; Acts 5:9; 1 Corinthians 7:5; 10:9-13; Hebrews 2:18; 4:15; James 1:2-4, 13-15.
The temptation of Jesus: Matthew 4:1-11; Mark 1:12-13; Luke 4:1-13.

WISDOM The expression of an attitude to life which is centred on God and his laws: Exodus 28:3; Deuteronomy 34:9; 1 Kings 3:5-14; Job 12:13; 28; Psalms 37:30; 104:24; Proverbs 1; 8; 9; Ecclesiastes 1:13-18; 2:12-26; Isaiah 11:2; Daniel 2:20-23; Matthew 13:54; Luke 2:52; 21:15; Acts 6:3; 1 Corinthians 1:17 - 2:16; 3:18ff.; Colossians 3:16; 2 Timothy 3:15; James 1:5; 3:13-18.

WORLD *The created universe; the earth:* 2 Samuel 22:16; Job 34:13; Psalms 24:1; 50:12; 90:2; Matthew 4:8; 16:26; John 1:9; Romans 5:12.
Mankind: Psalm 9:8; Isaiah 13:11; Luke 2:1; John 3:16-17; 8:26; 14:31; 1 Corinthians 1:21.
The present age: Matthew 24:3; 28:20; Luke 18:30; Ephesians 1:21.
The world in rebellion against God: John 7:7; 8:23; 14:17; 15:18-19; James 4:4; 1 John 2:15-17; 4:4-5; 5:4-5.

Nations and Peoples of Bible Lands

TERENCE MITCHELL

For the areas occupied by the various nations see the World of the Bible map, pp. 12-13.

AKKADIANS The northern neighbours of the Sumerians in 3rd-millennium Mesopotamia. From the Akkadian Semitic language Babylonian and Assyrian developed. As a place, Akkad is mentioned only in Genesis 10:10.

AMMONITES The inhabitants of the area of Transjordan which lay east of the Dead Sea end of the Jordan Valley. To the south lay Moab. Modern Amman stands on the site of the chief Ammonite city, Rabbath-Ammon (earlier Rabbah). The Israelites did not win their territory at the time of the conquest (Judges 11:5), but it was later partially occupied by the tribes of Reuben and Gad. The Ammonites were incorporated, successively, into the Assyrian, Babylonian and Persian Empires. But during their period of independence they formed a threat to the Israelites, at least until Maccabean times when the capital was known as Philadelphia (1 Maccabees 5:6).

AMORITES A Semitic-speaking people, stemming from the middle Euphrates area, who spread to Mesopotamia and Syria-Palestine, settling there in the late 3rd and early 2nd millennium BC. Their language, known only from personal names, is the earliest recorded example of West Semitic. They were prominent in the population of Mari, whose documents throw much light on patriarchal customs. After the conquest of Canaan by the Israelites, the Amorites who remained there were gradually absorbed (see 1 Samuel 7:14).

ARABIANS The Semitic-speaking nomadic and semi-nomadic inhabitants of the northern part of the Arabian peninsula, which adjoined the areas of settled civilization. During most of the 1st millennium BC, the Arabians appear mainly as raiders, but there was a continual drift of small numbers into the settled areas. And from the 3rd century BC onwards the region south-east of Palestine was occupied by one group of Arabs, the Nabataeans, who built up a flourishing civilization based on the incense trade (see Sabaeans) centring on Petra.

In New Testament times the Nabatean dominion extended to the area east of Damascus. where there seems to have been an agent of their king Aretas (2 Corinthians 11:32) Paul spent some time in Nabataean territory after his conversion (Galatians 1:17).

ARAMAEANS A Semitic-speaking people closely related to the Israelites (see Deuteronomy 26:5) who spread throughout Mesopotamia and Syria during the later part of the 2nd millennium BC, and are found in the early 1st millennium dominating such Syrian city-states as Damascus and Hamath (see also Cilicians) The Hebrew name 'Aram' is usually translated 'Syria'. but the Greek name Suria occurs in the New Testament.

ASSYRIANS The homeland of these neighbours of the Babylonians was north Mesopotamia. During the 2nd millennium, Assyria came under the rule of Amorites, and from about 1350 to 1100 BC built up a powerful state exercising some control as far west as the Mediterranean Sea. Its capital was then at Assur, but in 883 BC Ashurnasirpal II moved his capital to Kalhu (biblical Calah, modern Nimrud). His successors, including Shalmaneser III (858-824), Adad-nirari III (810-783), Tiglath-pileser III (or Pul; 744-727), Shalmaneser V (726-722) all of whom had contacts with Israel, continued there until Sargon II (721-705) founded a new capital at Dur-Sharrukin modern Khorsabad. His son Sennacherib (704-681) moved the capital to Nineveh. There it remained under Esarhaddon (680-669) Ashurbanipal (668-627); probably the Osnappar of Ezra 4:10), and other minor kings until its destruction in 612 BC by the Chaldeans and Medes.

BABYLONIANS The heirs of the Sumerians and Akkadians in southern Mesopotamia. Their capital city was Babylon. The best-known king of the 1st Babylonian dynasty (of Amorite stock; 18th century BC, roughly the time of Abraham) was Hammurabi, the author of a famous code of laws. During the early part of the 1st millennium BC, the Babylonians were subject to the Assyrians. But from 612 to 539 BC the Neo-Babylonian or Chaldean dynasty dominated Western Asia. Nebuchadnezzar (604-562). Amel-Marduk (biblical Evil-Merodach; 561-560), Nergal-shar-usar (biblical Nergal-Sharezer, Greek Neriglissar; 559-556). and Belshazzar were rulers of this dynasty mentioned in the Old Testament. Babylon fell to Cyrus the Persian in 539 BC.

CANAANITES The sedentary inhabitants of Palestine and southern Syria, who had a flourishing urban civilization in the 2nd millennium BC. The corrupt religion of Canaan criticized in the Old Testament, is illustrated in texts from Ugarit (modern Ras Shamra). Hebrew is a dialect of the Canaanite language (Isaiah 19:18) and the related Ugaritic language greatly helps our understanding of it

CARIANS An Indo-European-speaking people of south-west Asia Minor. They were used by the Israelites as mercenary troops in the 9th century BC (2 Kings 11:4, 19).

CHALDEANS As the Aramaeans spread across northern Mesopotamia. so the Chaldeans (related tribespeople) occupied the southern marshes. During the 9th and 8th centuries BC they often won control of Babylon (e.g. Merodach-baladan, 2 Kings 20:12ff.). After a long struggle with Assyria. the Chaldean dynasty established itself there in 626 BC.

CILICIANS The inhabitants of the area centring on Tarsus (Paul's native city). Cilicia (Kue) is mentioned as a source of horses for Solomon's trade with Syria (1 Kings 10:28-29). This passage seems.to indicate that Solomon obtained horses from Egypt and Cilicia. and chariots from Egypt. and traded them at a profit to the Hittite and Aramaean states of Syria.

CIMMERIANS A steppe people who crossed the Caucasus in the 8th-7th centuries BC, coming up against the Assyrians in north-west Persia, and overrunning the Phrygian and Lydian kingdoms in Asia Minor. They are mentioned in Ezekiel 38:6 (Gomer) in association with other northern peoples (see Phrygians).

CRETANS The inhabitants of the island of Crete, seat of the great Minoan civilization in the 3rd and 2nd millennia BC. In the Old Testament Crete is referred to as 'Caphtor' (Genesis 10:14; Deuteronomy 2:23). The Philistines are said to have come from the area under Cretan control (Jeremiah 47:4; Amos 9:7).

The Minoan civilization of Crete did not survive the Sea People upheavals (see Philistines) of the late 2nd millennium BC, and in the 1st millennium Crete was simply a part of the Greek cultural area. The Old Testament speaks of some of them, the 'Cherethites'. who settled near the Philistines in southern Palestine (1 Samuel 30:14). Some. like the Philistines, joined David's mercenary troops (2 Samuel 8:18; 15:18; 20:7. and see 1 Kings 1:38. 44). Cretans are mentioned among those present at Pentecost (Acts 2:11).

CYPRIOTES The inhabitants of the island of Cyprus, referred to in the old Testament by the ancient name 'Elishah' (Genesis 10:4; Ezekiel 27:7). This appears in other documents as Alashia. The Cypriotes are also sometimes referred to as Kittim (Genesis 10:4; Numbers 24:24).

Cyprus does not appear often in the Bible in this period. The name Kittim is applied to the island in Isaiah 23:1, 12, but it is qualified by 'coastlands' in Jeremiah 2:10 and Ezekiel 27:6, which suggests an extension to the adjacent mainland areas. In Daniel 11:30 it is used in a figurative way of Rome. In the New Testament the island of Cyprus figures frequently in Acts.

DEDANITES The inhabitants of Dedan, modern Al-'Ula. in north-west Arabia, who by about the 7th century BC were prospering from their position on the trade route to South Arabia (see e.g. Isaiah 21:13: Jeremiah 25:23: Ezekiel 25:13; 38:13). In about the 5th century BC the Minaeans established a trading colony at Dedan, and in about the 1st century BC it became part of the Nabataean dominion.

EDOMITES The southern neighbours of the Moabites, whose territory lay mainly to the east of the Wadi Arabah. They, like the Moabites, refused passage to the Israelites at the time of the conquest.

The Edomites continued hostile to the Israelites. In the 6th century, after the fall of Jerusalem, many immigrated to southern Judah, and were followed by others in later centuries, when their home territory became part of the Nabataean kingdom (see Arabians). Southern Judea came to be called Idumaea (1 Maccabees 4:29; 5:65), and the inhabitants Idumaeans (Mark 3:8). The Herods who ruled Judea in New Testament times were Idumaeans.

EGYPTIANS The inhabitants of Egypt, whose highly developed civilization matched that of Mesopotamia. When Abraham had contact with Egypt in the Middle Kingdom period (about 2100-1800 BC) its civilization was already over a thousand years old. It was probably during the Second Intermediate Period (about 1800-1600 BC) that Joseph and his people settled there. And the exodus took place under the New Kingdom (about 1600-1100 BC), probably in the time of the 19th dynasty pharaoh Ramesses II (about 1290-1224 BC). Israel is mentioned as one of the nations in Palestine on the so-called 'Israel Stele' of his successor Merneptah (about 1224-1220 BC).

By the 1st millennium BC, the great days of Egyptian civilization were over. A fresh attempt at Asiatic conquest was made in the 10th century by Sheshonq I (biblical Shishak; 1 Kings 11:29-40; 14:25-26), and Solomon traded with Egypt in the same century (see Cilicians). He also married a pharaoh's daughter. But though Egyptian rulers intervened in Palestine and Syria after this (2 Kings 19:9 – see Ethiopians; 23:29; 24:1-7; Jeremiah 37:5-19; 46:1-26; Ezekiel 17:11-21), Egypt was now a 'broken reed' (2 Kings 18:21; Isaiah 36:6). The country became successively part of the Persian, Hellenistic and Roman Empires.

ELAMITES The eastern neighbours of the Sumerians and Babylonians (Elam = modern Khuzistan in south-west Persia), whose capital, Susa, became important under their successors, the Persians.

Pilgrims from Elam were in Jerusalem for Pentecost (Acts 2:9).

ETHIOPIANS The southern neighbours of the Egyptians who inhabited, not modern Ethiopia, but the territory along the Nile from Aswan to Khartoum, the northern part of which corresponds to Nubia. This was known in ancient times as Cush.

In the 1st millennium, Ethiopia, with its capital at Napata, at times equalled the power of Egypt, its former ruler. In the 9th century the Egyptians employed an Ethiopian general against Palestine (2 Chronicles 14:9-15). In the 8th-7th centuries an Ethiopian dynasty (the 25th) took over Egypt and intervened in Palestine (2 Kings 19:9), and they continued to serve under the Saite (26th dynasty) pharaohs (Jeremiah 46:9). Ethiopia was at the furthest limit of the Persian Empire (Esther 1:1; 8:9), and

though its officials might travel in the Near East (Acts 8:27), it was too remote to be permanently ruled by the great powers.

GREEKS Known in the Near East by the name of their Asiatic territory, Ionia – the 'Javan' of the Old Testament (Isaiah 66:19; Ezekiel 27:13; Daniel 8:21; 10:20; 11:2; Zechariah 9:13). In the New Testament they are referred to by the name *hellenes*, Greeks (Romans 1:14, though this word was often used of Gentiles in general, e.g. John 7:35).

HITTITES An Indo-European-speaking people who established a civilization in central Asia Minor and controlled much of northern Syria in the 14th and 13th centuries. Their empire was destroyed by northern invaders (see Philistines) about 1200 BC. Many of the Hittites mentioned in the Old Testament were Neo- or Syro-Hittites.

After the destruction of the Hittite Empire in Asia Minor, some of the people migrated to north Syria where they dominated such city-states as Carchemish (see also Cilicia). These people, now known as Neo- or Syro-Hittites, were the biblical Hittites of the period of Israel's kings.

HURRIANS A northern people who spread through the Near East during the 2nd millennium BC. They were prominent in the population at Nuzi, where customs similar to those of the patriarchs are attested in 15th-century BC documents. They appear in the Bible as 'Horites' and probably 'Hivites' (the 'v' represents Hebrew w, which could be confused with r in later forms of the script.

LYDIANS An Indo-European-speaking people of western Asia Minor who succeeded to the territories of Phrygia, confronted Media, and succumbed to Persia in the 6th century BC. They are probably the 'Lud' of Isaiah 66:19; Jeremiah 46:9; Ezekiel 27:10; 30:5, though the associated names in the second and fourth of these passages might point to north Africa.

MANNAEANS: see Scythians.

MEDES An Indo-European-speaking people who controlled an empire in Persia and Asia Minor in the 7th and 6th centuries BC, from their capital Ecbatana, modern Hamadan, in north-west Persia. In 550 BC Cyrus of Persia incorporated Media into his growing empire. From then on, Medes held a prominent place in Persian life. On their presence at Pentecost, see Elamites.

MIDIANITES The southern neighbours of the Edomites, whose territory extended at times into the Hijaz of Arabia. They were camel-riding semi-nomads who were a threat to the Israelites in the time of Judges.

MOABITES The inhabitants of the area bounded on the north by Ammon, on the west by the Dead Sea, and on the south by Edom. The Moabites passed through much the same phases as the Ammonites (see above).

They were frequently in conflict with Israel. They refused to allow the Israelites to pass through their territory at the time of the conquest. Their own account of one episode in the 9th century is given on the Moabite Stone. The Moabite (or Mesha) Stone shows

that they spoke a Semitic-Canaanite language closely akin to Hebrew.

NABATAEANS: see Arabians.

PERSIANS An Indo-European-speaking people who conquered the Babylonians in the 6th century BC and went on to control an empire stretching from India to the Aegean and Egypt. Their main capital cities were Pasargadae and Persepolis in the mountains of south-west Persia, and the ancient Elamite capital Susa (biblical Shushan, Daniel 8:2; Nehemiah 1:1; Esther) in the lowland plain. Their liberally administered empire lasted until it became part of the still more extensive empire of Alexander the Great in the 4th century BC.

PHILISTINES Part of a group known as the Sea Peoples, who migrated into the Near East from the Aegean area in the 14th-13th centuries BC. They were repulsed from Egypt and settled on the southern coast of Palestine where they threatened the recently settled Israelites until they were finally conquered by David. The Philistines who had dealings with the patriarchs (Genesis 21, 26), were probably earlier, Aegean peoples, distinct from those of the late Bronze Age. The Philistines continued to occupy the southern coast of Palestine, and a contingent formed part of David's body-guard. They finally lost their independence to David (2 Samuel 5:25), and were probably largely assimilated, though they retained some cultural distinctiveness (see Nehemiah 13:24; 1 Maccabees 10:83-84).

PHOENICIANS The Semitic-speaking inhabitants of the Levant coast north of Palestine. They were active in east Mediterranean trade from the 11th century BC onwards, operating from such cities as Tyre, Sidon, and Byblos (1 Kings 5:18; Ezekiel 27:9). The name is Greek, *Phoinike*, probably meaning '(land of the) purple dye' (from *phoinos*, 'red'). They referred to themselves as Canaanites, whose descendants they were, and appear in the Old Testament as the people of Tyre, or, less commonly, Sidonians (e.g. 1 Kings 5:6).

PHRYGIANS An Indo-European-speaking people who occupied west central Asia Minor after the collapse of Hittite power, and established a kingdom there in the early 1st millennium BC. Phrygia was overrun by the Cimmerians in the 7th century BC, and subsequently became part of the Lydian kingdom. The Phrygians are probably to be identified with the Mushku of the Assyrian inscriptions and 'Meshech' of the Bible, who appear as a warlike northern people (Ezekiel 32:26; 38:2-3; 39:1).

SCYTHIANS A nomadic steppe people, a group of whom followed the Cimmerians over the Caucasus from south Russia into north-west Persia in the 7th century BC, where they became neighbours and allies of the Mannaeans.

This association is reflected in Jeremiah 51:27 where Urartians (Ararat), Mannaeans (Minni) and Scythians (Ashkenaz) are summoned against Babylon. For a time they rivalled the Medes, but eventually became part of their empire and that of the succeeding Achaemenids. The main body of

Scythians remained in south Russia.
SUMERIANS The early inhabitants of
Sumer, the southern part of Babylonia. and
the creators of Babylonian civilization,
which later absorbed and succeeded them
in southern Mesopotamia. Their great
period was during the 3rd millennium BC.
After about 2000 BC, their language was
replaced in common use by Akkadian. It
was, however, preserved as a scholarly
language, and in Sumerian literary texts,
down to Hellenistic times. The Sumerians
are not mentioned in the Bible, but 'Shinar'
in Genesis is probably the counterpart of
Sumerian *kengir*=Akkadian *sumeru*,
meaning the land of Sumer. In Genesis it
seems to refer to the whole of Babylonia.
SYRIANS: see Aramaeans.
URARTIANS A people speaking a language
related to Hurrian, who emerged as a
military power in the area of Armenia in the
9th century BC. They were possibly
descendants of Hurrians who had occupied
that area. They were a military threat to the
Assyrians with whom they were often at war.
Their chief god was Haldi, after whom some
authors have referred to them as Chaldians
(not to be confused with Chaldeans; see
above). Noah's ark is said to have landed on
the mountains of Ararat (Genesis 8:4), i.e.
somewhere in what was later Urartu, not
necessarily modern Mt Ararat, which only
received this name at a later date.

Who's Who in the Bible

A list of those who played a significant part in the Bible
narrative, with the most important Bible references.

AARON Moses' brother and spokesman;
first high priest of Israel: Exodus 4 - Numbers 33/pp.156ff. *Before Pharaoh:* Exodus
5ff. *Aaron's robes and consecration:*
Exodus 28 - 29; Leviticus 8. *The golden calf:*
Exodus 32. Atonement ritual: Leviticus 16.
Aaron and Miriam challenge Moses: Num-
bers 12. *Aaron's rod:* Numbers 17. *Death:*
Numbers 33:38-39.
ABEDNEGO One of Daniel's companions
exiled to Babylon: Daniel 1 - 3/pp.430,
432.
ABEL Second son of Adam and Eve;
brother of Cain: Genesis 4/p.129.
ABIATHAR Son of Ahimelech priest of Nob
who joined David; became joint high priest
with Zadok: 1 Samuel 22:20ff.
ABIGAIL Nabal's wife; later married David:
1 Samuel 25/pp.240-241.
ABIHU Son of Aaron; destroyed with
Nadab: Exodus 6:23; Leviticus 10/p.174.
ABIJAH Son of Jeroboam I: 1 Kings
14/p.264.
ABIJAH/ABIJAM Son of Rehoboam; king
of Judah: 1 Kings 15; 2 Chronicles 13/p.265.
ABIMELECH 1. King(s) of Gerar: Genesis
20; 26/pp.140, 143. **2.** Son of Gideon:
Judges 8:31ff.
ABIRAM Conspired against Moses with
Korah and Dathan: Numbers 16/p.189.
ABISHAG The girl from Shunem who
attended David: 1 Kings 1 - 2/p.251.
ABISHAI Brother of Joab and one of
David's thirty warriors: 1 Samuel 26:6ff./
p.241.
ABNER Sauls' army commander; killed by
Joab and Abishai: 1 Samuel 14:50 - 2
Samuel 3/pp.237-243.
ABRAHAM/ABRAM Father of the nation of
Israel; man of outstanding faith: Genesis
11:26 - 25:10/pp.135-142. *God's call:*
Genesis 12. *The meeting with Melchizedek:*
14. *God's covenant:* 17. *The 'sacrifice' of
Isaac:* 22. *Death:* 25:8.
ABSALOM Son of David; led a rebellion
against his father: 2 Samuel 13 - 18/pp.
246-248.
ACHAN Stoned for taking spoil from
Jericho: Joshua 7/p.211.
ACHISH King of Gath with whom David
took refuge: 1 Samuel 21; 27 - 29/pp.
239, 242.
ADAM The first man; created by God and
given charge of the Garden of Eden. By
his disobedience he brought sin and death
on the whole human race: Genesis 1 - 4;
see Romans 5:12ff. etc./pp. 127-128, 583ff.
ADONIJAH David's son who attempted to
seize the throne destined for Solomon:
1 Kings 1 - 2/pp. 251-252.
AGABUS Prophet who predicted famine
and Paul's imprisonment: Acts 11:27-30;
21:7-14/pp. 557-558, 566.
AGRIPPA Herod Agrippa II, who heard

Paul's defence at Caesarea: Acts 25:13 - 26:
32/p. 568
32/p. 568. See too article p. 540.
AHAB King of Israel (husband of Jezebel)
who seized Naboth's vineyard; opponent of
Elijah: 1 Kings 16:29 - 22:40/pp. 265-268.
AHASUERUS King of Persia who made
Esther his queen: Esther/pp. 313-315.
AHAZ Son of Jotham, king of Judah; father
of Hezekiah: 2 Kings 15:38ff.; 2 Chronicles
27:9ff.
AHAZIAH 1. Ahab's son; king of Israel: 1
Kings 22:40ff. **2.** Son of Joram, king of
Judah: 2 Kings 8:24ff.; 2 Chronicles
22:1ff./p. 298.
AHIJAH Prophesied to Jeroboam the revolt
of the ten tribes: 1 Kings 11: 29ff.; 14/p. 264.
AHIMAAZ Son of Zadok who passed
information to David during Absalom's
rebellion and brought news of victory:
2 Samuel 17:17ff.; 18/p. 248.
AHIMELECH Priest of Nob, killed for
assisting David: 1 Samuel 21 - 22/pp.
239-240.
AHITHOPHEL David's trusted adviser who
gave his support to Absalom: 2 Samuel
15:12 - 17:23/pp. 247-248.
ALEXANDER 1. Son of Simon of Cyrene:
Mark 15:21. **2.** Leader in Jerusalem: Acts
4:6. **3.** A Jew present during the riot at
Ephesus: Acts 19:33. **4.** A Christian who
lapsed: 1 Timothy 1:20. **5.** Opponent of Paul:
2 Timothy 4:14. (These may not all be
different people.)
AMASA Commander of Absalom's army;
killed by Joab; 2 Samuel 17:25; 20.
AMAZIAH Son of Joash, king of Judah: 2
Kings 12:21 - 14:21; 2 Chronicles 24:27ff./
p.276.
AMNON Son of David; raped Tamar and
was killed by Absalom: 2 Samuel 13/p.246.
AMON Son of Manasseh, king of Judah: 2
Kings 21; 2 Chronicles 33/p.282.
AMOS Prophet from Tekoa who declared
God's message to Israel: Amos/p.444.
ANANIAS 1. Disciple who tried to deceive
the church: Acts 5/p.552. **2.** Disciple at
Damascus sent to Saul: Acts 9/p.556. **3.**
High priest who laid charges against Paul:
Acts 23:2; 24:1.
ANDREW Peter's brother, also a fisherman;
one of the 12 apostles: Matthew 4:18, etc.;
John 1:40ff./pp.503, 535.
ANNA Prophetess in the temple at the time
Jesus was presented: Luke 2:36-38/p.516.
ANNAS Jewish high priest; father-in-law of
Caiaphas before whom Jesus stood trial:
John 18:13ff./p.547.
ANTIOCHUS Name of Seleucid kings of
Syria in the time between the Testaments:
pp.437, 571.
APOLLOS Jew from Alexandria instructed
by Priscilla and Aquila; powerful preacher
influencing the church at Corinth: Acts

18:24ff.; 1 Corinthians 1 - 4/pp.564, 590ff.

AQUILA AND PRISCILLA A Christian couple who instructed Apollos and served the church in various places: Acts 18; Romans 16:3, etc./pp.564, 588.

ARAUNAH/ORNAN The man whose threshing-floor David bought, site of the temple: 2 Samuel 24:16ff.; 1 Chronicles 21:15ff./p.289.

ARCHELAUS Son of Herod the Great; ruler of Judea: Matthew 2:22/p.476.

ARCHIPPUS Colossians 4:17; Philemon 2/p.625.

ARETAS Ruler of Arabia: 2 Corinthians 11:32/p.600.

ARISTARCHUS Paul's companion and fellow worker: Acts 19:29ff.; Colossians 4:10; Philemon 24/p.613.

ARTAXERXES King of Persia: Ezra 4:7ff.; Nehemiah 2:1/p.309.

ASA King of Judah: 1 Kings 15:8ff.; 2 Chronicles 14:1ff./pp.265, 297.

ASAHEL David's nephew; killed by Abner: 2 Samuel 2:18ff./pp.242-243.

ASAPH A Levite; leader of David's choir; named in the titles of some of the Psalms: 1 Chronicles 15:17ff.; 25:1ff./p.291.

ASHURBANIPAL King of Assyria: *pictures* pp.303, 395.

ATHALIAH Daughter of Jezebel who married Jehoram of Judah and seized the throne after her son's death: 2 Kings 11; 2 Chronicles 22/pp.276, 298-299.

AUGUSTUS First Roman emperor, who ordered the census which brought Mary and Joseph to Bethlehem: Luke 2:1.

AZARIAH Name of a number of individuals, notably the son of Amaziah, King of Judah: 2 Kings 14:21ff.; 2 Chronicles 26/p.276.

BAASHA Seized the throne of Israel from Jeroboam's son: 1 Kings 15:16ff.

BALAAM Prophet called on by Balak to curse the Israelites: Numbers 22:5 - 24:25/ p.190.

BALAK Moabite king who hired Balaam to curse Israel: Numbers 22:2 - 24:25/p. 190.

BARABBAS Robber released in preference to Jesus: Matthew 27:16ff., etc.

BARAK One of the Judges; with Deborah he defeated Sisera and the Canaanites: Judges 4:6ff.

BARNABAS A Levite from Cyprus; commissioned with Paul by the church at Antioch for missionary service: Acts 4:36; 9:27; 12:25ff./pp.552-553.

BARTHOLOMEW One of the 12 apostles: Matthew 10:3, etc.

BARTIMAEUS Blind man healed by Jesus: Mark 10:46ff./p.508.

BARUCH Jeremiah's secretary: Jeremiah 32:12ff./p.405.

BARZILLAI Loyal friend of David during Absalom's rebellion: 2 Samuel 17:27ff.; 19:31ff./p.249.

BATHSHEBA Wife of Uriah the Hittite; David committed adultery with her and later married her; mother of Solomon: 2 Samuel 11 - 12; 1 Kings 1 - 2/pp.245- 246.

BELSHAZZAR King of Babylon overthrown by the Persians: Daniel 5/pp.432-434.

BELTESHAZZAR Babylonian name given to Daniel: Daniel 1:7/p.431.

BENAIAH One of David's officers responsible for proclaiming Solomon king: 1 Kings 1 - 2/p.251.

BEN-HADAD The name of several rulers of Damascus: 1 Kings 15:18ff.; 20:1ff.; 2 Kings 6:24ff.; 8:7ff.; 13:3ff./p.266.

BENJAMIN Jacob's youngest son; Rachel died giving birth to him; father of the tribe of Benjamin which sided with Judah at the division of the kingdom: Genesis 35:18; 42 - 49/pp.142, 149-150.

BERNICE Sister of Herod Agrippa II; with him when he heard Paul's case at Caesarea: Acts 25:13ff.

BEZALEL The craftsman chosen to construct the tabernacle and its furnishings: Exodus 35:30ff.

BILDAD One of Job's three friends: Job 2:11, etc./p.320.

BILHAH Rachel's servant; mother of Dan and Naphtali: Genesis 29:29; 30:3, etc.

BOAZ Landowner of Bethlehem who became Ruth's husband and ancestor of David: Ruth 2 - 4/pp.226-228.

CAESAR Emperor of Rome: in the Gospels, Augustus (Luke 2:1) or Tiberius; in Acts, Claudius; elsewhere, Nero: Matthew 22:17ff.; John 19:12ff.; Acts 17:7; 25:8ff.; Philippians 4:22/pp. 571-573; *pictures:* Nero p.637; Domitian p.653.

CAIAPHAS High priest before whom Jesus stood trial: Matthew 26:3; Luke 3:2; John 18:13ff./pp.511, 547.

CAIN Eldest son of Adam and Eve, who killed his brother Abel: Genesis 4/p.129.

CALEB Sent to spy out Canaan; only he and Joshua of the twelve advised advance; in his old age he claimed possession of Hebron and drove out the Anakim: Numbers 13 - 14; Joshua 14 - 15/p.188.

CANAAN Son of Ham; cursed by his grandfather, Noah: Genesis 9:18ff./p.134.

CEPHAS See Peter.

CHEDORLAOMER King of Elam who headed a punitive raid against Sodom and Gomorrah; pursued and killed by Abraham: Genesis 14/p.137.

CLAUDIUS Emperor of Rome: Acts 11:28; 18:2/p.564.

CLAUDIUS LYSIAS Military tribune in Jerusalem who took Paul into custody: Acts 21:31 - 23:30/p.507.

CLEMENT Philippian Christian; Paul's fellow worker: Philippians 4:3.

CLEOPAS One of the two the risen Jesus met on the road to Emmaus: Luke 24:13ff.

CORNELIUS Roman centurion to whose household Peter was sent to preach the gospel: Acts 10/p.557.

CRESCENS Companion of Paul; sent to Galatia: 2 Timothy 4:10.

CRISPUS Convert at Corinth baptized by Paul: Acts 18:8; 1 Corinthians 1:14.

CUSHAN-RISHATHAIM Oppressor of Israel at the time of the Judges: Judges 3:7ff./ p.221.

CYRUS King of Persia who overthrew the Babylonians and returned the Jews from exile: Ezra 1:1ff. - 6:14; Isaiah 44:28ff.; Daniel 1:21/pp.306, 390, 431.

DAN One of Jacob's 12 sons and ancestor

of the tribe of Dan: Genesis 30:5-6, etc.

DANIEL Taken captive to Babylon as a young man and trained for service at court; interpreter of dreams and a visionary; one of the great Old Testament prophets: Daniel pp.430ff.

DARIUS 1. Darius the Mede who succeeded to the kingdom of Babylon after Belshazzar's death; known only from the book of Daniel: Daniel 5:31/p.434. **2.** Darius 1, king of Persia, under whom the temple was rebuilt: Ezra 4 - 6; Haggai 1:1; Zechariah 1:1/p.307. **3.** Darius II: Nehemiah 12:22.

DATHAN Rebelled against Moses with korah and Abiram: Numbers 16/p.189.

DAVID The shepherd boy who became Israel's second king and founded the royal line from which the Messiah was eventually born; composer/collector of many of the Psalms: 1 Samuel 16 - 1 Kings 2; 1 Chronicles 11 - 29/pp.238ff., 287ff. *Anointed king by Samuel:* 1 Samuel 16. *David and Goliath:* 17. *Friendship with Jonathan:* 18 - 20. *David on the run from Saul:* 19 - 31. *Lament for Saul and Jonathan:* 2 Samuel 1. *Capture of Jerusalem:* 5. *The ark brought to Jerusalem:* 6; 1 Chronicles 15. *God's promise of a lasting dynasty:* 2 Samuel 7; 1 Chronicles 17. *David and Bathsheba:* 2 Samuel 11 - 12. *Absalom's rebellion:* 15 - 18. *Arrangements for the temple:* 1 Chronicles 22ff. *Succession of Solomon and David's death:* 1 Kings 1 - 2:11; 1 Chronicles 29.

DEBORAH Prophetess in the time of the Judges who joined with Barak to overthrow Sisera: Judges 4 - 5/pp.221-222.

DELILAH Philistine woman who betrayed Samson: Judges 16/p.224.

DEMAS Paul's fellow worker who in the end deserted him: Colossians 4:14; 2 Timothy 4:10/pp.613, 622.

DEMETRIUS 1. Silversmith at Ephesus: Acts 19:24. **2.** Christian commended by John: 3 John 12/p.643.

DIANA Goddess of the Ephesians: Acts 19/p.565 *(with pictures).*

DINAH Jacob's daughter, whose rape by Shechem was cruelly avenged by Simeon and Levi: Genesis 34/p.146.

DIONYSIUS Member of the Areopagus council at Athens who became a Christian: Acts 17:34.

DIOTREPHES A self-seeking church leader denounced by John: 3 John 9-10/p.643.

DOEG Edomite servant of Saul who informed him that Ahimelech had helped David: 1 Samuel 21:7; 22:9ff./p.240.

DORCAS/TABITHA Woman noted for her good works, whom Peter raised from the dead: Acts 9:36ff.

DRUSILLA Jewish wife of the Procurator Felix, who heard Paul's case: Acts 24:24/ p.568.

EBED-MELECH Ethiopian servant of Zedekiah who saved Jeremiah's life: Jeremiah 38. 39:16ff./p.408.

EGLON King of Moab killed by Ehud: Judges 3/p.221.

EHUD Israelite champion who assassinated Eglon of Moab: Judges 3/p.221.

ELAH The name of a number of individuals. notably the son of Baasha king of Israel. assassinated by Zimri: 1 Kings 16/ p.265.

ELEAZAR Aaron's son; consecrated priest and put in charge of the Levites: Exodus 6:23; Leviticus 10; Numbers; Joshua 14:1. etc./pp.173ff.

ELI Priest and Judge at Shiloh who preceded Samuel: 1 Samuel 1 - 4/pp.231ff.

ELIAKIM Name of several individuals. the most notable being the steward over Hezekiah's household who negotiated with Sennacherib's officers: 2 Kings 18:18ff.; Isaiah.36.

ELIASHIB High priest in the time of Nehemiah; took part in rebuilding the city walls; later compromised with Nehemiah's enemies: Nehemiah 3:13.

ELIEZER Name of several individuals. notably Abraham's chief servant and adopted heir: Genesis 15:2.

ELIHU Angry young man in the story of Job: Job 32:2ff./p.325.

ELIJAH One of Israel's greatest prophets. contemporary with Ahab: 1 Kings 17 - 2 Kings 2/pp.265ff. *The drought:* 1 Kings 17. *Contest with the prophets of Baal:* 18. *The 'still, small voice':* 19. *The chariot of fire:* 2 Kings 2. *Elijah's appearance at the transfiguration of Christ:* Mark 9:4ff.

ELIMELECH Husband of Naomi: Ruth 1:2.

ELIPHAZ One of Job's three friends: Job 2:11, etc./pp.320ff.

ELISHA Elijah's successor as prophet of Israel: 1 Kings 19:16ff.; 2 Kings 2 - 9; 13/pp.266ff. *Elisha and the Shunammite woman:* 2 Kings 4. *Healing of Naaman:* 2 Kings 5.

ELIZABETH Wife of Zechariah and mother of John the Baptist: Luke 1/p.515.

ELKANAH Father of Samuel: 1 Samuel 1.

ELYMAS Magician who opposed Paul and Barnabas in Cyprus: Acts 13/p.558.

ENOCH Descendant of Adam's son Seth who 'walked with God' and was taken into his presence without dying: Genesis 5:18-24/p.131.

EPAPHRAS Paul's friend and fellow worker: Colossians 1:7, etc./p.611.

EPAPHRODITUS Christian sent to Paul by the Philippian church: Philippians 2:25ff./p.608-610.

EPHRAIM Son of Joseph; ancestor of the tribe of Ephraim: Genesis 41:52; 48:13ff., etc./p.150.

EPHRON Hittite from whom Abraham bought the cave of Machpelah: Genesis 23/p.141.

ERASTUS 1. Paul's assistant; sent to Macedonia with Timothy: Acts 19:22; 2 Timothy 4:20. **2.** City treasurer of Corinth: Romans 16:23/p.588.

ESARHADDON Succeeded Sennacherib as king of Assyria: 2 Kings 19:37.

ESAU Son of Isaac and Rebekah; twin brother of Jacob; bartered away his blessing and was cheated of his birthright: Genesis 25:25ff.; 27 - 28:9; 32 - 33; 36/pp. 143, 145-146.

ESTHER Jewish exile who became the queen of the Persian king Ahasuerus; heroine of the book of Esther/pp.313-315.

EUNICE Mother of Timothy: 2 Timothy 1:5.

EUTYCHUS Young man who fell from a window during Paul's sermon at Troas and was restored to life: Acts 20:9ff.

EVE The first woman; prompted by Satan to disobey God: Genesis 3/p.128.

EVIL-MERODACH Amel-marduk, king of Babylon, who released Jehoiachin from prison: 2 Kings 25:27; Jeremiah 52:31.

EZEKIEL Great Old Testament prophet and visionary whose prophecies to the Jewish exiles in Babylonia are recorded in the book of Ezekiel/pp.416ff. *Ezekiel's visions of God:* Ezekiel 1; 10. *The watchman:* 3; 33. *Death of Ezekiel's wife:* 24. *Valley of dry bones:* 37. *Vision of the temple:* 40ff. *The river of life:* 47.

EZRA Priest and scribe who returned to Jerusalem with a company of exiles; responsible for re-enforcing the Jewish law: Ezra 7 - 10; Nehemiah 8 - 9/pp.307-308. 310.

FELIX Roman procurator who kept Paul in prison at Caesarea: Acts 23:24 - 24:27/ pp. 567-568.

FESTUS Successor to Felix as procurator of Judea; heard Paul's case at Caesarea: Acts 25 - 26/p.568.

GABRIEL The angel sent to interpret Daniel's vision; to Zechariah to announce the birth of John the Baptist; to Mary to announce the birth of Jesus: Daniel 8:16; 9:21; Luke 1:19, 26/p.435.

GAD Son of Jacob and Leah's maid, Zilpah; ancestor of one of the tribes of Israel: Genesis 30:11; 49:19.

GAIUS 1. A Macedonian involved in the riot at Ephesus: Acts 19:29. **2.** Paul's companion on the journey to Jerusalem: Acts 20:4. **3.** A Corinthian whom Paul baptized: 1 Corinthians 1:14. **4.** The person to whom John wrote his third letter: 3 John 1/p.643. These may or may not be four different people.

Miracles of Jesus

	Matthew	Mark	Luke	John
Healing of physical and mental disorders				
Leper	8:2-3	1:40-42	5:12-13	
Centurion's servant	8:5-13		7:1-10	
Peter's mother-in-law	8:14-15	1:30-31	4:38-39	
Two Gadarenes	8:28-34	5:1-15	8:27-35	
Paralysed man	9:2-7	2:3-12	5:18-25	
Woman with a haemorrhage	9:20-22	5:25-29	8:43-48	
Two blind men	9:27-31			
Man dumb and possessed	9:32-33			
Man with a withered hand	12:10-13	3:1-5	6:6-10	
Man blind, dumb and possessed	12:22		11:14	
Canaanite woman's daughter	15:21-28	7:24-30		
Boy with epilepsy	17:14-18	9:17-29	9:38-43	
Bartimaeus. and another blind man	20:29-34	10:46-52	18:35-43	
Deaf and dumb man		7:31-37		
Man possessed, synagogue		1:23-26	4:33-35	
Blind man at Bethsaida		8:22-26		
Woman bent double			13:11-13	
Man with dropsy			14:1-4	
Ten lepers			17:11-19	
Malchus' ear			22:50-51	
Official's son at Capernaum				4:46-54
Sick man, Pool of Bethesda				5:1-9
Man born blind				9
Command over the forces of nature				
Calming of the storm	8:23-27	4:37-41	8:22-25	
Walking on the water	14:25	6:48-51		6:19-21
5,000 people fed	14:15-21	6:35-44	9:12-17	6:5-13
4,000 people fed	15:32-38	8:1-9		
Coin in the fish's mouth	17:24-27			
Fig-tree withered	21:18-22	11:12-14, 20-26		
Catch of fish			5:1-11	
Water turned into wine				2:1-11
Another catch of fish				21:1-11
Bringing the dead back to life				
Jairus' daughter	9:18-19, 23-25	5:22-24, 38-42	8:41-42, 49-56	
Widow's son at Nain			7:11-15	
Lazarus				11:1-44

GALLIO Proconsul of Achaia (and brother of Seneca the tutor of Nero) whose decision against the Jews who brought charges against Paul gave the church new freedom: Acts 18/pp.564, 573.

GAMALIEL Influential rabbi and member of the Sanhedrin who advised cautious handling of the apostles: Acts 5:34ff.; 22:3/p.553.

GEDALIAH Appointed governor of Judah by Nebuchadnezzar; assassinated after only a few months: 2 Kings 25; Jeremiah 39:14 - 41:18/pp.283, 409.

GEHAZI Servant of Elisha; punished for seeking reward from Naaman: 2 Kings 4 - 5; 8:4f./pp.273-274.

GERSHON Son of Levi; head of one of the three Levitical families: Exodus 6:16-17; Numbers 3:17ff./pp.185-186.

GESHEM An Arabian; one of Nehemiah's main opponents: Nehemiah 2:19; 6:1ff./p.309.

GIDEON Delivered Israel from the Midianites in the time of the Judges: Judges 6 - 8/p.222.

GOG Leader of invading northern peoples to be destroyed by God: Ezekiel 38 - 39/pp.426-427. 'Gog and Magog': quoted as symbol of the anti-God forces in the final onslaught: Revelation 20:8/p.656.

GOLIATH Philistine champion killed by David: 1 Samuel 17/p.238.

HABAKKUK Prophet whose puzzlement over God's use of the Chaldaeans to punish his people is recorded in the book of Habakkuk/pp.452-453.

HADADEZER/HADAREZER King of Zobah, defeated by David: 2 Samuel 8; 10; 1 Kings 11:23; 1 Chronicles 18 - 19.

HADASSAH Esther's earlier name.

HAGAR Sarah's Egyptian servant; mother of Ishmael: Genesis 16; 21/p.140.

HAGGAI Prophet who stirred the people to rebuild the temple after the return from exile: Haggai/p.455.

HAM Noah's son; father of a number of nations: Genesis 5:32; 9:18ff.; 10:6ff./pp.134-135.

HAMAN Villain of the book of Esther, who plotted against the Jews: Esther/pp.314-315.

HAMMURABI King of Babylon, compiler of a code of laws: picture p.202.

HANAMEL Jeremiah's cousin who sold him the field at Anathoth during the Babylonian invasion: Jeremiah 32/p.405.

HANANI Nehemiah's brother, who told him of the trouble in Jerusalem: Nehemiah 1:2/p.309.

HANANIAH False prophet denounced by Jeremiah: Jeremiah 28/p.405.

HANNAH Mother of Samuel: Samuel 1 - 2pp.231-232.

HAZAEL Seized the throne of Syria after assassinating Ben-hadad, following Elisha's prediction: 1 Kings 19:15-17; 2 Kings 8ff./pp.266, 274.

HEMAN Appointed by David as one of the leaders of the temple music: 1 Chronicles 16:41-42; 25/p.291.

HEROD 1. Herod the Great: Matthew 2; Luke 1:5. **2.** Herod Antipas: Matthew 14; Mark 6; Luke 3; 9; 23; Acts 4:27; 13:1. **3.** Herod Agrippa I: Acts 12/see special article, 'The Herod Family', p.540.

HERODIAS Wife of Herod Antipas who brought about the death of John the Baptist: Matthew 14; Mark 6; Luke 3:19/p.505.

HEZEKIAH One of Judah's most outstanding kings; contemporary of Isaiah; besieged in Jerusalem by the Assyrians: 2 Kings 18 - 20; 2 Chronicles 29 - 32; Isaiah 36 - 39/pp.281-282.

HILKIAH High priest at the time of Josiah; discovered the book of the law: 2 Kings 22 - 23; 2 Chronicles 34/p.282.

HIRAM King of Tyre, in alliance with David and Solomon; supplied cedar and skilled labour for the temple; joined with Solomon to operate a Red Sea trading fleet: 1 Kings 5; 9 - 10/pp.255, 258.

HOPHNI AND PHINEHAS Eli's unprincipled sons: 1 Samuel 2; 4/p.232.

HOSEA Prophet of God's love for his faithless people: Hosea/pp.438ff.

HOSHEA Last king of the northern kingdom of Israel: 2 Kings 17/p.279.

HULDAH Prophetess consulted by Hilkiah after he discovered the book of the law: 2 Kings 22:14ff.; 2 Chronicles 34:22ff.

HUSHAI David's friend who persuaded Absalom not to take Ahithophel's advice: 2 Samuel 15:32 - 17:15/pp.247-248.

HYMENAEUS Disciplined by Paul for unsettling people's faith with false teaching: 1 Timothy 1:20; 2 Timothy 2:17.

ISAAC Son of Abraham; father of Jacob and Esau: Genesis 21 - 35/pp.140ff. 'Sacrifice' of Isaac: Genesis 22. Wife for Isaac: 24. Blessing of Jacob: 27.

ISAIAH Great Old Testament prophet: 2 Kings 19 - 20; Isaiah/pp.281-282, 376ff. Call: Isaiah 6. Great Prophecies: the branch, Isaiah 4; Immanuel 7; the great light, a son is born, 9; a shoot from Jesse, wolf shall

Parables of Jesus

	Matthew	Mark	Luke
Lamp under a bushel	5:14-15	4:21-22	8:16; 11:33
Houses on rock and on sand	7:24-27		6:47-49
New cloth on an old garment	9:16	2:21	5:36
New wine in old wineskins	9:17	2:22	5:37-38
Sower and soils	13:3-8	4:3-8	8:5-8
Mustard seed	13:31-32	4:30-32	13:18-19
Tares	13:24-30		
Leaven (yeast)	13:33		13:20-21
Hidden treasure	13:44		
Pearl of great value	13:45-46		
Drag-net	13:47-48		
Lost sheep	18:12-13		15:4-6
Two debtors (unforgiving servant)	18:23-34		
Workers in the vineyard	20:1-16		
Two sons	21:28-31		
Wicked tenants	21:33-41	12:1-9	20:9-16
Invitation to the wedding-feast; man without a wedding-garment	22:2-14		
Fig-tree as herald of summer	24:32-33	13:28-29	21:29-32
Ten 'bridesmaids'	25:1-13		
Talents (Matthew); Pounds (Luke)	25:14-30		19:12-27
Sheep and goats	25:31-36		
Seedtime to harvest		4:26-29	
Creditor and the debtors			7:41-43
Good Samaritan			10:30-37
Friend in need			11:5-8
Rich fool			12:16-21
Alert servants			12:35-40
Faithful steward			12:42-48
Fig-tree without figs			13:6-9
Places of honour at the wedding-feast			14:7-14
Great banquet and the reluctant guests			14:16-24
Counting the cost			14:28-33
Lost coin			15:8-10
The prodigal son			15:11-32
Dishonest steward			16:1-8
Rich man and Lazarus			16:19-31
The master and his servant			17:7-10
The persistent widow and the unrighteous judge			18:2-5
The Pharisee and the tax collector			18:10-14

dwell with the lamb, 11 - 12; *desert shall blossom*, 35; *comfort my people*, 40; *'servant songs'*, 42; 49; 50; 52 - 53; 61; *arise, shine*, 60; *Sennacherib's invasion*: 36 - 39.
ISHBOSHETH Saul's son, made king by Abner: 2 Samuel 2 - 4/p.243.
ISHMAEL Son of Abraham and Hagar: Genesis 16 - 17; 25/pp.140,142.
ISRAEL Later name of Jacob, and the nation descended from him.
ISSACHAR Son of Jacob and father of one of the tribes of Israel: Genesis 30:18; 49:14f.
ITHAMAR Son of Aaron; priest of Israel: Exodus 6:23; Numbers 3ff./p.186.
ITTAI Philistine from Gath who stood by David during Absalom's rebellion: 2 Samuel 15; 18.

JABIN King of Hazor whose army was defeated by Deborah and Barak: Judges 4/p.222.
JACOB Son of Isaac who supplanted his elder brother Esau; father of the twelve tribes of Israel: Genesis 25 - 49/pp.142ff. *The birthright*: Genesis 25. *Isaac's blessing*: 27. *The dream at Bethel*: 28. *Jacob and Laban*: 29 - 31. *Jacob wrestles with God*: 32. *God's promise*: 35. *Journey to Egypt*: 44. *Blessing of his sons*: 49.
JAEL Wife of Heber who killed Sisera with a tent peg: Judges 4/p.223.
JAIRUS Ruler of the synagogue whose daughter Jesus restored to life: Mark 5:1ff./pp.504-505.
JAMES 1. Son of Zebedee, brother of John; one of the 12 apostles: Matthew 4:21f.; 10:2; 17:1ff.; Mark 10:35ff.; Acts 12:2/pp.503, 558. **2.** Son of Alphaeus: another of the apostles, probably the same as 'James the less': Matthew 10:3, etc. **3.** Brother of Jesus who became leader of the Jerusalem church; author of the letter of James: Matthew 13:55; Acts 12:17; 15:13ff.; 21:18; 1 Corinthians 15:7; Galatians 1:19; 2:9; James/pp.550, 560, 633-634.
JAPHETH One of Noah's three sons; ancestor of a number of nations: Genesis 5:32; 9:18ff.; 10:1ff./p.135.
JASON Paul's host who was held answerable for him at Thessalonica: Acts 17:5ff.
JEDUTHUN Appointed by David as one of the leaders of the temple music: 1 Chronicles 16:41-42; 25/p.291.
JEHOAHAZ 1. Son of Jehu, king of Israel: 2 Kings 13 - 14/p.276. **2.** Son of Josiah, king of Judah; deposed by Pharaoh Necho: 2 Kings 23:30ff.; 2 Chronicles 36/pp.283, 302.
JEHOASH King of Israel: 2 Kings 13/p.276; see also Joash.
JEHOIACHIN Son of Jehoiakim, king of Judah; taken to Babylon by Nebuchadnezzar, released from prison by his successor: 2 Kings 24; 25:27ff.; 2 Chronicles 36; Jeremiah 52:31ff./pp. 283, 302, 412.
JEHOIADA The name of a number of individuals, notably the chief priest responsible for the coup which dethroned Athaliah and placed Joash on the throne of Judah: 2 Kings 11 - 12; 2 Chronicles 23 - 24/pp.276, 299.
JEHOIAKIM Eliakim, son of Josiah, king of Judah; placed on the throne by Pharaoh

Necho; king who burnt Jeremiah's scroll of prophecies: 2 Kings 23:34ff.; 2 Chronicles 36; Jeremiah 22:18ff.; 26; 36/pp. 283, 302, 403, 405, 406.
JEHORAM/JORAM 1. Son of Ahab, king of Israel, killed by Jehu: 2 Kings 3; 8 - 9; 2 Chronicles 22/pp.272, 274. **2.** Son of Jehoshaphat, king of Judah: 2 Kings 8:16ff.; 2 Chronicles 21/pp.274, 298.
JEHOSHAPHAT Son of Asa, king of Judah; allied by marriage to Ahab of Israel; fought with him against the Syrians at Ramoth-gilead: 1 Kings 22; 2 Kings 3; 2 Chronicles 17 - 21/p.297.
JEHOSHEBA/JEHOSHABEATH Princess of Judah and wife of Jehoiada who saved the life of Joash: 2 Kings 11:2-3; 2 Chronicles 22:11-12/p.276.
JEHONADAB/JONADAB 1. One of David's family, involved in the rape of Tamar: 2 Samuel 13. **2.** Son of Rechab, who helped Jehu wipe out the worshippers of Baal: 2 Kings 10.
JEHU Anointed by God through Elisha to destroy Ahab's line and become king of Israel: 2 Kings 9 - 10/pp.274-276.
JEHUDI Officer at Jehoiakim's court who read Jeremiah's scroll to the king: Jeremiah 36.
JEPHTHAH The Judge whose vow resulted in the death of his daughter: Judges 11 - 12/p.223.
JEREMIAH Great prophet of Judah at the time of its fall to Babylon: 2 Chronicles 35:25; 36:12, 21-22; Jeremiah/pp.302-303, 396ff. *Call*: Jeremiah 1. *The potter*: 18 - 19. *The yoke of Babylon*: 27 - 28. *The new covenant*: 31. *Purchase of the field*: 32. *Reading of the scroll*: 36. *In the cistern*: 38. *Taken to Egypt*: 43.
JEROBOAM 1. Jeroboam 1, first king of the northern kingdom of Israel, who set up shrines to rival Jerusalem: 1 Kings 11:26 - 14:20/pp.263-264. **2.** Jeroboam II, one of Israel's most illustrious kings; social evils and empty ritual of his reign attacked by the prophets: 2 Kings 14:23-29; Amos 7/pp.277, 444.
JERUBBAAL Another name for Gideon.
JESSE David's father; grandson of Ruth and Boaz: 1 Samuel 16 - 17.
JESUS CHRIST See under Key Themes and Subjects and Events.
JETHRO/REUEL Moses' father-in-law: Exodus 2:16ff.; 3:1; 4:18; 18/p.164.
JEZEBEL Princess of Tyre and Sidon who married Ahab and introduced Baal worship in Israel; responsible for Naboth's death; thrown to her death on Jehu's orders: 1 Kings 16:31; 18:4, 13, 19; 19:1-2; 21; 2 Kings 9/pp.265ff.
JOAB Nephew of David and commander of his army; responsible for Abner's death; reconciled David and Absalom; supported Adonijah against Solomon: 2 Samuel 2 - 3; 10 - 11; 14; 18 - 20; 24; 2 Kings 1 - 2; also 1 Chronicles 11ff./pp.242-243, 247-252.
JOANNA One of the women who provided for Jesus and the 12; present on the resurrection morning: Luke 8:3; 24:10/pp.519, 521.
JOASH Rescued from Athaliah's massacre to become king of Judah; repaired the

temple: 2 Kings 11 - 12; 2 Chronicles 24/pp.276, 298-299.
JOB Central figure of the book of Job which explores the problem of suffering/p.319ff.
JOEL Prophet in the time of Uzziah, known only from the book of Joel/pp.442-443.
JOHANAN Jewish leader who warned Gedaliah of the plot to kill him; sought but ignored Jeremiah's advice about going to Egypt: Jeremiah 40 - 43.
JOHN 1. The apostle John, son of Zebedee, brother of James, whose teaching is recorded in the fourth Gospel, the letters of John, and Revelation: Matthew 4:21f; 10:2; 17:1ff.; Mark 5:37; 10:35ff.; Luke 9:49ff.; Acts 3 - 4/pp.503, 533ff., 551-552, 640ff., 645ff. **2.** John the Baptist, forerunner of the Messiah: Luke 1; 3; 7:18ff.; Matthew 3; 11; Mark 1; 6, etc.; John 1; 3:22ff./pp. 477, 482, 499, 516-517, 534, 536. **3.** John Mark, see Mark.
JONAH Prophet whose mission to Nineveh is recounted in the book of Jonah/p.448.
JONATHAN Eldest son of Saul; sworn friend of David: 1 Samuel 13 - 14; 18 - 20; 23:16-18; 31:2/pp.237-239, 242.
JORAM See Jehoram.
JOSEPH 1. Jacob's favourite son; one of the great Old Testament heroes: Genesis 30:24; 37 - 50/pp.146ff. *Joseph sold into Egypt*: Genesis 37. *Potiphar's wife*: 39. *In prison*: 40. *Pharaoh's dream*: 41. *Famine; Joseph and his brothers*: 42 - 45. *Death*: 50. **2.** Husband of Mary mother of Jesus: Matthew 1 - 2; Luke 1:27; 2/pp.475-476. **3.** Joseph of Arimathaea, secret disciple of Jesus who provided his tomb: Matthew 27:57ff.; Mark 15:43; Luke 23:50ff.; John 19:38ff./pp.513, 528.
JOSHUA Succeeded Moses as leader of Israel; led them into the promised land: mentioned from Exodus 17:9 on, but particularly the book of Joshua/pp.164, 194, 202, 209ff. *Victory against Amalek*: Exodus 17. *Spying out the land*: Numbers 13 - 14. *Appointed Moses' successor*: Numbers 27. *Moses places him in charge*: Deuteronomy 31; 34:9ff. *Crossing the Jordan*: Joshua 4. *Jericho*: 6. *Division of the land*: 13ff. *Joshua's charge to Israel*: 23 - 24.
JOSIAH King of Judah who embarked on thoroughgoing religious reform; killed fighting Pharaoh Necho at Megiddo: 2 Kings 21:24 - 23:30; 2 Chronicles 33:25 - 35:27/pp.282, 302.
JOTHAM Son of Uzziah, king of Judah: 2 Kings 15; 2 Chronicles 26 - 27/pp.279, 299.
JUDAH One of Jacob's 12 sons; ancestor of the royal tribe of Israel: Genesis 29:35; 37 - 38; 43ff.; 49:8-9/pp.147, 150.
JUDAS/JUDE Name of a number of individuals in the New Testament, among them: **1.** Judas son of James, one of the 12 apostles: Luke 6:16, etc./p.503. **2.** The brother of Jesus, who may have written the letter of Jude: Matthew 13:55. **3.** Judas Iscariot, who betrayed Jesus: Matthew 10:4; 26:14ff.; 27:3ff.; John 13; 18/pp.491, 493, 545.

KETURAH Abraham's second wife, after Sarah's death: Genesis 25:1ff./p.142.
KISH Father of King Saul: 1 Samuel 9:1ff.

KOHATH Son of Levi; head of one of the three Levitical families; ancestor of Moses: Exodus 6:16ff.; Numbers 3/pp. 185-186.

KORAH Levite who with Dathan and Abiram conspired against Moses and Aaron: Numbers 16/p.189.

LABAN Rebekah's brother; uncle to Jacob who out-played him at his own cunning game: Genesis 24:29; 28 - 30/pp.144-145.

LAMECH 1. Descendant of Cain: Genesis 4/p.129. **2.** Father of Noah: Genesis 5:28ff./p.131.

LAZARUS Brother of Martha and Mary; raised from the dead by Jesus: John 11 - 12:11/p.542.

LEAH Elder daughter of Laban; Jacob's wife and mother of six of his sons: Genesis 29:16 - 33:7/pp.144-145.

LEMUEL The king whose mother's teaching is set out in Proverbs 31:1-9/p.361.

LEVI One of Jacob's 12 sons; ancestor of the tribe which gave Israel their priests and ministers: Genesis 29:34; 34:25ff.; 49:5ff./pp.146, 150.

LOT Abraham's nephew who chose to live in Sodom and narrowly escaped destruction: Genesis 11:31 - 14:16; 19/pp.136. 139.

LUKE Author of the third Gospel and Acts; a doctor; companion of Paul in his missionary journeys: Colossians 4:14; 2 Timothy 4:11; Philemon 24/pp.514ff., 549ff., 613, 622.

LYDIA A business woman from Thyatira converted at Philippi: Acts 16:14-15/p.561.

MAGOG See Gog.

MALACHI Name or pseudonym of the author of the book of Malachi/pp.459-460.

MALCHUS Servant of the high priest; Peter cut off his ear when Jesus was arrested in the garden of Gethsemane: John 18:10.

MANASSEH 1. Joseph's son; ancestor of one of the tribes of Israel: Genesis 41:51; 48/p.150. **2.** Son of Hezekiah, king of Judah: 2 Kings 21; 2 Chronicles 33/pp.282, 300.

MANOAH Father of Samson: Judges 13/p.224.

MARK Author of the second Gospel; companion of Paul and Barnabas, also of Peter: Acts 12:12, 25; 13:13; 15:36ff.; Colossians 4:10; 2*Timothy 4:11; Philemon 24; 1 Peter 5:13/pp.499ff., 558, 560, 613, 622.

MARTHA Sister of Mary and Lazarus in whose home Jesus stayed: Luke 10:38ff.; John 11; 12:2/p.522.

MARY Name of a number of women in the New Testament. **1.** Mary the mother of Jesus and wife of Joseph: Matthew 1; 2:11; 13:55; Luke 1 - 2/pp.475-476. 514-516. **2.** Mary the sister of Martha - Lazarus, who anointed Jesus: Luke 10:39ff.; John 11; 12:3ff./pp.509, 522, 542. **3.** Mary Magdalene, who was healed by Jesus and was the first to see him after the resurrection: Matthew 27:55-56, 61; 28:1ff.; Mark 15:40ff.; Luke 8:2; John 20/p.548. **4.** Mary the mother of John Mark: Acts 12:12. **5.** Mary the mother of James, 'the other Mary', and Mary wife of Clopas—who are probably one and the same: Matthew 27:56, 61; 28:1; John 19:25.

MATTHEW Tax collector who became one of the 12 apostles and author of the first Gospel: Matthew 9:9; 10:3, etc./p.503.

MATTHIAS Chosen to take the place of Judas Iscariot as the twelfth apostle: Acts 1:15ff.

MELCHIZEDEK Priest and king of Salem who met and blessed Abraham: Genesis 14:18ff.; see Hebrews 5 - 7/pp.136, 628.

MENAHEM King of Israel: 2 Kings 15/p.278.

MEPHIBOSHETH Son of Saul's son Jonathan; honoured by David for Jonathan's sake: 2 Samuel 4:4; 9; 16:1ff.; 19:24ff./pp.245, 248, 249.

MERAB Saul's daughter, promised to David: 1 Samuel 14:49; 18:17ff.

MERARI Son of Levi; founder of one of the three Levitical families: Exodus 6:16ff.; Numbers 3/pp.185-186.

MERODACH-BALADAN Marduk-apla-iddina II, king of Babylon who sent an embassy to Hezekiah: Isaiah 39.

MESHACH One of Daniel's three companions in exile at Babylon; thrown into the fiery furnace but unharmed: Daniel 1; 2:49; 3/pp.430, 432.

METHUSELAH Longest lived of the patriarchs listed in Genesis 5/p.131.

MICAH/MICAIAH 1. Prophet in Isaiah's time whose prophecies we have in the book of Micah/pp.449-450. **2.** The Ephraimite who installed a Levite as priest to his house: Judges 17 - 18/p.225 **3.** The prophet summoned by Ahab: 1 Kings 22; 2 Chronicles 18/p.268.

MICHAEL The guardian angel of Daniel 10; 12:1; also Jude 9; Revelation 12:7/pp.436, 644.

MICHAL Saul's daughter; wife of David, who helped him escape Saul, but disapproved of him dancing before the ark: 1 Samuel 14:49; 18:20ff.; 19:11ff.; 2 Samuel 3:13-16; 6:16ff./pp.239, 243-244.

MIRIAM Elder sister of Moses and Aaron; sang in triumph at the crossing of the Red Sea; later punished with leprosy for rebellion against Moses: Exodus 2:4ff.; 15:20-21; Numbers 12; 20:1/pp.156, 162, 187, 190.

MORDECAI Cousin to Esther, who prompted her to act and save the Jewish people from massacre: Esther 2:5 - 10:3/pp.313-315.

MOSES Great leader and law-giver who led Israel out of Egypt to Sinai, and through the years of desert wandering: Exodus 2 - Deuteronomy 34/pp.155ff. *Birth, and upbringing by Pharaoh's daughter: Exodus 2. The burning bush: 3 - 4. The contest with Pharaoh: 7 - 12. Crossing of the Red Sea: 14. Water from the rock: 17; Numbers 20. Sinai; the law-giving: Exodus 19ff. The golden calf: 32. The spies: Numbers 13 - 14. Appointment of a successor: 27. Instruction to the people when they possess the land: Deuteronomy 6ff. Final charge to the nation: 31. Moses' blessing: 33. Death: 34.*

NAAMAN Syrian army commander healed of leprosy by Elisha: 2 Kings 5/p.273.

NABAL Husband of Abigail; landowner who refused David's request for hospitality: 1 Samuel 25/p.240.

NABOTH Killed so that Ahab could seize the vineyard he coveted: 1 Kings 21/p.268.

NADAB Aaron's son who, with Abihu, committed sacrilege and died: Leviticus 10/p.174.

NAHOR Abraham's brother who settled at Harran and became the ancestor of several Aramaean tribes: Genesis 11:27ff.; 22:20ff.; 24:10ff.

NAHUM Prophet whose prophecy against Nineveh is recorded in the book of Nahum/p.451.

NAOMI Mother-in-law of Ruth; from Bethlehem: Ruth/pp.226-228.

NAPHTALI One of Jacob's 12 sons; ancestor of one of the tribes of Israel: Genesis 30:8; 49:21.

NATHAN Prophet who delivered God's word to David and helped place Solomon on the throne: 2 Samuel 7; 12; 1 Kings 1; 1 Chronicles 17/pp.246, 251.

NATHANAEL One of the 12 apostles, probably the same as Bartholomew; from Cana: John 1:45-51; 21:2/pp.503, 535.

NEBUCHADNEZZAR/NEBUCHADREZZAR King of Babylon who captured Jerusalem and took the Judeans into exile; Daniel interpreted his dreams: 2 Kings 24 - 25; 2 Chronicles 36; Jeremiah 21:2 - 52:30; Ezekiel 26:7ff.; 29:18ff.; 30:10; Daniel 1 - 4/pp.283, 404, 406, 409-412, 424-425, 430-432.

NEBUZARADAN Nebuchadnezzar's captain of the guard at Jerusalem: 2 Kings 25; Jeremiah 39; 52.

NECHO Pharaoh who killed Josiah in battle at Megiddo, deposed Jehoahaz and put Jehoiakim on the throne: 2 Kings 23; 2 Chronicles 35:20 - 36:4/pp.282-283, 302.

NEHEMIAH Cup-bearer to the Persian king; returned to Jerusalem and organized the rebuilding of the walls; his memoirs are recorded in the book of Nehemiah/pp.309ff.

NERGAL-SHAREZER Senior official with Nebuchadnezzar's army: Jeremiah 39.

NICODEMUS The Jewish leader who came secretly to Jesus: John 3; 7:50ff.; 19:39/pp.536, 548.

NOAH Godly man saved from the flood which destroyed the rest of mankind; father of Ham, Shem and Japheth: Genesis 6 - 9/pp.131-134.

OBADIAH 1. Steward over Ahab's household who saved 100 prophets of God: 2 Kings 18. **2.** The prophet whose message against Edom is recorded in the book of Obadiah/p.447.

OBED Son of Ruth and Boaz; grandfather of David: Ruth 4:13ff.

OBED-EDOM Philistine in whose house the ark remained after Uzzah's death: 2 Samuel 6:10ff.; 1 Chronicles 13.

OG King of Bashan east of the Jordan conquered by the Israelites: Numbers 21:32ff.; Deuteronomy 3/pp.195-196.

OMRI Powerful king of Israel who made Samaria his capital: 1 Kings 16/p.265.

ONESIMUS Runaway slave; subject of Paul's letter to Philemon/pp.613, 625.

ONESIPHORUS Christian who helped Paul in prison: 2 Timothy 1:16ff.; 4:19.

ORNAN See Araunah.

ORPAH Daughter-in-law of Naomi: Ruth 1/p.226.

OTHNIEL One of the Judges: Judges 3:7-11/ p.221.

PASHUR Priest who put Jeremiah in the stocks: Jeremiah 20.

PAUL/SAUL Apostle to the Gentiles and author of 13 New Testament letters: Acts 7:58 - Philemon/pp.554, 556ff. *Stephen's martyrdom:* Acts 7:58ff. *Persecution of the church:* 8:3; 9:1ff. *Conversion:* 9 (22; 26). *First missionary journey:* 13 - 14. *Jerusalem council:* 15. *Second missionary journey:* 15:36 - 18:22. *Third missionary journey:* 18:23 - 20:37. *At Jerusalem; the arrest:* 21 - 23. *Caesarea; defence before Felix and Agrippa:* 24 - 26. *Voyage to Rome:* 27 - 28. See also the more personal passages in the letters: e.g. 2 Corinthians 1 - 2; 7; 11 - 12; Galatians 1:11 - 2:21; Philippians 1:12ff.; 3; 1 Thessalonians 2 - 3; 2 Timothy 4:6ff., etc.

PEKAH Seized the throne of Israel from Pekahiah: 2 Kings 15:25 - 16:5/p.279.

PEKAHIAH King of Israel assassinated by Pekah: 2 Kings 15:22-26/p.279.

PELATIAH Leader at Jerusalem whose death Ezekiel saw in a vision: Ezekiel 11/ p.419.

PENINNAH Elkanah's second wife, who taunted the childless Hannah: 1 Samuel 1/p.232.

PETER Apostle and leader of the early church: the Gospels; Acts 1 - 15; Galatians 1 - 2; 1 and 2 Peter/pp.486, 503, 527, 548, 550ff., 602, 635ff. *Call:* Matthew 4:18ff., etc. *Recognition of Jesus as Messiah:* Matthew 16:13ff., etc. *Presence at the transfiguration:* Matthew 17, etc. *Denial of Jesus:* Matthew 26:69ff., etc. *Jesus' charge:* John 21. *Sermon at Pentecost:* Acts 2. *Healing of the cripple at the temple:* 3. *Before the authorities:* 4. *Miraculous release from prison:* 5 and 12. *At Samaria:* 8:14ff. *Raising of Tabitha:* 9:36ff. *Vision, and visit to Cornelius:* 10. *At the Jerusalem council:* 15.

PHARAOH Title of the kings of Egypt. Notably the following: **1.** Abraham's pharaoh: Genesis 12:10ff. **2.** Joseph's pharaoh: Genesis 40ff./pp.149, 153. **3.** The pharaoh of the exodus: Exodus 5ff./pp. 153-154, 156ff. **4.** The pharaoh who gave Solomon his daughter in marriage: 1 Kings 9:16, etc. **5.** The pharaoh who sheltered Hadad: 1 Kings 11. **6.** Shishak, who aided Jeroboam and attacked Jerusalem: 1 Kings 11:40; 14:25ff.; 2 Chronicles 12/pp.154, 264, 296-297. **7.** So: 2 Kings 17:4. **8.** Tirhakah: 2 Kings 19:9; Isaiah 37:9/p.281. **9.** Necho (see above). **10.** Hophra: Jeremiah 44:30; Ezekiel 29:2/p.425.

PHILEMON Christian owner of the slave Onesimus to whom Paul wrote his letter/ p.625.

PHILIP 1. One of the 12 apostles: Matthew 10:3; John 1:43ff.; 6:5ff.; 12:21-22; 14:8/ p.535. **2.** Son of Herod the Great; husband of Herodias: Mark 6:17/p.505. **3.** Another son of Herod; tetrarch of Ituraea: Luke 3:1. **4.** Official and evangelist of the early church: Acts 6; 8; 21:8-9/pp.553, 555-556.

PHINEHAS 1. A priest; grandson of Aaron: Exodus 6:25; Numbers 25; 31:6; Joshua 22:13ff. **2.** Son of Eli; killed by the Philistines when the ark was captured: 1 Samuel 2:12ff.; 4/p.232.

PHOEBE Deaconess from Cenchreae: Romans 16:1-2/p.588.

PILATE Roman procurator of Judea who, fearing he would lose his position, allowed the Jews to crucify Jesus: Matthew 27; Mark 15; Luke 3:1; 13:1; 23; John 18 - 19/ see special article p.510.

POTIPHAR Officer of Pharaoh in whose household Joseph served: Genesis 37:36; 39/p.147.

PRISCILLA See Aquila and Priscilla.

PUBLIUS Head man on the island of Malta whose father Paul healed: Acts 27:7ff.

PUL Name for Tiglath-pileser as king of Babylon.

QUIRINIUS Governor of Syria when Jesus was born: Luke 2:2/p.516.

RABSARIS, RABSHAKEH, TARTAN Titles of Assyrian officials sent by Sennacherib to parley with Hezekiah and intimidate the people: 2 Kings 18 - 19; Isaiah 36 - 37/ p.281.

RACHEL Laban's daughter; Jacob's favourite wife; mother of Joseph and Benjamin: Genesis 29 - 35/pp.144-146.

RAHAB The Jericho prostitute who hid the two spies: Joshua 2; 6/p.209.

RAMESSES II Probably the pharaoh of the exodus (see Pharaoh): pp.153-155; *pictures* pp.160-161.

REBEKAH Wife of Isaac, brought to him by Abraham's servant; made Jacob her favourite son: Genesis 24 - 28/p.142.

REHOBOAM Solomon's son whose oppressive rule split the kingdom in two: 1 Kings 11:43 - 14:31; 2 Chronicles 9:31 - 12/16/ pp.263-264, 296.

REUBEN Eldest of Jacob's 12 sons who tried to save Joseph; ancestor of one of the tribes of Israel: Genesis 29:32; 30:14; 35:22; 37:42; 49:3f./p.146.

REUEL Another name for Jethro.

REZIN/REZON 1. Rezin, king of Syria, who attacked Judah and was killed by Tiglath-pileser: 2 Kings 15:37 - 16:9; Isaiah 7:1ff. **2.** Rezon, king of Damascus, who harassed Israel in Solomon's time: 1 Kings 11:23ff./ p.262.

RHODA The girl who answered the door to Peter after the angel had released him from prison: Acts 12:12ff.

RIZPAH Saul's concubine whose sons David gave to the Gibeonites to put to death: 2 Samuel 3:7; 21/pp.243, 250.

RUTH Moabite woman whose love for Naomi led her to Bethlehem, to become the wife of Boaz and great-grandmother of King David: Ruth/pp.226-228.

SALOME One of the women who accompanied Jesus and the disciples from Galilee; present at the crucifixion and on the resurrection morning: Mark 15:40-41; 16:1/p.513.

SAMSON Champion of Israel against the

Philistines in the time of the Judges: Judges 13 - 16/p.224.

SAMUEL Judge and prophet who anointed Israel's first two kings: 1 Samuel 1 - 4:1; 7 - 16; 19:18ff.; 25:1; 28/pp.231ff. *Birth:* 1 Samuel 1. *God speaks to him in the temple:* 3. *Israel asks for a king:* 8. *Samuel and Saul:* 9ff. *Samuel anoints David:* 16. *Death:* 25:1. *Saul calls up Samuel through the witch of Endor:* 28.

SANBALLAT Persistent opponent of Nehemiah: Nehemiah 2:10, 19; 4; 6/p.309.

SAPPHIRA With her husband Ananias, guilty of deceiving the church: Acts 5/p.552.

SARAH/SARAI Wife of Abraham; in old age, mother of Isaac: Genesis 11:29 - 23:19/pp. 136ff. *Sarah gives Hagar to Abraham:* Genesis 16. *The promise of a son:* 18. *Birth of Isaac:* 21. *Death:* 23:1.

SATAN See under Sin and evil in Key Themes.

SAUL 1. First king of Israel: 1 Samuel 9:2 - 31:13/pp.234ff. *Anointed king:* 1 Samuel 10. *Rejected for his disobedience:* 15. *Jealousy of David:* 18ff. *David spares his life:* 24; 26. *Consultation of the medium:* 28. *Death:* 31 (also 2 Samuel 1). **2.** See Paul.

SENNACHERIB King of Assyria whose army shut Hezekiah up in Jerusalem: 2 Kings 18:13ff.; 2 Chronicles 32; Isaiah 36:1ff./pp.281, 300.

SERGIUS PAULUS Pro-consul of Cyprus who asked to hear Paul's message: Acts 13:7ff./p.558.

SETH Son of Adam and Eve born after Abel's death: Genesis 4:25ff./p.129.

SHADRACH One of Daniel's three companions in exile at Babylon; thrown into the furnace but unscathed: Daniel 1; 2:49; 3/pp.430, 432.

SHALLUM Usurping king of Israel who reigned only a month: 2 Kings 15:10ff./ p.278. Also another name for Jehoahaz of Judah.

SHALMANESER Successor to Tiglath-pileser of Assyria who captured Samaria and took the Israelites into exile: 2 Kings 17.

SHAMGAR One of Israel's Judges: Judges 3:31; 5:6/p.221.

SHAPHAN Official of Josiah who reported to him the discovery of the book of the law: 2 Kings 22; 2 Chronicles 34.

SHEBNA(H) High official under Hezekiah who parleyed with Sennacherib's Assyrian delegation: 2 Kings 18 - 19; Isaiah 36 - 37.

SHECHEM Prince who raped Jacob's daughter Dinah: Genesis 34/p.146.

SHEM One of Noah's three sons; ancestor of a number of nations: Genesis 6:10 - 10:31/p.135.

SHESHBAZZAR Entrusted with treasure for the second temple, of which he laid the foundations: Ezra 1:8ff.; 5:14ff.

SHIMEI Benjaminite who cursed David at the time of Absalom's rebellion: 2 Samuel 16; 19; 1 Kings 2/p.248.

SHISHAK See Pharaoh.

SIHON Amorite king east of Jordan conquered by the Israelites: Numbers 21/p.190.

SILAS/SILVANUS A leader of the Jerusalem church who went with Paul on his missionary journeys and acted as his secretary for some of the letters to the churches: Acts 15:22 - 18:5; 2 Corinthians 1:19; 1 Thessalonians 1:1; 2 Thessalonians 1:1; 1 Peter 5:12/pp.560, 614, 638.

SIMEON 1. One of Jacob's 12 sons; ancestor of one of the tribes of Israel; left as hostage with Joseph in Egypt: Genesis 29:33; 34:25ff.; 42:24ff.; 49:5ff.pp.146, 150. **2.** The godly man present when Jesus was brought to the temple, whose prayer is known as the Nunc Dimittis: Luke 2:22-35/ p.516.

SIMON 1. Simon Peter: see Peter. **2.** Simon the Zealot, one of the 12 apostles: Matthew 10:4, etc.; Acts 1:13/p.503. **3.** One of Jesus' brothers: Matthew 13:55. **4.** Simon the leper, in whose house at Bethany Jesus was anointed: Matthew 26:6; Mark 14:3. **5.** A Pharisee: Luke 7:40ff. **6.** Simon of Cyrene who carried the cross: Matthew 27:32, etc. **7.** Simon Magus, who tried to buy the gift of the Spirit: Acts 8/p.555. **8.** Simon the tanner in whose house at Joppa Peter had his vision: Acts 9:43ff./ p.557.

SISERA Canaanite army commander killed by Jael: Judges 4 - 5.

SO See Pharaoh.

SOLOMON David's son; king of Israel in its golden age; gifted with great wisdom; builder of the temple; composer/collector of wise sayings: 2 Samuel 12:24; 1 Kings 1 - 11; 1 Chronicles 22:5 - 23:1; 28 - 2 Chronicles 9; Proverbs 1:1; 10:1; 25:1, etc./pp.251ff., 289ff...354ff., 362, 367-369. *Birth:* 2 Samuel 12:24. *Made co-regent:* 1 Kings 1. *Prayer for wisdom:* 1 Kings 3; 2 Chronicles 1. *Building of the temple:* 1 Kings 6 - 7; 2 Chronicles 3 - 4. *Dedication of the temple:* 1 Kings 8; 2 Chronicles 5 - 7. *Visit of the Queen of Sheba:* 1 Kings 10; 2 Chronicles 9. *Death:* 1 Kings 11:43; 2 Chronicles 10:31.

SOSTHENES Ruler of the synagogue at Corinth: Acts 18:17; perhaps the same man as named in 1 Corinthians 1:1.

STEPHANAS Corinthian Christian baptized by Paul: 1 Corinthians 1:16; 16:15ff./p.591.

STEPHEN One of the seven men chosen to take care of practical matters in the church; first Christian martyr: Acts 6 - 7/ pp.553-554.

TABITHA See Dorcas.

TAMAR 1. Daughter-in-law of Judah who bore him twin sons: Genesis 38. **2.** David's daughter raped by Amnon: 2 Samuel 13/ p.246.

TARTAN See Rabsaris.

TERAH Father of Abraham: Genesis 11:24ff./p.135.

THEOPHILUS Roman to whom Luke addressed his Gospel and Acts: Luke 1:3; Acts 1:1/pp.514, 550.

THOMAS One of the 12 apostles, who was absent when the others first saw the risen Christ: Matthew 10:3, etc.; John 11:16; 14:5; 20:24ff./p.548.

TIBERIUS Roman emperor: Luke 3:1.

TIGLATH-PILESER Powerful king of Assyria to whom Ahaz turned for help against Syria and Israel: 2 Kings 15:29; 16:7ff.; 2 Chronicles 28:16ff./pp.279, 300.

TIMOTHY Paul's young companion and fellow missionary, later with responsibility for the church at Ephesus; Paul sent him two letters on the subject of leadership in the churches: Acts 16:1ff.; 17:14; 18:5; 19:22; 20:4; 1 Corinthians 4:17; 16:10; 2 Corinthians 1:19; Philippians 2:19ff.; 1 Thessalonians 3:2ff.; 1 and 2 Timothy; Hebrews 13:23/pp.560-561, 608, 615, 618ff.

TIRHAKAH See Pharaoh.

TITUS Paul's companion and fellow missionary; smoothed things over with the Corinthian church; sent to Crete, where Paul sent him a letter of advice: 2 Corinthians 2:13; 7:6ff.; 8; 12:18; Galatians 2; 2 Timothy 4:10; Titus/pp.598, 599, 622-624.

TOBIAH An opponent of Nehemiah: Nehemiah 2; 4; 6; 13/pp.309, 312.

TROPHIMUS Ephesian Christian who went with Paul to Jerusalem: Acts 20:4; 21:29; 2 Timothy 4:20/p.622.

TYCHICUS Christian who went with Paul to Jerusalem; accompanied Onesimus to Colossae, taking Paul's letters: Acts 20:4; Ephesians 6:21; Colossians 4:7ff.; 2 Timothy 4:12; Titus 3:12/pp.613, 622.

URIAH/URIJAH 1. A Hittite warrior in David's army; husband of Bathsheba; sent to his death by David: 2 Samuel 11/p.245. **2.** Priest in Jerusalem: 2 Kings 16. **3.** Prophet in Jeremiah's time put to death by Jehoiakim: Jeremiah 26:20ff./p.405.

UZZAH Man who touched the ark as it was being moved from Kiriath-jearim and died: 2 Samuel 6/p.244.

UZZIAH Another name for Azariah.

VASHTI Queen whom Ahasuerus deposed: Esther 1/p.313.

ZACCHAEUS Tax collector who climbed a tree at Jericho to get a glimpse of Jesus: Luke 19:1-10/p.526.

ZACHARIAH,-IAS See Zechariah.

ZADOK Priest at David's court with Abiathar; founder of the line of Israel's high priests: 2 Samuel 15; 17:15; 19:11; 1 Kings 1; 2:25; 1 Chronicles, etc./p.251.

ZEBULUN One of Jacob's 12 sons; ancestor of one of the tribes of Israel: Genesis 30:20; 49:13/p.150.

ZECHARIAH, -IAS The name of a great number of people, notably the following: **1.** The prophet who, with Haggai, spurred the people on to rebuild the temple, and whose prophecies are recorded in the book of Zechariah/pp.456ff. **2.** The father of John the Baptist: Luke 1/pp.514-515.

ZEDEKIAH 1. Last king of Judah, whose rebellion brought Nebuchadnezzar's army and destruction on Jerusalem: 2 Kings 24 - 25; 2 Chronicles 36; Jeremiah 21; 32; 34; 37 - 39, etc./pp.283, 302. **2** A false prophet of Ahab's day: 1 Kings 22; 2 Chronicles 18.

ZEPHANIAH The prophet whose prophecies are recorded in the book of Zephaniah/ p.454.

ZERAH The Ethiopian who invaded Judah and was routed by Asa: 2 Chronicles 14:9-14/p.297.

ZERUBBABEL Leader in the return from exile and rebuilding of the temple: Ezra 2:2; 3 - 5; Haggai; Zechariah 4/pp. 455-456.

ZIBA Saul's servant who told David of Mephibosheth: 2 Samuel 9; 16/p.248.

ZILPAH Leah's servant who bore Jacob two sons: Genesis 29:24; 30:9-10.

ZIMRI Ruler of Israel for one week: 1 Kings 16/p.165.

ZIPPORAH Jethro's daughter; wife of Moses: Exodus 2:21; 4:24ff.; 18/pp.156, 164.

ZOPHAR One of Job's three friends: Job 2:11, etc./pp.321ff.

Gazetteer of Places

ABANA One of two rivers of Damascus mentioned by Naaman: 2 Kings 5:12.

ABEL-BETH-MAACAH Town in the north of Palestine, near Lake Huleh, to which Joab pursued Sheba: 2 Samuel 20; also 1 Kings 15:20/*Map* p.116C1.

ABEL-MEHOLAH Place to which Gideon pursued the Midianites; birthplace of Elisha: Judges 7:22; 1 Kings 19:16/*Map* p.222.

ABILENE Region around Damascus of which Lysanias was tetrarch: Luke 3:1/*Map* p. 464D1.

ACCAD Area and major city in Babylonia founded by Nimrod: Genesis 10:10.

ACHAIA Province of southern Greece governed from Corinth: Acts 18:12, etc./*Map* p. 579.

ACHOR Valley near Jericho where Achan was stoned: Joshua 7:24.

ADAM Where the River Jordan was blocked, allowing the Israelites to cross: Joshua 3:16/*Map* p.116C4.

ADMAH Near Sodom; one of the 'cities of the plain': Genesis 10:19; 14:2/*Map* p.137.

ADRAMYTTIUM Paul set sail for Rome in a ship from this port near Troy on the west coast of modern Turkey: Acts 27:2/*Map* p.567.

ADULLAM David, on the run from Saul, hid in a cave near this town in Judah: 1 Samuel 22:1; 2 Samuel 23:13/*Map* p.241.

AENON NEAR SALIM Where John baptized: John 3:23/*Map* p.464C3.

AHAVA River and place in Babylonia where Ezra camped: Ezra 8:15, 21, 31.

AI Site of one of Joshua's first battles in the promised land: Joshua 7 and 8/pp.213-214, *Map* p.116B4.

AIJALON An Amorite town; a city of refuge; fortified by Rehoboam: Joshua 19:42; 21:24; 1 Chronicles 6:69; 8:13, etc./*Map* p.116B5.

VALLEY OF AIJALON Where the sun 'stood still' while Joshua fought: Joshua 10/*Map* p.116.

ALEXANDRIA Major port in Egypt with a large Jewish element; home of Apollos: Acts 6:9; 18:24, etc./*Map* p.567.

AMMON State on the east of the Jordan; capital Rabbah, modern Amman; see Ammonites, in Nations and Peoples of Bible Lands/*Map* pp.12-13.

AMPHIPOLIS Town on Paul's route through northern Greece: Acts 17:1/*Map* p.560.

ANATHOTH Jeremiah's birthplace, just north of Jerusalem: Jeremiah 1:1/*Map* p.116B5 *Picture* p.397.

ANTIOCH 1. Important city on the river Orontes in Syria; major centre for the early church; base from which Paul and Barnabas journeyed: Acts 11; 13:1, etc./*Map* p.558.
2. Antioch in Pisidia; town visited by Paul on his first missionary journey: Acts 13:14ff./*Map* p.558 *Map* p.559.

ANTIPATRIS Paul was brought here under escort: Acts 23:31/*Map* p.464B4.

APHEK Here the Israelites lost the ark to the Philistines: 1 Samuel 4:1; also 29:1/*Map* p.116B4.

AR Chief town of Moab: Numbers 21:15/*Map* p.116C6.

ARABAH Rift valley running from the Sea of Galilee to the Gulf of Aqaba; the Sea of Arabah is the Dead Sea: Deuteronomy 1:1; 3:17, etc.

ARABIA Usually refers to north Arabia: see Arabians in Nations and Peoples of Bible Lands/*Map* pp.12-13.

ARAD Canaanite town in the Negev defeated by Joshua: Numbers 21:1; Joshua 12:14/*Map* p.116B6.

ARAM The name of states in southern Syria, especially Damascus: see also Aramaeans in Nations and Peoples of Bible Lands/*Map* pp.12-13.

ARARAT Mountains where the ark came to rest after the Flood; Lake Van area of Turkey and Armenia: Genesis 8:4/*Map* p.131.

AREOPAGUS Paul was brought before the council which formerly met on this hill (Mars hill) in Athens: Acts 17/*Picture* p.562.

ARGOB Part of the kingdom of Og in Bashan, east of the Jordan: Deuteronomy 3; 1 Kings 4:13/*Map* p.255.

ARMAGEDDON Assembling-place for the great final battle (see also Megiddo): Revelation 16:16.

ARNON River flowing into the Dead Sea from the east; boundary between the Amorites and Moab: Numbers 21:13, etc./*Map* p.196.

AROER Town on the north bank of the Arnon: Deuteronomy 2:36, etc.; 2 Kings 10:33/*Map* p.116C6.

ASHDOD Philistine town where the ark stood in the temple of Dagon: 1 Samuel 5; also 2 Chronicles 26:6; Isaiah 20:1, etc./*Map* p.116A5.

ASHER Territory of the tribe of Asher: Joshua 19:24-31/*Map* p.215.

ASHKELON Philistine town: Judges 14:19; 1 Samuel 6:17/*Map* p.116A5 *Picture* p.224.

ASHTAROTH, ASHTEROTH-KARNAIM Town sacked by Chedorlaomer; capital of Og of Bashan. Genesis 14:5; Deuteronomy 1:4, etc./*Map* p.116D2.

ASIA Roman province of which Ephesus was capital; western part of modern Turkey: Acts 19, etc./*Map* p.579.

ASSOS Sea-port on the west coast of modern Turkey: Acts 20:13/*Map* p.564.

ASSYRIA Country of north Mesopotamia; a great power in 9th-7th centuries BC – time of Isaiah, etc.; see Assyrians in Nations and Peoples of Bible Lands/*Map* pp.12-13.

ATAROTH Town east of Jordan: Numbers 32:3/*Map* p.116C5.

ATHENS Cultural centre of Greek civilization and university city, where Paul preached: Acts 17/*p.562 Map* p.560 *Picture* p.562.

ATTALIA Sea-port of Paul's first missionary journey, on the south coast of modern Turkey: Acts 14:25/*Map* p.558.

AZEKAH Town to which Joshua pursued the Amorites: Joshua 10:10.

BABEL Site of the great tower (Genesis 10:10) identified with Babylon.

BABYLON City on the Euphrates; became capital of Babylonia in southern Mesopotamia: 2 Kings 20:12ff.; Jeremiah 50, etc./*Map* p.304.

BASHAN Region east of the Sea of Galilee; kingdom of Og; famous for its cattle: Numbers 21:33; 32:33, etc./*Map* p.116C2.

BEERSHEBA Southernmost town of Israel, on the trade route to Egypt; Genesis 21:14, 31; 26:23ff.etc./*Map* p.116A6.

BENJAMIN Territory of the tribe of Benjamin: Joshua 18:11-28/*Map* p.215.

BEROEA Town in northern Greece where Paul preached: Acts 17:10/*Map* p.560.

BETHANY Home of Martha, Mary and Lazarus. just outside Jerusalem: John 11:1; 12:1/*Map* p.464B5 *Picture* p.546.

BETHEL Place of Jacob's dream; sanctuary-town which became an official shrine of the northern kingdom of Israel: Genesis 28; Judges 20:18, 26; 1 Samuel 7:16; 1 Kings 12:28ff.; Amos 7:10ff.. etc./*Map* p.116B4.

BETHESDA, BETHZATHA Pool in Jerusalem where Jesus healed an invalid: John 5:2/*Map* p.545 *Picture* p.538.

BETH-HORON (UPPER AND LOWER) Near the scene of Joshua's victory: Joshua 10:10/*Map* p.116B4.

BETHLEHEM Town a few miles south of Jerusalem; here Ruth settled and both David and Jesus were born: Ruth; 1 Samuel 16; 2 Samuel 23:13ff.; Matthew 2; Luke 2/*Map* p.116B5 *Pictures* pp.475, 516, 517.

BETHPHAGE Place near Bethany from which Jesus sent disciples to fetch the ass for his entry to Jerusalem: Mark 11:1/*Map* p.464B5.

BETHSAIDA Town on the shore of the Lake of Galilee; home of Philip. Andrew and Peter: John 1:44; Mark 8:22; Matthew 11:21/*Map* p.464C2.

BETH-SHAN Town on whose walls the Philistines hung Saul's body: 1 Samuel 31:10/*Map* p.116C3 *Picture* p.243.

BETH-SHEMESH Place to which the ark was returned by the Philistines: 1 Samuel 6; also 2 Kings 14:11/*Map* p.116B5 *Picture* p.233.

BETH-ZUR Town settled by Caleb's descendants; fortified by Rehoboam: 1 Chronicles 2:45; 2 Chronicles 11:7/*Map* p.116B6.

BITHYNIA Roman province bordering the Black Sea: Acts 16:7/*Map* p.579.

BOZRAH Town in Edom denounced by the prophets: Isaiah 34:6, etc.

CAESAREA Roman town on the coast of Palestine; residence of the procurators; home of Philip and of Cornelius: place where Paul was imprisoned: Acts 10; 11; 21; 23/*Map* p.464A3 *Picture* p.568.

CAESAREA PHILIPPI Town at the foot of Mt Hermon and source of the Jordan; near here Peter made his great confession of faith: Matthew 16:13ff./*Map* p.464C1.

CALAH One of the chief cities of Assyria, founded by Nimrod: Genesis 10:11/*Map* p.279.

CANA Village in Galilee where Jesus turned water into wine: John 2:1ff./*Map* p.464B2 *Picture* p.535.

CANÀAN Country settled by the Israelites, and Phoenician territory to the north; see Canaanites in Nations and Peoples of Bible Lands/*Map* pp.12-13. Genesis 11:31; Numbers 33:51, etc.

CAPERNAUM Town beside the Lake of Galilee; Jesus' base during his ministry: Matthew 4:13; Mark 1:21; Luke 7:1-10; 10:15, etc./*Map* p.464C2 *Picture* p.501.

CAPPADOCIA Roman province in what is now eastern Turkey: Acts 2:9; 1 Peter 1:1/*Map* p.579.

CARCHEMISH City on the Euphrates in northern Syria; here Nebuchadnezzar of Babylon defeated the Egyptians: Jeremiah 46:2/*Map* p.302.

CARMEL Range of hills jutting into the sea by the modern port of Haifa; scene of Elijah's contest with the prophets of Baal: 1 Kings 18:19ff.; also 2 Kings 2:25; 4:25/*Map* p.116B3 *Pictures* pp.266, 346.

CENCHREAE Harbour of Corinth: Acts 18:18; Romans 16:1/*Map* p.560.

CHALDEA South Babylonia; Abraham's family home; see Chaldeans in Nations and Peoples of Bible Lands: Genesis 11:28; Isaiah 48:20, etc./*Map* pp.12-13.

CHEBAR River in Babylonia beside which Ezekiel and the exiles settled: Ezekiel 1:1, etc.

CHERITH Brook beside which Elijah lived during the famine: 1 Kings 17:3/*Map* p.116C4.

CHINNERETH Another name for the Lake of Galilee (possibly because of its 'harp' shape), and town: Deuteronomy 3:17/*Map* p.116C2.

CHORAZIN Town in Galilee which Jesus condemned for its unbelief: Matthew 11:21/*Map* p.464C2.

CILICIA Roman province in what is now southern Turkey, with Tarsus as its capital: Acts 21:39/*Map* p.579.

COLOSSAE Town in what is now south-west Turkey; Paul wrote a letter to the church there: Colossians 1:2/p.611 *Map* p.579 *Picture* p.613.

CORINTH Leading city of southern Greece, where Paul founded a church: Acts 18/p.589 *Map* p.560 *Pictures* pp.592, 597.

CRETE Jews from Crete heard Peter's sermon at Pentecost; Titus was later in charge of the church there: Acts 2:11; Titus 1:5/*Map* p.623.

CUSH The Sudan: Genesis 10:6, etc./*Map* p.134.

CYPRUS Home of Barnabas; first stage on Paul's first missionary journey: Acts 4:36; 13:4/*Map* p.558.

CYRENE In Libya, north Africa; home of Simon who carried Jesus' cross: Matthew 27:32; also Acts 2:10; 11:20/*Map* p.551.

DALMATIA Roman province on the east of the Adriatic, where Titus preached: 2 Timothy 4:10/*Map* p.623.

DAMASCUS Leading city of Syria; home of

Naaman; visited by Elisha; denounced by the prophets; on his way to Damascus to persecute the church, Paul was converted: Genesis 15:2; 2 Kings 5; 8; Isaiah 17; Acts 9, etc./*Map* p.245 *Picture* p.556.

DAN Territory of the tribe of Dan; northern-most town of Israel in which Jeroboam set up a shrine: Joshua 19:40-48; 1 Kings 12:25ff./*Maps* pp. 215, 116C1 *Picture* p.263.

DEAD SEA See Salt Sea.

DECAPOLIS A group of free Greek cities, mainly south of the Sea of Galilee and east of the Jordan: Matthew 4:25; Mark 5:20; 7:31/*Map* p.464C3.

DEDAN See Dedanites in Nations and Peoples of Bible Lands/*Map* pp. 12-13.

DERBE Town in modern Turkey visited by Paul on the first and second missionary journeys: Acts 14; 16:1; 20:4/*Map* p.558.

DIBON Moabite town: Numbers 21:30; 32:34; Isaiah 15:2/*Map* p.116C6.

DOR Canaanite town in northern Palestine: Joshua 11: 1-2; 1 Kings 4:11/*Map* p.116B3.

DOTHAN Joseph's brothers sold him to the Midianites at Dothan; here Elisha was delivered from the surrounding Syrian army: Genesis 37:17; 2 Kings 6/*Map* p.116B3.

EBAL Mountain near Shechem on which the tribes were to stand to pronounce the curse on those who broke the law: Deuteronomy 11:29; Joshua 8:30/*Map* p.116B4 *Picture* p.296.

EDEN 'Garden' cradle of the human race, in Mesopotamia: Genesis 2:8.

EDOM Mountainous area south of the Dead Sea occupied by Esau's descendants; see Edomites in Nations and Peoples of Bible Lands: Genesis 32:3; Numbers 20:14ff.; 1 Samuel 14:47, etc.; Isaiah 34:5ff., etc./*Map* pp.12-13.

EDREI Town where Og was defeated: Numbers 21:33/*Map* p.116D3.

EGLON Town destroyed by Joshua: Joshua 10:34/*Map* p.212.

EGYPT See article pp.151-154 and Egyptians in Nations and Peoples of Bible Lands; the Brook of Egypt was the boundary between Israel and Egypt: Numbers 34:5, etc.

EKRON One of the five Philistine towns, where the ark was held; denounced by the prophets: 1 Samuel 5:10; Jeremiah 25:20, etc./*Map* p.116A5.

ELAH Valley where David slew Goliath: 1 Samuel 17:2/*Map* p.116B5.

ELAM Country east of Babylonia whose capital was Susa; see Elamites, in Nations and Peoples of Bible Lands: Genesis 14:1; Nehemiah 1:1; Isaiah 21:2, etc.; Acts 2:9/*Map* pp.12-13.

ELATH (ELOTH), EZION-GEBER Settlements at the northern end of the Gulf of Aqaba; here Solomon built his fleet: Deuteronomy 2:8; 1 Kings 9:26, etc./*Map* p.295.

EMMAUS On the day of his resurrection Jesus appeared to two disciples on their way to this village: Luke 24:13.

ENDOR Place in northern Israel where Saul consulted the medium: 1 Samuel 28:7/*Map* p.116B3.

ENGEDI Spring to the west of the Dead Sea where David took refuge: 1 Samuel 23:29, etc./*Map* p.116B6 *Picture* p.240.

EN-ROGEL Spring near Jerusalem; here Jonathan and Ahimaaz waited for news of Absalom; Adonijah was feasting here when Solomon was proclaimed king: 2 Samuel 17:17; 1 Kings 1:9.

EPHESUS Capital of the Roman province of Asia (western Turkey); important centre of the early church: Acts 18:19; 19; 20:17; Ephesians 1:1; Revelation 2:1-7/p.564 *Map* p.560 *Pictures* pp.565, 573, 593, 603. 605, 607, 646.

EPHRAIM Territory of the tribe of Ephraim: Joshua 16:4-10, etc./*Map* p.215.

EPHRATHAH Alternative name for Bethlehem.

ERECH Town in Babylonia: Genesis 10:10; Ezra 4:9.

ESHCOL Valley from which the spies brought back grapes: Numbers 13:23.

ESHTAOL Town mentioned in the story of Samson: Judges 13:25; 16:31/*Map* p.116B5.

ETHIOPIA Usually called Cush in the Old Testament – refers to the Sudan; see Ethiopians in Nations and Peoples of Bible Lands: 2 Kings 19:9; Isaiah 18:1, etc.; Jeremiah 38:7ff.; Acts 8:27ff./*Map* pp.12-13.

EUPHRATES Great river of Mesopotamia which flows from Turkey into the Persian Gulf, often called 'the River' in the Old Testament; one of the rivers of the garden of Eden: Genesis 2:14; 15:18, etc.

EZION-GEBER See Elath.

FAIR HAVENS Harbour in Crete on Paul's voyage to Rome: Acts 27:8/*Map* p.567.

GAD Territory of the tribe of Gad: Joshua 13/*Map* p.215.

GALATIA Roman province in what is now central Turkey, where Paul founded churches, to which he wrote: Acts 16:6; 18:23; Galatians 1:2/*Map* p.579 *Pictures* pp.601, 603.

GALILEE Region and Lake in northern Israel; home area of Jesus and a number of the disciples; centre of much of Jesus' ministry: 1 Kings 9:11; 2 Kings 15:29; Isaiah 9:1; Luke 4:14; 5:1ff.; 8:22ff.; John 21, etc.; Acts 9:31/p.500 *Map* p.464B3 *Pictures* pp. 18, 326, 328, 336, 351, 478-480, 502, 504, 539, 543, 548.

GATH One of the five Philistine towns; home of Goliath; later refuge of David: Joshua 11:22; 1 Samuel 5:8; 17:4; 21:10ff. etc./*Map* p.233.

GATH-HEPHER Place from which Jonah came: 2 Kings 14:25/*Map* p.116B2.

GAZA One of the Philistine towns; features in the story of Samson: Joshua 13:3; Judges 16; 1 Samuel 6:17, etc./*Map* p.116A6.

GEBA Town which features in the exploit of Jonathan and his armour-bearer; northern limit of Judah: 1 Samuel 14; 2 Kings 23:8; Nehemiah 11:31/*Map* p.116B5.

GEBAL Phoenician town of Byblos in Lebanon; provided workmen for the temple: Joshua 13:5; 1 Kings 5:18/*Map* p.424.

GENNESARET Another name for the Lake of Galilee.

GERAR Town in southern Israel ruled by Abimelech in Abraham's day: Genesis 10:19; 20:1ff. etc./Map p.116A6.

GERIZIM Mountain opposite Mt Ebal near Shechem where blessing was pronounced on those who kept the law; place of Jotham's parable, and later of the Samaritan temple: Deuteronomy 27:12; Judges 9:7; John 4:20/Map p.116B4 Picture p.296.

GESHUR Region and town in southern Syria; Absalom took refuge here, in his mother's home: Joshua 12:5; 2 Samuel 3:3; 13:38, etc./Map p.245.

GETHSEMANE Garden across the Kidron Valley from Jerusalem where Jesus went on the night of his arrest: Matthew 26:36; John 18:1, etc./Map p.545 Picture p.547.

GEZER Joshua campaigned against this Canaanite town; Pharaoh gave it to Solomon, who fortified it: Joshua 10:33. etc.; 1 Kings 9:15-16/p.259 Map p.212 Picture p.251.

GIBEAH Town a few miles north of Jerusalem; home of Saul: Judges 19: 1 Samuel 10:5, 10, 26ff.; 13; 14; 23:19, etc./Map p.116B5.

GIBEON The inhabitants of this town tricked Joshua into an agreement, which Saul later broke; David and Ishbosheth's men fought here; sanctuary in Solomon's day, where the tabernacle was kept: Joshua 9; 2 Samuel 2:12ff.; 20:8; 21; 1 Kings 3:4ff.; 1 Chronicles 21:29/Map p.116B5 Picture p.409.

GIHON One of four rivers of the garden of Eden; also a spring outside Jerusalem where Solomon was anointed king and from which Hezekiah channelled water by a tunnel into the city: Genesis 2:13; 1 Kings 1:38; 2 Chronicles 32:30/Map and picture p.301.

GILBOA Ridge of hills where Saul gathered his army for the battle against the Philistines in which he and Jonathan died: 1 Samuel 28:4; 31, etc./Map p. 116B3.

GILEAD Israelite land east of the Jordan: famous for its flocks and spices; region from which Jair, Jephthah and Elijah came: Genesis 37:25; Joshua 17:1; Judges 10:3; 11; 1 Kings 17:1; Song of Solomon 4:1/Map p.255.

GILGAL Place near Jericho where the Israelites marked the crossing of the Jordan; site of an important shrine; on Samuel's circuit as Judge: Joshua 4:20; Judges 3:19; 1 Samuel 7:16; 10:8, etc.; 2 Samuel 19:15; Hosea 4:15, etc./Map p.116C5.

GOMORRAH Town at the southern end of the Dead Sea violently destroyed for its wickedness: Genesis 14; 19; Isaiah 1:9-10, etc.; Matthew 10:15, etc./Map p.137.

GOSHEN Region of the Egyptian delta where Jacob and his family settled: Genesis 45:10; Exodus 8:22, etc./Map p. 163.

GOZAN Town in northern Mesopotamia annexed by the Assyrians, to which the Israelites were deported: 2 Kings 17:6;19:12.

GREAT SEA Name used throughout the Old Testament for the Mediterranean.

GREECE Alexander's conquests brought Israel under Greek control (with the rest of the eastern Mediterranean) and under the influence of Greek civilization, culture and thought; see Greeks in Nations and Peoples of Bible Lands: Daniel 11: John 12:20; Acts 6; 17; 18/Maps pp. 12-13, 304.

HABOR Tributary of the Euphrates; Gozan stood on its banks: 2 Kings 17:6.

HAMATH Hama on the River Orontes in Syria; ideal northern limit of Israel; conquered by Assyria: Joshua 13:5; 2 Samuel 8:9; 1 Kings 8:65; 2 Kings 17:24; 18:34, etc./Map p.411.

HARRAN Town in north Mesopotamia to which Abraham went on the first stage of his journey to Canaan; where Jacob served Laban; later dominated by Assyria: Genesis 11:31; 12:4-5; 29:4, etc.; 2 Kings 19:12/Map p. 137.

HAROD Spring where Gideon camped and chose the small force which defeated the Midianites: Judges 7:1/Map p.222.

HAZOR Important Canaanite city in the north of Israel; Joshua defeated Jabin of Hazor and destroyed the city; the army of a later Jabin of Hazor was defeated by Deborah and Barak; rebuilt and fortified by Solomon; fell to Assyria: Joshua 11; Judges 4; 1 Kings 9:15: 2 Kings 15:29/pp.213-214, 259/Map p.116C2 Pictures pp.25, 277.

HEBRON Early name Kiriath-arba; in the Judean hills; base of Abraham and the patriarchs, who were buried in the cave of Machpelah; conquered by Caleb; David's first capital; where Absalom staged his rebellion: Genesis 13:18; 23; 35:27; Joshua 14:6-15; 2 Samuel 2:1-4; 15:9-10; etc./Map p. 116B6 Pictures pp.143, 244.

HELIOPOLIS (ON) Sacred city of the sun god in ancient Egypt: Genesis 41:45; Jeremiah 43:13/Map p. 147.

HERMON 9,000ft mountain on the borders of Israel, Lebanon and Syria; also called Sirion; it snows from part of the source of the Jordan; probably the mountain where Jesus was transfigured: Joshua 12:1, etc.; Psalms 42:6; 133:3; Matthew 17:1, etc./Map p.464C1 Picture p.506.

HESHBON Moabite, Amorite and later Israelite town east of the Jordan: Numbers 21:25ff., etc./Map p.116C5.

HIERAPOLIS Town with hot medicinal springs in the Lycus Valley (western Turkey) near Laodicea and Colossae; Epaphras may have founded the church there: Colossians 4:12-13/Map p.579 Picture p.650.

HINNOM Valley outside Jerusalem; in the time of the prophets Molech was worshipped here, with child sacrifice; later a place where corpses and refuse were burned; it provided the name for hell— Gehenna: 2 Kings 23:10; Jeremiah 7:31-32, etc./Map p.248 Picture p.249.

HOREB Another name for Mt Sinai.

HORMAH Here, because of their disobedience, the Israelites were defeated by the Canaanites: Numbers 14:45; also 21:3; Joshua 15:30, etc./Map p.116B6.

IBLEAM Town in the north of Israel where Jehu killed Ahaziah: Joshua 17:11-12; 2 Kings 9:27; 15:10/Map p.116B3.

ICONIUM Modern Konya in Turkey; Paul preached here on his first missionary journey: Acts 13:51; 14:19-21/Map p.558.

IDUMAEA Edom, including part of Judah after the exile; the Herod family were Idumaeans/Map p.464A7.

ILLYRICUM Roman province in what is now Yugoslavia, where Paul preached: Romans 15:19/Map p.579.

ISRAEL The land occupied by the twelve tribes; after the split, the northern kingdom, excluding Judah and Benjamin/Maps pp.116, 464.

ISSACHAR Territory of the tribe of Issachar: Joshua 19:17-23/Map p.215.

ITURAEA Philip's tetrarchy north-east of the Sea of Galilee: Luke 3:1/Map p.464C1.

JABBOK Tributary flowing into the Jordan from the east, beside which Jacob wrestled with the angel; boundary of Ammon: Genesis 32:22ff.; Numbers 21:24/Map p.116C4.

JABESH-GILEAD Town east of the Jordan which features in Judges 21 and the story of Saul: 1 Samuel 11; 31:11-13/Map p.116C4.

JAVAN Coastlands and islands occupied by the Ionians (Greeks).

JAZER Amorite town captured by the Israelites; famous for its vines: Numbers 21:32; 1 Chronicles 26:31; Isaiah 16:8-9/Map p.247.

JEBUS Early name for Jerusalem: Joshua 18:28, etc.

JERICHO Town with a fresh-water spring in the desert north of the Dead Sea, guarding fords of the Jordan, to which Joshua sent the spies; Israel's first great victory in the promised land was at Jericho; features in Judges and the Elijah-Elisha story; here Jesus gave Bartimaeus his sight, and Zacchaeus was converted; in the parable of the Good Samaritan, the Jew was attacked on the Jerusalem-Jericho road: Joshua 2; 6; Judges 12:13; 2 Kings 2; Mark 10:46; Luke 19:1ff.: 10:30/pp.213-214 Map p.116C5 Pictures pp.84, 85, 208, 272, 389.

JERUSALEM Probably the 'Salem' of which Melchizedek was king; taken from the Jebusites by David; became capital and holy city of Israel, and of the southern kingdom of Judah after the split; here Solomon built the temple; besieged by the Assyrians in Hezekiah's reign; besieged and destroyed by the Babylonians; Zerubbabel rebuilt the temple after the exile; Nehemiah rebuilt the walls; city and temple were despoiled and desecrated by Antiochus Epiphanes; when the Romans took over the Greek Empire, Jerusalem remained subject; Herod rebuilt the temple; here Jesus was presented as a baby, and came when he was 12; he visited Jerusalem during his ministry; his trial, crucifixion and resurrection all took place here; in Jerusalem the church came into being at Pentecost, and from here it spread far and wide; here too the council on the position of the Gentiles was held: Genesis 14:18; 2 Samuel 5; 1 Kings 6; 2 Kings 18; 19; 25; Ezra 5; Nehemiah 3ff.; Luke 2; 19:28 - 24, etc.; John 5, etc.; Acts 2; 15/*Maps* pp.248, 116B5 *Pictures* pp.246, 249, 292-293, 308, 312, 337, 372, 401, 404, 406, 415, 489, 511, 526, 527, 528, 545, 552, back endpaper. *Reconstruction* p.471.

JEZREEL Town and valley in northern Israel where Ahab had his palace and Naboth his vineyard; the wounded Joram came to Jezreel; Jezebel died here: 1 Samuel 29:1; 1 Kings 18:45-46; 21; 2 Kings 8:29; 9:30-37/*Map* p.116B3.

JOPPA Sea-port in Israel (modern Jaffa); where Jonah embarked; here Peter had his dream and Cornelius sent for him: 2 Chronicles 2:16; Jonah 1:3; Acts 9:36ff.; 10 *Map* p.116A4.

JORDAN Israel's chief river, flowing through the Sea of Galilee to the Dead Sea; the Israelites crossed the river to enter the promised land; David fled back across it from Absalom; Naaman washed in the Jordan and was healed; John baptized the people, and Jesus, in the Jordan: Joshua 3; 2 Samuel 17:22ff.; 2 Kings 2:6-8, 13-14; 5; Mark 1:5, 9, etc./*Map* p.116C *Pictures* pp.273, 368, 334, 500.

JUDAH Territory of the tribe of Judah, of which the hill-country of Judah and the wilderness of Judea (bordering the west side of the Dead Sea) form part; later the name of the southern kingdom: Joshua 15; 1 Kings 12:21, 23/*Map* p.215. See pictures under Judea.

JUDEA Greek and Roman name for Judah; sometimes includes, sometimes excludes, Galilee and Samaria: Luke 4:44; 3:1, etc./*Map* p.464B5 *Pictures* pp.17, 241, 389, 394, 525.

KADESH-BARNEA An oasis in the desert south of Beersheba; in this general area most of Israel's years of desert wandering were spent: Numbers 13:26; 20:1, 14; 33:36, etc.; Joshua 14:7/*Map* p.163.

KEDESH Canaanite town in Galilee conquered by Joshua; home of Barak: Joshua 12:22; Judges 4:6; also 2 Kings 15:29, etc./*Map* p.116C1.

KEILAH Town David saved from Philistine attack, and where he took refuge: 1 Samuel 23/*Map* p.241.

KIDRON Valley between Jerusalem and the Mount of Olives; David crossed it, fleeing from Absalom; Jesus crossed it to Gethsemane: 2 Samuel 15:23; 1 Kings 15:13; 2 Kings 23:4; John 18:1/*Map* p.248 *Pictures* pp.249, 401.

KING'S HIGHWAY Road running from the Gulf of Aqaba, east of the Dead Sea, to Syria; Edom refused Moses access to it: Numbers 20:17, etc./*Map* p.196.

KIR, KIR-HARESETH Fortified town in Moab: 2 Kings 3; Isaiah 15:1; 16:7/*Map* p.116C6.

KIRIATHAIM Place east of Jordan allotted to Reuben; later in Moabite hands: Joshua 13:19; Jeremiah 48:1/*Map* p.116C6.

KIRIATH-ARBA Earlier name for Hebron.

KIRIATH-JEARIM Chief town of the Gibeonites; where the ark was kept for 20 years before David took it to Jerusalem: Joshua 9; 1 Samuel 6:19 - 7:2/*Map* p.116B5 *Picture* p.234.

KISHON River referred to in the story of Barak's victory, and Elijah's slaughter of the prophets of Baal; flows into the sea north of Mt Carmel: Judges 5:21; 1 Kings 18:40/*Map* p.116B2.

KITTIM Name for Cyprus; later for east Mediterranean coastlands generally.

KUE Region of what is now southern Turkey (Cilicia) from which Solomon imported horses: 1 Kings 10:28/*Map* p.295.

LACHISH Important fortified town in the foot-hills south-east of Jerusalem; features in the story of the conquest; the place where Amaziah was assassinated; a target of Assyrian and Babylonian attack: Joshua 10; 2 Kings 14:19; 18:14, 17; Jeremiah 34:7/*Map* p.116A6 *Pictures* pp.83, 283.

LAODICEA Town in the Lycus Valley of present-day western Turkey; Paul's letter to the Colossians was also to be taken to the church there; one of the seven churches addressed by John in Revelation: Colossians 2:1; 4:13-16; Revelation 1:11; 3:14-22/*Map* p.579 *Picture* p.649.

LEBANON The modern country and its mountain range; famous for its cedars (used in building the temple) and its fruit: 1 Kings 5:6; Psalm 72:16; Isaiah 2:13, etc./*Pictures* of cedars pp.253, 330.

LIBNAH Fortified lowland town taken by Joshua; revolted against Joram; attacked by Sennacherib: Joshua 10:29-30; 2 Kings 8:22; 19:8, etc./*Map* p.116A5.

LO-DEBAR Place east of Jordan where Mephibosheth lived: 2 Samuel 9:4/*Map* p.116C3.

LUD See Lydians in Nations and Peoples of Bible Lands/*Map* pp.12-13.

LUZ Former name of Bethel.

LYCIA Region in what is now south-west Turkey: Acts 27:5/*Map* p.579.

LYDDA Old Testament and modern Lod, near Jaffa: Acts 9:32, 35/*Map* p.464B5.

LYSTRA Timothy's home town; where Paul healed a cripple and was acclaimed as a god (not far from Konya in modern Turkey): Acts 14:6ff.; 16/*Map* p.558.

MAACAH Region south-east of Mt Hermon, mentioned in David's campaigns: Joshua 12:5; 2 Samuel 10/*Map* p.245.

MACEDONIA Roman province of northern Greece, including Philippi, Thessalonica and Beroea: Acts 16:9ff.; 20:1ff.; 2 Corinthians 9, etc./*Map* p.567.

MAHANAIM Place east of the Jordan near the River Jabbok; mentioned in the story of Jacob's return; headquarters of David during Absalom's rebellion: Genesis 32:2; 2 Samuel 17:24, etc./*Map* p.245.

MAKKEDAH Joshua captured the town and killed five Amorite kings in a nearby cave: Joshua 10:16ff./*Map* p.116B5.

MALTA Here Paul was shipwrecked on the way to Rome: Acts 27:39 - 28:10/*Map* p.567 *Picture* p.568.

MAMRE Place close to Hebron where Abraham stayed: Genesis 13:18; 18:1; 23:17, etc.

MANASSEH Territory of the tribe of Manasseh: Joshua 13:29-31; 17:7-13/*Map* p.215.

MAON Town near which David took refuge

from Saul and where Nabal lived: 1 Samuel 23:24; 25:2/*Map* p.116B6.

MARESHAH Town fortified by Rehoboam, near which Asa defeated Zerah of Ethiopia: 2 Chronicles 11:8; 20:37; 14:9; Micah 1:15/*Map* p.116A6.

MEDIA North-west Iran; subject to Assyria; ally of Babylonia; brought under control by Cyrus; partner in the Medo-Persian confederation; see Medes, in Nations and Peoples of Bible Lands/*Map* pp.12-13.

MEGIDDO Joshua defeated the king of this Canaanite city which dominates the pass through the Carmel hills; its strategic position has made it the site of numerous battles, hence its symbolical use as Armageddon (Har-Magedon, hill of Megiddo) in Revelation; Sisera was defeated near here; Solomon fortified the city; Ahaziah died here; so also did Josiah, killed in the battle against Pharaoh Necho: Joshua 12:21; Judges 5:19; 1 Kings 9:15; 2 Kings 9:27; 23:29/p.259 *Map* p.116B3 *Pictures* pp.207, 270, 299, 655.

MEMPHIS Ancient capital of Egypt: Jeremiah 2:16; 46:14, etc./*Map* p.151.

MESOPOTAMIA Land between the Tigris and Euphrates; the term is often extended to include Babylonia to the south; includes Harran and Paddan-aram where some of Abraham's family settled: Genesis 24:10; Deuteronomy 23:4, etc.; Acts 2:9/*Map* p.13.

MICHMASH Where Saul's army mustered against the Philistines: 1 Samuel 13:2; 14/*Map* p.116B5.

MIDIAN Region of north-west Arabia; see Midianites in Nations and Peoples of Bible Lands; Moses stayed here after escaping from Pharaoh; Gideon routed invaders from Midian: Exodus 2:15; Judges 6, etc./*Map* pp.12-13.

MILETUS Sea-port where Paul spoke to the elders from Ephesus: Acts 20:15, 17; also 2 Timothy 4:20/*Map* p.564.

MITYLENE Paul's ship put in here, at the island of Lesbos, on his way to Jerusalem: Acts 20:14/*Map* p.564.

MIZPAH The name (meaning watch-tower) denotes a number of different places: primarily one near Jerusalem where the Israelites assembled in the time of Samuel and the Judges; here Saul was presented as king; later fortified by Asa; residence of Gedaliah: Judges 20:1; 1 Samuel 7:5ff.; 10:17; 1 Kings 15:22; 2 Kings 25:23/*Map* p.116B5.

MOAB Country east of the Dead Sea; see Moabites in Nations and Peoples of Bible Lands; home of Ruth; in constant conflict with Israel; frequently denounced by the prophets: Ruth 1; 2 Samuel 8:2; 2 Kings 3; Isaiah 15, etc./*Map* pp.12-13.

PLAINS OF MOAB Where the Israelites assembled before crossing the Jordan: Numbers 22:1; 35:1, etc./*Map* p.116C5.

MOREH The hill where the Midianites encamped against Gideon: Judges 7:1/*Map* p.116B3 *Picture* p.223.

MORESHETH, MORESHETH-GATH Home of the prophet Micah: Micah 1:1, 14.

MORIAH Mountains where Abraham was told to go to sacrifice Isaac; the site of Jerusalem: **MT MORIAH**: site of Solomon's

temple: Genesis 22:2; 2 Chronicles 3:1.
MOUNT OF OLIVES Hill overlooking Jerusalem; David fled this way from Absalom; from it Jesus entered Jerusalem in triumph, and wept over the city; on its slopes was Gethsemane; the village of Bethany lay on the far side; the mountain of the ascension: 2 Samuel 15:30; Zechariah 14:4; Luke 19:29, 37, 41; 22:39; Acts 1:12, etc./ *Map* p.545 *Picture* p.550.
MYRA Port on Paul's journey to Rome: Acts 27:5/ *Map* p.567.
MYSIA Region Paul passed through on his way to Troas: Acts 16:7-8/ *Map* p.560.

NAIN Place in Galilee where Jesus restored the widow's son to life: Luke 7:11/ *Map* p.464B3 *Picture* p.518.
NAPHTALI Territory of the tribe of Naphtali in Galilee: Joshua 19:32-39/ *Map* p.215.
NAZARETH Town in Galilee where Joseph and Mary lived; Jesus' home: Luke 1:26ff.; 2:39, 51; 4:16ff., etc./ *Map* p.464B2 *Pictures* pp.476, 517.
NEAPOLIS Port near Philippi in northern Greece (modern Kavalla): Acts 16:11/ *Map* p.560.
NEBO Town and mountain in Moab from which Moses viewed the promised land and where he died: Deuteronomy 32:49-50; 34:1ff./ *Map* p.116C5.
NEGEV Arid region in the far south of Israel merging with Sinai, on the route to Egypt; here the patriarchs led their flocks, and the Israelites wandered before entering Canaan: Genesis 20:1, etc. Numbers 13:17; 21:1, etc./ *Map* p. 163 *Pictures* pp. 16, 184, 188, 193, 392-393.
NILE Great river of Egypt on which its whole economy rested; occurs in Pharaoh's dream; here the Hebrew babies were drowned and Moses was hidden; polluted in the plagues; often mentioned by the prophets: Genesis 41:1ff.; Exodus 1:22; 2:3ff.; 7:14ff.; Isaiah 18:2. etc./ *Map* p.151.
NINEVEH City which became capital of Assyria in Sennacherib's reign; Jonah was sent to save it; Nahum prophesied against it; when it fell to the Babylonians the power of Assyria crumbled: Genesis 10:11; 2 Kings 19:36; Jonah 1:2; 3; Nahum 1:1/ *Map* p.279.
NOB Place where David came to Ahimelech, and took Goliath's sword; its priests were killed by Doeg: 1 Samuel 21; 22/ *Map* p.241.

ON Another name for Heliopolis in Egypt.
OPHIR Country of unknown location famous for its gold: 1 Kings 9:28, etc.

PADDAN-ARAM Where Laban lived, in north Mesopotamia: Genesis 28:2, etc./ *Map* p.137.
PAMPHYLIA Region in what is now south-western Turkey, including Perga: Acts 2:10; 13:13/ *Map* p.579.
PAPHOS Town in the south-west of Cyprus visited by Paul on the first missionary journey: Acts 13:6ff./ *Map* p.558 *Picture* p.595.
PARAN Desert area near Kadesh-barnea which the Israelites passed through after

the exodus: Numbers 10:12, etc./ *Map* p.163.
PATMOS Island off the coast of Turkey where John had his visions: Revelation 1:9/ *Map* p.646.
PENUEL Beside the River Jabbok, where Jacob wrestled with the angel: Genesis 32:22ff./ *Map* p.116C4.
PERGA Paul's first mainland stopping-place in what is now Turkey: Acts 13:13, 14:25/ *Map* p.558.
PERGAMUM Town of one of the seven churches to which John wrote: Revelation 1:11; 2:12-17/ *Map* p.646 *Pictures* pp 647, 654.
PERSIA Country which conquered Media and overthrew Babylon to establish an empire which continued until the conquests of Alexander the Great; Cyrus king of Persia allowed the Jews to return from exile; Esther was queen of Persia: Ezra 1:1; Esther 1:3; Daniel 8:20; 10:1, etc./ see Persians in Nations and Peoples of Bible Lands/ *Map* pp.12-13.
PHILADELPHIA Town of one of the seven churches to which John wrote: Revelation 1:11; 3:7-13/ *Map* p.646 *Picture* p.649.
PHILIPPI Roman colony in northern Greece, on the great Egnatian highway first place in Europe where Paul established a church; here an earthquake set him free from prison; later he sent a letter to the church at Philippi: Acts 16; 20:6; Philippians/ p.608 *Map* p.560 *Pictures* pp.36 560, 609.
PHILISTIA Land of the Philistines on the coast of Israel; see Philistines in Nations and Peoples of Bible Lands/ *Map* pp.12-13.
PHOENICIA Country on the coast north of Israel whose chief towns were Tyre and Sidon: Obadiah 20; Mark 7:24ff.; Acts 11:19; 15:3/ *Map* p.383.
PHOENIX Harbour in Crete: Acts 27:12/ *Map* p.567.
PHRYGIA Region of what is now western-central Turkey, including Pisidian Antioch and Iconium, towns visited on Paul's first missionary journey: Acts 2:10; 13:14ff.; 16:6/ *Map* p.560.
PISGAH One of the peaks of Mt Nebo/ *Map* p.196.
PISIDIA Mountainous region of inland Turkey: Acts 13:14; 14:24/ *Map* p.558.
PITHOM One of the delta store-cities built for Pharaoh by Israelite slaves: Exodus 1:11
PONTUS Roman province bordering the Black Sea; Jews from here were in Jerusalem at Pentecost; Aquila's home area: Acts 2:9; 18:2; 1 Peter 1:1/ *Map* p.579.
PTOLEMAIS Greek name for Acco: Acts 21:7/ *Map* p.464B2.
PUT An African country, probably part of Libya: Jeremiah 46:9; Ezekiel 27:10, etc.
PUTEOLI Italian port where Paul landed on his way to Rome: Acts 28:13/ *Map* p.567.

RAAMSES One of the delta store-cities built for Pharaoh by Israelite slaves: Exodus 1:11/ *Map* p.163.
RABBAH Capital city of Ammon (modern Amman): Deuteronomy 3:11; 2 Samuel 12:26; 17:27; Jeremiah 49:2, etc./ *Map* p.116C4.

RAMAH Town to the north of Jerusalem; place of Rachel's tomb; mentioned in connection with Deborah, the story of the Levite, fortifications of Baasha and Asa, and Jeremiah's release: Matthew 2:18; Judges 4:5; 19:13; 1 Kings 15:17, 22; Jeremiah 40:1/ *Map* p.221.
RAMOTH-GILEAD City of refuge east of the Jordan which featured in wars with Syria; chief of Solomon's districts; here Ahab was killed in battle and Jehu anointed: Joshua 20:8; 1 Kings 4:13; 22:ff.; 2 Kings 8:28ff.; 9/ *Map* p.116D3.
RED SEA 'Sea of reeds' crossed by the Israelites at the exodus; see p.163.
REPHAIM Valley where David fought the Philistines: 2 Samuel 5:18. etc.
REUBEN Territory of the tribe of Reuben: Joshua 13:15-23/ *Map* p.215.
RHEGIUM Italian port where Paul's ship put in: Acts 28:13/ *Map* p.567.
RIBLAH This town on the Orontes was the military base of Pharaoh Necho and later of Nebuchadnezzar; here Zedekiah was blinded and his sons killed: 2 Kings 23:33; 25:6-7.
ROME Capital of the Roman Empire, Jews from Rome were in Jerusalem on the day of Pentecost; later Claudius expelled them; Paul wrote to the Christians at Rome, planned to visit them, and eventually reached the city as a prisoner: Acts 2:10; 18:2; Romans 1:7, 15; Acts 28/p.581 *Pictures* pp.570, 587.

SALAMIS Town in Cyprus visited by Paul and Barnabas: Acts 13:5/ *Map* p.558 *Picture* p.558.
SALEM See Jerusalem.
SALT SEA Old Testament name for the Dead Sea/ *Pictures* pp.139, 140.
SALT Valley where David defeated the Edomites: 2 Samuel 8:13/ *Map* p.245.
SAMARIA Built by Omri as capital of the northern kingdom of Israel; Ahab added a temple and palace; besieged by Syria; denounced for its wealth and corruption by the prophets; besieged and captured by the Assyrians; after this Samaria becomes the name of the general area. 1 Kings 16:24, 32; 22:39; 2 Kings 6:24; Amos 3:9ff. etc.; 2 Kings 17; Nehemiah 4:2; John 4:4ff. etc./ *Map* p.116B4 *Pictures* pp.271, 274, 333.
SARDIS Town of one of the seven churches to which John wrote: Revelation 1 11; 3:1-6/ *Map* p.646 *Picture* p.648.
SEIR Another name for Edom.
SELA Capital of Edom, probably on the same site as Petra: Isaiah 16:1.
SELEUCIA Port of Antioch from which Paul set out on his first missionary journey: Acts 13:4/ *Map* p.558.
SENIR Another name for Mt Hermon, or a nearby peak.
SEPHARVAIM People from this town conquered by the Assyrians were brought to Samaria: 2 Kings 17:24; 18:34.
SHARON Coastal plain of Israel: Isaiah 35:2, etc./ *Map* p.116B4 *Picture* p.18.
SHEBA Arabian country whose queen visited Solomon: 1 Kings 10.
SHECHEM Important ancient town near Mt Gerizim; features in the stories of Abraham

and Jacob, Joshua's renewal of the covenant, and Gideon's son Abimelech; first capital of the northern kingdom: Genesis 12:6; 33:18; 34; 37:12ff.; Joshua 24; Judges 9; 1 Kings 12, etc./Map p.116B4 *Pictures* pp.146, 218, 296.

SHILOH Sanctuary-town where Eli was priest and Hannah made her vow; here the ark was kept, and Samuel received his call; probably destroyed by the Philistines: 1 Samuel 1-4/Map p.116B4 *Picture* p.232.

SHINAR Another name for Babylonia.

SHITTIM Israelite camp from which the spies were sent to Jericho; probably where the Balaam episode occurred, and Joshua was appointed Moses' successor: Joshua 2:1; 3:1; Numbers 22ff.; 25ff./Map p.116C5.

SHUNEM Where the Philistines camped for the battle of Gilboa; town from which Abishag came; where Elisha stayed and restored a child to life: 1 Samuel 28:4; 1 Kings 1:3; 2 Kings 4/Map p.116B3.

SHUR Desert region to which Hagar fled and through which the Israelites passed: Genesis 16:7; Exodus 15:22/ Map p.163.

SIDDIM Valley where Chedorlaomer fought the kings of the plain: Genesis 14:3/Map p.137.

SIDON Phoenician port and merchant city, linked with Tyre; condemned by the prophets; visited by Jesus: Genesis 49:13; 1 Kings 17:9; Isaiah 23, etc.; Matthew 15:21; Luke 6:17; Acts 27:3/Map p.215.

SILOAM Pool in Jerusalem to which Hezekiah channelled water through a rock tunnel from the Gihon spring; here Jesus sent the blind man for healing: 2 Kings 20:20; John 9:7/p 301.

SIMEON Territory of the tribe of Simeon: Joshua 19/Map p.215

SINAI Mountain in the Sinai peninsula where Moses received the law and the people worshipped the golden calf; also the surrounding area of desert: Exodus 19ff./Map p.163 *Picture* p.165.

SMYRNA Modern Izmir in Turkey; town of one of the seven churches to which John wrote: Revelation 1:11; 2:8-11/Map p.646 *Picture* p.647.

SODOM Notorious town at the south of the Dead Sea where Lot settled; destroyed with Gomorrah: Genesis 14; 19/Map p.137.

SUCCOTH First stopping-place on the Israelites' journey from Egypt: Exodus 12:37/ Map p.163. Also a town where Jacob stopped, and which refused help to Gideon: Genesis 33:17; Judges 8/Map p.116C4.

SUSA Capital of Elam where the Persian kings spent part of the year: Ezra 4:9; Nehemiah 1:1; Esther 1:2/Map p.305

SYCHAR Samaritan town; site of Jacob's well: John 4:5-6/Map p.464B4.

SYENE Modern Aswan in Egypt: Isaiah 49:12; Ezekiel 29:10.

SYRACUSE Town in Sicily where Paul stayed on the way to Rome: Acts 28:12/ Map p.567.

SYRIA In the Old Testament, the Aramaean (later Syrian) land whose capital was Damascus; at times the ally, often the enemy of Israel; see Aramaeans in Nations and Peoples of Bible Lands; in the New Testament the Roman province of which Palestine was part/Map p.464C1.

TAANACH Canaanite town near which Barak fought Sisera: Joshua 12:21; Judges 5:19/ Map p.116B3.

TABOR Distinctive mountain in the plain of Jezreel where Barak gathered his forces to fight Sisera: Judges 4/Map p.116B3 *Picture* p.222.

TAHPANHES Delta town in Egypt to which Jeremiah was taken: Jeremiah 43:7-8/ Map p.408.

TARSHISH Far-off destination of Jonah, and source of minerals; may be Tartessus in Spain; the phrase 'ship of Tarshish' describes the vessel rather than its destination: Jonah 1:3; Isaiah 23:6; Ezekiel 38:13, etc.

TARSUS Important town in what is now southern Turkey; birth-place of Paul: Acts 9:11, 30; 21:39/Map p.558.

TEKOA Town in the Judean hills from which the wise woman came to David; home of Amos: 2 Samuel 14; Amos 1:1/Map p.377.

TEMAN Part of Edom; its inhabitants were famous for their wisdom; home area of Job's friend Eliphaz: Jeremiah 49:7; Job 2:11/Map p.411.

THEBES Capital city of Egypt sacked by the Assyrians: Jeremiah 46:25; Nahum 3:8/ Map p.151.

THESSALONICA Important city of northern Greece (modern Thessaloniki) evangelized by Paul; he wrote two letters to the church there: Acts 17; 1 and 2 Thessalonians/p.614 Map p.560 *Picture* p.616.

THYATIRA Home town of Lydia who was converted at Philippi; one of John's letters to the seven churches was addressed to Thyatira: Acts 16:14; Revelation 1:11; 2:18-29/Map p.646 *Picture* p.648.

TIBERIAS Spa town on the west shore of the Sea of Galilee, built by Herod Antipas and named after the Emperor Tiberius: John 6:23/Map p.464C2.

TIGRIS Second great river of Mesopotamia: Genesis 2:14.

TIMNAH Home of Samson's Philistine wife: Judges 14/Map p.116A5.

TIMNATH-SERAH Town where Joshua was buried: Joshua 24:30/Map p.116B4.

TIRZAH Former Canaanite town which became the early capital of the northern kingdom of Israel: Joshua 12:24; 1 Kings 14:17; 15:21, etc./Map p.116B4.

TISHBE Home of Elijah, in Gilead: 1 Kings

17:1/ Map p.116C4.

TOB Aramaean region north-east of Israel mentioned in connection with Jephthah and David: Judges 11:3; 2 Samuel 10:6/ Map p.245.

TOPHETH Place of child-sacrifice in the Valley of Hinnom.

TRACHONITIS Area north-east of Israel in Herod Philip's tetrarchy: Luke 3:1/Map p.464D2.

TROAS Port near Troy in north-west Turkey, used several times by Paul; here he had his dream of the man from Macedonia, and restored Eutychus to life: Acts 16:8ff.; 20:5ff.; 2 Corinthians 2:12/Map p.560.

TYRE Phoenician sea-port and city-state on the coast of Lebanon; famous centre of trade; Hiram of Tyre supplied David and Solomon with timber and materials for the temple; Jezebel was the daughter of a king of Tyre and Sidon; the prophets condemned Tyre's pride and luxury: 2 Samuel 5:11; 1 Kings 5; 9:10-14; 16:31; Isaiah 23, etc./Map p.116B1 *Pictures* pp.252, 566.

UR Famous city in south Babylonia; family home of Abraham: Genesis 11:28ff. etc./ Map p.137.

UZ Home country of Job, probably in the region of Edom: Job 1:1.

ZAREPHATH Town belonging to Sidon, where Elijah stayed; here he restored the widow's son to life: 1 Kings 17:8ff./Map p.267.

ZEBOIIM Town at the south of the Dead Sea, destroyed with Sodom and Gomorrah: Genesis 10:19; 14; Deuteronomy 29:23/ Map p.137.

ZEBULUN Territory of the tribe of Zebulun: Joshua 19:10-16/ Map p.215.

ZIKLAG Town taken by the Philistines and given to David by Achish; raided by the Amalekites: 1 Samuel 27:6; 30/Map p.241.

ZIN Area of desert near Kadesh-barnea where the Israelites wandered after the exodus: Numbers 13:21; 20:1; 27:14, etc./ Map p.163.

ZION One of the hills of Jerusalem; David's city; also stands for Jerusalem as the city of God's temple/Picture p.337.

ZIPH Area to which David fled from Saul; but the men of the town betrayed him: 1 Samuel 23:14ff./Map p.241.

ZOAN/TANIS Ancient town in the Egyptian delta: Numbers 13:22; Isaiah 19:11, etc./ Map p.151.

ZOAR Town near Sodom to which Lot fled escaping destruction: Genesis 13:10; 14:2, 8; 19:18ff./ Map p.137.

ZOBAH Somewhere in the region of Damascus; Aramaean kingdom defeated by David: 2 Samuel 8:3; 10:6; 1 Kings 11:23/ Map p.245.

ZORAH Birth place of Samson: Judges 13:2; 16:31/Map p.225.

Prayers of the Bible

Subjects and Events

Acknowledgements

TEXT
The article *Using the Bible in Archaeology,* p. 259, is adapted from a BBC2 television programme, 'Hazor, City of the Bible', 27 May 1972, with the kind permission of Prof. Yigael Yadin. The help of Miss Mary Hart in preparing *Key Themes* material in Part Four is acknowledged.

GRAPHICS
Graphic design of the charts on pp. 22-3, 30-1, 75, 78, 104-5, 106-7, 108-9, 112-13, 118-121, 132, 153, 284-5, by Tony Cantale. Maps on pp. 19, 116, 131, 236, 377, 464 by Arka Graphics.
The relief model used for the maps of Israel was made by Dupliterre; other relief models used by kind permission of Oxford University Press.

PICTURES
All photographs were taken by David Alexander (except those acknowledged separately below), including the following taken with help and permission as shown:
Agricultural Museum, Jerusalem: p. 141 (waterskin)
Archaeological Museum, Istanbul: pp. 110, 301, 390, 427, 567, 620, 632 (both)
British and Foreign Bible Society, London: pp. 70, 73, 76, 77, 88 (scroll)
British Museum, London: pp. 11, 15, 43, 67, 82, 86 (hieroglyph, cuneiform), 87 (potsherd), 136, 143, 148, 149 (dream manual), 152, 153, 156, 159 (book), 160, 161, 162 (dagger), 170 (tassel), 200, 215, 221, 232, 239, 257, 258, 264, 277, 278, 281, 303, 313, 314, 353, 355, 356, 365, 386, 390 (relief), 413, 417, 423, 431, 432, 434, 436, 509, 524, 577, 598, 607, 609, 622, 635, 637 (ornament), 642
Church's Ministry among the Jews: pp. 179, 488, 522, 525
Convent of the Sisters of Nazareth, Israel: p. 46
Vernon Durrant: p. 159
Damascus Museum, Syria: p. 507
Ecce Homo Convent, Jerusalem: pp. 406, 526, 527
Ephesus Museum, Selçuk, Turkey: pp. 565, 603
Haifa Music Museum and Amli Library, Israel: pp. 187, 210, 238, 349, 433

Hatay Archaeological Museum, Antakya, Syria: pp. 141 (ram's head), 344, 637 (coin), 641
Hazor Museum, Israel: p. 25
Israel Department of Antiquities and Museums: pp. 85, 94, 154, 162 (figure), 170 (bull), 173, 235, 262 (seal), 266, 270, 536
Izmir Archaeological Museum, Turkey: pp. 590, 591, 619, 653
Megiddo Museum, Israel: p. 207
Museum of Biblical Antiquities, Amsterdam: pp. 166, 167, 169, 256, 288, 471, 496, 628

Other pictures have been supplied by the following:
Ashmolean Museum, Oxford: pp. 268, 271, 418 (Department of Antiquities)
Barnaby's Picture Library: p. 135
The Bible Society: pp. 41, 54
British Museum: pp. 86 (Hebrew), 87 (Aramaic, Greek), 88 (papayrus, codex), 130, 133, 149 (Egyptian figure), 163, 202, 253 (ivory), 262, 275, 280, 282, 291, 323, 331, 335, 338, 388, 395, 408, 419, 445, 612, 632
Camera Press, London: pp. 26, 28, 44, 63, 95, 101 (pigeon), 102 (serpent), 171, 511, 544
George Cansdale: pp. 101 (partridge), 503
Peter Clayton: p. 233
Fritz Fankhauser: p. 62
Haifa Maritime Museum, Israel: pp. 260-1, 569, 610
Sonia Halliday Photographs/Sonia Halliday: pp. 227, 351, 361, 444, 565, 582, 595, 617; *Jane Taylor:* pp. 93, 336
Nigel Hepper: all pictures on pp. 97-100 except data-palm, olive, acacia
Maurice Chuzeville/Louvre Museum: p. 202
Alistair Duncan/MEPhA: p. 218
Alan Millard: pp. 83, 186, 267, 268, 290
Observer Magazine (Transworld Feature Syndicate): p. 366
Picturepoint: p. 433
Royal Jordanian Airline: p. 447
Shell International Petroleum Co. Ltd: p. 443
Ronald Sheridan: p. 180
Staatliche Museen zu Berlin: p. 412
D. J. Wiseman: p. 239
ZEFA: pp. 53, 63, 65
Zoological Society of London: pp. 102 (scorpion), 103 (bear)